T0353651

Lecture Notes in Computer Science 15506

Founding Editor

Juris Hartmanis

The series Lecture Notes in Computer Science (LNCS), including its subseries Lecture Notes in Artificial Intelligence (LNAI) and Lecture Notes in Bioinformatics (LNBI), has established itself as a medium for the publication of new developments in computer science and information technology research, teaching, and education.

LNCS enjoys close cooperation with the computer science R & D community, the series counts many renowned academics among its volume editors and paper authors, and collaborates with prestigious societies. Its mission is to serve this international community by providing an invaluable service, mainly focused on the publication of conference and workshop proceedings and postproceedings. LNCS commenced publication in 1973.

Marco Comuzzi · Daniela Grigori ·
Mohamed Sellami · Zhangbing Zhou
Editors

Cooperative Information Systems

30th International Conference, CoopIS 2024
Porto, Portugal, November 19–21, 2024
Proceedings

 Springer

Editors
Marco Comuzzi 🆔
Ulsan National Institute of Science
and Technology
Ulsan, Korea (Republic of)

Mohamed Sellami 🆔
Institut Polytechnique de Paris
Paris, France

Daniela Grigori 🆔
Paris Dauphine - PSL University
Paris, France

Zhangbing Zhou 🆔
University of Geosciences
Beijing, Beijing, China

ISSN 0302-9743   ISSN 1611-3349 (electronic)
Lecture Notes in Computer Science
ISBN 978-3-031-81374-0   ISBN 978-3-031-81375-7 (eBook)
https://doi.org/10.1007/978-3-031-81375-7

Preface

The International Conference on Cooperative Information Systems (CoopIS 2024), held November 19–21 in Porto, Portugal, marked the 30th edition of this established conference series. Since its inception in 1993 in Rotterdam, Netherlands, CoopIS has consistently gathered researchers and professionals from around the world. Over the years, CoopIS has strengthened its role as a key international forum for discussions around cooperative information systems and their impact on technical, economic, and societal domains.

Cooperative Information Systems (CISs) facilitate cooperation between individuals, organisations, smart devices, and systems of systems, by providing flexible, scalable and intelligent services to enterprises, public institutions, and user communities. CISs enable seamless information exchange and cooperation across physical and digital boundaries, drawing from interdisciplinary areas like distributed systems, collaborative decision-making, enterprise architecture, and conceptual modeling. In recent years, several innovative technologies have emerged (Cloud Computing, Service-Oriented Computing, the Internet of Things, Linked Open Data, Semantic Systems, Collective Awareness Platforms, Blockchain, Processes as a Service, etc) that enable the next generation of CISs.

CoopIS 2024 received 78 paper submissions from 31 countries of which 16 were accepted and published as full papers. A double-blind paper review was performed for each submission by at least 3 members of the International Program Committee, which was composed of established researchers and domain experts.

The conference program was enriched by keynote talks from distinguished experts in the field: Paul Grefen (Eindhoven University of Technology, Netherlands) and Barbara Weber (University of St.Gallen, Switzerland).

In addition to the main sessions, CoopIS 2024 featured a Demo Track led by Demo Track Chairs Marwa Elleuch (Orange Labs, France) and Marwan Hassani (Eindhoven University of Technology, Netherlands), offering a platform for practical demonstrations of innovative CIS applications and solutions.

The program for this conference required the dedicated effort of many people. Firstly, we must thank the authors, whose research efforts are herewith recorded. Next, we thank the members of the Program Committee and the auxiliary reviewers for their diligent and professional reviewing. We would also like to deeply thank the invited speakers for their invaluable contribution and for taking the time to prepare their talks. Finally, a word of appreciation for the hard work of the Institute for Systems and Technologies of Information, Control and Communication (INSTICC); organizing a conference of this level is a task that can only be achieved by the collaborative effort of a dedicated and highly competent team.

We hope you all had an exciting and inspiring conference. We hope to have contributed to the development of our research community, and we look forward to having additional research results presented at the next edition of CoopIS.

November 2024

Marco Comuzzi
Daniela Grigori
Mohamed Sellami
Zhangbing Zhou

Organization

Conference Co-chairs

Mohamed Sellami   Institut Polytechnique de Paris - Télécom
SudParis, SAMOVAR, France

Zhangbing Zhou   China University of Geosciences, Beijing

Program Co-chairs

Marco Comuzzi   Ulsan National Institute of Science and
Technology, Republic of Korea

Daniela Grigori   Paris DauphinePSL University, France

Program Committee

Han van der Aa	University of Vienna, Austria
Marco Aiello	University of Stuttgart, Germany
Ahmed Awad	British University in Dubai, UAE
Banu Aysolmaz	Technische Universiteit Eindhoven, Netherlands
Isabel Azevedo	ISEP, Portugal
Eduard Babkin	National Research University "Higher School of Economics", Russian Federation
Khalid Belhajjame	PSL, Paris-Dauphine University, LAMSADE, France
Salima Benbernou	Université Paris Cité, France
Hayet Brabra	Télécom SudParis, France
Cristina Cabanillas	University of Seville, Spain
Luis Camarinha-Matos	New University of Lisbon, Portugal
Paolo Ceravolo	University of Milan, Italy
Richard Chbeir	Université de Pau et des Pays de l'Adour, France
Carlo Combi	Università degli Studi di Verona, Italy
Pavlos Delias	Democritus University of Thrace, Greece
Joyce El Haddad	Paris Dauphine University - PSL, France
Rik Eshuis	Eindhoven University of Technology, Netherlands
Marcelo Fantinato	University of São Paulo, Brazil
Chiara Di Francescomarino	University of Trento, Italy

Luciano García-Bañuelos	Tecnológico de Monterrey, Mexico
Laura Genga	Eindhoven University of Technology, Netherlands
Nikolaos Georgantas	Inria, France
Chirine Ghédira Guégan	IAE - Jean Moulin Lyon 3 University, France
María Gómez López	Universidad de Sevilla, Spain
Jose Gonzalez	University of Seville, Spain
Laura González	Universidad de la República, Uruguay
Mohamed Graiet	University of Monastir, Tunisia
Georg Grossmann	University of South Australia, Australia
Mirian Halfeld-Ferrari	University of Orleans, LIFO, UR4022, France
Lazhar Hamel	University of Monastir, Tunisia
Anett Hoppe	TIB Leibniz Information Centre for Science and Technology; L3S Research Centre, Leibniz Universität Hannover, Germany
Stefan Jablonski	University of Bayreuth, Germany
Andres Jimenez Ramirez	University of Seville, Spain
Slim Kallel	University of Sfax, Tunisia
Dimka Karastoyanova	University of Groningen, Netherlands
Kais Klai	Université Sorbonne Paris Nord, France
Matthias Klusch	German Research Center for Artificial Intelligence (DFKI) GmbH, Germany
Maria Leitner	University of Regensburg, Germany
Francesco Leotta	Sapienza University of Rome, Italy
Teng Long	China University of Geosciences (Beijing), China
Jiangang Ma	Federation University Australia, Australia
Zakaria Maamar	University of Doha for Science and Technology, Qatar
Amel Mammar	Télécom SudParis, SAMOVAR-CNRS, France
Qizhong Mao	ByteDance, USA
Rabia Maqsood	NUCES, Pakistan
Raimundas Matulevicius	University of Tartu, Estonia
Lin Meng	Ritsumeikan University, Japan
Philippe Merle	Inria, France
Giovanni Meroni	Technical University of Denmark, Denmark
Nizar Messai	University of Tours, France
Enrique Moguel	University of Extremadura, Spain
Sellami Mokhtar	Higher Institute of Technological Studies of Jendouba, Tunisia
Alex Norta	Tallinn University of Technology, Estonia
Selmin Nurcan	Institut D'administration Des Entreprises De Paris - Université Paris I - Panthéon Sorbonne, France
Hervé Panetto	University of Lorraine, France

Manfred Reichert	Ulm University, Germany
Kate Revoredo	Humboldt Universität zu Berlin, Austria
Sonja Ristic	University of Novi Sad, Serbia
Mattia Salnitri	Politecnico di Milano, Italy
Michael Sheng	Macquarie University, Australia
Johannes De Smedt	KU Leuven, Belgium
Pnina Soffer	University of Haifa, Israel
Jacopo Soldani	University of Pisa, Italy
Francesco Tiezzi	Università degli Studi di Firenze, Italy
Nick van Beest	CSIRO, Australia
Genoveva Vargas-Solar	CNRS, France
Lena Wiese	Independent Researcher, Germany
Karolin Winter	Eindhoven University of Technology, Netherlands
Sami Yangui	INSA, University of Toulouse, France
Jian Yu	Auckland University of Technology, New Zealand
Sebastiaan van Zelst	Celonis Labs GmbH., Germany
Zhangbing Zhou	CUG Beijing, China

Additional Reviewers

Jaime Arias	CNRS, LIPN, Université Sorbonne Paris Nord, France
Frederique Biennier	INSA Lyon, France
Karam Bou-chaaya	Expleo Group, France
Marwa Boulakbech	University of Tours, France
Henrique Caetano	University of São Paulo, Brazil
Wei Cao	Research and University of Stuttgart, Germany
Umberto Costa	Université Sorbonne Paris Nord, Brazil
Elias Entrup	TIB - Leibniz Information Centre for Science and Technology, Germany
Mohammad Mustafa Ibrahimy	TLU.ee, Estonia
Wang Lingchen	Université d'Orléans, France
Alessandro Marcelletti	University of Camerino, Italy
Nada Mimouni	CNAM Conservatoire national des arts et métiers, France
Rebecca Morgan	University of South Australia, Australia
Evelyn Navarrete	TIB - Leibniz Information Centre for Science and Technology, Germany
Christoph Nirschl	University of Regensburg, Germany
Hadi Novandish	TLU.ee, Estonia
Hanene Ochi	ECE, Ecuador

Nathalie Pernelle	Université Sorbonne Paris Nord, LIPN, France
Sara Pettinari	Gran Sasso Science Institute, Italy
Tobias Pfaller	AIT Austrian Institute of Technology, Austria
Michael Reinstein	University of Regensburg, Germany
Nan Sai	Eindhoven University of Technology, Netherlands
Ratan Sebastian	TIB - Leibniz Information Centre for Science and Technology, Germany
Mozhgan Vazifehdoostirani	Eindhoven University of Technology, Netherlands
Dinesh Reddy Vemula	University of Stuttgart, Germany

Invited Speakers

| Paul Grefen | Eindhoven University of Technology, Netherlands |
| Barbara Weber | University of St.Gallen, Switzerland |

Machine Learning and Generative AI in BPM: Recent Developments and Emerging Challenges

Barbara Weber

University of St. Gallen, Switzerland

Abstract. This keynote presentation explores the integration of Machine Learning and Generative AI within Business Process Management (BPM), focusing on recent developments and emerging challenges. Generative AI holds potential for improving automation efficiency and democratizing process design and -analysis. In addition, it facilitates innovative problem-solving, enables conversational BPM, and allows to tap into novel data sources. With the third wave of BPM emphasizing data-led processes, AI technologies, including machine learning and natural language processing, are driving significant advancements in AI-augmented BPM including process automation and process mining. Attendees will gain insights into the transformative impact of AI on BPM, recent developments, and key challenges.

Brief Biography

BarbaraWeber is Full Professor for Software Systems Programming and Development and Director at the Institute of Computer Science at the University of St. Gallen (HSG), Switzerland since 2019. Since February 2024 she is additionally Vice-President for Studies and Teaching at HSG. Before joining HSG, Barbara held a full professorship at the Technical University of Denmark and led the Section for Software and Process Engineering for 3 years. Before moving to Denmark, Barbara worked for over 15 years for the University of Innsbruck where she started her research career and obtained her doctorate and habilitation degrees. Barbara's research interests include human and cognitive aspects in software and process engineering, process modeling and mining. Together with her team, she focusses on the development and evaluation of software artifacts. This includes topics in the areas of source code analysis, the Internet of Things, and process mining to study and build eventdriven software systems that adapt based on the user's behavior and context. On these and other topics, Barbara published around 200 peer-reviewed papers and articles in scientific journals. Barbara is part of the BPM and CAiSE Steering Committee and served as PC chair for BPM 2013, CAiSE 2019, EASE 2021, ICPM 2022 and was general chair of BPM 2015.

Contents

Knowledge Graphs and Knowledge Engineering

Predictive Process Monitoring

Services and Cloud

Short Papers

Invited Speakers

Business Models, Business Processes and Information Systems: A Dynamic Network View

Paul Grefen[1,2](✉) (iD)

[1] Eindhoven University of Technology, Eindhoven, Netherlands
p.w.p.j.grefen@tue.nl
[2] Eviden Digital Transformation Consulting, Amstelveen, Netherlands

Abstract. The business world is becoming increasingly networked: organizations engage in increasingly complex collaborations, such as global supply networks and service delivery networks. Consequently, organizations need to define their positions in these networks, both in intention and execution. At the same time, we see that the business world is becoming increasingly dynamic: the context in which collaborations function is prone to change more frequently, caused by global market changes, changing customer requirements, and rapid digital technology developments. Consequently, organizations have to anchor the ability to change in their core business DNA. These two developments imply that organizations must be able to define and operationalize their position in complex, dynamic networks. This requires an agile, outside-in approach at three interconnected levels: the business model level defining what to achieve, the business process level defining how to achieve this, and the business information system level defining how to support this. Many frameworks, methods, and architectures have been proposed that address aspects of the required approach, but few cover the complete business model to information system infrastructure spectrum. The few that do cover this spectrum often lead to very complex specifications, like in the field of enterprise architecture. This paper presents an approach that aims at supporting the complete spectrum without sacrificing conceptual elegance. The approach is based on the BASE/X framework that has been developed and tested with industry in the past decade-and-a-half. We present our learnings from this period.

Keywords: Collaborative business model · Interorganizational business process · Cooperative information system · Networked business · Business agility · BASE/X

1 Introduction

The business world is becoming increasingly networked [30], both in the for-profit and non-profit sectors. Business organizations engage in increasingly complex collaborations, such as global supply networks [7, 23] and service delivery networks [24]. In many situations, the execution of business processes in these collaborations gets an

M. Comuzzi et al. (Eds.): CoopIS 2024, LNCS 15506, pp. 3–17, 2025.
https://doi.org/10.1007/978-3-031-81375-7_1

increasingly real-time character. Also, the effects of globalization [23] on the one hand and mass-customization [25] on the other hand play a progressively dominant role in modern business. These developments call for the deployment of automated solutions to efficiently and effectively manage the business complexity and time pressure on the business execution.

At the same time, we see that the business world is becoming increasingly dynamic [23]: the context in which collaborations function is prone to change more frequently. This is caused by global market changes, changing customer requirements, and rapid technology developments – the latter mostly in the digital field. Consequently, organizations must not only change but anchor the ability to change in both their core business DNA and in their digital business systems landscape.

These two developments imply that organizations must be able to define and operationalize their position in complex, dynamic, IT-enabled networks. They must keep positioning themselves in swiftly evolving competitive playing fields and at the same time keep executing their processes in an efficient way. This requires an agile, outside-in approach at three interconnected levels: the business model level defining what to achieve, the business process level defining how to achieve this, and the business information system level defining how to support this.

Many proposals have been made for frameworks, methods, and architectures that address aspects of the required approach, but few cover the complete spectrum from business model to information system infrastructure. The few that do cover the spectrum often lead to overly complex specifications, like in the field of enterprise architecture. This paper presents an approach that aims at supporting the complete spectrum without sacrificing conceptual elegance. The approach is based on the BASE/X framework that has been developed and tested with industry in the past decade-and-a-half.

This paper has a retrospective character. As a basis, it provides a global overview of our approach to show how we have connected the three mentioned levels while taking the networked character of business and business agility as the main points of departure. Using this overview, this paper next describes where the approach worked well and where we faced challenges. Therefore, the contribution of this paper is a connection between the main elements of our approach and an experience report on the application of these elements.

The structure of this paper is as follows. In Sect. 2, we present a conceptual model in which we link and contextualize the main elements at the three interconnected levels mentioned above: business models, business processes, and information systems. In doing so, we explicitly aim at networked, cooperative structures. In Sect. 3, we briefly explain the BASE/X framework, which is the basis for the approach presented next. Section 4 presents our take on business models and the way these business models are mapped to business processes – addressing the first pair of the levels mentioned above. The agility in this approach is based on the concept of business services, which we discuss in Sect. 5. Section 6 then presents the mapping of business processes and business services onto cooperative information systems – addressing the technical side of the second pair of the levels mentioned above. Section 7 outlines our experience in the past decade-and-a-half with the presented approach, explaining what has been achieved but also where things proved harder than anticipated. We end this paper in Sect. 8 with conclusions and a brief look forward. As it is impossible to show all details of our work in the past years in this one paper, the bibliography provides ample links to more detailed work on our approach and experience.

2   Business Models, Processes and Information Systems

As stated in the introduction section, this paper revolves around the connection between three levels in networked digital business management: business models, business processes, and information systems. These three levels are shown in the conceptual model in Fig. 1, which is an extended version of the conceptual model of the BASE/X framework [11].

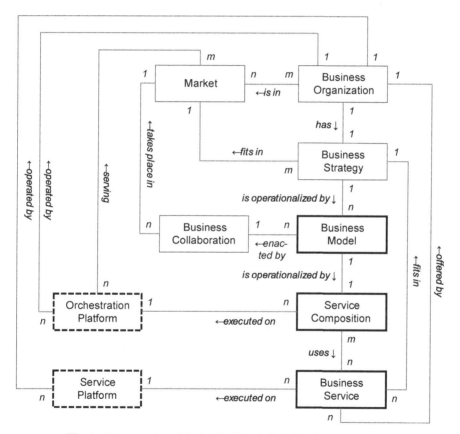

Fig. 1. Conceptual model of a distributed digital business ecosystem.

The conceptual side of the three levels is represented by the three classes with bold, solid boxes in the bottom-right of the figure. The concept of *business model* speaks for itself for now. The concept of *service composition* is the service-oriented version of the concept of business process (BASE/X is strongly service-based as we explain in the next section). The concept of *business service* refers to a customer-facing business function (or capability, if you prefer). We use this concept to represent the conceptual aspect of information systems, interpreted as a collection of business functions at the networked level. The technical (execution) aspect is limited to two levels only, as business models cannot be directly executed on a digital platform (at least in our understanding of the concepts). These two levels are represented by the two classes with bold, dashed boxes at the bottom-left of the figure. Service compositions are executed on *orchestration platforms* (or business process management platforms), business services on *service (execution) platforms*.

To give the five discussed classes in the conceptual model the networked character (i.e., to specialize them for a cooperative context), we need to contextualize them with the other classes in the model. They show that a networked business model is enacted by a *business collaboration* that takes place in a *market* (or business ecosystem) context. A *business organization* is a player in the market, defining its position in its *business strategy*. This strategy is the umbrella under which business models are defined. The market and business collaboration concepts are networked (distributed) by definition (without providing the definitions here), forcing the other concepts to have a networked character as well.

The conceptual model of Fig. 1 shows *what* the ingredients in our world of thinking are, but not *how* we bring these concepts to live to support networked business in practice. For that we need a business engineering approach, which we discuss in the next section.

3 The BASE/X Framework

The BASE/X framework is the main result of the CoProFind project, which was a direct, four-year collaboration between industry and academia with direct funding from industry. BASE/X is a business engineering framework that takes the then emerging paradigm of service-dominant business [17, 28] as the starting point for its design. The basic design of BASE/X is defined in a technical report [10], underpinned in a PhD thesis [15], and its concepts are further extended in a set of four later PhD theses [3, 4, 8, 22] and a set of publications, part of which is cited in this paper.

The structure of the BASE/X business modeling framework is shown in Fig. 2 [11]. The main structure is a pyramid consisting of four layers. The top layer (S) describes the business strategy (as also shown as a concept in Fig. 1) [16]. It describes the evolving identity of a business organization in its business ecosystem. The second layer describes the networked business models that operationalize the business strategy (as also shown in Fig. 1) [26]. Given a strategy, they are defined in an agile way. Note that a strategy can be operationalized by multiple business models, each of which describes a specific value proposition for a specific customer segment. The third layer of the pyramid describes the networked service compositions that each form the operationalization of a single business model. Each service composition is specified as an inter-organizational business process composed of business services. Given a set of business services in a catalog, a composition can be defined in an agile way. The bottom layer of the pyramid contains the business services that are used in service compositions – both internal and external services. Internal services are owned by an organization; external services are provided by a partner in a network. Business services encapsulate business resources and hence evolve, based on requirements from the business strategy. This means that BASE/X is a bi-speed business design approach (as illustrated by the two circular arrows in Fig. 2): a slower, strategic design loop defines the business strategy and business services; a faster, tactic design loop defines the business models and service compositions, based on an existing business strategy and a set of business services [11]. To align the execution of the two design loops, there are two confrontation points between the loops as shown in Fig. 2 one to align the goals and one to align the means.

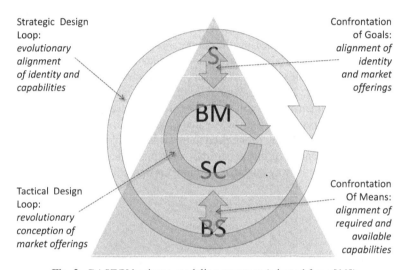

Fig. 2. BASE/X business modeling structure (adapted from [11]).

The business strategy of an organization pertains to a single organization and is not distributed across organizations. Hence, it is not networked in our use of the term in this paper. Obviously, a strategy can be based on a networked market to be the basis for business models [4]. As the concept of strategy is not networked in itself, we do not further discuss it in this paper and start our further discussion with the business model layer below.

4   From Business Models to Business Process Models

Business models define the 'why' of networked digital application scenarios: they explain why organizations participate in these scenarios with a certain role. To relate a networked business model and a networked business process, the business model should explicitly identify the organizations that participate in the model (the actors) and the parts of the process executed by each organization (the activities). To be truly networked, the business model should have an ecosystem-centric perspective, not an organization-centric perspective (like for example the original Business Model Canvas technique [19]). In other words, it should start with specifying the relations between the actors on the network level (i.e., represent an outside-in way of thinking), not with specifying a single organization as a focal point and then elaborating the interactions with other actors (i.e., represent an inside-out way of thinking). For this reason, we have developed the business model radar (BMR) as the main technique for specifying business models in the BASE/X approach (in the second layer of Fig. 2).

The graphical format of the BMR technique is shown in Fig. 3 (a more formal description is provided in [9]). The center point of the technique is the *value-in-use* that is produced (co-created) by the network for the identified customer (which represents a class of customers, or a well-described segment of a class of customers). Around the value-in-use, the actors participating in the business model are positioned as pie slices. In the inner ring, the *actor value proposition* of each actor specifies its contribution to the central value-in-use. In the middle ring, the *actor coproduction activity* specifies for each actor what the activity is to produce its actor value proposition. The specifications in this ring are the basis for the construction of the service composition for the business model (in the third layer of Fig. 2). In the outer ring, the *costs and benefits* are specified for each actor, both with financial and non-financial natures. These are obviously important from the business perspective as they are related to key performance indicators (KPIs) of business organizations [9] and hence need to be evaluated rigorously [8], but they are less important in the context of this paper: they determine the business feasibility of a business model, but not the way the business model is operationalized.

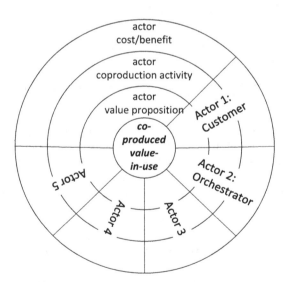

Fig. 3. Business Model Radar (adapted from [11]).

The specification of the service composition is in essence the service-oriented variant of an inter-organizational business process model [1]. According to the BASE/X philosophy, the service composition contains a control flow that links business services (in the bottom layer of Fig. 2) as process activities. These business services are selected from a catalog, which is defined in the strategic design loop of Fig. 2.

In designing the service composition, two hurdles need to be taken. The first hurdle is the fact that the BMR does not contain any temporal ordering between coproduction activities. Hence, we need to map a declarative activity specification to an imperative process specification. The second hurdle is that coproduction activities in a BMR are typically specified at a higher abstraction and aggregation level than business services. Hence, we need to refine and concretize the specification of the coproduction activities, which we can label as a mapping through vertical decomposition [13].

To guide the mapping of a business model to a service composition, a structured method (SDBMOM) has been developed [21, 22]. An overview of the structure of the method is shown in Fig. 2. In this figure, we see that the method is used to map the actors and activities of a BMR into a service composition (equivalent to a conceptual process model), by infusing the information from a business service catalog (listing the available capabilities of the networked ecosystem to use in the activities of the process model) and a specification of the customer experience (customer journey), providing the basis for the control flow of the business process (Fig. 4).

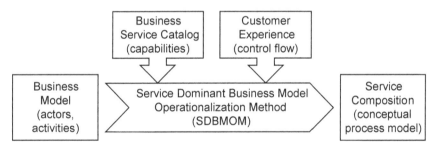

Fig. 4. Overview of SDBMOM method (adapted from [21]).

The service composition created by the method is always an inter-organizational business process, as it is executed by a set of autonomous organizations (the actors in the business model that is the input to the method). In a next step (not covered here for reasons of brevity), the conceptual process model is mapped to an executable process model for deployment in a business process management environment.

5 Identifying and Allocating Business Services

For the SDBMOM method described in Sect. 4 to work, it is essential to have a catalog of well-defined business services (in the bottom layer of Fig. 2). As we have seen in Sect. 3, business services are derived from the specification of a business strategy, such that they become reusable across business models.

The identification and design of business services is not a simple task, however, that needs to take several design concerns into consideration. For this reason, a multi-concern method for the structured identification of business services was designed [2, 3]. This method is built on a set of eleven business concerns that delineate the characteristics of a well-shaped business service. The structure of the method is shown in Fig. 5. It maps a value proposition in four steps to a set of business service specifications, using among other approaches the Strategic Dependency (SD) and Strategic Rationale (SR) Modeling from the i* framework [6, 29].

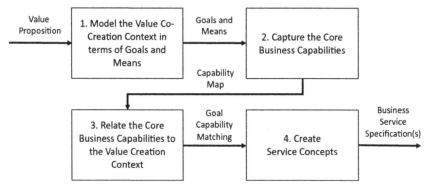

Fig. 5. Overview of method for the identification of business services (from [2]).

The method described above is a basis for identifying business services, but not yet for allocating these in the networked business ecosystem: the question is whether they should be offered (and hence often developed) by the 'owner' of a business strategy or by one of the partners in the business ecosystem. For answering this question, we use the decision tool shown in Fig. 6. The vertical dimension distinguishes between business services that are essential for the support of a strategy (the 'must-haves') and business services that bring an added value (the 'nice-to-haves'). The horizontal dimension distinguishes between services with a very specific functionality and services with a more-or-less standardized functionality. This matrix provides a first guidance for the allocation of business services in a business network from the perspectives of the individual actors in the network.

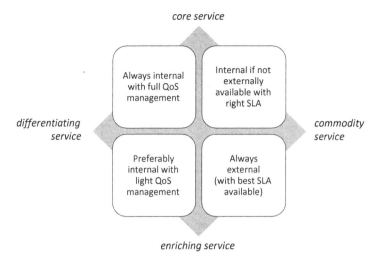

core service

differentiating service

commodity service

enriching service

Always internal with full QoS management

Internal if not externally available with right SLA

Preferably internal with light QoS management

Always external (with best SLA available)

Fig. 6. Business service allocation matrix (adapted from [21]).

6   From Business Processes and Services to Digital Platforms

So far, we have discussed the conceptual side of things, i.e., the concepts with the bold, solid boxes in Fig. 1. To go the technical (execution) aspect (the bold, dashed boxes in Fig. 1, we need to take a look at an architecture for distributed business execution platforms. To have an architecture model that covers our complete story, we use the reference architecture of the BASE/X approach [10]. It is shown in Fig. 7. The architecture is organized along the same four levels as the BASE/X business modeling structure shown in Fig. 2.

The technical elements in the conceptual model of Fig. 1 are the service orchestration platform and the service execution platform. These coincide with the business process management system (BPMS) respectively the managed service platform (MSP) in Fig. 7. The BPMS is complemented with a service mash-up platform (Mash, which is not so relevant for this paper) and a database management system (DBMS) that manages the SC-level process data for the BPMS in an operational data store (ODS, typically a relational DBMS). The MSP manages the internal business services but is connected by an enterprise service bus (ESB) bridge to external business services that are offered by partners in a business model, such that they can be orchestrated by the BPMS. Likewise, internal business services can be orchestrated by a BPMS of a partner in the case that this partner is the orchestrator of the business model (as in the BMR concept discussed in Sect. 4).

At the business model (BM) level, we see a (business model execution) dashboard, a tactical decision support system (DSS), a tactical data warehouse (T-DW) and the tactical ETL logic that loads data from the ODS and external data sources into the T-DW. These facilities accommodate the (re)design of business models and cater for the tactical design loop in Fig. 2. This loop is supported by a 'data loop' in the architecture that includes the ESB. A similar structure exists at the business strategy (S) level – this

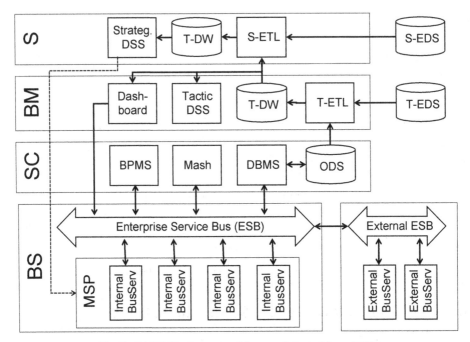

Fig. 7. BASE/X reference architecture (adapted from [10]).

structure supports the strategic design loop in Fig. 2. The tactical design loop is executed relatively frequently to support business agility (the need for which we have addressed in the introduction of this paper) and should preferably have full system support, including direct online reconfiguration of service compositions from the tactical dashboard. The strategic design loop is executed less frequently and hence, full system support is not always needed: reconfiguration of business services can be performed on a more offline, manual basis (hence, the feedback flow in the strategic loop is shown dashed in Fig. 7).

7   A Decade-and-a-Half of Experience

In the previous sections, we have outline our approach to integrating networked business models, business processes and information systems, as it has been elaborated in the past decade-and-a-half. In this section, we turn our attention to our experiences with the application of this approach in more or less the same period. As the initial development of BASE/X was financed by and executed in close collaboration with industry, the experiences could start early in the development process. Below, we first present the experiences with the conceptual side of our approach, then with the technical side.

7.1 Using the Conceptual Side of the Approach

We discuss our experience with the conceptual side of our approach (represented by the bold, solid boxes in Fig. 1 per level: business models, service compositions (business processes), and business services.

We can report success with the application of the networked business model concept and the corresponding business model radar (BMR) technique: they have been applied in many cases, covering many domains. For example, we have experience with some 15 application contexts resulting in 21 business models in only the smart mobility domain in the period 2015–2018 [27]. Other domains in which the BMR has been applied cover smart manufacturing, automotive, healthcare, agriculture, and even motorsports, among others. Cases have been elaborated with the BMR for research, teaching and commercial services. This often happened in a business model ideation phase of business (re)design using interactive workshops with stakeholders. The BMR approach and technique have been evaluated positively in general, often informally but with a more formal evaluation in the smart mobility domain [27]. The intuitive approach of the BMR technique has contributed to the positive reception. We have some experience with the structured evaluation of the viability of business models [8].

We have experience with the elaboration of service compositions from business models, but mostly in a research context [22]. In some cases, this could build on direct input from business practice, e.g., in the car leasing domain [15]. In doing so, we have not always followed the method presented in Sect. 4, for the simple reason that it was not yet available at the time. In the academic research and education domain (i.e., in designing the operational structure of an academic institute), we have developed a set of simple business process models from business models with practitioners. Developing full service compositions is a task, however, that takes considerable effort and preferably requires the availability of a business service catalog – which is not trivial, as outlined below.

We have elaborated several business service catalogs in research [3], sometimes with direct input from practice, e.g., in the car leasing domain [15]. We have not always used the method presented in Sect. 5, again for the simple reason that it was not yet available at the time, so needed to work more intuitively. The definition of well-structured and complete catalogs of business services in a practical business context has proven hard. Many business professionals are not used to think in terms of modular business services, despite the fact that they often acknowledge the value of the concept to drive business agility. An important aspect is the selection of the appropriate aggregation level of business services in terms of functionality: if business services are too large, agility is hampered; if business services are too small, the complexity of service compositions becomes too great. This issue is analogous to the question about the level of modularity in (physical) systems engineering, where an optimum level of modularity is found to stimulate innovativeness [14]. Even though we have both a formal method available for business service identification and design [3] and a more practice-oriented set of criteria for identifying business services [11, choosing the optimal granularity of business services remains a hard task.

7.2 Using the Technical Side of the Approach

We discuss our experience with the technical aspect of our approach (represented by the two bold, dashed boxes in Fig. 1) in a more general sense, as the two individual elements in isolation do not make much sense in an application scenario. Hence, we take the architecture of Fig. 7 as a starting point here.

It has turned out hard to map the BASE/X reference architecture of Fig. 7 to information system landscapes in business practice. We can identify two main reasons for this from the architectural point of view. Firstly, applying the reference architecture cannot easily be done in a stepwise fashion: to use the BASE/X approach in a full-blown way, a substantial part of the reference architecture needs to be covered in an initial development step. This is obviously quite a threshold to step over in practice – and something we have probably underestimated at the very beginning of the development of the approach. The question remains whether it is practically possible to make a major business paradigm switch (in our case to networked, service-dominant business) without a major business systems overhaul. Secondly, our approach is built on flexibly composing business services, which requires a high level of modularization in digital business support. In a business world in which networked business is usually supported by interconnecting large, off-the-shelve commercial enterprise systems (like ERP and CRM systems), there is not so much room for the required level of modularization. Consequently, we cannot report on any full-blown implementation of the architecture in Fig. 7.

For the design and evaluation of business models, several digital prototype tools have been developed, which are in the scope of the BM layer of Fig. 7. An example is a tool for the concretization of the value model designed in a BMR [8]. A prototype of a business service catalog tool was also developed in collaboration with industry, which fits in the BS layer of Fig. 7. These prototype tools all have a stand-alone character from a technical point of view: they can be clearly placed in the conceptual landscape of our approach, but have not been technically integrated into a system following the reference architecture of Fig. 7. One of the main reasons for this is the effort required to develop tools with more integration – this fits badly in the scope (and goals) of a research group at a university.

8 Conclusions

In the current economy, we observe a trend that moves from an interest in 'pure products' towards an interest in the value that the use of products brings. One can think for example of the development of shared resource business models and ecosystems (like B2C car sharing ecosystems and B2B shared service facilities). This trend often goes under the flag of servitization in business ecosystems [30], i.e., encapsulating resources in value-producing services, and sometimes even under the flag of outcome-based models [5, 12, 18], i.e., focusing on the value of services in terms of customer KPIs. The trends of growing complexity and dynamicity of markets has only become stronger since the start of the research reported in this paper. From these observations, the relevance of a framework like BASE/X appears to have only grown.

Nevertheless, a framework like BASE/X requires a different approach on all the levels that we have discussed in this paper: it requires a business paradigm shift. This approach does not align easily with the standard (or even legacy) approach found in most existing business organizations. The alignment for a holistic approach like BASE/X is also hard because it entails both business-oriented and technology-oriented aspects. Consequently, two types of audience have to be convinced at the same time. Other integrated frameworks that address business and technology aspects have also shown problems with widespread adoption, like the ebXML case [20]. Approaches that can be labeled as 'stand-alone' and address an element in an overall spectrum, like the business model canvas [19], have shown greater success in attracting widespread attention and adoption.

In practice, we see business (and also non-profit) organizations struggling with adapting to changing market conditions. Often, this is caused by a traditional business paradigm that is woven through all levels of both the organization and its digital infrastructure – a paradigm that hence is very hard to substantially modify or even completely replace with a new one. From this point of view, the approach presented in this paper is rather abstract, as it does not connect to a specific business domain. In current work on outcome management as a way to support value-driven business [12], we try and stay closer to specific domains to avoid this 'abstraction gap' – both in terms of concepts and digital system landscapes.

Nevertheless, the networked business model concept and the BMR technique as discussed in Sect. 4 remain popular to this date and are used frequently in our research ecosystem and around, both for research purposes and for business model ideation in practice. Sessions with the BMR often lead to valuable insights for the involved stakeholders, certainly where ecosystems are complex. Implementing the conceived business models in full in practice with digital support, however, remains a big step that is not easy to take.

Acknowledgments. All colleagues and students are thanked that have contributed through the years to the development of the BASE/X approach and related methods and techniques.

Disclosure of Interests.   The author has no competing interests to declare that are relevant to the content of this article.

References

1. van der Aalst, W.: Loosely coupled interorganizational workflows: modeling and analyzing workflows crossing organizational boundaries. Inf. Manag. **37**(2), 67–75 (2000). https://doi.org/10.1016/S0378-7206(99)00038-5
2. Adali, O.E., et al.: A multi-concern method for identifying business services: a situational method engineering study. In: Enterprise, Business-Process and Information Systems Modeling. Springer (2020). https://doi.org/10.1007/978-3-030-49418-6_15
3. Adali, O.E.: Transformation of value propositions into resource re-configurations through the business services paradigm. PhD Thesis. Eindhoven University of Technology (2021)
4. Berkers, F.: Realizing digital platform business strategy through design requirements for business models. PhD Thesis. Eindhoven University of Technology (2023)
5. Connerty, M., Navales, E., Kenney, C., Bhatia T.: Manufacturing companies need to sell outcomes, not products. Harvard Business Review (2016)

6. Dalpiaz, F., Franch, X., Horkoff, J.: iStar 2.0 Language Guide. CoRR, abs/1605.0 (2016). http://arxiv.org/abs/1605.07767

7. Gereffi, G., Lee, J.: Why the world suddenly cares about global supply chains. Supply Chain Manag. **48**(3), 24–32 (2012). https://doi.org/10.1111/j.1745-493X.2012.03271.x

8. Gilsing, R.: Supporting service-dominant business model evaluation in the context of business model innovation. PhD Thesis. Eindhoven University of Technology (2020)

9. Gilsing, R., et al.: Defining business model key performance indicators using intentional linguistic summaries. Softw. Syst. Model. **20**, 965–996 (2021). https://doi.org/10.1007/s10 270-021-00894-x

10. Grefen, P., Lüftenegger, E., van der Linden, E., Weisleder, C.: BASE/X - business agility through cross-organizational service engineering. Beta WP414, Eindhoven University of Technology (2013)

11. Grefen, P.: Service-Dominant Business Engineering with BASE/X: Business Modeling Handbook. Amazon CreateSpace, North Charleston (2015)

12. Grefen, P., et al.: Towards customer outcome management in smart manufacturing. Machines **11**, 636 (2023). https://doi.org/10.3390/machines11060636

13. Jiang, Y., Xiao, N., Zhang, Y., Zhang, L.: A novel flexible activity refinement approach for improving workflow process flexibility. Comput. Ind. **80**, 1–15 (2016). https://doi.org/10.1016/j.compind.2016.03.002

14. Lau, A., Yam, R., Tang, E.: The impact of product modularity on new product performance: mediation by product innovativeness. Prod. Innov. Manag. **28**(2), 270–284 (2011). https://doi.org/10.1111/j.1540-5885.2011.00796.x

15. Lüftenegger, E.: Service-dominant business design. PhD Thesis. Eindhoven University of Technology (2014)

16. Lüftenegger, E., Comuzzi, M., Grefen, P.: Designing a tool for service-dominant strategies using action design research. Serv. Bus. **11**, 161–189 (2017). https://doi.org/10.1007/s11628-015-0297-7

17. Lusch, R., Vargo, S., O'Brien, M.: Competing through service: insights from service-dominant logic. Retailing **83**(1), 5–18 (2007)

18. Ng, I., Xin Ding, D., Yip, N.: Outcome-based contracts as new business model: the role of partnership and value-driven relational assets. Ind. Mark. Manage. **42**(5), 730–743 (2013). https://doi.org/10.1016/j.indmarman.2013.05.009

19. Osterwalder, A., Pigneur, Y.: Business Model Generation. Wiley, Hoboken (2010)

20. Rebstock, M., Fengel, J., Paulheim, H.: Ontologies-Based Business Integration. Springer, Cham (2008)

21. Suratno, B., Ozkan, B., Turetken, O., Grefen, P.: A method for operationalizing service-dominant business models into conceptual process models. In: Business Modeling and Software Design. Springer (2018).https://doi.org/10.1007/978-3-319-94214-8_9

22. Suratno, B.: A method for operationalizing service-dominant business models. PhD Thesis. Eindhoven University of Technology (2020)

23. Tallman, S., Luo, Y., Buckley, P.: Business models in global competition. Glob. Strateg. J. **8**(4), 517–535 (2018). https://doi.org/10.1002/gsj.1165

24. Tax, S., McCutcheon, D., Wilkinson, I.: The service delivery network (SDN): a customer-centric perspective of the customer journey. Bus. Manag. **16**(4), 454–470 (2013). https://doi.org/10.1177/1094670513481108

25. Tiihonen, J., Felfernig, A.: An introduction to personalization and mass customization. Intell. Inf. Syst. **49**, 1–7 (2017). https://doi.org/10.1007/s10844-017-0465-4

26. Turetken, O., Grefen, P.: Designing service-dominant business models. In: 25th European Conference on Information Systems, pp. 2218–2233 (2017). https://aisel.aisnet.org/ecis2017_rp/141/

27. Turetken, O., Grefen, P., Gilsing, R., Adali, O.E.: Service-dominant business model design for digital innovation in smart mobility. Bus. Inf. Syst. Eng. **61**, 9–29 (2019). https://doi.org/10.1007/s12599-018-0565-x
28. Vargo, S., Lusch, R.: Evolving to a new dominant logic for marketing. Marketing **68**(1), 1–17 (2004)
29. Yu, E.: Modelling strategic relationships for process reengineering. Univ. Toronto (1995). https://doi.org/10.1007/11603412
30. Zhang, K., et al.: Servitization in business ecosystem: a systematic review and implications for business-to-business servitization research. Technol. Anal. Strateg. Manag. **35**(11), 1480–1496 (2021). https://doi.org/10.1080/09537325.2021.2010698

Processes and Human-in-the-loop

Using Eye-Tracking to Detect Search and Inference During Process Model Comprehension

Amine Abbad-Andaloussi[1(✉)], Clemens Schreiber[2], and Barbara Weber[1]

[1] University of St. Gallen, St. Gallen, Switzerland
{amine.abbad-andaloussi,barbara.weber}@unisg.ch
[2] Karlsruhe Institute of Technology, Karlsruhe, Germany
clemens.schreiber@kit.edu

Abstract. Understanding process models involves different cognitive processes. These processes typically manifest in users' visual behavior and thus can be captured using eye-tracking. In this paper, we focus on the detection of two very essential behaviors: information search and inference. Using a set of eye-tracking features allowing to discern these two behaviors, we train several machine learning (ML) models to predict whether the user is involved in a search phase or an inference one. Following a cross-validation approach inspired by the leave-one-out method, our ML models attain 85% precision, 82% recall, and an F1 score of 80%. The outcome of this work enables the creation of novel adaptive systems, detecting whether the user is involved in a search or inference phase and accordingly providing adequate support. Moreover, it opens up new opportunities to better understand how different process model, tool, user and task-related factors affect users' search and inference behaviors.

Keywords: Process model comprehension · Eye-tracking · Search behavior · Inference behavior · Machine learning

1 Introduction

Comprehending process models is essential for performing a wide range of technical and managerial activities [14,44]. For the former, tasks such as maintenance, process redesign, and enhancement rely heavily on the ability to understand the existing models [44]. On the managerial side, understanding these models is vital for eliciting requirements and enhancing communication between IT professionals and domain specialists [14,23]. With the rapid pace at which processes nowadays have to change to cope with evolving users' needs, modelers must maintain a comprehensive understanding of existing process models to effectively enhance their capabilities. Additionally, although process models can be created automatically through techniques such as process mining [36] or generative artificial intelligence (AI) [13], the need to understand these automatically generated models and to ensure their correctness is still crucial.

© The Author(s), under exclusive license to Springer Nature Switzerland AG 2025
M. Comuzzi et al. (Eds.): CoopIS 2024, LNCS 15506, pp. 21–38, 2025.
https://doi.org/10.1007/978-3-031-81375-7_2

The literature on process model comprehension can be divided into two streams. The former covers studies investigating the factors influencing the understanding of process models (e.g., [1,6,10,27,31,33,34,39,43,44]), while the latter proposes approaches designed to support the comprehension of these models (e.g., [8,24,32,40]). Our work extends this research stream by laying the foundations for novel adaptive systems that provide context-specific support to users in real-time. Specifically, we focus on the detection of two distinct behavioral phases during process model comprehension: *search* and *inference*. Search denotes the identification and separation of relevant from non-relevant information [41], while inference refers to the creative process of deriving new knowledge following the recognition of task-relevant information [25]. Providing context-specific support during process comprehension tasks depends highly on the behavioral phase a user is involved in. For information search, the user may need extra guidance towards the information relevant to solving the task at hand, whereas for inference processes, showing relevant concepts and additional contextual information would be more beneficial.

To detect search and inference, we train new machine learning (ML) models and evaluate their ability to distinguish these two behaviors. Our first research question can be formulated as follows *RQ1. To what extent can we detect users' search and inference behaviors from eye-tracking data during process model comprehension tasks?* Subsequently, we investigate the importance of each of the used eye-tracking measures in estimating users' behavior by answering the following research question *RQ2. What eye-tracking features are important for inferring users' search and inference behaviors?* Our ML models form the core component of adaptive systems that can support users in real-time. Therefore, the training and evaluation of these models, including the investigation of the most predictive features denote the primary focus of this paper.

In a nutshell, throughout this work, we conduct an eye-tracking study where we instruct participants to perform search and inference in a specific order during comprehension tasks. Such an approach provides us with the ground truth denoting phases where users are either conducting search or inference. This ground truth (i.e., serving as labels) is used together with the collected eye-tracking measures (i.e., serving as features) in the training of our ML models following a supervised ML approach. Then, to evaluate our ML models' capability to detect search and inference, we use a special cross-validation approach inspired by the leave-one-out method. Therein, the ML models are tested with eye-tracking data from participants and tasks not previously used in the training set. As a result, our ML models attain 85% precision, 82% recall and a 80% F1 score. Moreover, our findings demonstrate a trade-off between the performance of the ML models and the window length at which the selected eye-tracking features are computed.

Our work has diverse implications in both online and offline settings. In the former, upon the detection of users' search and inference behavioral phases, context-adaptive systems can react in real-time to provide targeted support to users based on the phase they are involved in. In the latter, detecting users' search and inference phases can help to delve deeper into their characteristics and studying how different model, task, user and tool-related factors affect these behavioral phases. The remainder of this paper is structured as follows. Section 2 and Sect. 3 introduce the background and related work respectively. Sect. 4 explains our research method. Section 5 and Sect. 6 present and discuss the findings respectively. Section 7 summarizes this work and sets the path for future research.

2 Background

This section describes the theoretical underpinnings relevant to our study. Section 2.1 presents the theories underlying search and inference behaviors respectively. Section 2.2 introduces eye-tracking and presents the measures allowing to differentiate search and inference behaviors.

2.1 Search and Inference

Search and *inference* manifest with distinct behaviors during comprehension tasks [24]. Search involves distinguishing relevant from irrelevant information [41]. In process comprehension, this translates into identifying activities in the process model that are either *task-relevant* or *task-irrelevant* [31]. Search activities consume valuable resources including time and cognitive effort. Thus, users typically cease once they believe they have acquired sufficient information to complete the given task [11]. In tasks involving process model comprehension, this means a user will stop the search process once they identify all the task-relevant process activities, assuming that these activities are clearly identifiable in the process model [11]. *Cognitive stopping rules* [12] are typically used in this context by users to evaluate the sufficiency of collected information and upon that decide when to stop the search. For tasks that are structured and can be broken down into parts, users commonly rely on a particular stopping rule known as *mental lists* [11]. This rule consists of maintaining a mental checklist of necessary elements that must be located before ending the search [12]. For instance, when a user is asked to determine how some activities within the process model interconnect, then relying on this stopping rule implies holding a mental list of the activities that must be identified in the model before investigating how they interconnect. Once this list of activities is identified, the search phase is complete.

Inference involves generating new insights through the creative process of interpreting the identified relevant information [25]. This process is closely linked to reasoning, where the integration of newly extracted information with pre-existing knowledge takes place [24].

Search and inference have been explored within various cognitive frameworks. For example, Kim et al. [24] identified *perceptual* and *conceptual* processes as two main processes involved in understanding diagrammatic representations such as graphical models. The perceptual process (related to information search) focuses on the search and recognition of pertinent information, whereas the conceptual process (related to inference) is concerned with reasoning and the derivation of insights from the models. Similarly, according to multimedia learning theory [28], after relevant information is selected during the search phase, it is organized and integrated with existing knowledge in the inference phase.

Our study aims at discerning search and inference using the eye-tracking measures that will be introduced in Sect. 2.2. Throughout the design and execution of our study, we formulate our experiment tasks in such a way that the task-relevant information can be clearly recognized in the process models. Also, we instruct our participants to continue with search until they have found all task-relevant information to foster the mental list stopping rule [12]. These design decisions are meant to facilitate the separation between search and inference behavioral phases in the users' data as will be explained in Sects. 4.1 and 4.2.

2.2 Using Eye-Tracking to Detect Search and Inference Behaviors

Eye-tracking has many applications. Notably, it allows detecting visual and behavioral patterns, which might otherwise, not be clear based on verbal protocols [22]. In the field of process modeling, eye-tracking is well-established as it has been successfully used in numerous studies investigating different aspects associated with users' visual behavior (e.g., [3, 10, 15, 19, 32, 34, 35, 37, 42]). Among the popular eye-tracking concepts referred to in this field are: *fixations, saccades, areas of interest (AOI)* and *scan-paths*.

A fixation occurs during an interval characterized by eye movements of very low velocity, indicating that the pupil is still on a particular point within the visual field [22]. A saccade refers to rapid eye movements that indicate the pupil is transitioning from one position (i.e., a fixation) to another within the visual field [22]. Areas of interest can be defined in a stimulus (e.g., process model), to analyze how often a specific area (e.g., a process model activity) is entered, left and revisited [22]. Lastly, a scan-path denotes a sequence of fixations or visits to AOIs, reflecting the visual path followed by the user when engaging with an artifact (e.g., a process model) [22].

The literature comprises a number of eye-tracking measures that can be used to differentiate search and inference behaviors. The *average fixations duration* calculates the mean duration of fixations within a specified time frame [22]. This measure is typically lower during information screening and scanning as part of a search process, than when performing mental processing as part of an inference process [22]. In [17], Glöckner et al. assigned fixed thresholds to *short fixations* (of duration < 250 ms) and *long fixations* (of duration >= 500 ms) to differentiate superficial processing common in information search from deep mental processing associated with inference processes. Accordingly, authors in the literature have split their fixations into short and long (following Glöckner thresholds) to study the underlying cognitive processes [37].

Besides fixations, saccades can also provide interesting insights allowing to differentiate search and inference behaviors. The *average saccade amplitude* calculates the mean distance that saccades cover over a specific time frame [22]. This measure tends to decrease when users are deeply engaged in a thorough inspection of an object [22].

Scan-path precision is another key measure distinguishing between search and inference behaviors. It calculates a ratio that divides the number of fixations landing on the task-relevant AOIs (e.g., process model activities) over the total number of fixations on the entire artifact [31]. Scan-path precision reveals the degree to which users concentrate on task-relevant activities [31]. During the search phase, users are engaged in identifying the task-relevant activities from a broader array of irrelevant ones. Consequently, their fixations may land on both relevant and irrelevant activities of the process model, which results in a lower scan-path precision ratio. In contrast, after identifying all relevant activities, users tend to focus exclusively on this set of activities, during the inference phase. This, in turn, leads to significantly higher scan-path precision.

Following these theoretical underpinnings, we use the average fixation duration, proportions of short and long fixations (to all fixations), average saccade amplitude and scan-path precision computed over specific time windows to differentiate search and inference behaviors in our eye-tracking data (cf. Section 4.3).

3   Related Work

In the literature, several authors have investigated users' behavior to understand the strengths and pitfalls associated with different process model representations (e.g., [1,6,10,31,39,43]) and task types (e.g., [27,33,35,44]). As a result, a number of insights (e.g., [10,33,35]), guidelines (e.g., [31,43]) and frameworks (e.g., [1,27,39, 44]) have emerged within this research stream, notably on users' reading strategies [31], visual routines [39], attention distribution [6,31], cognitive integration [10] and task performance [27,33,35]. In turn, another stream of research focusing on developing techniques to support process model comprehension has emerged (e.g., [8,24,32,40]). Our study fits within this latter stream of research. In this vein, for instance, Kim et al. [24] showed that both perceptual and conceptual integration processes (related to search and inference respectively, cf. Sect. 2.1) can be facilitated by visual cues and contextual information. Visual cues are applied to emphasize the relation between the elements in different diagrams, and contextual information provides a general overview of the dependencies between multiple diagrams within a system. Another support mechanism, also based on visual cues, was tested by Winter et al. [40]. In their study, novices were provided with visual guidance based on experts' eye movements recorded while they were engaging with process models. In this way, the novices' attention was guided toward the relevant areas of the process models which affected positively their comprehension of the models at hand. From a task-perspective, Petrusel et al. [32] used task-specific visual cues to facilitate process model understanding. The applied visual cues consisted of coloring the task-relevant elements and doing layout adjustments. Both visual cues had a positive impact on task performance. Dynamic visualization techniques such as animations were also investigated for their support in problem-solving tasks involving process models. As shown in a study by Aysolmaz and Reijers [8], applying color transformations to indicate the status-changes of activities contributes to a better comprehension of process models.

As mentioned in Sect. 1, our work extends the existing research on supporting the comprehension of process models by establishing the basis for novel adaptive systems that can provide context-specific support based on users' behavior. This foundation is achieved through the development of ML models capable of discerning whether a user is engaged in information search or inference. Once deployed, these models could infer users' behavior and thereby enable more targeted support strategies tailored to fulfil specific user needs.

4   Research Method

4.1   Study Design

Material. The experiment involves a series of *model fragments* that represent various aspects of a logistics process and a collection of *comprehension tasks* designed to prompt participants to engage with these fragments. Since in real-world settings, systems comprise multiple components, which are modeled separately [24], we selected a process model consisting of multiple fragments. Hence, the comprehension tasks could refer to single fragments of the process model or to different fragments. This way, it is possible to observe extensive search behavior since the relevant information for the comprehension tasks could be distributed across multiple fragments. To further emphasize the need for inference, we decided to use the fragment-based modeling approach introduced in [21]. This approach is well suited to model systems, consisting of multiple components. However, in some circumstances, it requires extensive mental effort to infer information distributed over several fragments [34].

In a nutshell, the fragment-based modeling approach [21] uses a subset of the standard BPMN notation [30]. It allows to model separate process fragments, which are implicitly connected by data objects. A data object is always described by its name and its state. If a data object is assigned as an input for a task, this task can only be executed if the data object is in the required state. If a data object is assigned as an output of a task, the task execution leads to a state change of the data object. All possible state changes and their interdependence are additionally depicted in a data-object lifecycle [21].

Using the fragment-based approach, our logistics process is segmented into six process model fragments. These fragments are linked through three data objects, for which the state changes are modeled in their respective life cycles. A portion of this process is illustrated in Fig. 1, while the full process is available in our online appendix[1]. The design of the process fragments adheres to established process modeling guidelines [9,29], ensuring that each fragment has a well-organized layout and a reasonable number of activities and gateways (ranging from two to four parallel or exclusive gateways and six to eight activities). The fragments have overall comparable essential and accidental complexity levels [3,7]. To minimize the influence of specialized domain knowledge, activity names are phrased in layman's terms.

The experimental setup includes eight tasks that ask the participants to examine relationships (such as sequence flow, repetition, exclusiveness, or concurrency) between process activities either located inside the same process model fragment (termed *local tasks*) or distributed over multiple fragments (termed *global tasks*). This design allows the tasks to capture various workflow patterns at both local and global scales, thereby reflecting realistic process model comprehension scenarios. The tasks were presented as statements written based on the template shown in Fig. 2. The participants were asked to evaluate the correctness of these statements considering the process behavior encoded in the model fragments. In the statements, the names of the activities relevant to solving the tasks were put into quote marks to facilitate their recognition in the process model fragments during the search phase (cf. Sect. 2.1). Additionally, to minimize any poten-

---

[1] See https://github.com/aminobest/COOPIS2024BehaviorDetection.

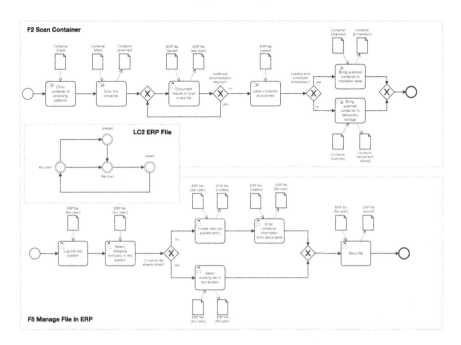

Fig. 1. A fraction of the process model used in the experiment (i.e., designed using the fragmented-based approach [21]). **The complete model and a high-resolution version of this figure can be accessed in our online appendix**[1].

tial learning effects, each task was designed to focus on different aspects of the model fragments used. The materials deployed in our experiment are available online[1].

Participants. The experiment covered 46 participants (22 from the University of St Gallen, 17 from Karlsruhe Institute of Technology, 4 from the research institute Forschungszentrum für Informatik FZI in Karlsruhe and 3 from Promatis i.e., a German IT company). The participants ranged in age from 20 to 50 years, with the majority (63%) falling within the 20–30 age bracket. They came from diverse backgrounds: 22 were engaged in academic research, 17 were students at various stages of their bachelor's and master's degree programs, and 7 worked in the IT industry. Regarding their familiarity with BPMN, as rated on a scale from 1 (unfamiliar) to 7 (very familiar), 48% of the participants reported high familiarity (scores of 5 to 7), while 42% indicated low familiarity (scores of 1 to 3). To prepare the participants for the experiment, they were all uniformly trained on the BPMN concepts used in this study and the fragment-based approach. Before beginning the main experiment, their comprehension was assessed using a set of test tasks similar to those they would encounter during the experiment. All of them passed the test tasks. Detailed demographic information about the participants is available in our online appendix[1].

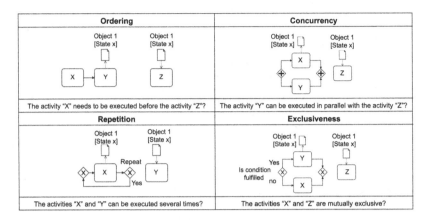

Fig. 2. Task template used in the experiment. **A higher resolution of this figure is available in our online appendix**[1].

4.2 Experiment Procedure

The experiment was conducted in individual eye-tracking lab sessions, each lasting approximately one hour. All participants provided signed consent for their involvement and all collected data was anonymized to ensure no identifiable information could be traced back to the individuals. Initially, a familiarization phase introduced each participant to the relevant BPMN concepts and the fragment-based modeling approach [21]. Following this familiarization, a quiz was administered to assess their understanding of the covered concepts and thus confirm their readiness for the experiment. The participant, then completed screening and demographic forms to respectively ensure their physical ability to participate in an eye-tracking experiment and to gather basic demographic data (e.g., gender, age range, familiarity with the concepts). Before data collection started, each participant was positioned in front of the eye-tracking device. They received instructions on the data collection process, including a directive to minimize head movements, and then underwent device calibration to accurately track their gazes. Each participant was also instructed against forming an overarching understanding of the entire process model (including the six fragments and three life cycles) from the first task. Instead, they were requested to approach each task independently, focusing on identifying task-relevant activities (in the different models) first and then investigating their relationships. This approach was intended to reinforce the use of the mental list stopping rule during the search phase (cf. Section 2.1) by prompting participants to first locate all relevant activities before deducing their connections in the inference phase. The data collection was conducted within the data collection framework EyeMind [4], using the research-grade Tobii Pro X3-120[2] eye-tracker. Therein, each participant was presented with a series of tasks in randomized order. After each task, they were asked to explain their answers and complete a self-assessment questionnaire to evaluate the

---

[2] See https://go.tobii.com/X3UM.

task's perceived difficulty. For the current data analysis, only the eye-tracking data is analyzed.

4.3 Data Analysis

To address RQ1 (cf. Sect. 1) we train and test a set of ML models. Therein, we follow an inductive segmentation approach to differentiate between the search and inference phases in our data. This segmentation serves as a foundation for training our ML models to distinguish these phases effectively. We then assess the performance of these models across various scenarios. Afterward, to address RQ2 (cf. Sect. 1), we examine the extent to which each of the used eye-tracking features contributes to the predictions of the trained ML models.

Data Segmentation Approach (RQ1). An overview of this analysis is illustrated in Fig. 3. ① The process begins by organizing the collected eye-tracking data into distinct trials. Each trial encompasses the data from one participant engaging with a specific task (for example, participant P10 performing task T3, participant P11 performing task T3). ② Next, a specific point, referred to as a cut-mark, is determined within each trial. This cut mark corresponds to the point in time when the participant has located all the task-relevant activities. The cut marks were automatically derived through the automated detection of AOIs (corresponding to process activities in this context) provided by EyeMind [4], along with supplied information about which activities were relevant to each specific task. ③ The trial is then segmented into two parts: the segment before the cut-mark (i.e., Phase 1) and the segment after the cut-mark (i.e., Phase 2). ④ Subsequent to this segmentation, the eye-tracking measures presented in Sect. 2.2 are calculated for each segment. As depicted in Fig. 3, comparisons between Phase 1 and Phase 2 reveal that Phase 1 exhibits shorter average fixation durations, a higher ratio of short fixations, a lower ratio of long fixations, reduced scan-path precision and smaller average saccade amplitudes than Phase 2. ⑤ Using the Wilcoxon signed-rank paired test (which compares paired data without imposing normality requirements), significant statistical differences are confirmed between the measures in Phase 1 and Phase 2. ⑥ Considering these observed trends in the eye-tracking measures, in line with the theoretical foundations introduced in Sect. 2.2, and taking into account the instructions given to the participants (cf. Sect. 4.2), it is reasonable to infer that Phase 1 likely represents search behavior, while Phase 2 represents inference behavior. It is worthwhile to mention that while the inferential statistics validate the assumption that the participants generally followed the given instruction by first conducting search and then inference, there might have been instances where this instruction was not strictly adhered to. This threat to validity is discussed in Sect. 6.

ML Training and Benchmarking (RQ1). This part aims at developing and benchmarking ML models predicting whether the user is conducting search or inference based on the eye-tracking measures introduced in Sect. 2.2. In the context of adaptive systems, a key requirement for these predictions would lie in the ability of the ML models

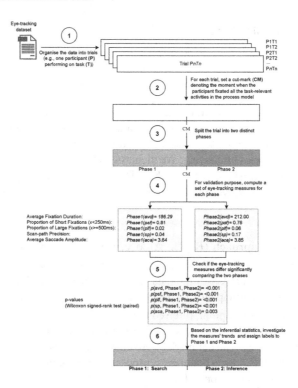

Fig. 3. The inductive segmentation approach. **A higher resolution of this figure is provided in our online appendix**[1].

to infer users' behavior with low latency. In turn, this would enable timed online support depending on whether the user is searching for information or inferring insights from the process models (cf. Sect. 1). To evaluate the extent to which one can go fine-grained in time, while still having good model performance, we train and benchmark our ML models with features (i.e., eye-tracking measures) collected at window intervals ranging from 5 s to 60 s, with an increment of 5 s. Our ML training and benchmarking approach is summarized in Fig. 4. ① Firstly, we segment the data of the search and inference phases into windows with a fixed length (e.g., 5 s). ② Afterwards, for each window, we compute a set of features capturing the average fixation duration, proportion of short fixations and proportion of long fixations, scan-path precision and average saccade amplitude at the level of each window. Then, we assign each window the label of its parent phase (e.g., a window in the search phase will be assigned a *search* label), which is used in the next step to train the machine learning model. ③ Using a supervised learning approach, we train a classifier (i.e., a random forest implementation in Scikit-learn[3] with n_estimators=300 and max_depth=5) to predict the windows labels based on the given eye-tracking features. We choose random forests considering the

---

[3] https://scikit-learn.org/stable/modules/generated/sklearn.ensemble.RandomForest Classifier.html.

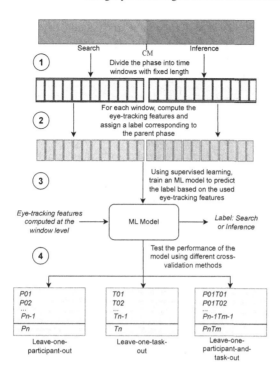

Fig. 4. Model training and testing. **A higher resolution of this figure is available in our online appendix**[1].

enhanced performance of ensemble methods [20] and the ability of random forests to return the importance of each of the features used in their training.

We rely on a cross-validation approach inspired by the leave-one-out method to test and benchmark the performance of our ML Models in different scenarios (i.e., similar to [5,16]). ④ The leave-one-participant-out approach consists of training the model with the data of all participants (in Set P) except one (i.e., $\{P_1...P_{n-1}\} \in P$) of whom the data is used to test the model (i.e., $P_n \in P$). Likewise, the leave-one-task-out approach consists of training the model with the data of all tasks (in Set T) except one (i.e., $\{T_1...T_{n-1}\} \in T$) of which the data is used to test the model (i.e., $T_n \in T$). Lastly, the leave-one-participant-and-task-out approach consists of training model with the data of all participants and all tasks (in Set $P \times T$), except one combination (i.e., $\{P_1T_1...P_{n-1}T_{m_1}\} \in P \times T$), which is used to test the model (i.e., $P_nT_m \in P \times T$). This cross-validation approach allows validating the performance of the model when predicting search and inference behaviors for new participants, new tasks and new participants performing new tasks for which the data were not used in the training of the model. As performance measures, we use precision, recall and F1 score (similar to [16]). The results of our benchmarking showing the performance of our ML models with data segmented in time windows of different lengths (in the range [5 s, 60 s]) are reported in Fig. 5, Sect. 5.

Feature Importance (RQ2). This part aims at studying the extent to which each of the used eye-tracking measures contributes to the predictions of the trained ML models. To this end, we rely on the feature importance metric given by the used random forest implementation[3]. This metric computes the *"Mean Decrease Impurity (MDI)"* which refers to "the total decrease in node impurity [...] averaged over all trees of the ensemble [i.e., the random forest] [38]". We compute the feature importance metric in each cross-validation scenario (i.e., leave-one-participant-out, leave-one-task-out, leave-one-participant-and-task-out) and window length (5 to 60 s). Note that this computation assigns a ratio to each feature (i.e., eye-tracking measure) used in training the model, with these ratios collectively summing up to 1 in each individual analysis (with a different cross-validation scenario and window length). Since the feature importance values do not vary much across the different cross-validation scenarios, we average the values across all the scenarios and plot the aggregated results for each window length (cf. Fig. 6, Sect. 5).

Our full analysis is documented in the Python Notebooks available in our appendix[1].

5 Findings

ML Models' Performance (RQ1). The performance of our ML models considering the different cross-validation scenarios introduced in Sect. 4.3 (i.e., leave-one-participant-out, leave-one-task-out, leave-one-participant-and-task-out) is shown in Fig. 5. For each scenario, the performance measures (i.e., precision, recall and F1 score) are reported over the different applied window sizes.

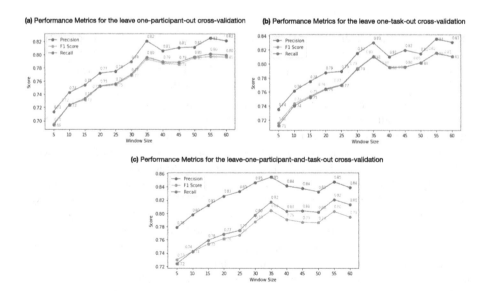

Fig. 5. Performance measures for the different cross-validation scenarios. **A higher resolution of this figure is available in our online appendix**[1].

In all the cross-validation scenarios, there is a consistent trend showing that the performance of the ML models increases until it reaches a peak at a window size of 35 s. At this point, the best performance is observed in the ML model based on the leave-one-participant-and-task-out strategy, achieving a precision of 85%, a recall of 82%, and an F1 score of 80%. The performance metric values in other cross-validation scenarios (i.e., leave-one-participant-out and leave-one-task-out) remain nevertheless similar to one of the leave-one-participant-and-task-out scenario. Following this peak, the performance in terms of precision, recall, and the F1 scores remains relatively steady.

Features' Importance (RQ2). The importance scores of the features used in the training of our ML models are depicted in Fig. 6 together with the different window lengths at which these features were extracted. The scan-path precision is the most predictive feature (average importance ratio: 0.58), followed by the proportion of long fixations (0.17), then the average fixation duration (0.10), the average saccade amplitude (0.08) and finally the proportion of short fixations (0.05). From Fig. 6, it also emerges that generally the obtained importance scores do not vary much when changing the window length. Overall, these results highlight the importance of the scan-path precision and the proportion of long fixations in differentiating the search and inference behaviors in time windows of different lengths.

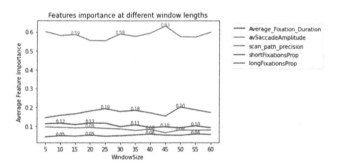

Fig. 6. Features importance at different window lengths. **A higher resolution of this figure is available in our online appendix**[1].

6   Discussion

The results presented in Sect. 5 show that our ML models can classify whether users are involved in a search or inference behavior. The performance, reflected by the precision, recall, and F1 scores, varies with window size. Notably, the 35-second mark reflects the peak point at which these metrics reach 85%, 82% and 80% respectively. Beyond this point, increasing the window size does not enhance the performance significantly (cf. Fig. 5). Therefore, a window size of 35 s can be optimal to reach a good performance when predicting whether a user is engaged in search or inference behavior. If our ML models are integrated into a system designed to detect users' behaviors based on eye-tracking data, for example, it would take at least 35 s to identify a user's behavior reliably. While it is possible to reduce this detection time, doing so would affect the ML model's performance. For instance, reducing the window to 5 s results in a performance of approximately 70% in terms of precision, recall, and F1 scores. This highlights a fundamental trade-off between window size and model performance. Hence, one should weigh the specific needs of their application when selecting the optimal window size and accordingly balance the demand for rapid detection of users' behavior with the necessity for robust predictions.

Regarding the importance of the features computed in the training of our ML models, the scan-path precision and the proportion of long fixations take the lead (cf. Fig. 6). Therefore, they represent the key predictors for search and inference phases during process model comprehension.

Threats to Validity. Our approach underlies a number of assumptions, which may threaten the validity of our study. Particularly, the inductive behavioral analysis explained in Sect. 4.3, assumes a clear cut between search and inference phases in the participants' behavior, such that they are first searching for all the task-relevant activities in the process model fragments and then inferring the answer to the given task. This assumption may not always hold true especially if people intertwine search and inference phases when engaging with process models. As this behavior would result in a more complex inductive data analysis and training of our ML models, we have opted for a simpler experiment design where (1) the tasks are formulated in a way that the relevant activities are marked explicitly in the text (in quotemarks, cf. Sect. 4.1) and (2) the participants are instructed to search for the relevant activities and then infer their relationship (cf. Sect. 4.2). This way, we enforced a clear cut between search and inference phases. Although there is no strict evidence that all the participants followed the given instruction in all tasks, the inferential statistics (cf. Fig. 4) confirm that this pattern was followed to a large extent. At prediction time, our ML models are also expected to provide accurate predictions of the search and inference phases, if the cuts between the two phases are less clear as long as search and inference behavior do not overlap completely. Testing this hypothesis would require a follow-up eye-tracking study, where concurrent think-aloud techniques [22] can be used to triangulate participants' behavior with their insights.

Moreover, not all behavioral patterns associated with search and inference can be captured using our eye-tracking measures. For instance, people tend to fixate empty spaces when coordinating the visual image with their mental model [18]. This behavior can be incorporated within the inference phase as it reflects the process of integrating new information (extracted from the process model) with existing knowledge (as part of the mental model) to derive an answer to the given task (cf. Sect. 2.1). However, the scan-path precision measure would suggest an inconsistent behavior since the fixations will not land on the task-relevant activities and thus the scan-path precision would be relatively low. To capture similar behavior accurately, a more fine-grained analysis is required which can be conducted as part of future work.

Another potential limitation is associated with the labels assigned to the windows at different time granularities. While the inferential tests confirm that the used eye-tracking measures significantly differentiate search and inference phases, these measures were computed at the whole phase level. Moving into time windows with reduced time granularity, we cannot guarantee that the windows are totally free of noise (e.g., partial search behavior in an inference phase). However, we expect this noise to be marginal and thus without significant impact on the goodness of the assigned labels, especially when the windows are large enough. It also remains to be tested, whether our ML models would perform adequately on other test sets, for instance, when users are performing search and inference on process models in other process modeling notations. Our study provides a good basis and starting point for inferring search and inference behaviors but more research is needed to ensure the reliability of our ML models in other settings.

Implications. Addressing the limitations pointed out in this section would enhance the performance of the proposed ML models, opening up a wide array of potential applications. In an online setting, detecting whether users are involved in information search or inference can help to provide timed and targeted support. For instance, the system can accordingly raise the saliency of the task-relevant parts in the process model to support the search process, or provide documentation and explain the relevant concepts to support the inference process. Therein, generative AI and large language models (LLMs) can be used to generate context-specific documentation and explanations. Besides process modeling, such a system can be useful in supporting software development tasks but could also find applications in e-learning platforms to help with information search and the inference of new insights when studying new material. In offline settings, the detection of search and inference behavioral phases can help isolate them and study how they are influenced by different model and tool properties as well as various task types and user profiles. For instance, one can explore how novices and experts differ in their search and inference behavior, or investigate how different model representations (e.g., hybrid models [2]) or tool features (e.g., customized sub-process navigation [26]) affect the speed and accuracy of these behaviors.

7   Conclusion and Future Work

In this paper, we propose a set of ML models using eye-tracking features to differentiate search and inference phases in users' behavior when performing comprehension tasks on process models. The performance indicators demonstrate the ability of our ML models to detect these phases, while the analysis of features' importance suggests that the scan-path precision measure and the proportion of long fixations are the best predictors among the used eye-tracking features.

Following the reflections made in Sect. 6, a follow-up study capturing users' behavior in a more open setting where participants can freely intertwine search and inference phases is deemed important as future work to test our ML models in this different and more realistic environment. Therein, considering also various comprehension tasks and process modeling notations could contribute to more robust ML models. Additionally, by using concurrent think-aloud [22] in the new data collection, we can isolate search and inference phases more clearly and deepen our analysis of the underlying cognitive processes. Another important line of research would be to study the impact of different model, tool, task and users' characteristics on search and inference phases. Our data allows us, particularly, to delve into the impact of task type since our experiment material covers both local and global tasks (cf. Sect. 4.1).

References

1. Abbad-Andaloussi, A.: A framework for enhancing the modeling and comprehension of declarative process models. Ph.D. thesis (2021)
2. Abbad-Andaloussi, A., Burattin, A., Slaats, T., Kindler, E., Weber, B.: On the declarative paradigm in hybrid business process representations: a conceptual framework and a systematic literature study. Inf. Syst. **91**, 101505 (2020)
3. Abbad-Andaloussi, A., Burattin, A., Slaats, T., Kindler, E., Weber, B.: Complexity in declarative process models: metrics and multi-modal assessment of cognitive load. Expert Syst. Appl. **233**, 120924 (2023)
4. Abbad-Andaloussi, A., Lübke, D., Weber, B.: Conducting eye-tracking studies on large and interactive process models using eyemind. SoftwareX **24**, 101564 (2023)
5. Abbad-Andaloussi, A., Soffer, P., Slaats, T., Burattin, A., Weber, B.: The impact of modularization on the understandability of declarative process models: a research model. In: Information Systems and Neuroscience (NeuroIS), Springer (2020)
6. Abbad-Andaloussi, A., Zerbato, F., Burattin, A., Slaats, T., Hildebrandt, T.T., Weber, B.: Exploring how users engage with hybrid process artifacts based on declarative process models: a behavioral analysis based on eye-tracking and think-aloud. Softw. Syst. Model. **20**, 1437–1464 (2021)
7. Antinyan, V.: Evaluating essential and accidental code complexity triggers by practitioners' perception. IEEE Softw. **37**(6), 86–93 (2020)
8. Aysolmaz, B., Reijers, H.A.: Animation as a dynamic visualization technique for improving process model comprehension. Inf. Manage. **58**(5), 103478 (2021)
9. Becker, J., Rosemann, M., Von Uthmann, C.: Guidelines of business process modeling. In: Business Process Management: Models, Techniques, and Empirical Studies, pp. 30–49. Springer (2002)
10. Bera, P., Soffer, P., Parsons, J.: Using eye tracking to expose cognitive processes in understanding conceptual models. MIS Q. **43**(4), 1105–1126 (2019)
11. Browne, G.J., Pitts, M.G.: Stopping rule use during information search in design problems. Organ. Behav. Hum. Decis. Processes **95**(2) (2004)
12. Browne, G.J., Pitts, M.G., Wetherbe, J.C.: Cognitive stopping rules for terminating information search in online tasks. MIS quarterly, pp. 89–104 (2007)
13. van Dun, C., Moder, L., Kratsch, W., Röglinger, M.: Processgan: supporting the creation of business process improvement ideas through generative machine learning. Decis. Support Syst. **165**, 113880 (2023)
14. Figl, K.: Comprehension of procedural visual business process models: a literature review. Bus. Inf. Syst. Eng. **59**, 41–67 (2017)
15. Franceschetti, M., Abbad-Andaloussi, A., Schreiber, C., A. López, H., Weber, B.: Exploring the cognitive effects of ambiguity in process models. In: International Conference on Business Process Management, Springer (2024)
16. Fritz, T., Begel, A., Müller, S.C., Yigit-Elliott, S., Züger, M.: Using psycho-physiological measures to assess task difficulty in software development. In: Proceedings of the 36th International Conference on Software Engineering (2014)
17. Glöckner, A., Herbold, A.K.: Information processing in decisions under risk: evidence for compensatory strategies based on automatic processes. MPI collective goods preprint (2008/42) (2008)

18. Grant, E.R., Spivey, M.J.: Eye movements and problem solving: guiding attention guides thought. Psychol. Sci. **14**(5), 462–466 (2003)
19. Gulden, J., Burattin, A., Andaloussi, A.A., Weber, B.: From analytical purposes to data visualizations: a decision process guided by a conceptual framework and eye tracking. Softw. Syst. Model. **19**, 531–554 (2020)
20. Han, J., Pei, J., Tong, H.: Data Mining: Concepts and Techniques. Morgan Kaufmann (2022)
21. Hewelt, M., Weske, M.: A hybrid approach for flexible case modeling and execution. In: Business Process Management Forum: BPM Forum 2016, Rio de Janeiro, Brazil, 18–22 September 2016, Proceedings 14, pp. 38–54. Springer (2016)
22. Holmqvist, K., Nyström, M., Andersson, R., Dewhurst, R., Jarodzka, H., van de Weijer, J.: Eye Tracking: a comprehensive guide to methods and measures. OUP Oxford (2011)
23. Indulska, M., Green, P., Recker, J., Rosemann, M.: Business process modeling: perceived benefits. In: Conceptual Modeling - ER conference, Springer (2009)
24. Kim, J., Hahn, J., Hahn, H.: How do we understand a system with (so) many diagrams? cognitive integration processes in diagrammatic reasoning. Inf. Syst. Res. **11**(3), 284–303 (2000)
25. Larkin, J.H., Simon, H.A.: Why a diagram is (sometimes) worth ten thousand words. Cogn. Sci. **11**(1), 65–100 (1987)
26. Lübke, D., Ahrens, M.: Towards an experiment for analyzing subprocess navigation in bpmn tooling (2022)
27. Mandelburger, M.M., Mendling, J.: Cognitive diagram understanding and task performance in systems analysis and design. MIS Q. **45**(4), 2101–2157 (2021)
28. Mayer, R.E.: Human nonadversary problem solving. Human and machine problem solving, pp. 39–56 (1989)
29. Mendling, J., Reijers, H.A., van der Aalst, W.M.: Seven process modeling guidelines (7pmg). Inf. Softw. Technol. **52**(2), 127–136 (2010)
30. OMG, O.M.G.: Business process modeling notation v 2.0 (2006). https://www.omg.org/spec/BPMN/2.0/
31. Petrusel, R., Mendling, J.: Eye-tracking the factors of process model comprehension tasks. In: Salinesi, C., Norrie, M.C., Pastor, Ó. (eds.) Advanced Information Systems Engineering, CAiSE Conference (2013)
32. Petrusel, R., Mendling, J., Reijers, H.A.: Task-specific visual cues for improving process model understanding. Inf. Softw. Technol. (2016)
33. Ritchi, H., Jans, M.J., Mendling, J., Reijers, H.A.: The influence of business process representation on performance of different task types. J. Inf. Syst. (2019)
34. Schreiber, C., Abbad-Andaloussi, A., Weber, B.: On the cognitive effects of abstraction and fragmentation in modularized process models. In: Business Process Management: 21st International Conference, BPM 2023, Utrecht, Netherlands, 11–15 September 2023 (2023)
35. Schreiber, C., Abbad-Andaloussi, A., Weber, B.: On the cognitive and behavioral effects of abstraction and fragmentation in modularized process models. Inf. Syst. **125**, 102424 (2024)
36. Van Der Aalst, W.: Process mining: data science in action, vol. 2. Springer (2016)
37. Wang, W., Chen, T., Indulska, M., Sadiq, S., Weber, B.: Business process and rule integration approaches–an empirical analysis of model understanding. Inf. Syst. **104**, 101901 (2022)
38. Wang, Y., Pan, Z., Zheng, J., Qian, L., Li, M.: A hybrid ensemble method for pulsar candidate classification. Astrophys. Space Sci. **364**, 1–13 (2019)
39. Winter, M., Neumann, H., Pryss, R., Probst, T., Reichert, M.: Defining gaze patterns for process model literacy-exploring visual routines in process models with diverse mappings. Expert Syst. Appl. **213**, 119217 (2023)
40. Winter, M., Pryss, R., Probst, T., Reichert, M.: Applying eye movement modeling examples to guide novices' attention in the comprehension of process models. Brain Sci. **11**(1), 72 (2021)

41. Wolfe, J.M.: Guided search 2.0 a revised model of visual search. Psychonomic Bull. Rev. **1**, 202–238 (1994)
42. Zimoch, M., Mohring, T., Pryss, R., Probst, T., Schlee, W., Reichert, M.: Using insights from cognitive neuroscience to investigate the effects of event-driven process chains on process model comprehension. In: International Conference on Business Process Management, pp. 446–459. Springer (2017)
43. Zimoch, M., Pryss, R., Schobel, J., Reichert, M.: Eye tracking experiments on process model comprehension: lessons learned. In: EMMSAD 2017 Essen, Germany, pp. 153–168. Springer (2017)
44. Zugal, S.: Applying cognitive psychology for improving the creation, understanding and maintenance of business process models. Ph.D. thesis, University of Innsbruck (2013)

Conversationally Actionable Process Model Creation

Nataliia Klievtsova[1(✉)], Timotheus Kampik[2], Juergen Mangler[1],
and Stefanie Rinderle-Ma[1]

[1] TUM School of Computation, Information and Technology, Technical University of Munich,
Munich, Germany
{nataliia.klievtsova,juergen.mangler,stefanie.rinderle-ma}@tum.de
[2] SAP Signavio, Berlin, Germany
timotheus.kampik@sap.com

Abstract. With the recent success of large language models, the idea of AI-augmented Business Process Management systems is becoming more feasible. One of their essential characteristics is the ability to be conversationally actionable, allowing humans to interact with the system effectively. However, most current research focuses on single-prompt execution and evaluation of results, rather than on continuous interaction between the user and the system. In this work, we aim to explore the feasibility of using chatbots to empower domain experts in the creation and redesign of process models in an effective and iterative way. In particular, we experiment with the prompt design for a selection of redesign tasks on a collection of process models from literature. The most effective prompt is then selected for the conducted user study with domain experts and process modelers in order to assess the support provided by the chatbot in conversationally creating and redesigning a manufacturing process model. The results from the prompt design experiment and the user study are promising w.r.t. correctness of the models and user satisfaction.

Keywords: Process discovery · Process models · Large language models · Process improvement · Conversations

1 Introduction

Business process modeling is an approach to describe how businesses execute their operations [10] by using graphical constructs to describe and implement the business logic. The utilization of a standardized notation such as Business Process Model and Notation (BPMN 2.0[1]) typically improves operational efficiency, significantly minimizes errors, and enhances communication and collaboration. One of the primary challenges is the extensive training and skill development required for best-practice utilization of BPMN by various stakeholders within an organization, such as domain experts and process designers/modelers. The successful creation of best-practice models [33] can be facilitated either by extensive collaboration between domain experts and modelers, or by investing in training programs for domain experts, so that they can do the modeling themselves.

---

[1] www.omg.org/spec/BPMN/2.0.

© The Author(s), under exclusive license to Springer Nature Switzerland AG 2025
M. Comuzzi et al. (Eds.): CoopIS 2024, LNCS 15506, pp. 39–55, 2025.
https://doi.org/10.1007/978-3-031-81375-7_3

While collaborations help to avoid the implementation of special training programs and ensure that BPMN models are well designed [33], they can also lead to a "dilemma between process modeler and domain expert" as there is no or only limited knowledge overlap between them, i.e., there exists a communication gap. The process modeler lacks specific domain knowledge, while the domain expert may have only limited knowledge of process model notations [28]. The constant need to transfer the domain knowledge to process modelers is especially burdensome for organizations continuously undergoing adaptations caused by internal or external changes, i.e., when business processes need to be designed or redesigned to improve their day-to-day execution performance [7]. Hence, it is crucial to find a simple and effective way to generate, manipulate, and evaluate process models, minimizing the communication effort of domain experts.

Conversational process modeling (CPM) [23] aims to maximize the involvement of domain experts in the creation of process models and hence to minimize the communication effort between domain experts and process modelers [27]. Specifically, CPM refers to the iterative process of creating process models based on process descriptions and conversations between domain experts and chatbots, until the created models reach a certain quality level and become sufficiently mature to fulfill their purpose. This paper advances our previous work on CPM [23,24] by providing an in-depth evaluation of whether domain experts can design and redesign a process model in a conversationally actionable manner, i.e., in interaction with a chatbot instead of a process modeler.

In Sect. 2, we explore the process of process model creation from the perspective of a domain expert by employing Large Language Models (LLMs) as a conversational tool that substitutes the process modeler. Section 3 demonstrates the capabilities of LLMs, such as GPT-4, for model redesign and refinement, in connection with the textual representation of graphical notation of the process model using the JavaScript-based visualization library Mermaid.js. In particular, we experiment with different redesign tasks based on change patterns from literature [39] for finding the most effective prompt design. At this, effectiveness is assessed based on the syntactic and semantic correctness of the resulting process models. Moreover, a user study is conducted to assess the quality of the LLM-redesigned models regarding user satisfaction, model completeness and correctness, layouting and the quality of the selected graphical representation (see Sect. 4). Section 5 discusses related work and Sect. 6 concludes the paper.

2   Conversationally Actionable Process Model Creation

One future direction in business process management is the development of AI-augmented process-aware information systems, i.e., systems that act in an autonomous, adaptive, explainable, and *conversationally actionable* way [9,12]. In the following, we examine the aspect of how to make process models creation conversationally actionable, i.e., allowing domain experts to create and redesign process models interactively in a conversation with the system via a chatbot. To this end, we start with an analysis of the process of process model creation as currently applied and realized as interaction between domain expert and process modeler. We show how this process can be transformed into the conversationally actionable process model creation (CAPMC) approach, based on interaction between domain expert and chatbot.

2.1 Interaction in Process Model Creation

A common issue in process model creation is the complexity of the modeling notation, making it challenging for domain experts, as they possess the knowledge about their application domains and typically lack modeling knowledge [36]. The latter hinders the creation of correct models as well as the analysis of models for errors. This leads to substantial efforts being spent on training domain experts in process modeling, diverting resources away from solving business problems, such as simplifying, enhancing, and optimizing these processes [36].

One typically used remedy strategy is to team up the domain expert with a process modeler who has extensive knowledge on how to create correct process models and typically lacks knowledge about the application domain. The process modeler then creates the process model based on her interpretation of the knowledge provided by the domain experts [22]. The cooperation between a process modeler and a domain expert can be established in multiple ways distinguished by diverse methods of information gathering about a process. According to [13] there are three types of discovery methods, i.e., evidence-based discovery, interview-based discovery, and workshop-based discovery.

In all cases, a process modeler can either play (1) an active role (i.e., direct communication) performing one-on-one interviews with domain experts, or (2) facilitate a series of modeling sessions in which several domain experts come together to negotiate a common view of the global process model [22]. Additionally the process modeler can act (3) as passive observer, studying the evidence to get familiar with certain parts of a process and its environment, and to formulate hypotheses [13]. Direct process modeling interaction (1) is depicted in Fig. 1. Here, the interpretation of the process description and the changes provided by the domain expert are interpreted by the process modeler which might lead to validity errors due to misunderstandings and the modeler being agnostic of the application domain.

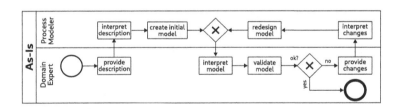

Fig. 1. Interaction between Domain Expert and Process Modeler (1).

2.2 Chatbot vs Process Modeler: Does the Difference Matter?

Process model creation is generally most efficiently conducted when domain knowledge can be accessed immediately by individuals directly involved in the process. This helps reduce the risk that the modeling expert becomes a bottleneck for capturing process knowledge [22].

Natural text-based language is one of the preferred process representations among domain experts, primarily due to lack in experience and knowledge in process modeling [2,26]. Therefore, it is necessary to develop a framework where domain experts can create and iteratively refine a model using natural language, in a human-like conversational manner and without the involvement of a (human) process modeler. This is realized in the Conversational Process Modeling (CPM) framework introduced in our previous work [23]; the core CPM process is depicted in Fig. 2[2]. Task `refine description/model` is a complex task and the underlying sub process defines the iterative interaction between text to model (T2M) transformation performed by a chatbot and model interpretation and its redesign via process description adjustment performed by a domain expert. A process model is created based on a process description and it is reviewed and adjusted multiple times before it is used further. We refer to this iterative and continuous interplay between model generation and its interpretation as *Conversationally Actionable Process Model Creation*, defined in Concept 1.

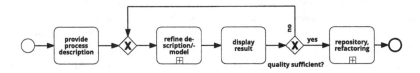

Fig. 2. Conversational Process Modeling, abstracted from [23].

Concept 1 (Conversationally Actionable Process Model Creation). *Conversationally Actionable Process Model Creation (CAPMC) refers to the continuous translation and interpretation of modeling artifacts utilized during the real-time interaction between a chatbot and different stakeholders involved in process design. With real-time we refer here to the immediate, live exchange of messages as in a human-like communication. Under these circumstances, stakeholders interact with the chatbot using domain-specific natural language (**conversationally**), and the chatbot reacts to their requests (**actionable**), translating them into process models (**process model creation**).*

CAPMC, as realized by interactions between domain expert and chatbot is depicted in Fig. 3. Note that according to Concept 1, further stakeholders such as the process modeler can be involved in CAPMC, as well. In this work, we aim at contrasting traditional process model creation with process modeler as depicted in Fig. 1 with CAPMC without process modeler as depicted in Fig. 3. In the latter case, the domain expert provides her knowledge in the form of a process description. Based on the process description, the chatbot creates an initial process model. The model is then interpreted and validated by the domain expert. If the validation fails, changes are provided by the domain expert to the chatbot. The model is then again interpreted and validated by the domain expert. This change and validate cycle is repeated until the model reaches a certain validation quality. Note that for soundness checks of the model, at each point, the process modeler and/or automatic soundness checks can be applied.

We compare CAPMC with chatbot (cf. Fig. 3) to traditional process model creation with process modeler (cf. Fig. 1). Starting with the effort of the domain expert, she is supposed to conduct the same tasks for both approaches, i.e., `interpret model`,

---

[2] We abstract from the tasks referring to storing and refactoring of process models which can be targeted in future work.

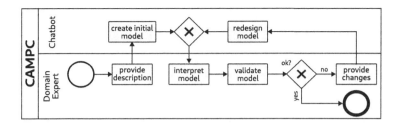

Fig. 3. CAMPC between Domain Expert and Chatbot.

`validate model`, and `interpret model`. Moreover, when modeling without a human process modeler, the domain expert can face several issues such as lack of specialized skills, technical problems handling modeling tools, modeling errors, and as follow intensive time commitment. Furthermore, complexity management and maintenance of the model, communication issues with other participants who rely on the model, as well as the limitations when using BPMN modeling tools (e.g., interoperability, user interface complexity, insufficient functionality, lack of customization, and inadequate technical documentation, etc.) can also lead to problems.

However, the utilization of a chatbot offers advantages at multiple levels that help overcome the limitations mentioned above. First, while a domain expert communicates with the chatbot instead of a process modeler, there tasks `interpret description` and `interpret changes` (cf. Fig. 1) become obsolete, and consequently, additional documentation or conversations to prevent substantial errors and failures are not required [22]. Second, one of the primary challenges, i.e., finding a common language between modeling language and domain-specific natural language [34], is effectively overcome. Third, a direct involvement in process model design encourages a sense of psychological ownership, which has been demonstrated to positively impact not only affective commitment but also the quality of the model [16].

CAPMC with chatbot is expected to only create models that adhere to the syntactic correctness requirements of the used process modeling notation. This prevents the domain expert from introducing syntactic errors and allows her to focus solely on the semantic aspects of process modeling. The domain expert can immediately inspect and interpret a created model. As soon as an error or an inconsistency is detected, the domain expert can promptly refine the model. The advantage of this form of interaction is that the domain expert can interact with the chatbot as frequently as desired, without fear of negative judgment from the chatbot [19]. Since the models are created based on text provided by the domain expert, any occurring errors or mistakes can be considered a part of the learning process, contributing to the development of modeling skills and process thinking. Furthermore, there is evidence that a manual analysis of the created models and the documented interactions between domain expert and chatbot can assist novice analysts in the creation and optimization of these models [38].

3   Model Redesign for LLMs

As depicted in Fig. 3, in CAPMC, the domain expert is interacting with the chatbot where the chatbot serves as interface to an underlying LLM performing tasks `create` `inital model` and `redesign model`. We have provided LLM-based methods for creating process models from text, i.e., process descriptions, in our previous work [23,24]. In the following, we focus on task `redesign model` based on LLMs, i.e., the selection of suitable graphical representations and prompt engineering.

Selection of Graphical Representation: The context window of an LLM refers to the maximum number of tokens that can be put into the model at a time. This number is limited because LLMs are trained with a fixed length of training sequences [20]. Most regular large language models have a context window limit between 1,000 and 8,000 tokens. Due to its complexity, a simple BPMN model with 4 tasks in XML representation might exceed 4,000 to 8,000 tokens [1]. However, most of the information provided in this representation is not specific to the process content, i.e., specifies, for example, the layouting or the boilerplate overhead on diagram and element levels. Therefore, a simplified abstract representation of the BPMN model is required to enable process model generation and direct visualization of the output from an LLM in a user-friendly manner. We select Mermaid.js (MER) as our representation format because it is widely used, well-documented, and yields consistent results during model generation (see Fig. 4). Moreover, Mermaid.js performs well in model creation from text as shown in our previous work in [24].

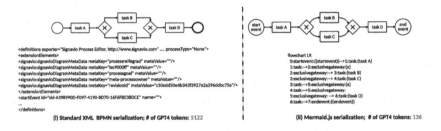

Fig. 4. Business Process represented via BPMN2.0 and Mermaid.js.

Prompt Engineering: The construction of a prompt to guide LLMs in performing a required task in the most efficient way, known as prompt engineering, is typically used to avoid fine-tuning [29]. This approach makes general-purpose LLMs more task-specific [3]. For initial model generation, we utilize the prompt provided in [24], which yields good results in terms of completeness and correctness of the created process model. For model redesign, we adopt the structure of this prompt and create rules defining the desired output format of the redesigned model. Figure 6 depicts the final structure of the prompt for process model redesign. The prompt consists of three parts: [1] provided changes, [2] additional information, and [3] the actual task that should be executed by the LLM. Central for the redesign are the changes provided by the domain expert based on her assessment of the current process model. Change of process models can be represented in different ways, e.g., based on change patterns [39]. CAPMC allows changes to be stated in natural language. Assume, for example, a current process model where tasks A, B, and C form a sequence, and the domain expert states the following change: "task A should be executed in parallel with tasks B and C" (see Fig. 5).

Fig. 5. Model Redesign utilizing Chatbot.

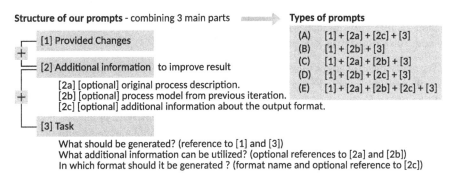

Fig. 6. Prompt Structure and Types of Prompts.

Based on the combination of the elements described in each part in Fig. 6, we developed five prompts[3]. The changes [1], specified by the user for model redesign, and the actual task to be performed by the LLM [3] are included in each prompt. Optional information [2] is inserted in various combinations to explore its influence on the quality of the LLM-generated output.

Prompt Selection: To select the most suitable prompt for model redesign, we define four redesign tasks in natural language as representatives for common change and adaptation patterns (AP), i.e., insertion and deletion of tasks (AP1 and AP2 from [39]) where insertion is further varied into conditional (AP10) and parallel (AP9) insertion. During prompt selection, we focus on these change patterns as the simplest building blocks that enable users to create and redesign process models [40] and because most modeling environments rely on these fundamental operations. In future work, we plan to incorporate more change patterns into.

The prompt selection is then performed in two rounds. First, we apply the synthetic redesign tasks to 7 different process models, ensuring that the redesign tasks are similar for each model regardless of the model complexity and domain (Round 1). Then, we focus on a single process model, adjust the redesign tasks according to its specific description, and apply the best prompts identified from the first round (Round 2). Applying the synthetic redesign tasks to different process models from different domains (Round 1) aims at selecting the most effective prompts for model redesign across different domains providing a broad evaluation. Round 2 is supposed to ensure performance for process model redesign within a more specific context. Moreover, the redesign tasks for Rounds 1 and 2 are designed to be straightforward and uniform serv-

---

[3] https://github.com/com-pot-93/campc/tree/main/prompt_engineering.

ing to create a common ground despite potential differences in phrasing during communication with real domain experts.

Round 1: The following 4 synthetic redesign tasks are utilized for Round 1:

(a) add a task'dummy task 1' after the second task;
(b) delete the third task in the model;
(c) add an alternative branch with the task'dummy task 2' for the second task;
(d) add a task'dummy task 3' parallel to the first task;

We apply these changes to multiple process descriptions to evaluate how effectively these changes are adapted by an LLM[4]. We utilize GPT-4, as currently it is considered one of the leading LLMs. As process descriptions, we utilize examples from the PET dataset [5] describing processes from multiple domains. The processes comprise between 3 and 11 tasks, at least 2 events, exclusive and parallel gateways, and involve 2 or more participants. Figure 7 depicts an "original" process model, e.g., a created process model in a certain iteration of the CAPCM interaction between domain expert and chatbot. Assume that the domain expert assesses the model and notes that a task D is missing after the first task and specifies this as the change shown in Fig. 7 (middle part at the top), using change template example (a) with taks D as dummy task.

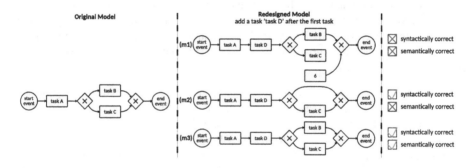

Fig. 7. Syntactic and Semantic Correctness of a Model.

A redesign task is then assessed w.r.t. its *syntactic* and *semantic* correctness where it is assumed that the original model is a valid mermaid.js model according to the Mermaid.js specification[5]. We assume that a redesign task can be applied to a given model, i.e., the preconditions as stated in [35] are fulfilled, e.g., one can only delete a task that exists in the model. A redesign task is considered *syntactically correct* if, after its execution, the newly created model is again a valid mermaid.js and adheres to the predefined output format as specified in the prompt. Moreover, a redesign task is considered *semantically correct* if it fulfills the post-conditions as stated in [35], e.g., tasks are added at the intended position. Moreover, the LLM should not hallucinate w.r.t. change, i.e., create effects that are not specified in the redesign task such as inserting arbitrary

---

[4] https://lmsys.org/blog/2023-06-22-leaderboard/.
[5] https://mermaid.js.org/syntax/flowchart.html.

tasks. In Fig. 7, created model (m1) is syntactically not correct due to node 6 having no incoming edge and semantically not correct as 6 was inserted, but not specified in the redesign task.

We start with checking syntactic correctness of the created model, i.e., verify if the model is valid and check whether its textual notation adheres to the predefined output format[6]. If syntactic correctness is satisfied, we evaluate whether the changes specified in the redesign task were performed correctly by the LLM. We check if the desired element was added, if it was added in the correct position, and if all accompanying attributes were added correctly (i.e., if gateways were also added by parallel tasks or decisions). Additionally, we check if other elements in the model remain unchanged.

During evaluation, prompt A was excluded since its design utilizes only a textual process description and a redesign task as input. This causes complications because, before submitting the output model to the LLM for the next iteration, we need to convert it into a textual description to maintain the modifications made.

Table 1 summarizes the evaluation results. The best results are achieved with prompt B, where all created models are syntactically correct and the application of redesign tasks (a) and (b) achieve also 6 out of 7 semantically correct models. Redesign tasks (c) and (d) result in a low number of semantically correct process models. Prompt C shows the lowest performance, creating a limited number of syntactically correct models in comparison to the other prompts. The greater the number of changes made to the model, the more the current model deviates from the original process description. We suggest that inconsistencies between the original process description and the redesign task result in dubious outcomes. Prompt E also results in syntactically correct models and is obviously less prepared to deal with deleting tasks as Prompt B, though it has the largest amount of additional information. Prompt D creates a limited number of semantically correct models (see Table 1).

Table 1. Prompt Selection Assessment: Round 1 (7 Models).

	Prompt B		Prompt C		Prompt D		Prompt E	
	syntactic	semantic	syntactic	semantic	syntactic	semantic	syntactic	semantic
(a)	7	6	7	6	7	6	7	6
(b)	7	6	7	4	7	5	7	4
(c)	7	2	5	3	6	0	7	3
(d)	7	0	4	0	6	0	7	0
sum	28	14	23	13	26	11	28	13

Generally, we can see that easier redesign tasks (a) and (b) show a better performance than the more sophisticated ones for conditional (c) and parallel insert (d). Most of the semantic errors occur due to a misinterpretation of the redesign task (e.g., the task is inserted in the wrong position, or the wrong task is deleted, or additional task is deleted).

---

[6] https://github.com/com-pot-93/campc/blob/main/prompt_engineering/prompts.txt.

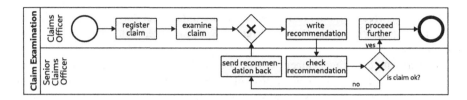

Fig. 8. Claim Handling Process.

Table 2. Prompt Selection Assessment: Round 2 (1 Model).

	Prompt B		Prompt C		Prompt D		Prompt E	
	syntactic	semantic	syntactic	semantic	syntactic	semantic	syntactic	semantic
(a)	1	0	1	0	1	0	1	0
(b)	1	1	1	0	1	1	1	1
(c)	1	0	1	0	1	1	1	1
(d)	1	1	1	1	1	1	1	1
sum	4	2	4	1	4	3	4	3

Round 2: As most of the tasks, are designed in a general manner to be applicable to all use cases, we perform one more round of evaluation of the created models with only one PET example describing a claim examination[7]. The process comprises 6 tasks, 1 decision point, and involves 2 participants (see Fig. 8). This time, the redesign tasks are defined as follows:

(a) add one task "login to the system" after the second task;
(b) delete the first task in the model;
(c) add an alternative branch with the task "claim is examined by senior officer" for the second task;
(d) make examination claim tasks parallel;

Prompt C shows the lowest performance. Also prompt B generates a limited number of semantically correct models (see Table 2). Using prompt B, it is also impossible to achieve the correct syntactic structure of the model, as soon as redesign tasks attempt to integrate elements that were not previously introduced in the model, as it has no access to detailed rules for the desired output format of the model. Both prompt D and E yield same results, even though prompt E requires the largest number of input tokens for to perform the task.

The comparable performance of prompts D and B (only 1 semantically correct model less) and prompts E and C (2 semantically correct models less), indicate that by employing a process model rather than a textual process description as input can result in better outcomes. The ability of prompt B and C to generate a rather high amount

---

[7] Process description: https://github.com/com-pot-93/campc/blob/main/pet_examples/process_descriptions/3_3.txt.

of syntactically correct models without detailed description of the desired output format suggests a creditable self-learning capability of the LLM, enabling redesign of the model solely based on the structure of the input model itself.

The quality of the refined model does not only depend on supplementary information but also on the provided redesign task. Based on two rounds of iterations, it can be seen that it is better to refer to the tasks by their names rather than by their sequence numbers to achieve better results. Also, when adding parallel or alternative branches, it is important to not only define where the branch starts, but also to explicitly mention where the branch should end. Overall, we consider Prompt D as most suitable for the user study.

Limitations: The prompt selection evaluation faces several threats to validity that could affect the generalizability, and fairness of the results. Primarily, the range of BPMN constructs investigated in this work is limited and does not include elements, such as pools, lanes, and specialized gateways. Secondly, the (Round 1) evaluation is conducted on a small dataset of only seven process models, which have a rather simplistic nature. This limitation restricts the ability to generalize findings to more complex and diverse processes. In the (Round 2) evaluation, only one model is used, making it unclear whether performance differences are caused due to the use of activity labels individually for this particular process model or other contextual factors related to the LLM' and prompt's design. Additionally, the prompts themselves may introduce ambiguity due to used formulations. Potential biases in the design of synthetic tasks, combined with a subjective evaluation of correctness, further threaten the validity and overall robustness of the findings.

4   User Study

To reduce the influence of biases and limitations when evaluating the quality of models created and redesigned by LLMs, a survey involving domain experts from the manufacturing sector with extensive knowledge of the selected use case and process modelers, i.e., students and professionals with different modeling backgrounds is conducted. This direct interaction with participants helps to assess the real usability and effectiveness of the chatbot beyond quantitative assessments. Insights into how users perceive and interact with the LLMs to generate content can provide valuable information for further improvements. Participants are asked to create a process model for a use case from manufacturing, utilizing natural language via a conversational user interface. No instructions, tutorials, or additional supplementary materials are given to the participants to avoid influencing their behavior during interaction with the chatbot.

Participant Background: The survey includes 10 participants categorized into domain experts and process modelers. All respondents are familiar with graphical modeling languages such as UML, ER, or BPMN. Process modelers (5 out of 10 respondents) are considered proficient, having applied modeling languages in multiple industry projects, while domain experts are only slightly familiar with modeling languages through books or individual projects.

Use Case: The use case represents a genuine manufacturing process ensuring the automated production and inspection of GV12 valve-lifters to maintain quality standards, with a focus on detecting chip formation on the workpiece surface. A batch of workpieces is automatically produced and inspected to ensure the quality of each produced piece. To facilitate efficient monitoring and decision-making throughout the production cycle the process includes data collection, compression, and analysis.

Conversational Interface: In order to generate the model, we employ the prompt along with one of the textual representations from [23]. To update the model, we utilize the prompt designed and evaluated in Sect. 3. As background LLM, we select GPT-4 due to its superior performance compared to other LLMs. A user interacts with the LLM using natural language, and the LLM returns a model created in the selected representation. It is important to mention that in an integrated prototype during graphical model generation using LLMs out of text, the textual representation of the model is not visible to a user. In the experiment, only flow objects as start and end events, tasks, exclusive and parallel gateways and sequence flows are considered. All respondents create an initial model and subsequently have the opportunity to perform changes in up to 3 iterations to the model. To prevent any influence on the decision making process and behavior of the participants, they are unaware of the limitation of 3 attempts.

User Study Results[8]: To assess the process models created and redesigned by the LLM in interaction between user and chatbot, the participants are presented questions about their satisfaction with the chatbot, the correctness and completeness of the models, labeling and layouting, and visual representation of the model[9]. Since only half of the participants are experienced process modelers, we first aim to investigate whether an association between modeling experience and the level of users' satisfaction exists (see Fig. 9(a)). Both variables are categorical, each comprising five levels (see Fig. 9(c)).

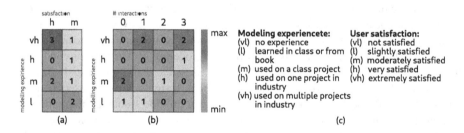

Fig. 9. User Study Results: Modeling Experience, User Satisfaction and # Interactions.

It is expected that individuals with less modeling experience are more likely to be satisfied with the final model, while those with more experience are more likely to express dissatisfaction. However, based on the distribution of satisfaction levels among participants according to their experience we can observe that participants with both low

---

[8] The detailed study results: https://github.com/com-pot-93/campc/tree/main/user_study/study.
[9] https://github.com/com-pot-93/campc/tree/main/user_study.

(l) and high (h) levels of modeling experience achieve a moderate level of satisfaction (m) during chatbot interaction. Meanwhile, individuals with moderate (m) and very high (vh) modeling experience reach both moderate (m) and high (h) levels of satisfaction. Given the limited sample size, no clear relationship between these three variables can be seen. At the same time, there is not enough evidence to definitively say that there is no association between them. Given that 30% of all participants expressed satisfaction with the initial model, another 30% were satisfied with the model obtained after the first redesign, and only 40% engaged in 2 or 3 iterations furthermore, we move forward to investigate the relationship between the level of modeling experience and the number of iterations performed by participants to refine the model (see Fig. 9(b)). We assume that participants with greater modeling experience tend to redesign the model more frequently than those with lower levels of experience.

Generally, we can say that participants with very high (vh) and high (h) experience are more likely to perform more interactions with the chatbot to refine the originally generated model (1 and 3 interactions), while participants with low (l) experience tend to have fewer interactions (0 and 1 interactions). There seems to be a relationship between experience level and the number of interactions, where participants with higher experience tend to communicate with the chatbot more intensively. However, due to the small sample size, these observations should be interpreted cautiously.

General Observations: In general, among the 10 respondents, the lowest level of satisfaction with the final model was *moderate* (m), while the highest level was *very satisfied* (h). 90% of all participants assert that they have obtained a correct model (i.e., consistent with the provided process description), with 70% also claiming that their models are complete (i.e., all the tasks from the provided process description are included in the model). Also, 7 out of 10 respondents confirm that generated models are structurally correct (i.e., consistent with the BPMN 2.0 standard). Only 1 out of 10 respondents mentions to have observed hallucinations, i.e., extra modeling elements provided by LLM that are not included in the process description.

9 out of 10 participants consider the labeling of the final model as appropriate, indicating that task, gateway, and event labels are easily comprehensible. Comparable to model satisfaction, the lowest level of satisfaction with the visual representation of the final model was *moderate* (m), while the highest level was *very satisfied* (h). However, only 60% of all respondents expressed satisfaction with the auto-layouting and with the set of pre-selected BPMN elements (start and end events, tasks, exclusive and parallel gateways, and sequence flow).

Prompting Style: When creating the initial models, 8 out of 10 users provided regular "story-like" text descriptions. Only 2 users attempted to operate with tasks and keywords. Initially proposed redesign tasks referred to the insertion and deletion of tasks, as well as parallel and conditional embedding (i.e., AP1, AP2, AP9, and AP10 change patterns [39]). However, none of the participants involved in model redesign utilized insertion, deletion of tasks, and conditional embedding. They primarily referred to parallelization (A9). In addition to AP9, participants also mentioned change patterns such as the replacement of elements, loop embedding, and changing conditions (AP4, AP8, and AP13 [39]).

The fact that the participants did not utilize simple change patterns may indicate that the LLM can successfully detect atomic modeling elements (tasks) and their sequence in the process. However, it struggles to identify more complex constructs related to the relationships between these elements. The achievement of a relatively high level of satisfaction during model creation, despite the fact that the utilized redesign tasks differ from those defined by participants, indicates that the prompt engineering was successful.

Our synthetic redesign statements were designed in a general manner, referring to the tasks by their sequence numbers. However, all participants found it easier to mention the task labels. This is possibly because the uniqueness of the task labels led to less misunderstanding for humans. During prompt selection, we add only one redesign task per call. It turns out that all participants also use this strategy, focusing on one change at a time. Adding only one redesign task per call seems to help maintain clarity, reduce errors, and simplify debugging.

Limitations: Given the relatively small sample size, the study results should be interpreted with caution. With half of the respondents identified as process modelers and the other half as domain experts, there is a potential impact of response biases or misinterpretation of questions. Moreover, factors like the length and complexity of the survey could impact the involvement and the responses accuracy of respondents. Also, prior user experiences and expectations can influence not only their interaction with the LLM but also their perception of the generated results. Furthermore, the variability caused by the probabilistic nature of the LLM can lead to some issues related to reproducibility (i.e., the results of the user study referring to the quality of the generated models cannot be consistently replicated).

5 Related Work

Several studies address the communication gap between domain experts and process modelers, e.g., [11, 28, 30–32]. They can be distinguished into the following two strategies, i.e., a) developing specific guidelines and recommendations and b) designing specific systems, tools, and notations for the modeling process by b1) requiring the user to adapt to predefined input formats and system rules or b2) enabling users to interact with the system using a familiar way of communication (i.e., natural language). Several works propose (a) recommendations and guidelines for different labeling styles and their use in process modeling practice [30], for changing a process model to a behavior-equivalent and more understandable model [31], and for having more efficient and effective interactions during model development [11]. Examples of approach (b.1) include a computer-based questioning system called "Process Interviewer" [28], BPMN-SBVR business vocabularies and rules converters [32], an interactive tabletop interface with tangible building blocks [22], and the design of simplified BPMN to reduce the difficulty domain experts face in learning and understanding other notations [36]. Approach b.2 can benefit from the shift in Business Process Management caused by the advancements in NLP and GenAI. This shift focuses on intelligent decision-making, NLP, and increased human-computer interaction, transforming classical BPM systems into AI-augmented Business Process Management systems [17]. These systems become conversationally actionable, meaning they can proactively communicate with human agents about process-related actions, goals, and intentions using natural language [12]. This interaction can be enhanced via the integration of intelligent chatbot functions for improved communication within the BPM framework, promoting collaboration [17]. The systems can lead conversations in a multi-turn nature, considering context and incorporating utterances from previous turns to achieve a higher degree of user engagement [9]. Currently, as mentioned in [4, 8, 18, 21, 37], there is an increasing interest in the potential benefits for the entire BPM domain arising from employing LLMs, particularly in process model generation. For instance, [6] proposes extracting process elements and relations using prompts with varying levels of pre-knowledge. In [15], the generation of an entire model with a specific level of abstraction is presented. Additionally, [25] generates complete BPMN models using LLM and POWL (Partially Ordered Workflow Language). [14] utilizes the JSON format to enhance LLMs' ability to generate not only BPMN models, but also Entity-Relationship (ER) and UML class diagrams. However, most existing approaches focus solely on single-time interactions, where the user is able to receive a final artifact from the system, but is not able to adjust it. So far, the multi-turn conversational capabilities of LLMs for process model generation have received little attention and have not yet been thoroughly explored in the Business Process Management domain.

6 Conclusions

In this work, we explore whether LLM-based chatbots can effectively support domain experts during the redesign of process models in continuous interaction via a conversational user interface to overcome the communication gap between domain experts and process modelers. The continuous interaction is based on redesign tasks of the models. To this end, we conducted a prompt design experiment for process model redesign tasks. The selected prompt was then applied in a user study with domain experts and process modelers on a manufacturing process model. It can be seen that the quality of a model redesign is highly dependent not only on a prompt design but also on how the redesign task is described and the complexity of the task itself. 90% of all participants assert that they have produced a correct model, meaning it is consistent with the provided process description. Additionally, 70% of participants claim that their models are complete, including all expected tasks from the process description, and structurally correct, adhering to the BPMN 2.0 standard. Future research will focus on two primary directions. The first will explore multiple change patterns and more complex datasets to address the increasing complexity of real-world scenarios. The second direction will emphasize evaluating and integrating knowledge about user behavior to improve the quality of human-chatbot communication, better meeting the needs of domain experts. Additionally, observing this communication as a learning process for domain experts may help develop their modeling skills and foster *process thinking* through active engagement in process model creation.

References

1. Ali, M., et al.: Tokenizer choice for LLM training: negligible or crucial? arXiv preprint arXiv:2310.08754 (2023)
2. Azevedo, L.G., Rodrigues, R.D.A., Revoredo, K.: BPMN model and text instructions automatic synchronization. In: Enterprise Information System, pp. 484–491 (2018)
3. Bakker, M., et al.: Fine-tuning language models to find agreement among humans with diverse preferences. Adv. Neural. Inf. Process. Syst. **35**, 38176–38189 (2022)
4. Beheshti, Aet al.: ProcessGPT: transforming business process management with GenAI. In: Web Services, pp. 731–739 (2023)
5. Bellan, P., van der Aa, H., Dragoni, M., Ghidini, C., Ponzetto, S.P.: PET: an annotated dataset for process extraction from natural language text tasks. In: Business Process Management Workshops, pp. 315–321 (2022)
6. Bellan, P., Dragoni, M., Ghidini, C.: Extracting business process entities and relations from text using pre-trained language models and in-context learning. In: Enterprise Design, Operations, and Computing, pp. 182–199 (2022)
7. Beverungen, D.: Exploring the interplay of the design and emergence of business processes as organizational routines. Bus. Inf. Syst. Eng. **6**(4), 191–202 (2014)
8. Busch, K., Rochlitzer, A., Sola, D., Leopold, H.: Just tell me: Prompt engineering in business process management. In: Enterprise, Business-Process and Information Systems Modeling, pp. 3–11 (2023)
9. Casciani, A., Bernardi, M.L., Cimitile, M., Marrella, A.: Conversational systems for AI-augmented business process management. In: Research Challenges in Information Science, pp. 183–200 (2024)
10. DaSilva, C.M., Trkman, P.: Business model: what it is and what it is not. Long Range Plan. **47**(6), 379–389 (2014)
11. Doren, A., Markina-Khusid, A., Cotter, M., Dominguez, C.: A practitioner's guide to optimizing the interactions between modelers and domain experts. In: Systems, pp. 1–8 (2019)
12. Dumas, M., et al.: AI-augmented business process management systems: a research manifesto. ACM Trans. Manag. Inf. Syst. **14**, 1–19 (2022)
13. Dumas, M., Rosa, M.L., Mendling, J., Reijers, H.A.: Fundamentals of Business Process Management. Springer, Heidelberg (2013)
14. Fill, H., Fettke, P., Köpke, J.: Conceptual modeling and large language models: impressions from first experiments with chatGPT. Enterp. Model. Inf. Syst. Archit. Int. J. Concept. Model. **18**, 3 (2023)
15. Grohs, M., Abb, L., Elsayed, N., Rehse, J.: Large language models can accomplish business process management tasks. CoRR abs/2307.09923 (2023)
16. Gutschmidt, A., Lantow, B., Hellmanzik, B., Ramforth, B., Wiese, M., Martins, E.: Participatory modeling from a stakeholder perspective: on the influence of collaboration and revisions on psychological ownership and perceived model quality. Softw. Syst. Model. **22**, 1–17 (2022)
17. Hildebrand, D., Rösl, S., Auer, T., Schieder, C.: Next-generation business process management (BPM): a systematic literature review of cognitive computing and improvements in bpm (2024)
18. Jessen, U., Sroka, M., Fahland, D.: Chit-chat or deep talk: prompt engineering for process mining. CoRR abs/2307.09909 (2023)
19. Jieon Lee, D.L., Gil Lee, J.: Influence of rapport and social presence with an AI psychotherapy chatbot on users' self-disclosure. Int. J. Hum.–Comput. Interact. **40**(7), 1620–1631 (2024)

20. Jin, H., et al.: LLM maybe longLM: Self-extend LLM context window without tuning. CoRR abs/2401.01325 (2024)
21. Kampik, T., et al.: Large process models: business process management in the age of generative AI. CoRR (2023)
22. Kannengiesser, U., Oppl, S.: Business processes to touch: engaging domain experts in process modelling, vol. 1418 (2015)
23. Klievtsova, N., Benzin, J., Kampik, T., Mangler, J., Rinderle-Ma, S.: Conversational process modelling: state of the art, applications, and implications in practice. In: Business Process Management Forum, pp. 319–336 (2023)
24. Klievtsova, N., Mangler, J., iik, T., Benzin, J.V., Rinderle-Ma, S.: How can generative AI empower domain experts in creating process models? In: Wirtschaftsinformatik (2024). (accepted)
25. Kourani, H., Berti, A., Schuster, D., van der Aalst, W.M.P.: PromoAI: process modeling with generative AI. ArXiv abs/2403.04327 (2024)
26. Leopold, H., van der Aa, H., Pittke, F., Raffel, M., Mendling, J., Reijers, H.: Searching textual and model-based process descriptions based on a unified data format. Softw. Syst. Model. **18** (04 2019)
27. Leopold, H., Mendling, J., Polyvyanyy, A.: Supporting process model validation through natural language generation. IEEE Trans. Software Eng. **40**(8), 818–840 (2014)
28. Ley, D.: Approximating process knowledge and process thinking: acquiring workflow data by domain experts. In: 2011 IEEE International Conference on Systems, Man, and Cybernetics, pp. 3274–3279 (2011)
29. Liu, P., Yuan, W., Fu, J., Jiang, Z., Hayashi, H., Neubig, G.: Pre-train, prompt, and predict: a systematic survey of prompting methods in natural language processing. ACM CSUR **55**(9) (2023)
30. Mendling, J., Reijers, H., Recker, J.: Activity labeling in process modeling: empirical insights and recommendations. Inf. Syst. **35**(4), 467–482 (2010)
31. Mendling, J., Reijers, H., Aalst, W.: Seven process modeling guidelines (7PMG). Inf. Softw. Technol. **52**, 127–136 (2010)
32. Mickeviciute, E., Butleris, R., Gudas, S., Karciauskas, E.: Transforming BPMN 2.0 business process model into SBVR business vocabulary and rules. Inf. Technol. Control. **46**, 360–371 (2017)
33. Mursyada, A.: The role of business process modeling notation in process improvement: a critical review. Adv. Qual. Res. (2024)
34. Odeh, Y.: BPMN in engineering software requirements: An introductory brief guide. In: International Conference on Information Management and Engineering (2017)
35. Rinderle-Ma, S., Reichert, M., Weber, B.: On the formal semantics of change patterns in process-aware information systems. In: ER, pp. 279–293 (2008)
36. Solís-Martínez, J., Espada, J.P., Pelayo G-Bustelo, B.C., Lovelle, J.M.C.: BPMN MUSIM: approach to improve the domain expert's efficiency in business processes modeling for the generation of specific software applications. Expert Syst. Appl. **41**(4, Part 2), 1864–1874 (2014)
37. Vidgof, M., Bachhofner, S., Mendling, J.: LLMs for business process management: opportunities and challenges. In: BPM Forum, pp. 107–123 (2023)
38. Wang, B., Wang, C., Liang, P., Li, B., Zeng, C.: How LLMs aid in UML modeling: an exploratory study with novice analysts. ArXiv abs/2404.17739 (2024)
39. Weber, B., Reichert, M., Rinderle-Ma, S.: Change patterns and change support features - enhancing flexibility in process-aware information systems. Data Knowl. Eng. **66**(3), 438–466 (2008)
40. Weber, B., Zeitelhofer, S., Pinggera, J., Torres, V., Reichert, M.: How advanced change patterns impact the process of process modeling. CoRR abs/1511.04060 (2015)

Event Log Extraction for Process Mining Using Large Language Models

Vinicius Stein Dani[1(✉)], Marcus Dees[2], Henrik Leopold[3], Kiran Busch[3],
Iris Beerepoot[1], Jan Martijn E. M. van der Werf[1], and Hajo A. Reijers[1]

[1] Utrecht University, Princetonplein 5, 3584 CC Utrecht, The Netherlands
{v.steindani,i.m.beerepoot,h.a.reijers}@uu.nl
[2] Uitvoeringsinstituut Werknemersverzekeringen, Amsterdam, The Netherlands
marcus.dees@uwv.nl
[3] Kühne Logistics University, Großer Grasbrook 17, 20457 Hamburg, Germany
{henrik.leopold,kiran.busch}@the-klu.org

Abstract. Process mining is a discipline that enables organizations to discover and analyze their work processes. A prerequisite for conducting a process mining initiative is the so-called event log, which is not always readily available. In such cases, extracting an event log involves various time-consuming tasks, such as creating tailor-made structured query language (SQL) scripts to extract an event log from a relational database. With this work, we investigate the use of large language models (LLMs) to support event log extraction, particularly by leveraging LLMs ability to produce SQL scripts. In this paper, we report on how effectively an LLM can assist with event log extraction for process mining. Despite the intrinsic non-deterministic nature of LLMs, our results show the potential of future LLM-assisted event log extraction tools, especially when domain and data knowledge are available. The implementation of such tools can increase access to event log extraction to a broader range of users within an organization by reducing the reliance on specialized technical skills for producing relational database query scripts and minimizing manual effort.

Keywords: Process mining · Event log extraction · Relational database · Prompt engineering · Large language model · LLM · Assistance

1 Introduction

Process mning is a discipline that helps organizations to discover and analyze their work processes [2]. A prerequisite for conducting any process mining initiative is the so-called event log, which is not always readily available. When it is not, extracting an event log involves laborious, time-consuming tasks [19]. The event log extraction is particularly challenging when an organization needs to extract event logs for continuously changing purposes. For instance, new demands emerging from various departments can make the replication of event log extraction strategies impractical. In such a situation, new database query scripts must be designed for each demand, which further increases the time needed for event log extraction. As a result, organizations have to wait longer to gain insights from their data.

M. Comuzzi et al. (Eds.): CoopIS 2024, LNCS 15506, pp. 56–72, 2025.
https://doi.org/10.1007/978-3-031-81375-7_4

Large language models (LLMs) emerged as tools capable of analyzing and generating text, offering potential applications in different domains and research fields [11,16,21]. These models have demonstrated capabilities in natural language processing tasks, including text generation, translation, and summarization [25,26]. In the context of process mining, studies have shown the potential and applicability of LLMs [3,12]. For example, in [3] the authors shown the applicability of LLMs to process analysis-related tasks, while in [12] the authors have demonstrated how LLMs can be used for assisting on process modeling tasks. Moreover, different studies experimented with using LLMs to map natural language questions on a given relational database into ready-to-use SQL queries [9]. Considering this, it may be beneficial to use LLMs for event log extraction, what has not been explored before.

With this in mind, we argue that SQL query generation from natural language text using LLMs can potentially reduce the manual effort required for event log extraction. We hypothesize that this automation can streamline the event log extraction process by reducing the dependency on specialized technical skills from business analysts, making event log extraction more accessible to a broader range of users within an organization. Although LLMs are non-deterministic, their flexibility enables a quick adaptation to the continuously changing scenarios of different demands coming from a variety of departments. We argue that as new data-related requirements emerge, these models can quickly generate the appropriate relational database queries for event log extraction without the need for major reprogramming efforts. By integrating LLMs into the event log extraction workflow, having human-computer collaboration, organizations can increase their ability to quickly extract event logs, thereby gaining timely insights and getting more quickly to their decision-making moments based on the discovered process.

Against this background, we develop this work to answer the following research question: *"How effective are LLMs in assisting the event log extraction from relational databases?"* For this purpose, we assess state-of-the-art LLMs' performance against a number of structurally different relational databases and prompt engineering strategies. To do so, we leverage an experimental setup that executes each available prompt against each available database, extracts the LLM-generated SQL script from the LLM response, executes the generated SQL script against the database, and compares the LLM-assisted generated event log against a gold standard, outputting similarity scores by means of precision, recall, and F1-score. Despite the intrinsic non-deterministic nature of LLMs, our results show that LLMs (particularly GPT-4o) can effectively assist in the event log extraction from relational databases when domain and data knowledge are available.

The remainder of this paper is structured as follows. In Sect. 2, we discuss the background of this work. Then, in Sect. 3, we present our experimental setup. In Sect. 4, we report on the acquired results of this work, while in Sect. 5 we provide a discussion and recommendations based on our findings. Finally, Sect. 6 concludes the paper.

2 Background

In this section, we first provide a brief introduction into process mining. Then, we discuss LLMs and prompt engineering strategies.

2.1 Process Mining

Process mining is a discipline that enables organizations to discover and analyze their work processes. This is possible by leveraging the available data in an event log format. In its simplest form, an event log is a comma-separated file containing a list of events with at least the following three attributes: CaseID, ActivityID, and timestamp. The CaseID represents a process instance, i.e., a particular trace of the execution of a process; the ActivityID represents an activity that was performed in the context of a particular trace or multiple traces; and the timestamp represents the exact moment in which an activity was performed [2, 14]. For example, consider Table 1. In this table, we have two cases, A and B, of a purchase-to-pay process. In case A, three activities happened in the following temporal order "Create purchase order", "Receive goods", and "Pay invoice". In case B, there are only two activities: "Create purchase order", and "Pay invoice". In this example, one can see that in case B, the goods were not received, and a root-cause analysis can be conducted to understand whether this is an expected behavior or not.

What is important to note is that extracting such an event log often requires a significant amount of manual effort [19]. It typically involves an iterative process, in which SQL scripts are developed to integrate all required data in the target event log.

2.2 Large Language Models and Prompt Engineering

In recent years we have seen the insurgence of a variety of LLMs. Some are advertised as open-source, without actually sharing training data [10,22]. Others as proprietary, and claim that the data they used to train their models are public, which is not necessarily always the case [8,17,18]. What is a commonality for all widely available –publicly or privately– LLMs, is their intrinsic non-deterministic nature. A number of approaches to improve the effectiveness of LLMs have been produced in the form of prompt engineering strategies. For example, in [23] the authors propose a prompt engineering strategy titled *chain-of-thought*, which breaks down tasks into intermediate steps. In [27],

Table 1. Example event log.

CaseID	ActivityID	Timestamp
A	Create purchase order	2023-10-26 10:17:33
B	Create purchase order	2023-10-27 06:03:19
A	Receive goods	2023-10-29 14:36:01
A	Pay invoice	2023-10-30 19:03:26
B	Pay invoice	2023-11-21 10:14:59

the authors propose a prompt strategy titled *tree-of-thought*, which explores multiple reasoning paths to respond to a prompt, potentially leading to more robust and creative solutions. In [4], the authors introduce the *few-shot examples* prompt strategy, which uses examples of how a desired task should be performed. In addition, in [24] the authors present a prompt engineering strategy titled *persona*, which elicits how to ask an LLM to behave in a certain way (e.g., as a process mining expert) while answering to the input prompt. In this work, we leverage these prompt engineering strategies.

A variety of studies have shown the applicability of LLMs in a number of domains and purposes [5,11,16,21], including SQL script generation [9] and process mining [3,12]. To the best of our knowledge, what has not been explored is the applicability of LLMs in assisting the event log extraction. With this work we provide a robust and methodological assessment of the performance of LLMs in assisting the event log extraction from relational databases.

3 Experimental Setup

In this section, we describe our experimental setup to assess how effective LLMs can be in assisting the event log extraction from relational databases. To this end, in Sect. 3.1, we provide an overview of our approach. In Sect. 3.2, we present the materials used in this work, which are composed by a number of LLMs, databases, prompts, and gold standard event logs. Finally, in Sect. 3.3 we elaborate on the analysis of the results, i.e., the comparison between a gold standard event log and its generated counterpart.

3.1 Overview

Figure 1 depicts the architecture of our experimental setup, which expects the following input objects: (i) an *LLM* to be evaluated; (ii) a *database* from which an event log can be extracted; (iii) a *prompt engineering strategy* to instruct an LLM about the event log extraction task; (iv) a *gold standard* event log to serve as a benchmark for comparison against the LLM-assisted generated event log. Upon receiving the expected input objects, our architecture automatically proceeds as follows: on the given *LLM*, it executes the *prompt*, appending to the prompt the *database* structure, and a request to generate an SQL script as an output. Then, the LLM-generated SQL script is extracted from the LLM response and executed against the database to produce the LLM-assisted event log generation. Next, the LLM-assisted generated event log is compared against the gold standard event log for the particular database, and similarity metrics are calculated. Finally, results can be manually analyzed and reported.

3.2 Materials

We define an architecture that handles four main input-objects: (i) a collection of different *LLMs* to be evaluated; (ii) a variety of *databases* from which event logs can be extracted; (iii) different *prompt engineering strategies* to instruct an LLM about the event log extraction task; and, (iv) *gold standard* event logs, which are previously known event logs extracted from each relational database to serve as a benchmark for

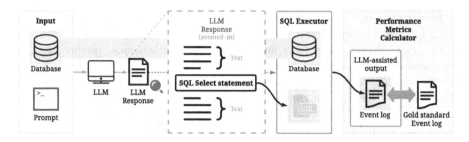

Fig. 1. Overview of our approach.

comparison against the LLM-assisted generated event log. Next, we present further details about the materials used in this work[1].

LLMs. In this work, we evaluated four different OpenAI models: GPT 3.5-turbo, 4, 4-turbo, and 4o. We chose OpenAI models because they have demonstrated capabilities in natural language processing and code generation-related tasks [9,25,26], and because of its wide adoption [20].

An important aspect to have in mind regarding GPT is that OpenAI enables users of their LLM API to reduce the intrinsic non-deterministic nature of their models. This can be done by setting a feature called *temperature*[2] to zero. To minimize the randomness of the LLM responses we did so. Still, we learned that the LLM did not always produce the same output given the same input. We executed each test case (i.e., the combination of a prompt with a particular database) three times, averaging the results.

Databases. For the database selection, we aimed at choosing databases featuring diverse foreign key relations among the tables, as well as varied event identification types, such as one event per row versus multiple events per row. In addition, we also aimed at databases with different sizes in terms of the number of tables and columns. What is more, we created two simplified versions for each selected database. We did so to enhance the generalizability of our findings, thus making our work more reliable in terms of our performance assessment of LLM-assisted event log extraction. The database selection also considered the prompt size limitations of the LLMs. For this work, we selected four databases: a synthetic purchase-to-pay (P2P) database, a real ERP system database [15], the BPI2016 Challenge database [6], and a real-life database from UWV (the Dutch Employee Insurance Agency). Table 2 outlines key characteristics of these selected databases. Versions 1 and 2 of each database are simplified versions of their version 3. Next, we delve into further details about each selected database:

- *P2P.* A synthetic purchase-to-pay database, inspired by [15], to serve as a basis for initial assessment of our experimental setup. This database particularly contributed to our understanding of the nuances in the differences between the LLM-assisted generated event log and the gold standard. It contains high-level information about

---

[1] https://github.com/KiriBu10/event-log-extraction-for-process-mining.

[2] https://platform.openai.com/docs/guides/text-generation/.

orders, invoices, payments and shipment, and enables the event data understanding under two case notions related to the order and the invoice. Creating an event log for this database is straightforward due to the presence of only one-to-many foreign key relationships among the tables. Also, each table holds one event per record. Thus, each table represents events related to one particular ActivityID. The ActivityID of an event is therefore defined as the table name. In the most complex version of the database, version V3, also two tables are present containing clicks and configurations that have no relation with any of the other tables. These tables are added to observe how the LLM deals with unrelated information that is given as input.

– *ERP.* A real ERP system database fragment, as first used by Li et al. [15]. This database holds more information about orders, invoices, payments, and shipments, such as order items, shipment items, and many-to-many relations between order and invoice. In addition, this database has information about the customer. Thus, this database has three possible case notions, related to order, invoice, and customer. Creating an event log for this database is equivalent to the P2P database, with the difference that it holds many-to-many foreign key relationships among the tables. The ActivityID is determined by the table name.

– *BPI2016.* A database based on the BPI Challenge of 2016 [6]. In the BPI Challenge of 2016 a dataset was used with several types of customer contact data from UWV. The database contains clicks on the UWV website from logged-in users and of not logged-in users, messages sent through the website, calls to the call center and com-

Table 2. Characteristics of the databases used in this work.

Database	Version	# Tables	# Columns	# Case notions	# Timestamps	# Activity IDs	# Events per gold standard	Has foreign keys
P2P	V1	2	5	2	1	0	8	Yes
	V2	4	11	2	1	0	13	Yes
	V3	6	19	2	1	0	13	Yes
ERP	V1	3	13	3	1	0	6	Yes
	V2	5	18	2	1	0	5	Yes
	V3	9	32	3	1	0	12	Yes
BPI2016	V1	3	42	2	>1	>1	30	No
	V2	2	35	2	1	>1	250	Yes
	V3	5	77	2	>1	>1	280	Yes
UWV	V1	2	7	1	1	1	11	No
	V2	3	17	2	>1	1	33	No
	V3	5	23	2	>1	1	43	No

plaints from customers. This database has two case notions, i.e., website sessions with a SessionID and the customers with a CustomerID. Creating an event log for this database poses a different challenge when compared to the previous ones, as there are tables with multiple events per record. In this case, the ActivityID is determined by the column names instead of the table name.

– *UWV.* The UWV database is taken from a typical claim handling process executed by UWV. It combines tables from different information systems used in the execution of the process. It contains a table with letters sent to customers, a table with calls to the customer, a table with calls from customers and a table with timestamps per step in the claim handling process. The two case notions in the database are the customer and the claim handling session, i.e., one customer can have multiple claim handling sessions. Creating an event log for this database poses different challenges when compared to the previous databases, as there are no explicit foreign key relationships among the tables and there are tables with multiple events per record.

Prompts. Inspired by the rise of a variety of prompt engineering strategies, Table 3 shows seven prompts used in this work. The first five prompts are prompt strategies inspired by literature [4,23,24,27]. The sixth and seventh prompts, are prompts collaboratively engineered by the authors of this study. The sixth prompt leverages process mining and event log extraction-related knowledge in an attempt to improve the LLM-based event log extraction assistance. The seventh prompt leverages database-specific knowledge. On top of these prompt strategies, a number of statements are always appended to each prompt in the context of this work, in order to fit our automated experimental setup. These statements form the *Baseline* prompt, and include statements such as *"write an SQL statement with the columns: CaseID, ActivityID and timestamp"* and *"return only the complete SQL query, nothing else should be part of the response"*. Apart from these statements, we conducted several experiments to test different database-specific statements, such as *"each record in each table represents at least one event"* and *"if a table contains multiple columns containing a datetime format, then each of these datetime values is an event"*, for the UWV database; or, *"when a table does not have a column that contains the selected case notion, combine the necessary tables to obtain this case notion"*, for the BPI2016 database.

Gold Standards. In the context of this work, the *gold standard* is an event log previously known to contain all the process instances of a particular case notion. Two researchers were involved in manually creating the gold standards separately. They wrote the SQL queries to extract the gold standard event log for each database, and assessed each others work with the help of a third researcher.

To ensure the gold standards are created in a similar fashion, we first determined a common strategy. For example, we assume that each record in a table is an event, except when multiple timestamps are present. In that case each timestamp in a record defines an event. Secondly, when there is no column present that could serve as the ActivityID, then the name of the table is used as the ActivityID. When multiple timestamps exist in a table, we use the name of the table concatenated with the name of each respective timestamp column as ActivityID. We added elements of our gold standard construction strategy to the *process mining knowledge* prompt (prompt 6).

Table 3. Examples of prompts used in this work. Prompts 1 to 5 are based on prompt engineering strategies from literature. Prompts 6 and 7 are based on process mining, and domain and data knowledge, respectively.

ID	Prompt
1	**Baseline** This prompt consists of the database schema and the prompt elements "write a SQL statement with the columns: CaseID, ActivityID and timestamp" and "return only the complete SQL query". All other prompts used in this work consist of the Baseline prompt, expanded with another particular prompt.
2	**Persona** [24] Act as a Process Mining Specialist that is an expert in event log extraction.
3	**Few-shot example** [4] Consider the following example of how an event log looks like when extracted from a database with two tables: {Table A} {Table B} {Extracted event log}
4	**Chain-of-thought** [23] Take a deep breath and think step-by-step in silence.
5	**Tree-of-thought** [27] Consider three experts are collaboratively answering a request using a tree-of-thoughts method. Each one of the three experts will share their thought process in detail, taking into account the previous thoughts of others and admitting any errors. They will iteratively refine and expand upon each others' ideas, giving credit where it's due. The process continues until a conclusive answer to the request is found. The request is the following.
6	**Process mining knowledge.** [Note: *This prompt is built using knowledge about process mining and event log-related concepts such as case notion, activity labels, and timestamps.*]
7	**Custom-made.** [Note: *For each database version, a fully customized prompt is created using domain and data knowledge.*]

3.3 Performance Assessment

To analyse and assess the performance of the LLM-assisted generated event log, we compare the responses for different combinations of database and prompt against the gold standard defined for the database. In this work, we use three performance metric calculation (PMC) strategies:

PMC_1. Inspired by [1], we calculate the precision, recall, and F1-score by directly comparing the LLM-extracted event log L against the gold standard event log G. We identify true positives (TP), false positives (FP), and false negatives (FN) as follows: TP as $G \cap L$, FP as $L \setminus TP$, and FN as $G \setminus TP$. In the context of this work, a TP is defined as an event in L that also occurs in G, with exactly the same CaseID, ActivityID, and timestamp.

PMC_2. Inspired by our observation that often when the F1-score is zero in preliminary results using PMC_1, which is caused by ActivityIDs that do not match, we devised PMC_2. In PMC_2, we calculate the relaxed F1-score considering a partial match between an event in L and an event in G, ignoring the ActivityID. For example, consider an event as a triple (CaseID, ActivityID, and timestamp), event l_i as (1001, "Create order", 2024-06-02 12:37:40) in L, and event g_i as (1001, "order", 2024-06-02 12:37:40) in G. In the relaxed F1-score calculation, we accept l_i as equal to g_i. Note that the number of events in the comparison of the generated event log with the gold standard event log can become smaller when the ActivityID is ignored. Sometimes the ActivityID is the only distinguishing element between two or more events. This effect is due to the set abstraction we use in the comparison and has an impact on the calculation of the F1-score since the number of FNs can decrease.

PMC$_3$. In further observations we identified that often when the F1-score is zero for PMC$_1$, this is caused by ActivityIDs that do not perfectly match syntactically, but should do so semantically. We used the Levenshtein distance [13] to calculate the minimum number of edits necessary to transform the event from L to an event in G. For each event, all elements are first concatenated, e.g., the event (1001, "Create order", 2024-06-02 12:37:40) from L becomes "1001;Create order;2024-06-02 12:37:40". This transformation is also done for all events from G. Next, for each event in L the distance to each event in G is calculated. The similarity is expressed as 1 minus the ratio between the number of edits and the length of the longest of the two strings that are being compared, i.e., the gold standard value and the generated value. If the similarity value is above a threshold value of 0.75, we consider the match a TP; otherwise, it is an FP. The number of FPs is calculated based on the size of the larger of the two event logs minus the number of TPs. Inspired by [7], we selected the 0.75 threshold experimentally. We manually identified that the balance between semantically similar words was higher for the 0.75 thresholds than, for example, when using 0.8, which means that if we had used 0.8 as a threshold, we would not have classified as TP events that should have been classified as such.

4   Results

In this section, we discuss the results of our experiments. Table 4 provides an overview of the results[3]. We show the results for GPT 4o, which was overall the best performing LLM used in this work. In total, we ran 252 API calls, as we had 84 test cases (four databases times three versions per database times seven prompts) that were executed three times each. In 25 out of 84 test cases (29.8%), the LLM produced different results in the three runs. Differences between the runs for a test case could be either small, indicating that only some of the events have changed in the result, or also large. In Table 4 we provide the average scores.

In the following sections, we report on the results of our experiments for each specific database, providing detailed findings that form the basis for our discussion section. Mind that whenever we say *generated event log* we refer to the *LLM-assisted generated event log*.

---

[3] We focus on the F1-scores since precision and recall were very close in most cases.

Table 4. Evaluation summary of database versions, with F1-scores for the three different Performance Metric Calculations (PMC). The $-\infty$ symbol is used when no valid event log was returned by the LLM. The greyscale cell-background goes from black (F1-score equals to zero) to white (F1-score equals to one).

Database	Prompt	V1			V2			V3		
		PMC_1	PMC_2	PMC_3	PMC_1	PMC_2	PMC_3	PMC_1	PMC_2	PMC_3
P2P	1	0.000	1.000	1.000	0.000	0.769	0.769	0.000	0.667	0.647
	2	0.000	1.000	1.000	0.000	0.769	0.769	0.000	0.606	0.588
	3	0.500	1.000	1.000	0.769	0.769	1.000	0.448	0.458	0.631
	4	0.000	1.000	1.000	0.000	0.769	0.769	0.588	0.667	0.765
	5	0.000	1.000	1.000	0.000	0.462	0.615	0.000	0.606	0.588
	6	0.000	1.000	0.000	0.000	1.000	0.000	0.449	0.449	0.590
	7	1.000	1.000	1.000	1.000	1.000	1.000	1.000	1.000	1.000
ERP	1	0.000	0.000	0.400	0.261	0.655	0.744	0.000	0.182	0.583
	2	0.000	0.133	0.204	0.210	0.210	0.886	0.000	0.182	0.167
	3	0.267	0.400	0.526	1.000	1.000	1.000	0.250	0.250	0.417
	4	0.000	0.000	0.000	0.089	0.267	0.838	0.000	0.182	0.472
	5	0.000	0.000	0.400	0.364	0.364	1.000	0.000	0.182	0.306
	6	0.000	0.000	0.278	0.000	0.000	0.140	0.000	0.000	0.000
	7	1.000	1.000	1.000	1.000	1.000	1.000	1.000	1.000	1.000
BPI2016	1	0.067	1.000	0.067	0.000	0.000	1.000	0.005	0.671	0.260
	2	0.067	1.000	0.067	0.000	0.000	1.000	0.000	0.671	0.038
	3	0.000	1.000	0.233	0.000	0.421	0.011	0.000	0.671	0.043
	4	0.067	1.000	0.067	0.000	0.000	1.000	0.000	0.671	0.038
	5	0.045	1.000	0.122	0.211	0.211	1.000	0.000	0.671	0.029
	6	0.022	0.799	0.038	0.000	0.000	1.000	$-\infty$	$-\infty$	$-\infty$
	7	1.000	1.000	1.000	1.000	1.000	1.000	1.000	1.000	1.000
UWV	1	1.000	1.000	1.000	0.333	1.000	1.000	0.435	0.959	0.913
	2	1.000	1.000	1.000	0.333	1.000	1.000	0.435	0.959	0.913
	3	0.000	0.259	0.187	0.000	1.000	0.879	0.000	0.959	0.877
	4	1.000	1.000	1.000	0.333	1.000	1.000	0.435	0.959	0.913
	5	1.000	1.000	1.000	0.331	0.943	0.510	0.435	0.959	0.913
	6	1.000	1.000	1.000	1.000	1.000	1.000	0.920	0.959	0.935
	7	1.000	1.000	1.000	1.000	1.000	1.000	1.000	1.000	1.000

4.1 P2P Database

The P2P database is a synthetic database which incorporates two case notions (order and invoice). A key challenge for the LLM regarding this database is to select one case notion and write an appropriate SQL query. In the *custom-made* prompt (prompt 7) we specify a case notion, but for all other prompts the LLM chooses one. Figure 2 shows the F1-scores for three versions of the P2P database. For PMC_1 (cf., Fig. 2a), prompt 7 is the only one reaching an F1-score of 1, meaning only the *custom-made* prompt performs well. The other prompts perform poorly, with prompts 3, 4, and 6 reaching F1-scores between 0.4 and 0.8 and prompts 1, 2, and 5 doing the worst at zero. For PMC_2 (cf., Fig. 2b), the LLM is performing much better, with perfect F1-scores for V1 and scores for V2 generally varying between 0.8 and 1.0 (with the exception of prompt 5). V3 does not perform as well, with F1-scores generally between 0.4 and 0.7, but with a perfect score for prompt 7. For PMC_3 (cf., Fig. 2c), all F1-scores are equal or higher than the F1-scores of PMC_2, except for the *process mining knowledge* prompt (prompt 6). Again, F1-scores are highest for V1, followed by V2, and then V3.

For PMC_1, all prompts but the custom-made prompt perform badly due to the LLM adding "_created" to the ActivityID (e.g., the LLM generates an ActivityID "order_created" instead of "order"). Note that we did not ask the LLM to add this in any prompt, nor did we include it in our gold standard, which as a logical choice simply uses table names as ActivityIDs when no dedicated ActivityID column is available.

The mismatch in the ActivityIDs between the generated event log and the gold standard may also explain why the PMC_2 and PMC_3 scores are better for all prompts. PMC_2 ignores ActivityIDs, while PMC_3 does not require that ActivityIDs match 100% to be considered a true positive. Figure 2b shows that when the ActivityID is ignored, the F1-scores are all above zero.

Another pattern that can be observed is the relation between database complexity (V3 being more complex than V2, which is more complex than V1) and the F1-score, with more complex databases reaching lower scores. This implies that next to a mismatch on ActivityID other mismatches are present. Further examining the generated event logs reveals that either the case notion is not correctly derived (e.g., some events have InvoiceID as the CaseID instead of OrderID), or the generated event log incorporates irrelevant events. In other words, events from tables that are present in the DB schema but do not have a relation with an order (e.g., click events from a customer).

Mismatches in case notion and inclusion of irrelevant events also affect the PMC_3 scores, shown in Fig. 2c. Most PMC_3 F1-scores are equal or higher than the PMC_2 F1-scores. Apparently the ActivityIDs are close enough to the gold standard ActivityIDs to not negatively impact the F1-score. This means that the match between the ActivityIDs of the generated event logs are above the threshold of 0.75. This is not the case for the *process mining knowledge* prompt in combination with the databases V1 and V2. None of the ActivityIDs of the generated event log come close enough to the gold standard which results in an F1-score of zero. This is caused by the prompt itself, which requests the LLM to create an ActivityID by concatenating the table name and the column name in the situation that no other columns exist that could be the ActivityID. However, this should only be done when at least two timestamp columns are present in a table. Otherwise the name of the table should be used as the ActivityID. In this case we only have one timestamp column, hence the LLM applied the wrong part of the prompt.

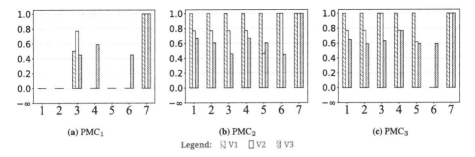

Fig. 2. P2P F1-scores for the different used prompts and PMCs.

4.2 ERP Database

The ERP database has a similar complexity to the P2P database, as can be observed from the characteristics of both databases in Table 2. The biggest differences are the additional tables, the many-to-many foreign key relationships among the tables, and an extra case notion. The additional tables represent order lines, payment lines, and shipment lines, which are respectively related to orders, payments, and shipments. These additional tables are needed to connect, for example, payments to invoices. In the P2P database this information was part of the payment table.

The F1-scores for the three versions of the ERP database are shown in Fig. 3. The scores of PMC_1 are similar to those of the P2P database, with prompt 7 performing perfectly, but the other ones performing poorly with many F1-scores at zero. V2 of the database is performing slightly better, with a perfect F1-score for prompt 3 and 7 but scoring below 0.4 for the other ones. We see similar results for PMC_2, which performs slightly better, and PMC_3, which performs best in terms of the ERP database. However, both perform worse than in the P2P database. Overall, the F1-scores for V2 are generally better than for V1 and V3. Prompt 7 consistently reaches F1-scores of 1, while the performance of the other prompts varies greatly.

From the results of PMC_2 (cf., Fig. 3b), we gather that even ignoring the ActivityID is not enough to generate an event log close to the gold standard. Only the *custom-made* prompt performs perfectly, as it was designed to do. This indicates that it is possible to

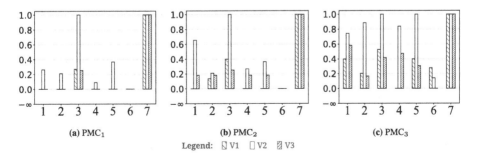

Fig. 3. ERP F1-scores for the different used prompts and PMCs.

write an effective prompt to support the event log extraction for the ERP database. Moreover, the ERP database V2 stands out in all the F1-scores in Fig. 3. Considering that V2 is a less complex and V3 is the most complex database, we again notice that there is a relation between the complexity of the database and the F1-scores, as F1-scores for less complex databases are generally higher. In addition, we notice that the prompt type also matters, as different prompts yield different F1-scores for the ERP database. Prompt type 3 (*Few-shot example*) relatively performs best compared to the other prompt engineering strategies.

4.3   BPI2016 Database

The complexity in the BPI2016 databases comes from having multiple columns that can serve as ActivityID and multiple timestamp columns per table, giving the LLM more options to choose from. Figure 4 shows the different PMCs for the three versions of the BPI2016 database. The F1-scores for PMC_1 are the lowest of all the four databases, with all database versions performing poorly except prompt 7, which again scores perfectly. There is even one F1-score that could not be calculated, namely prompt 6, which is depicted in the figure as a negative value. The performance for PMC_2 varies greatly, with V1 scoring perfectly on all prompts except prompt 6, where it scores 0.8. V3 scores around 0.7 for prompts 1 through 5 but again scores negatively for prompt 6. V2 performs worst, with many F1-scores at zero. This is different for PMC_3, where V2 performs well, with F1-scores of 1 for all prompts except 3. Prompt 7 again scores perfectly, but all other prompts perform badly for V1 and V3, all scoring lower than 0.3.

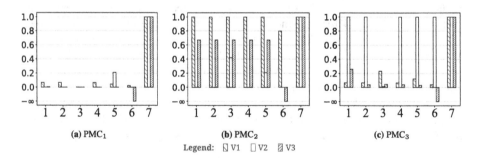

(a) PMC_1 (b) PMC_2 (c) PMC_3

Legend: ▨ V1   ☐ V2   ▨ V3

Fig. 4. BPI2016 F1-scores for the different used prompts and PMCs.

As for the F1-scores that could not be calculated: the reason is that the LLM did not return a valid SQL statement. Without a valid SQL statement an event log cannot be generated. The generated SQL statement included a join of two tables that both contained the column *page_action_detail*. This column was selected as the ActivityID. Unfortunately, the SQL SELECT statement did not specify from which table this column should be taken. This resulted in an *ambiguous column* error.

Figures 4b and 4c show the influence of the ActivityID on the calculated F1-scores. The values of the PMC_2 (cf., Fig. 4b) are at least 0.6, except for the database V2. This implies that for the V1 and the V3 databases when the ActivityID is left out of the match, the generated event log resembles the gold standard event log. The inverse of Fig. 4b is visible in Fig. 4c. In this case, database V2 has high F1-scores for nearly every prompt, while V1 and V3 have low scores. This effect is caused by the composition of the BPI2016 database versions. V1 contains questions, messages and complaints. V2 contains website clicks for customers who are known because they logged in and clicks from unknown customers. V1 and V2 have disjunct sets of tables. In V3 all the tables from V1 and V2 are combined.

Figure 4b also shows that the LLM is capable of retrieving the correct CaseID and timestamps for V1 and V3. Looking into the generated SQL statement for V2, it is revealed that the LLM choose the wrong CaseID, i.e., SessionID instead of CustomerID. In the PMC_3 F1-scores in Fig. 4c the ActivityID plays a role once more. Even though the LLM selected the wrong CaseID for V2, the match is considered perfect, judging by the F1 scores of 1 for almost every prompt. This turns out to be an artifact from the Levenshtein distance comparison that is used in our PMC_3. The SessionID for each event is very close to the CustomerID, i.e., both columns contain numbers that appear to be very similar. The match result is just above the threshold for recording a TP. If the threshold would be lowered, then Fig. 4c would resemble Fig. 4a. Finally, the PMC_3 F1-scores for V1 and V3 in Fig. 4c are low because the LLM selected the wrong column as ActivityID. The values of this column are, even with PMC_3, not similar enough to the ActivityIDs in the gold standard.

In conclusion, the LLM does not seem to handle the BPI2016 database well. Either the wrong CaseID is selected (for V2) or the wrong ActivityID is selected (for V1 and V3). For the timestamp, the correct column is selected by the LLM. The complexity of this database mostly comes from having multiple columns that can serve as ActivityID.

4.4   UWV Database

The UWV database is from a typical claim handling process as executed by UWV. It combines tables from different information systems used in the execution of the process. The complexity of this database lies in the lack of direct connections between the tables, as there are no tables containing foreign keys. Next to that, there is one table containing multiple timestamp columns. Each of these columns represents a different event.

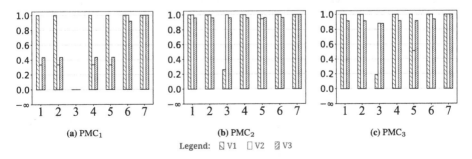

(a) PMC_1 (b) PMC_2 (c) PMC_3

Legend: V1   V2   V3

Fig. 5. UWV F1-scores for the different used prompts and PMCs.

Figure 5 contains all PMC F1-scores for the UWV databases. Most of the F1-scores have the maximum possible value of 1. V1 especially, performs well, scoring 1 for all prompts across PMCs, except for prompt 3 where it scores below 0.3 for all three PMCs. V2 and V3 perform very well for PMC_2 and PMC_3, mostly nearing the maximum scores, but experience more difficulty with PMC_1, where they score below 0.5 for prompts 1 through 5.

For all three PMCs, the LLM is capable of generating an event log that is in line with the gold standard. In addition to the *custom-made* prompt (prompt 7), the *process mining knowledge* prompt (prompt 6) also performs well. For the UWV database V1, most prompts work well, except for the *few-shot example* prompt (prompt 3), which generates incorrect SQL statements referencing orders and payments not present in the database. This only occurs for the UWV database V1. For the other database versions the *few-shot example* prompt (prompt 3) is interpreted as an example, as it should be.

5   Discussion

After executing a variety of prompt strategies against a number of databases with different structural characteristics, we have acquired two major insights. First, we learned that prompt engineering strategies per se are not enough for effective LLM-assisted event log extraction. Our results show that LLMs cannot fully autonomously identify effectively what the desired event log should look like, nor what case notion should be considered. Second, we learned that domain and data knowledge can make LLM-assisted event log extraction effective. What is interesting is that having domain and data knowledge, and being able to transfer those to the LLM, can yield effective LLM-assisted event log extraction. Particularly, if there is previous knowledge available about which specific tables hold which event data, or if the LLM is provided with a couple of examples of how the event log extraction should be performed, the outcome of the LLM-assisted event log extraction becomes more effective.

Based on these findings, we can make three specific recommendations to support the effective use of LLM-assisted event log extraction:

R1 - Combine prompt engineering strategies with domain and data knowledge. Prompt engineering strategies such as *persona*, *few-shot examples*, *tree-of-thought* or *chain-of-thought* should be combined with domain and data knowledge to produce more effective results. Considering only the *custom-made* prompts, which leverages domain and data knowledge, LLM-assisted event log extraction could produce useful event logs in 100% of the times (36 out of 36 runs). In the context of our work, an event log is considered useful if its F1-score is above 0.75 for either PMC_1, PMC_2 or PMC_3.

R2 - Do not rely on the first generated event log. If domain and data knowledge are not readily available, be ready to test the generated event log and go back to the LLM for refinement of the event log extraction. Considering our results for all prompts (and not only for the *custom-made* prompt), LLM-assisted event log extraction can produce useful event logs in 68.3% of the times (172 of the 252 runs).

R3 - Use LLM-assisted event log extraction with parsimony. If you do not know how to extract event logs and you need to start analyzing some particular process data, you can leverage LLM-assisted event log extraction considering the recommendations R1 and R2. However, for more stable and precise process analysis, double-check the event log extraction with a domain or data expert.

6 Conclusion

In this paper, we presented a first experimental setup to investigate the effectiveness of LLMs in assisting event log extraction from a relational database. We showed that there is no one-fits-all prompt engineering strategy solution for databases with different structural characteristics and that domain and data knowledge is still needed to yield satisfactory results. We also showed that if domain and data knowledge is available, one can actually benefit from an LLM-assisted event log extraction, as it can create and adapt SQL scripts fast, enabling business analysts to get to the process discovery and analysis step for process mining faster. Our findings, therefore, show the potential for LLM-assisted event log extraction. They pave the way for future *human-as-a-tool* in a human-LLM interaction event log extraction system, where the user is actively asked by the LLM for clarifications about domain and data related ambiguities, to diminish the error-proneness inherent in event log extraction.

Naturally, our work is not without limitations. While our analysis involved multiple databases to enhance robustness of our experiment, the relatively small database sample size may impact the generalizability of our findings. Also, because of the limitations imposed by the prompt length. We, however, used a diverse range of prompts and databases to ensure a systematic selection process to cover varied scenarios. Moreover, we established clear data collection and analysis protocols, which ensured consistency and reduced individual bias in the interpretation of data. While we do not claim to provide a complete set of test cases, with this work we provide an architectural basis for future research to systematically assess other combinations of databases, prompts, performance metric calculations, and large language models in assisting event log extraction for process mining.

In future work, we aim at incorporating our findings into a multi-agent framework for event log extraction, where data from different sources can be jointly considered, and an LLM-assisted generation of object-centric event logs can also be investigated.

Acknowledgements. Part of this research was funded by NWO (Netherlands Organisation for Scientific Research) project number 16672.

References

1. van der Aa, H., Leopold, H., Reijers, H.A.: Comparing textual descriptions to process models - the automatic detection of inconsistencies. Inf. Syst. **64**, 447–460 (2017)
2. van der Aalst, W.M.P.: Process mining: Discovery, conformance and enhancement of business processes, Springer (2011)
3. Berti, A., Schuster, D., van der Aalst, W.M.P.: Abstractions, scenarios, and prompt definitions for process mining with LLMs: a case study. In: Business Process Management Workshops, Springer (2024)

4. Brown, T., et al.: Language models are few-shot learners. In: Advances in Neural Information Processing Systems (NeurIPS), vol. 33. Curran Associates (2020)
5. Busch, K., Rochlitzer, A., Sola, D., Leopold, H.: Just tell me: prompt engineering in business process management. In: BPMDS, Springer (2023)
6. Dees, M., van Dongen, B.F.: BPI challenge 2016 (2016)
7. Dijkman, R., Dumas, M., Dongen, van, B., Käärik, R., Mendling, J.: Similarity of business process models: metrics and evaluation. Inf. Syst. **36** (2011)
8. Finlayson, M., Ren, X., Swayamdipta, S.: Logits of API-Protected LLMs leak proprietary information. ArXiv **2403.09539** (2024)
9. Gao, D., et al.: Text-to-SQL empowered by large language models: a benchmark evaluation. Proc. VLDB Endowment **17**(5), 1132–1145 (2024)
10. Jiang, A.Q., et al.: Mistral 7B. ArXiv **2310.06825** (2023)
11. Kasneci, E., et al.: ChatGPT for good? On opportunities and challenges of large language models for education. Learn. Ind. Differ. **103** (2023)
12. Kourani, H., Berti, A., Schuster, D., van der Aalst, W.M.P.: Process modeling with large language models. In: Enterprise, Business-Process and Information Systems Modeling, Springer (2024)
13. Levenshtein, V.I.: Binary codes capable of correcting deletions, insertions, and reversals. Soviet Phys.-Doklady **10**(8) (1966)
14. Li, C.Y., et al.: Rectify sensor data in IoT: a case study on enabling process mining for logistic process in an air cargo terminal. In: Cooperative Information Systems (CoopIS), pp. 293–310. Springer (2024)
15. Li, G., de Murillas, E.G.L., de Carvalho, R.M., van der Aalst, W.M.P.: Extracting object-centric event logs to support process mining on databases. In: Information Systems in the Big Data Era, Springer (2018)
16. Mustroph, H., Winter, K., Rinderle-Ma, S.: Social network mining from natural language text and event logs for compliance deviation detection. In: Cooperative Information Systems (CoopIS), pp. 347–365. Springer (2024)
17. Nasr, M., et al.: Scalable extraction of training data from (production) language models. ArXiv **2311.17035** (2023)
18. Ollion, É., Shen, R., Macanovic, A., Chatelain, A.: The dangers of using proprietary LLMs for research. Nat. Mach. Intell. **6**(1), 4–5 (2024)
19. Stein Dani, V., et al.: Towards understanding the role of the human in event log extraction. In: Business Process Management Workshops, Springer (2022)
20. Teubner, T., Flath, C.M., Weinhardt, C., van der Aalst, W., Hinz, O.: Welcome to the era of ChatGPT, et al. Bus. Inf. Syst. Eng. **65**(2), 95–101 (2023)
21. Thirunavukarasu, A.J., Ting, D.S.J., Elangovan, K., Gutierrez, L., Tan, T.F., Ting, D.S.W.: Large language models in medicine. Nat. Med. 1930–1940 (2023)
22. Touvron, H., et al.: Llama 2: open foundation and fine-tuned chat models. ArXiv **2307.09288** (2023)
23. Wei, J., et al.: Chain-of-thought prompting elicits reasoning in large language models. In: Advances in Neural Information Processing Systems (NeurIPS), vol. 35, pp. 24824–24837. Curran Associates (2022)
24. White, J., et al.: A prompt pattern catalog to enhance prompt engineering with ChatGPT. ArXiv **2302.11382** (2023)
25. Wu, Y.: Large language model and text generation, pp. 265–297. Springer (2024)
26. Yang, J., et al.: Harnessing the power of LLMs in practice: a survey on ChatGPT and beyond. ACM Trans. Knowl. Disc. Data **18**(6) (2024)
27. Yao, S., et al.: Tree of thoughts: Deliberate problem solving with large language models. In: Advances in Neural Information Processing Systems (NeurIPS), Curran Associates (2023)

Process Analytics and Technology

All Optimal k-Bounded Alignments Using the FM-Index

Astrid Rivera-Partida[1]([✉]), Abel Armas-Cervantes[2][iD], Luciano García-Bañuelos[1][iD], and Luis Rodríguez-Flores[1][iD]

[1] Tecnologico de Monterrey, Monterrey, Mexico
A01324504@tec.mx
[2] The University of Melbourne, Melbourne, Australia

Abstract. Alignments are a popular technique in process mining to compare pairs of process executions. Given a pair of process executions, an optimal alignment represents the commonalities with the minimum number of differences. Compared process executions are event sequences representing process model runs or traces in an event log. Alignments are used in different process mining operations, such as conformance checking and comparison of event logs, *a.k.a.* variants analysis or log delta analysis. Given an event sequence, several optimal alignments can exist, but the majority of alignment techniques focus on computing a single (optimal) solution. Often, it is due to the exponential complexity associated to the computation of all optimal alignments. To tackle this problem, we present a novel approach to compute all k-bounded optimal alignments, which uses a text indexing technique called FM-Index. Given a k, our approach computes optimal alignments with up to k differences. The approach is evaluated in the context of conformance checking and variants analysis using synthetic and real-life event logs. The results show the feasibility to compute all optimal alignments in a reasonable time.

Keywords: All optimal alignments · Conformance checking · Variant analysis · FM-index

1 Introduction

Process mining is a family of methods that aim to extract valuable insights into business processes from *event logs*. These event logs are records of historical process executions gathered by information systems [1], where a process execution is recorded as a sequence of activity instances (*a.k.a. events*) called a *trace*. There are various operations in process mining where pairs of event sequences need to be compared for similarities and differences. For instance, in conformance checking, a process model (expected behaviour) is compared against an event log (observed behaviour). Then, it is necessary to determine the most likely process model execution – *a.k.a. run* – that generated every trace in the event log. A technique used for conformance checking is alignments [5]. An optimal alignment represents the commonalities and differences between an event log trace and a process model run – also represented as a sequence of events. It is optimal because the number of differences between such sequences is minimized. Alignments

M. Comuzzi et al. (Eds.): CoopIS 2024, LNCS 15506, pp. 75–92, 2025.
https://doi.org/10.1007/978-3-031-81375-7_5

are also used in other operations, such as in log delta analysis [15] where alignments are computed between traces of two different event logs – this operation is also called variants analysis.

Given two event sequences, an alignment describes the differences using two edit operations (insertion and deletion of events) to transform one sequence into the other. Such edit operations carry a cost and the total cost of an alignment is the sum of the edit operations. When the edit operations carry a cost of 1, the notion of alignment is similar to the well-known Levenshtein distance between a pair of strings. In conformance checking, algorithms frame the construction of optimal alignments as a search problem with an exponential time complexity in the size of the trace and the model [9]. To reduce the search space, existing algorithms implement different heuristics, such as A* heuristics and shortest path algorithms [5,12], or use decomposition techniques [16]. Often, the focus is on the computation of a single optimal alignment for an event sequence, but several optimal alignments can exist [4]. When the computation of all-optimal alignments is of interest, a complete exploration of the search space is required. Existing techniques for computing alignments can be adapted to compute all optimal alignments, albeit with a significant increase in memory usage and execution times. Due to this complexity, some approaches have resorted to approximate results, e.g., [31,32] compute approximate several (not all) optimal alignments.

This paper presents an approach to compute all optimal k-bounded alignments. The approach uses an FM-Index [14], an indexing technique that allows for fast queries. Our approach receives two families of event sequences as input – a reference behaviour and a set of queries – and a value k. After indexing the reference behaviour, all k-bounded optimal alignments are computed for each sequence in the queries. These optimal alignments have the minimal cost that does not surpass k. To show the potential of our approach, the evaluation is performed in the context of conformance checking and variants analysis using synthetic and real-life event logs.

The remainder of the paper is structured as follows. Section 2 discusses previous work. Section 3 introduces existing concepts that serve as a theoretical foundation for our work. Section 4 presents our approach, and describe how to use it for conformance checking and variants analysis. We describe the results of our experiments in Sect. 5. Lastly, Sect. 6 concludes the paper, addressing the limitations of the approach, and providing an outlook for future research.

2   Related Work

The concept of alignment was introduced in [4] for conformance checking. The authors use an A* heuristic to optimize the computation of one optimal alignment. It consists of searching the shortest path by traversing the state space of the synchronous product between each trace in the log and a process model. Other works, such as [5,12], have developed improvements to the mentioned approach. While the technique can be adapted to compute all optimal alignments, it comes at the expense of significantly increasing the memory footprint.

In [17] the alignment problem is reformulated as an automated planning problem. This approach outperforms [4,5] in larger datasets and, depending on the design of the planning system, it can provide either optimal or approximate solutions. A generalization of alignments is presented in [15]. Such work computes optimal alignments over partial orders, and not over total orders like in the case of event sequences. Such approach also uses an A* heuristic similar to [4].

Approximate alignments propose a trade-off between accuracy and performance to cope with the complexity of computing optimal alignments. The technique in [31] frames the computation of alignments as an Integer Linear Programming problem; however, the algorithm does not guarantee optimality. Further research [32] proposes a technique to find approximate several (not all) optimal alignments using a genetic algorithm. In a related line of research, [28] uses a subset of the process model's behavior for the computation of alignments. The result of the alignments heavily depends on the selected subset. In [27], the error bounds are quantified for such approximate alignments, which can be used to assess the approximation and to select the most appropriate subset.

In the context of conformance checking, other strategies have been implemented, such as model decomposition. The work in [2] presents a divide-and-conquer approach, where the model is broken down into smaller model fragments, and each fragment is aligned separately. The approach in [21] splits the model into single-entry and single-exit (SESE) fragments and aligns each fragment to a corresponding part of the event log. However, it only yields partial alignments. To overcome this limitation, the technique developed in [16] recomposes complete optimal alignments from partial alignments. Another approach is [25], where an input event log and a process model are represented as automata. The approach decomposes the process model into sequential components, and a product automaton is computed for each component separately. Then, the automata are recomposed to compute all optimal alignments.

3   Background

This section establishes the background of the paper. The first two subsections present event logs (Subsec. 3.1) and alignments(Subsec. 3.2), respectively. Finally, concepts related to string processing algorithms are reviewed, FM-Index (Subsec. 3.3) and backward search in the FM-Index (Subsec. 3.4).

The technique presented in this paper for computing alignments can be applied to any pair of event sequences (traces or runs). For consistency, let us present our technique using event log traces. In Sect. 4, we show how this technique can be applied for both conformance checking and variants analysis.

3.1   Traces and Event Logs

Event logs record historical business process executions. A process execution is captured in the log as a trace, which is a sequence of events (activity instances). In a trace, events are ordered by their time of occurrence. For each event, the event log must contain three key pieces of information: case it belongs to, its time of occurrence (usually completion time), and the name of the activity it represents; but other information can be recorded – such as, start time or resource who executed the activity. In this paper we assume only the three key pieces of information are present. Let us define some notation next.

Let $\mathcal{A}$ be the universe of activity labels. Then, an *event* is represented as a tuple $e = (t, a, c)$ where t is the timestamp, $a \in \mathcal{A}$ is the activity label, and c is the case id. The timestamp, activity and case id of an event e can be accessed as $e.t$, $e.a$ and $e.c$, respectively. A *trace* is a non-empty ordered sequence of events $\sigma = \langle e_1, \ldots, e_n \rangle$ such that $\forall i \in [1 \ldots n-1] e_i.c = e_{i+1}.c \wedge e_i.t \leq e_{i+1}.t$.

A pair of traces are considered as the same *trace variant* if they have the same number of events, which are instances of the same activities, and they were observed in the same order of occurrence. Then, an *event log L*, or *log* for short, is defined as a multiset of traces because it can contain several occurrences of the same trace variant. However, in this work we consider the event logs as sets of traces containing only trace variants.

3.2   Alignments

Alignments [3] were originally defined as a comparison between an event log trace and a process model run. We consider alignments in more general terms.

In this work, an alignment between two traces σ_1, σ_2 consists of a sequence of *moves*, which are pairs of events (e, e'). There are two types of moves: *synchronous* and *sequence* moves.

1. A *synchronous* move is a pair of events (e, e'), such that $e.a = e'.a$, and $e \in \sigma_1$ and $e' \in \sigma_2$. Synchronous moves represent pairs of events matched because they represent the same activity.
2. A *sequence* move (e, e') is used to make a move in either of the compared sequences, such that either (a) $e = \gg \wedge e' \in \sigma_2$, or (b) $e \in \sigma_1 \wedge e' = \gg$, where $\gg$ represents no counterpart. A sequence move can be interpreted as an edit operation, which can be an insertion or a deletion and, in traditional alignments jargon, it defines a move on model or a move on log.

Please note that a sequence move can be applied to either of the sequences compared and it carries a cost. Usually, the alignments of interest are *optimal* – those with the least number sequence moves. In the remainder of the paper, when we talk about alignments we refer to optimal alignments. Figure 1 shows a simple example of an alignment between two traces $\langle a, c, b, d \rangle$ and $\langle a, b, d \rangle$, where $\gg$ represents a sequence move for c because it cannot be matched in the bottom trace. The rest of the events can be matched with synchronous moves.

3.3   The FM-Index

In our approach, the computation of alignments is performed on top of a special data structure called FM-Index [14]. The latter is a text index, built on top of several auxiliary data structures, which enables the implementation of fast string processing techniques. We leverage the FM-Index as the foundation for designing the fast sequence alignment technique that we present in this work.

$$\begin{array}{c|c|c|c}
a & c & b & d \\
\hline
a & \gg & b & d
\end{array}$$

Fig. 1. Alignment between $\langle a, c, b, d \rangle$ and $\langle a, b, d \rangle$.

The FM-Index of a string T is a tuple (BWT, SA, C, Occ), where BWT is the Burrows-Wheeler transform of T, SA is a suffix array of T, and C/Occ are auxiliary arrays. In the following, we describe each element in the FM-Index.

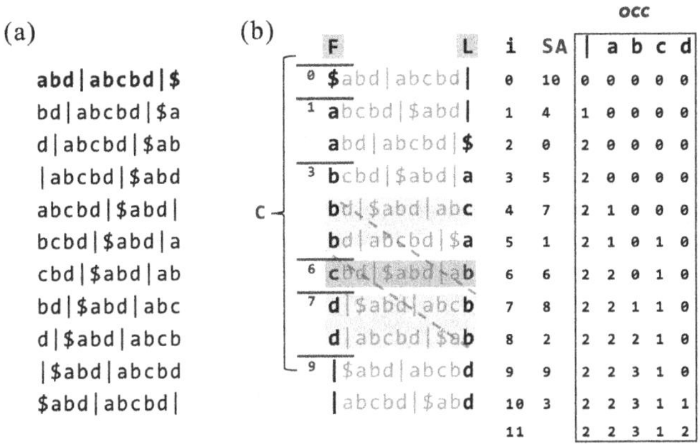

(a)

```
abd|abcbd|$
bd|abcbd|$a
d|abcbd|$ab
|abcbd|$abd
abcbd|$abd|
bcbd|$abd|a
cbd|$abd|ab
bd|$abd|abc
d|$abd|abcb
|$abd|abcbd
$abd|abcbd|
```

(b)

	F	L	i	SA	a	b	c	d
0	$abd|abcbd|		0	10	0	0	0	0
1	abcbd|$abd|		1	4	1	0	0	0
	abd|abcbd|$		2	0	2	0	0	0
3	bcbd|$abd|a		3	5	2	0	0	0
	bd|$abd|abc		4	7	2	1	0	0
	bd|abcbd|$a		5	1	2	1	0	1	0
6	cbd|$abd|ab		6	6	2	2	0	1	0
7	d|$abd|abcb		7	8	2	2	1	1	0
	d|abcbd|$ab		8	2	2	2	2	1	0
9	|$abd|abcbd		9	9	2	2	3	1	0
	|abcbd|$abd		10	3	2	2	3	1	1
			11		2	2	3	1	2

Fig. 2. Computation of the BWT for abd|abcbcd|$ (a) Matrix of circular shifts (b) Sorted matrix, index i, SA, C and Occ.

Burrows and Wheeler [8] describe a text transformation (BWT) as part of a technique for data compression. Using a reversible permutation, the BWT rearranges characters in a text string to achieve better compression ratios in comparison to using the original string. Let us explain how to compute the BWT for an input text T. We assume that T is drawn from an alphabet $\Sigma \setminus \{\$\}$. For convenience, the alphabet includes the sentinel character $, which serves to mark the end of the text and is the smallest symbol in Σ.

Figure 2 depicts the procedure to compute the BWT for T= abd|abcbd|$. A left circular shift of a string s is another string resulting from removing the first character in s and moving it to the end. For instance, bd|abcbd|$a is the first circular shift of abd|abcbd|$. All the circular shifts of an input string are computed and collected in a matrix (Fig. 2a). Then, they are sorted lexicographically to form the matrix in Fig. 2b. In the following, we will refer to the sorted matrix as the Burrows-Wheeler Matrix (BWM). We keep only the first and last columns of BWM, which we will refer to as F and L, respectively. The rest of the columns are discarded. The BWT of T is obtained from column L, i.e., ||$acabbbdd in Fig. 2b.

The suffix array (SA) is another text index intimately related to the BWT. The SA is an array of integers storing the positions of all sorted suffixes of T. The sorted suffixes of T correspond to the ordered circular shifts in BWM up to $, so each character in F (first column in Fig. 2b) matches the first character of a suffix. The SA is the array of integers representing F and it stores the positions of all sorted suffixes of T. Figure 2 includes a column with the SA of our sample string abd|abcbd|$. We can easily check in Fig. 2b that T[10 :][1] is the smallest lexicographical suffix of T (i.e., "$"), followed

---

[1] With abuse of notation, we will use T[i:] to denote the suffix of T starting at position i, T[$i:j$] to denote the substring between positions i and j, and T[:j] to refer to the prefix of T up to position j.

by T[4 :] (i.e., "abcbd|$"), so on and so forth. Several linear time algorithms exist in the literature (e.g., [24]) to compute the SA of a string. For a text T, the BWT can be computed using the SA as follows: $BWT[i] = T[SA[i] - 1]$ **if** $SA[i] > 0$ **else** $. The arrays C and Occ are discussed in the following subsection.

3.4   Backward Search in the FM-Index

We now describe how to search for a substring using the FM-Index. As explained in the following section, in our context, the substring is a trace that needs to be found in the reference behaviour. By way of example, we search for acbd in abd|abcbcd|$ using the information from Fig. 2. The search occurs backwards, thus we start by locating the last symbol of the query string, i.e., d, in the column F of BWM, resulting in an interval in SA. The indexes of an interval can be checked in column i in Fig. 2b. For instance, we say that d occurs in the interval $[7, 8]$[2] of F. So, we proceed by looking for the second symbol, i.e., b, over the same interval but now over column L, see rows 7 and 8 highlighted in orange in Fig. 2b. However, only two occurrences of b are selected in L, leaving out of the analysis the other b(Fig. 2b, highlighted in red). Our search goes back to column F, including only the second and third occurrences of b in the interval $[4, 5]$ in F. Because the rotations are lexicographically sorted all bs appear in a block that starts in row 3. Note that the order of occurrence of symbols in the original string is preserved in BWM's columns L and F.

Note that the backward search relies on mapping the occurrences of symbols over L to blocks residing over F. The mapping can be implemented by precomputing information that can be stored in auxiliary data structures and using the following functions:

– Occ(T, c, i)[3] returns the number of occurrences of symbol c in T$[: i]$,
– C(T, c) returns the overall number of symbols in T that are lexicographically smaller than c.

For convenience, the function LF(T, c, i) $\triangleq$ C(T, c) + Occ(T, c, i) is used, where "LF" stands for "Last to First mapping". Occ and C are implemented just as arrays as shown in Fig. 2. Using function LF, backward search can be implemented as shown in Algorithm 1. Please note that because the representation of Occ and C as arrays may have

---

Algorithm 1. Backward search over Burrows-Wheeler transform.

1: **function** BASICBACKWARDSEARCH(BWT, Q, f, g)
2:     **for** $\alpha \in$ REVERSE(Q) **while** f < g **do**
3:         f, g ← LF(BWT, α, f), LF(BWT, α, g)
4:     **end for**
5:     **return** $[f, g)$
6: **end function**

---

[2] To avoid confusion with citations, we use $[\ ]$ and $(\ )$ to represent closed and open intervals with the usual meaning.
[3] Occ is also referred to as RANK in some sources.

high memory requirements, other data structures are preferred, such as the wavelet tree (see [8]). In fact, our prototype uses wavelet trees for memory efficiency.

We now replay the example in Fig. 2 using LF. Note that the array OCC has a capacity of $|T| + 1$ to capture the number of occurrences of all the symbols correctly. In the example, d occurs 2 times in the indexed string, this is asserted only in the last position of OCC. BASICBACKWARDSEARCH is called with the value of the BWT, the query string Q = acbd and the indexes $f = 0$ and $g = 11$ ($[\![0, 11[\![$, using an open interval), meaning that we are covering the entire indexed string. Table 1 summarizes all the intermediate results. In the first row, we have that d is the symbol that we are searching for, such that OCC(BWT, d, 0) is 0 and C(BWT, d) is 7 and, hence LF(BWT, d, 0) is 7. Next, we compute LF(BWT, d, 11), which results in 9. Thus, the first iteration results in the open interval $[\![7, 9[\![$. The next iteration with symbol b then sets f to 7 and g to 9.

Table 1. LF mapping.

α	f	OCC(BWT,α,f)	C(BWT,α)	LF(BWT,α,f)	g	OCC(BWT,α,f)	C(BWT,α)	LF(BWT,α,g)
d	0	0	7	7	11	2	7	9
b	7	1	3	4	9	3	3	6
c	4	0	6	6	6	1	6	7
a	6	2	1	3	7	2	1	3

The last iteration results with the empty interval $[\![3, 3[\![$, which signals a failure in the search, i.e., the query string acbd is not a substring of the indexed string. In general, the procedure stops whenever it finds an empty interval.

4 Approach

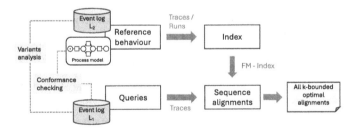

Fig. 3. Overview of the approach.

The overview of our approach is shown in Fig. 3. The approach requires a reference behaviour to be queried, a set of queries for which all optimal alignments are needed, and a value k. Given a query Q and the reference behaviour T, the approach outputs all optimal alignments of Q with a cost of at most k. As detailed in Subsect. 4.2, this approach can be used for variants analysis (log-to-log comparison) and conformance checking (model-to-log comparison). Depending on the operation, the reference behaviour can be either a family of traces representing the process model's behaviour or another event log.

The approach starts by identifying the set of event labels in the reference behaviour and defining an alphabet for indexing, e.g., english characters. In our case, this reference behaviour is a set of traces, which is formatted to construct the FM-Index using two special characters "|" and "$" as the trace/run separator and end of input, respectively. When computing the alignments for a trace, the events on the trace are labeled according to the alphabet produced during the indexing of the reference behaviour. Then, the FM-Index is used to compute all k-bounded optimal alignments, as detailed in the rest of the section.

4.1   All Optimal k-Bounded Alignments

Our approach to computing sequence alignments is based on the well-known approach to global sequence alignment using dynamic programming. First, a matrix that summarizes the cost of an alignment is computed, considering two possibilities: a synchronous move (the symbols being analyzed in both sequences match); and a sequence move, i.e., a symbol is skipped in either of the compared sequences. The size of the matrix depends on the size of the sequences being aligned. Assume we want to align sequences $S1$ and $S2$, then we need to build a matrix of size $(|S1| + 1) \times (|S2| + 1)$.

The approach above, however, aligns two sequences at a time and we need to align the trace against all traces in the reference behaviour. Instead of repeating the procedure once per run, which would be extremely costly, using the backward search over the BWT allows us to align the trace against multiple runs at a time. Moreover, to enumerate all the optimal alignments with at most k edit operations, we traverse and prune the search space using heuristics similar to the well-known branch-and-bound algorithm, as shown in Algorithm 2, which is an adaptation of the algorithm presented in [26].

Algorithm 2 clearly combines elements from the backward search over the FM-Index, the sequence alignment, and those to implement a branch and bound approach. The LF mapping over the BWT in line 14 and the recursive call in line 25 (instead of an explicit loop) implement the backward search over the FM-Index (Algorithm 1)[4]. The rules for updating the cost matrix, as used in sequence alignment – e.g., the Needleman–Wunsch algorithm [23] – are defined in line 17. Finally, the condition in line 19, i.e. all values in the cells of the row being calculated holding a value greater than k, stops the search for an alignment according to the branch-and-bound strategy.

Algorithm 2 Walk-Through. To illustrate how the algorithm works, let us compute the alignment of trace acbd against the set of concatenated runs abd|abcbd|$, same example used in Subsect. 3.4. We will be frequently referring to the BWM, arrays OCC and C, and columns F and L information in Fig. 2. We consider $k = 2$ and, hence, the cost matrix M will have a size of 5×7 as illustrated in Fig. 4.

The cost matrix is created in line 6 of Algorithm 2. Then, the first row and column of M are initialized, i.e., $M[i, 0] = i, \forall i \in [\![0, |\sigma| + k + 1]\!]$; and $M[0, j] = j, \forall j \in [\![0, |\sigma| + 1]\!]$. Since we are interested in aligning complete traces, we start by searching the interval

---

[4] We use a cost of 1 for moves and 0 for matching but other costs are possible. The use of ∞ for replacement implies preference for a combination of insertion and deletion.

Algorithm 2. All Optimal k-Bounded Alignments.

```
 1: Global BWT, SA, Occ, C, M, Solns
 2: procedure INIT(Runs)
 3:     BWT, SA, Occ, C ← BUILDFM(Runs)
 4: end procedure
 5: function CHECKCONF(σ, k)
 6:     M ← INITMATRIX(|σ| + k + 1, |σ|)
 7:     Solns ← ∅                                                          ▷ Empty priority queue
 8:     f, g ← LF("l", 0), LF("l", |σ| + 1)
 9:     BACKWARDSEARCH(REVERSE(σ), k, f, g, 1)
10:     return TAKEALLOPTIMAL(Solns)                                       ▷ Return only the optimal alignments
11: end function
12: function BACKWARDSEARCH(Q, k, f, g, row)
13:     for c ∈ Σ do                                                       ▷ In lexicographical order
14:         f', g'← LF(BWT, c, f), LF(BWT, c, g)
15:         if f' >= g' then continue
16:         for col ← 1, |Q| + 1 do
```

$$17: \quad M[\text{row, col}] \leftarrow \min \left(\begin{array}{l} M[\text{row - 1, col - 1}] \text{ if } Q[\text{row}] = c \text{ else } \infty \\ M[\text{row - 1, col}] + 1 \\ M[\text{row, col - 1}] + 1 \end{array} \right)$$

```
18:         end for
19:         if ∀j ∈ ⟦1, |Q|⟧, M[row, j] > k then continue
20:         localK ← min_{j ∈ ⟦1, |Q|⟧}(M[row,j])
21:         if M[row, |Q|] = localK then
22:             OFFER(Solns, BUILDSOLUTION(⟦f', g'⟧, row, col))
23:             k ← localK
24:         else
25:             k ← min(k, BACKWARDSEARCH(Q, k, f', g', row + 1))
26:         end if
27:     end for
28:     return k
29: end function
```

---

associated with symbol "l", that is, the end-of-trace mark. Then, BACKWARDSEARCH is called with the inverted trace to query.

The algorithm proceeds by filling the cells of the cost matrix M using the information already stored thereof. In line 13, we select a candidate symbol from the alphabet Σ, and in lines 14–15 we check if the candidate corresponds with a valid extension (i.e. if the LF mappings result in a non-empty interval). If the extension is not valid, then we skip the current symbol and consider the next one. In this example, only d will be a valid extension. We can check in the BWM of Fig. 2 that "l" appears in the last two rows of BWM in column F, whereas column L has two ds in the same rows. That means that "l" is only preceded by ds in all the runs. We now compute the content of $M[1,1]$, highlighted in Subfig. 4a with a background in orange. To this end, we use the content of the three surrounding cells, highlighted in yellow. Applying the rule in line 17, we have that $M[1,1] = min(M[0,0]$ **if** $c = $ 'd' **else** $\infty, M[0,1] + 1, M[1,0] + 1)$. In this case, the candidate symbol corresponds with the one in the column, i.e., d, hence $M[1,1] = min(0,2,2) = 0$. The same rule is applied to the rest of the columns until completing the row. The next line to consider is 25, where the procedure BACKWARD-SEARCH is recursively called, with f', g' updated to values 7 and 9, respectively, indicating that we have to work with the next row. Row number 3 is computed similarly.

An interesting case appears when the algorithm reaches row number 3 (highlighted with blue font color). By analyzing the set of indexed runs, one can see that b is preceded by two different symbols, namely a and c. We assume that the symbols are drawn from Σ in alphabetical order. Thus, the first symbol to be processed is a. Interestingly, once row 4 gets filled we reach the stop condition for procedure BACKWARDSEARCH, i.e., the value in the last column is less than or equal to all other values in the working row (see Subfig. 4b). Such stop condition is checked in line 21. This means that a¢bd is a possible alignment with a sequence move (same as in Fig. 1). We assume that function BUILDSOLUTION computes the textual form of the alignment, by traversing the M from cell $M[3,4]$ to cell $M[0,0]$, following the path with lowest cost all along (the path specified with red arrows Subfig. 4b), "applying" the rules of line 17 but inversely. With the solution, we also store the number of edit operations required by the alignment (1 in this case) and the SA interval. All the alignments found by the algorithm are stored in a priority queue called Solns. Later, in line 10, the procedure will return all the optimal alignments found.

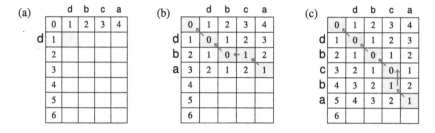

Fig. 4. Sample cost matrices to illustrate Algorithm 2.

Once a solution is found, the algorithm "backtracks" to the closest row where multiple extensions exist. In our example, this corresponds to row 3 where, after processing a, the algorithm still must explore the extension with c. Subfig. 4c presents the cost matrix computed when considering c, case where the alignment abcbd is found with 1 sequence move operation. Please note that the algorithm backtracks in line 22 whenever we reach the point where the row has alignments with more than k edit operations. It is worth noting that Algorithm 2 updates k when an alignment with fewer edit operations than k is found. This *dynamic adjustment* of k occurs in lines 23 and 25. In the first case, the update occurs right after finding an alignment. In the latter case, k is updated after returning from a recursive call, when k was updated down in the chain of recursion.

Note that the FM-Index can also do forward search by computing the BWT and all the other auxiliary data structures over the reverse of the original string. We refer the reader to [26] for additional details.

Complexity Analysis. Computing the sequence alignment of two sequences using dynamic programming is known to have a time complexity of $O(mn)$, where m and n are the lengths of the input sequences. The space complexity is also of $O(mn)$. We consider the space complexity a very important characteristic of this method, when we compare it with exponential space required by any A*-based methods. Moreover, in our case $m = n+k$ because of the bound on the number edit operations. It is also worth noting that the complexities depend on the size of the input trace and on k and not in the length of the runs.

The matrix is potentially computed for every indexed run, each resulting in an alignment. However, each alignment is not necessarily an optimal one because the exploration of the solution space is determined by the order in which each partial solution is extended, i.e., each symbol in lexicographical order in line 13.

Clearly, the number of alignments that can be computed for two sequences is exponential. The worst-case scenario corresponds to the case where an alignment required k insertions, resulting in a sequence of length $n + k$. There are thus $\binom{n+k}{k}$ possibilities to choose the match/mismatch positions in the alignment. Recall that alignments with more edit operations than k will be pruned as a result of the branch-and-bound strategy used by the algorithm. Moreover, we consider that the dynamic adjustment of k can potentially improve the perceived overall performance of the method. In fact, the method showed acceptable execution times and the exponential complexity was not observed.

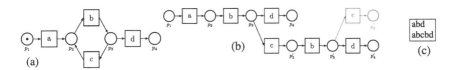

Fig. 5. (a) Petri net, (b) Causally compl. prefix unfolding, and (c) Runs.

4.2   FM-Index for Process Mining

Variants Analysis. Variants analysis compares pairs of event logs to find similarities and differences. For instance, the event logs of fast process executions could be compared against the event logs of slow process executions. The insights from such comparison can be used to find root causes leading to delays. Alignments have been previously used for variants analysis, see [33] for a survey and classification. To use our approach, an event log is used as a reference behaviour, while the other is considered as the set of traces to be queried.

Conformance Checking. Conformance checking is one of the main operations in process mining. In this operation, an event log and a process model are compared, where the model defines the reference behaviour and the traces in the event log are the queries to check for. To use our approach for conformance checking, the process model's behaviour must be captured as an event log to build the FM-Index. There are different strategies to generate an event log from a process model, such as simulation or unfoldings [19,20]. In this work, we use Petri net unfoldings to generate "complete" event logs from the process models. Petri nets is a formal model for concurrent systems that offers an intuitive graphical representation and a precise mathematical definition. In the following, we assume the reader is familiar with Petri nets, an introduction to this formalism can be found in other works, e.g. [22]. Let us recap only the basics on Petri nets.

Figure 5a shows a Petri net N, where transitions (boxes) carry a label – name of the activity it represents – but transitions can also be silent (usually labeled as τ). Places (circles) represent the states of the Petri net and can contain tokens (black dot). A distribution of tokens in a Petri net is a *marking*. A transition t is *enabled* at a marking and can *fire* if every place in its preset contains a token. Firing t leads to a new marking, where a token is removed from each place in the preset of t and a token is added to each place in the postset of t. While places can contain any number of tokens, in this work we consider only *safe* Petri nets, i.e., every place can contain at most one token. In Fig. 5a, the initial marking is $\{p_1\}$ and the final marking is $\{p_4\}$; once a token reaches the final marking, no transition can be enabled. When transitions fire successively from an initial marking, they form a firing sequence and if it reaches the final marking, it is called a *run*. For instance, a firing sequence that is a run in N is $\langle a, b, d \rangle$.

In the presence of loops, a Petri net represents infinite behaviour. Complete unfolding prefixes [19, 20] are finite prefixes representing the partial order semantics of a Petri net. These prefixes are acyclic and contain only forward conflict (places can have only one incoming arc, but they can have several outgoing arcs). Due to this restriction, the complete prefix of a Petri net requires having several transitions and places instantiations, which are called events and conditions, respectively. There are various strategies to construct a prefix unfolding (e.g., [6, 13]). In this work, we use [6] to compute a prefix unfolding that is complete with respect to causal relations. I.e., an unfolding stops once a marking already contained in the prefix is found, and the activities executed to reach such marking are the same. We refer to this last unfolding technique as *causally complete prefix unfolding*. We use this approach to capture at least one loop execution. Note, however, that loops can be unfolded any arbitrary number of times as required.

For example, Fig. 5b shows the causally complete prefix unfolding of N (Fig. 5a). In this unfolding, p_2'' is called the cut-off condition (a marking in the Petri net for which an equivalent marking already exists in the prefix). In this example, p_2'' is cut-off because p_2' represents the same marking and both markings are reached through the execution of activities $\{a, b, c\}$. Please note that p_2 is also the same marking as p_2' and p_2'', however p_2 is caused by $\{a, b\}$, and p_2' and p_2'' are caused by $\{a, b, c\}$. A causally complete prefix unfolding contains complete and incomplete runs. In the example shown in Fig. 5b, the complete runs are $\langle a, b, d \rangle$ and $\langle a, b, c, b, d \rangle$ because they reach the final marking represented by places p_4 and p_4'. In an unfolding, a complete run can be a partial order when concurrent transitions are present, thus the interleaved representations of the complete runs are used to build the FM-Index.

5 Evaluation

We implemented our approach on top of an open-source implementation of the FM-Index[5] that supports backward and forward search as described in [29]. The prototype[6]

---

[5] https://www.uni-ulm.de/in/theo/research/seqana.

[6] https://github.com/AstridRivPar/Alignment-FMIndex.git.

is implemented in C++ and uses wavelet trees to implement the LF mapping functions. All the experiments were executed in a Windows 10 laptop with an Intel Core i7-6700HQ CPU at 2.60 GHz, with 8 GB of RAM.

5.1 Datasets

The approach was tested using three public datasets, 5 model-log pairs in total. First, we took 3 synthetic models and event logs from [18]. The model/log **G** is acyclic and highly concurrent, **E** and **F** have cycles. The second dataset is the BPI Challenge 2012 (BPIC12) [11], which contains historical process executions of a loan application process. It consists of 13,087 traces. The events in this dataset have three different prefixes "A", "O" and "W". The used model is a Petri net manually derived from the event log and it was taken from the lab handouts of Chap. 12^7 of the book [9]. The model includes duplicated tasks but only captures activities with prefixes "A" and "O", thus we filtered out all the events with the prefix "W" from the log, leaving 576 trace variants. Finally, the last dataset was generated from an information system managing Road Traffic Fines (RTF) [10] in an Italian municipality. The dataset has 150,370 traces and 231 trace variants. The model selected for this dataset was discovered with a neural network-based discovery technique [30]. The model has a complex synchronization of two parallel paths within an unstructured loop. Details of the datasets are given in Table 2. For each log, #tr is the number of traces, #utr is the number of unique traces (trace variants), and the Min, Max and Mean are the minimum, maximum and average number of events per trace. For models, #runs represent the number of complete runs extracted from its unfolding, $|\Sigma|$ is the number of activity labels, $|BWT|$ is the size of the indexed string, and the Min, Max and Mean are the minimum, maximum and average number of events per run. Please note that for our approach only trace variants are considered.

Table 2. Characteristics of the datasets used in our experiments.

Dataset	Event log					Process model					
	#tr	#utr	Events per trace			#runs	$|\Sigma|$	$|BWT|$	Events per run		
			Min	Max	Mean				Min	Max	Mean
E	1000	98	6	22	7.02 ± 2.21	72	10	649	6	10	8 ± 2
F	1000	24	8	23	8.78 ± 1.72	12	10	127	8	11	9.50 ± 1.57
G	1000	144	9	9	9.0	144	10	1441	9	9	9.0
BPIC12	13087	576	3	38	7.04 ± 5.25	311	17	5131	3	18	15.50 ± 2.31
RTF	150370	231	2	20	3.73 ± 1.64	707	11	9130	3	14	11.91 ± 1.78

5.2 Conformance Checking

Experimental Setup. In a first experiment, the set of unique traces of each dataset was aligned against the corresponding indexed runs. Each experiment was run five times to compute the average execution time. For each dataset, we performed a series of experiments, each with a different k, starting with a value of zero and incrementing by one until optimal alignments for all traces were found.

---

^{7} https://conformancechecking.win.tue.nl/cc_book/in-the-lab/in-the-lab-chapter-12.

We considered a variant of the experiments using a fixed value for k and the other one where k was dynamically adjusted. We refer to those variants as "unoptimized" and "optimized", respectively. Finally, we tried a backward search (BW) as described in the previous sections and implemented a forward (FW) by building the FM-index over the reversed concatenated reference behaviour.

Table 3. Execution times for (a) Conformance checking with synthetic datasets, (b) Log-to-log comparison.

Dataset	Times(s)		
	PM4Py	FW	BW
E	0.392	0.036	0.056
F	0.104	0.003	0.005
G	0.531	0.042	0.043

(a)

Dataset	Times(s)		
	PM4Py	FW	BW
BPIC12	19.873	1.263	1.692
RTF	1.906	0.450	0.451

(b)

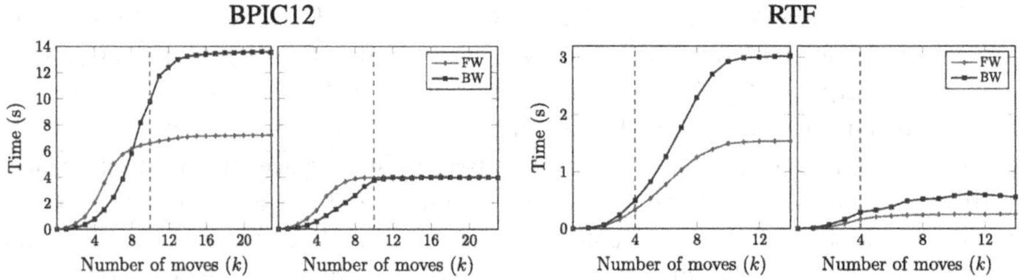

(a) Unoptimized   (b) Optimized   (c) Unoptimized   (d) Optimized

Fig. 6. Execution times for our approach with BPIC12 and RTF.

Results (Synthetic Datasets). Table 3a summarizes the execution times for synthetic datasets. As a reference, in column 1, we included the execution times for PM4Py [7], using the "alignment-based replay between the event log and a Petri net". However, the comparison is not straightforward: (1) PM4Py is implemented in Python, our prototype in C++; (2) the times for PM4Py includes the computation of the synchronous product between the log and the Petri net, whereas for our prototype we discount the time required for building the FM-index and we only report the times for the alignment; (3) PM4Py computes only one optimal alignment, while our prototype computes all of them. One interesting case is that of dataset G, where there is a big difference in execution times, PM4Py took 0.531 s and our approach took 0.042 and 0.043 s in the backward and forward search. Seemingly, the high degree of concurrency induces high computational costs in the case of PM4Py. In the case of our prototype, all the interleavings are computed beforehand thus reducing some of the overhead.

Results (Real-World Datasets). In the case of BPIC12, the maximum value for k was 23. Interestingly, FW search was twice as fast as BW search in the unoptimized version (cf., k kept constant), as shown in Figs. 6a-b. In contrast, better execution times were obtained when the value of k was dynamically adjusted by the algorithm, but the BW search was as performant as the FW search. We noticed that this behaviour results from the fact that discrepancies in traces with 9+ sequence moves occurred mostly at the end of the trace, thus forcing BW search to compute almost fully the cost matrices. This overhead seems to be reduced by the dynamical updates of k. The execution times for RTF, shown in Figs. 6c-d were faster in the version with optimization (cf., dynamically adjusting k), but showed better performance on FW search than on BW search. By manually checking, we could observe that the cases with 5+ discrepancies presented them uniformly distributed in the timeline represented by a trace. However, we believe other hidden factors impact the overall execution times, which need further investigation. Note that PM4Py required 22.16 s for processing BPIC12, i.e., 5X slower than our implementation, and 2.17 s for RTF, i.e., 4X slower than our prototype. The time required for building the FM-Index is small (e.g., 3.5 s in the case of the RTF, and even less for the others). The approach in [32] computes approximate several (not all) optimal alignments. Unfortunately, their implementation is not available and it was not possible to compare against it. However, they use the same RTF event log and report an average of 1.41 approximate optimal alignments per trace, which contrasts with the average of 7.97 optimal alignments found by our approach. Similarly, our approach found an average of 5.97 optimal alignments for BPIC12 and 1.0 optimal alignment for E, F, and G.

5.3 Log-to-Log Alignment

Experimental Setup. This experiment consisted of iteratively aligning a trace against all the other unique traces in an event log. Table 3b presents times for BPIC12 (max $k = 9$) and RTF (max $k = 3$). Here, we used PM4Py's "Alignments between logs" method. Surprisingly, PM4Py was not only slower than our approach but also failed to find optimal alignments for 53/576 traces on BPIC12, and 154/231 traces on RTF. We prepared bubble charts with the results of this experiment. Each unique trace is represented by a bubble in the plot and the value over the Y-axis shows the length of the trace. The diameter of the bubble is proportional to the number of computed optimal alignments, and the number of sequence moves (k) is color encoded. We believe that this visualization could help in process standardization, i.e., traces having a large bubble are good candidates for standardization.

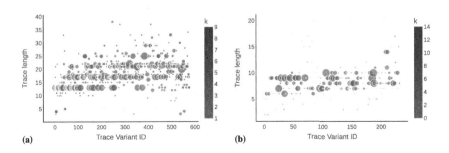

Fig. 7. Bubble charts for log-to-log alignment, a) BPIC12, and b) RTF.

6 Conclusions and Future Work

We presented an approach to compute all k-bounded optimal alignments. To show the potential of the approach, it was tested in the context of conformance checking and log variant analysis. In contrast to previous work, our method returns all the (k-bounded) optimal alignments and not only few approximations. The use of an upper-bound k, i.e., maximum number of sequence moves allowed by the algorithm, plays an important role not only in pruning the state space explored by the method but also reduces the overall memory footprint which, in turn, results in very competitive running times. Since the technique works on sequential executions (runs/traces), when used for conformance checking, a log from the model needs to be computed, for example using unfolding techniques. As an avenue for future work, we aim at lifting this limitation by combining the FM-Index with other auxiliary data structures, e.g., event structures, not only to allow loop reentrancy but also to provide additional information to produce intuitive feedback to end-users. Another avenue for future work is the extension of the approach to compute alignments for very large datasets.

Acknowledgments. This work received funding from the Swiss National Science Foundation, Grant No. IZSTZ0 208497 (ProAmbitIon project). Astrid Rivera-Partida is doctoral fellow with CVU 1007189, funded by Mexico's government (CONAHCyT).

References

1. van der Aalst, W.M.P.: Process Mining - Discovery. Springer, Conformance and Enhancement of Business Processes (2011)
2. van der Aalst, W.M.P.: Decomposing petri nets for process mining: a generic approach. Distrib. Parall. Databases **31**(4), 471–507 (2013)
3. van der Aalst, W.M.P., Adriansyah, A., van Dongen, B.F.: Replaying history on process models for conformance checking and performance analysis. WIREs Data Mining Knowl. Discov. **2**(2), 182–192 (2012)
4. Adriansyah, A.: Aligning observed and modeled behavior. Phd Thesis, Technische Universiteit Eindhoven, Mathematics and Computer Science (2014)
5. Adriansyah, A., van Dongen, B.F., van der Aalst, W.M.P.: Conformance checking using cost-based fitness analysis. In: EDOC, pp. 55–64. IEEE Comp Soc (2011)
6. Armas-Cervantes, A., Baldan, P., Dumas, M., Garcia-Bañuelos, L.: Diagnosing behavioral differences between business process models: an approach based on event structures. Inf. Syst. **56**, 304–325 (2016)
7. Berti, A., van Zelst, S.J., Schuster, D.: Pm4py: a process mining library for python. Softw. Impacts **17**, 100556 (2023)
8. Burrows, M., Wheeler, D.: A block-sorting lossless data compression algorithm. Technical Report, number 124, Digital Equipment Corporation (1994)
9. Carmona, J., van Dongen, B.F., Weidlich, M.: Conformance checking: foundations, milestones and challenges. In: van der Aalst, W.M.P., Carmona, J. (eds.) Process Mining Handbook, LNBIP, vol. 448, pp. 155–190. Springer (2022)

10. de Leoni, M., Mannhardt, F.: Road traffic fine management process. https://doi.org/10.4121/uuid:270fd440-1057-4fb9-89a9-b699b47990f5
11. van Dongen, B.: BPI challenge 2012. https://doi.org/10.4121/uuid:3926db30-f712-4394-aebc-75976070e91f
12. Dongen, B.F.: Efficiently computing alignments. In: Weske, M., Montali, M., Weber, I., vom Brocke, J. (eds.) BPM 2018. LNCS, vol. 11080, pp. 197–214. Springer, Cham (2018). https://doi.org/10.1007/978-3-319-98648-7_12
13. Esparza, J., Römer, S., Vogler, W.: An improvement of McMillan's unfolding algorithm. Formal Methods Syst. Des. **30**(2), 285–310 (2002)
14. Ferragina, P., Manzini, G.: Opportunistic data structures with applications. In: FOCS, pp. 390–398. IEEE Computer Society (2000)
15. García-Bañuelos, L., van Beest, N., Dumas, M., Rosa, M.L., Mertens, W.: Complete and interpretable conformance checking of business processes. IEEE Trans. Software Eng. **44**(3), 262–290 (2018)
16. Lee, W.L.J., Verbeek, H.M.W., Munoz-Gama, J., van der Aalst, W.M.P., Sepúlveda, M.: Recomposing conformance: closing the circle on decomposed alignment-based conf. checking in process mining. Inf. Sci. **466**, 55–91 (2018)
17. de Leoni, M., Marrella, A.: Aligning real process executions and prescriptive process models through automated planning. Expert Syst. Appl. **82**, 162–183 (2017)
18. Lu, X.: Handling duplicated tasks in process discovery by refining event labels. https://doi.org/10.4121/uuid:ea90c4be-64b6-4f4b-b27c-10ede28da6b6
19. McMillan, K.L.: Symbolic model checking. Kluwer (1993)
20. Montanari, U., Rossi, F.: Contextual occurence nets and concurrent constraint programming. In: Int. Wksp. Graph Transfer in Computer Science, LNCS, vol. 776, pp. 280–295. Springer (1993)
21. Munoz-Gama, J., Carmona, J., van der Aalst, W.M.P.: Single-entry single-exit decomposed conformance checking. Inf. Syst. **46**, 102–122 (2014)
22. Murata, T.: Petri nets: Properties, analysis and applications. Proc. of the IEEE **77**(4), 541–580 (1989)
23. Needleman, S.B., Wunsch, C.D.: A general method applicable to the search for sim. in the amino acid sequence of two proteins. J. Mol. Biol. **48**, 443–453 (1970)
24. Nong, G., Zhang, S., Chan, W.H.: Linear suffix array construction by almost pure induced-sorting. In: 2009 Data Compression Conference, pp. 193–202 (2009)
25. Reißner, D., Armas-Cervantes, A., Conforti, R., Dumas, M., Fahland, D., Rosa, M.L.: Scalable alignment of process models and event logs: an approach based on automata and s-components. Inf. Syst. **94**, 101561 (2020)
26. Renders, L.: Approximate Sequence Alignment using the Bidirectional FM-index. Ph.D. thesis, Ghent University (2020)
27. Sani, M.F., Kabierski, M., van Zelst, S.J., van der Aalst, W.M.P.: Model-independent error bound estimation for conformance checking approximation. In: BPM Workshops, LNBIP, vol. 492, pp. 369–382. Springer (2023)
28. Fani Sani, M., van Zelst, S.J., van der Aalst, W.M.P.: Conformance checking approximation using subset selection and edit distance. In: Dustdar, S., Yu, E., Salinesi, C., Rieu, D., Pant, V. (eds.) CAiSE 2020. LNCS, vol. 12127, pp. 234–251. Springer, Cham (2020). https://doi.org/10.1007/978-3-030-49435-3_15
29. Schnattinger, T., Ohlebusch, E., Gog, S.: Bidirectional search in a string with wavelet trees and bidirectional matching statistics. Inf. Comput. **213**, 13–22 (2012)
30. Sommers, D., Menkovski, V., Fahland, D.: Process discovery using graph neural networks. In: ICPM, pp. 40–47. IEEE Comp Soc (2021)

31. Taymouri, F., Carmona, J.: A recursive paradigm for aligning observed behavior of large structured process models. In: La Rosa, M., Loos, P., Pastor, O. (eds.) BPM 2016. LNCS, vol. 9850, pp. 197–214. Springer, Cham (2016). https://doi.org/10.1007/978-3-319-45348-4_12
32. Taymouri, F., Carmona, J.: An evolutionary technique to approximate multiple optimal algns. In: BPM, LNCS, vol. 11080, pp. 215–232. Springer (2018)
33. Taymouri, F., Rosa, M.L., Dumas, M., Maggi, F.M.: Business process variant analysis: survey and classification. Knowl. Based Syst. **211**, 106557 (2021)

Unsupervised Anomaly Detection of Prefixes in Event Streams Using Online Autoencoders

Zyrako Musaj and Marwan Hassani$^{(\boxtimes)}$ (iD)

Eindhoven University of Technology, Eindhoven, The Netherlands
m.hassani@tue.nl

Abstract. In this work we address the problem of unsupervised online detection of anomalies in traces of logs. Our input is an event log containing multiple traces where each trace is an ordered and finite sequence of activities. This problem presents a significant challenge due to the need to identify abnormal sequence patterns without the benefit of labeled data or the advantage of being able to forget individual event data since an instance is represented by a specific *sequence* of events. This requires methods that can adapt to evolving data streams and provide timely and accurate anomaly detection while efficiently managing limited memory resources. This paper presents an efficient unsupervised-learning method for online anomaly detection. We leverage a limited data structure to store prefixes. Event stream prefixes are transformed into vector representations using word2vec or one-hot encoding, which are fed into an online autoencoder. The discrepancy between input and output generates a reconstruction error, serving as an anomaly score. We also introduce Progressive Anomaly Labelling (PAL), a dynamic method for real-time anomaly detection which helps in labelling suffixes as anomalous once their prefix is labelled as such. Our approach excels in detecting control-flow and data-flow anomalies, early anomaly identification, and reduced execution time, outperforming state-of-the-art online anomaly detection techniques. The implementation and the datasets are publicly available at https://github.com/zyrako4/sequence-online-ad.

Keywords: Unsupervised online anomaly detection · Event streams

1 Introduction

In recent years, process mining has gained attention for analyzing and enhancing business processes using event logs [1]. These event logs are invaluable for process analysis. However, these logs can contain anomalies, which are deviations from the expected sequence, and these anomalies can significantly affect process models and decision-making [3]. Consider a scenario where a manufacturing process experiences unexpected delays or a financial transaction process encounters unusual patterns. Identifying these anomalies in real-time can be pivotal for ensuring smooth operations. Researchers have explored various anomaly detection approaches, yet a substantial portion of them operates in an offline mode, which restricts their real-time applicability. This limitation raises a critical issue: how can we detect anomalies in real-time event streams, where

© The Author(s), under exclusive license to Springer Nature Switzerland AG 2025
M. Comuzzi et al. (Eds.): CoopIS 2024, LNCS 15506, pp. 93–110, 2025.
https://doi.org/10.1007/978-3-031-81375-7_6

events are continuously generated and processed, ensuring prompt anomaly identification while managing limited memory resources?

Online anomaly detection in event streams is vital for several reasons. Firstly, it enables the early identification of anomalies in process execution, allowing for swift corrective actions, which can be crucial in contexts where errors can lead to significant consequences. Secondly, online detection provides real-time insights into process behavior, facilitating timely decision-making. However, this domain poses several challenges. One major challenge is the limited amount of memory available for analysis. Unlike offline methods that can process entire event logs, online detection must operate within memory constraints. These restrictions can also be implied by external privacy regulations (i.e. GDPR) that prohibit the unconditional storage of data. This requires efficient techniques to manage and analyze event data as it arrives. Furthermore, real-world event streams can be vast and diverse, making it challenging to design an online anomaly detection system that is both accurate and computationally efficient.

Autoencoders are a type of neural network that has shown promise in capturing complex patterns in data, including anomalies. Historically, autoencoders have been avoided in the context of online anomaly detection due to concerns about their computational efficiency. Their application in online settings has been limited due to the potential computational demands, especially when dealing with event streams that produce a high volume of sequences. Therefore, this paper proposes an innovative unsupervised-learning online anomaly detection framework that leverages autoencoders while addressing these efficiency challenges. This framework focuses on detecting anomalies on a prefix level, which is essential for maintaining context in event streams. We maintain a sliding window for recent events. To improve existing methods, we experiment with various encoding techniques, such as one-hot encoding and word2vec, and denoising autoencoders to improve the efficiency of anomaly detection without the need for prior labels.

The main contributions of this paper can be summarized as:

- An online autoencoder architecture for the detection of the anomalies in sequences of event streams,
- performing an early anomaly detection on a prefix level (and not only on a full trace level),
- detecting event sequence anomalies (control-flow anomalies) and event attribute anomalies (data-flow anomalies),
- conducting extensive experimental evaluation that shows the superiority of the contributed framework against state-of-the-art anomaly detection methods.

The remainder of this paper is organized as follows: Sect. 2 gives some required background to introduce the main framework. Section 3 delves into the relevant research to the addressed problem. In Sect. 4, we outline the methodology employed in this work, while Sect. 5 describes the experimental setup and presents the results of our experimental evaluation in several aspects. Finally, in Sect. 6, we draw conclusions based on our findings and propose potential directions for future research.

2 Preliminaries

The basics of process mining is formed by the notion of an *event* and an *event log*. An event log L is a multiset of traces where each trace σ is a finite ordered sequence of events $\sigma = <e_1, \ldots, e_k>$. An activity a_j is an attribute of event e_j for $j \in [1, k]$ which reflects the name of the activity being recorded when e_j happened. An event might record multiple attributes, not just the name of an activity.

An event is a specific action in a process, e.g. *Receive Payment*. An event attribute is additional details about an event, e.g. the user who did the event *Bob*. The event sequence refers to the ordered set of events, e.g., *Receive new Order* → *Receive Payment* → *Pack order*. Lastly, a trace is the complete history of events for a case, e.g., from *Receive New Order* to *Confirm Delivery*.

Definition 1 (Prefix and Suffix). *Given a trace* $\sigma = <e_1, \ldots, e_k>$ *and a positive integer* $i < k$, *a prefix of the trace is* $p = <e_1, \ldots, e_i>$.

A superset of the prefix, called suffix and denoted by s, is a sequence $p_{s_j} = \langle e_1, \ldots, e_{i+j} \rangle \supseteq p$, *which extends the prefix by adding additional events, for all* $j \in 1, \ldots, k - i$.

Figure 1 presents various types of sequences. It is important to note that whenever the term 'trace' is used, it specifically refers to a complete trace.

Definition 2 (Event Stream). *Given a universe of observable events* U, *an event stream is an infinite sequence of events* $e_n = (c, t, a)$, *where c is the case identifier, t is the timestamp, and a is the activity label. The stream is defined as* $S : \mathbb{N}_{\geq 0} \to U$, *where each* $e_n \in U$ *is an observable unit indexed by* n.

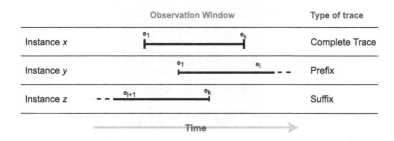

Fig. 1. Types of sequences depending on the observation window.

Given a dynamic, possibly infinite, event stream $\mathcal{E} = e_1, e_2, \ldots$, the objective of online anomaly detection is to detect events, event sequences (prefixes), or full traces that follow patterns deviating "substantially" from the observed "norms" of the event sequences or traces of the evolving process. Formally: let $\mathcal{S}^+ = \{(p^{(i)}, y^{(i)}) | \forall i \in \mathbb{N}\}$ be a set of potentially infinite sequence of tuples each consisting of a prefix $p^{(i)}$ and a corresponding anomaly label $y^{(i)} \in \{0, 1\}$. Additionally, let $\mathcal{S} = \{(p^{(i)}, y^{(i)}) | \forall i \in \{1, \ldots, I\}\}$ be a sub-sequence of previously observed prefixes. Let $\mathcal{A} = \{p^{(i)} | y^{(i)} =$

$1, i \in \{1, \ldots, I\}\}$ be the set of anomalies in $\mathcal{S}$, where $\frac{|A|}{I} \ll 0.5$. Also, let $\mathcal{S}_{train}$ and $\mathcal{S}_{valid}$ be disjoint subsets of $\mathcal{S}$.

Definition 3 (Online Anomaly Detection of Sequences in Event Streams). *Given a validation protocol $\mathcal{V}$ and an arbitrary anomaly detection function $g : U \rightarrow \{0, 1\}$ that was trained on $\mathcal{S}_{train}$, the objective of the online anomaly detection can be defined as:*

$$min_g \mathcal{V}(\mathcal{L}_c, \mathcal{S}_{valid}, g(.; \mathcal{S}_{train})), \qquad (1)$$

where $\mathcal{L}_c$ denotes a classification loss that quantifies the similarity of the true label $y^{(i)}$ and the prediction $\hat{y}^{(i)} = g(p^{(i)})$. We use test-then-train as a validation protocol $\mathcal{V}$.

The encoding of prefixes or traces refers to the process of representing and converting sequences of events, which may contain categorical or structured data, into a suitable data representation that can be efficiently analyzed and utilized by computational methods.

3 Related Work

The field of anomaly detection on event logs has witnessed significant growth in recent years, offering methods to detect anomalies at both the trace level, which concerns the order and occurrence of activities in a process trace, and the event level, which focuses on the attribute values of individual events. These methods leverage various approaches that do not require labeled data. However, the research on anomaly detection in event streams (real-time setting) is relatively limited.

Ko and Comuzzi [14] define offline event log anomaly detection as the processing of event logs as a batch of data, whereas online event log anomaly detection involves processing events as a continuous stream of data that becomes available for analysis as soon as they are logged during the process execution. In essence, offline detection is performed retrospectively, while online detection occurs in real-time. The latter entails the continuous monitoring of event streams or event logs, detecting deviations from expected patterns, and providing timely alerts or interventions [26]. However, this setting introduces additional challenges to the design of event log anomaly detection methods, such as the limited number of recent events available for analysis due to the finite memory assumption [14].

Tavares et al. [23] introduced an online anomaly detection method comprising a conversion phase extracting case features from traces and time intervals, followed by the use of the DenStream algorithm [6] for identifying irregular activity sequences or time intervals. Setiawan et al. [22] proposed a different approach involving graph creation for incoming events, simplifying graphs by removing infrequently visited edges and checking for inter-arrival time violations. However, this method requires clean training data, posing challenges for real-life scenarios, and does not handle attribute-based anomalies.

The most recent study done in the field is the one of Ko and Comuzzi [14]. Their method operates in an online setting, adopting a window-based approach. They explore prefix-length and trace-level encodings, favoring prefix-length encoding for its better accuracy and speed. The anomaly scores are calculated using the statistic leverage, an information-theoretic measure. However, the trace-level method involves zero padding, creating biases in the scoring process by favoring longer traces over shorter ones. They introduce a weighting factor based on trace length to mitigate this bias.

Autoencoder-based anomaly detection methods, like PW-AE by Cazzonelli and Kulbach [7], have shown promise in data streams. PW-AE addresses gradual adaptation issues by assigning higher weight to anomalous data during model training. Although effective, for online anomaly detection, generating a unified representation of traces using appropriate encoding methods is crucial. Encoding methods play a vital role in transforming event data into feature vectors that can be efficiently processed by autoencoders, demonstrating their potential as effective unsupervised methods for this task. Therefore, our framework similarly leverages autoencoders to tackle these challenges in online anomaly detection.

Table 1. State-of-the-art anomaly detection methods classification of unsupervised approaches ($\sim$ = Other, * = Competitor in the experimental evaluation cf. Sect. 5).

Method	Paper	Online	Encoding	Control Flow	Data Flow
Probabilistic	Li and van der Aalst [16]	✗	$\sim$	✓	✗
	Bezerra and Wainer [2]	✗	$\sim$	✓	✗
	Choi et al. [8]	✓	$\sim$	✓	✗
	Cuzzocrea et al. [9]	✗	$\sim$	✓	✗
	Böhmer and Rinderle-Ma [3]	✗	$\sim$	✓	✓
	Böhmer and Rinderle-Ma [4]	✗	$\sim$	✓	✓
Distance based	van Zelst et al. [27]	✓	$\sim$	✓	✗
	Junior et al. [12]	✗	word2vec	✓	✗
	Setiawan et al. [22]	✓	$\sim$	✓	✗
	Rullo et al. [20]	✗	word2vec	✓	✓
Information theoretic	Ko and Comuzzi [13]	✗	one-hot	✓	✗
	Ko and Comuzzi* [14]	✓	one-hot	✓	✗
Neural networks based	Nolle et al. [18]	✗	one-hot	✓	✓
	Nolle et al. [19]	✗	one-hot	✓	✓
	Nguyen et al. [17]	✗	one-hot	✓	✓
	Guan et al. [10]	✗	$\sim$	✓	✓
	OAE (ours)	✓	one-hot word2vec	✓	✓

Table 1 outlines unsupervised methods in process anomaly detection. Most works target offline scenarios, with only a few tackling online anomaly detection, primarily focusing on control-flow anomalies. In contrast, our work (OAE) addresses both online challenges and data-flow anomalies. Additionally, our evaluations emphasize prefix-length analysis, unlike the prior trace-level focus in existing literature.

4   OAE Framework

Our Framework consists of four key stages, as illustrated in Fig. 2: (1) maintaining a sliding window for observed traces in the event stream, which we discuss in Sect. 4.1, (2) encoding the prefix seen for each case, detailed in Sect. 4.2, (3) utilizing the autoencoder architecture as explained in Sect. 4.3, and (4) computing the anomaly score and performing classification to identify anomalous instances as discussed in Sect. 4.4. Algorithm 1 provides the pseudocode for executing the framework.

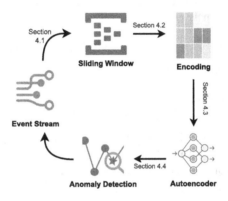

Fig. 2. Our online anomaly detection framework.

4.1   Trace-Level Sliding Window

Similar to other online anomaly detection methods found in the literature, it is practical to initiate decisions regarding trace anomalies only after a sufficient number of events have been accumulated. To address this, we adapt the *Grace Period* (GP) [15], $GP \in \mathbb{N}^+$, which signifies the count of traces for which at least 2 events have been recorded, mathematically $GP = |\sigma : pref(\sigma, 2) \neq \bot|$. For example, setting $GP = 100$ implies that online anomaly detection commences after receiving the first event only when at least the first 2 events of 100 distinct traces have been received.

In addressing the challenge of managing finite memory resources in online data analysis, methods such as non-incremental event stream analysis commonly employ a sliding window approach. This technique focuses solely on a subset of the most recently received observations for analysis. In the context of processing event streams, we introduce a case-based sliding window strategy, designed to retain in memory only the events associated with a limited number of recent cases. Initially, up to the point of reaching the GP, we store all events encountered in the stream within this sliding window. However, upon reaching GP, with each new event, we monitor whether the sliding window has surpassed its defined limits in terms of traces and events. In cases where these limits are exceeded, we initiate the removal of the oldest event (the event with the earliest timestamp) in the SW to make room for the new incoming event.

4.2 Encoding Methods

Before each instance of the event stream (i.e. an event sequence of any length) is used as an input for the autoencoder, it needs to be transformed into a suitable form, as stated in Sect. 2. In this work, we investigate two different encoding methods: one-hot encoding and word2vec encoding.

One-Hot Encoding. One-hot encoding is not only the most commonly used encoding method in online settings, but also one of the few methods that considers attributes, making it the prevalent choice among existing approaches. In this method, we employ an n-dimensional vector to represent each attribute (e.g., event name, user, day), where n corresponds to the number of distinct activities found in the event log. For encoding a specific activity, we utilize a one-hot vector, where the corresponding dimension is set to one, and all other dimensions are set to zero. The same approach is applied to encode each event attribute, resulting in a one-hot vector for the activity and one for each attribute associated with that event. These vectors are then combined by concatenating them into a unified representation. For instance, if the activity vectors are labeled as $a_1, a_2, ..., a_n$, and the only event attribute available is the user, with corresponding user vectors $u_1, u_2, ..., u_n$, the resulting concatenated vector would be $a_1 \| u_1 \| a_2 \| u_2 \| ... \| a_n \| u_n$, where $\|$ denotes concatenation.

Word2vec Encoding. The word2vec embedding [12,20] employs a two-layer neural network that compresses input attributes into a compact set of columns, effectively reducing their dimensionality. This neural network aims to reconstruct linguistic contexts of words, implying that the learned embedding is based on neighboring words. If a group of words consistently appears close to certain words, their embeddings will become similar. In the context of our study, we view each attribute as a word, and the entire case can be comparable to a sentence. By applying this analogy, word2vec captures meaningful relationships between attributes within the event log data, enabling effective anomaly detection. Word2vec provides a vector representation for each word, and to construct the full sentence vector, we have different options for mapping the input words. In this paper we use a two-step aggreggation technique, where we average the attribute vector representations to form the event vector representation and then concatenate them to form the prefix representation.

Let $p = e_1, e_2, e_3...e_m$ denote a prefix of length m, where each event consists of the activity name and other event attributes. Let us suppose we have only the user as an event attribute. Given a vector size n, word2vec would represent each attribute of the event $\mathbf{e}_i$ as the mean of the corresponding activity vector $\mathbf{a}_i = [\mathbf{a}_{i,1}, \mathbf{a}_{i,2}, \ldots, \mathbf{a}_{i,n}]$ and the user attribute vector $\mathbf{u}_i = [\mathbf{u}_{i,1}, \mathbf{u}_{i,2}, \ldots, \mathbf{u}_{i,n}]$. The vector representation of the event $\mathbf{e}_i$ would be the element-wise mean of the two vectors:

Algorithm 1. Online Anomaly Detection using Autoencoders (OAE).

1: E : stream of events, W_c: maximum number of traces in SW, W_e: maximum number of events in SW, $after\_GP \leftarrow False$, T : a threshold on anomaly score
2: **for** $e_i \in E$ **do**
3:     $SlideSW andAddEvent(e_i)$ ▷ Section 4.1
4:     **if** not after_GP **then**
5:         **if** $|SW| \geq GP$ **then**   ▷ Check GP conditions
6:             $after\_GP \leftarrow True$
7:             $initiateAutoencoder(SW)$
8:         **end if**
9:     **else**   ▷ Anomaly Detection Activated
10:        $P \leftarrow Encoding(SW_i)$ ▷ Section 4.2
11:        $score \leftarrow getAnomalyScore(P)$ ▷ Section 4.4
12:        **if** $score \geq T$ **then**
13:            $label(P_i) \leftarrow$ anomalous
14:        **else**
15:            $label(P_i) \leftarrow$ normal
16:        **end if**
17:    **end if**
18:    Increment SW_e by 1
19:    Increment prefix of trace t
20: **end for**

$$\mathbf{e}_i = \left[\frac{\mathbf{a}_{i,1} + \mathbf{u}_{i,1}}{2}, \frac{\mathbf{a}_{i,2} + \mathbf{u}_{i,2}}{2}, \ldots, \frac{\mathbf{a}_{i,n} + \mathbf{u}_{i,n}}{2} \right] \tag{2}$$

where each component of $\mathbf{e}_i$ is the average of the corresponding components in $\mathbf{a}_i$ and $\mathbf{u}_i$. This representation captures the combined information of both the activity and the user attribute for each event in the business process sequence.

The vector representation of the entire prefix p would be obtained by concatenating the event vectors $\mathbf{e}_1, \mathbf{e}_2, \ldots, \mathbf{e}_m$:

$$\text{Prefix Representation: } \mathbf{p} = \mathbf{e}_1 \| \mathbf{e}_2 \| \ldots \| \mathbf{e}_m \tag{3}$$

This results in a single vector that captures the information of all events in the business process sequence.

Word2vec, with its capacity to create dense vectors that effectively capture semantic relationships, is well-suited for autoencoders in anomaly detection. Its ability to capture context and semantic meaning without extensive hyperparameter tuning aligns perfectly with the unsupervised nature of autoencoders, making it an ideal choice for encoding. Because feed-forward neural networks have a fixed-size input, we must apply one more step of pre-processing. To force all encoded trace vectors to have the same size, we pad all vectors with zeros, so each vector has the same size as the longest vector (i.e., the longest trace) in the event log.

4.3   Online Autoencoder

In classification tasks the desired output of the neural network will be a class label $\hat{y}^{(i)}$. However, one can also train a neural network without the use of class labels. This is especially helpful when no labels exist. Autoencoders are neural networks that do not rely on labels and are what we deployed in our method. The explanation in Definition 3 includes supervised approaches, however we limit our analysis to unsupervised online anomaly detection methods. An autoencoder is trained in an unsupervised fashion, as it is trained to reproduce its own input $(p^{(i)})$.

Obviously, a neural network, if given enough capacity and time, can simply learn the identity function of all examples in the training set. To prevent a neural network from doing that, we apply a dropout technique which randomly deactivates some of the neurons in a layer during training, forcing the network to learn more robust and generalized representations. This technique helps to avoid overfitting, where a model memorizes the training data without capturing meaningful patterns.

In addition to dropout, another technique is enforcing a bottleneck, where one of the hidden layers is very small, limiting the information flow and preventing the autoencoder from simply learning the identity function.

Our proposed method is based on a denoising autoencoder, utilizing dropout and a bottleneck to learn robust and noise-free representations of the input data. The autoencoder consists of an input and an output layer with linear units, along with 2 hidden layers with rectified linear units. These training parameters remain consistent across different event logs, while the size of the hidden layer is adjusted based on the specific event log. Specifically, the number of neurons in the hidden layer is set to half the size of the input layer. The activation function for the output layer is set to hyperbolic tangent function. For the real-life datasets, we opt for using only 1 hidden layer, as suggested by Nolle et al. [18].

To initiate the score calculation for the most recent event sequence, we start by invoking the reconstruction function $r\theta$ on the input $p^{(i)}$. This involves a forward pass through the autoencoder to generate a reconstruction, denoted as $\hat{p}^{(i)}$. Next, we compute the reconstruction loss $\mathcal{L}^i$ as $\mathcal{L}(p^{(i)}, \hat{p}^{(i)})$. To account for potential variations in average reconstruction losses, we apply a post-processing function π to scale $\mathcal{L}^i$, resulting in the anomaly score $z^{(i)}$, explained in Sect. 4.4. Next, the autoencoder is trained using the back-propagation algorithm [21], where the encoded event sequence serves as both the input and the label, to optimize the model's parameters. The test-then-train nature of applied validation protocol $\mathcal{V}$ (c.f Definition 3), ensures a high sensitivity to concept drifts. Figure 3 presents a simplified version of the architecture.

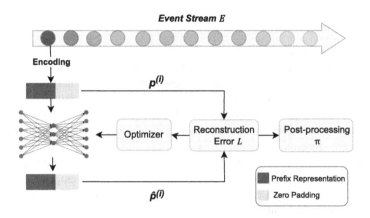

Fig. 3. Autoencoder trained to replicate encoded prefixes in E.

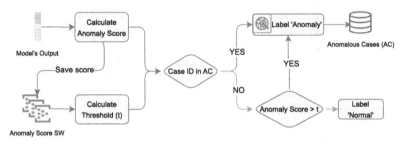

Fig. 4. Flowchart of the PAL method for online anomaly detection and the preceding anomaly scoring process. AC is the window of anomalous cases.

4.4 Anomaly Score

The autoencoder computes the reconstruction error, which helps in determining in an event prefix is anomalous. This error, which we call the anomaly score, measures the difference between the input prefix and its reconstructed version, using mean squared error (MSE) as a metric. The threshold for anomaly detection is dynamically determined based on the sliding window of the most recent anomaly scores. The threshold considers both the mean and standard deviation of the scores within this window, with the parameter alpha (α) influencing its sensitivity. A higher alpha value results in a more conservative approach, while a lower value increases sensitivity. Mathematically the threshold can be expressed as:

$$\tau = \mu + \alpha * std \tag{4}$$

Progressive Anomaly Labeling. To accommodate varying trace lengths and prevent anomalies due to the zero-padding, we maintain separate windows for different prefix lengths. This approach ensures that anomalies are detected consistently across traces of different lengths, as it prevents anomalies from being influenced by padding. Furthermore, we introduce the Progressive Anomaly Labeling (PAL) method, which continuously monitors the event stream for anomalies. PAL operates by tracking anomalous cases in a dynamic window and labeling new suffixes within these cases as anomalies in real-time. When a prefix is marked as anomalous, its case identifier is saved in a window of anomalous cases. Subsequently, whenever a new event from the same case is encountered, the suffix is immediately labeled as anomalous, regardless of whether its anomaly score exceeds the threshold. This process is illustrated in Fig. 4.

PAL significantly enhances the efficiency of the autoencoder and improves real-time anomaly detection by adapting to evolving patterns. By saving the case identifier of anomalous prefixes and labeling new suffixes immediately, PAL eliminates the need to re-evaluate the anomaly score for every new event, reducing redundant computations and enabling faster identification. This method leverages historical knowledge to ensure timely and precise detection of anomalies while allowing the model to focus on relevant sections of the event stream. Consequently, the processing speed and responsiveness of the autoencoder are greatly improved.

5   Experimental Evaluation

In this section, we present the setup and then the experimental results. An open source implementation of OAE together with datasets and results are available under: https://github.com/zyrako4/sequence-online-ad.

5.1   Experimental Setup

The following subsections outline our experimental setup for evaluating the proposed framework. We cover the event logs used, including injected anomalies, and detail the hyperparameters for the autoencoder and encoding methods.

Datasets.   To evaluate model-agnostic anomaly detection in event logs, researchers commonly introduce anomalies into existing event logs to simulate real-world scenarios. Artificial datasets, with manually injected anomalies into assumed clean logs, are valuable for testing detection algorithms. The artificial datasets in this study were created using the PLG2 tool [5] by simulating five distinct process models (small, medium, large, huge, and wide), originally proposed in [18]. To add variability, a set of users was randomly generated for each process, and subsets of users were assigned to specific activities within each process model. A likelihood graph was then constructed to establish dependencies between activities and attributes. Subsequently, event logs were generated from these process models by randomly sampling variants of the process with replacement. Each process model was generated with two attributes. In addition to artificial events logs, we also used the Hospital Billing[1] event log containing events about the billing of medical services that have been obtained from the ERP system of a regional hospital, and the Business Process Intelligence Challenge 2012[2] and 2013[3]

---

[1] https://data.4tu.nl/datasets/5ea5bb88-feaa-4e6f-a743-6460a755e05b.

[2] https://data.4tu.nl/datasets/533f66a4-8911-4ac7-8612-1235d65d1f37.

[3] https://data.4tu.nl/articles/dataset/BPI_Challenge_2013_incidents/12693914.

event log representing a loan application process and an incident management process from Volvo IT respectively. Details are presented in Table 2.

Table 2. Summary of descriptive statistics for experimental event logs.

Name	#Logs	#Cases	#Events	#Activities	#Attr.
Small	3	10k	110k–116k	41	2
Medium	3	10k	73k–84k	65	2
Large	3	10k	123k–137k	85	2
Huge	3	10k	90k–99k	108–109	2
Wide	3	10k	79k–84k	63–69	2
Hospital	1	10k	50k	16	0
BPIC13	3	66k	7.5k	25	4
BPIC12	1	13k	288k	73	2

In our study, we focus on six anomaly patterns that are likely to occur as genuine root causes in real-world scenarios. The anomalies, represented by one or more anomaly patterns, are injected into the logs that are assumed to be clean. Datasets include 10%, 20% or 30% anomalous cases. It's important to emphasize that our model is entirely unsupervised, and we introduce these predefined anomalies solely for evaluation purposes. These six anomaly patterns, illustrated in Fig. 5, include:

– Early - a sequence of at most 2 events are executed too early (skipped later).
– Late - a sequence of 2 or fewer events are executed too late.
– Insert - 3 or less random activities are inserted in the case.
– Skip - a sequence of 3 or less necessary events is skipped.
– Rework - a sequence of 3 or less necessary events is repeated after its occurrence.
– Attribute - an incorrect attribute value is set in 3 or fewer events.

Fig. 5. Examples of anomaly types.

Hyperparameters. The parameters used play a significant role in influencing the performance and effectiveness of the anomaly detection process, making this section an essential part of the evaluation and analysis of the framework.

Firstly, we investigated the impact of word2vec hyperparameters, particularly the number of dimensions and window size, which are known to have significant effects. Our findings indicate that varying vector sizes has minimal impact on performance. Hence, we adopt a vector size of 100 and a window size of 5. We utilize smaller vector and window sizes, as they require fewer computational resources while still maintaining a high level of representational capacity.

The training of the autoencoder employs the Adam optimizer, the parameters of which are set to $\beta_1 = 0.9$ and the learning rate is set at 0.0001. Additionally, a dropout of 0.5 is applied between all layers to prevent overfitting. In terms of the threshold's alpha value (Equation (4)) and the sliding window size for anomaly scores, we experimented with values of $\{0.1, 0.5, 1\}$ and $\{2000, 6000, 10000\}$ respectively. Our testing revealed that utilizing an alpha value of 0.1 and a window size of 6000 demonstrated the most optimal performance across all test datasets. To implement these strategies, we used Gensim for word embeddings (word2vec), Scikit-learn for one-hot encoding, and TensorFlow for the autoencoder architecture.

Evaluation Measures. Imbalanced data in anomaly detection challenges traditional accuracy-based evaluation methods. To comprehensively assess model performance, it's essential to consider true positives (correctly flagged anomalies), false positives (normal instances misclassified as anomalies), false negatives (anomalies misclassified as normal), and true negatives (correctly identified normal instances). Precision (accuracy of positive predictions) and recall (proportion of actual positives predicted) are crucial. To strike a balance between them, the F-score metric (cf. Eq. 5) is employed in the literature, integrating both aspects with a parameter (typically set to 1 for equal importance).

$$\text{F-score} = \frac{(1 + \beta^2) \times \text{Precision} \times \text{Recall}}{(\beta^2 \times \text{Precision}) + \text{Recall}} \tag{5}$$

5.2   Performance Results

We conducted a comprehensive evaluation of our proposed method, starting with a comparison of the two encoding methods employed. Figure 6 demonstrates that the word2vec encoding consistently outperforms the one-hot encoding across most of the event logs. While the difference between their performances is subtle, word2vec consistently exhibits advantage in anomaly detection. The bars representing word2vec encoding consistently yield higher F-scores. This suggests that word2vec encoding excels in capturing more relevant information and contextual nuances within the event logs, ultimately enhancing its anomaly detection capabilities. However, it's worth noting that one-hot encoding performs marginally better for the *small* dataset, possibly due to its limited range of attribute values in this particular dataset. Word2vec excels in larger corpora of words, which explains its strong performance in this context.

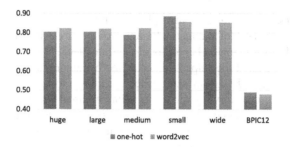

Fig. 6. Performance of each encoding method across datasets.

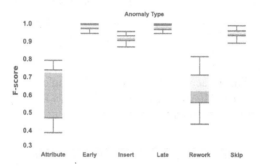

Fig. 7. Boxplots depicting the F-score distribution for different anomaly types across all synthetic event logs, utilizing word2vec.

Next, we conduct an ablation study to assess the impact of the PAL component in our framework. We compare the performance of utilizing PAL against using only the autoencoder's reconstruction error and threshold to classify instances. Initially, we noticed that using the latter led to higher F-scores than employing the PAL method. A detailed analysis by prefix length (cf. Fig. 8) showed that not using PAL performed better for shorter prefixes in event logs like huge and large (prefix length ≤ 4). However, for event logs like small and wide, both approaches performed similarly for short prefixes, while medium event logs performed better with PAL. This discrepancy in performance arises because shorter prefixes constitute a larger portion of event logs, contributing to the higher overall F-score when not using PAL. Conversely, PAL consistently outperformed the other approach for longer prefix lengths. PAL's adaptability to evolving anomaly patterns enabled it to excel in identifying abnormalities in the event stream, especially in real event logs, where longer prefixes are common.

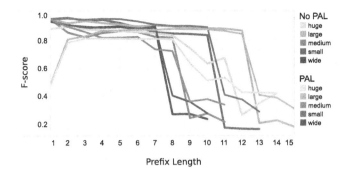

Fig. 8. F-Score wrt prefix length for each of the artificial logs.

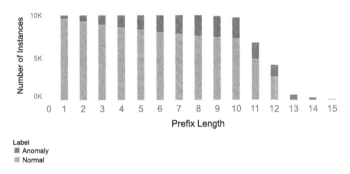

Fig. 9. Number of instances and distribution of normal and anomalous ones across prefix lengths on the *large* dataset.

Furthermore, Fig. 8 reveals a trend of decreasing average performance with the increase in prefix length. This could be influenced by the varying number of traces with different lengths in the datasets. This is illustrated in Fig. 9, where the number of instances notably decreases after a prefix length of 10. Additionally, the distribution of anomalies among the prefixes could play a role in influencing the overall performance trends. We notice that prefix lengths greater than 12, are all anomalous.

Our further analysis examined performance variations among six anomaly types (Fig. 7). Attribute anomalies posed the greatest challenge, as they do not heavily impact the control-flow perspective. However, the results indicate a moderate ability for the detection of such anomalies. Rework anomalies ranked second in difficulty, largely due to their association with higher length prefixes, as discussed earlier.

Conversely, the autoencoder excelled in identifying control-flow anomalies, well-captured by word2vec encoding. It notably detected insert and skip anomalies, as they significantly impact the context of activities. For example, a skipped activity alters the context of the entire sequence, and word2vec effectively identifies this deviation.

5.3 Runtime Results

An important aspect to consider when choosing an encoding method is the time it takes to process each instance using that method. For all experiments, we used GPU utilizing the MPS backend with a Python 3.10 environment. Table 3 provides the average encoding time for each prefix using one-hot encoding and word2vec embedding. As expected, one-hot encoding is generally faster in every dataset since it doesn't require a training process like word2vec. However, focusing solely on the encoding time doesn't provide a complete picture of the overall processing time for anomaly detection. Interestingly, despite one-hot encoding being faster for encoding individual prefixes, the overall anomaly detection time using word2vec is lower than one-hot encoding in every event log. This suggests that the extra time spent on training word2vec during encoding is offset by faster detection times. A notable contrast emerges when examining the BPIC12 dataset, revealing a nearly tenfold increase in processing time.

Table 3. Average encoding and execution time comparison when using the different encoding methods.

	Encoding Time [s]		Processing Time [s]	
	word2vec	one-hot	word2vec	one-hot
huge	0.016	0.015	0.030	0.044
large	0.017	0.015	0.032	0.043
medium	0.016	0.014	0.025	0.029
small	0.016	0.014	0.028	0.030
wide	0.016	0.014	0.024	0.028
BPIC12	0.196	1.608	2.117	19.87

Table 4. F-score and processing time for the leverage method and our proposed framework ran on the same datasets. The best results are highlighted in bold.

Event Log	Leverage [14]		W2V-OAE	
	F-score	Time [s]	F-score	Time [s]
Huge	0.63	0.73	0.824	0.030
Large	0.65	0.59	0.822	0.032
Medium	0.54	0.44	0.825	0.025
Small	0.51	0.28	0.857	0.028
Wide	0.51	0.67	0.854	0.024
Hospital	0.29	1.38	0.477	1.024
BPIC13	0.18	0.46	0.516	0.360

5.4 Comparison with the State-of-the-Art

The only work directly addressing the same problem as this work is the one by Ko and Comuzzi [14], making them our main competitors. Table 4 presents the results obtained on all the artificial and real event logs, focusing on both anomaly detection performance and computational complexity. The findings demonstrate that our proposed framework outperforms our competitor [14] in every scenario. Not only do we achieve very high performance in anomaly detection, but our method also exhibits, on average, over three times faster end-to-end running times.

6 Conclusions

In this paper we introduced an event stream anomaly detection framework and conducted a comprehensive evaluation to assess its effectiveness. We explored two different encoding methods, where word2vec emerged as a superior choice, demonstrating exceptional performance and efficiency. Word2vec's ability to capture semantic relationships among events without extensive tuning enhances anomaly detection. One key contribution of our framework is the leverage of the autoencoders for online anomaly detection, showing high accuracy and sensitivity. The dynamic threshold approach efficiently adapted to varying prefix lengths, enhancing overall system performance. Additionally, we introduced Progressive Anomaly Labelling (PAL), a novel method for continuous monitoring and timely anomaly identification.

The choice of the encoding method was orthogonal to the contributed architecture. As such, one possible future direction is to test the performance with other encoding methods. Additionally, we would like to address the cold start issue while collecting the minimal number of prefixes. Finally, we want to elaborate on our method to combine it with an online concept drift detection method [11], and continual learning models (see [24] and [25]) to detect changes in the underlying distributions and avoid catastrophic forgetting.

References

1. van der Aalst, W.: Process Mining: The Missing Link, pp. 25–52. Springer, Heidelberg (2016)
2. Bezerra, F., Wainer, J.: Algorithms for anomaly detection of traces in logs of process aware information systems. Inf. Syst. **38**(1), 33–44 (2013)
3. Böhmer, K., Rinderle-Ma, S.: Multi-perspective anomaly detection in business process execution events. In: OTM, pp. 80–98. Springer (2016)
4. Böhmer, K., Rinderle-Ma, S.: Mining association rules for anomaly detection in dynamic process runtime behavior and explaining the root cause to users. Inf. Syst. **90**, 101438 (2020)
5. Burattin, A.: PLG2: multiperspective processes randomization and simulation for online and offline settings. arXiv preprint arXiv:1506.08415 (2015)
6. Cao, F., Estert, M., Qian, W., Zhou, A.: Density-based clustering over an evolving data stream with noise. In: SDM, pp. 328–339 (2006)
7. Cazzonelli, L., Kulbach, C.: Detecting anomalies with autoencoders on data streams. In: PKDD, pp. 258–274 (2022)

8. Choi, S., Youm, S., Kang, Y.S.: Development of scalable on-line anomaly detection system for autonomous and adaptive manufacturing processes. Appl. Sci. **9**(21), 4502 (2019)
9. Cuzzocrea, A., Folino, F., Guarascio, M., Pontieri, L.: Deviance-aware discovery of high-quality process models. AJAIT **27**(07), 1860009 (2018)
10. Guan, W., Cao, J., Zhao, H., Gu, Y., Qian, S.: WAKE: a weakly supervised business process anomaly detection framework via a pre-trained autoencoder. IEEE Trans. Knowl. Data Eng. **36**(6), 2745–2758 (2024)
11. Huete, J., Qahtan, A.A., Hassani, M.: PrefixCDD: effective online concept drift detection over event streams using prefix trees. In: COMPSAC, pp. 328–333 (2023)
12. Junior, S.B., Ceravolo, P., Damiani, E., Omori, N.J., Tavares, G.M.: Anomaly detection on event logs with a scarcity of labels. In: ICPM, pp. 161–168 (2020)
13. Ko, J., Comuzzi, M.: Detecting anomalies in business process event logs using statistical leverage. Inf. Sci. **549**, 53–67 (2021)
14. Ko, J., Comuzzi, M.: Keeping our rivers clean: information-theoretic online anomaly detection for streaming business process events. IS **104**, 101894 (2022)
15. Ko, J., Comuzzi, M.: A systematic review of anomaly detection for business process event logs. Bus. Inf. Syst. Eng. 1–22 (2023)
16. Li, G., van der Aalst, W.M.: A framework for detecting deviations in complex event logs. Intell. Data Anal. **21**(4), 759–779 (2017)
17. Nguyen, H.T.C., Lee, S., Kim, J., Ko, J., Comuzzi, M.: Autoencoders for improving quality of process event logs. ESA **131**, 132–147 (2019)
18. Nolle, T., Luettgen, S., Seeliger, A., Mühlhäuser, M.: Analyzing business process anomalies using autoencoders. Mach. Learn. **107**(11), 1875–1893 (2018). https://doi.org/10.1007/s10994-018-5702-8
19. Nolle, T., Seeliger, A., Mühlhäuser, M.: BINet: multivariate business process anomaly detection using deep learning. In: BPM 2018, pp. 271–287 (2018)
20. Rullo, A., Guzzo, A., Serra, E., Tirrito, E.: a framework for the multi-modal analysis of novel behavior in business processes. In: IDEAL 2020, pp. 51–63 (2020)
21. Rumelhart, D.E., Hinton, G.E., Williams, R.J.: Learning representations by back-propagating errors. Nature **323**(6088), 533–536 (1986)
22. Setiawan, W., Thounaojam, Y., Narayan, A.: GWAD: greedy workflow graph anomaly detection framework for system traces. In: SMC, pp. 2790–2796 (2020)
23. Tavares, M., et al.: Leveraging anomaly detection in business process with data stream mining. ISYS **12**(1), 54–75 (2019)
24. Verbeek, T., Hassani, M.: Handling catastrophic forgetting: online continual learning for next activity prediction. In: CoopIS (2024, to appear)
25. Verbeek, T., Yao, R., Hassani, M.: Task-free continual learning with dynamic loss for online next activity prediction. In: ICPM Workshops (2024, to appear)
26. van Zelst, S.J., Bolt, A., Hassani, M., van Dongen, B.F., van der Aalst, W.M.: Online conformance checking: relating event streams to process models using prefix-alignments. Int. J. Data Sci. Anal. **8**, 269–284 (2019)
27. van Zelst, S.J., Sani, M.F., Ostovar, A., Conforti, R., La Rosa, M.: Detection and removal of infrequent behavior from event streams of business processes. Inf. Syst. **90**, 101451 (2020)

Autoencoder-Based Detection of Delays, Handovers and Workloads over High-Level Events

Irne Verwijst[1], Robin Mennens[2], Roeland Scheepens[2], and Marwan Hassani[1(✉)]⑩

[1] Eindhoven University of Technology, Eindhoven, The Netherlands
`i.verwijst@student.tue.nl, m.hassani@tue.nl`
[2] UiPath, Eindhoven, The Netherlands
`{robin.mennens,roeland.scheepens}@uipath.com`

Abstract. Detecting delays, anomalous work handovers, and high workloads is a challenging process mining task that is typically performed at the case level. However, process mining users would benefit from analyzing such behaviors at the process level where instances of such behavior are called high-level events. We propose a novel framework for high-level event mining that leverages anomaly detection and clustering methods to identify and analyze high-level events in an unsupervised setting. Our framework, called High-level Event Mining Machine Learning Approach (HEMMLA), utilizes an autoencoder-based anomaly detection method and requires no predefined time window or anomaly thresholds. An extensive experimental evaluation over real and synthetic datasets highlights the high scalability of our approach. An additional user study over real datasets underlines the ability of our framework to detect more interesting and explainable anomalies than the state-of-the-art.

Keywords: Process mining · Dynamic process behavior · Anomaly detection · Clustering · High-level events ·

1 Introduction

Process Mining aims to offer insights into a process by mining a so-called event log, which can then be analyzed by experts. Such experts often aim to understand and optimize the process by reducing costs, inefficiencies, delays, and high workloads.

Analysis in process mining is typically done at the process instance (case) level. For example, descriptive statistics over observed events are employed [6] by averaging throughput times. Process instances, however, do not run in isolation. For example, one overworked resource can cause delays in numerous process instances. Therefore, instead of analyzing individual instances of the process, we require a broader, more high-level perspective. Through this high-level perspective, we aim to bring these undesired high-level behaviors to light. These behaviors typically surface in particular areas of the process and at a specific time. We call an instance of this high-level behavior a high-level event.

Figure 1 shows the flow of a process from activity to activity. In high-level event mining, instead of analyzing the behavior of a certain activity, we are specifically interested in the behavior across activities. The figure shows three instances of high-level

M. Comuzzi et al. (Eds.): CoopIS 2024, LNCS 15506, pp. 111–128, 2025.
https://doi.org/10.1007/978-3-031-81375-7_7

behavior. Each of these instances, indicated by a colored box, reflects a high-level event of a different type. Based on industry specifications and a user study, this work considers three behavior types: handover, delay, and workload. A handover is characterized by the resources of events. In Fig. 1 we observe two high-level handovers, indicated by the blue boxes. The events within these boxes show unusual combinations of activities and resources in short time windows. Delays are events that show an exceptional waiting time. The high-level delay of Fig. 1 includes four transitions. A workload is defined by an overloaded or underloaded resource. *Resource 3* executes an unusual number of events on the right-hand side of Fig. 1, which we define as a high-level workload. Each high-level event has a time window that indicates when the behavior occurred. Detecting high-level events is not a trivial task as it is difficult to determine which process executions are undesired with respect to the data.

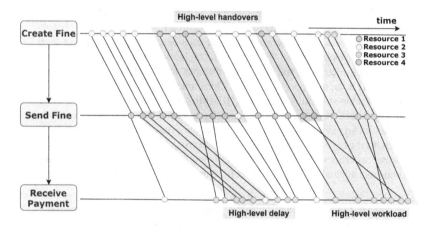

Fig. 1. A visual representation of high-level events of the types handover, delay, and workload. The high-level handovers on the segment (Create Fine, Send Fine) has unusual resource-activity combinations. The high-level delay on the segment (Send Fine, Receive Payment) shows slower progress of four transitions. The high-level workload is characterized by an abnormal number of events for a certain resource. (Color figure online)

To the best of our knowledge, no process mining industry vendor currently allows users to analyze high-level events. Cases can be analyzed in isolation or data can be aggregated to get a summarized view, but no vendor allows users to analyze specific high-level behavior across cases. Furthermore, high-level event mining has only been recently discussed in the literature [2] and is, therefore, a new area being explored in the industry.

The contribution of this work is the development of a novel framework HEMMLA, which discovers high-level events based on delay, handover, and workload in an event log. Although this work focuses on three behaviors, the approach can be extended to other types of behavior. The framework leverages the machine learning autoencoder model for anomaly detection and DBSCAN from the clustering domain for high-level event mining. Our approach is flexible in terms of parameters and input and can be adjusted to a user's requirements. We extensively evaluated HEMMLA using synthetic and real datasets including a user study with process mining users. Lastly, we show that HEMMLA is at least as good as the state-of-the-art by Bakullari et al. [3] while delivering better high-level delays and operating without rigid parameters. Additionally, the unsupervised nature of our work facilitates an evaluation based on common metrics.

Section 2 positions the paper and sheds a light into the related literature, Sect. 3 introduces the related definitions and formulates the problem. In Sect. 4, we introduce our framework HEMMLA, which we then extensively evaluate in Sect. 5. In Sect. 6, we conclude the paper with an outlook.

2 Related Work

In the literature, the concept of system-level or high-level events is fairly recent. Classical process mining techniques that analyze performance along individual cases cannot detect phenomena bounded in time and location. Toosinezhad et al. [22] show that undesired high-level behavior can be detected across different process instances at the segment level. The focus of their work was on dynamic bottlenecks and on detecting cascades of blockages and high loads. Wimbauer et al. [23] take the approach of Toosinezhad et al. [22] further with an online and unsupervised approach named PErrCas. Firstly, instead of partitioning the log into specific time windows, cascades are created incrementally with incoming outlier events. Secondly, clustering with DBSCAN takes place on the constructed cascades to discover patterns in the cascades [23]. PErrCas only detects dynamic delays. Denisov [6] applies high-level event mining on Baggage Handling Systems, where the event log is modeled in a process, queue, and resource dimension. In his method, blockages are detected and a root-cause analysis is conducted to discover problems in the system.

Other methods encode high-level behavior into new features that capture congestion [10, 19]. Pourbafrani et al. [17] do not encode observations as additional features for prediction purposes. Instead, each sequence of recurring outlier observations represents an explicit variant of high-level behavior, which is a trait of the process itself.

Bakullari et al. initially introduced a framework for high-level event mining, establishing a basis for the definition of different features related to congestion patterns [1]. Building upon this, Bakullari et al. , in their subsequent work, extended the scope of identifiable high-level events and refined the method of correlating them. The refined method incorporated six different behavioral types, each focusing on a unique aspect of the event data [3]. Recently, Bakullari et al. [2] have refined their work on high-level event mining with an overview of existing work and challenges.

Anomaly detection has been studied extensively in the field of process mining on the level of traces and prefixes. Nolle et al. [13] was one of the first solutions making usage of autoencoders for unsupervised trace anomaly detection. Musaj and Hassani [12] designed an efficient model to detect anomalies online on the prefix level. In our work, we utilize autoencoder too but over high-level events and we advance both [13] and [12] by using state-of-the-art encoding methods that turned to be more suitable for high-level events. Trace clustering has been actively addressed in the literature e.g. in

[5]. In our work, we apply a density-based clustering approach to group similar anomalous high-level by incorporating also their anomalousness values extracted from in the output of the autoencoder.

3 Definitions and Problem Formulation

To define the high-level events of handover, delay, and workload formally, we first define the necessary background on high-level event mining. We assume that our input events are records of activities that happened within a specific case and at a specific point in time, i.e., the standard event notion in process mining.

Here, we split our three behavior types into two groups. Handover and delay that are defined by transitions, and, workload which is defined by events. For the segment level, we define a high-level segment behavior as the group of transitions on a segment that was flagged anomalous for a specific type. A high-level event is a set of anomalous events (workload) or transitions (handover and delay) within a time window.

Definition 1 (Transition, Segment). *Let $\#_{attr}(e)$ be a function that returns the attribute value of event e's $attr = \{act, res, ts\}$ with act being the activity name, res the resource and ts the timestamp. A transition t is a pair of directly-follows events of a trace. For a pair of events (e_1, e_2) with $\#_{act}(e_1) \Rightarrow_{Log} \#_{act}(e_2)$ we define a transition as $t = (e_1, e_2)$. A segment is defined as $s = (act_1, act_2)$ where $\#_{act}(e_1) = act_1$ and $\#_{act}(e_1) = act_2$. S is the set of all segments.*

Definition 2 (Coordinate [3]). *A coordinate is a tuple $co = (s, \theta)$ referring to a position in space; segment s, and time; window pair $\theta = [tx_1, tx_2]$.*

In Fig. 1 a segment is $(CreateFine, SendFine)$. Given the time window $[tx_1, tx_2]$, a corresponding coordinate is $((CreateFine, SendFine), [tx_1, tx_2])$.

Definition 3 (High-Level Segment Behavior) *Let $\mathcal{U}_{types}$ be the universe of behavior types and let $s = (act_1, act_2)$ be a segment. $hlb \in \mathcal{U}_{types} \times S \to T$ is a function that assigns a set of transitions T to a combination of a type and a segment. $hlb(type, s) = \forall_{t \in T}\{t = (e_1, e_2)|\#_{act}(e_1) = act_1 \wedge \#_{act}(e_2) = act_2 \wedge t \in \mathcal{A}\}$. Each high-level segment behavior is a group of anomalous transitions on a segment with the same type.*

A high-level segment behavior in Fig. 1 is for example $(Handover, (CreateFine, SendFine), [e_1, e_2, ..., e_{12}])$ where $[e_1, e_2, ..., e_{12}]$ are the six transitions in the two blue highlights.

Definition 4 (High-Level Event). *A high-level event is defined as $hle = (type, E, T, \theta)$ with behavior type $type \in \mathcal{U}_{types}$, E a set of events, T the transitions of E. $E \in \mathcal{A}$ and $|E| \geq min\_e(type)$. $min\_e(type)$ is a predefined minimum number of elements per type. $\theta = [\#_{ts}(e_1), \#_{ts}(e_n)]$ where $\forall e \in E, \#_{ts}(e_1) \leq ts(e) \leq \#_{ts}(e_n)$. A high-level event on the segment-level with $s = (act_1, act_2)$ requires $T \neq \emptyset \wedge T \subseteq hlb(type, s)$.*

From the high-level segment behavior $(Handover, (CreateFine, SendFine),$ $[e_1, e_2, ..., e_{12}])$ two high-level events are identified, the two individual blue boxes in Fig. 1.

Given the definitions of high-level segment behavior, we can define high-level handovers and delays. To quantify a handover, we first define what a single handover implies. Handover from one activity to the next is defined as one resource directly following another resource on a segment.

Definition 5 (Handover). *Given segment* $s = (act_1, act_2)$ *and transition* $t = (e_1, e_2), Handover(e_1, e_2) = (\#_{res}(e_1), \#_{res}(e_2))$ *where* $\#_{res}(e_1) \neq \#_{res}(e_2)$

High-level delays are characterized by the time from one activity to the next. For this, we define the measure of elapsed time, which specifies this time.

Definition 6 (Elapsed Time). *Given segment* $s = (act_1, act_2)$ *and transition* $t = (e_1, e_2)$ *with* $\#_{act}(e_1) = Act_1, \#_{act}(e_2) = Act_2$ *and* $\#_{ts}(e_2) \geq \#_{ts}(e_1)$, *the elapsed time* $elapsed\_time(e_1, e_2) = \#_{ts}(e_2) - \#_{ts}(e_1)$.

While delay conceptually implies a high waiting time, we might also be interested in high-level events where the time between a segment is significantly lower than anticipated. Hence, our definition includes a higher and lower bound on the elapsed time.

Definition 7 (High-Level Handover, High-Level Delay). *Let* $set = \{handover, delay\} \in \mathcal{U}_{types}$. *For each type* $\in set$, *we observe a high-level event on coordinate* $co = (s, \theta)$ *with transitions* $T \subseteq hlb(type, s)$ *if and only if* $\forall_{t \in T}\ t \in \mathcal{A}$ *and* $|T| \geq min\_e(type)$. $\theta = [\#_{ts}(e_1), \#_{ts}(e_n)]$ *where* $\forall e \in E, \#_{ts}(e_1) \leq ts(e) \leq \#_{ts}(e_n)$.

While sophisticated methods exist for workload analysis, defining workload on the segment level gives ambiguous results about the busyness of a resource. This is because a resource's workload is not bound by the busyness of a resource on a segment. Therefore, workload is defined as the number of events performed by a resource in a specific time frame. For simplicity reasons, the time frame for the workload is set to one day.

Definition 8 (Workload). *Let* R *be the set of resources of event log* L. *Given resource* $r \in R$, *the workload* $W(r, \theta)$ *of a resource given time window* $\theta = [tx_1, tx_2]$ *is* $|\{e \in L | tx_1 \leq \#_{ts}(e) \leq tx_2 \wedge \#_{res}(e) = r\}|$.

Definition 9 (High-Level Workload). *Let* r *be a resource in* R. *We observe a high-level workload* hle_w *for events* E *in time window* $\theta = [tx_1, tx_2]$ *if* $\forall_{e \in E} \#_{res}(e) = r, W(r, \theta)$ *is anomalous and* $|E| > min\_e(workload)$.

High-level event mining involves the task of detecting dynamic behavior that significantly deviates from the established distribution. These dynamic behaviors are identified through anomaly detection (Definition 10). On the segment level, we call these high-level segment behaviors (Definition 3). The goal is to detect high-level events (Definition 4) at similar timestamps.

Definition 10 (Anomaly Detection). *Let X be a set of all high-level events of a specific type. The objective of anomaly detection is to detect a subset of $\mathcal{A} \in X$ that "substantially" deviates from the observed "norms" of the data. Let $\mathcal{S} = \{(x_i, y_i) | \forall i \in \{1, ..., |X|\}\}$ be the set of X including corresponding anomaly labels $y_i \in \{0, 1\}$. In that case, $\mathcal{A} = \{x_i | y_i = 1, i \in \{1, ..., |X|\}\}$ is the set of anomalies in $\mathcal{S}$, where $\frac{|\mathcal{A}|}{|X|} \ll 0.5$. Note that our autoencoder model uses a tiny portion of labeled normal data for learning.*

To determine the hle's for behavior types $handover, delay$, and $workload$ the first objective is to determine the set of anomalies $\mathcal{A}$. The second is to cluster these anomalies for each type separately using meaningful features such that they can be effectively presented to users. We use a density-based clustering mainly because we do not want to restrict the number of clusters. Formally, for a $HLE_{behavior}$, we use a distance measure d, and some combination of clustering parameters $p \in \mathcal{P}$ over the extracted and existing features of $a \in \mathcal{A}$ to extract several clusterings $\mathcal{C}_p = \{C_{p_1}, C_{p_2}, ..., C_{|\mathcal{C}_p|}\}$ for each $p \in \mathcal{P}$. Since we rely on unsupervised machine learning to determine the anomalies, we will not have labels to determine the best clustering. Therefore, we will use internal evaluation measures [8] to select the best $\mathcal{C}_p \forall p \in \mathcal{P}$ that, using d: (1) maximizes the similarities of the anomalies $a \in \mathcal{A}$ inside each of its clusters $C_{p_i} \forall i$, and, (2) maximizes the dissimilarities between $a \in \mathcal{A}$ that belong to different clusters (C_{p_i} & $C_{p_j} \forall i \neq j$).

4   High-Level Detection of Handovers, Delays and Workloads

In this section, we introduce HEMMLA, our machine learning approach to high-level event mining of handovers, delays, and workloads. Figure 2 depicts the steps of HEMMLA.

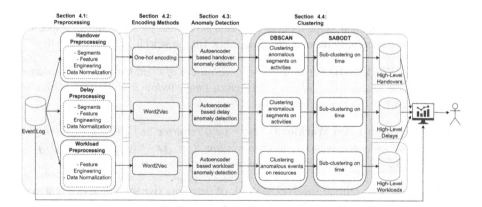

Fig. 2. High-level Event Mining Machine Learning Approach HEMMLA. Each high-level behavior type has customized and configurable steps.

We first preprocess and encode the data for each specific behavior. We then perform anomaly detection leveraging an autoencoder model. The anomaly detection returns anomalies of handover, delay, and workload. Because the behaviors correspond to different attributes of the data, three different models with different inputs and parameters were developed. To extract high-level events from the anomalies, we deploy the clustering algorithm DBSCAN [18] to group anomalies based on common attributes. Finally, our algorithm SABODT divides the clusters into high-level events based on a maximum timestamp difference. The clustered outliers are then presented to the user together with their outlierness values and by referring to involved traces and events.

4.1 Preprocessing the Event Log

Each high-level behavior type requires slightly different preprocessing, as this allows the following HEMMLA steps to detect different types of behaviors.

Intuitively, handover anomalies represent combinations of activities and resources that are unusual. As a first consideration, the combination of the resource and activity of an event influence the handover on a segment. Secondly, the complete combination of the two activities and two resources shows a handover anomaly on a segment. Therefore, we designed two attributes that indicate the frequencies of the combinations between activities and resources: *counts_to* and *counts_all*. We define *counts_to* by:

$$counts\_to_{ij} = \sum_{m=1}^{n} \mathbf{1}(a_m = a_i \wedge r_m = r_j) \tag{1}$$

where a_m is the *activity_to* and r_m is the *resource_to* of the m-th record, a_i and r_j are the unique activity and resource to be counted, and n is the total number of rows. The identity function $\mathbf{1}$ returns 1 if the condition is satisfied. *counts_all* is defined as:

$$counts\_all_{ijkl} = \sum_{m=1}^{n} \mathbf{1}(a_m^f = a_i^f \wedge a_m^t = a_j^t \wedge r_m^f = r_k^f \wedge r_m^t = r_l^t) \tag{2}$$

where the superscript f is the "from" event and t is the "to" event. *counts_to* and *counts_all* are min-max normalized.

The elapsed time (Definition 6) represents the time from one activity to the next. Delays represent deviations in the elapsed time. Hence, the attribute elapsed time is added in the delay preprocessing step. The *elapsed_time* is normalized based on the samples with the same *activity_from* and *activity_to*.

Workload is defined as the number of activities that a resource performs within a certain time window (cf. Definition 8). To represent a low or high workload, we want to understand what a "normal" workload is for a resource. Therefore, we use the attribute: *difference* that measures the deviation in the workload. This attribute specifies the difference between the current workload and the average workload of a resource:

$$difference_{ij} = |w_{ij} - mean_i| \tag{3}$$

where w_{ij} is the *workload* of resource i in the j-th time window, and $mean_i$ is the average of the total workload for resource i. We chose days as the window size for the workload. The attributes *workload* and *difference* are normalized for each unique resource.

4.2 Encoding Methods Used For High-Level Behavior

In this paper, we explore two encoding methods of our segments: one-hot encoding and Word2Vec [11]. One-hot encoding has been a popular method because of its simplicity, explainability, expressiveness, and encoding speed [20]. However, because of the high dimensional space of one-hot encoding and its relatively low F1-score, other methods such as the NLP-based encoding method Word2Vec have also become popular. In Word2Vec encoding we can decide on the size of the encoded vector, where the length of one-hot encoded vectors is based on the number of alternatives of an attribute. Word2Vec can correctly capture attributes in the context of event logs and demonstrates a better performance than classic encoding methods [21]. In Sect. 5 we evaluate the performance of one-hot encoding and Word2Vec on handover, delay, and workload anomalies. Other NLP-based encoding methods such as GloVe [15] and ELMo [16] could have been alternatively utilized. Even fine-tuned, pre-trained LLMs could have been used for the encoding. We limit the choices however on efficient methods that showed to be suitable for the framework purposes. Similarly, we opted against the embedding method Act2Vec [4], as it has mainly been tested on control flow problems, while we focus on data flow.

4.3 Anomaly Detection of Handovers, Delays and Workloads

In the anomaly detection step of our approach, our goal is to find behavior that does not conform with the general workings of our process. The model must deduce the difference between normal and anomalous behavior based on the patterns in the preprocessed data. Training the model is therefore done in an unsupervised fashion. One type of neural network that does not rely on labels is the autoencoder model [13]. Autoencoders are trained to reconstruct their input. This reconstruction capability allows autoencoders to capture the underlying structure of normal data, allowing us to detect anomalous behavior. For these reasons, the autoencoder model was selected for HEMMLA. To prevent the model from overfitting, we add dropout layers between each hidden layer.

While the input for the autoencoder is different for each behavior, the network architecture and hyperparameters of the autoencoder model remain the same.

In the preprocessing step of HEMMLA (Sect. 4.1), we created separate datasets for each behavior. The encoding step turns the categorical attributes into numerical representations (Sect. 4.2). The input for the autoencoder is different for each high-level behavior type. For each behavior, we have specifically selected certain attributes as input because these attributes comprise the data that we want to detect anomalies on. In the colored boxes of Fig. 3 the attributes per behavior are specified.

For handover anomalies, the goal is to find anomalies based on the combinations of the activities and resources, therefore these attributes are included. Furthermore, the count attributes are added to capture additional information for the model to learn from. We found that *counts_to* and *counts_all* had a positive influence on the anomaly detection. A delay is characterized by the time between two activities, therefore the three attributes that are used to detect delay anomalies are the activities and the elapsed time. For the workload, we are interested in anomalous workloads of resources. The workload attribute represents the busyness of a resource. To aid the model in learning the right representation of a low or high workload, we additionally give it the *difference* attribute.

Classification of a sample as an anomaly is based on the anomaly score. Using the autoencoder, HEMMLA computes a reconstruction error for each sample (represented on a segment for handover and delay, and an event for workload). This calculated error serves as the anomaly score. For each sample x_i, HEMMLA determines the anomaly label as depicted in Fig. 3. As depicted in the figure, if the MSLE of x_i and the reconstruction $\hat{x}_i$ is more than the mean μ and standard deviation σ of the training data reconstruction errors, we determine that x_i is an anomaly.

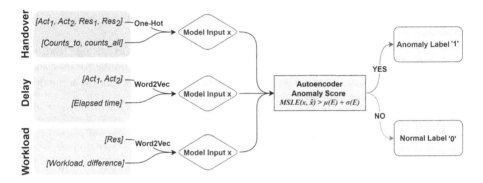

Fig. 3. Flowchart of anomaly detection for high-level behaviors. (Color figure online)

4.4 Clustering the Anomalies

The output labels of the autoencoder give us all events on segments (delay, handover) and events (workload) that are anomalous based on the anomaly score. As we aim to discover accurate and meaningful high-level events, we want to find clusters of anomalies based on their behavior type and timestamps. Therefore, the clustering step of HEMMLA is two-fold. First, a global clustering method is used based on the activity and/or resource attributes of each behavior type's anomalies. For example, for handover, in Fig. 1 the first clustering step groups all transitions on the segment $(CreateFine, SendFine)$ into one cluster. Second, these clusters are further divided into subclusters based on a maximum time delta between the timestamps of anomalies. Using this strategy we ensure that we encapsulate the anomalies into clusters that represent a combination of activities or resources that have high similarity and also occur close in time. In Fig. 1 this means that the two individual blue boxes are identified.

DBSCAN is a very popular clustering algorithm [18] and has the advantages that it does not require a pre-defined number of clusters, and it identifies outliers as noise, instead of forcing them into clusters. DBSCAN takes two required parameters: ϵ and $min\_samples$. Both of these parameters largely influence the clustering of DBSCAN and selecting the appropriate values for these parameters is complicated. Therefore, we implemented a coarse-to-fine method that efficiently finds the best configuration of DBSCAN parameters. The coarse-to-fine method works by discretizing the available value range of each parameter into a "coarse" grid of values. The "coarse" grid is used to estimate the effect of increasing or decreasing the value of that parameter. After selecting the most promising value, a "finer" search is performed to optimize it even further. The initial ranges of values for ϵ and $min\_samples$ are [0.05, 0.5, 1.5] and [max(3, (#behavior specific anomalies * 0.001))].

After running DBSCAN, we use Subcluster Assignment Based on Timestamp Difference (SABODT) to further split into subclusters based on a max time delta Δ between the timestamps of anomalies. Intuitively, anomalies within Δ time from each other end up in the same subcluster. Each final cluster with at least a minimum number of anomalies is a high-level event. This minimum number is configurable for each behavior. If we were to set the minimum number of anomalies to three for the high-level events in Fig. 1, the blue box with only two transitions would not be included in the output.

The result of HEMMLA is an enriched version of the input event log. Both the anomaly detection and clustering steps add labels to the event log in the form of additional attributes. Process mining users can leverage this enriched event log to analyze individual anomalies or high-level events.

5   Experimental Evaluation of HEMMLA

This section outlines the experimental setup and results of the proposed framework HEMMLA. First, we present an overview of the (synthetic) event logs that were used in the experiments. Then, we evaluate each part of HEMMLA separately. Also, we compare our high-level delays, handovers, and workloads to the approach of Bakullari *et al.* [3]. Their method is the only work that is conceptually comparable to HEMMLA. Therefore, it is selected for the evaluation. The comparison of the two methods is based on the evaluation strategy in Bakullari *et al.* [3] their work. Lastly, we present a user study. Due to confidentiality reasons, we currently can not share the source code of HEMMLA.

5.1   Dataset Generation

To evaluate an approach to anomaly detection in event logs, it is common to introduce anomalies into synthetic datasets that simulate real processes. Artificial datasets offer an effective setting for evaluating anomaly detection algorithms since we initially assume the event logs to be free of anomalies. The anomalies that are injected in the event logs establish a clear "gold standard" for the specific anomalies that we aim to detect.

For the evaluation of HEMMLA, five process models were used to simulate event logs: *p2p, small, medium, large, huge*. All models were initially proposed by Nolle *et al.* [14]. All models except *p2p* originally included activity names in the form of *Activity* with a letter of the alphabet. As this does not represent a realistic process, and Word2Vec works by processing words, the activity names were replaced with more realistic ones. In addition to the synthetic datasets, we use the real dataset BPIC2017[1], three GitHub datasets from the industry. The details regarding each dataset are outlined in Table 1.

---

[1] https://data.4tu.nl/articles/dataset/BPI_Challenge_2017/12696884.

Table 1. Overview of synthetic and real datasets statistics.

no.	name	model	#cases	#events	#activities	#resources
1	p2p_30k	p2p	30k	244933	13	20
2	small_30k	small	30k	260349	20	20
3	medium_30k	medium	30k	157870	32	20
4	large_10k	large	10k	112609	42	20
5	large_30k	large	30k	337641	42	20
6	large_50k	large	50k	562408	42	20
7	large_100k	large	100k	1125180	42	20
8	huge_30k	huge	30k	223176	53	20
	GitHub_Team_1	–	1261	15010	11	30
	GitHub_Team_2	–	2491	17817	11	54
	GitHub_Team_3	–	2467	24972	12	49
	BPIC2017	–	22861	688059	41	147

To inject high-level events for handover and delay into the synthetic event logs, anomalies are injected in consecutive randomly sized time windows to make sure anomalies happen close in time. We select a random group of activities that occur in such a window and divide them into two subgroups, where each subgroup will be modified to facilitate handover and delay anomalies. For each activity in the delay subgroup, the events in the time window with this activity are delayed. Consequently, all succeeding events of the affected cases are shifted. For each activity in the handover subgroup, the resources belonging to the events in the time window with this activity are changed to resources that never perform the activity. We create high-level workloads by first finding the days where significantly more occurrences of an activity took place. We pick such days to prevent such days from becoming false positives. For these days we assign all events with the frequently occurring activity to one resource, thereby creating a high workload for this resource. The resource that receives this high workload is a resource that is assigned to this activity.

5.2 Performance Evaluation

For each component of HEMMLA that contributes to the detection of high-level events, we want to evaluate the performance. We use the F_1-score [7] as our main evaluation metric for the output of the autoencoder model. For the clustering steps of HEMMLA, we use the silhouette score and the Adjusted Rand Index [7].

In Sect. 4 we mentioned that we explored two encoding methods: one-hot encoding and Word2Vec. We discuss the results of comparing the two encoding methods for the three high-level behavior types. Given this experiment, we decided on the encoding method for each of our three high-level behavior types. The length of the Word2Vec vectors for the features of delay and workload is set to 100. For handover, it is set to 200 because we have four features to encode. These vectors are relatively large because we want them to have full expressivity capability. Figure 4 shows the F_1-score of the anomaly detection predictions using Word2Vec and one-hot encoding. Five different synthetic datasets with 30k cases were used to evaluate the encoding methods (see Table 1). The figure reveals that Word2Vec outperforms one-hot encoding for the behavior types delay and workload across all five synthetic datasets. Reversely, one-hot encoding outperforms Word2Vec for the handover data. We suspect that Word2Vec is unable to embed the features due to a lack of context. Because one encoding method outperforms the other for all three behaviors we conclude the use of the best-performing encoding method for each behavior. Hence, any handover is encoded with one-hot encoding, and delays and workloads are encoded with Word2Vec, as can be seen in Fig. 2.

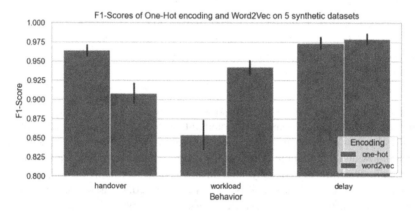

Fig. 4. F_1-scores of one-hot encoding and Word2Vec for handover, delay, and workload anomalies of datasets 1, 2, 3, 5, and 8 from Table 1.

In designing the training loop of our autoencoder model, we observed that the training time was very long. Therefore, we evaluated whether we could use less training data without losing accuracy. In Fig. 5 the impact of using 5%, 10%, and 80% training data on the *small_30k* dataset is shown. This experiment illustrates that we can decrease the dataset size while maintaining a certain score. It is not meant as an experiment to tune the dataset size. The F_1-score of 10% training data compared to 80% training data is higher for all behavior types. Furthermore, the training time of using 80% training data is about five times as much as using 10%. Given these observations, we decided that using only 10% training data has a positive effect on HEMMLA. We opted against using 5% training data because of the large differences between the results and the expected negative effect on larger process models.

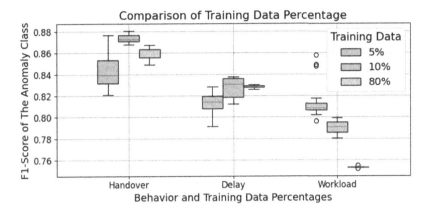

Fig. 5. Impact of different training dataset sizes on the F_1-score.

In the implementation, the autoencoder model as described in Sect. 4.3 is run for 25 epochs with a batch size of 64. These settings are the same for each high-level behavior type and each dataset. We evaluate the F_1-score for the five different synthetic datasets with 30k cases. In Fig. 6 we show the scores. All scores are high, where the handover and delays are detected with the highest scores. The workload anomalies are slightly more difficult to distinguish. There seems to be no clear pattern in the difference of the scores for the different datasets. This might be due to the nature of the process models and the distribution of the datasets.

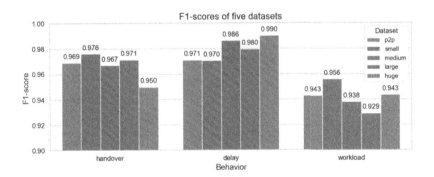

Fig. 6. Autoencoder $F1$-scores for datasets 1, 2, 3, 5, and 8 from Table 1.

The silhouette score is used as an internal clustering evaluation measure to evaluate the clustering by DBSCAN and indicates the quality of the clusters. A high score indicates dense and well-separated clusters. In Fig. 7 we show the silhouette score of the synthetic datasets with 30k cases and BPIC2017 (see Table 1). We can investigate both synthetic and real-life datasets, which broadens our judgment of the performance. The silhouette scores are all very close to 1, which is the maximum possible value.

This indicates that DBSCAN is capable of making clusters that are distinct and of high quality.

To evaluate the last step of HEMMLA, the high-level events generation method SABODT, we use the adjusted Rand Index. The Adjusted Rand Index (ARI) measures the similarity between two clusterings. The "gold standard" labels that were generated in the dataset generation are compared to the final cluster labels given by the last step of HEMMLA. In Fig. 8 the scores are shown for the synthetic 30k cases datasets.

We observe that the high-level delays are detected with the highest score, this means that HEMMLA was able to find high-level delays that are true to our data. The ARI scores of the high-level handovers and high-level workloads are significantly less and vary per dataset. However, the scores still represent a certain level of similarity to the "gold standard" since a completely random clustering is characterized by the value 0. One of the reasons why the scores are lower for high-level handovers and workloads is the data generation procedure. A high-level delay is created by significantly increasing the duration of a set of activities, creating a clear outlier. High-level handovers and workloads, however, both concern resources. Modifying resources to create high-level workload for example inherently also changes the handovers occurring. Therefore, such high-level events are not as clearly distinguishable.

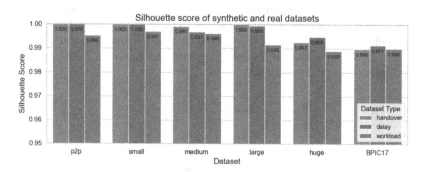

Fig. 7. Silhouette scores of six datasets (datasets 1, 2, 3, 5, 8, and BPIC17 from Table 1). y-axis adjusted to start at 0.95.

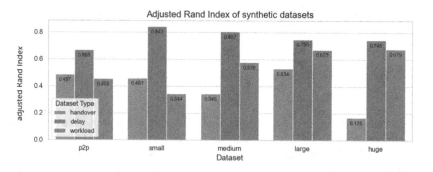

Fig. 8. Adjusted Rand Index of datasets 1, 2, 3, 5, and 8 from Table 1.

Running Time Analysis. The goal of the running time analysis is to gain insights into the scalability of HEMMLA for the convenience of end users. Additionally, we are interested in the individual running times of the anomaly detection, clustering (DBSCAN), and subclustering (SABODT) steps of HEMMLA. Figure 9 shows the running times of four datasets from the *large* process model. Each line represents the running time of a step in HEMMLA, including the total time. We have seen similar effects on the running time for datasets with other underlying process models. For the running time analysis of HEMMLA, we used a 2x AMD EPYC 7513 @ 2.60GHz and 32GBs of RAM divided into four CPUs.

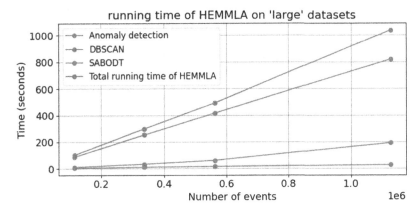

Fig. 9. Running times for each step of HEMMLA on multiple dataset sizes of the underlying process model *Large*. (datasets 4, 5, 6, and 7 from Table 1).

Table 2. Participating and not participating cases in high-level segment behavior (Delay, (W_Call after offers | suspend, W_Call after offers | resume)) with regard to throughput time.

	thr. time	Participating	Not Participating
Bakullari *et al.*	≤10 days	12 (6,63%)	4623 (27,31%)
	10–30 days	138 (76,24%)	10575 (62,48%)
	≥30 days	31 (**17,13%**)	1727 (10,20%)
	total: 17106	*181*	*16925*
HEMMLA	≤10 days	0 (0,0%)	5081 (30,01%)
	10–30 days	66 (37,93%)	10253 (60,55%)
	≥30 days	108 (**62,07%**)	1598 (9,44%)
	total: 17106	*174*	*16932*

HEMMLA Compared to the State-of-the-Art. Bakullari *et al.* [3] evaluate high-level events of the BPIC2017 dataset by investigating the correlation between the *outcome* and *throughput time* of cases, and the high-level events. To understand how HEMMLA

performs compared to the method by Bakullari *et al.*, we followed this evaluation approach too, although this is only one component of our output. In Table 2 we show such a
comparison. In the table, every case that is *participating* traverses the segment *(W_Call
after offers | suspend, W_Call after offers | resume)* and is present in a high-level delay.
Not participating cases also traverse the segment but are not part of a high-level delay.
We observe a significant difference in the *participating* cases, particularly in the ≥ 30
days class. This difference indicates that HEMMLA was better at discovering the high-
level delays in cases that actually have a higher throughput time on the segment. Where
possible, we performed more comparisons like the above. We found no other significant
differences between the two methods. This indicates that HEMMLA performs better for
delays and at least as good for the other high-level behavior types, while being considerably more scalable for finding more interesting anomalies of further types in larger
datasets.

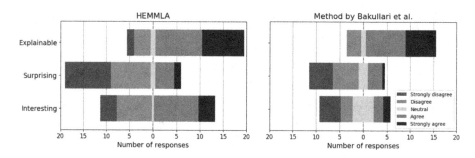

Fig. 10. Likert scales indicating the responses of process mining users on high-level events.

In addition to the previous comparison, we presented eight process mining users
from different departments with high-level events from both approaches on three real-
life GitHub datasets and a Purchase-to-Pay dataset. In each interview a user was asked
to score high-level events. Both high-level events from HEMMLA and the method of
Bakullari *et al.* were presented, without mentioning the method itself. Overall, users
appreciated the high-level events because it gives them a starting point for performance
analysis. This indicates that high-level event mining would be a valuable addition to
industry tools as well. In Fig. 10 the Likert scale results of the interestingness, surpris-
ingness, and explainability of the presented high-level events are given. The method of
Bakullari *et al.* did not produce any high-level delays for the used datasets, indicating
a lower number of responses in the respective Likert Scale. At first glance, the results
for HEMMLA and the method of Bakullari *et al.* are similar. We observe that both
approaches showed explainable high-level events and that the majority of high-level
events were not surprising. The largest contrast between the two methods is the interestingness. HEMMLA produced many more high-level events that were interesting to
the users.

6   Conclusion and Outlook

In this work, we introduced HEMMLA, a novel machine learning based anomaly detection and clustering framework for high-level event mining. HEMMLA is implemented currently for three high-level behaviors: handover, delay, and workload. The framework can be easily extended to other high-level behaviors on both the event and segment level.

Based on the experimental evaluation, HEMMLA provides high-level events that are at least as good at those discovered by Bakullari *et al.* [3]. Users generally found the discovered high-level events by HEMMLA more interesting. Furthermore, while the method of Bakullari *et al.* requires the selection of multiple parameters and a fixed time window, HEMMLA is significantly less influenced by its parameters. Lastly, HEMMLA detects many more high-level events than the method by Bakullari *et al.*.

As a future work, further optimizing parameters used in the autoencoder could further enhance its performance. Other, transformer-based anomaly detection methods could deliver promising results. Additionally, we plan to explore further, more advanced encoding methods such as GloVe [15] and ELMo [16], and pre-trained language models. Finally, we plan to apply multi-perspective anomaly detection methods over high-level events and combine those with concept drift detection methods [9] to obtain explainable results to the end users.

References

1. Bakullari, B., van der Aalst, W.M.P.: High-level event mining: a framework. In: ICPM, pp. 136–143 (2022)
2. Bakullari, B., van der Aalst, W.M.P.: High-level event mining: overview and future work (2024)
3. Bakullari, B., Thoor, J.V., Fahland, D., van der Aalst, W.M.P.: The interplay between high-level problems and the process instances that give rise to them. In: BPM Forum, pp. 145–162 (2023)
4. De Koninck, P., vanden Broucke, S., Weerdt, J.: act2vec, trace2vec, log2vec, and model2vec: representation learning for business processes. In: BPM, pp. 305–321 (08 2018)
5. De Weerdt, J.: Trace clustering. In: Encyclopedia of BD Tech, pp. 1–6 (2018)
6. Denisov, V.V.: Process mining for systems with shared resources and queues process modeling, conformance checking, and performance analysis (2023)
7. Han, J., Kamber, M., Pei, J.: Data Mining: Concepts and Techniques. Elsevier Science (2011)
8. Hassani, M., Seidl, T.: Using internal evaluation measures to validate the quality of diverse stream clustering algorithms. Vietnam. J. Comput. Sci. **4**(3), 171–183 (2017)
9. Huete, J., Qahtan, A.A., Hassani, M.: PrefixCDD: effective online concept drift detection over event streams using prefix trees. In: COMPSAC, pp. 328–333 (2023)
10. Klijn, E.L., Fahland, D.: Identifying and reducing errors in remaining time prediction due to inter-case dynamics, pp. 25–32. Institute of Electrical and Electronics Engineers Inc. (2020). https://doi.org/10.1109/ICPM49681.2020.00015
11. Mikolov, T., Chen, K., Corrado, G., Dean, J.: Efficient estimation of word representations in vector space. In: ICLR Workshops (2013)
12. Musaj, Z., Hassani, M.: Unsupervised anomaly detection of prefixes in event streams using online autoencoders. In: CoopIS (2024, to appear)
13. Nolle, T., Luettgen, S., Seeliger, A., Mühlhäuser, M.: Analyzing business process anomalies using autoencoders. Mach. Learn. **107**, 1875–1893 (2018)

14. Nolle, T., Luettgen, S., Seeliger, A., Mühlhäuser, M.: BINet: multi-perspective business process anomaly classification. Inf. Syst. **103**, 101458 (2022)
15. Pennington, J., Socher, R., Manning, C.D.: GloVe: global vectors for word representation. In: Empirical Methods in Natural Language Processing (EMNLP), pp. 1532–1543 (2014)
16. Peters, M.E., et al.: Deep contextualized word representations (2018). https://arxiv.org/abs/1802.05365
17. Pourbafrani, M., van der Aalst, W.M.: Extracting process features from event logs to learn coarse-grained simulation models. In: CAiSE, pp. 125–140 (2021)
18. Schubert, E., Sander, J., Ester, M., Kriegel, H.P., Xu, X.: DBSCAN revisited, revisited: why and how you should (still) use DBSCAN. ATDS **42**(3) (2017)
19. Senderovich, A., Francescomarino, C.D., Maggi, F.M.: From knowledge-driven to data-driven inter-case feature encoding in predictive process monitoring. Inf. Syst. **84**, 255–264 (2019)
20. Tavares, G.M., Oyamada, R.S., Barbon, S., Ceravolo, P.: Trace encoding in process mining: a survey and benchmarking. Eng. Appl. Artif. Intell. **126**, 107028 (2023)
21. Tavares, G.M., Barbon, S.: Analysis of language inspired trace representation for anomaly detection. In: CCIS, pp. 296–308 (2020)
22. Toosinezhad, Z., Fahland, D., Köroğlu, O., van der Aalst, W.M.P.: Detecting system-level behavior leading to dynamic bottlenecks (2020)
23. Wimbauer, A., Richter, F., Seidl, T.: PErrCas: process error cascade mining in trace streams. In: PM Workshops, pp. 224–236 (2022)

Process Improvement

SwiftMend: An Approach to Detect and Repair Activity Label Quality Issues in Process Event Streams

Savandi Kalukapuge(✉) ⓘ, Arthur H. M. ter Hofstede ⓘ, and Moe T. Wynn ⓘ

Queensland University of Technology, Brisbane, Australia
savandi.kalukapuge@hdr.qut.edu.au,
{a.terhofstede,m.wynn}@qut.edu.au

Abstract. Process mining (PM) techniques extract insights from event logs to discover, monitor, and improve business processes. The quality of input data significantly impacts the reliability and accuracy of these insights. Existing approaches to detect and repair these issues are limited to offline data pre-processing. Given the potential of real-time process analysis to provide valuable business-related insights, online PM has gained interest. However, process-data quality (PDQ) issues in process event streams (PES) beyond anomalous events or traces have not yet been addressed. Existing PDQ management approaches lack the adaptability and incremental processing capabilities necessary for streaming event data and evolving processes. This paper presents a novel approach for dynamically detecting and repairing synonymous, polluted, and distorted activity labels in PES, which are common issues affecting the quality of PM outcomes. By incrementally maintaining stabilised activity control-flow context using memory-efficient approximate data structures, the approach detects and merges similar labels or splits dissimilar labels on the fly. An incremental hierarchical clustering algorithm, incorporating decaying and forgetting mechanisms, is employed for the dynamic repair of similar activities, ensuring efficiency and adaptability. The approach is validated using publicly available real-life logs from two hospitals.

Keywords: Online process mining · Process data quality · Synonymous label · Distorted label · Polluted label

1 Introduction

Process mining (PM) has traditionally utilised algorithms in historical, end-to-end business processes stored in information systems, known as event logs [2]. The insights extracted from these logs are then used to discover, control, and improve the associated processes [2]. With the advent of big data and the increasing volume of real-time business process transactions, there is a growing interest in online PM [7]. Techniques in this area enable the monitoring and analysis of running business processes, i.e., process event streams (PES), in real-time, facilitating the prompt elicitation of knowledge for operational excellence [7]. Activity label issues are particularly critical in online process mining due to the real-time nature of data processing [4,27]. Inconsistent or

© The Author(s), under exclusive license to Springer Nature Switzerland AG 2025
M. Comuzzi et al. (Eds.): CoopIS 2024, LNCS 15506, pp. 131–149, 2025.
https://doi.org/10.1007/978-3-031-81375-7_8

erroneous labels can lead to immediate misinterpretations of ongoing processes, potentially resulting in incorrect decisions or actions [6,31]. Unlike offline analysis, there's limited opportunity for retrospective correction, making robust, on-the-fly detection and repair essential [7,36]. Online PM techniques have been applied to various tasks, e.g. process discovery [34], conformance checking [35], decision mining [29], predictive process monitoring [10], concept drift [25] and anomaly detection [16], demonstrating their potential to provide valuable insights into dynamic business processes. However, the quality of the analysis results heavily depends on the quality of the input data. Poor process-data quality (PDQ) can lead to unreliable outcomes such as inaccurate process models, misleading conformance-checking results, and incorrect performance indicators used for decision-making [6]. Some typical PDQ problems have been systematised into a collection of event log imperfection patterns [31]. Techniques have been developed in offline PM to detect and repair event log imperfection patterns, e.g. related to activity labels [27] and timestamps [12], and other PDQ problems, e.g. related to log incompleteness [23] and outliers [14]. Early detection of PDQ issues in PES is crucial for online PM, enabling timely corrective actions [7]. However, analysing these high-velocity streams in near real-time presents challenges such as noise, incorrect attributes, and incompleteness [7]. While data stream mining offers quality management techniques [13,24], these are not directly applicable to PM due to a fundamental difference: stream analysis focuses on individual events, whereas online PM conducts analysis at the case level, considering temporal event sequences [2,7]. Despite some techniques addressing outlier detection in online PM [16,36], comprehensive research on the multifaceted nature of PDQ issues in PES remains lacking. Challenges include selective memory constraints, varying event arrival rates, high volume and velocity of events, and diverse attribute sources [7].

To address this research gap, we propose a novel approach for detecting and repairing label quality issues in PES. Our approach focuses on three activity label imperfection patterns [31]: Synonymous (e.g., *'Flight Departed'* and *'Flight Take Off'*), Polluted (e.g., *'Submit Request 534 by User1'* and *'Submit Request 675 by User2'*), and Distorted (e.g., *'Send inv'* and *'Send inv.'*). The manifestations of these issues in PES (see Fig. 1) stem from various organisational, human, and technical factors [4]. These issues need to be addressed to avoid problematic PM analysis outcomes. The approach's key features:

- Real-time imperfect label pattern detection using approximate data structures;
- Activity similarity reassessment through causal/parallel stability metrics;
- Semantic activity clustering via customised incremental hierarchical clustering;
- Frequency- and recency-based label selection for the dynamic repair of activities;
- Adaptive historical data retention through customised decay/forgetting mechanisms.

The approach was evaluated using two publicly available real-life event logs processed as streams with injected label issues, comparing against an existing offline technique and assessing performance under various configurations.

The paper is structured as follows. Section 2 reviews related work, while Sect. 3 discusses the approach. Section 4 presents the implementation and the evaluation results, and Sect. 5 concludes with summarised findings and avenues for future research.

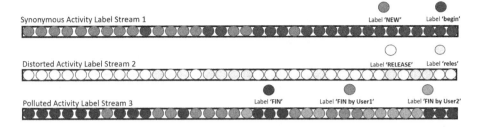

Fig. 1. Synonymous, distorted, and polluted activity label manifestations in PES.

2   Related Work

Data Quality Management in PM. Despite PM's widespread adoption, PDQ issues and the complexity of managing large-scale business processes in modern settings hinder effective analysis. To address this, PM researchers have implemented PDQ management techniques to characterise, identify, and rectify PDQ issues in event logs, primarily from an offline perspective. The Process Mining Manifesto [3] discussed the importance of input PDQ in PM, providing a one-to-five-star maturity rating to classify event logs based on their quality, while Bose et al. [6] introduced an event log quality framework with four classifications of issues: missing, incorrect, imprecise, and irrelevant data. Suriadi et al. [31] further consolidated eleven well-known imperfection patterns that describe quality issues when working with event logs, building on Bose et al.'s classification. Regarding approaches for detection and repair of PDQ issues in offline PM, various techniques have been developed: Nguyen et al. [23] used autoencoders for handling missing/outlier event attributes, Fischer et al. [12] proposed an extensible framework to automatically detect and quantify accuracy, completeness, consistency, and uniqueness, and Sadeghianasl et al. [27,28] implemented a gamified crowdsourcing approach to contextually detect and collaboratively repair semantically identical but syntactically different labels. Other techniques include fuzzy mining for clustering semantically similar activities [15], NLP-based approaches for detecting label anomalies [1], and multi-perspective label refinement frameworks [9]. However, these techniques cannot be readily transposed to streaming contexts for quality management in online PM.

Online PM. The majority of online PM techniques were developed for automated process discovery, implementing efficient algorithms [34] or adapting existing ones to online settings [8]. Online conformance checking [35], decision mining [29], and predictive process monitoring [10] focusing on compliance issues, decision rule amendments, and forecasting process input data (respectively) have also been explored. Several methods have been proposed to detect process drifts from event or trace streams, utilising various techniques such as adaptive [19] and sliding [18] windows, statistical tests [18,25], and feature/behavioural abstractions [25]. These empirically validated analysis techniques regard their input – PES – as flawless. However, we assume that there may be quality issue patterns in PES similar to those found in event logs [6]. Current techniques focusing on PES quality primarily address anomaly detection and removal, such as Tavares et al.'s [32] approach using trace-activity and timestamp descriptors, Ko and Comuzzi's [16] method using statistical leverage, and van Zelst et al.'s [36] use of prefix-based probabilistic automata. However, these studies disregard the detection of specific quality issues in process attributes, predominantly focusing on marking entire events or traces as abnormal.

Data Stream Quality Management. The data stream mining field has various techniques to effectively address quality issues in event streams, such as detecting outliers and noise [13], removing duplicates [13], and imputing missing data [30]. Researchers have proposed frameworks and methods for managing quality in general data streams, utilising quality dimensions [24], metrics [24], and on-the-fly quantification [33]. These approaches employ a range of techniques, including (among others) control schemes [33], correlation statistics [26], and a-priori knowledge [17]. However, PES differ from general data streams in their need to maintain case-level coherence and correlation, preserve process semantics, and handle complex temporal dependencies between events, which are crucial for accurate process mining analyses [2]. For example, in an order processing system, events like 'Order Received', 'Payment Confirmed', and 'Order Shipped' would all be correlated to a single order case. Thus, these techniques are not specifically tailored to detect and repair quality issues manifesting in PES.

3   *SwiftMend* Approach

Three key rationales underpin the design of the *SwiftMend* approach. First, it leverages the *control-flow perspective* to detect similar activities and label issues, as it provides the most influential information about an activity's context within a process [27]. This context-based approach, as used by Sadeghianasl et al. [27], recognises that activities are best understood through their contextual relationships rather than label text alone. Second, *stability* is emphasised in control-flow contextual behaviours, ensuring only the most reliable relationships among similar labels are considered for detection and repair, with weak relations treated as anomalies [5]. Third, a *representative label selection* mechanism is used to emit the most frequent and recent label from clustered similar activities based on the assumption that correct data consistently outweighs incorrect data or errors in real-world PES [2,3,21,31]. SwiftMend concurrently detects and repairs three label imperfection patterns within PESs: Synonymous (similar control-flow contexts), Polluted (stable base with fluctuating details), and Distorted (approximate matching). Adjustable similarity thresholds allow prioritisation of specific patterns, balancing sensitivity between distorted and more distinct labels.

Our approach consists of six components (see Fig. 2). These components work in concert to address the challenges of streaming process-data: (1) The case/activity context storage (refer to Sect. 3.1) efficiently captures evolving process behaviours, enabling real-time updates of directly-follows relations. (2) Control-flow stability checking (refer to Sect. 3.2) ensures that only reliable activity relationships influence label repair, filtering out noise inherent in streaming data by employing two stability measures: causal and parallel relation stability. (3) The similarity change identification mechanism (refer to Sect. 3.3) dynamically detects changes in activity patterns through footprint comparisons, triggering reassessment when necessary. (4) Incremental clustering (refer to Sect. 3.4) allows for adaptive grouping of similar activities, accommodating the continuous nature of streaming data. (5) The representative label selection (refer to Sect. 3.4) prioritises frequent and recent labels, assuming correct labels tend to dominate over time. Finally, (6) the decay/forgetting mechanisms (refer to Sect. 3.5), inspired by the lossy counting algorithm [20], balances the need for historical context with adaptability to recent changes, which is crucial for handling evolving processes in resource-constrained environments.

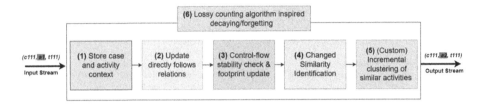

Fig. 2. Schematic Overview of the *SwiftMend* Approach.

3.1   Storing Case/Activity Context and Updating Directly Follows Relations

Algorithm 1 manages activity similarities in PES using parameters including detection window *dtWindow*, reference window *refWindow*, causality thresholds (θ_1^{upper}, θ_1^{lower}), parallelism thresholds (θ_2^{upper}, θ_2^{lower}), and similarity threshold (θ). Lines 1–3 initialize global data structures[1]. Line 5 extracts events from the input stream *inputStream* $\in (CaseID \times Act \times Timestp)^*$, and Line 6 updates relevant counters and timestamps. The override function $\oplus$ [11] is used for these amendments. The activity counter is updated (Line 8) or initialised (Line 16) depending on whether that activity has already been seen as part of the current case. We use projection operators π_i ($1 \leq i \leq n$) (e.g., on Line 10) on any relation $R \subseteq A_1 \times A_2 \times \ldots \times A_n$ to extract all elements of A_i that participate in R, i.e., $\pi_i(R) = \{a_i \in A_i \mid \exists a_1 \in A_1, \ldots a_{i-1} \in A_{i-1}, a_{i+1} \in A_{i+1}, \ldots a_n \in A_n[(a_1, a_2, \ldots, a_n) \in R]\}$. Lines 9–15 initialize the footprint matrix and update cluster-related structures for new activities. For existing cases (Line 17), it updates the directly-follows relation (*dflw*) and re-evaluates causal and parallel relations (Lines 18–24), potentially leading to footprint updates and activity similarity reassessment via Algorithm 2 (Line 23). The algorithm handles both new (Lines 26–27) and existing cases, initializing or updating relevant structures

---

[1] Global data structures include *lastAct* (last seen activity for each case), *cntr* (distinct case counters), *aLstSn* (last seen timestamp of each activity), *distAct* (distinct activity counters), *dflw* (directly-follows relations), *ftpr* (current footprint), *ftpr* (previous footprint), *InflPairs* (influencing activity pairs for clustering), *pairSim* (current activity pair similarities), *actToClus* (map of activities to their cluster representative), and *mClust* (currently merged clusters).

as needed, and ensures continuous evaluation of activity relationships throughout the stream processing.

Algorithm 1. StreamActivityManagement.

Global Input: $dtWindow \in \mathbb{N}$, $refWindow \in \mathbb{N}_0$, $inputStream \in (CaseID \times Act \times Timestp)^*$, $\theta_1^{upper} \in [0, 1]$,
$\theta_1^{lower} \in [0, 1]$, $\theta_2^{upper} \in [0, 3]$, $\theta_2^{lower} \in [0, 3]$, $\theta \in [0, 1]$
Output: $outputStream \in (CaseID \times Act \times Timestp)^*$

1 **Global Variables:** $lastAct: CaseID \rightarrowtail Act$, $cntr: CaseID \rightarrowtail \mathbb{N}_0$ such that $dom(lastAct) = dom(cntr)$,
   $aLstSn: Act \rightarrowtail Timestp$, $distAct: Act \times CaseID \rightarrow \mathbb{N}$, $dflw: Act \times Act \times CaseID \rightarrow \mathbb{N}$, $actPairs: Act \times Act$,
   $ftpr: Act \times Act \rightarrow \{0, 1, 2, 3\}$, $pvFtpr: Act \times Act \rightarrow \{0, 1, 2, 3\}$, $InflPairs: Act \times Act \rightarrow$
   $\mathbb{R}$, $actToClus: Act \rightarrow Act$, $pairSim: Act \times Act \rightarrow \mathbb{R}$, $mClust: Act \rightarrow \mathcal{P}(Act)$, $evtCntr \in \mathbb{N}_0$,
   $cThreshold \in \mathbb{N}_0$; $evtCntr, cThreshold \leftarrow 0$;
2 $lastAct, cntr, aLstSn, Timestp, distAct, dflw, ftpr \leftarrow \varnothing$;
3 $pvFtpr, InflPairs, actToClus, pairSim, mClust \leftarrow \varnothing$;
4 **while** *true*:
5     $(c, a, t) \leftarrow inputStream(evtCntr)$;   // Fetch new event from stream
6     $evtCntr \leftarrow evtCntr + 1, aLstSn \leftarrow aLstSn \oplus \{(a, t)\}$;   // Update last seen timestamp for activity
7   **if** $(a, c) \in dom(distAct)$:
8        $distAct(a, c) \leftarrow distAct(a, c) + 1$; // If already seen, increment activity count for case
9   **else:**
10   **if** $a \notin \pi_1(dom(distAct))$:
11         $ftpr[a, a] \leftarrow 0$;   // Initialise footprint for completely new activity
12   **foreach** $Acti \in \pi_1(dom(distAct))$ **do**
13           $ftpr[Acti, a] \leftarrow 0; ftpr[a, Acti] \leftarrow 0$;   // Initialise new footprint positions
14         $actToClus \leftarrow actToClus \cup \{(a, a)\}$; // Assign activity representative as its own
15         $mClust \leftarrow mClust \cup \{(a, \{a\})\}$; // Assign new activity to its own cluster
16       $distAct \leftarrow distAct \cup \{((a, c), 1)\}$;   // Initialise activity count from new case
17   **if** $c \in dom(lastAct)$:
18   **if** $(lastAct(c), a, c) \in dom(dflw)$:
19         $dflw \leftarrow dflw \oplus \{((lastAct(c), a, c), dflw(lastAct(c), a, c) + 1)\}$;   // Update directly-follows
20   **else:**
21         $dflw \leftarrow dflw \cup \{((lastAct(c), a, c), 1)\}$; // Add new directly-follows relation
22       $cntr \leftarrow cntr \oplus \{(c, cntr(c) + 1)\}$;   // Update case counter
23   SIMILARITYCHANGEMANAGEMENT$(lastAct(c), a)$;   // Trigger algorithm 2
24       $lastAct \leftarrow lastAct \oplus \{(c, a)\}$;   // Update last seen activity
25   **else:**
26       $lastAct \leftarrow lastAct \cup \{(c, a)\}$;   // Initialise last seen activity of new case
27       $cntr \leftarrow cntr \cup \{(c, cThreshold)\}$;   // Initialise counter of new case
28   **if** $evtCntr$ **div** $dtWindow \neq cThreshold$:
29       $actPairs \leftarrow \varnothing$;
30       $casesToForgt \leftarrow \{c' \in dom(cntr) \mid cntr(c') \leq cThreshold - refWindow\}$;   // Cases to forget
31       $lastAct \leftarrow casesToForgt \lhd lastAct$;   // Forget cases with their last seen activities
32       $cntr \leftarrow casesToForgt \lhd cntr$;   // Forget cases with their counters
33       $actPairs \leftarrow actPairs \cup \{(a, b) \mid (a, b, c') \in dom(dflw) \wedge c' \in casesToForgt\}$;   // Get affected directly following activity pairs
34       $distAct \leftarrow \{(a, c') \mid a \in Act \wedge c' \in casesToForgt\} \lhd distAct$; // Remove activity counts
35       $dflw \leftarrow \{(a, b, c') \mid a, b \in Act \wedge c' \in casesToForgt\} \lhd dflw$;   // Remove directly follows counts
36   **foreach** $actPair \in actPairs$ **do**
37   SIMILARITYCHANGEMANAGEMENT $(\pi_1(actPair), \pi_2(actPair))$;   // Trigger algorithm 2
38       $cThreshold \leftarrow evtCntr$ **div** $dtWindow$;   // Update cThreshold for next detection window
39   **if** $a \in \bigcup ran(mClust)$:
40   **let** $b \in Act$ **such that** $a \in mClust(b)$; // Get representative activity from merged cluster
41       $outputStream(evtCntr) \leftarrow (c, b, t)$; // Output event with representative activity

3.2 Control-Flow Stability Checking and Footprint Updates

When triggered, Algorithm 2 updates the footprint (which consists of activity ordering relations) based on the strength of the causal/parallel relationship between the last seen activity (α) and the current activity that directly follows it (β). For any pair of activities $\alpha, \beta \in \pi_1(dom(distAct))$, exactly one direct ordering relation holds [2]: 'Causes' ($\alpha \rightarrow \beta$), 'Caused by' ($\beta \rightarrow \alpha$), 'Concurrent' ($\alpha \parallel \beta$), and 'Exclusive/Choice' ($\alpha \# \beta$). These relations are used to populate the footprint matrix $ftpr$ location with regard to the two activities $ftpr[\alpha, \beta]$ and are represented in Algorithm 2 by numeric values: 1 for $\rightarrow$, 2 for $\leftarrow$, 3 for $\parallel$, and 0 for $\#$ (Lines 5, 7, 9, and 11). Our approach considers the support for the changing causal and parallel relationships between two activities and asserts their strength before updating the $ftpr$. The two measures ((1) from van Zelst et al. [34] and (2) custom derived) used to compute the direct causality and parallelism strength are as follows:

$$Direct\ Causality(a,b) = \frac{|a > b| - |b > a|}{|a > b| + |b > a| + 1} \in [-1, 1] \tag{1}$$

$$Direct\ Parallelism(a,b) = \frac{\max(|a > b|, |b > a|)}{\min(|a > b|, |b > a|)} \in [3, 2] \tag{2}$$

where $|\alpha > \beta|$ represents the frequency of β observed directly after α. Algorithm 2 updates footprint locations using these causal and parallel measures, guided by the configurable upper and lower stability thresholds [5]. These thresholds control footprint update frequency and reflect only stable, strongly supported relations. When neither causal nor parallel thresholds are met, the footprint location is set to 0, indicating exclusivity (#). For example: if $causality(\alpha, \beta) \geq \theta_1^{upper}$, it updates the causal relationship on location $[\alpha, \beta]$ to 1, and on location $[\beta, \alpha]$ to 2; if $causality(\alpha, \beta) \leq -\theta_1^{upper}$, it does the reverse, i.e. 1 is assigned to location $[\beta, \alpha]$ and 2 to location $[\alpha, \beta]$; if $parallelism(\alpha, \beta) \leq \theta_2^{upper}$, it updates locations $[\alpha, \beta]$ and $[\beta, \alpha]$ to 3 indicating a parallel relationship; and if $causality(\alpha, \beta) < \theta_1^{lower}$ or $parallelism(\alpha, \beta) \geq \theta_2^{lower}$, it updates locations $[\alpha, \beta]$ and $[\beta, \alpha]$ to 0 to reflect that exclusive relationships hold (Lines 4–11).

3.3 Identifying Changed Similarities Between Activities

Algorithm 2 focuses on footprint relationship changes between activities and determines the need for re-clustering (handled in Lines 12–19). In Line 13, X_α is assigned the set of activities $x \in Act$ where the previous or current footprint location between α and β ($pvFtpr[\alpha, \beta]$ and $ftpr[\alpha, \beta]$) matches that between x and β in those respective footprints. Similarly, X_β is constructed for matching footprint locations between β and α, and $x \in Act$ and α. Activities in set X_α and X_β are used to compare with α and β, respectively, for similarity changes. For each activity γ in $\{\alpha, \beta\}$ and each activity η in X_γ, the algorithm checks if (Lines 15–17): (1) The similarity between the current footprint row of γ and η is defined ($\downarrow$) and non-zero (2) The similarity between the previous footprints of γ and η is defined and non-zero (3) The similarity between the previous and current footprints of γ and η is defined and has changed. Line 17 employs short-circuit evaluation for AND (**&&**) and OR (∥) operations, potentially avoiding expensive computations. If any of the above conditions hold, the *InflPairs* set is updated with the pair (γ, η) and their new similarity value. The rows of the footprint are accessed using the notation $ftpr[\gamma,]$, where γ represents the activity label. The similarity function (3) below compares the similarity between the corresponding positions within the footprint rows of γ ($ftpr[\gamma,]$) and η ($ftpr[\eta,]$), i.e., how control-flow relationships of activity γ with other activities compare to those of activity η.

$$Sim(\gamma, \eta) = \frac{|\{(i,j) \mid 1 \le j \le n \wedge ftpr[\gamma,j] = ftpr[\eta,j] \wedge (ftpr[\gamma,j] \ne \# \vee ftpr[\eta,j] \ne \#)\}|}{|\{(i,j) \mid 1 \le j \le n \wedge (ftpr[\gamma,j] \ne \# \vee ftpr[\eta,j] \ne \#)\}|}, \quad (3)$$

where $n = |\pi_1(dom(distAct))|$ and rows of the footprint matrix are accessed using the expressions $ftpr[\gamma,]$ and $ftpr[\eta,]$, where γ and η represent the activity labels. This function ensures that exclusive relations are not considered[2]. Algorithm 2 resets the *pvFtpr* variable to an empty set if the *InflPairs* set is non-empty. In that case, it triggers Algorithm 3 to cluster the influencing pairs and clears the *InflPairs* set (Lines 19–22).

3.4 (Custom) Incremental Clustering of Similar Activities

Algorithm 3 updates new pair similarities (Lines 1–5), clusters activities (Line 6 and Lines 8–18), reassesses cluster memberships (Lines 19–28), and finally reassesses and updates cluster centroids (Lines 29–40). An adapted version of agglomerative hierarchical clustering [22] is chosen due to several key advantages: its hierarchical structure allows flexible grouping at various similarity levels, not requiring a predefined number of clusters, efficient incremental updates, and preservation of cluster history. It uses the single linkage criterion for cluster merging, which is highly sensitive to close similarities and ideal for detecting similar elements with slight variations [22]. For instance, the algorithm might initially group *'Register request'* and *'Regis R'* into *ClusterA*, but can dynamically adjust by merging *'Submit request'* or splitting clusters as the process evolves and similarity scores change, accommodating changes and integrity. The algorithm selects a cluster's most appropriate representative label based on the highest frequency and recency (Line 37), accurately reflecting the dominant activity label. Lines 39–41 of Algorithm 1 handle activities that should be represented as another activity before being emitted onto the *outputStream*. If the current activity a belongs to a cluster with more activities (stored in *mClust*), the algorithm replaces a with its cluster's representative activity b (Line 40) in *outputStream*.

3.5 Lossy Counting Algorithm Inspired Decaying/Forgetting

Rather than using a window-based method having disadvantages such as biases and inefficient summarisation due to rigidity [7], our approach uses the problem reduction approach [7] to adapt to recent and frequent activity label representations without fixed window constraints, maintaining an accurate and up-to-date context. This is achieved through a customised version of the lossy counting algorithm [20] (Algorithm 1 Lines 28–38), where the algorithm divides PES into detection windows to manage their unboundedness. This component induces the other components (see Fig. 2)

---

[2] Mutual exclusion from other activities doesn't imply activity identity.

Algorithm 2. SimilarityChangeManagement(α, β).

Input: $\alpha, \beta \in Act$
1 **Initialization:**
2 X_α, X_β : *Sets of Act*;
3 $X_\alpha, X_\beta \leftarrow \varnothing$;
4 **if** $causality(\alpha, \beta) \geq \theta_1^{upper}$:
5     $pvFtpr \leftarrow ftpr; ftpr[\alpha, \beta] \leftarrow 1; ftpr[\beta, \alpha] \leftarrow 2$;   `// Causal`
6 **elif** $causality(\alpha, \beta) \leq -\theta_1^{upper}$:
7     $pvFtpr \leftarrow ftpr; ftpr[\alpha, \beta] \leftarrow 2; ftpr[\beta, \alpha] \leftarrow 1$;   `// Inverse causal`
8 **elif** $parallelism(\alpha, \beta) \leq \theta_2^{upper}$:
9     $pvFtpr \leftarrow ftpr; ftpr[\alpha, \beta] \leftarrow 3; ftpr[\beta, \alpha] \leftarrow 3$;   `// Parallel`
10 **elif** $causality(\alpha, \beta) < \theta_1^{lower}$ **or** $parallelism(\alpha, \beta) \geq \theta_2^{lower}$:
11     $pvFtpr \leftarrow ftpr; ftpr[\alpha, \beta] \leftarrow 0; ftpr[\beta, \alpha] \leftarrow 0;$`// No significant relation`
12 **if** $ftpr \neq pvFtpr$:
    `// Get similarity changed activity pairs with matching locations`
    $X_\alpha \leftarrow \{x \mid x \in Act \setminus \{\alpha\} \wedge (pvFtpr[\alpha, \beta] = pvFtpr[x, \beta] \vee ftpr[\alpha, \beta] = ftpr[x, \beta])\}$;
    $X_\beta \leftarrow \{x \mid x \in Act \setminus \{\beta\} \wedge (pvFtpr[\beta, \alpha] = pvFtpr[x, \alpha] \vee ftpr[\beta, \alpha] = ftpr[x, \alpha])\}$;
13   **foreach** $\gamma \in \{\alpha, \beta\}$ **do**
14   **foreach** $\eta \in X_\gamma$ **do**
15   **if** $(sim(ftpr[\gamma,], ftpr[\eta,]) \downarrow$ **&&**
            $sim(ftpr[\gamma,], ftpr[\eta,]) \neq 0) \parallel (sim(pvFtpr[\gamma,], pvFtpr[\eta,]) \downarrow$ **&&**
            $sim(pvFtpr[\gamma,], pvFtpr[\eta,]) \neq 0) \parallel (sim(pvFtpr[\gamma,], pvFtpr[\eta,]) \downarrow$ **&&**
            $sim(ftpr[\gamma,], ftpr[\eta,]) \downarrow$ **&&**
            $sim(pvFtpr[\gamma,], pvFtpr[\eta,]) \neq sim(ftpr[\gamma,], ftpr[\eta,]))$:
16             $InflPairs \leftarrow InflPairs \cup \{(\gamma, \eta, sim(ftpr[\gamma,], ftpr[\eta,]))\}$;
17     $pvFtpr \leftarrow \varnothing$;
18 **if** $InflPairs \neq \varnothing$:
19   INCREMENTAL-AH-CLUSTERING();   `// Trigger algorithm 3`
20     $InflPairs \leftarrow \varnothing$;

---

to maintain their contextual information as the process evolves. The additional parameter of reference window *refWindow* is used to have flexibility in the degree of influence of historical information, allowing for efficient management of data structures with bounded memory usage. When set to 0, case information forgetting is triggered immediately at each detection window boundary. When set to 1, information from the previous window is retained, while forgetting is triggered after two detection windows are completed. This balances memory efficiency and long-term dependency capture. At Line 28, frequency forgetting tasks are triggered when the current event count *evtCntr* divided by the *dtWindow* differs from *cThreshold* (detection window boundary). When this condition is met, the algorithm identifies cases to forget based on the values of *cThreshold* and *refWindow* (Line 30). It then removes related data from the *lastAct*, *cntr*, and *dflw* data structures (Lines 31–35), using domain subtraction $\lhd$ [11]. If there are directly

Algorithm 3. Incremental-AH-Clustering.

```
 1  foreach (α, β, s) ∈ InflPairs do
 2  │  if (β, α) ∈ dom(pairSim):
 3  │  │  │  pairSim ← pairSim ⊕ {((β, α), s)} ;   // Update new (β, α) similarities
 4  │  else:
 5  │  │  │  pairSim ← pairSim ⊕ {((α, β), s)};   // Update new (α, β) similarities

 6  clusterActivities();                    // Invoke reclustering of activities
 7  reassessMembers();                      // Invoke reassessment of cluster members
 8  Function clusterActivities():
 9  │  repeat
10  │  │     updated ← false;
11  │  │     foreach (actA, actB) ∈ dom(pairSim) do
12  │  │     │  if pairSim(actA, actB) ≥ θ:
13  │  │     │  │  centroidA ← actToClus(actA);
14  │  │     │  │  centroidB ← actToClus(actB);
15  │  │     │  │  if centroidA ≠ centroidB and
16  │  │     │  │     allMemSim(actA, mClust(centroidB), θ) and
       │  │     │  │     allMemSim(actB, mClust(centroidA), θ):
16  │  │     │  │     │  mClust ← ({centroidB} ◁ mClust) ⊕
       │  │     │  │     │     {(centroidA, mClust(centroidA) ∪ mClust(centroidB))};
17  │  │     │  │     │  updated ← true;

18  │  until not updated;
19  Function reassessMembers():
20  │  foreach c ∈ ran(mClust) do
21  │  │     membersToRemove ← ∅;
22  │  │     foreach a ∈ c do
23  │  │     │  if not allMembersSimilar(a, c\{a}, θ):
24  │  │     │  │  membersToRemove ← membersToRemove ∪ {a};
25  │  │     │  │  mClust ← mClust ⊕ {(a, {a})};
26  │  │     │  │  actToClus ← actToClus ⊕ {(a, a)};

27  │  │     if c\membersToRemove ≠ ∅:
28  │  │     │  reassessCentroids(c\membersToRemove);  // Invoke reassessment of
       │  │     │     cluster representative

29  Function reassessCentroids(cluster):
30  │  Initialize maxCt ← 0, centroid ∈ Act;
31  │  foreach act ∈ cluster do
32  │  │     Initialize currCt ← 0;
33  │  │     foreach case ∈ π₂(dom(distAct)) do
34  │  │     │  if (act, case) ∈ dom(distAct):
35  │  │     │  │  currCt ← currCt + distAct(act, case);

36  │  │     if currCt ≥ maxCt && ((aLstSn(act) > aLstSn(centroid)) ∨
       │  │        centroid = ⊥):
37  │  │     │  centroid ← act, maxCt ← currCt;

38  │  mClust ← mClust ⊕ {(centroid, cluster)};           // Update new cluster
39  │  foreach act ∈ cluster do
40  │  │     actToClus ← actToClus ⊕ {(act, centroid)};        // Assign new
       │  │        representative
```

following activity pairs to be forgotten, they will be assigned to *actPair* (Line 33). Algorithm 2 is invoked at Line 37, for each activity pair $(\pi_1(actPair), \pi_2(actPair))$ (here projection is used on a tuple rather than a set of tuples). The *cThreshold* variable (number of completed detection windows) is incremented by one whenever a detection window boundary is passed (Line 38). This new value is assigned to the starting counter of newly observed cases in the next window, thus handling the decaying process (Line 27).

4   Implementation and Evaluation

We have implemented our *SwiftMend* approach as a prototype using Java and used the event logs simulated as PES by timestamp order. The solution is released as a plugin in the open-source PraeclarusPDQ framework[3]. All experiments were executed on an AMD Ryzen 7 CPU (8 cores, 16 threads) 4.2 GHz system with 32 GB RAM (64 bit), running Windows 11 with JVM 21 version where initial and maximum heap space being 524 MB and 8.36 GB respectively. The experiments[4] was conducted in two phases.

4.1   Experimental Design

In the first experimental phase, we configured *SwiftMend* to behave as an offline approach and evaluated it against a baseline offline approach by Sadeghianasl et al. [27], namely *SynonymousLabelRepair*, as it is the most mature approach to contextually detect similar labels at the time of writing. The metrics utilised for this comparative analysis were recall, precision, and F-score. This experimental setup allowed us to evaluate *SwiftMend*'s accuracy in detecting similar activity labels in logs that resulted from a variety of modifications to two real-life event logs, which are:

1. The Hospital Billing log[5]: Contains 451,359 events, 100,000 cases, and 18 activity labels. We used the same 40 logs randomly generated (five logs per each of eight types of renaming variations) as originally used by the baseline approach [27], simulating various levels of activity imperfections.
2. The Sepsis log[6]: Contains 1,050 cases, 15,214 events, and 16 distinct activities. While this log is from a BPI challenge, we chose to include it due to its relevant characteristics for our study, particularly its feature of several activity labels with identical meanings. We compared our approach's performance using two ground truths: one considering "Release C", "Release D", and "Release E" as variants of patient discharge [27], and another additionally including "Release A" and "Release B" as confirmed by Mannhardt and Blind [21].

---

[3] https://github.com/praeclaruspdq/PraeclarusPDQ.
[4] The complete experimental results can be accessed online through https://github.com/Savandi/ SwiftMend.
[5] https://data.4tu.nl/articles/dataset/Hospital_Billing_-_Event_Log/12705113.
[6] https://data.4tu.nl/articles/dataset/Sepsis_Cases_-_Event_Log/12707639.

The second phase involved a sensitivity analysis to evaluate the applicability of detecting and repairing activity label issues in PES using the Hospital Billing log. We selected six distinct activity labels with varying occurrence frequencies (22% to 0.4%) from the original 18, considering the rest as outliers. These labels were systematically renamed to create 50 versions of the log, each featuring synonymous, distorted, or polluted manifestations of a selected label[7]. We analysed detection window sizes from 0.1% to 25% of the total log, acknowledging that real-world implementations would use absolute sizes. The analysis described here focuses on (1) the influence of different detection windows on approach accuracy and (2) the performance of various reference windows for small, medium, and large detection windows. Our primary metric was the mismatch percentage of renamed events per 1,000 events (see Sect. 4.2) between the ground truth and output streams. We used the optimised similarity and stability thresholds to minimise this percentage and enable the balance between recent and historical contexts.

4.2 Results

Baseline Comparison – Renamed Frequency Levels: Table 1 shows the averaged affected activities, affected event percentage, and accuracy values for *SwiftMend* and *SynonymousLabelRepair* for the 40 hospital billing log variants. For example, log $H_{40,50}$ (7 affected activities, 20.909% affected events) achieved precision 1.0, recall 0.858, and F-score 0.92357. Settings include similarity threshold $\theta = 0.7$, full log detection window, and no reference windows. Key observations are delineated below:

– Our approach outperforms the baseline for logs with high percentages of affected events (max. F-score 0.92 vs. baseline's 0.78).
– For our approach, the percentage of affected events and the number of affected activities increasing first leads to a performance (F-score) improvement, then to a decline (though with an F-score of approx. 0.84, it still seems acceptable for approx. 50% affected events and 18 (i.e. all) affected activities).
– *SwiftMend* factors in the frequency of each directly follows relation and performs stability checks on causal and parallel relations before updating the footprint (thus, mostly, detected labels are all true positives – higher precision and recall), unlike the baseline, which updates the footprint based on even a single occurrence of a directly follows relation (detected labels include both true and false positives – lower precision and recall).
– The log with the lowest percentage of affected events (0.017% for $H_{20,0.1}$) causes insurmountable problems for both approaches (with an F-score of 0 in both cases). Recall is low for both approaches for the log with the second lowest percentage of affected events, as is precision for the baseline. With sparse data, *SwiftMend*'s advantage of using directly follows relation frequencies and causal/parallel stability checks is less effective, but so is the baseline's use of single occurrences for updating footprint relations.

---

[7] Renaming ranges were based on the overall event count, as the *dtWindow* parameter determines the batch of consecutive events processed together.

Baseline Comparison – Similarity Thresholds: Table 2 depicts the accuracy results for our approach and the baseline for the $H_{40,30}$ log and the Sepsis log, with similarity thresholds (θ) of 0.7, 0.8, and 0.9. Key findings include:

- For $H_{40,30}$, *SwiftMend* outperformed the baseline, with a peak F-score of 0.82.
- Both approaches showed decreasing F-scores as θ increased from 0.7 to 0.9, indicating fewer identified similar labels with stricter thresholds.
- For the Sepsis log, with the exception of the precision at $\theta = 0.7$ for the ground truth of [21], *SwiftMend* detected less or no labels as similar due to infrequent ($<1\%$) labels. As our approach aims to repair labels, it prioritises highly supported relationships for identifying similar labels. Less frequent labels, lacking sufficient contextual information and support, are treated as outliers and excluded from cohesive cluster formation of similar elements.

Table 1. Results for the Hospital Billing logs with different imperfect label frequencies.

Log	Aff Acts	Affected Events	% Affected Events	SwiftMend			SynonymousLabelRepair		
				Precision	Recall	F-score	Precision	Recall	F-score
$H_{20,0.1}$	2.6	79.4	0.017	0	0	0	0	0	0
$H_{20,10}$	4	11234.2	2.488	0.80	0.250	0.38095	0.40	0.100	0.1600
$H_{20,30}$	4	38574.6	8.546	1	0.650	0.78788	0.62	0.550	0.5829
$H_{40,30}$	7	58308	12.918	1	0.690	0.81657	0.88	0.433	0.5807
$H_{40,50}$	7	94378.8	20.909	1	0.858	0.92357	0.85	0.714	0.7774
$H_{60,50}$	11	138396.2	30.662	1	0.784	0.87892	0.85	0.600	0.7034
$H_{80,50}$	14	173395	38.416	1	0.726	0.84125	0.95	0.642	0.7683
$H_{100,50}$	18	225684	50.001	1	0.722	0.83856	0.98	0.611	0.7537

Table 2. Results of different similarity (θ) thresholds: (a) = 0.7, (b) = 0.8, and (c) = 0.9.

Log	Approach	(a)			(b)			(c)		
		Precision	Recall	F-score	Precision	Recall	F-score	Precision	Recall	F-score
$H_{40,30}$	*SynonymousLabelRepair(Control flow)*	0.8800	0.4333	0.5666	0.8000	0.2380	0.3542	0	0	0
	SwiftMend	1	0.6900	0.8165	1	0.3100	0.4732	0.4000	0.0560	0.0982
Sepsis	*SynonymousLabelRepair(Control flow)*	0.2000	0.3333	0.5099	0.5000	0.3333	0.3999	0.5000	0.3333	0.3999
	SwiftMend	0.2500	0.3300	0.2844	0	0	0	0	0	0
	SwiftMend (Ground Truth of [21])	0.6709	0.2097	0.3195	1	0.1000	0.1818	1	0.1000	0.1818

SwiftMend differs from the baseline approach [27] by treating low-frequency labels as potential outliers unless they meet strict stability thresholds, effective in scenarios with varying levels of label imperfections. Our approach requires multiple occurrences before updating the footprint, in contrast to the baseline, which doesn't account for control-flow relation frequencies of infrequent labels. Additionally, *SwiftMend* requires *all* cluster members to be similar above a defined threshold rather than a pairwise approach, comparing two activity label similarities. These features contribute to more controlled and accurate label grouping, reducing noise and improving precision in similarity assessment, as automatic label repair is the final goal.

Influence of Detection Window: Figure 3 illustrates mismatch percentages across five detection window sizes for synonymous (A), distorted (B), and polluted (C) issue manifestation variations of the 'CHANGE DIAGN' label and the key observations are:

- Smaller detection windows (0.10% and 0.50% of the stream) showed lower mismatch percentages and quicker adaptability compared to larger windows (15.00% and 25.00% of the stream). Mismatches reduce over time (reaching 0%) for all windows.
- When multiple versions of the label coexist, fluctuations in mismatch percentages occur due to changing frequencies and strict cluster grouping.
- Synonymous labels (A) show increasing mismatch percentages as the new label is introduced. Distorted labels (B) maintain very low mismatch percentages (below 0.05%) with a brief spike that's quickly repaired. Polluted labels (C) exhibit consistent fluctuations throughout the coexisting period.
- Spontaneous minor spikes are observed (in (B) and (C)), indicating the dynamic nature of the repair process in response to changing label frequencies and similarities.

Influence of Reference Window: Figure 4 illustrates the mismatch percentage of a stream with synonymous label issue manifestations in 'RELEASE' events for four reference windows (0, 1, 2, 3) across three detection window sizes: small (451 events, 0.1%), medium (22568 events, 5%), and large (112840 events, 25%). Below are the key insights:

- Small detection window (451 events):
  • Exhibits high variability with frequent spikes across all reference windows.
  • Mismatch percentages range from 0% to 0.15%.
  • Shows rapid adaptability but with increased volatility.
- Medium detection window (22568 events):
  • Displays an initial period of low mismatch followed by a sustained plateau around 0.15%.
  • Shows less variability compared to the small window.
  • Stabilises towards the end of the stream.
- Large detection window (112840 events):
  • Demonstrates minimal impact from different reference windows.
  • Maintains a consistent mismatch percentage (0.15%−0.17%) for most of the stream.
  • Exhibits the longest stabilisation period, with changes occurring gradually.

SwiftMend demonstrates adaptability to various label issue manifestations, with performance heavily influenced by detection and reference window sizes. Smaller detection windows (0.10% to 0.50% of the stream) show higher responsiveness and quicker adaptability but with increased volatility. Larger windows (15.00% to 25.00%) provide more stability at the cost of slower adaptation to changing issue manifestations with comparatively higher mismatches. Reference windows significantly impact smaller detection windows, while their influence diminishes with larger detection windows.

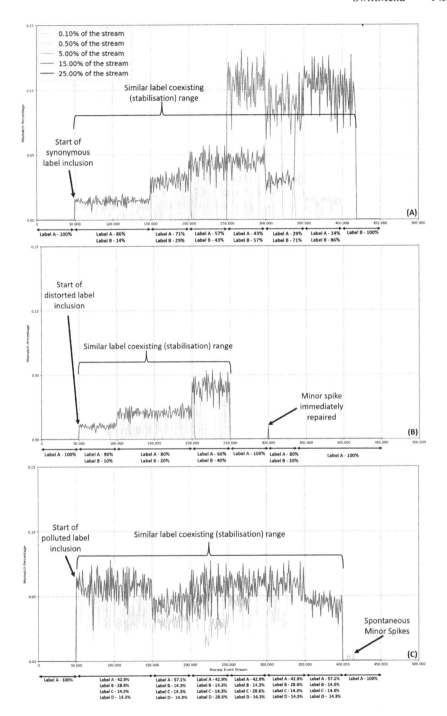

Fig. 3. Mismatch percentages for the label 'CHANGE DIAGN' across different detection window sizes (0.10% to 25.00%) under synonymous (A), distorted (B), and polluted (C) issue manifestations.

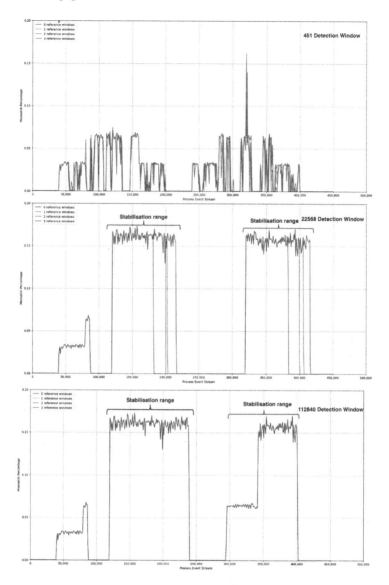

Fig. 4. Mismatch percentages for synonymous label manifestations of label 'RELEASE' events across three detection window sizes: small (451 events), medium (22568 events), and large (112840 events). Each subplot shows the impact of four reference windows.

Optimal label repair is achieved with smaller detection windows combined with carefully selected reference windows, which can maintain low mismatch percentages even for complex label issues. These configurations[8] balance responsiveness and stability,

---

[8] For the computations shown in Sub-sect. 4.2, we have considered 0.8 and 0.7 as the causality upper (θ_1^{upper}) and lower (θ_1^{lower}) thresholds and 2 and 3 as the parallelism upper (θ_2^{upper})

allowing *SwiftMend* to reduce synonymous, distorted, and polluted label mismatches over time.

Time Performance: The time required to store contextual information, extract activity similarities, and performance dynamic clustering using *SwiftMend* per event ranges from a minimum of 0.0013 ms to a maximum of 0.218 ms, with an average of 0.0634 ms across both logs. These results demonstrate that the method is scalable and suitable for PES analysis.

5   Conclusion

Our research addresses a critical gap in online PM by introducing *SwiftMend*, an approach to detect and repair activity label quality issues in PES. The method employs memory-efficient approximate data structures and an incremental hierarchical clustering algorithm with decaying mechanisms, enabling on-the-fly analysis of synonymous, polluted, and distorted labels. Validation using real-life hospital logs demonstrated *SwiftMend*'s effectiveness in detecting and repairing activity label issues in PES in the healthcare domain, outperforming the baseline, particularly for logs with higher percentages of affected events. The sensitivity analysis revealed *SwiftMend*'s adaptability to various label issue manifestations, with average mismatch percentages below 20% (i.e., accuracy above 80%) across different scenarios. A trade-off was observed between detection and reference window sizes: smaller windows allowed quicker adaptation, while larger windows provided more stability but slower responsiveness. These results showcase *SwiftMend*'s potential for improving activity label quality in PES. We acknowledge limitations, including challenges in handling infrequent labels, potential vulnerabilities when invalid labels dominate, and a primary focus on the control-flow perspective. Future work is required to address these limitations by developing methods for low-frequency events, maintaining model integrity under low-quality label dominance, incorporating additional process perspectives (e.g., resource, time, and data), and expanding strategies to manage a broader range of quality drifts from heterogeneous PES across multiple domains. Our approach (and any future extensions) may benefit from further experimentation with more artificial and real-life logs exhibiting a wide variety of characteristics.

References

1. van der Aa, H., Leopold, H., Reijers, H.A.: Detecting inconsistencies between process models and textual descriptions. In: BPM 2015. LNCS, vol. 9253, pp. 90–105. Springer (2015)
2. van der Aalst, W.M.P.: Process Mining - Data Science in Action, 2nd edn. Springer (2016)
3. van der Aalst, W.M.P., et al.: Process mining manifesto. In: BPM. LNCS, vol. 99, pp. 169–194. Springer (2011)
4. Andrews, R., et al.: Root-cause analysis of process-data quality problems. J. Bus. Anal. 5(1), 51–75 (2022)

---

and lower (θ_2^{lower}) thresholds, respectively. Except for the evaluation shown in Table 2, we have considered the similarity threshold (θ) = 0.7 for the other experiments to maintain similar execution conditions.

5. Bifet, A., et al.: Mining frequent closed graphs on evolving data streams. In: ICKDDM, pp. 591–599. ACM (2011)
6. Bose, J.C., et al.: Wanna improve process mining results? In: CIDM, pp. 127–134. IEEE (2013)
7. Burattin, A.: Streaming process mining. In: Process Mining Handbook. LNCS, vol. 448, pp. 349–372. Springer (2022)
8. Burattin, A., et al.: Control-flow discovery from event streams. In: CEC, pp. 2420–2427. IEEE (2014)
9. Conforti, R., Dumas, M., García-Bañuelos, L., La Rosa, M.: Beyond tasks and gateways: discovering BPMN models with subprocesses, boundary events and activity markers. In: BPM 2014. LNCS, vol. 8659, pp. 101–117. Springer (2014)
10. Cuzzocrea, A., et al.: Predictive monitoring of temporally-aggregated performance indicators of business processes against low-level streaming events. Inf. Syst. **81**, 236–266 (2019)
11. Edmond, D.: Information Modelling: Specification and Implementation. Prentice Hall, New York (1992)
12. Fischer, D.A., et al.: Towards interactive event log forensics: detecting and quantifying timestamp imperfections. Inf. Syst. **109**, 102039 (2022)
13. Geisler, S., et al.: Ontology-based data quality management for data streams. ACM J. Data Inf. Qual. **7**(4), 18:1–18:34 (2016)
14. Ghionna, L., et al.: Outlier detection techniques for process mining applications. In: ISMIS. LNCS, vol. 4994, pp. 150–159. Springer (2008)
15. Günther, C.W., van der Aalst, W.M.P.: Fuzzy mining - adaptive process simplification based on multi-perspective metrics. In: BPM. LNCS, vol. 4714, pp. 328–343. Springer (2007)
16. Ko, J., Comuzzi, M.: Keeping our rivers clean: information-theoretic online anomaly detection for streaming business process events. Inf. Syst. **104**, 101894 (2022)
17. Lim, H., et al.: Research issues in data provenance for streaming environments. In: SIGSPATIAL, pp. 58–62. ACM (2009)
18. Lu, Y., Chen, Q., Poon, S.: A robust and accurate approach to detect process drifts from event streams. In: BPM 2021. LNCS, vol. 12875, pp. 383–399. Springer (2021)
19. Maaradji, A., et al.: Detecting sudden and gradual drifts in business processes from execution traces. IEEE Trans. Knowl. Data Eng. **29**(10), 2140–2154 (2017)
20. Manku, G.S., Motwani, R.: Approximate frequency counts over data streams. In: VLDB, pp. 346–357. Morgan Kaufmann (2002)
21. Mannhardt, F., Blinde, D.: Analyzing the trajectories of patients with sepsis using process mining. In: CAiSE. CEUR, vol. 1859, pp. 72–80 (2017)
22. Narita, K., et al.: Incremental hierarchical clustering for data insertion and its evaluation. Int. J. Softw. Innov. **8**(2), 1–22 (2020)
23. Nguyen, H.T.C., et al.: Autoencoders for improving quality of process event logs. Expert Syst. Appl. **131**, 132–147 (2019)
24. Oliveira, Ó., Oliveira, B.: An extensible framework for data reliability assessment. In: ICEIS, pp. 77–84. SCITEPRESS (2022)
25. Ostovar, A., et al.: Robust drift characterization from event streams of business processes. ACM Trans. Knowl. Discov. Data **14**(3), 30:1–30:57 (2020)
26. Qi, D., et al.: On-line monitoring data quality of high-dimensional data streams. J. Stat. Comput. Simul. **86**(11), 2204–2216 (2016)
27. Sadeghianasl, S., ter Hofstede, A.H.M., Wynn, M.T., Suriadi, S.: A contextual approach to detecting synonymous and polluted activity labels in process event logs. In: OTM 2019. LNCS, vol. 11877, pp. 76–94. Springer (2019)
28. Sadeghianasl, S., et al.: Collaborative and interactive detection and repair of activity labels in process event logs. In: ICPM, pp. 41–48. IEEE (2020)

29. Scheibel, B., Rinderle-Ma, S.: Decision mining with time series data based on automatic feature generation. In: CAiSE. LNCS, vol. 13295, pp. 3–18. Springer (2022)
30. Sibai, R.E., et al.: Assessing and improving sensors data quality in streaming context. In: ICCCI. LNCS, vol. 10449, pp. 590–599. Springer (2017)
31. Suriadi, S., et al.: Event log imperfection patterns for process mining: towards a systematic approach to cleaning event logs. Inf. Syst. **64**, 132–150 (2017)
32. Tavares, G.M., et al.: Overlapping analytic stages in online process mining. In: SCC, pp. 167–175. IEEE (2019)
33. Yang, W., et al.: Computing data quality indicators on big data streams using a CEP. In: IWCIM, pp. 1–5. IEEE (2015)
34. van Zelst, S.J., et al.: Event stream-based process discovery using abstract representations. Knowl. Inf. Syst. **54**(2), 407–435 (2018)
35. van Zelst, S.J., et al.: Online conformance checking: relating event streams to process models using prefix-alignments. Int. J. Data Sci. Anal. **8**(3), 269–284 (2019)
36. van Zelst, S.J., et al.: Detection and removal of infrequent behavior from event streams of business processes. Inf. Syst. **90**, 101451 (2020)

Towards Fairness-Aware Predictive Process Monitoring: Evaluating Bias Mitigation Techniques

Mickaelle Caldeira da Silva$^{(\boxtimes)}$ ⓘ, Marcelo Fantinato ⓘ, and Sarajane Marques Peres ⓘ

School of Arts, Sciences and Humanities, University of São Paulo, Sao Paulo, SP, Brazil
{mickaelle.caldeira,m.fantinato,sarajane}@usp.br

Abstract. Predictive process monitoring (PPM) faces fairness issues due to biases in historical data, causing discriminatory practices. Balancing fairness and performance in PPM is crucial but underexplored, possibly requiring the adaptation of ML fairness techniques to process mining. This study assesses Reweighing, Adversarial Debiasing, and Equalized Odds Postprocessing to reduce discrimination in PPM models and understand their trade-offs. Using synthetic event logs of a hiring process with varying discrimination levels, we analyzed the models' performance and fairness metrics. Reweighing improved fairness with minimal performance loss, Adversarial Debiasing greatly boosted fairness but reduced accuracy and recall, and Equalized Odds Postprocessing kept performance without notable fairness gains. Our study offers insights into applying fairness techniques in PPM, advancing equitable and effective predictive models.

Keywords: Process mining · Prediction · PPM · Fairness

1 Introduction

Predictive process monitoring (PPM) faces significant challenges related to fairness, similar to those encountered in other machine learning (ML) applications. These challenges stem primarily from the reliance on historical data from business process executions, which often contain societal biases and prejudices [15]. As a result, predictions that are technically effective may nonetheless perpetuate imbalances and even discriminatory practices within business processes.

Ensuring fairness in PPM is complex and critical. While distributing predictions fairly between protected and non-protected groups seems fair, it can reduce model performance and, in turn, its relevance and applicability. Conversely, optimizing the model solely for performance can reproduce or introduce imbalances and discriminatory practices [13]. Thus, it is essential to strike a balance that promotes fairness without significantly sacrificing model performance, ensuring decisions based on effective and fair predictive models [20].

The balance between performance and fairness has been explored in ML, but remains underexplored in process mining. Moreover, ML techniques often do not translate well to process mining. To our knowledge, only one study tackles discrimination in process mining in a limited way, employing a single post-processing technique to

M. Comuzzi et al. (Eds.): CoopIS 2024, LNCS 15506, pp. 150–166, 2025.
https://doi.org/10.1007/978-3-031-81375-7_9

the results of the basic C4.5 algorithm in WEKA [20]. This study modestly reduces discrimination at the cost of precision, illustrating the challenge of balancing fairness and performance also in PPM.

In this paper, we present an exploratory study evaluating three ML techniques designed to reduce discrimination in PPM models: Reweighing, Adversarial Debiasing, and Equalized Odds Postprocessing. Our results demonstrate the utility of each technique in mitigating discrimination, as well as the trade-offs between performance and fairness. The feasibility of these techniques was confirmed, as the findings provided valuable insights into their applicability in the context of process mining. This study contributes to the understanding of how to enhance fairness in business processes, offering a pathway for more equitable and effective PPM.

This paper is organized as follows: Sect. 2 presents some background concepts used in this paper; Sect. 3 provides information on the research design of our exploratory study; Sect. 4 discusses the results related to the analysis of performance and fairness metrics of different PPM models; Sect. 5 summarizes our contributions and highlights the research paths raised from the exploratory study.

2 Theoretical Background

2.1 Process Mining and PPM

A business process consists of a set of activities executed in coordination within an organizational and technical environment, aimed at achieving a specific business goal [24]. Process mining is an interdisciplinary field at the intersection of data science and process science. Its purpose is to discover, monitor, and improve real processes by extracting knowledge from event logs available in corporate information systems [1].

As summarized by Sousa et al. [23], following van der Aalst [1], process mining relies on the concepts of event, case, trace, log, and attribute. An *event* is the occurrence of a process activity at a given time, performed by a given resource, at a given cost. A *case* corresponds to a process instance and comprises events, each uniquely linked to a case. A *trace* is a mandatory *attribute* of a case, representing a finite sequence of events where each event appears only once. An *event log* is a set of cases such that each event is unique within the event log. Events in the event log include non-mandatory *attributes* such as identifier, timestamp, activity, resource, and cost. Cases can also have non-mandatory *attributes*, often related to domain-specific data.

Process mining has been instrumental in enabling organizations to manage their business processes through descriptive, predictive, and prescriptive approaches [2]. Among these, predictive process monitoring (PPM) focuses on predicting the future of ongoing cases [14]. Typical predictions include process outcomes, estimated completion times, and the sequence of upcoming activities [8]. PPM approaches leverage historical data from past process executions to generate these predictions. These approaches consist of two main phases: the training phase, where a predictive model is developed based on historical data, and the prediction phase, where the model is used to predict the future of ongoing cases.

2.2 Fairness in PPM

Process mining, like any method related to data science, relies on data to perform its tasks. In PPM approaches, this data can reveal patterns that may inadvertently reproduce societal biases and discriminatory treatment against protected groups. Protected groups are populations safeguarded by laws and policies due to historical and systemic discrimination, including those defined by race, gender, age, disability, and other characteristics [21]; while, in ML, a protected attribute is any information that can infer personal or demographic characteristics sensitive from an ethical and social standpoint [16]. Therefore, PPM approaches must be adjusted to avoid reinforcing discriminatory patterns and to maximize fairness in decision-making within business processes.

Fairness definitions are divided into two main groups [7]:

- *Group Fairness*: seeks equality in specific metrics across protected groups. This approach does not require assumptions about the data and is easily verifiable but often fails to ensure fairness for subgroups or individuals.
- *Individual Fairness*: applies equal treatment to similar individuals, based on the principle that *similar individuals should be treated similarly*. This approach faces practical challenges due to assumptions about similarity and relationships between individuals' characteristics and labels.

Three main factors can lead to discrimination in ML [7]. First, bias in training data reflects human and social prejudices, which algorithms can replicate. Second, the focus on minimizing average error in algorithms often benefits majority groups, leading to unequal error rates across different populations. Lastly, exploring data for improving ML can impact certain subgroups or violate ethical standards in specific contexts.

There are three approaches to mitigate discrimination in ML, each applied at a different stage of the ML process [10]:

- *Preprocessing*: This approach reduces bias before training by adjusting the distributions of sensitive attributes or applying specific transformations to remove prejudice from the training data. It is flexible, as it does not constrain the choice of subsequent ML methods.
- *In-Processing*: This approach incorporates fairness during model training. It integrates fairness constraints into the model's optimization functions, aiming to balance performance and fairness by addressing dominant characteristics and varied distributional effects.
- *Postprocessing*: This approach enhances fairness by refining the model's results. It applies transformations to the trained model's outputs, such as altering predictions, to ensure balanced performance across different protected groups. Its main advantage is simplicity, requiring only access to the model's results and sensitive attributes without modifying the ML algorithms.

While preprocessing and postprocessing approaches can adjust input data or model outputs, they cannot directly influence the model's learning process. Additionally, these techniques may reduce model interpretability, as the transformations made might not be explainable. In contrast, in-processing approaches integrate fairness into the learning process, enabling the simultaneous optimization of both performance and fairness.

3 Exploratory Study Design

This exploratory study is structured in two main phases. Initially, a descriptive analysis examines the characteristics and distribution of attributes in the event logs, identifying preliminary patterns and potential indicators of discrimination in the underlying process. In the subsequent phase, these identified patterns support the evaluation of predictive models, which are assessed for both performance and fairness.

3.1 Process Model and Event Log

Our study utilizes synthetic event logs for a recruitment process, provided by Pohl and Berti [18] and detailed by Pohl et al. [19]. The dataset comprises three event logs, each with 10,000 cases and representing different degrees of discrimination. These event logs simulate the entire recruitment process, from initial candidate evaluation to the final decision-making stage, resulting in either a job offer or candidate rejection.

The event logs include attributes like age, citizenship, German proficiency, gender, religion, years of education, and an unspecified protected attribute. These are key for profiling candidates but can lead to bias if misused. Table 1 presents basic statistics for a quantitative overview of the event logs.

Table 1. Basic statistics of the event logs (adapted from [19]).

Event log	Number of events	Number of cases	Number of variants	Number of activities
hiring_log_high	63,869	10,000	386	12
hiring_log_medium	69,054	10,000	382	12
hiring_log_low	72,094	10,000	296	12

Figures 1, 2 and 3 show the discovered process model as a directly-follows graph (DFG) for the three event logs, generated using the Python PM4Py package [5].

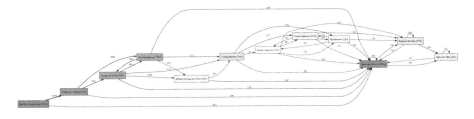

Fig. 1. Process model discovered from the high-discrimination event log.

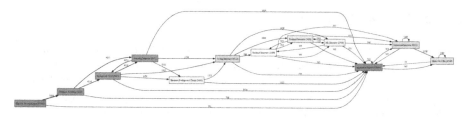

Fig. 2. Process model discovered from the medium-discrimination event log.

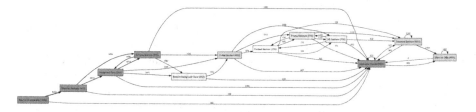

Fig. 3. Process model discovered from the low-discrimination event log.

In Fig. 1, the process discovered for the high-discrimination event log starts with the activity *Hand In Job Application*, followed by evaluation and interview stages. Candidates may undergo various technical interviews, such as *Coding Interview*, *Backend Interview*, *Frontend Interview*, and *ML Interview*, each focusing on technical skills relevant to the position. The final stage is the *Behavioral Interview*, which assesses the candidate's behavioral competencies. The process concludes with either *Make Job Offer* or *Application Rejected*.

The high-discrimination process model (in Fig. 1) shows higher rejection rates early on, particularly after the *Telephonic Screening* and *Screening Interview*, and proportionally more candidates being rejected in subsequent stages. Conversely, for the medium- and low-discrimination process models (in Figs. 2 and 3, respectively), more candidates progress through the initial stages, although the overall rejection rate remains high. In the low-discrimination process model, candidates are more evenly distributed throughout the process, with more reaching the final stages and receiving job offers. In summary, increasing discrimination reduces the likelihood of candidates being considered until the end of the recruitment process.

3.2 Descriptive Analysis

The first phase of this study involves a descriptive analysis to identify discriminatory attributes in recruitment event logs. To determine case outcomes, cases ending with *Make Job Offer* were marked *positive*, while cases ending in *Application Rejected* were marked *negative*. Table 2 shows the distribution of case outcomes for each event log.

To determine whether specific candidate characteristics significantly impact recruitment outcomes, we analyzed the distribution of each attribute in relation to case outcomes. Additionally, we examined the frequency of transitions between activities to identify stages of the recruitment process associated with discriminatory bias, correlating these transitions with attributes indicating discrimination within the process.

3.3 Preprocessing

These preprocessing actions were taken to ensure data integrity, prevent overfitting, and guarantee generalization. Table 2 shows the values resulting from preprocessing.

One-Hot Encoding of Transitions. Each possible transition between two activities in the process was represented as a unique column in the dataset, with 1 or 0 indicating, respectively, the occurrence or non-occurrence of a given transition for each case. For example, if the attribute *Hand In Job Application → Application Rejected* is set to 1, it means that activity *Hand In Job Application* followed by activity *Application Rejected* occurred in the case. This transformation enables predictive models to analyze the relationships between sequential activities.

Encoding of Categorical Attributes. Categorical attributes, including binary characteristics of the candidates, were converted from boolean to binary numerical values (1 for true and 0 for false). The attributes encoded this way are: *German speaking, gender, citizen, protected,* and *religious.*

Categorization of Numerical Attributes. Numerical attributes, such as age and years of education, were converted from continuous to discrete data. The *age* attribute was segmented into categories: childhood (0–12), adolescence (13–17), youth (18–24), young adult (25–34), middle-aged adult (35–49), mature adult (50–64), and older adult (65+). The *yearsOfEducation* attribute was categorized into groups reflecting levels of formal education: no formal education (0), elementary education (1–8); secondary education (9–12), higher education (13–16), and graduate education (17+). Numerical data was discretized to reduce attribute complexity and improve the interpretability of categories, especially for life stages related to age and educational levels.

Removal of Duplicates. Exact duplicates were removed, keeping only the first occurrence. Conflicting duplicates, where identical data led to different outcomes, were completely removed from the dataset. This approach promotes data integrity and prevents the over-representation.

Table 2. Case outcome before and after preprocessing.

Before preprocessing				
Event log	Number of cases	Case outcome		Disparate impact
		Positive	Negative	
hiring_log_high	10,000	2,430	7,570	0.12
hiring_log_medium	10,000	3,461	6,539	0.30
hiring_log_low	10,000	2,981	7,019	0.60
After preprocessing				
Event log	Number of cases	Case outcome		Disparate impact
		Positive	Negative	
hiring_log_high	4,128	1,707	2,421	0.22
hiring_log_medium	4,544	2,191	2,353	0.43
hiring_log_low	4,616	2,605	2,011	0.70

3.4 Predictive Models

Considering the recruitment process, the goal of the PPM was to predict whether a given ongoing case would be finalized as *Make an Offer* or *Application Rejected*. To achieve this, a baseline predictor was created without consideration for fairness. Subsequently, a series of approaches aimed at mitigating discrimination in predictive models was applied. The open-source library AI Fairness 360 (AIF360) [4] was used to implement these approaches. AIF360 includes techniques developed by the research community to detect and mitigate biases in ML models. The implemented approaches encompass preprocessing, in-processing, and postprocessing methods, addressing different stages of the model implementation cycle to minimize the impact of historical biases on final decisions.

Bias mitigation methods were selected based on Bellamy et al. [4], who evaluated fairness techniques from the AIF360 library with Random Forest and Logistic Regression models. In this experiment, one method from each category—preprocessing, in-processing, and postprocessing—was chosen for its ability to improve fairness with minimal accuracy impact. To maintain consistency and comparability, Random Forest was used as both the baseline model and the fairness-aware model.

Baseline Model (BSL). The initial model used the Random Forest classifier, known for modeling complex attribute interactions. Random Forest was chosen as the baseline model due to its robustness, ability to handle large datasets with higher dimensionality, and resistance to overfitting. Hyperparameter optimization was conducted using Scikit-learn's *GridSearchCV* to maximize the F1-score, with 3-fold cross-validation to enhance generalization and performance on unseen data. The tuned hyperparameters included the number of estimators (50, 100, 200), tree depth (None, 10, 20, 30), minimum samples required to split a node (2, 5, 10), minimum samples at a leaf node (1, 2, 4), use of bootstrap samples (True, False), and class weighting ('balanced' and 'balanced_subsample').

Reweighing (RWG) [preprocessing]. This technique adjusts the weights of training instances to ensure equal representation of protected and non-protected groups, aiming to mitigate biases in the protected attribute [12]. In the AIF360 toolkit [3], instance weights are adjusted according to the representativeness of each group and label in the dataset. It corrects imbalances in the training data before model training. In this application, the adjusted data were used to train a new Random Forest classifier, with hyperparameter optimization via GridSearchCV, using the same parameter grid and 3-fold cross-validation as the baseline model to maintain consistency.

Adversarial Debiasing (ADB) [in-processing]. This technique uses adversarial learning to reduce bias in predictive models. Two models are trained simultaneously: a predictor based on input features and an adversary that detects bias in these predictions. The adversary forces the predictor to learn fair patterns not influenced by protected attributes [25]. In the toolkit AIF360 [3], both the predictor and adversarial models are implemented using straightforward artificial neural network architectures. In this application, the AIF360's *ADB* classifier was used instead of the Random Forest classifier. Parameters were manually tuned to balance performance and bias mitigation. These included the number of epochs (100), the number of hidden units (100), and the adversary's loss weight adjusted for high (0.12), medium (2.62), and low (3.1) bias levels.

Equalized Odds (EOP) [postprocessing]. This technique adjusts model predictions to meet the criterion of EO between different groups [11,17]. It focuses on making TPR and FPR equal between groups defined by protected attributes, promoting fairer distribution of predictions. In the AIF360 toolkit [3], predictions are adjusted using linear programming to optimally change predicted labels, aiming to minimize differences between the metrics. In this application, the same Random Forest classifier and hyperparameter optimization via GridSearchCV were applied. After obtaining initial predictions, *EOP* was used to adjust the labels and mitigate bias.

3.5 Evaluation of Fairness in PPM

Event logs were temporally divided based on case completion dates for training and testing. Cases completed before an automatically determined cutoff date, representing 80% of the data, were allocated to the training set, while those completed afterward, representing 20%, were assigned to the test set. Additionally, balancing was performed to ensure a proportional distribution of the target variable in both the training and test sets. This simulates a realistic prediction scenario, ensuring the model is evaluated on future cases that were not available during training.

The model included the categorical variables *German speaking, gender, citizen, protected*, and *religious*. Transitions between activities were also incorporated, excluding those leading to the final activity to prevent information leakage. To avoid redundancy, one category each was excluded from *age* and *yearsOfEducation*, as categorizing numeric variables naturally creates a reference group. In total, 37 attributes were used for model training.

The performance of PPM models was evaluated based on accuracy, recall, precision, and F1-score, offering a comprehensive view of the model's ability to make correct predictions. Additionally, group fairness metrics were employed to evaluate the model's effectiveness in detecting and mitigating biases between protected and non-protected groups. The group fairness metrics used are:

Demographic Parity. This group fairness metric requires that the probability of a positive outcome be the same for both protected and non-protected groups, regardless of their characteristics [6]. Equation 1 express this metric mathematically. While demographic parity promotes equal treatment among groups, it can lead to less accurate predictions or overlook differences in outcome prevalence among groups [6].

$$P(\hat{Y} = 1 \mid A = a) = P(\hat{Y} = 1 \mid A = b) \tag{1}$$

where $P(A)$ represents a protected attribute, while $P(a)$ and $P(b)$ represent different groups within that attribute. Parity is achieved when the probabilities of predicting $P(\hat{Y} = 1)$, or a positive outcome, are identical for both groups.

In this study, demographic parity was examined through the disparate impact (DI) indicator. DI is calculated as the ratio of positive outcome rates between the protected and non-protected groups (see Eq. 2). A DI value of 1 indicates no disparity, meaning outcomes are equal between groups. A DI value less than 1 indicates that the protected group is disadvantaged compared to the non-protected group. Conversely, a DI value greater than 1 indicates that the protected group is advantaged compared to the non-protected group [6].

$$DI = \frac{P(\hat{Y} = 1 \mid A = a)}{P(\hat{Y} = 1 \mid A = b)} \tag{2}$$

The hiring rate for protected groups must be at least 80% of that for non-protected groups [9]. Additionally, DI is expected to fall within the range $\tau \leq DI \leq \frac{1}{\tau}$. Therefore, if $\tau = 0.8$ represents the minimum threshold for bias against protected groups, then 1.25 represents the maximum threshold for undue favoritism towards protected groups [22].

Equalized Odds (EO). This group fairness metric requires that the true positive rate (TPR) and the false positive rate (FPR) be similar between groups [6]. It has two perspectives:

- **Equality of Opportunity.** This refers to the equality of the TPR between groups— the probability of an individual receiving a true positive result should be the same across all groups. This criterion is relevant in contexts such as loans or job offers, where it is important to ensure that deserving individuals are not unjustly excluded. Equation 3 expresses this metric mathematically.

$$P(\hat{Y}=1 \mid A=a, Y=1) = P(\hat{Y}=1 \mid A=b, Y=1) \tag{3}$$

- **Predictive Equality.** This refers to the equality of the FPR between groups—the probability of an individual receiving a false positive result should be the same across all groups. This criterion is crucial in contexts where it is important to minimize errors that harm innocent individuals, such as avoiding wrongful arrests. Equation 4 expresses this metric mathematically.

$$P(\hat{Y}=1 \mid A=a, Y=0) = P(\hat{Y}=1 \mid A=b, Y=0) \tag{4}$$

For equality of opportunity, EO was determined by subtracting the TPR values of the protected group from those of the non-protected group. Similarly, for predictive equality, EO was determined by subtracting the FPR values between these groups. For both, a difference of 0 shows that the TPR or FPR are equal for both groups, representing an ideal scenario [6].

4   Analysis of Results

4.1   Descriptive Analysis

This section explores data distribution and attributes that might influence recruitment outcomes, aiming to highlight potential discrimination factors by examining candidate characteristics and their transitions between activities.

Figures 4, 5, and 6 display the proportion of positive and negative outcomes for each attribute in the high-, medium- and low-discrimination event logs, respectively. While most attributes show consistent proportions of positive and negative outcomes relative to the overall data distribution, the *protected* attribute shows differing proportions between such outcomes across the discrimination levels.

In the high-discrimination event log, there are marked disparities in the proportions of positive and negative outcomes for the protected attribute, with a significantly higher incidence of negative outcomes for the protected group. The medium-discrimination event log exhibits less pronounced disparities, yet still shows a higher proportion of negative outcomes for the protected group. Conversely, the low-discrimination event log demonstrates a balanced distribution of positive and negative outcomes, indicating a recruitment process with minimal discrimination against the protected attribute.

Figure 7 displays the frequency of transitions between activities for the high-discrimination recruitment event log, distinguishing candidates from the protected group (*True*) and non-protected group (*False*). The data reveal two critical patterns indicating that candidates from the protected group encounter substantial obstacles throughout the recruitment process: (1) their representation decreases sharply in the later stages, and (2) transitions involving rejection have a higher proportion of protected group candidates compared to other transitions. These patterns suggest that protected group candidates have fewer opportunities to progress and secure job offers.

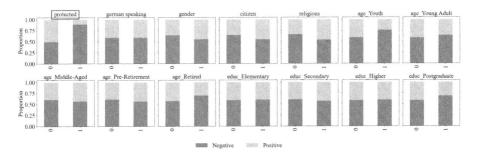

Fig. 4. Proportions of positive and negative outcome by attributes from the high-discrimination event log.

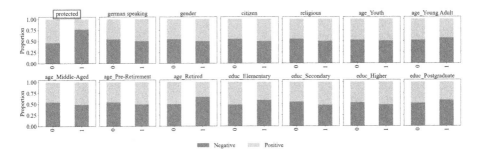

Fig. 5. Proportions of positive and negative outcome by attributes from the medium-discrimination event log.

For instance, when comparing transition *Hand In Job Application → Telephonic Screening* to *Telephonic Screening → Background Check* and *Telephonic Screening → Screening Interview*, a noticeable decline in the proportion of candidates from the protected group is evident in the latter stages, indicating potential early-stage discrimination. Additionally, transition *Hand In Job Application → Application Rejected* shows a significantly higher rejection rate for protected group candidates at the initial stage, further indicating early-stage bias in the hiring process. At more advanced stages in the process, such as transitions *Screening Interview → Coding Interview* and *Backend Interview → Behavioral Interview*, candidates from the non-protected group predominantly dominate. In contrast, transition *Behavioral Interview → Make Job Offer* reveals a notably lower proportion of candidates from the protected group, indicating that few candidates from this group receive job offers. Conversely, transitions involving rejections, such as *Telephonic Screening → Application Rejected* and *Extensive Background Check → Application Rejected*, disproportionately affect candidates from the protected group.

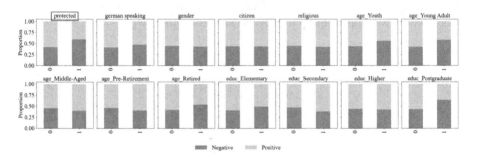

Fig. 6. Proportions of positive and negative outcome by attributes from the low-discrimination event log.

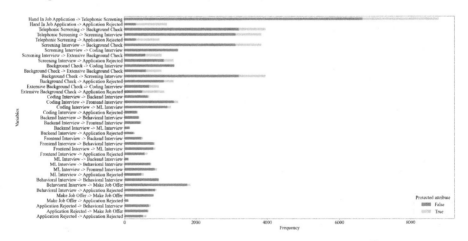

Fig. 7. Transitions between activities for the high-discrimination recruitment event log, distinguishing candidates from protected and non-protected groups (transitions are presented from top to bottom, ordered from the most initial to the most final).

A consistent pattern appears in the medium- and low-discrimination event logs, showing unbalanced representation of protected group candidates in various process transitions. Bias against these candidates persists in the process simulation but is less pronounced in the medium-discrimination event log and further reduces in the low-discrimination event log.

This analysis of the recruitment process across three event logs demonstrates that discrimination is linked to the protected attribute. As discrimination decreases, equality for protected group candidates significantly improves. Consequently, the approaches for reducing discrimination in PPM, discussed in the following section, specifically target the protected attribute.

4.2 Evaluation of Fairness in PPM

Tables 3, 4, and 5 compare performance and fairness metrics for four predictive models (*BSL, RWG, ADB,* and *EOP*) across high-, medium- and low-discrimination event logs, respectively. The results reveal distinct trade-offs between performance and fairness for each predictive model, varying with the discrimination level in each event log.

For the high-discrimination event log (see Table 3), *BSL* performed well but faced significant fairness issues, with a DI of only 0.19 and imbalances in TPR and FPR between protected and non-protected groups, as indicated by EO. Conversely, *ADB* greatly improved fairness metrics, especially DI and EO-FPR, but at the cost of a significant drop in performance metrics, particularly accuracy and recall. A recall value of 0.35 indicates that, despite the model's improved fairness, it often fails to correctly identify positive cases, resulting in a high number of false negatives. In correlation with the significant decline in recall, the fairness metric EO-TPR also deteriorated substantially. This deterioration is likely due to the model generating a high number of false negatives for the non-protected group in an attempt to improve DI. As a result, the number of true positives for the non-protected group decreased, leading to a distortion in this metric. *RWG*, on the other hand, reached a more balanced approach, achieving moderate fairness improvements, with DI still below 0.8, while incurring minimal performance loss. The EO-TPR of 0.00 stands out, indicating perfect equality in TPR between groups. Finally, while *EOP* maintained high performance, it failed to deliver satisfactory results in terms of fairness. The values of DI and EO-TPR are similar to those of *BSL*, and EO-FPR worsened, indicating that the post-processing strategy was ineffective in reducing discrimination for this case.

Figure 8 shows the DI disparity for the high-discrimination event log, revealing significant discrimination by *BSL, RWG,* and *EOP*. These three models predict lower positive outcomes for candidates from the protected group compared to the non-protected group. Notably, *ADB* stands out, slightly reversing this proportion, reflecting DI slightly greater than 1. Although *RWG* and *EOP* did not achieve a DI of 0.8, both models showed an improvement compared to the original distribution of the high-discrimination event log, which had a DI of 0.12 before pre-processing (see Table 1) and a DI of 0.22 after pre-processing (see Table 2).

Table 3. Comparison of performance and fairness metrics among predictive models for high-discrimination event log.

Type	Metric	BSL	RWG	ADB	EOP
Performance	Accuracy	0.90	0.88	0.69	0.87
	Precision	0.83	0.80	0.81	0.78
	Recall	0.97	0.96	0.35	0.97
	F1-Score	0.89	0.87	0.48	0.86
Fairness	Disparate impact (DI)	0.19	0.35	1.03	0.18
	Equalized odds (EO)–TPR	0.16	0.00	0.65	0.17
	Equalized odds (EO)–FPR	0.17	0.07	0.05	0.26

For the medium-discrimination event log (see Table 4), *BSL* performed well again, exhibiting now fewer significant fairness issues. This is evidenced by a DI of 0.52, but still below the desired minimum of 0.8, and smaller imbalances in TPR and FPR between protected and non-protected groups, as indicated by EO. Figure 9 demonstrates the reduced DI disparity produced by *BSL* compared to Fig. 8. Although discrimination

Table 4. Comparison of performance and fairness metrics among predictive models for medium-discrimination event log.

Type	Metric	BSL	RWG	ADB	EOP
Performance	Accuracy	0.89	0.88	0.87	0.83
	Precision	0.85	0.84	0.90	0.75
	Recall	0.94	0.94	0.81	0.95
	F1-Score	0.89	0.89	0.85	0.84
Fairness	Disparate impact (DI)	0.52	0.66	0.72	0.45
	Equalized odds (EO)–TPR	0.09	0.02	0.13	0.09
	Equalized odds (EO)–FPR	0.04	0.05	0.09	0.22

Table 5. Comparison of performance and fairness metrics among predictive models for low-discrimination event log.

Type	Metric	BSL	RWG	ADB	EOP
Performance	Accuracy	0.91	0.91	0.87	0.86
	Precision	0.90	0.90	0.97	0.84
	Recall	0.94	0.95	0.80	0.95
	F1-Score	0.92	0.92	0.88	0.89
Fairness	Disparate impact (DI)	0.68	0.79	1.05	0.62
	Equalized odds (EO)–TPR	0.11	0.03	0.14	0.12
	Equalized odds (EO)–FPR	0.01	0.01	0.18	0.13

is still present, it is notably less pronounced. Although *BSL*, *RWG*, *EOP*, and *ADB* did not achieve a DI of 0.8, all models showed an improvement compared to the original distribution of the medium-discrimination event log, which had a DI of 0.30 before pre-processing (see Table 1) and a DI of 0.43 after pre-processing (see Table 2). *ADB* demonstrated mixed results for this event log. On one hand, it maintained accuracy and even improved precision compared to *BSL*, with only a drop in recall, which was less severe than for the high-discrimination event log. However, this model did not significantly enhance fairness, as indicated by a DI below 0.8 and an EO-FPR higher than *BSL*.

Figure 9 shows that *ADB* failed to equalize prediction proportions for both groups of the protected attribute, unlike the high-discrimination event log. *RWG* consistently demonstrated the best balance between performance and fairness. While the performance metrics of *BSL* were nearly maintained, *RWG* significantly enhanced fairness metrics. Although the DI did not approach the ideal minimum of 0.8, the EO-TPR exhibited a near-perfect difference of just 0.02. *EOP* again, while maintaining high performance, failed to deliver satisfactory results in terms of fairness. The EO-TPR is equal to that of *BSL*, but DI and EO-FPR even worsened, indicating that the post-processing strategy was ineffective in reducing discrimination in this case as well.

As for the low-discrimination event log (see Table 5), the pattern observed in previous event logs continues, indicating that even with minimal bias, different strategies still struggle to balance performance and fairness effectively. Only *ADB* managed to achieve a DI above 0.8, but this came at the cost of reduced performance, particularly recall, which negatively impacted the EO-TPR and EO-FPR fairness metrics. In contrast, *RWG* maintained steady performance but did not meet the DI threshold of 0.8, even in a low bias scenario. However, it showed improvement compared to the original distribution of the low-discrimination event log, which had a DI of 0.60 before pre-

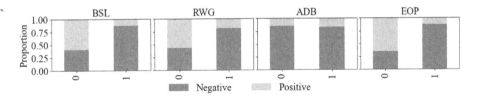

Fig. 8. Proportion of positive and negative predictions for the protected attribute for high-discrimination event log (0 represents the non-protected group and 1 the protected group).

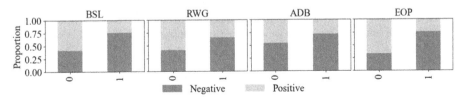

Fig. 9. Proportion of positive and negative predictions for the protected attribute for medium-discrimination event log (0 represents the non-protected group and 1 the protected group).

processing (see Table 1) and a DI of 0.70 after pre-processing (see Table 2). Additionally, *RWG* achieved excellent EO-TPR and EO-FPR values. Lastly, *EOP* again produced the least favorable results. Figure 10 illustrates the reduced DI disparity across the four models (*BSL*, *RWG*, *ADB*, and *EOP*) compared to Figs. 8 and 9. While discrimination persists for *BSL*, *RWG*, and *EOP*, it is less pronounced, whereas *ADB* predicts slightly more positive outcomes for the protected group than for the non-protected group.

The comparison of predictive models at varying discrimination levels reveals specific performance and fairness characteristics. In this experiment, *RWG* slightly reduced accuracy and precision to enhance three fairness metrics, achieving a better performance-fairness balance as discrimination decreased. Conversely, *ADB* excelled in improving the DI fairness metric, showing its ability to balance predictions more equally across different groups. However, this improvement in fairness significantly reduced performance metrics, particularly accuracy and recall. The drop in accuracy suggests the model's reduced capability to correctly predict outcomes, while low recall indicates a failure to identify a substantial proportion of true positives. Moreover, the EO-TPR and EO-FPR fairness metrics did not yield satisfactory results, likely correlating with the decline in recall. Although *EOP* kepted high recall, its precision and fairness metrics, such as DI, remained limited. Additionally, all applied techniques improved the DI compared to the original distribution of the event logs.

These results align with Bellamy et al. [4]: *Reweighing (RWG)* improved fairness with minimal accuracy loss, *Adversarial Debiasing (ADB)* enhanced fairness but reduced accuracy and recall, and *Equalized Odds Postprocessing (EOP)* had minimal impact on both fairness and accuracy. Overall, the experiments revealed that both performance and fairness corrections tend to improve as discrimination in event logs decreases. This improvement can be attributed to the reduced need for adjustments to correct existing biases, allowing techniques like *RWG* and *ADB* to operate more effectively without significantly compromising performance. These findings suggest that starting with a more balanced and representative dataset is crucial for implementing effective and fair discrimination mitigation techniques.

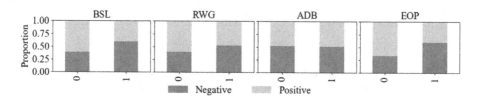

Fig. 10. Proportion of positive and negative predictions for the protected attribute for low-discrimination event log (0 represents the non-protected group and 1 the protected group).

5 Conclusion

In this paper, we examined the impact of three discrimination mitigation approaches—Reweighing, Adversarial Debiasing, and Equalized Odds—on PPM in various discriminatory contexts. We compared these approaches against a baseline using performance and fairness metrics. The results highlight the utility and feasibility of each approach. Utility is demonstrated through the distinct benefits in discrimination mitigation and performance, aiding in selecting the most appropriate model for specific business scenarios. Feasibility is confirmed as the findings provide insights into the applicability of these approaches in the PPM context, enhancing the understanding of fairness improvement in process mining.

However, this study has limitations. It analyzes a limited number of discrimination mitigation approaches and uses a single synthetic event log dataset. Additionally, the metrics used, while widely recognized, do not capture all nuances of fairness and performance. The findings indicate that models like Adversarial Debiasing, although effective in improving fairness metrics, often experience significant reductions in other performance metrics such as recall and accuracy.

This study opens several avenues for future research, including exploring bias mitigation approaches that better balance fairness and performance specifically in process mining contexts. Applying these techniques to a broader range of event logs, including real-world data, is another direction to validate generalization. Investigating business process improvements to mitigate discrimination and developing prescriptive monitoring models to proactively address it are also needed. Finally, integrating these models' outputs into visualization tools can make the analysis of fairness and performance results more intuitive and accessible for end users.

References

1. van der Aalst, W.M.P.: Process Mining: Data Science in Action, 2nd edn. Springer, Heidelberg (2016)
2. van der Aalst, W.M.P.: Process mining: a 360 degree overview. In: van der Aalst, W.M.P., Carmona, J. (eds.) Process Mining Handbook. LNBIP, vol. 448, pp. 3–34. Springer, Cham (2022)
3. Bellamy, R.K.E., Dey, K., Hind, M., et al.: AI fairness 360 (AIF360) (2024). Repository. https://github.com/Trusted-AI/AIF360
4. Bellamy, R.K., et al.: AI fairness 360: an extensible toolkit for detecting and mitigating algorithmic bias. IBM J. Res. Dev. **63**(4/5), 4-1 (2019)
5. Berti, A., van Zelst, S.J., van der Aalst, W.M.P.: PM4Py web services: easy development, integration and deployment of process mining features in any application stack. In: Demonstration Track at BPM 2019, pp. 174–178 (2019)
6. Castelnovo, A., Crupi, R., Greco, G., Regoli, D., Penco, I.G., Cosentini, A.C.: A clarification of the nuances in the fairness metrics landscape. Sci. Rep. **12**(1), 4209 (2022)
7. Chouldechova, A., Roth, A.: A snapshot of the frontiers of fairness in machine learning. Commun. ACM **63**(5), 82–89 (2020)
8. Di Francescomarino, C., Ghidini, C.: Predictive process monitoring. In: van der Aalst, W.M.P., Carmona, J. (eds.) Process Mining Handbook. LNBIP, vol. 448, pp. 320–346. Springer, Cham (2022)
9. Equal Employment Opportunity Commission: Uniform guidelines on employee selection procedures, USA (1978). https://www.govinfo.gov/content/pkg/CFR-2011-title29-vol4/xml/CFR-2011-title29-vol4-part1607.xml
10. Hajian, S., Domingo-Ferrer, J.: A methodology for direct and indirect discrimination prevention in data mining. IEEE Trans. Knowl. Data Eng. **25**(7), 1445–1459 (2012)

11. Hardt, M., Price, E., Srebro, N.: Equality of opportunity in supervised learning. In: Annual Conference on Neural Information Processing Systems, pp. 3315–3323 (2016)
12. Kamiran, F., Calders, T.: Data preprocessing techniques for classification without discrimination. Knowl. Inf. Syst. **33**(1), 1–33 (2012)
13. Liu, W., Liu, F., Tang, R., Liao, B., Chen, G., Heng, P.A.: Balancing between accuracy and fairness for interactive recommendation with reinforcement learning. In: 24th Pacific-Asia Conference on Advances in Knowledge Discovery and Data Mining, pp. 155–167. Springer (2020)
14. Maggi, F.M., Di Francescomarino, C., Dumas, M., Ghidini, C.: Predictive monitoring of business processes. In: 26th International Conference on Advanced Information Systems Engineering, pp. 457–472. Springer (2014)
15. Mannhardt, F.: Responsible process mining. In: van der Aalst, W.M.P., Carmona, J. (eds.) Process Mining Handbook. LNBIP, vol. 448, pp. 373–401. Springer, Cham (2022)
16. Mehrabi, N., Morstatter, F., Saxena, N., Lerman, K., Galstyan, A.: A survey on bias and fairness in machine learning. ACM Comput. Surv. **54**(6), 1–35 (2021)
17. Pleiss, G., Raghavan, M., Wu, F., Kleinberg, J., Weinberger, K.Q.: On fairness and calibration. In: Annual Conference on Neural Information Processing Systems, pp. 5680–5689. Springer (2017)
18. Pohl, T., Berti, A.: (Un)fair process mining event logs (2023). Dataset. https://doi.org/10.5281/zenodo.8059488
19. Pohl, T., Berti, A., Qafari, M.S., van der Aalst, W.M.P.: A collection of simulated event logs for fairness assessment in process mining. In: Demonstration & Resources Forum at BPM 2023, pp. 87–91 (2023)
20. Qafari, M.S., van der Aalst, W.M.P.: Fairness-aware process mining. In: International Conference on Cooperative Information Systems, pp. 182–192. Springer (2019)
21. Romei, A., Ruggieri, S.: A multidisciplinary survey on discrimination analysis. Knowl. Eng. Rev. **29**(5), 582–638 (2014)
22. Saleiro, P., et al.: Aequitas: a bias and fairness audit toolkit. preprint arXiv:1811.05577 (2018)
23. de Sousa, R.G., Peres, S.M., Fantinato, M., Reijers, H.A.: Concept drift detection and localization in process mining: an integrated and efficient approach enabled by trace clustering. In: 36th Annual ACM Symposium on Applied Computing, pp. 364–373. ACM (2021)
24. Weske, M.: Business Process Management: Concepts, Languages, Architectures, 3 edn. Springer (2019)
25. Zhang, B.H., Lemoine, B., Mitchell, M.: Mitigating unwanted biases with adversarial learning. In: Proceedings of the 2018 AAAI/ACM Conference on AI, Ethics, and Society, pp. 335–340. ACM (2018)

Knowledge Graphs and Knowledge Engineering

A User-Driven Hybrid Neuro-Symbolic Approach for Knowledge Graph Creation from Relational Data

Jan-David Stütz[1,2]([✉]) [ID], Oliver Karras[3] [ID], Allard Oelen[3] [ID], and Sören Auer[2,3] [ID]

[1] Robert Bosch GmbH, Gerlingen, Germany
jan-david.stuetz@de.bosch.com
[2] Leibniz University Hannover, Hanover, Germany
[3] Leibniz Information Centre for Science and Technology (TIB), Hanover, Germany
{oliver.karras,allard.oelen,soeren.auer}@tib.eu

Abstract. In all kinds of organizations, relational data is prevalent and ubiquitous in a plethora of systems. However, the integration and exchange of such data is cumbersome, time-consuming, and error-prone. Semantic technologies, such as ontologies, KGs, and linked data, were developed to facilitate this but require comprehensive technical skills and complex methods for mapping relational data to semantic formalisms. Naturally, this process lacks speed, scalability, and automation. This work presents a novel user-driven neuro-symbolic approach to transform relational data into KGs. In our approach, users are supported by neural models (in particular Large Language Models) and symbolic formalisms (ontologies and mappings) to automate various mapping tasks and thus speed up and scale up the transformation from relational to linked data. We implemented our approach in a comprehensive intelligent assistant dubbed LXS. Our experimental evaluation, conducted primarily with participants from the Robert Bosch GmbH, demonstrates enhanced mapping quality compared to manual creation, a competitive application, and AI-only generations. Additionally, it significantly reduces user interaction time by nearly half, independent of the user's experience level. Also, qualitatively, users appreciated the attractiveness and novelty of the user interface. Furthermore, the neuro-symbolic approach of LXS contributes to a more trustworthy human-AI interaction since it keeps users in the loop and provides transparency in the transformation process.

Keywords: Neuro-symbolic · Knowledge graph creation · HCI

1 Introduction

In the modern data-driven landscape, organizations generate vast amounts of data, often stored in relational databases. This relational data usually serves as the backbone of decision-making processes, is required to meet legal obligations, or forms the foundation for crucial research and analysis in various fields. However, the actual value of this data can only be unlocked when it is transformed into a more structured and interconnected form, such as Knowledge graphs (KGs) [25]. KGs offer a rich semantic representation that enables organizations to derive valuable insights, enhance data integration, and support advanced analytics and data handling, even on a large scale [14]. Furthermore, Zou and Hitzler et al. highlight the importance of KGs for a more trustworthy Artificial Intelligence (AI) by utilizing KGs as the foundation of knowledge for AI-driven applications [16,29]. This way, AI-driven applications can provide a higher level of transparency and, moreover, enable those applications to increase their performance and results. Although KGs offer great potential, transforming from relational data to KGs encounters various difficulties. Traditional methods for this conversion frequently involve a significant amount of manual work, require domain-specific expertise, and are sensitive to human errors [4,5,9,15,26]. As a result, the process of transforming from relational data to KGs is perceived to be particularly time-consuming and error-prone [4,5,9,15,26]. These characteristics limit the widespread adoption of KGs, especially in organizations where the expertise for transforming relational data to KGs is scarce or not readily available.

Current research proposes approaches for the desired transformation, that are based on mappings or annotations and link data only using a provided Graphical User Interface (GUI) [4]. Even though this already reduces the complexity and indicates a decrease in mental workload, it does not scale since the mappings are still done manually [8,9]. To address these constraints, enhance efficiency in terms of speed and scale, and minimize common human-made errors, we have created LXS (which stands for "Large Language Model meets Semantic Web"). LXS leverages a user-driven neuro-symbolic approach for creating KGs from relational data. Using LXS, users subsequently create and validate the mappings required to generate the KG. Those mappings are generated by neural models that are enhanced through symbolic formalisms and support users with plausibility checks.

The within-subject study comparison, the between-subject analysis, the interviews, and the User Experience Questionnaire (UEQ) prove that LXS effectively speeds up and scales up the KG generation while providing trust in the AI generations and maintaining a pleasant UX.

The remainder of this work presents the current state of relevant research in Sect. 2, proposes our approach in Sect. 3, describes our methodology in Sect. 4, presents the results in Sect. 5 and it's discussion in Sect. 6. We finalize this work with a conclusion and proposal for future work in Sect. 7.

2   Related Work

2.1   Human-in-the-Loop AI Applications

Applications in the area of neural networks gained considerable attention through the latest introductions in Generative AI [10]. LLMs are utilized in different domains, such as psychology, literature, and health care to generate text mostly from domain-specific knowledge provided through texts [23,27,28].

AI-powered applications can lack trust and acceptance. Therefore the work of Kaur et al. provides an overview of different approaches to increase trust and acceptance of applications by putting the human before-, in-, or over-the-loop [18]. Amershi et al. extend this work by exploring human-in-the-loop case studies and proposing new ways for human-in-the-loop learning systems while also describing challenges to move forward in this field [1].

Building on these concepts, the Human-in-the-loop application developed by Du et al. assists human writers by providing text suggestions based on an LLM that users can accept or reject [12]. This process aims to enhance text quality and improve the model's suggestions by incorporating user feedback [12].

2.2 Symbolic and Neuro-Symbolic Applications

One characteristic of symbolic approaches is representing and manipulating knowledge using formal languages and language items, referred to as symbols [16]. Ontologies and KGs belong to the symbolic part of neuro-symbolic AI. In order to transform relational databases into KGs, mapping rules are required. RML, which is an extension of R2RML (RDB to RDF Mapping Language), is one possible way to map relational data in a declarative approach. Therefore, database table columns are declared as subjects and objects while the definition of predicates links them. Those links are based on the underlying ontology, which provides the desired structure of the KG. At the Robert Bosch GmbH (Bosch), computer scientists usually do this task manually. However, some tools that are similar in their core functionality but differ in features, visual representation, and interactions, like JUMA [8] RMLEditor, RMLx Visual Editor, and Spread2RML support that process with a GUI. The developers of those applications argue that R2RML has a steep learning curve, where creating mappings is time-consuming and syntactically heavy in various cases [4,5,9,15,26]. They further argue that their work shows good usability results and highlights users' reduced mental workload, indicating that the visual representation was helpful in the creation of R2RML mappings [5,9,15,26]. We created a structured comparison to show that they all combine the abstraction of the actual mappings into a visual representation [4].

Even though they successfully abstract RML (or R2RML) expertise, they lack automation, speed, and scalability since the process is still done manually, not just by writing actual code but by using a GUI. Those applications also do not provide the possibility to directly create the KG since they do not include built-in processors like SDM-RDFizer [17]. This means that people who want to transform from relational to linked data must first generate the rules manually using a GUI and later use another tool to process the mappings to verify the results.

The neuro-symbolic AI combines the approaches of neural networks and symbolic techniques and so can eradicate the weaknesses of the introduced approaches [16]. Some applications aim to annotate tables semantically and perform cell and column annotation and relationship identification while others propose a combination of embeddings, ontology matching, and lookups for approaches that, for example, predict Wikipedia infoboxes [7,13,21]. Opasjumruskit et al. propose an application that extracts information based on ontologies using modern Natural Language Processing (NLP) methods and is so considered a human-in-the-loop application focusing more on symbolic techniques [24]. Their application, called OntoHuman, annotates text in documents via NLP based on ontology information and further tries to improve the underlying ontology while providing verification and collaboration features [24].

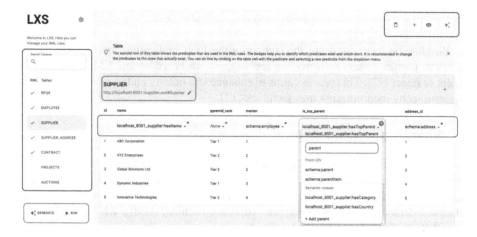

Fig. 1. Screenshot of the application. Blue rectangle: table selection; purple rectangle: delete RML rule for this table, add mapping for one column, view RML rule in turtle, generate RML rule for the selected table; brown rectangle: table name and the corresponding found ontology class; red rectangle: properties; green rectangle: possible options of properties dropdown; pink rectangle: generate all RML rules for every table and process the RML rules. (Color figure online)

We have presented various human-in-the-loop approaches and applications in the field of neuro-symbolic AI. To the best of our knowledge, neuro-symbolic approaches have not been utilized for RML rule generation yet.

3 Approach

LXS is an approach for transforming a relational database into a KG by utilizing LLMs while offering a rich GUI to users, which is shown in Fig. 1[1]. Since LLMs tend to hallucinate [6,20] and to ensure transparency, reproducibility, and trustworthiness, we propose a human-in-the-loop approach, visually outlined and described in Fig. 2, that breaks down larger tasks into smaller ones and further indicates the plausibility of AI-generated items (e.g. properties or classes). Therefore, the AI only generates suggestions and calculates the plausibility for each relevant small step so that users can verify, validate, and apply each suggestion quickly and independently from other items. As a result, the application keeps track of AI generations, plausibility, and human validation for later scrutinizing.

To include users in that loop, the neural engine generates the first draft of an RML rule. Therefore, users trigger the creation by defining the input selection. While the neural engine's task is to create those RML rules, the symbolic engine's task is to provide enough suitable context for the neural engine. Thus, the symbolic engine ranks the previously processed ontology snippets based on their semantic similarity to the user input. Those ontology snippets, together with the database schema and the user-set prefixes,

---

[1] We published LXS here: https://github.com/J-x-D/lxs-db2kg.

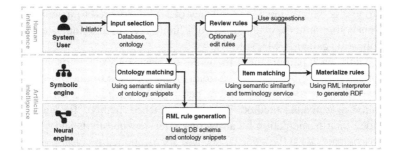

Fig. 2. Process of creating and editing RML rules, which are triggered by users, later processed and prepared by the symbolic engine, and then drafted by the neural engine so that users can afterward review and, if needed, edit using the symbolic engine.

are sent to the neural engine, which can then generate a first draft of an RML rule. In the following, users receive the RML rule draft for the triggered input, which is based on the database schema, the semantically best-fitting ontology snippets, and the set prefixes. This approach can be classified as a modern Retrieval-Augmented Generation (RAG) approach, in which the symbolic engine's retrieval and the neural engine's generation processes work in tandem. After receiving the first RML rule draft, users can review the generated classes, properties, and connections. Therefore, the application indicates the plausibility calculated by the symbolic engine for the drafted item directly at each item. In the case of a misfit or no plausibility, users can still edit each individual part of the draft. For the editing, the symbolic engine repeats the same process as before - finding the best-fitting ontology snippets based on semantic similarity to the user's search term. In addition, the symbolic engine also accesses external services to provide vocabularies from terminology services. The symbolic engine then sends the processed best-fitting ontology snippets and suggestions from the external terminology services to the user. Thus, users can select from those curated options the best-fitting one. The review and editing process continues until all tables are correctly defined and mapped according to the users' preferences. As a final step, users trigger the transformation of the relational data into the KG using the symbolic engine.

4 Methodology

4.1 Study Design

To provide a comprehensive evaluation, we conducted a within-subject study comparison and a between-subject study analysis. In all parts of our study, participants had to transform either a real-world-oriented database about suppliers or a made-up database in the university context into a KG. It has to be noted that the supplier example is considered larger but less complex, while the university example is considered smaller but more complex. Throughout the evaluation, we focused exclusively on assessing RML rules, as we consider this approach more practical than comparing resulting KGs.

Participants involved in the within-subject study comparison had the task of creating RML rules manually and utilizing LXS. Since coding RML rules manually is considered the state-of-the-art process of transforming relational databases into KGs at Bosch, we aimed to assess the efficiency and efficacy of LXS compared to manual RML rule creation. This is similar to the evaluation Crotti Junior et al. used to indicate the benefits of their application called JUMA [8].

Consequently, each participant of the within-subject study comparison participated in a 90-min structured meeting. The session began with an introduction to the experiment, followed by a 30-min task where participants generated a KG using either the application or a manual method. They then switched methods for another 30 min and concluded their participation by answering interview questions and filling out the UEQ. All participants used the same device and approved their recording of voices and screens. Further, all participants had the same experiment conductor and interviewer. They also had the chance to ask questions about the procedure and tasks before the experiment began.

Each participant was randomly categorized into one of the four groups. Specifically, 14 participants created RML rules for a university database, while 16 created rules for a supplier database. Each group was further divided into two parts: one half started with manual coding, and the other half began with LXS.

For the manual creation, the participants had to code RML rules in a predefined code editor. Additionally, we provided a database schema diagram and uploaded the ontology to an online ontology viewer to give a visual representation.

The interview questions were about their eventually experienced exhaustion, increased efficiency, application guidance, difficulties, opinions, and improvements. Further, they were asked about their experience levels in RML and the semantic web, if they would use the tool in their daily business, and which method of KG generation, in their opinions, provided better results. As a last step, all participants completed the UEQ developed by Laugwitz et al. [19]. We published all the provided study materials, interviews, and results [3].

The between-subject study analysis focuses on investigating differences in LXS and the RMLEditor. We chose RMLEditor since the developers and authors of the associated paper were involved in creating the specification of RML [11]. To the best of our knowledge, the paper belonging to the RMLEditor is also the most cited paper describing a tool to create RML rules.

Since the RMLEditor can not connect to an existing database but allows processing CSV files, we exported the data to CSV files and provided images describing the relation of those files (covering the initial database schema). All participants in the between-subject study analysis who created RML rules utilizing the RMLEditor received the RMLEditor-explaining video, a detailed task description, the needed CSV files and their relations, and ontology visualizations.

Similar to the participants who tested LXS, they had a time limit of 30 min to complete the desired task and had to estimate their experience levels and fill out the UEQ afterwards.

In additional to the within-subject study comparison and the between-subject study analysis, we generated RML rules solely by AI. The AI-only generations were created based on the number of participants for each database of the within-subject study comparison. We generated those RML rules using LXS but did not adjust or improve the generated RML rules further. Since various factors influence generation time, we consider time measurements for AI-only generations unnecessary and consequently did not measure them.

Hypotheses. Our research attempts to investigate the effectiveness of four distinct procedures: using the LXS application versus manually creating RML rules, AI-only generations, and creations using the RMLEditor. Central to this exploration are the hypotheses that guide our investigation, which are listed below.

$H1_0$: There is no difference between the quality of RML rules created using LXS and manual coding.

$H2_0$: There is no difference between the quality of RML rules created using LXS and established non-AI-supported RML creation applications.

$H3_0$: There is no difference between the time needed for RML rules created using LXS and manual coding.

$H4_0$: There is no difference between the time needed for RML rules created using LXS and established non-AI-supported RML creation applications.

$H5_0$: There is no difference between the quality of RML rules created using LXS and AI-only creations.

The corresponding alternative hypotheses assume that there is a difference.

Dependent and Independent Variables. In our study, we defined and examined two key variables to evaluate the impact of different approaches for creating the RML rules. The independent variables for our hypotheses are the database example (supplier or university) and the creation type of the RML rules (LXS, manual coding, and RMLEditor). The dependent variable, on the other hand, depends on the null hypothesis and is thus either the quality of the RML rules or the time needed to generate them using LXS.

By analyzing the relationship between these two variables, we aim to uncover valuable insights into whether the tool choice significantly influences performance in RML rule creation and, if so, to what extent. This exploration will provide us with a deeper understanding of the relative values of each approach in the context of our study.

4.2 Sample

In total, we conducted the within-subject study comparison with 31 participants. All of them volunteered after a call for participation in various mailing lists. We did not provide sufficient information for the first participant to complete the study successfully. Consequently, the data from this participant was excluded. Accordingly, we adjusted the study introduction and provided additional guidance throughout the entire experiment. As a result, we conducted the experiment and the following interview with UEQ with 30 people from six different organizations, including profit-driven companies and research institutes from two countries. Of those 30 participants, five identify as women and 25 as men and are from different ages. All of them have some experience in computer science, while their experience levels range from junior to expert. In total, 26 interviews were held in German and four in English.

We made another call for participation in various mailing lists for the between-subject study analysis. In total, ten volunteers were assigned the task of creating RML rules utilizing RMLEditor. Two of them identify as women, eight as men, and they have different experience levels. Eight volunteers work for Bosch, and two for a research institute in the area of neuro-symbolic AI (Leibniz Information Centre for Science and Technology).

4.3 Data Analysis

For every participant in the within-subject study comparison, we collected two files. The first contains the RML rules created manually, and the second contains the RML rules generated utilizing LXS. All participants of the between-subject study analysis emailed their created RML rules along with the completed interview and UEQ. The RML rules in all those files were evaluated and compared to the ideal solutions.

The ideal solutions are RML rules coded and reviewed by three experts in the field of Semantic Web and RML from two different organizations. A point schema was applied to compare the built RML rules to the ideal solutions, which we published with all the collected data [3]. This point scheme is based on the errors users have made with the manual coding. After assigning the points to each RML rule file, we analyzed the results and compared them to the data collected from the interview and the UEQ using Spearman, a t-test for two independent means, and common statistical methods.

The conducted interview questions are qualitative data that have to be handled differently. Therefore, we applied the content analysis proposed by Mayring et al. to find and further categorize the participant's answers to our conducted interviews [22]. The initial category system was established by extracting meaningful segments from the responses and subsequently providing abstract summaries within appropriate categories. After coding 30% of the data, we reviewed and, in some cases, incorporated categories into broader terms. A final refinement of the category system was performed after completing the coding of the entire dataset. To ensure coding reliability, a second employee from Bosch independently coded the data. In cases where differing interpretations arose, both coders engaged in discussions until a consensus was reached. In general, our main focus was evaluating the application, even though we also asked about difficulties when coding manually.

5 Results

5.1 RML Rules Validation

We divided all participants of the within-subject study comparison into four groups. Independent from the used database, half of the participants either started with LXS or coded the rules manually. As desired, there is no quality difference based on the order in which users created the RML rules. Nevertheless, this is different regarding the databases participants used. Table 1 shows the mean results compared to the ideal solution of all participants grouped by the database they have transformed. Concretely, it represents the differences between users' performances for the supplier and university

Table 1. Comparison of the results attained by the study participants in generating RML rules, both through the utilization of LXS and manual coding for their respective databases.

Database	LXS (%)	AI (%)	Coding (%)	RMLEditor (%)
Supplier	95.60	87.64	45.74	26.36
University	87.02	72.93	61.90	48.42

Table 2. Comparison of RML rule quality and time efficiency among the investigated tools: evaluating the performance shift compared to LXS baseline. Metrics incorporate both database variants.

Tool	Mean (%)	Deviation (%)	Mean (min)	Deviation (min)
LXS	91.81	–	17:14	–
AI	80.29	−8.58	–	–
Coding	53.82	−37.99	29:50	+12:36
RMLEditor	37.39	−54.42	28:20	+11:06

databases. While the LXS results for the supplier database were better than those for the university database when coded manually, they were the opposite.

Table 1 further shows the achieved quality for the AI-only generations and utilizing RMLEditor. As can be seen, LXS clearly provides the best results in terms of RML rule quality. On the other hand, the other investigated tool, RMLEditor, provides the worst RML rule quality results. Those are even worse than the manually coded RML rules, while the AI-only generations are the closest to the LXS-achieved results.

Table 2 shows the calculated mean independent of the transformed database and the change in quality and duration compared to the performance of LXS. There, you can see that even though coding manually and using RMLEditor take almost the same amount of time, the manually coded RML rules deliver higher-quality RML rules.

The high-quality results for LXS and the lower-quality results in RML rule quality for coding manually and utilizing RMLEditor are further still present when the results are grouped by different experience levels. Figure 3 shows the performance achieved by each experience level group for LXS, coding manually, and utilizing RMLEditor. The figure shows that the quality of the RML rules created with LXS is stable and independent of the experience levels in RML and the semantic web. Further, the results show no significant difference or correlation between the different experience levels.

All participants had to stop coding the RML rules after 30 min, except one who finished the RML rule generation after 25 min. For the LXS and RMLEditor usage, the duration of RML rule generation was different. In Table 3, we divided all participants into five groups based on the time needed for the RML rule creation. As the table shows, each group has no significant difference in the results. Consequently, there is no correlation between the quality of the RML rules created and the time needed for their creation. In all groups, the mean time spent using LXS was 17:14 min, 29:50 min while coding manually, and 28:20 min utilizing RMLEditor. Even though there are differences in the time a participant used the application, there is no correlation between the experience level and the usage time of the application.

Table 3. Results using the application and the time needed to fulfill the task.

Duration	LXS (%)	LXS Count	RMLEditor (%)	RMLEditor Count
5–10	91.79	5	–	0
10–15	91.88	7	–	0
15–20	92.65	8	70.17	1
20–25	89.07	6	36.36	1
25–30	92.54	4	33.42	8

Nevertheless, statistical analyses of all created RML rules and time measures show a significant difference in quality and time, dependent on the tool used to create the RML rules. This can be seen in Table 4. We used the t-test for two independent means as a testing method with Bonferroni-Holm correction to counteract the problem of multiple testing by adjusting each calculated p-value considering the number of performed tests. The corrected p-values reveal a significant improvement in quality and time when using LXS compared to manual coding, AI-only generations, and RMLEditor. Therefore, we can reject all null hypotheses and consequently accept all alternative hypotheses.

In the interview, we asked all the participants of the within-subject study comparison which of the two tasks was more exhausting. The data shows that even people who felt more exhausted while using the application still achieved better results. There is further no significant indication that the experience level influences exhaustion, even though the data tends to indicate that the application is more exhausting for more experienced participants in the semantic web.

During those interviews, we also asked about their estimation of which of the two methods of creating RML rules, in their opinion, provided better results. The only participant who assumed his manually coded results were better than the ones from the application actually achieved equal results. This participant was further the most experienced in RML and the semantic web. Besides that, two other participants achieved even better results with the manual coding than with the application. Those two people who achieved better results specified themselves as rather and very inexperienced in RML and the semantic web. Further mentionable correlations do not exist.

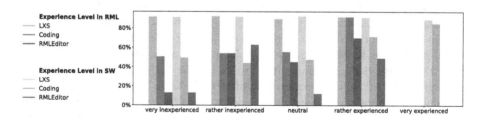

Fig. 3. Comparison of the achieved quality across experience levels in RML and the semantic web: the bars illustrate the quality achieved with LXS and the manual coding for different experience levels in RML and the semantic web, with the number of people represented as lines belonging to each group.

5.2 User Experience Questionnaire

The evaluation of the UEQ is done as suggested by the formulas provided by Laugwitz et al. In their provided benchmark, LXS achieves above-average results in all categories, with three of six scales in the category good and two of six in excellent. Table 5 indicates the benchmark results and their interpretation, while the published in-depth UEQ analysis details each scale's answer distribution and includes the mean and deviations of the supercategories [3].

While LXS achieved overall satisfying results in the UEQ, the analysis of the UEQ completed for the RMLEditor revealed an overall and consistent bad user experience. In fact, all scales score negatively and, based on the analysis provided by Laugwitz et al., are rated as bad. For a comprehensive comparison, we added the achieved scores for both LXS and RMLEditor, to the Table 5.

5.3 Qualitative Interview

The qualitative interview was only part of the within-subject study comparison. We coded those qualitative data according to Mayring et al. and published the found categories [3]. The found categories largely reflect the structure of the questionnaire since we specifically asked for enhancements and their difficulties. This means that the categories mainly belong to one of those questionnaire focuses. Since there were many questions users could answer openly, we collected all sayings that fit into one category independently from the question asked. Therefore, the frequency of mentions does not correlate with the number of individuals and number of questions asked. As a result, questions can be influenced by participants who argue very positively or very negatively in many questions.

As concretely discussed in the following section, some found categories can influence or depend on others. The counted frequency of the categories also indicates an overall positive impression of LXS. Although the focus was on collecting data about the application, two categories also concern manual coding. For the categories "Labor-Intensive Task" and "Manual Labor Challenges", we focused exclusively on the sayings that target the difficulties and characteristics of manual coding of the RML rules.

Table 4. Results for the different hypotheses. The column *Corrected p* presents the p-values resulting from the Bonferroni-Holm correction.

Hypothesis	Tool A	Tool B	Focus	p	Corrected p	Accept/Reject
$H1_0$	LXS	Coding	Quality	0.00001	<0.001	Reject
$H2_0$	LXS	RMLEditor	Quality	0.00001	<0.001	Reject
$H3_0$	LXS	Coding	Time	0.00001	<0.001	Reject
$H4_0$	LXS	RMLEditor	Time	0.00001	<0.001	Reject
$H5_0$	LXS	AI-only	Quality	0.000012	<0.001	Reject

Table 5. Comparison of Evaluation Metrics for LXS and RMLEditor based on the UEQ analysis tool.

Scale	Mean LXS	Benchmark Comparison to LXS	Mean RMLEditor	Benchmark Comparison to RMLEditor
Attractiveness	1.90	Excellent	−0.72	Bad
Perspicuity	1.60	Above Average	−0.68	Bad
Efficiency	1.62	Good	−0.28	Bad
Dependability	1.62	Good	−0.55	Bad
Stimulation	1.41	Good	−0.65	Bad
Novelty	1.62	Excellent	−0.33	Bad

6   Discussion

6.1   Results

The results presented in Table 1 and Table 2 clearly show that LXS, in comparison to AI-only generations, manual coding and utilizing RMLEditor, provides better RML rules in terms of quality. As a result, we suggest exchanging the current state-of-the-art manual coding in favor of LXS. This applies to Bosch and all the other companies that manually code their RML rules and have a similar experience level for their employees.

Table 3 shows already that there is no impact on the results independent from a user's experience level. This means that even very inexperienced users can quickly achieve high-quality results, and thus, more people can transform relational data into KGs. On the other hand, it would be ideal if at least the very experienced users in RML or the semantic web created the desired perfect results and so reached 100% correctness compared to the ideal solution in a short time. Nevertheless, the high-quality achievements of the inexperienced users show that the application abstracts RML successfully since we could not detect advantages for participants who are more experienced in RML or the semantic web. This applies even if you consider that very inexperienced users utilizing LXS achieved better results than experienced users using RMLEditor.

Participants described the application as user-friendly. This and the presented results confirm our objective of designing LXS as a suitable human-in-the-loop application for transforming relational data into KGs. Since our evaluation also indicates that using a UI is beneficial to AI-only generations, we recommend using applications that keep humans in the loop during the RML rule creation process. Nevertheless, our research shows that the AI-only generations based on our approach are already better than the ones created manually or using a currently existing application (RMLEditor). This information is especially useful for people experienced in RML. Based on our findings, they could apply our approach to draft RML rules and edit them manually using a code editor. Nevertheless, we recommend using an application like LXS since it offers a streamlined process with different possibilities for editing, storing, and even processing the RML rules.

The two provided databases differed in their schema, so the corresponding ontologies naturally differ in complexity. Since the supplier example was longer but less complex and the university example accordingly shorter but more complex, the results shown in Table 1 outline a first tendency that LXS scales better for less complex examples. Nevertheless, we want to highlight again that the supplier database is based on a real-world database schema. On the other hand, since more complex databases and ontologies lead to worse AI generations (as seen in Table 1), more user interactions are necessary to create ideal RML rules. Although LXS provided all the necessary features for ideal solutions, many users did not utilize them. Analyzing the interviews revealed that participants would rather regenerate the RML rules entirely than manually create the missing items and their relationships. In the interview, some people mentioned that they did not know what to do and trusted the regenerated drafts more than their manual work. Some experienced participants noted that they wanted to code manually in case of a missing item. Since those participants also regenerated the RML rules, this probably also relates to a higher trust in the AI generation than in their own interactions with the application on the provided abstracted level. Accordingly, trust in the application has to be seen as two-sided. While trust in the AI generations is assumed to be relatively high throughout all experience levels, it is relatively low for manually creating missing or misfitting items. Another reason to avoid manually creating missing or misfitting items could be the low perspicuity of those interaction features. Since the UEQ benchmark also shows only an above-average score in the category "perspicuity", we propose improving interaction features for manual item creation.

Based on the interview answers, the application is sometimes mentioned as slow compared to other web applications but still efficient compared to manual creation. The UEQ confirms the efficiency, probably also due to the comparison to manual creation. Besides the differences in interpretation of efficiency, the interview also reveals a lack of domain knowledge regarding the example's context (database schema and ontology), as well as in the task of creating RML rules in general, which leads to insecurities and ambiguities. This is probably considered a typical user experience for first-time users of applications. Nevertheless, the UEQ completed regarding LXS scores high in almost all categories which is especially a valuable insight compared to RMLEditor. Comparing the UEQ outcomes for LXs and RMLEditor allows us to conclude that our approach to visualizing RML rules is superior to RMLEditor's graph view. The interviews also revealed that some categories naturally depend on each other. So can "Trust based on Experience" only be achieved if "Skepticism and Learning Barriers" are a previous state of a participant's mind. One way to eliminate "Skepticism and Learning Barriers" is by providing features that are classified into the category of "Validation and Confirmation", like the direct mapping of, for example, properties to their columns. Nevertheless, implementing suggestions summarized in the category "Identified Enhancements" would probably decrease the "Unpleasant User Experience" and increase overall user satisfaction and performance.

6.2 Study Design

The results presented in Sect. 5 and discussed in Sect. 6.1 show the advancement of LXS in time and quality compared to the RML rules of AI-only generations, utilizing

RMLEditor and manual coding. Applying different evaluation guidelines could characterize the strengths and weaknesses of the application even further. Another way to evaluate the application is to analyze the resulting KG. We decided not to follow this approach since syntax errors would lead to no KG generation at all. Since we expected many inexperienced participants in the study beforehand, this approach would not provide transparent insights. More experienced users would also have strengthened the results further. On the other hand, the study participants represent real-world coverage even in a Fortune 500 company like Bosch, where entire departments work with semantic technologies. Even though the real-world supplier example relied on a database schema provided by a department working with semantic technologies, more and different examples could lead to different results. In the controlled experiment setting, everything, from the database schema to the ontology, was prepared for the participants. A case study, where users bring their databases and ontologies, could lead to even more realistic results. We decided against a case study due to such studies' time- and cost-intensive nature.

Since we did not know how the application performed, we planned the interview for the within-subject study comparison to compare LXS with the manual coding. Since the application clearly outperformed the manual coding, we would conduct a different interview in the retrospective, focusing more on a user's mental workload while interacting with LXS.

Even though we compared the participants' UEQ answers with their interview answers and results, we could not find relevant correlations. Nevertheless, we want to note that the UEQ could be partially biased due to the direct comparison between the application usage and the manual coding. Specifically, the question about efficiency is probably influenced by the fact that coding manually took considerably longer than using the application to create the RML rules. Compared to other UIs, the application and its RML generations through button clicks are probably relatively slow.

As previously mentioned, we decided to compare LXS to manual coding, which is considered state-of-the-art at Bosch. Nevertheless, the outcome of the comparison of an AI-supported application like LXS to manual coding provides expectable results. The between-subject study analysis balances this comparison weakness, but it would still be beneficial if the participant size were equal. Concretely, it would be best also to have 30 participants who used RMLEditor for their RML rule creations. Even though there are differences in participant sizes, we consider the conducted study as valid. The additional comparison to the AI-only generations further shows that a UI can provide even higher-quality results, consequently considered valuable comparison information.

6.3   Additional Remarks

In general, some mistakes using LXS could have been avoided if the users had trusted the application more. They often did not change items even though the application indicated the drafted items were not plausible. Since users also struggled with handling the application, an introduction tutorial to LXS could have been advantageous. This way, users would learn and understand the application better. Some participants further mentioned that they would like a view that allows them to see the ontology alongside the database schema. This mapping of the user-provided ontologies and the database schema can directly indicate which table and columns are mapped to the corresponding classes and properties in the ontologies. This would also solve a concern related to trust. Even though the users' trust is important for the acceptance of the application in general, it also comes with some risks. If the AI generations do not fit the wanted ideal solution, but the trust in the generations is too high, the quality of the KGs probably decreases. Accordingly, we suggest to optimize the plausibility check. Concretely, we consider using a dynamic value instead of a binary one. This way, users are encouraged to evaluate the generated items skeptically. As a result, visual mapping of classes and properties in ontologies to database tables and columns, together with an improved and dynamic plausibility check, could facilitate an even more trustworthy AI.

Another way of improving the application is by applying the Human-AI-Guidelines, formulated by Microsoft [2]. Especially since the UEQ revealed that the perspicuity has space for improvements, the guidelines would probably provide users with more explicit interactions and feedback. In general, the UEQ indicated strengths that can be obtained but also weaknesses that should be improved.

LXS is ambiguously rated in the "slow/fast" category [3]. To improve speed and quality, we suggest a self-hosted, fine-tuned LLM. Better neural engine results save time by reducing corrections and interactions, likely enhancing UX, especially if users can utilize the wait time effectively. However, user involvement is essential for maintaining trust in AI generations and allowing interventions. In conclusion, self-hosting a fine-tuned LLM would reduce costs and thus be more attractive for organizations that want to transform their relational data into KGs, even though the costs are already relatively small. Compared to the costs of hiring experts for the transformation, LXS outperforms the manual work in an experiment setting in terms of time and quality. Thus, using the application results in better, cheaper, and faster KG creations.

7   Conclusion and Future Work

Due to the steadily increasing need for KGs in recommender systems, question-answering applications, and as a knowledge base for AI-driven applications, existing relational data should be transformed into KGs. In this work, we presented a user-driven hybrid neuro-symbolic approach to KG creation from relational data. Our experimental evaluation showed a significant increase in transformation quality (9% compared to AI-only generations, 38% compared to manual coding, and 54% compared to the RMLEditor) while reducing the user interaction time to create those rules by almost half. This leads to faster and qualitative better KG creations at Bosch. By interviewing all participants, we demonstrated that the application derived from our approach generates high levels of user trust besides providing high-quality and fast results. Nevertheless, the interviews also indicate potential ways for improvement. The same applies to the evaluation of the UEQ, which is better in every of the UEQ's scales than the also investigated RMLEditor but still leaves room for improvement, especially in the scale perspicuity.

Concretely, we encourage further development to increase the quality of the neural engine's first draft since users do not interact with the created rules further if the first draft is already satisfying and indicated as plausible. Since the application already covers the transformation from relational data into KGs and relational data is considered structured data, future developments in neuro-symbolic AI could focus on unstructured data. The proposed approach, together with new enhancing implementations, could lead to a more knowledge-driven world by leveraging KGs in various use cases.

Acknowledgements. We gratefully acknowledge the support of Luca Mario Ziegler Felix and Selamawit Gegziabher in designing and developing LXS.

References

1. Amershi, S., Cakmak, M., Knox, W.B., Kulesza, T.: Power to the people: the role of humans in interactive machine learning. AI Mag. **35**(4) (2014). https://doi.org/10.1609/aimag.v35i4.2513
2. Amershi, S., et al.: Guidelines for human-AI interaction. In: CHI Conference on Human Factors in Computing Systems (2019)
3. Anonymous: Appendix to the paper "a user-driven hybrid neuro- symbolic approach for knowledge graph creation from relational data" (2024). https://doi.org/10.5281/zenodo.10915049
4. Anonymous: Comparison of RML creation applications (2024). https://doi.org/10.48366/R703669, https://orkg.org/comparison/R703669
5. Aryan, P.R., Ekaputra, F.J., Kiesling, E., Tjoa, A.M., Kurniawan, K.: RMLx: mapping interface for integrating open data with linked data exploration environment. In: 1st International Conference on Informatics and Computational Sciences (2017). https://doi.org/10.1109/ICICOS.2017.8276347
6. Azamfirei, R., et al.: Large language models and the perils of their hallucinations. Crit. Care **27**(1), 120 (2023). https://doi.org/10.1186/s13054-023-04393-x
7. Biswas, R., Türker, R., Bakhshandegan-Moghaddam, F., Koutraki, M., Sack, H.: Wikipedia infobox type prediction using embeddings. In: 1st Workshop on Deep Learning for Knowledge Graphs and Semantic Technologies. CEUR Workshop Proceedings, vol. 2106 (2018)
8. Crotti Junior, A., et al.: Juma: an editor that uses a block metaphor to facilitate the creation and editing of R2RML mappings. In: The Semantic Web: ESWC 2017 Satellite Events. Springer (2017)
9. Crotti Junior, A., et al.: Juma uplift: using a block metaphor for representing uplift mappings. In: IEEE 12th International Conference on Semantic Computing (2018). https://doi.org/10.1109/ICSC.2018.00037
10. Currie, G.M.: Academic integrity and artificial intelligence: is chatGPT hype, hero or heresy? Seminars Nucl. Med. **53**(5) (2023). https://doi.org/10.1053/j.semnuclmed.2023.04.008
11. Dimou, A., Vander Sande, M., Colpaert, P., Verborgh, R., Mannens, E., Van de Walle, R.: RML: a generic language for integrated RDF mappings of heterogeneous data. Ldow **1184** (2014)
12. Du, W., Kim, Z.M., Raheja, V., Kumar, D., Kang, D.: Read, revise, repeat: a system demonstration for human-in-the-loop iterative text revision. In: 1st Workshop on Intelligent and Interactive Writing Assistants. Association for Computational Linguistics (2022). https://doi.org/10.18653/v1/2022.in2writing-1.14
13. Efthymiou, V., Hassanzadeh, O., Rodriguez-Muro, M., Christophides, V.: Matching web tables with knowledge base entities: from entity lookups to entity embeddings. In: d'Amato, C., et al. (eds.) ISWC 2017. LNCS, vol. 10587, pp. 260–277. Springer, Cham (2017). https://doi.org/10.1007/978-3-319-68288-4_16

14. Fensel, D., et al.: Introduction: What is a Knowledge Graph? Springer (2020). https://doi.org/10.1007/978-3-030-37439-6_1
15. Heyvaert, P., et al.: RMLEditor: a graph-based mapping editor for linked data mappings. In: The Semantic Web. Latest Advances and New Domains. Springer (2016)
16. Hitzler, P., Eberhart, A., Ebrahimi, M., Sarker, M.K., Zhou, L.: Neuro-symbolic approaches in artificial intelligence. Natl. Sci. Rev. **9**(6) (2022). https://doi.org/10.1093/nsr/nwac035
17. Iglesias, E., Jozashoori, S., Chaves-Fraga, D., Collarana, D., Vidal, M.E.: SDM-RDFizer: an RML interpreter for the efficient creation of RDF knowledge graphs. In: 29th ACM International Conference on Information & Knowledge Management. ACM (2020). https://doi.org/10.1145/3340531.3412881
18. Kaur, D., Uslu, S., Rittichier, K.J., Durresi, A.: Trustworthy artificial intelligence: a review. ACM Comput. Surv. **55**(2) (2022). https://doi.org/10.1145/3491209
19. Laugwitz, B., et al.: Construction and evaluation of a user experience questionnaire. In: Holzinger, A. (ed.) HCI and Usability for Education and Work. Springer, Heidelberg (2008)
20. Lee, K., Firat, O., Agarwal, A., Fannjiang, C., Sussillo, D.: Hallucinations in neural machine translation (2019). https://openreview.net/forum?id=SkxJ-309FQ
21. Liu, J., Troncy, R.: Dagobah: an end-to-end context-free tabular data semantic annotation system. In: SemTab@ ISWC (2019)
22. Mayring, P., et al.: Qualitative content analysis. Companion Qual. Res. **1**(2) (2004)
23. Montagna, S., Ferretti, S., Klopfenstein, L.C., Florio, A., Pengo, M.F.: Data decentralisation of LLM-based chatbot systems in chronic disease self-management. In: PACM Conference on Information Technology for Social Good. ACM (2023). https://doi.org/10.1145/3582515.3609536
24. Opasjumruskit, K., Böning, S., Schindler, S., Peters, D.: OntoHuman: ontology-based information extraction tools with human-in-the-loop interaction. In: Luo, Y. (ed.) CDVE 2022. LNCS, vol. 13492, pp. 68–74. Springer, Cham (2022). https://doi.org/10.1007/978-3-031-16538-2_7
25. Peng, C., Xia, F., Naseriparsa, M., Osborne, F.: Knowledge graphs: opportunities and challenges. Artif. Intell. Rev. **56**(11) (2023). https://doi.org/10.1007/s10462-023-10465-9
26. Schröder, M., et al.: Spread2RML: constructing knowledge graphs by predicting RML mappings on messy spreadsheets. In: 11th on Knowledge Capture Conference. ACM (2021). https://doi.org/10.1145/3460210.3493544
27. Shakeri, H., et al.: SAGA: collaborative storytelling with GPT-3. In: Conference on Computer Supported Cooperative Work and Social Computing. ACM (2021). https://doi.org/10.1145/3462204.3481771
28. Xiao, Z., Liao, Q.V., Zhou, M., Grandison, T., Li, Y.: Powering an AI chatbot with expert sourcing to support credible health information access. In: 28th International Conference on Intelligent User Interfaces (2023)
29. Zou, X.: A survey on application of knowledge graph. In: Journal of Physics: Conference Series, vol. 1487. IOP Publishing (2020)

Assisted Data Annotation for Business Process Information Extraction from Textual Documents

Julian Neuberger[1]($\boxtimes$) , Han van der Aa[2] , Lars Ackermann[1] , Daniel Buschek[1] ,
Jannic Herrmann[1], and Stefan Jablonski[1]

[1] University of Bayreuth, Bayreuth, Germany
{julian.neuberger,lars.ackermann,daniel.buschek,
jannic.herrmann,stefan.jablonski}@uni-bayreuth.de
[2] University of Vienna, Vienna, Austria
han.van.der.aa@univie.ac.at

Abstract. Machine-learning based generation of process models from natural language text process descriptions provides a solution for the time-intensive and expensive process discovery phase. Many organizations have to carry out this phase, before they can utilize business process management and its benefits. Yet, research towards this is severely restrained by an apparent lack of large and high-quality datasets. This lack of data can be attributed to, among other things, an absence of proper tool assistance for business process information extraction dataset creation, resulting in high workloads and inferior data quality. We explore two assistance features to support dataset creation, a recommendation system for identifying process information in the text and visualization of the current state of already identified process information as a graphical business process model. A controlled user study with 31 participants shows that assisting dataset creators with recommendations lowers all aspects of workload, up to -51.0%, and significantly improves annotation quality, up to $+38.9\%$ in F_1 score. We make all data and code available to encourage further research on additional novel assistance strategies.

Keywords: Business process management · Process information extraction · Natural language processing · Human computer interaction

1 Introduction

Business process management (BPM) can provide organizations with many benefits by improving their regular operating procedures. Organizations looking to utilize these benefits first need to discover and model their business processes, which is a very time consuming, and therefore expensive task [13]. To alleviate this, researchers in the BPM community use the information contained in natural language process descriptions from sources like quality management handbooks, documentation of standard operating procedures, or employee notes to automatically generate formal process models [4]. While this area is actively researched [1,5,8,11,13,28], new and innovative approaches are quite rare. One reason is the limited availability of data to develop, train, and assess approaches in BPMN contexts [18]. Recent initiatives aim to mitigate this issue, providing a gold-standard dataset for the process information extraction task—PET [9]. With

M. Comuzzi et al. (Eds.): CoopIS 2024, LNCS 15506, pp. 186–203, 2025.
https://doi.org/10.1007/978-3-031-81375-7_11

this dataset, systems for extracting process information can be developed, e.g., machine learning models for extraction are trained, and subsequently evaluated. Extracted information is then the basis for automated model generation methods, allowing fully automated process model generation from process descriptions. Still, PET contains only 45 process descriptions, which is not enough to train deep neural networks [28], although they have been shown to be well suited for similar tasks in other areas [6]. Even techniques based on pretrained large language models are affected by the lack of data, as rigorous evaluation on many different data sources is essential to assess their practicality, especially in light of the large variation in terms of the structure, style, and contents of textual documents that contain process information [2].

The lack of suitable data for process information extraction tasks can in part be attributed to the effort required to establish gold standard annotations. Such annotations are a critical requirement for both training and evaluation of information extraction approaches. However, manually annotating process information in textual process descriptions involves elaborate guidelines [9] and considerable ambiguity [3,12], making it time consuming and mentally taxing. Figure 1 shows two sentences of a process description from the PET dataset, fully annotated with the gold-standard process information. Note, that annotating these sentences requires identifying 14 process-relevant elements, and 16 dependencies between them, in just these two sentences, where the average description in PET has 9.27 sentences [9]. We discuss the task in detail in Sect. 3.1 and how to circumvent this complexity in Sect. 3.2. Additionally, depending on the annotation schema, some of these annotations are not intuitive, e.g., "*decides*", which would intuitively be annotated as an *activity*, underlining the need for annotation guidelines mentioned above.

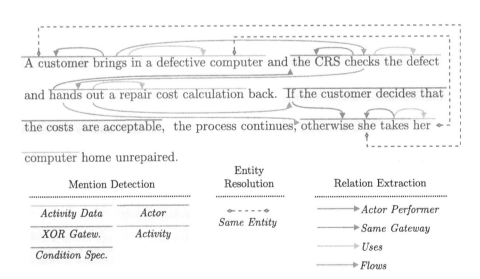

Fig. 1. The first two sentences of document *doc-1.2* in the PET dataset, fully annotated with entity mentions, entity references, and relations.

Recognizing this issue, we explore how dataset creators (*annotators*) can be assisted in their data annotation task, so that their workload is lightened, while simultaneously improving the quality of their extractions. Therefore, in this paper, we propose and evaluate the benefits of two assistance features that can support human annotators: (1) AI-based recommendations, which allow annotators to quickly tackle trivial parts of the annotation task—as well as receive suggestions for less trivial aspects—and (2) the use of a visualizations of the currently annotated information through a graphical process model, which allows annotators to observe the process that they have so far captured. Note that, although the task of text annotation is generic, the assistance features are tailored to the specifics of text annotations for process information extraction.

We implement both assistance features in a prototypical annotation tool that we use as a basis for a rigorous user study with 31 participants, ranging from modeling novices to experts, to assess the effectiveness and efficiency of the proposed features. Code[1] and data[2] are made publicly available to the research community, to allow others to efficiently and effectively annotate their own datasets, but also encourages exploration of additional assistance features. The main insights from this study are as follows.

1. Assisting annotators with suggestions made by artificial intelligence systems is observed to make annotating process relevant information in textual process descriptions significantly easier. This results in a significant reduction of key workload metrics by more than one half (-51.0%). At the same time, assistance improves the quality of extracted information measured in F_1 score by up to $+0.224$ ($+38.9\%$).
2. The use of assistance features is recognized to considerably reduce the gap between novice and experienced process modelers in annotation tasks. Specifically, complete beginners can reach annotation quality comparable to expert annotators, speeding up the training process for new data annotators considerably. This insight shows that annotation features can help assembling larger data annotation teams, and speeds up the creation of new datasets in the space of business process model extraction from natural language text.

The rest of this paper is structured as follows. In Sect. 2, we discuss related work on process information extraction, relevant user studies, and annotation tools. In Sect. 3, we present our concept behind a tool built specially for annotating textual process descriptions, its implementation in a research prototype, and the assistance features. In Sect. 4 we describe the design and execution of the user study. We present results for this study in Sect. 5. We conclude the paper in Sect. 6, summarizing, discussing limitations, and describing future work.

2 Related Work

Work related to this paper can be roughly categorized into three sections.

Business Process Information Extraction. The last decades have seen various approaches to the task of extracting process relevant information from natural language text, including systems based on expert-defined rules [1,8,11,30], data-driven

---

[1] see https://github.com/JulianNeuberger/assisted-process-annotation.
[2] see https://zenodo.org/doi/10.5281/zenodo.12770686.

ones [5,9,28], and systems based on pretrained generative large language models [8,21,27]. We use approaches from [28] and [9] in our work to implement annotation recommendations. Many of the works mentioned also propose data annotation schemata tailored towards specific modeling languages, such as [1,30] for declarative process modeling, towards different task descriptions, such as [29] for information extraction from process relevant sentence fragments, or towards other stages in the process life cycle, e.g., process redesign [25].

We focus on PET, as it is heavily biased towards the current industry standard, BPMN, and the to date largest available dataset. PET was extended with the notion of entity identities [28], i.e., the task of resolving multiple mentions of the same process element across the textual description to a single one. This is important for properly modeling business objects and process participants, which would otherwise be duplicated in the generated model. In this paper we use this extended version of PET.

User Studies. Schützenmeier et al. [32] present a user study on the cognitive effort of understanding declarative process models, though they do not consider data annotation, but process simulation and verification. Rosa et al. [31] develop and evaluate a tool for business process modelling which assists users by identifying core BPMN 2.0[3] elements and highlighting them in the process description. Our work, in contrast, aims to be a step towards alleviating the data scarcity problem in business process model generation from text, by making data annotation easier. In a study of similar size to ours, the authors evaluate the usefulness of the *BPMN Sketch Miner* for process modelling based on textual descriptions with visual representations of process elements [16]. While their study mainly focuses on usability and subjective values, ours also considers objective measures.

Annotation Tools. Both our concept and implementation for assisted process-relevant information annotation are related to a number of annotation tools. These can usually be used to annotate text for use in Named Entity Recognition (NER), Entity Matching and Resolution (ER), or Relation Extraction (RE), tasks which are similar to business process information extraction (compare definition in Sect. 3). Still, these tools are not designed with characteristics of business process descriptions in mind, including but not limited to, the high information density present in such descriptions, its inherent ambiguity (see Sect. 1), and the target down-stream task, i.e., generation of a formal and graphical process model. Additionally, unlike in the NLP community, data annotators for process information extraction are often times experts in BPM, but not in NLP, and therefore can benefit from purposeful simplifications in the annotation tool. In the following we will describe several notable examples of multi-purpose Natural Language Processing (NLP) data annotation tools, from which we drew inspiration and how our proposed concept differs from them.

Doccano [26] provides features useful for collaborative data annotation, creating datasets in multiple languages, and comparing annotations between annotators. Label Studio [34] supports more machine learning domains, e.g., computer vision, and audio processing. This makes the tool even more multi-purpose and less bespoke, compared to our research prototype. The authors already have experience annotating textual busi-

---

[3] https://www.omg.org/bpmn/, accessed July 4, 2024.

ness process descriptions using Label Studio [5], which is integrated into our concept for assisted annotation (Sect. 3). Finally, INCEpTION [20] uses *recommenders* to make suggestions for new annotations, which would fit our requirement for AI-based annotation recommendations, but to the best of the author's knowledge can not be extended to show the current state of annotation as a BPMN model. The authors of [20] did not investigate the effectiveness of recommendations for text annotation, and while a positive effect seems plausible, we are interested in proving and quantifying this effect.

3 Concept for Assisted Annotation

This section outlines our concept for assisted data annotation. First, we define the task of annotators in Sect. 3.1. Based on this we motivate the need for more efficient and effective data annotation and derive assistance features in Sect. 3.3. Finally, we describe our research prototype implementation in Sect. 3.4.

3.1 The Process Information Extraction Task

Ultimately, human annotators have to complete the process information extraction task to annotate process descriptions with process-relevant information. Therefore, we define this task in the following. Consider, for example, document *doc-1.2* from the PET dataset describing the process of a computer repair. Figure 1 shows this document fully annotated with all process relevant information, which consists of three major categories. First, *Mentions* of process relevant entities in PET are continuous sequences of text with a given type, for example, *Actors* (process participants, "a customer"), *Activity Data* (business objects, "a computer"), or *XOR Gateways* (decision points, often indicated by "if", "otherwise"). The last example illustrates, why we call detecting and extracting such mentions *Entity Mention Detection* (MD) and not *Named Entity Recognition* (NER). Named Entities are defined by either proper names (e.g., persons, locations) or natural kind terms (e.g., enzymes, species) [22]. "If" or "otherwise" do not fall into this definition, which is why we use the more relaxed definition of (non-named) entities and the detection of their mentions within the text [35]. Mentions are then resolved to *Entities*, i.e., clustered, allowing subsequent model generation steps to only render a single process element, instead of multiple (one for each of its mentions). This task is called *Entity Resolution* (ER) and is closely related with co-reference and anaphora resolution [33]. *Relations* between mentions define how these elements interact with each other. PET defines, for example, *Flow* (order of task execution), *Uses* (association between a task and the business object it uses), or *Actor Performer* (assigning a process participant as executor of a given task).

3.2 Annotation Workflow

As we discussed in Sect. 1, annotating the process relevant information contained in textual process descriptions is a complex task and very demanding for the human performing the annotation, as it requires attention to three sub-tasks, as outlined in the previous Sect. 3.1. We therefore split the task into its sub-tasks MD, ER, and RE. While this partially alleviates the issue of complexity, it will also allow us to assist annotators in these sub-tasks differently, and analyze how assistance features help during a specific sub-task. Figure 2 depicts the resulting workflow. After the annotator submits a natural language process description, they are then asked to select mentions (MD), resolve entities (ER), and define relations between mentions (RE), in three separate steps. Finally, all information is shown again, so that the annotator may reconcile any errors.

While this workflow reduces the complexity of process information annotation by splitting it up into smaller tasks, the overall complexity remains high. High density of information makes annotating very confusing, especially for beginners. The example in Fig. 1 contains a total of 40 words, of which only eight are not part of one of the 14 entity mentions (20%), while also containing 14 relations between them. From previous annotation experience in other tools (see Sect. 2), we know that this can be partially mitigated by splitting the task into smaller sub-tasks, e.g., focusing on a subset of entity and relation types, or by annotating the categories from above one after the other. Based on this experience we defined a *workflow*, which we describe in Sect. 3.2. High information density and the resulting complexity of displaying this information also motivates us to find ways to visualize the information better, and help the user focus on information they potentially would miss otherwise. This results in two assistance features, *visualization* and *recommendation*, which we describe in Sect. 3.3.

3.3 Assistance Features

In one of our preliminary studies two assistance features were identified as promising candidates for improving the efficiency, quality, and user experience of annotation documents for the process information extraction task.

AI-Based Annotation Recommendations. Building on the progress that has already been made in the development of automated information extraction approaches for mentions, entities, and relations, we can present the user with recommendations for these elements. Interviews with BPM experts during the preliminary study and our review of related work (Sect. 2) suggested that recommendations can be a powerful tool for speeding up annotation in trivial cases and provide useful ideas in non-trivial ones. We used an approach based on conditional random fields for extracting mentions, as presented by Bellan et al. [9], with code from [28], a pretrained neural co-reference resolver for entities [28], and a relation extraction approach based on gradient boosting on decision trees [28]. All trainable approaches were trained with 80% of the available data (36 documents) and the rest was held out for use during the user study. Recommendations are shown during the appropriate workflow steps and can be confirmed, discarded, edited, or marked for later review. The extraction approaches we use are limited in their understanding of business processes, and as such have no real world knowledge that could help during extracting process information from unseen descriptions. This means recommendations can be flawed, but are enough to effectively support data annotation (Sect. 5).

Visual Result Representation. Second, the information that a human annotator marks in a textual process description is always process relevant, i.e., a perfect annotation results in a model that perfectly reflects the process description. This shows how a human annotator may benefit from a graphical process model as a visualization of the currently annotated information, as any missing information is reflected in the (therefore incomplete) graphical process model. Visualizing the current state of annotation involves three major stages. First, in the ***Consolidation*** stage, we assign conditions to their respective paths in the process, merge mentions of entities, and find the closest actor in the text left of activities that are not explicitly assigned one. In the second stage, the ***Vertex*** stage, we create process elements for all mentions, e.g., *Tasks, Data Objects, Swimlanes*, etc. The final ***Linking*** stage connects related elements, e.g., successive tasks and gateways with *Sequence Flows*, if they are located in the same Pool, or *Message Flows* between them. We also create *Data Associations* between Data Objects and Tasks, adding the label of the Data Object to the label of the Task, for labels like *"send a mortgage offer"*. In this way the graphical process model is generated and layouted automatically, and as such has limitations that might affect its usefulness, which we discuss in Sect. 6.

3.4 Implementation

We have implemented our concept in a usable research prototype. It consists of a user-facing web application, implemented in JavaScript, using React[4].

A backend server provides NLP pre-processing functionality, such as tokenization and the information extraction approaches for the recommendation assistance feature. It is implemented in Python 3.11, using spaCy[5] for pre-processing. When the user inputs a textual process description, it is first sent to this server to pre-process the text. The result is then displayed in the web application. In each of the annotation sub-tasks defined in Sect. 3.2 the relevant information is extracted by the backend server and presented to the annotator as recommendations. The backend server is also responsible for storing annotation results. A second backend server is used for visualizing the current annotations by generating a formal process model in BPMN and its graphical representation. We implement this using Java 17 and the Camunda Model API[6]. Both back-end servers expose any functionality using REST interfaces, which the user-facing web application can query. Figure 2 shows the workflow in the web application, as well as the communication between servers.

4 Study Design

We conducted a user study with 31 participants to assess the effectiveness of the two assistance features, based on several measures in scenarios of varying assistance. Both measures and scenarios are defined later in this section. We focus our efforts on answering the following three key research questions.

RQ1. Which annotation assistance features or combinations lower the workload of annotating process information?

RQ2. Which annotation assistance features or combinations improve the quality of annotations?

---

[4] https://react.dev/, last accessed July 11, 2024.

[5] https://spacy.io/, last accessed July 11, 2024.

[6] https://docs.camunda.org/manual/7.21/user-guide/model-api/bpmn-model-api/, last accessed July 11, 2024.

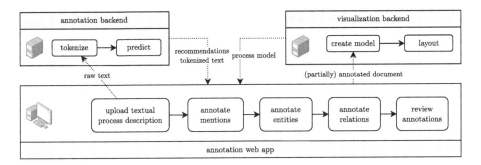

Fig. 2. Visualization of the workflow and general architecture of our implementation.

RQ3. Which annotation assistance bridge the gap in annotation quality between beginner annotators and those with BPMN experience?

The general setup of this study is as follows. All supplementary material, such as the questionnaires and resulting data can be found online, see Sect. 1.

Study Procedure. Each participation within our user study, is structured into three blocks. First, general demographic information is collected, and the task and annotation tool are explained to the participant, which involved giving a brief tutorial and a small guided annotation task, without any assistance features enabled. This task is only done for training purposes and is not evaluated later. Next, the participant has to complete four annotation scenarios, which we describe later in this section. After each scenario a short questionnaire is conducted, aimed at collecting user opinion, sentiment, and feedback concerning the scenario they just completed. The last block involves a questionnaire to gather general feedback and data regarding overall user preferences.

Measures. We measure the effectiveness of assistance features using several metrics aimed at *objective* and *subjective* values. For objective values we measure the time a user takes to annotate a document and the quality of mention, entity, and relation annotations, each measured with the F_1 score. Subjective values are derived from the NASA Task Load Index (TLX), which is widely used for measuring the workload during or right after performing a task [15]. The NASA-TLX can be used in many different contexts, and was also already used to evaluate information systems [7]. It defines a total of six dimensions that measure different aspects of workload. We used the four relevant to our study.

mental demand: How much the annotator has to focus on the task
uncertainty: How uncertain the annotator is of their annotations
effort: How much work is needed to complete the task
frustration: How frustrated the annotator is with the task

We excluded physical and temporal demands, to focus on the subjective metrics most relevant to our research questions. While *physical* demand is not completely irrelevant (think of mouse movements), it is far less informative than the other measures. Regarding *temporal* demands we refer to our objective measure of task completion time. Note that compared to the original definition of the NASA-TLX, we rephrase *performance* to measure the *uncertainty* of an annotator with their annotation results. Additionally to the NASA-TLX, we also asked users to share their experiences with the tool and assistance features in a questionnaire using 5-point Likert items [17].

Annotation Scenarios. We assess the efficiency and effectiveness of annotators in four scenarios. Scenario *(A)* entails no assistance, besides the workflow defined in Sect. 3.2 and serves as a baseline. Scenario *(B)* visualizes the current state of annotation, and *(C)* gives recommendations for annotations made by an artificial intelligence system. Finally, scenario *(D)* combines both assistance features.

Documents in PET contain 168 words on average, which took experts in a preliminary experiment as much as 25 min to annotate. We therefore decided to instead only use fragments of documents, containing two sentences. These fragments were carefully selected by measuring the number of mentions, relations, as well as their types. We selected fragments from documents *doc-1.2*, *doc-3.6*, *doc-8.3*, and *doc-9.2*. Document fragments are part of the supplementary material for this paper and available in the repositories mentioned in Sect. 1.

To avoid carry-over effects, i.e., confounding variables such as familiarity with the task after completing a scenario and therefore performing better in the next one, we use the Balanced Latin Square method [19]. This method systematically produces sequences of the scenarios described above, so that each scenario appears as the first one in the sequence equally often, as well as two scenarios preceding or succeeding one another equally often. Users are assigned a sequence of scenarios in a round-robin fashion, compare Fig. 3a. This setup minimizes the number of scenarios each user has to perform while addressing carry-over effects between scenarios, such as increasing familiarization with the annotation task.

5   Results

In this section we will describe our observations during the experiments described in Sect. 4, starting with an overview of study participants. We had respondents of various age, education, and field of work. 39% have not obtained a university degree, or did not pursue higher education, while 39% completed either Masters or PhD studies. The majority (71%) of participants work in a technical field, i.e., computer science, engineering, or mathematics. Figure 3b shows a detailed break-down of demographic characteristics of participants.

5.1   Subjective Measures

As described in Sect. 4, we measure four subjective sub-metrics of the NASA-TLX— mental demand, uncertainty, effort, and frustration—across four different assistance scenarios. We then used a repeated measure ANOVA [10] to find if there are statistically significant differences in the four assistance scenarios defined in Sect. 4. A repeated measure ANOVA can be used to test if two ore more non-independent samples (measurements) are from the same distribution, measured by $p \in [0, 1]$. In our case, we test for differences in workload between annotation assistance scenarios. We reject the Null hypothesis (no difference) and accept the alternative one (difference exists) when $p < 0.05$.

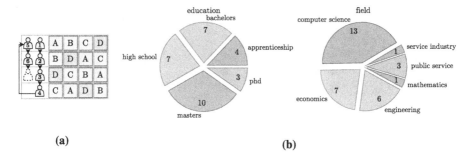

Fig. 3. Assigning annotators to a sequence of scenarios based on a balanced Latin square (left), and demographic information about user study participants (right).

Repeated measures ANOVA assumes sphericity in data, i.e., the difference in metrics for all combinations of two scenarios have the same variance. This assumption can be tested with Mauchly's test for sphericity [24]. Data for three out of four metrics violated the assumption of sphericity ($p < 0.05$). We use the Greenhouse-Geisser correction [14] to account for this. Even then, our observations show that each one of the four workload metrics are affected by changing how annotators are assisted by our annotation tool and the differences are statistically significant with $p < 0.001$.

Since the repeated measures ANOVA indicated a difference in the NASA-TLX metrics when using different assistance features, we ran six post-hoc tests, looking for the differences between each combination of two features, e.g., measurements for non-assisted annotation (scenario A in contrast to only recommendations (scenario C). We corrected all p values using Bonferroni's method [23] for running multiple tests. Intuitively, running many tests increases the likelihood of finding statistically significant differences in one of them, even though there is none. This correction multiplies the P-value with the number of tests, to account for this increased likelihood. Table 4 in Sect. A reports details.

In summary, no assistance feature at all (scenario A) is statistically significantly worse than either only recommendations (scenario C) or both assistance features combined D). Surprisingly, assisting annotators with a visualization of the information they found in the text (i.e., the generated graphical process model, scenario B) was not found to help with reducing the workload.

Compared to no assistance, assisting the annotator with recommendations reduced mental demand by 24.7 (-34.6%), effort by 22.4 (-34.2%), and frustration by 20.5 (-51.0%). Uncertainty is best lowered by combining recommendations with visualizations, which reduces it by 24.4 (-44.8%), according to our observations. Note, that we found no statistically significant effect on any sub-metric when comparing recommendations (scenario C) to the combination of recommendations and visualizations (scenario D). Similarly, we could not observe a difference between non-assisted annotation (scenario A) and just visualization of annotated information (scenario B). This indicates that only visualizing the currently annotated process-relevant information is not enough to reduce the workload of the annotation task. Contrary, recommendations are a way to reduce it by up to to nearly 50%. Some limitations apply to our findings concerning the quality of the graphical process representation, which we discuss in Sect. 6.

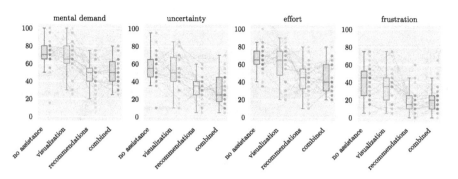

Fig. 4. Subjective measures for each of the four scenarios from Sect. 4.

Figure 4 aggregates our data for each sub-metric into plots, showing values for each participant and scenario as strip plots, where the values of a given participant are connected by lines. Additionally the data points are aggregated into box plots, showing the data mean, 25th and 75th percentiles as box, and the rest of the distribution as whiskers, excluding outliers. The plots mirror the general observations we drew from Table 4, and shows that recommendations and the combination of both assistance features help best with reducing the workload of data annotators. Overall, the ordering of assistance features in terms of reducing the workload is obvious from the plots. No assistance (scenario A) and visualizations only (scenario B) share the spot for least useful, while recommendations and the combination of features seem to be equally useful in lowering the workload of process information annotation, thus answering research question **RQ1**.

5.2 Objective Measures

As discussed in Sect. 1, our goal with assisting data annotators is twofold. The previous Sect. 5.1 discussed metrics that are subjective, i.e., are based on the experiences of a data annotator. On the other hand, assisting annotators also affects the quality of annotations. We measured a total of four objective metrics, which we presented in detail in Sect. 4. These are the F_1 scores for annotated mentions, entities, and relations, as well as the total time a given annotator needed to complete annotating a document fragment. An aggregate of the data we obtained is shown in Fig. 5 as a plot, similar to the one we showed and explained in Sect. 5.1. Detailed results are listed in Table 2 in Appendix A.

Again, using a repeated measure ANOVA we found significant effects on the annotation quality measured in F_1 when using different assistance features during the annotation of mentions ($p < 0.001$) and relations ($p < 0.001$). The annotation quality of entities was not affected ($p = 0.450$), which may be caused by the low number of entities[7], as well as the fact that we count an entity only as correct, if contains all expected mentions. This means errors by the annotator during MD propagate to the ER task.

---

[7] On average, fragments used in the user study only contained one entity that needed resolution, i.e., there are at least two entity mentions referring to the same entity.

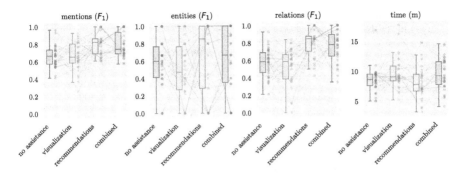

Fig. 5. Objective measures for each of the four scenarios from Sect. 4.

Furthermore, we did observe a statistically significant difference in the time an annotator needs to annotate a document ($p = 0.011$), but during post hoc tests we could only explain this with a statistically significant difference between the assistance features *visualization* (B) and *recommendations* (scenario C), where the latter speeds up completion times by about 1.5 min (see Table 3 in the Appendix A).

Several participants remarked during the user study, that identifying relations and classifying them correctly is a very challenging task. These participants were mostly inexperienced with BPM and BPMN and thus greatly benefited from the recommendation assistance feature. We can observe this across all participants, as the post hoc tests for relation annotation quality show. Comparing scenario A (no assistance) against scenario C (recommendations only), we see a statistically significant ($p = 0.001$) increase in F_1 of 0.224 (+38.9%). Using the visualization does not seem to have a significant effect compared to no assistance at all ($p = 1.000$), but is significantly worse than using recommendations (-0.259, $p < 0.001$) or using both assistance features (-0.204, $p < 0.001$).

The same analysis can be made for the task of mention detection. Participants of our user study seem to benefit most from recommendations, when compared to no assistance at all ($p < 0.001$), with an improvement of 0.141 (+21.4%). Visualization has no statistically significant effect ($p = 1.000$) compared to no assistance at all. Using only visualization has an adverse effect compared to just recommendations ($p < 0.001$) with a decrease in F_1 of 0.141. Similar to Sect. 5.1, this effect can be attributed to limitations in our graphical process model, which we discuss in Sect. 6, or a user's familiarity with BPMN (Sect. 5.3).

This also answers research question **RQ2.**, as recommendations seem to be the best choice for improving the quality of annotations. Notably, for all three tasks the annotation recommendations themselves are of lower quality than the average annotations by a human annotator assisted by recommendations (scenario C). Human review improved the F_1 score of annotations by +0.100 for MD, +0.181 for ER, and +0.151% for RE, showing how humans assisted by AI-based systems can perform better than each part in isolation.

Table 1. Independent Samples T-Test for the hypothesis that objective scores for annotations by *novices* are lower than those by *experts*.

		t	df	p^a
mentions	no assistance	−1.950	20.691	0.032 *
	recommendations	0.023	23.041	0.509
	visualization	−1.166	23.984	0.128
	combined	−1.463	24.491	0.078
relations	no assistance	−1.800	25.072	0.042 *
	recommendations	0.664	21.132	0.743
	visualization	−1.182	28.000	0.124
	combined	−0.590	20.711	0.281

*, **, *** statistically significant results of increasing degrees.
^{a}P-value following Welch's test.

5.3 Effects of Annotator Experience

We asked participants for their experience with BPMN, measured in years. With this information, we now investigate if a user's experience with BPMN influences how much they can benefit from assistance. To this end we split the data into two groups—*experts*, which we define for the purposes of this analysis as participants with at least one year of BPMN modeling experience, and *novices*, which are the remaining study participants. This split results in 10 experts and 18 novices. We hypothesize that annotations by *novices* are worse in terms of F_1 score compared to those by *experts*. Table 1 lists results for an independent samples T-Test.

We can confirm our assumption that BPMN experience improves the quality of mention (MD) and relation annotations (RE), for un-assisted annotation (scenario A). In all assisted scenarios (B, C, D) we have to reject our hypothesis, i.e., *novices* no longer produce worse annotations than *experts*, from which we infer that the two assistance features can indeed bridge the gap in annotation quality caused by differences in experience with BPMN. We therefore answer **RQ3.** with *annotation recommendations*, *visualizations*, and *combined assistance*.

6   Conclusion

In this section we will reiterate the core contribution of this paper, the limitations of the user study we conducted, and we describe our plans for future work.

Core Contributions. This paper presents an in-depth exploration on the usefulness of two features for assisting data annotators in the domain of business process information extraction. A user study with 31 participants shows that annotation recommendations reduce certain workload aspects by up to −51.0% (**RQ1.**). We find that recommendations obtained by a system based on machine learning improve annotation quality as much as +38.9% (**RQ2.**). The same recommendations bridge the gap in annotation quality between beginner and expert annotators, promising easier assembly of annotation teams by means of shorter training times (**RQ3.**). We make all data and code publicly available.

Limitations. First, we focused our study on two assistance features, to ensure its feasibility, while also guaranteeing methodological correctness. Investigating more assistance features would either increase participation times, or limit each participation to a subset of scenarios. Next, while we could not observe statistically significant effects of any assistance features on the quality of entity resolution annotations, we cannot eliminate the possibility that this caused by errors propagated from the MD task. Our automated method used for generating and layouting a graphical process model from the process information (annotations) used for the visualization assistance feature has limitations in terms of structure, accuracy stemming from the employed heuristics, and clarity of generated labels. This may affect its usefulness, as these limitations may make the graphical model harder to understand, especially for untrained annotators. Finally, we only present and analyze a sub-set of the data collected during the user study. For example, we recorded all user interaction with the tool, such as when a recommended annotation is discarded, or a new annotation is created. These logs constitute valuable data for improving the workflow for annotating process relevant data in textual process descriptions.

Future Work. Our future work is mainly concerned with eliminating the limitations we discussed in the previous Sect. 6. As such we plan to improve the implementation of our annotation tool, e.g., improve the way relations are displayed. We also plan to extend our analysis of the data we already obtained during this user study, e.g., by evaluating the interaction logs. This data can be very valuable to learn how annotators interact with the annotation tool, and give indications on how to improve the workflow, or which parts of the interface are still unintuitive. Furthermore, we want to explore better annotation recommendation methods, as this feature seems to have a consistently positive effect. We plan to evaluate integrating incremental training, as soon as annotators have submitted a document. Finally we would like to extend the user study to new assistance features, in addition to comparing different workflows and user interface options. The initial findings regarding how experts benefit in different ways from assistance features, compared to novice users, motivate us to conduct a targeted study to find ways to properly assist users of different experience levels.

Disclosure of Interests. The authors have no competing interests to declare that are relevant to the content of this article.

A Appendix

Table 2. Post hoc comparisons of assistance features on objective metrics. Largest statistically significant absolute difference to unassisted annotation is set in **bold**. We abbreviate mean difference with MD and standard error with SE.

			MD	SE	t	p_{bonf} [a]
mentions	no assistance	recommendations	**−0.141**	0.037	−3.774	0.002 **
		visualization	−0.000	0.037	−0.008	1.000
		both	−0.132	0.037	−3.529	0.014 **
	recommendations	visualization	0.141	0.037	3.766	0.005 **
		both	0.009	0.037	0.244	1.000
	visualization	both	−0.132	0.037	−3.522	0.004 **
entities	no assistance	recommendations	−0.068	0.097	−0.706	1.000
		visualization	0.080	0.097	0.825	1.000
		both	−0.038	0.097	−0.398	1.000
	recommendations	visualization	0.148	0.097	1.532	0.775
		both	0.030	0.097	0.309	1.000
	visualization	both	−0.118	0.097	−1.223	1.000
relations	no assistance	recommendations	**−0.224**	0.049	−4.524	<.001 ***
		visualization	0.025	0.049	0.842	1.000
		both	−0.179	0.049	−3.691	0.002 **
	recommendations	visualization	0.259	0.049	5.367	<.001 ***
		both	0.055	0.049	0.834	1.000
	visualization	both	−0.204	0.049	−4.533	<.001 ***

*, **, *** statistically significant results of increasing degrees.

[a] P-value adjusted for comparing a family of six using Bonferroni correction.

Table 3. Post hoc comparisons of assistance features on completion time. We abbreviate mean difference with MD and standard error with SE.

			MD	SE	t	p_{bonf} [a]
time (s)	no assistance	recommendations	23.778	30.528	0.779	1.000
		visualization	−67.621	30.528	−2.215	0.176
		both	−56.082	30.528	−1.837	0.418
	recommendations	visualization	−91.399	30.528	−2.994	0.022 *
		both	−79.860	30.528	−2.616	0.063
	visualization	both	11.539	30.528	0.378	1.000

*, **, *** statistically significant results of increasing degrees.

[a] P-value adjusted for comparing a family of six using Bonferroni correction.

Table 4. Post hoc comparisons of assistance features on subjective metrics. Largest statistical significant absolute difference to unassisted annotation for a given metric is set in **bold**. We abbreviate mean difference with MD and standard error with SE.

			MD	SE	t	p_{bonf}[a]
mentaldemand	no assistance	recommendations	**24.677**	3.521	7.009	<.001 ***
		visualization	4.194	3.521	1.191	1.000
		both	21.290	3.521	6.047	<.001 ***
	recommendations	visualization	−20.484	3.521	−5.818	<.001 ***
		both	−3.387	3.521	−0.962	1.000
	visualization	both	17.097	3.521	4.856	<.001 ***
uncertainty	no assistance	recommendations	21.129	3.558	5.938	<.001 ***
		visualization	4.677	3.558	1.314	1.000
		both	**24.355**	3.558	6.844	<.001 ***
	recommendations	visualization	−16.452	3.558	−4.623	<0.001 ***
		both	3.226	3.558	0.907	1.000
	visualization	both	19.677	3.558	5.530	<.001 ***
effort	no assistance	recommendations	**22.419**	3.710	6.043	<.001 ***
		visualization	5.000	3.710	1.348	1.000
		both	21.129	3.710	5.695	<.001 ***
	recommendations	visualization	−17.419	3.710	−4.695	<.001 ***
		both	−1.290	3.710	−0.348	1.000
	visualization	both	16.129	3.710	4.347	<.001 ***
frustration	no assistance	recommendations	**20.484**	3.655	5.604	<.001 ***
		visualization	3.548	3.655	0.971	1.000
		both	18.548	3.655	5.074	<.001 ***
	recommendations	visualization	−16.935	3.655	−4.633	<.001 ***
		both	−1.935	3.655	−0.530	1.000
	visualization	both	15.000	3.655	4.104	<.001 ***

*, **, *** statistically significant results of increasing degrees.
[a]P-value adjusted for comparing a family of six using Bonferroni correction.

References

1. van der Aa, H., Di Ciccio, C., Leopold, H., Reijers, H.A.: Extracting declarative process models from natural language. In: CAiSE (2019)
2. van der Aa, H., Leopold, H., Mannhardt, F., Reijers, H.A.: On the fragmentation of process information: challenges, solutions, and outlook. In: International Workshop on Business Process Modeling, Development and Support (2015)
3. Van der Aa, H., Leopold, H., Reijers, H.A.: Checking process compliance against natural language specifications using behavioral spaces. IS (2018)
4. Ackermann, L., et al.: Recent advances in data-driven business process management (2024)
5. Ackermann, L., Neuberger, J., Jablonski, S.: Data-driven annotation of textual process descriptions based on formal meaning representations. In: CAiSE (2021)

6. Ackermann, L., Neuberger, J., Käppel, M., Jablonski, S.: Bridging research fields: an empirical study on joint, neural relation extraction techniques. In: CAiSE (2023)
7. Bagozi, A., Bianchini, D., De Antonellis, V., Garda, M., Melchiori, M.: Personalised exploration graphs on semantic data lakes. In: On the Move to Meaningful Internet Systems: OTM 2019 Conferences: Confederated International Conferences: CoopIS, ODBASE, C&TC 2019, 21–25 October 2019, Rhodes, Greece (2019)
8. Bellan, P., Dragoni, M., Ghidini, C.: Extracting business process entities and relations from text using pre-trained language models and in-context learning. In: EDOC (2022)
9. Bellan, P., Ghidini, C., Dragoni, M., Ponzetto, S.P., van der Aa, H.: Process extraction from natural language text: the PET dataset and annotation guidelines. In: NL4AI (2022)
10. Bergh, D.D.: Problems with repeated measures analysis: demonstration with a study of the diversification and performance relationship. Acad. Manage. J. (1995)
11. Ferreira., R.C.B., Thom., L.H., Fantinato., M.: A semi-automatic approach to identify business process elements in natural language texts. In: ICEIS (2017)
12. Franceschetti, M., Seiger, R., López, H.A., Burattin, A., García-Bañuelos, L., Weber, B.: A characterisation of ambiguity in BPM. In: International Conference on Conceptual Modeling (2023)
13. Friedrich, F., Mendling, J., Puhlmann, F.: Process model generation from natural language text. In: CAiSE (2011)
14. Greenhouse, S.W., Geisser, S.: On methods in the analysis of profile data. Psychometrika (1959)
15. Hart, S.G.: Nasa-task load index (NASA-TLX); 20 years later. In: Proceedings of the Human Factors and Ergonomics Society Annual Meeting (2006)
16. Ivanchikj, A., Serbout, S., Pautasso, C.: From text to visual BPMN process models: design and evaluation. In: Proceedings of the 23rd ACM/IEEE International Conference on Model Driven Engineering Languages and Systems (2020)
17. Joshi, A., Kale, S., Chandel, S., Pal, D.K.: Likert scale: Explored and explained. Br. J. Appl. Sci. Technol. (2015)
18. Käppel, M., Schönig, S., Jablonski, S.: Leveraging small sample learning for business process management. Inf. Softw. Technol. (2021)
19. Kim, B.G., Stein, H.H.: A spreadsheet program for making a balanced Latin square design. Rev. Colombiana Ciencias Pecuarias (2009)
20. Klie, J.C., Bugert, M., Boullosa, B., de Castilho, R.E., Gurevych, I.: The inception platform: machine-assisted and knowledge-oriented interactive annotation. In: Proceedings of the 27th International Conference on Computational Linguistics: System Demonstrations (2018)
21. Kourani, H., Berti, A., Schuster, D., van der Aalst, W.M.: Process modeling with large language models. arXiv preprint arXiv:2403.07541 (2024)
22. Li, J., Sun, A., Han, J., Li, C.: A survey on deep learning for named entity recognition. IEEE Trans. Knowl. Data Eng. (2020)
23. Ludbrook, J.: Multiple comparison procedures updated. Clin. Exp. Pharmacol. Physiol. (1998)
24. Mauchly, J.W.: Significance test for sphericity of a normal N-variate distribution. Ann. Math. Stat. (1940)
25. Mustansir, A., Shahzad, K., Malik, M.K.: AutoEPRS-20: extracting business process redesign suggestions from natural language text. In: ASE (2020)
26. Nakayama, H., Kubo, T., Kamura, J., Taniguchi, Y., Liang, X.: doccano: text annotation tool for human (2018). https://github.com/doccano/doccano
27. Neuberger, J., Ackermann, L., van der Aa, H., Jablonski, S.: A universal prompting strategy for extracting process model information from natural language text using large language models (2024). https://arxiv.org/abs/2407.18540

28. Neuberger, J., Ackermann, L., Jablonski, S.: Beyond rule-based named entity recognition and relation extraction for process model generation from natural language text. In: CoopIS (2023)

29. Qian, C., et al.: An approach for process model extraction by multi-grained text classification. In: CAiSE (2020)

30. Quishpi, L., Carmona, J., Padró, L.: Extracting annotations from textual descriptions of processes. In: BPM 2020 (2020)

31. Rosa, L.S., Silva, T.S., Fantinato, M., Thom, L.H.: A visual approach for identification and annotation of business process elements in process descriptions. Comput. Stand. Interfaces (2022)

32. Schützenmeier, N., Käppel, M., Fichtner, M., Jablonski, S.: Scenario-based model checking of declarative process models. In: ICEIS (2023)

33. Sukthanker, R., Poria, S., Cambria, E., Thirunavukarasu, R.: Anaphora and coreference resolution: a review. Inf. Fusion (2020)

34. Tkachenko, M., Malyuk, M., Holmanyuk, A., Liubimov, N.: Label studio: data labeling software (2020-2022). https://github.com/heartexlabs/label-studio

35. Xu, M., Jiang, H., Watcharawittayakul, S.: A local detection approach for named entity recognition and mention detection. In: Proceedings of the 55th Annual Meeting of the Association for Computational Linguistics (Volume 1: Long Papers) (2017)

FleX: Interpreting Graph Neural Networks with Subgraph Extraction and Flexible Objective Estimation

Duy Nguyen[1,2], Thanh Le[1,2], and Bac Le[1,2(✉)]

[1] Faculty of Information Technology, University of Science, Ho Chi Minh City, Vietnam
22c11004@student.hcmus.edu.vn, {lnthanh,lhbac}@fit.hcmus.edu.vn
[2] Vietnam National University, Ho Chi Minh City, Vietnam

Abstract. Graph Neural Networks (GNNs) have shown remarkable results in graph-related tasks, yet interpreting their decision-making process remains challenging. Most existing methods for interpreting GNNs focus on finding a subgraph that preserves the model's predictions. However, removing edges alters the original structure, making the optimization process heavily dependent on the loss function. In this paper, we propose FleX, a novel approach that transcends these limitations by using a distillation model to estimate prediction values after subgraph extraction. Our method combines implicit and explicit edge masking techniques to identify the most relevant subgraph. We introduce a flexible loss estimation strategy that allows for a more robust optimization process. Experimental results demonstrate that FleX outperforms most existing Graph XAI models across various benchmark datasets, achieving superior performance in interpreting GNNs. This approach enhances the interpretability of GNNs while maintaining high accuracy, contributing to more trustworthy and explainable graph-based machine learning models.

Keywords: Graph neural network · Graph explainability · Graph knowledge distillation · Subgraph extraction

1 Introduction

Graph Neural Networks (GNNs) have emerged as a powerful and versatile solution for analyzing graph-structured data across various domains. GNNs employ various types of layers, including Graph Convolution Layers (GCN [3], GAT [17], GraphConv [10]), Graph Pooling Layers (SAGPooling [4]), and Graph Normalization Layers (Batch Normalization [2], Instance Normalization [16]). Their innovative message passing mechanism, which propagates and aggregates information from neighboring nodes through linear and non-linear transformations, enables GNNs to effectively capture complex relational information inherent in graph structures. This self-learning attribute, analogous to CNNs in image processing, allows GNNs to autonomously learn and synthesize essential features crucial for decision-making, surpassing traditional approaches that rely on hand-crafted features. The adaptability and feature learning capacity of GNNs have led to their widespread application and superior performance in diverse

M. Comuzzi et al. (Eds.): CoopIS 2024, LNCS 15506, pp. 204–221, 2025.
https://doi.org/10.1007/978-3-031-81375-7_12

fields, including social network analysis [18], biology [26], chemistry [23] and recommendation system [7, 11]. This broad applicability underscores the significant impact of GNNs in advancing graph analysis and their potential to uncover subtle patterns and relationships across a wide spectrum of graph-based problems.

While GNNs have demonstrated impressive accuracy across various tasks, they face a significant challenge in terms of interpretability. This opaqueness stems from their complex architecture and the intricate nature of graph-structured data, making it difficult to elucidate the decision-making process. The lack of interpretability represents a barrier to understanding, impeding trust, complicating error analysis, and potentially concealing harmful biases. Developing methods to balance high performance with interpretability has become a crucial criterion for evaluating and deploying modern AI models. This pursuit not only aims to enhance reliability and foster trust in GNN-based systems but also opens avenues for refining model architectures and training procedures.

In case of GNN model interpretation, there are two primary approaches: feature importance and subgraph identification. Feature importance method seeks to pinpoint the input characteristics that wield the most influence over the model's output, shedding light on the comparative importance of various graph properties. Subgraph identification aims to isolate a critical portion of the graph that plays a pivotal role in shaping the model's decisions. This method draws parallels with saliency mapping in image analysis but is tailored to graph structures. However, as previously noted, graph-based explanations encounter unique hurdles in terms of human comprehension. Unlike images or text, where explanations can be more easily linked to concepts people understand, the abstract nature of graph relationships often proves challenging for intuitive interpretation. As a result, the effectiveness of graph explanations is typically gauged through quantitative measures rather than qualitative human evaluation. This dependence on metrics highlights the persistent challenge in making machine-generated graph explanations more accessible and meaningful to human understanding.

In this paper, we introduce a novel method for explaining Graph Neural Networks through an innovative subgraph extraction technique. Our approach systematically reduces the original graph to a more compact form while preserving the essential decision-making process of the initial model. We use the distillation model as a flexible loss estimator combine with edgemask learning. This mechanism not only enhances the comprehensibility of GNN predictions but also potentially unveils critical substructures that drive the model's decision-making process. The proposed method addresses the ongoing challenge of interpretability in graph-based machine learning, offering a solution that maintains model accuracy while significantly improving explainability.

The main contributions of this paper are as follows:

– We propose a novel GNN explanation model that integrates subgraph mask learning with flexible loss estimation using a distillation model.
– We use a strategy to evaluate the importance of nearest neighbors in graph explanations.
– We provide a comprehensive evaluation of our model on both synthetic and realistic datasets, offering comprehensive analysis and thorough insights into its performance.

2   Related Work

Recent advancements in explanations for GNNs, exemplified by models like GNNExplainer and XGNN, have necessitated comprehensive classification systems. We adopt the classification framework by Yuan et al. [24], which categorizes graph-based XAI models into instance-level and model-level explanations. Instance-level explanation such as GNNExplainer [22], GradCAM [12, 14], GraphMask [13], PGExplainer [8, 9], DeepLIFT [15], aim to provide specific explanations for each prediction made by the GNN. Taking node classification as an example, given a GNN f, graph $\mathcal{G}$, and target node v, we aim to identify a subgraph $\mathcal{G}_s$ that preserves f's output for v. This subgraph G_s serves as an explanation by highlighting the most influential parts of the original graph that contribute to the model's prediction for the specific node.

GNNExplainer, an instance-level explanation method, uses a softmask strategy with learnable parameters to explain GNN predictions. It generates explanations through subgraph extraction and feature importance identification by learning specific masks. The model treats the original graph as noisy and denoises it while preserving mutual information. Unlike our method, GNNExplainer employs the output of a pretrained GNN as feedback for generating explanations which will be affected when an edge or node is removed from the graph.

GradCAM is another method that uses gradients to identify saliency maps. While this approach can be effective for image data, it often performs poorly when applied to graphs due to their typically high sparsity. Additionally, attention mechanisms have been proposed as a means to interpret graph neural networks. However, previous experimental results have largely shown that these attention-based methods are not particularly effective in explaining GNNs.

GraphMask is a model that shares similarities with our proposed approach. It introduces an edge masking mechanism by learning a classifier to determine which edges can be removed at each GNN layer. Additionally, GraphMask replaces eliminated edges with a learnable baseline to compensate for missing information. However, a key difference between GraphMask and FleX lies in the application of this learnable baseline. However, a sufficiently powerful learnable baseline could potentially interfere with the edge mask learning process, potentially leading to the unintended removal of important edges.

XGNN [25], to the best of our knowledge, is the only model that falls under the category of model-level explanations for GNNs. Its primary objective is to identify a common graph pattern that serves multiple inputs. However, model-level approaches typically provide explanations at a high level of abstraction. This, coupled with the scarcity of research in this domain, has resulted in a lack of effective evaluation methods and clear research directions for model-level explanations. The limited exploration in this area presents both challenges and opportunities for developing comprehensive frameworks to assess and advance model-level explanation techniques for Graph Neural Networks.

3   Proposed Method

3.1   Edge Masking with Learnable Parameter Strategy

Given a graph $\mathcal{G}$ with a set of node features $\mathbf{X}$ and a pre-trained GNN model f, our objective is to find a subgraph $\mathcal{G}_s$ that maximally preserves the prediction results of model f on the original graph. In this context, $\mathcal{G}_s$ is considered an explanation for the GNN model f. Various methods exist for identifying this subgraph $\mathcal{G}_s$. However, our approach utilizes learnable parameters, similar to the proposals in predecessor models such as GNNExplainer and GraphMask.

Our hypothesis stems from the observation that the output of a GNN reflects its intended outcome. A typical GNN model f comprises multiple layers that aggregate information from neighboring nodes. The layers closer to the output contain the most condensed information learned by the model, crucial for its decision-making process. Building on this concept, we posit the existence of a reverse process. This process takes as input the output of the penultimate layers of the GNN and, through a series of computations, identifies the important neighboring vertices that contribute to the meaningful features in the model's prediction process. We term this process "Explicit masking". This reverse process aims to trace back from the concentrated information in the later layers to determine which neighboring nodes and their features were most influential in forming these high-level representations. By doing so, we can potentially uncover the critical substructures within the graph that drive the model's predictions. Figure 1 shows the edge masking process in details.

Formally, let u and v be two vertices in the graph, e_u, e_v correspond to the embeddings of u and v obtained from the final GNN layer. An edge $e_{u,v}$ between these vertices is defined as:

$$e_{u,v} = \gamma z_{u,v} + (1 - \gamma) h_{u,v} \qquad (1)$$

where $0 \leq \gamma \leq 1$ act as a hyper parameter to normalize the result.

The term $z_{u,v}$ is referred to as "soft edge masking". We compute this value using a learnable neural network that takes as input the features from the final layer of the GNN. Formally $z_{u,v}$ is follow as Eq. 2:

$$z_{u,v} = \sigma(W L_z(e_u))[v] \qquad (2)$$

where σ denotes to sigmoid function, L denotes to linear transformation with ReLU6 activation and W denotes to learnable parameter.

Similarly to z(u, v), the term $h_{u,v}$ serves to measure the similarity between nodes u and v in vector space. This is based on the assumption that if two nodes are similar, the probability of them forming an edge is higher. Formally, we can express this as:

$$h_{u,v} = \sigma(L_u(e_u) L_v(e_v)^T) \qquad (3)$$

where σ denotes to sigmoid function, L denotes to linear transformation with ReLU6 activation.

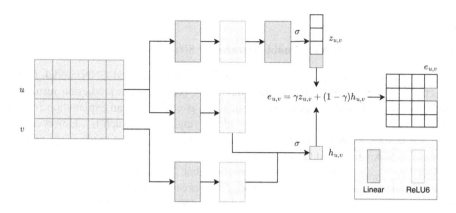

Fig. 1. Edge mask learning process, σ denotes to sigmoid activation function.

By combining soft edge masking, node similarity, and the implicit mask, we provide the explainer model with a multi-perspective approach to identifying relevant graph connections. Soft edge masking discerns which edges contribute significantly to vertex feature synthesis, enabling the elimination of less important edges, while node similarity prioritizes and retains semantically related edges. Additionally, the implicit mask—a learnable parameter—addresses the limitation of relying solely on GNN output data by learning implicit contributions of edges that may affect node features indirectly, such as through data normalization, thereby enhancing the model's explanation capabilities.

The concept of an implicit mask arises from the hypothesis that the explainer alone may not possess sufficient capacity to fully represent the complex structure of a graph given the current input data. The process of translating from model output to an explanation subgraph inherently involves information loss. Therefore, introducing an additional component to compensate for this incompleteness becomes essential. Motivated by this hypothesis, we introduce a learnable parameter with dimensions matching those of the adjacency matrix. This parameter is designed to automatically optimize through the explainer training process. By incorporating this implicit mask, we aim to enhance the explainer's ability to capture and represent intricate graph structures that may not be fully conveyed by the explicit input data alone. In that case, the edgemask formula can be rewritten as follows:

$$e_{u,v} = \frac{1}{2}(\gamma z_{u,v} + (1 - \gamma)h_{u,v} + \sigma(I[u, v])) \qquad (4)$$

where σ denotes to sigmoid function, $I[u, v]$ denotes to the value of implicit edgemask between vertices (u, v).

The process of learning the edge mask in our model is optimized through gradient descent. However, this approach presents challenges in ensuring that the resulting adjacency matrix remains symmetric. Moreover, this learning process may potentially introduce new edges that were not present in the original graph structure. To address these issues, we implement a normalization procedure on the obtained adjacency matrix. This step serves two critical purposes:

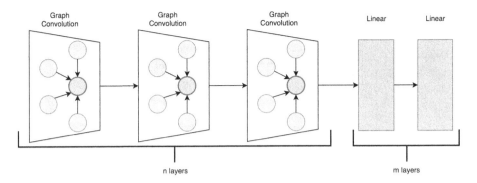

Fig. 2. GNN model architecture.

- Ensuring symmetry: We enforce symmetry on the learned edge mask to maintain consistency with the undirected nature of the original graph.
- Constraining edge set: We restrict the edges in the normalized mask to be a subset of the original graph, preventing the introduction of dic connections.

The normalization of the edge mask is formulated as follows:

$$e_{u,v} = \frac{1}{2}(e_{u,v} + e_{v,u})A[u,v] \tag{5}$$

where A denotes to adjacency matrix.

3.2 Soft Objective Estimator

Hence, the task of dropping edges without affecting predictions presents a significant challenge. Our objective is to achieve $f(\mathcal{G}) \approx f(\mathcal{G}_s)$, where $\mathcal{G}$ is the original graph and $\mathcal{G}_s$ is the subgraph. However, this condition makes it exceptionally difficult for the model to reach an optimal state. To address this, GraphMask proposes a mechanism to replace the removed edges with a learnable baseline, formulated as: $f(\mathcal{G}) \approx f(\mathcal{G}_s) + b$. However, this approach presents a potential drawback. If the learnable baseline b becomes sufficiently powerful, it may dominate the contribution of the discovered subgraph $\mathcal{G}_s$. This is problematic because b is not utilized in the actual prediction process. Consequently, this can adversely affect the quality and relevance of the identified subgraph.

Leveraging the core concept of GraphMask while avoiding the pitfall of having two independently trained components, we propose a more flexible mechanism for estimating the objective function. Our approach utilizes a distilled model [19,20] based on the GNN that requires explanation. This method allows us to reformulate the objective of finding the optimal subgraph as follows: $f(\mathcal{G}) \approx f_s(\mathcal{G}_s)$. Where f_s is distillation model distilled from GNN f. Figure 2shows the architecture of both the student and teacher GNN models. The student model has fewer layers than the teacher model.

The distilled model f_s is a refined version of the original GNN, designed to achieve a comparable level of performance with a significantly reduced number of parameters. This streamlined architecture, while maintaining accuracy, necessitates that the distilled

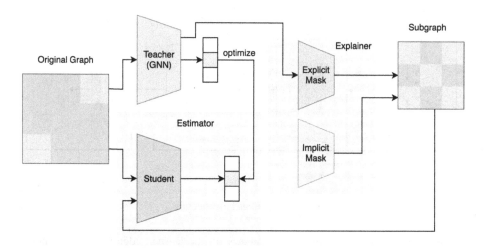

Fig. 3. The FleX model consists of two main components: distillation and explainer. The distillation component includes a "Teacher" GNN for specific tasks and a "Student" GNN, which has fewer parameters and is trained on the Teacher's output. The Student model then acts as a loss estimator to guide the Explainer's learning process.

model learns to efficiently represent the most crucial information from the larger model. In the context of Graph Neural Networks, we posit that the key aspect the distilled model focuses on is the structure of important subgraphs. This aligns perfectly with our objective of finding explanatory subgraphs for the GNN's decisions. Through the distillation process, the model implicitly learns to focus on the most relevant subgraph structures, effectively performing a form of feature selection at the graph level. The subgraphs that the distilled model deems important for its predictions are likely to be the same subgraphs that provide the best explanations for the original GNN's decisions.

3.3 The FleX Framework

Based on the ideas discussed, we have synthesized and constructed a unified framework to address the challenge of explaining Graph Neural Networks (GNNs). Figure 3 presents a detailed illustration of our framework, which we have designed with two primary components: the Explainer and the Estimator. Explainer is responsible for identifying and extracting the most relevant subgraph from the input graph that meaningful and consistent with the GNN output. The Estimator is a distilled version of the original GNN model in order to evaluate the effectiveness of the subgraph identified by the Explainer.

In our framework, both the Estimator and the Explainer are trained simultaneously. This concurrent training approach ensures that when one model undergoes minor changes, the other can promptly adapt, thereby accelerating the overall training process. This synergistic training mechanism is crucial for maintaining the balance and effectiveness of our explanation framework.

The training process begins with the Estimator, which is designed to emulate the behavior of the original GNN model. This is achieved by optimizing the following loss function:

$$\mathcal{L}_s = \sum_{i=1}^{N} y_t * (y_t - y_s) + \sum_{i=1}^{N} \sum_{j=1}^{C} -y_t^j log(y_s^j) + \sum_{i=1}^{N} (y_t^c - y_s^c) \qquad (6)$$

where y_t, y_s is the probality of GNN and estimator prediction respectively. y^j is the prediction probability at class j, y^c is the true prediction of GNN model.

To ensure that the Estimator can learn multiple objectives simultaneously, we employ a composite loss function consisting of three components. This multifaceted approach allows us to capture various aspects of the original GNN's behavior and prediction characteristics. The first component ensures overall output similarity, capturing the general behavior of the GNN. The second component focuses on maintaining consistent class predictions between the two models. The last component emphasizes accuracy for the correct class, recognizing that discrepancies in other class probabilities are less critical for our explanatory goals.

Following the training of the Estimator, it is employed to evaluate the loss associated with the explanation subgraph generated by the Explainer. As previously introduced, the Estimator is designed to capture important graph patterns of the original GNN, with the expectation that these patterns will correspond to the explanation subgraph. This establishes a causal relationship where the expected output of the Explainer aligns with the expected input of the Estimator. To optimize this process, we have designed a loss function with two components:

$$\mathcal{L}_e = \sum_{i=1}^{N} \sum_{j=1}^{C} -y_t^j log(y_s^j) + \sum_{i=1}^{N} (y_t^c - y_s^c) \qquad (7)$$

where components of Eq. 7 are the same as those of Eq. 6, except that y_s is now computed using the explanation subgraph on the estimator instead of the original graph.

Our current model design successfully achieves two primary objectives. Firstly, the model learns to represent important subgraphs effectively by leveraging the expected output of the original GNN in combination with an implicit mask. This approach allows us to capture and supplement information that the explanation model might otherwise miss. The implicit mask serves as a mechanism to compensate for the inherent limitations of the explainer in fully representing complex graph structures. Second, our model addresses the challenge of removing edges without significantly affecting the original output. This is accomplished through the use of a distillation model for estimation purposes. The distilled model, serving as an Estimator, allows us to evaluate the impact of edge removals more accurately and efficiently.

3.4 Rebalancing Subgraph Estimation

One of the distinctive features of our model is its approach to estimating subgraph masks. Rather than predicting discrete values, our model generates continuous mask

Algorithm 1. The rebalancing algorithm refines the nearest neighbors.

Input: adjacency matrix $\mathbf{A}$, subgraph mask $\mathbf{M}$, target explanation node v_i, k
Output: normalized $\mathbf{M}$
1: **for** $v_j \in \mathcal{N}_i$ **do**
2:    $e_{i,j} \leftarrow max(e_{i,j}, A_{i,j})$
3: **end for**
4: **return** M

Table 1. The statistics of datasets.

Dataset	#nodes	#edges	#features	#classes
BA-Shapes	700	2,050	10	4
BA-Community	1,400	4,460	10	8
Tree-Grid	1,231	1,565	10	2
Tree-Cycles	871	981	10	2
Cora	2,708	10,556	1,433	7
CiteSeer	3,327	9,104	3,703	6

values. This approach may lead to the phenomenon of "introduced evidence". While this issue could potentially be addressed by employing a Gumbel-Sigmoid function to convert continuous values into discrete ones, we argue that such a step is unnecessary. The very nature of removing less significant edges from the graph inherently alters the graph structure from its original context. Moreover, the fundamental operation of Graph Neural Networks involves weighted summation of neighboring vertices. Consequently, when an edge is removed, there is an inherent need to compensate for this loss to restore the initial equilibrium. This can be achieved by adjusting the weights of the remaining edges in the graph, effectively redistributing the importance across the network.

Furthermore, our current optimization method, which is gradient-based, focuses solely on minimizing the loss function without considering the nature or structure of the added graph components. This approach implicitly treats all edges as equally important. However, we propose that nearest neighbors and vertices within k-hops should be given higher priority when predicting the subgraph. Specifically, we argue that the most critical graph structure, which has the greatest influence on the model's decision-making process, consists of the immediate neighborhood (k = 1) of each node. Therefore, we introduce an additional rebalancing step, which involves reintroducing nearest neighbors that were initially removed from the explanatory subgraph. By doing so, we aim to assess the effectiveness and validity of our hypothesis regarding the importance of local graph structure. This rebalancing mechanism allows us to preserve the significance of proximal connections. Algorithm 1 introduces the working mechanism of the process. Note that the rebalancing trick can only be applied to instance-level explanations. For model-level explanations, since there is no target node, it cannot be applied.

4 Experiment Results

4.1 Datasets

To comprehensively evaluate our model and provide diverse perspectives, we conducted experiments and assessments using both synthetic and realistic datasets. The synthetic datasets are widely used benchmarks for evaluating the effectiveness of GNN Explanation models. We employed four primary synthetic datasets: BA-Shapes, BA-Community, Tree-Grid, and Tree-Cycles. These datasets, introduced in the GNNExplainer paper [22], are artificially generated with predefined ground truths.

The BA-Shapes dataset is based on the Barabási-Albert (BA) graph, where house-like motifs are attached to the initial BA graph. The BA-Community dataset builds on this by merging two BA-Shapes graphs, forming a more complex network with two distinct communities. Both the Tree-Grid and Tree-Cycles datasets are derived from a binary tree structure but differ in the motifs added. In Tree-Cycles, 6-cycle node motifs are attached, creating cyclic patterns, while Tree-Grid introduces 3×3 grid motifs, adding localized grid-like substructures to the tree.

In certain contexts, predefined ground truths are not available, as the alignment between explanations and ground truths often depends more on the GNN model itself. Moreover, not all datasets come with readily available ground truths. To address these limitations and provide a more comprehensive evaluation, we extended our assessment to include realistic datasets, specifically Cora and CiteSeer [21]. These datasets are well-suited for node classification tasks, offering an appropriate number of vertices without predetermined ground truths. In these cases, the effectiveness of our explanatory model is estimated solely through various metrics, ensuring a fair and efficient evaluation. This approach allows us to test our model's performance in more complex, real-world scenarios, providing insights into its practical applicability and robustness across different types of graph data. Table 1 we show the statistic of evaluation datasets.

4.2 Evaluation Method and Setup

There are two primary approaches to evaluating the effectiveness of Graph Neural Network explanations: plausibility and faithfulness. Plausibility is assessed using predefined ground truths, requiring human intervention to define reasonable explanations. However, this is challenging for graph-structured data, and not all datasets have well-defined ground truths. Consequently, this method faces difficulties in real-world applications where such truths are often unavailable, highlighting the need for alternative evaluation strategies for diverse and realistic scenarios.

Faithfulness evaluation, on the other hand, measures how accurately an explanation reflects the model's output without requiring ground truth labels. This method compares the explanation's output with that of the original model, allowing for an assessment of whether the explanation captures the essence of the model's decision-making. Its independence from ground truth data makes it viable for real-world applications where such labels may be scarce. By focusing on the alignment between the explanation and the model's behavior, faithfulness evaluation provides a robust framework for assessing the quality and reliability of GNN explanations, enhancing trust and understanding in graph-based AI systems.

Based on the characteristics of faithfulness evaluation, we have chosen to employ this method to assess the effectiveness of our model. To provide a comprehensive comparison, we also retrained several popular explanation methods, including GNNExplainer, PGExplainer, GraphMask, GradCAM, and DeepLIFT which implemented on PyG [1] and DIG [6] library. We then utilized faithfulness metrics to compare these established methods with our proposed model. These model will be train on different level sparsity from {0.5, 0.6, 0.7, 0.8, 0.9}.

In our methodology, we first train a GNN model from scratch until it achieves optimal performance. For the baseline models, we trained using the default hyperparameters provided by the libraries, only adjusting the learning rate. In the case of FleX, we initially fixed the sparsity at 0.5 and then trained and searched for optimal model parameters, including the learning rate and the embedding dimensions of the graph convolution layers. Once the optimal parameters were determined, we fixed these parameters and ran the model at higher sparsity levels. In the previous step, when training the classification model, we found that the best performance was achieved with three graph convolution layers and two linear feed-forward layers. Consequently, when designing the student model, we reduced this to two graph convolution layers and one feed-forward layer. In our study, we also included the model-level XGNN for comparative analysis. However, since XGNN does not inherently provide a model for node classification tasks, we implemented a modified version to address this limitation. We rewriting the XGNN algorithm by altering the rule set of the graph generator.

4.3 Metrics

To evaluate the effectiveness of graph neural network explanation models, we employ two primary metrics: Fidelity [5,24] and Inverse Fidelity [5,24]. These metrics are used in conjunction with Sparsity, defined as $1 - \frac{m}{M}$ where m is the number of edges in explanatory subgraph, M is the number of edge in the original graph. Sparsity quantifies the extent of edge removal from the original graph when generating explanations. A well-performing explanatory model is expected to achieve high Fidelity and Inverse Fidelity scores while maintaining a sufficiently high level of Sparsity.

Fidelity (Fidelity+) is a metric designed to quantify the degree of change in model predictions when comparing the original graph to a modified version where the importance subgraph has been masked out. The higher Fidelity+ the better model. Fidelity+ defined as:

$$\text{Fidelity+} = \frac{1}{N} \sum_{i=1}^{N} (f(\mathcal{G}_o)^{y_i} - f(\mathcal{G}_o \backslash \mathcal{G}_s)^{y_i}) \tag{8}$$

where $y_i = \mathbf{argmax} f(\mathcal{G})$, $\mathcal{G}_o$ denotes to original graph and $\mathcal{G}_s$ denotes to explanatory subgraph.

Inverse Fidelity (Fidelity−) in contrast measuring the extent to which the explanation subgraph preserves the model's predictive outcome compared to the original graph. The Fidelity− should be low as much as possible. Fidelity− defined as:

$$\text{Fidelity−} = \frac{1}{N} \sum_{i=1}^{N} (f(\mathcal{G}_o)^{y_i} - f(\mathcal{G}_s)^{y_i}) \tag{9}$$

Table 2. Experimental results on generating a single subgraph to explain the entire model prediction on synthesis dataset. F+ denotes to Fidelity+ and F− denotes to Fidelity−.

Model	BA-Shapes			BA-Community			Tree-Grid			Tree-Cycles		
	F+	F−	EC	F+	F−	EC	F+	F−	EC	F+	F−	EC
XGNN	0.279	0.669	0.313	0.252	0.656	0.268	0.247	0.572	0.410	0.238	0.412	0.587
FleX	**0.338**	**0.509**	**0.482**	**0.303**	**0.500**	**0.435**	**0.438**	**0.534**	**0.461**	**0.265**	**0.403**	**0.597**

Table 3. Experimental results on generating a single subgraph to explain the entire model prediction on realistic dataset.

Model	Cora			CiteSeer		
	Fidelity+	Fidelity−	EC	Fidelity+	Fidelity−	EC
XGNN	**0.181**	0.428	0.537	0.139	0.337	0.528
FleX	0.177	**0.367**	**0.599**	**0.143**	**0.263**	**0.608**

Explanation Confidence (EC) [5] is a normalized variant of Fidelity− computed by dividing score by the prediction probability on the original graph:

$$EC = \frac{1}{N} \sum_{i=1}^{N} \frac{|f(\mathcal{G}_o)^{y_i} - f(\mathcal{G}_s)^{y_i}|}{f(\mathcal{G}_o)^{y_i}} \tag{10}$$

4.4 Results and Analysis

We initially evaluated FleX at the model level, conducting experiments to identify a single, common subgraph that explains instance predictions across the entire graph. Tables 2 and 3 present detailed results from our experimental runs on two models, we report the average values obtained at different sparsity levels.

Our experimental results demonstrate that our model outperforms XGNN across most benchmarks, with the exception of Fidelity+ on the Cora dataset. Despite this single instance, the overall findings indicate that our model exhibits superior capability in detecting important graph structures compared to the XGNN algorithm. Notably, for real-world datasets such as Cora and CiteSeer, these results highlight our model's proficiency in handling practical, complex data. This performance establishes a crucial foundation for exploring significant structures within graphs through our explanatory model. The ability to effectively process real-world datasets not only validates the robustness of our approach but also paves the way for more insightful and applicable graph analysis in various domains.

FleX demonstrates remarkable improvements across various datasets and metrics, particularly in comparison to XGNN. Notably, it achieves a substantial 16.8% enhancement in explanation confidence on the BA-Community dataset, showcasing its superior ability to generate meaningful explanations for complex community structures. Additionally, FleX exhibits an impressive 8% improvement on the CiteSeer dataset, underlining its effectiveness in handling real-world citation networks. Beyond these stand-

Table 4. Experimental results on instance-level explanation on synthesis dataset. F+ denotes to Fidelity+ and F− denotes to Fidelity−. FleX* is the version of FleX that using rebalancing trick. GE denotes to GNNExplainer, GM denotes to GraphMask, PGE denotes to PGExplainer, DLIFT denotes to DeepLIFT.

Model	BA-Shapes			BA-Community			Tree-Grid			Tree-Cycles		
	F+	F−	EC	F+	F−	EC	F+	F−	EC	F+	F−	EC
GE	0.410	0.732	0.259	0.304	0.687	0.2442	0.497	0.571	0.420	**0.473**	0.422	0.577
GM	0.404	0.696	0.2948	0.297	0.659	0.270	0.413	0.572	0.419	0.247	0.422	0.578
PGE	0.263	**0.405**	**0.593**	0.202	0.607	0.349	<u>0.513</u>	<u>0.391</u>	**0.600**	0.379	**0.298**	**0.701**
DLIFT	<u>0.507</u>	0.901	0.085	<u>0.648</u>	<u>0.372</u>	<u>0.576</u>	0.506	0.561	0.431	0.299	0.350	0.659
GCAM	0.496	0.614	0.375	0.492	0.405	0.529	0.370	0.583	0.406	0.375	0.429	0.571
FleX	0.346	<u>0.459</u>	<u>0.534</u>	0.340	0.398	0.546	0.417	**0.387**	<u>0.484</u>	0.261	<u>0.300</u>	**0.701**
FleX*	**0.741**	0.460	0.524	**0.731**	**0.357**	**0.583**	**0.558**	0.521	0.470	<u>0.412</u>	0.386	0.614

Table 5. Experimental results on realistic dataset with instance-level explanation.

Model	Cora			CiteSeer		
	Fidelity+	Fidelity−	EC	Fidelity+	Fidelity−	EC
GNNExplainer	0.097	0.395	0.571	0.031	0.344	0.547
GraphMask	0.190	0.473	0.491	0.174	0.396	0.482
PGExplainer	0.093	0.544	0.421	–	–	–
DeepLIFT	<u>0.554</u>	<u>0.043</u>	**0.947**	<u>0.340</u>	<u>0.040</u>	<u>0.919</u>
GradCAM	0.222	0.337	0.632	0.022	0.331	0.555
FleX	0.209	0.136	0.849	0.165	0.074	0.900
FleX*	**0.603**	**0.029**	<u>0.935</u>	**0.380**	**−0.032**	**1.0**

out performances, FleX consistently outperforms XGNN across most metrics, with improvements ranging from 1% upwards.

A significant distinction between FleX and XGNN lies in their subgraph generation strategies. While XGNN generates subgraphs based on the current graph state and employs reinforcement learning to enhance its inference capabilities, this approach lack the global view of original graph. In contrast, our FleX model is designed to have a comprehensive view of the entire graph context through the adjacency matrix. This holistic perspective enables FleX to generate more accurate and contextually relevant explanations.

We also conducted an evaluation of the explanatory capabilities at the instance level. In this experimental setup, each node in the graph was individually analyzed to determine its unique explanatory subgraph. The results, averaged across various sparsity levels are presented in Tables 4 and 5. We have emphasized the best results in bold and underlined the second-best outcomes.

The experimental results demonstrate that FleX achieves superior performance across most datasets, consistently ranking in the top two positions in our comparative analysis. In contrast, other models typically excel only on specific datasets. This broad-based effectiveness indicates that FleX is versatile and well-suited for application

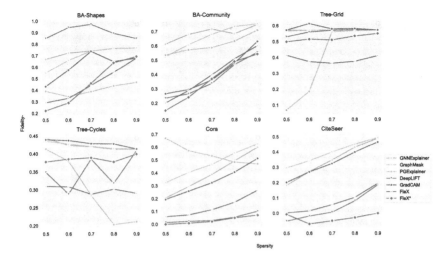

Fig. 4. Comparision of Fidelity− metric on various sparsity level.

across diverse graph datasets. Notably, our proposed model exhibits exceptional performance on the BA-Community dataset. The intrinsic nature of this dataset, comprising two identical graphs, presents a unique challenge: the generated subgraph must not only reflect the model's output but also capture the community information to which each node belongs. FleX's outstanding performance in this context provides strong evidence of its ability to preserve crucial connections within the graph structure.

To provide a more detailed analysis of our model's behavior, we visualized the experimental results using the Fidelity− metric across various sparsity levels. This visualization, presented in Fig. 4, aims to assess the stability and effectiveness of our model as the number of edges pruned in the explanatory subgraph increases.

As sparsity increases, indicating a greater number of edges removed from the graph, the explanatory subgraph's representational capacity diminishes, leading to a gradual decline in model performance. Ideally, a robust explanation model should maintain stability under minor input perturbations. The visualization in Fig. 4 reveals that FleX exhibits relative stability across most datasets, with exceptions in BA-Shape and BA-Community. Notably, our model demonstrates consistent performance on real-world datasets such as Cora and CiteSeer, where most other models, except DeepLIFT, show instability. This stability on complex, real-world data underscores FleX's practical applicability. Furthermore, the results indicate that PGExplainer is the least stable model in this experiment, particularly evident in its performance on Tree-Grid and Tree-Cycles datasets, where the performance curve shows a large slope.

In additionally, we similarly visualized Fidelity+ to evaluate the model's effectiveness on this metric. A notable aspect of FleX* is its nearest-neighbor preservation mechanism, which creates isolated vertices in the masked-out graph across all sparsity levels, resulting in a linear representation. As illustrated in Fig. 5, this strategy yields remarkably high Fidelity+ scores, underscoring the critical role of immediate neighbors in GNN explanations. The GNN mechanism primarily focuses on aggregating features

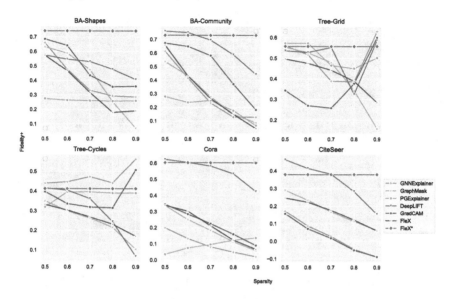

Fig. 5. Model effectiveness on Fidelity+ metric.

from nearby neighbors, and our results strongly suggest that closer neighbors are pivotal in explaining GNN behavior. This finding aligns with the fundamental principles of GNNs, where the most proximate nodes often contribute most significantly representation.

When comparing FleX and FleX*, it is evident that the rebalancing trick significantly enhances the performance of the base FleX model. Specifically, on certain datasets such as BA-Shapes and Cora, this improvement can result in up to a 40% increase in Fidelity+. This performance boost stems from the inherent behavior of the models: FleX faces challenges in determining the optimal node order when deciding which edges to include in the explanation graph. In contrast, FleX* addresses this issue by reconnecting edges that were erroneously removed, thereby improving the overall explanation quality. This suggests that for graph explanation tasks, it is crucial to prioritize edges closer to the target node. However, our current approach retains all edges, which may be unnecessary, as evidenced by the model's marginal performance improvement over GNNExplainer on the Tree-Cycles dataset. This highlights the need for further development of the algorithm to selectively retain only the most critical edges.

5   Conclusion

In this paper, we introduce a novel approach to explaining graph neural networks by identifying critical subgraphs that significantly influence model output. Our methodology employs a distillation model to estimate the loss function between the original model's performance on the full graph and its performance on the explanatory subgraph.

This approach effectively addresses the probability inconsistency issue often encountered when making predictions on subgraphs. Experimental results demonstrate our model's robust performance across a wide range of benchmarks, including both synthetic and real-world datasets. This versatility distinguishes our approach from existing methods that often excel only on specific data types. Notably, our model shows particularly strong performance at low sparsity levels, efficiently capturing essential graph structures with minimal information.

Furthermore, we propose a new hypothesis regarding the significance of nearest neighbors in graph explanations. Preliminary experiments provide compelling evidence for this approach's viability, suggesting its potential to substantially enhance FleX's performance. This finding not only offers a promising direction for advancing graph explanation techniques but also illuminates the fundamental nature of Graph Neural Networks, underscoring the critical role of local structural information in their decision-making processes. Despite these promising results, our model faces challenges, such as performance degradation at higher sparsity levels, which presents opportunities for future research.

However, the model still has numerous parameters that can be optimized to yield superior results. For instance, the proposed rebalancing trick to reconnect critical edges between the target node and its current neighboring vertices is currently fixed. If this algorithm could be expanded to encompass a k-hop neighborhood, it could potentially enhance and improve model performance significantly. Moreover, the current explanatory model can only be effectively evaluated through quantitative metrics, which may sometimes remain abstruse to human interpretation. Therefore, improving the model to generate interpretable ground truths could substantially enhance its explainability.

Acknowledgments. This research is funded by Vietnam National Foundation for Science and Technology Development (NAFOSTED) under grant number 102.05-2023.44.

References

1. Fey, M., Lenssen, J.E.: Fast graph representation learning with PyTorch Geometric. In: ICLR Workshop on Representation Learning on Graphs and Manifolds (2019)
2. Ioffe, S., Szegedy, C.: Batch normalization: accelerating deep network training by reducing internal covariate shift. In: Proceedings of the 32nd International Conference on International Conference on Machine Learning, ICML 2015, vol. 37, pp. 448–456 (2015)
3. Kipf, T.N., Welling, M.: Semi-supervised classification with graph convolutional networks. In: International Conference on Learning Representations (ICLR) (2017)
4. Lee, J., Lee, I., Kang, J.: Self-attention graph pooling. In: Proceedings of the 36th International Conference on Machine Learning (2019)
5. Li, P., Yang, Y., Pagnucco, M., Song, Y.: Explainability in graph neural networks: an experimental survey (2022)
6. Liu, M., et al.: DIG: a turnkey library for diving into graph deep learning research. J. Mach. Learn. Res. **22**(240), 1–9 (2021). http://jmlr.org/papers/v22/21-0343.html
7. Liu, Z., Wan, M., Guo, S., Achan, K., Yu, P.S.: BasConv: aggregating heterogeneous interactions for basket recommendation with graph convolutional neural network. In: Proceedings of the 2020 SIAM International Conference on Data Mining, pp. 64–72 (2020)

8. Luo, D., et al.: Parameterized explainer for graph neural network. In: Advances in Neural Information Processing Systems, vol. 33 (2020)
9. Luo, D., et al.: Towards inductive and efficient explanations for graph neural networks. IEEE Trans. Pattern Anal. Mach. Intell. (2024)
10. Morris, C., et al.: Weisfeiler and leman go neural: higher-order graph neural networks. In: Proceedings of the Thirty-Third AAAI Conference on Artificial Intelligence and Thirty-First Innovative Applications of Artificial Intelligence Conference and Ninth AAAI Symposium on Educational Advances in Artificial Intelligence (2019). https://doi.org/10.1609/aaai.v33i01.33014602
11. Mu, N., Zha, D., He, Y., Tang, Z.: Graph attention networks for neural social recommendation. In: 2019 IEEE 31st International Conference on Tools with Artificial Intelligence (ICTAI), pp. 1320–1327 (2019). https://doi.org/10.1109/ICTAI.2019.00183
12. Pope, P.E., Kolouri, S., Rostami, M., Martin, C.E., Hoffmann, H.: Explainability methods for graph convolutional neural networks. In: 2019 IEEE/CVF Conference on Computer Vision and Pattern Recognition (CVPR), pp. 10764–10773 (2019). https://doi.org/10.1109/CVPR.2019.01103
13. Schlichtkrull, M.S., Cao, N.D., Titov, I.: Interpreting graph neural networks for NLP with differentiable edge masking. In: International Conference on Learning Representations (2021). https://openreview.net/forum?id=WznmQa42ZAx
14. Selvaraju, R.R., Cogswell, M., Das, A., Vedantam, R., Parikh, D., Batra, D.: Grad-CAM: visual explanations from deep networks via gradient-based localization. In: 2017 IEEE International Conference on Computer Vision (ICCV), pp. 618–626 (2017). https://doi.org/10.1109/ICCV.2017.74
15. Shrikumar, A., Greenside, P., Kundaje, A.: Learning important features through propagating activation differences. In: Proceedings of the 34th International Conference on Machine Learning, vol. 70, pp. 3145–3153. JMLR.org (2017)
16. Ulyanov, D., Vedaldi, A., Lempitsky, V.: Instance normalization: the missing ingredient for fast stylization (2017). https://arxiv.org/abs/1607.08022
17. Veličković, P., Cucurull, G., Casanova, A., Romero, A., Liò, P., Bengio, Y.: Graph attention networks. In: International Conference on Learning Representations (2018)
18. Wu, L., Sun, P., Hong, R., Fu, Y., Wang, X., Wang, M.: SocialGCN: an efficient graph convolutional network based model for social recommendation. ArXiv (2018)
19. Yang, C., Liu, J., Shi, C.: Extract the knowledge of graph neural networks and go beyond it: an effective knowledge distillation framework. In: Proceedings of the Web Conference 2021, pp. 1227–1237 (2021). https://doi.org/10.1145/3442381.3450068
20. Yang, Y., Qiu, J., Song, M., Tao, D., Wang, X.: Distilling knowledge from graph convolutional networks. In: 2020 IEEE/CVF Conference on Computer Vision and Pattern Recognition (CVPR), pp. 7072–7081 (2020). https://doi.org/10.1109/CVPR42600.2020.00710
21. Yang, Z., Cohen, W.W., Salakhutdinov, R.: Revisiting semi-supervised learning with graph embeddings. In: Proceedings of the 33rd International Conference on International Conference on Machine Learning, vol. 48, pp. 40–48 (2016)
22. Ying, R., Bourgeois, D., You, J., Zitnik, M., Leskovec, J.: GNNExplainer: generating explanations for graph neural networks. In: Advances in Neural Information Processing Systems, vol. 32, pp. 9240–9251 (2019)
23. You, J., Liu, B., Ying, R., Pande, V., Leskovec, J.: Graph convolutional policy network for goal-directed molecular graph generation. In: Proceedings of the 32nd International Conference on Neural Information Processing Systems, pp. 6412–6422 (2018)
24. Yuan, H., Yu, H., Gui, S., Ji, S.: Explainability in graph neural networks: a taxonomic survey. IEEE Trans. Pattern Anal. Mach. Intell. 5782–5799 (2023). https://doi.org/10.1109/TPAMI.2022.3204236

25. Yuan, H., Tang, J., Hu, X., Ji, S.: XGNN: towards model-level explanations of graph neural networks. In: Proceedings of the 26th ACM SIGKDD International Conference on Knowledge Discovery & Data Mining, pp. 430–438 (2020). https://doi.org/10.1145/3394486.3403085
26. Zitnik, M., Agrawal, M., Leskovec, J.: Modeling polypharmacy side effects with graph convolutional networks. Bioinformatics 457–466 (2018)

Predictive Process Monitoring

Handling Catastrophic Forgetting: Online Continual Learning for Next Activity Prediction

Tamara Verbeek and Marwan Hassani[✉][ID]

Eindhoven University of Technology, Eindhoven, The Netherlands
t.a.m.verbeek@student.tue.nl, m.hassani@tue.nl

Abstract. Predictive business process monitoring focuses on predicting future process trajectories, including next-activity predictions. This is crucial in dynamic environments where processes change or face uncertainty. However, current frameworks often assume a static environment, overlooking dynamic characteristics and concept drifts. This results in *catastrophic forgetting*, where training while focusing merely on new data distribution negatively impacts the performance on previously learned data distributions. Continual learning addresses, among others, the challenges related to mitigating catastrophic forgetting. This paper proposes a novel approach called Continual Next Activity Prediction with Prompts (CNAPwP) which adapts the DualPrompt algorithm for next-activity prediction to improve accuracy and adaptability while mitigating catastrophic forgetting. New datasets with recurring concept drifts are introduced, alongside a task-specific forgetting metric that measures the prediction accuracy gap between initial and subsequent task encounters. Extensive testing on both synthetic and real-world datasets shows that this approach outperforms five competing methods, demonstrating its potential applicability in real-world scenarios. An open source implementation of our method together with datasets and results are available under: https://github.com/TamaraVerbeek/CNAPwP.

Keywords: Process mining · Next-activity prediction · Concept drift · Catastrophic forgetting · Continual learning

1 Introduction

Recent emphasis on predictive process monitoring highlights its critical importance by enabling organizations to predict the future trajectories of individual process instances dynamically [2,3]. Predictive business process monitoring offers decision support that empowers organizations to make adjustments to their processes. In predictive process monitoring, next activity prediction holds significant relevance due to its ability to anticipate and plan for future actions within business processes. This predictive capability enables proactive management of resources, ensuring they are deployed effectively to meet upcoming demands. For example, accurate next activity prediction in customer service enables organizations to plan ahead, optimize resources, and reduce response times, leading to more efficient operations and improved customer satisfaction [23].

Offline predictive process monitoring involves two main phases: training and testing. Performing next activity prediction in an online setting offers distinct advantages over

M. Comuzzi et al. (Eds.): CoopIS 2024, LNCS 15506, pp. 225–242, 2025.
https://doi.org/10.1007/978-3-031-81375-7_13

offline methods. In an online environment, predictive models continuously learn and adapt in real-time as new data streams in, more accurately reflecting the current state of operations. This dynamic approach allows organizations to respond swiftly to changing conditions and optimize processes continuously, whereas offline methods typically rely on static datasets that may not capture evolving patterns and trends effectively [6,9,23].

A significant challenge in online next activity prediction arises from adapting to new concepts following shifts in data distribution. While real-time model updates enable responsiveness to evolving trends and operational changes, they also introduce the risk of *catastrophic forgetting* [8]. This phenomenon occurs when the prediction model overwrites previously learned information with a new data distribution, potentially leading to a loss of accuracy or reliability in predicting next activities when refacing previously learned data distributions. Balancing dynamic model updates with the retention of critical historical knowledge is crucial, especially given constraints such as storage limitations and privacy concerns that prevent organizations from retaining all historical data indefinitely. Developing robust online prediction models requires efficient use of historical data while integrating new information. In process mining, recurring drifts from factors such as seasonal changes or shifts in customer behavior make it essential to prevent catastrophic forgetting. Neglecting recurring tasks would compromise the model's long-term performance.

Only recently algorithms have been developed for online predictive process monitoring [7] and specifically for online next activity prediction [9,23]. In contrast, numerous algorithms already exist for online image classification that avoid catastrophic forgetting, including [8,17,21,22]. By leveraging the techniques utilized in such algorithms, there is potential to create high-performance online next activity prediction models for this purpose. Unlike independent data points in classification, next activity prediction requires capturing temporal dependencies, which presents unique challenges.

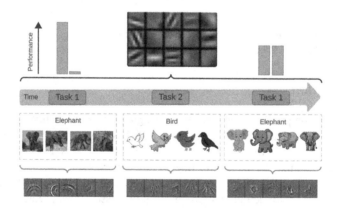

Fig. 1. A continual learning setup where two tasks are sequentially learned. The second appearance of Task 1 implies a domain change from photographs to drawings.

Continual learning, also known as lifelong learning, plays a crucial role in enhancing the effectiveness of online prediction models. This concept facilitates the retention of previously learned information while integrating new insights, thereby maintaining a comprehensive understanding of the data distribution landscape. By leveraging task-specific and task-invariant features, continual learning helps to mitigate catastrophic forgetting. Figure 1 illustrates a stream of animal image classification tasks. Initially, the model classifies elephant photographs, followed by a task classifying bird drawings. Typically, an online model forgets how to classify elephants when switching to birds. In the performance depicted for the occurrences of *Task 1*, we observe a decline after learning *Task 2* when the model is compelled to deal again with the first task. However, by identifying task-invariant features, such as distinguishing between photographs and drawings, we have the potential to preserve valuable information for the subsequent reappearance of the initial task, for instance when involving elephants depicted in drawings. By understanding the distinctions between photographs and drawings and incorporating task-specific insights about elephants, we improve the model's ability to classify representations of elephants in drawings accurately. These features can be incorporated as prompts. A prompt is an additional piece of information provided to the model to guide its learning or inference process. By using prompts that highlight task-specific and task-invariant features, we can maintain the contextual knowledge necessary for effectively addressing evolving tasks, ensuring continued success in classification, particularly when faced with domain shifts in a task.

In this paper, we propose a framework called Continual Next-Activity Prediction with Prompts (CNAPwP) with components for handling temporal dependencies, capturing long-term patterns, and incorporating memory and context into the learning process. The key contributions of this work include: (i) introducing an innovative framework that combines general and expert prompts for dynamic adaptation and learning from streaming data, (ii) developing the "task-specific forgetting" evaluation metric to assess the retention and the degradation of task-specific knowledge, (iii) creating new datasets that are specifically tailored for evaluating online predictive process monitoring, and, (iv) conducting a comprehensive experimental evaluation which demonstrates that CNAPwP significantly outperforms existing methods in dynamic environments.

The remainder of this paper is structured as follows: in Sect. 2, we review related literature; in Sect. 3, we explain foundational concepts and define the problem; in Sect. 4, we present our framework; in Sect. 5, we discuss evaluation criteria and analyze results; and finally, we conclude with remarks in Sect. 6.

2 Related Work

At its core, continual learning seeks to equip machine learning models with the ability to continuously learn and adapt over time, similar to how humans acquire and refine knowledge throughout their lives. Within this framework, researchers have explored various methodologies, each offering unique perspectives and strategies. These approaches include memory-based, architecture-based, regularization-based, and prompt-based methods.

Memory-based approaches, inspired by human cognition and memory systems, focus on storing and retrieving past experiences or knowledge. These methods can be broadly classified into two categories. The first involves retaining actual past experiences, as demonstrated by techniques such as Experience Replay [17], iCaRL [16],

DynaTrainCDD [9], Maximally Interfered Retrieval [15], and Gradient Episodic Memory [12]. The second category, on the other hand, generates past experiences during training, with Generative Replay [10] serving as a key example.

Regularization-based methods aim to prevent catastrophic forgetting by constraining weight updates during training. This constraint is typically achieved by evaluating the importance of each parameter for previously learned tasks. For example, Elastic Weight Consolidation [8] determines parameter significance, while Synaptic Intelligence [24] imposes penalties during the training of new tasks to preserve essential knowledge. Alternatively, the importance of parameters can be assessed based on their impact on output sensitivity, with selective penalties applied to critical parameters to mitigate forgetting, as seen in Learning without Forgetting [11].

Architecture-based approaches prioritize adjusting the neural network's structure to integrate new data while preserving existing knowledge. One approach involves dynamic architectures, which expand the network by adding more neurons or layers for each task. This allows the model to continuously grow and adapt without forgetting previous knowledge, as exemplified by methods such as Progressive Neural Networks [18] and Dynamic Neural Networks [5].

Prompt-based approaches, a more recent addition to the continuum, introduce a novel perspective on continual learning challenges. These methods entail attaching static or adaptable "instructions", also referred to as prompts, to direct the model's behavior. These prompts can take various forms, such as specific input patterns, embeddings, or task-specific tokens, and they help the model recall and apply knowledge from earlier tasks. Examples of prompt-based approaches include Learning to Prompt [22] and DualPrompt [21].

We will delve deeper into DualPrompt [21], since our approach adopts a modified version of it. DualPrompt is a continual image classification method, inspired by prompting techniques commonly used in natural language processing to guide models toward desired results [21]. This approach is particularly useful for sequence-like data, as it helps the model understand the underlying structure and the relationships within the sequences. It comprises two key components: G-Prompt and E-Prompt, which learn task-invariant and task-specific knowledge, respectively. The architecture of Dual-Prompt involves multiple Multi-Head Self-Attention (MSA) layers, with G-Prompt and E-Prompt integrated into these layers. The **G-Prompt** is a shared parameter for all tasks, applied during both training and testing to capture general knowledge. The **E-Prompt** on the other hand contains a set of task-specific parameters, each linked to a learnable key representing the task's unique features. These prompts are strategically attached to different layers of the model, with G-Prompt typically at shallower layers and E-Prompt at deeper layers. This setup leverages the varying levels of feature abstraction in the layers. Two prompting functions can be used to combine the prompts with embedding features. In **Prompt Tuning**, prompts are attached to the input tokens of each layer, increasing the output length. In **Prefix Tuning**, the prompt is split and attached to specific tokens, maintaining the same output length as the input. During inference, an input is transformed to identify the closest task key and the associated E-Prompt using cosine similarity. The shared G-Prompt and matched E-Prompt are then attached to multiple MSA layers to produce the model's output. During training, the E-Prompt and G-Prompt are jointly trained with the classifier based on the task identity.

TFCLPM [20] is the first continual learning model specifically designed for predictive process mining. It utilizes a memory-based approach to store hard samples and a dynamic loss to predict next activities while mitigating catastrophic forgetting.

Outside continual learning, innovative methodologies have emerged in offline next-event prediction. The state of the art in offline next-activity prediction is evolving through advancements in deep learning architectures, attention mechanisms, hybrid modeling approaches, and the integration of Generative Adversarial Networks (GANs), enhancing sequence generation and capturing complex temporal dependencies [19]. Studies explore incremental techniques to update predictive models with new process execution data. Pauwels et al. [14] compare various update strategies, including retraining with and without hyperoptimization and incremental updates, demonstrating the effectiveness of incremental updates in maintaining model quality while offering real-time adaptability.

To efficiently store traces, prefix trees [6] offer a robust solution. These trees, represented as simple graphs, organize event sequences efficiently, with each node representing an event and edges connecting sequential events. As events occur, nodes are either created or their frequencies updated, capturing unique event sequences for individual cases.

3 Preliminaries and Problem Formulation

In this section we delve into formulating the problem of utilizing continual learning in process prediction. We aim to develop an algorithm that continuously processes an event stream $S = \{e_1, e_2, ...\}$ as events are generated, where an event $e = (c, a, t, v_1, ..., v_A)$ is a tuple of case identifier c, activity label a, timestamp t, and the values of other event attributes $v_1, ..., v_A$. A case refers to a single instance of the process being analyzed or executed, encompassing all events, their attributes, and contextual information associated with that instance. A trace $\sigma^{(i)} = \langle e_{1i}, ..., e_{ni} \rangle$ denotes any finite sequence over the set of all events. Without loss of generality and since we are dealing merely with event logs, the terms trace and case are used interchangeably in the remainder of the paper and refer to the sequence of activities within the instance. A stream S contains multiple traces.

Given $\sigma^{(i)}$, the prefix represents the sequence of activities executed up to a certain point in a trace's lifecycle. The prefix of length k is defined by $\sigma_{\leq k}^{(i)} = \langle e_{1i}, ..., e_{ki} \rangle$. On the other hand, a suffix refers to the part of a trace that occurs after a particular event in that trace. Given $\sigma^{(i)}$, the suffix of events of length k is defined by $\sigma_{>n-k}^{(i)} = \langle e_{(n-k)i}, ..., e_{ni} \rangle$. For each event e that occurs in stream S, we want to predict the next activity name of event $e_{(k+1)i}$ happening at the beginning of suffix $\sigma_{>n-k}^{(i)}$ based on the prefix $\sigma_{\leq k}^{(i)}$.

Definition 1 (Next activity prediction). *Let there be a sample of prefixes of sequences* $\mathcal{P} = \{\sigma_{\leq k}^{(i)}\}_{i=1}^{i=m}$ *where* $2 \leq k < |\sigma^{(i)}|$ *is the prefix length and* m *is the sample size.*

Given a prefix of an events sequence $\sigma_{\leq k}^{(i)}$, the next activity prediction is $\hat{a}_{(k+1)i}$ of activity $a_{(k+1)i}$ happening at the beginning of suffix $\sigma_{>n-k}^{(i)}$.

To continuously predict the next activity in a stream, we must engage in online next activity prediction.

Definition 2 (Online Next Activity Prediction). *Assume we aim to perform ongoing predictions of the next activity on a stream of events. Upon the arrival of each new event e_{ki}, we continuously utilize the prefix $\sigma_{\leq k}^{(i)}$ to predict the subsequent activity $a_{(k+1)i}$.*

A stream S encompasses multiple learning tasks, each having several traces.

Definition 3 (Learning Task). *A model will learn a learning task $\mathcal{T}_n$ with a corresponding dataset $\mathcal{D}_n$ for $n \in [1, ..., \mathcal{N}]$ where $\mathcal{N}$ is the number of learning tasks. Let $\mathcal{T}_p$ and $\mathcal{T}_r$ represent two distinct learning tasks, where $p \neq r$. This indicates that $\mathcal{T}_p$ and $\mathcal{T}_r$ belong to different processes or data, implying there is no relationship between these learning tasks.*

In the context of a stream of events involving multiple learning tasks, the distribution evolves over time, necessitating continuous updates to the prediction model. Within a learning task, the domain may change. In such cases, we seek a prediction model that can adapt to this shift, enabling domain incremental learning.

Definition 4 (Domain Incremental Learning). *In domain incremental learning, all tasks share the same set of outputs $\mathcal{Y}$, i.e., $\mathcal{Y}_n = \mathcal{Y}_1 \forall n \in \mathcal{N}$. The objective is to learn all tasks while the joint probability between input and output changes.*

Domain incremental learning focuses on adapting the prediction model to variations within the same task. However, in many scenarios, the model must also handle entirely new tasks that are distinct from previously encountered ones. This necessitates a special form of incremental learning, known as *task* incremental learning.

Definition 5 (Task Incremental Learning). *In task incremental learning, two tasks $\mathcal{T}_n, \mathcal{T}_m$ where $n, m \in [1, ..., \mathcal{N}]$ have no correspondence to each other if $n \neq m$. Each task has unique objectives and is associated with a separate process, necessitating the model to acquire new patterns, features, or behaviors.*

Changes in the domain and the emergence of new tasks both result from concept drifts.

Definition 6 (Concept Drift [4]). *A concept drift between timestamps t_0 and t_1 is defined as $\exists X : p_{t_0}(X, y) \neq p_{t_1}(X, y)$ where p_{t_0} denotes the joint distribution at time t_0 between the set of input variables X and the target variable y.*

A task repeating multiple times is called a recurrent concept drift.

Definition 7 (Recurrent Concept Drifts). *A recurrent concept drift implies repeated changes in tasks, with the possibility of cycles that bring the system back to the original task.*

When updating the model after a concept drift, the goal is to utilize as much data as possible. If a task reappears, it is advantageous to have stored data about this task, ensuring that it is not forgotten. However, this poses challenges such as storage limitations or privacy concerns. This often prevents keeping all past data, but relying only on recent data introduces bias and causes catastrophic forgetting [1].

Definition 8 (Catastrophic Forgetting [8]). *Let there be a model at any point in time that has learned a sequence of T learning tasks. When faced with the $(T + 1)$th task, the model tends to forget how to predict the next activities of the T previously learned tasks.*

This phenomenon poses a significant challenge in dynamic environments. To address the issue of catastrophic forgetting, continual learning enables models to retain and incorporate knowledge from previous tasks while learning new ones.

Definition 9 (Continual Learning [9]). *Let there be a model at any point in time that has learned a sequence of T learning tasks. When faced with the $(T + 1)$th task, the model can leverage the past knowledge in the knowledge base to help learn this task. The objective is to optimize the performance of the new task while minimizing the decrease in performance on the previous tasks.*

By compiling the definitions, we arrive at the following definition for a continual learning algorithm used to predict the next activity.

Definition 10 (Continual Learning for Next Activity Prediction). *Consider a model that has learned to predict the next activities for an event stream S. Throughout S, concept drifts may occur which refer to the alteration in the learning task. The event stream contains a sequence of T learning tasks. A learning task for next activity prediction is defined by a sample of prefixes of sequences P. Given a prefix of an events sequence $\sigma_{\leq k}^{(i)}$, the model has to predict the activity $\hat{a}_{(k+1)i}$ occurring at the beginning of the suffix $\sigma_{>n-k}^{(i)}$.*
When presented with the $(T + 1)$th task, the model must accurately predict the activities for this new task without suffering from catastrophic forgetting.

The solution to the challenges of continual learning in process prediction models must meet several key requirements. Firstly, it should efficiently utilize an input event stream S consisting of multiple learning tasks T, as defined in Definition 3, and predict next activities accurately in near-real-time, as described in Definition 2. Secondly, the solution should accommodate both domain and task incremental learning, mentioned in Definitions 4 and 5, respectively, allowing for seamless integration of shifts in the domain and the emergence of new tasks. Additionally, the solution must exhibit the capability to perform next activity predictions while remaining robust to concept drifts, mentioned in Definition 6. Moreover, the solution should aim to reduce catastrophic forgetting, as defined in Definition 8, particularly when tasks recur in the stream, as defined in Definition 7. In essence, the algorithm should incorporate continual learning for predicting next activities, as defined in Definition 10.

4   Continual Next-Activity Prediction with Prompts (CNAPwP)

In the section, we provide an overview of the CNAPwP architecture by detailing its components. The implementation is available on github[1]. Figure 2 shows the framework architecture for training and testing the prediction model.

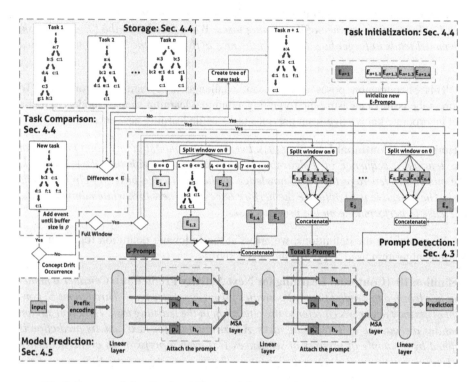

Fig. 2. Framework for Continual Next-Activity Prediction with Prompts (CNAPwP).

4.1   Preprocessing

Preprocessing involves **initial data reduction**, where unnecessary columns are removed from the event log to reduce noise, focusing on essential attributes such as case, event, resource, and completion time. If events are missing key attributes, the corresponding cases are excluded from the dataset. Attributes representing the resource should be retained if present. Next, **data is ordered chronologically** to represent a real-time data stream, and afterward, the completion time attribute is deleted. Next, for each new event, **a prefix is generated**. The approach checks whether the case has appeared within the window of events. If the case is found and there are sufficient events to match the prefix size, the prefix is formed. If there are insufficient events, the prefix is padded with "None" values. If the case is new and not previously encountered, a prefix composed entirely of "None" values is created. Once the prefix is defined, the next activity

---

[1] https://github.com/TamaraVerbeek/CNAPwP.

is assigned as the new event. Events outside the defined window are disregarded in this process. After generating the prefixes, the next step involves **encoding** both the prefix and the next activity. The prefix is one-hot encoded, generating sparse input vectors that are effective for handling high-dimensional categorical data, whereas the next activity is ordinally encoded, offering a compact and efficient representation.

4.2   Window Handling

The process starts by importing an event log and extracting key attributes necessary for predicting the next activity. These attributes are converted into a continuous event flow, transmitting events until the entire log is analyzed. Events are sequenced by activity completion order, allowing new cases to begin while others are still ongoing. As each event arrives, it is added to a dynamic window that accumulates events until it reaches its capacity, defined by γ. The optimal value of this parameter is established based on the experiment outlined in Sect. 5.4. Once full, the window operates on a 'first-in, first-out' basis, maintaining a consistent size to manage the sequence of events effectively.

4.3   Window Updating and Prompt Detection

When γ events accumulate, an update is initiated, as depicted in the green segment of Fig. 2. This ensures the model remains current with the evolving event stream, maintaining a dynamic framework ready to process new events seamlessly. After accumulating γ events, the data is partitioned into buckets based on prefix lengths θ. Each bucket represents a specific range of prefix lengths, ensuring a uniform distribution. Figure 2 illustrates that there are four buckets, with the first containing solely empty prefixes and the second containing prefixes ranging in length from 1 to 3, for example. During initialization, bucket ranges are selected based on optimal values. Data of a specific prefix length is added to buckets until a significant discrepancy occurs, ensuring each bucket has a comparable number of values. With the window data segmented into buckets, the next phase updates all method parameters, including the G-Prompt, the bucket-specific E-Prompts, the task-specific E-Prompt, and the model weights. Data is batched by bucket, with each batch containing data from a single bucket. Data from each bucket is used solely for updating the parameters within its corresponding bucket-specific E-Prompt. The task-specific E-Prompt, G-Prompt, and weights receive updates across all batches. The cross-entropy loss is used for updating the weights and parameters of the G-Prompt and E-Prompt:

$$\text{CrossEntropyLoss} = -\sum_{i=1}^{N} y_i \log(\hat{y}_i) \tag{1}$$

where N is the number of classes, y_i and $\hat{y}_i$ are the true and predicted probabilities for class i, respectively. Both the G-Prompt and E-Prompt are concatenated with the model to facilitate these targeted updates. An ablation study experiment, detailed in Sect. 5.5, is conducted to validate the use of both the G-Prompt and E-Prompt.

4.4 Concept Drift Detection

Routine weight and parameter updates continue until a concept drift is detected. CNAPwP assumes these shifts are anticipated, triggering a task recognition mechanism upon encountering a drift index. After a concept drift, a specified number of events ρ is stored in a prefix tree, as depicted in the yellow segment of Fig. 2. The optimal value of ρ is established through an experiment outlined in Sect. 5.4. The prefix tree of the new task is compared with the prefix trees of stored tasks, as shown in the purple section of Fig. 2. The comparison focuses on identifying overlaps and unique sequences between them. A high degree of overlap and fewer unique sequences in the new task's prefix tree indicate greater similarity between the trees. A dissimilarity ratio is then calculated to measure how distinct the tasks are, with the lowest ratio indicating the stored task most similar to the new task. For each dataset, an $\mathcal{E}$ value is established according to the dissimilarity between its constituent tasks. If the similarity between the new task and any of the stored tasks is less than $\mathcal{E}$, the model will utilize the E-Prompts associated with that task. The optimal value for $\mathcal{E}$ for each dataset is determined in an experiment outlined in Sect. 5.4.

If none of the stored tasks are similar to the new task, our model does not overfit to only previously seen tasks and, as such, initializes parameters for the new task, as depicted in the pink segment of Fig. 2. This involves setting up the E-Prompt parameters for the new task and each bucket, which are initialized randomly. A new prefix tree is also created to characterize the task and is stored together with the tasks already in storage. As events stream in, they are added to the prefix tree until it reaches 500 events, enough to capture the task's essence for future comparisons.

4.5 Prediction Model

A Multi-Head Self-Attention mechanism is utilized for next activity predictions. The Multi-Head Self-Attention mechanism enhances next activity prediction by capturing complex dependencies and relationships between events, allowing the model to weigh the significance of past activities effectively. This approach enables the model to handle variable-length sequences efficiently while extracting diverse features, leading to more accurate predictions based on historical patterns. The prediction model of the approach is depicted in the blue segment of Fig. 2.

The prefix of each input event from the event stream is used as the model input. During preprocessing, each event's prefix is converted into a one-hot encoded array with dimensions $[k, num\_events]$, where k is the prefix length and num_events is the number of distinct events. Therefore, the encoded prefix of the event is initially determined. Subsequently, this encoded prefix undergoes a series of layers, ultimately resulting in a prediction of the next activity. The model consists of duplicated linear layers and Multi-Head Self-Attention layers. Linear layers take inputs of size $input\_size$ and produce outputs of $3 \times input\_size$, allowing prompt attachment via Prefix Tuning. For further details on Prefix Tuning, please refer to [21]. These outputs are then processed by a Multi-Head Self-Attention layer with softmax activation and dropout regularization. Outputs from the Multi-Head Self-Attention layers feed into a dense layer with matching input and output sizes, equivalent to the number of events times the prefix length.

Finally, the output passes through a softmax layer, converting it into a probability distribution over possible activities. The activity with the highest probability is predicted as the next activity.

During inference, the G-Prompt and E-Prompt are appended to the input of the Multi-Head Self-Attention layers. The G-Prompt remains consistent across all inputs, while the E-Prompt is determined by the task recognition mechanism. The task linked with the input event is identifiable due to the mechanism activated after a concept drift, as explained in Sect. 4.4. The bucket-specific E-Prompt is chosen based on the prefix size σ of the input event. This bucket-specific E-Prompt is combined with the task-specific E-Prompt and applied to the input using a designated prompting function, such as Prefix Tuning. The justification of selecting the prompting function is based on the related experiment described in Sect. 5.4.

5 Experimental Evaluation

5.1 Evaluation Metrics

Typically, studies rely on metrics such as accuracy and running time to assess performance. However, these metrics often fall short of capturing the longitudinal performance of our model, which can vary significantly over time. We will explore alternative evaluation metrics that offer a more nuanced understanding of our model's performance dynamics over extended periods.

Accuracy at a given event index is a performance metric used to assess the effectiveness of a predictive model at a specific position within the sequence of events. In mathematical terms, if we denote γ as the size of the average accuracy window, and $\hat{y}_j$ as the predicted activity label of an event at index j based on preceding events, with y_j representing the actual activity at index j, the accuracy at index i can be expressed as:

$$accuracy_i = \frac{1}{\gamma} \sum_{j=i-\gamma}^{i} 1\{\hat{y}_j = y_j\}. \qquad (2)$$

The formula computes the ratio of correct predictions from j up to event index i, averaging the predictions in the window.

Average accuracy is calculated by averaging across all events to determine if each activity is predicted correctly. To calculate the average accuracy, we have the following formula:

$$accuracy = \frac{1}{\mathcal{N}} \sum_{j=0}^{\mathcal{N}} 1\{\hat{y}_j = y_j\}. \qquad (3)$$

where $\mathcal{N}$ is the total number of events in the stream. In both cases, $1\{\cdot\}$ denotes the indicator function, yielding 1 if its argument holds and 0 otherwise.

Task-specific forgetting is the difference in the accuracy of predictions when the task is encountered for the first time compared to the accuracy during subsequent encounters. For each task and each appearance of a task, we compute the following:

$$task\_accuracy(n, a) = \mathcal{R}_{t_n, t_{n1}} - \mathcal{R}_{t_n, t_{na}}. \qquad (4)$$

236 T. Verbeek and M. Hassani

where n is the task, $\mathcal{R}_{t_n, t_{ni}}$ is the accuracy of task t_n after encountering it for the ith time, and $a > 1$ is the appearance of the subsequent task, except for the first task.

The **running time** is computed by taking the difference between the end time and the start time.

5.2 The Datasets

We provide an overview of the datasets utilized in our study, comprising a diverse selection of both real-world and synthetic datasets.

To generate sudden concept drift datasets, the following scheme was employed: for each concept, $\mathcal{N}$ examples are sampled. The samples of each concept are concatenated to form a new event log, alternating between the concepts. Consequently, a sudden concept drift is introduced at every $\mathcal{N}$ events.

To replicate the occurrence of a drift in a log, the authors of [13] created a reference set of 72 event logs by modifying various parameters. They systematically modified a base model by applying one of twelve simple change patterns. Using the Business Process Drift data, three datasets were generated, each with different lengths and characteristics. The first dataset, RandomTasks, consists of seven distinct tasks arranged in batches without any specific order. Each batch contains all tasks, and the entire dataset is made up of four batches, totaling $80,406$ events. The second dataset, ImbalancedTasks, includes four tasks that occur with varying frequencies, with each task appearing between one and four times, totaling $30,754$ events. The third dataset, RecurrentTasks, features four distinct tasks that recur within the same loop multiple times, totaling $100,739$ events.

Moreover, we utilize a real dataset called Recurrent BPIC2015, which is a recurrent dataset generated from actual data collected across five different municipalities. Each task within BPIC2015 corresponds to data from a specific municipality. This recurrent BPIC2015 dataset comprises $32,016$ events.

5.3 The Competitors

The model's performance is compared against five competitors, including two baseline methods: Landmark and Incremental Update (w = Last Drift). In the **Landmark** approach [14], the model retrains from scratch with each new data window. In the **Incremental Updating (w = Last Drift)** approach [14], the model updates based on historical data up to the last observed concept drift.

In addition to these, three state-of-the-art methods are used as competitors. The method **DynaTrainCDD** [9] distinguishes itself through its advanced concept drift detection algorithm called PrefixTreeCDD. It continually monitors process data for deviations and utilizes Prefix Trees to represent and analyze process sequences efficiently. These detected drifts dynamically dictate the frequency of updates and the selection of datasets for retraining. **TFCLPM** [20] dynamically updates its model based on a retraining dataset that combines recent events with hard samples. It is processed through a Single Dense Layer model using a dynamic loss function that incorporates Mean Squared Error and Memory Aware Synapses to mitigate significant parameter changes. The approach using **GANs** [19] is constructed upon the principle of establishing a competitive game between two entities, each represented by a Recurrent Neural Network (RNN). Throughout the training process, one player gradually learns to generate event sequences that closely resemble those observed in the training data, while the other player evaluates the realism of this prediction.

To ensure a fair comparison, all approaches are adapted into a multi-layer self-attention model. Additionally, the model in the GAN-based approach is initially trained on 500 events and then continuously updated with each new window of events.

5.4 Parameter Selection

Three parameters are fine-tuned for CNAPwP. The `window_size` specifies the dimensions of the window, the `buffer_size` denotes the capacity of the buffer, and the `threshold` sets the criteria for deciding whether new data pertains to an existing task or necessitates the initialization of a new task. All parameter configurations are assessed by measuring the average accuracy of the resulting predictions and the running time. Table 1 lists the parameter values that yielded the best performance.

Table 1. The final parameter settings for all datasets.

Dataset	window_size γ	buffer_size ρ	threshold ε
RandomTasks	250	100	0.5
ImbalancedTasks	500	100	0.6
RecurrentTasks	250	150	0.6
Recurrent BPIC2015	250	100	0.8

5.5 Ablation Study

To confirm the effectiveness of using both the E- and G-prompts, an ablation study compares the average accuracy on the `RecurrentTasks` dataset under four conditions: using only the E-prompt, using only the G-prompt, using neither prompt, and using both prompts (CNAPwP). For the baseline with no prompts, a model is trained on the initial 500 events, after which its layer weights are frozen, leaving only the classification head trainable.

Table 2. Average accuracy value for each condition on the `RecurrentTasks` dataset.

Condition	CNAPwP	E-Prompt	G-Prompt	No Prompt
Average Accuracy	**78.90%**	77.30%	77.07%	70.86%

Table 2 displays the accuracy values for the four distinct conditions. The condition employing both the E- and G-prompts achieves the highest accuracy on the `RecurrentTasks` dataset. From this, we can conclude that using both prompts yields the best results.

Prompting Function. The original DualPrompt study compared two prompting functions: Prefix Tuning and Prompt Tuning [21]. We compared average accuracy and running time for each dataset and prompting function. Prefix Tuning generally had higher accuracy and lower running time. Consequently, Prefix Tuning was chosen for all further experiments.

5.6　Results

Table 3 provides a comprehensive overview of the average accuracies across all datasets and methods.

Table 3. Average accuracy and standard deviation (after 5 runs of each method over each dataset). **Bold** indicates the highest accuracy, *italic* indicates the second-highest accuracy, and underlined indicates the third-highest accuracy.

Method	Dataset			
	RandomTasks	ImbalancedTasks	Recurrent BPIC2015	RecurrentTasks
CNAPwP (Ours)	**81.33%** ± 0.39	79.66% ± 0.71	*66.18%* ± 0.31	**78.90%** ± 0.24
DynaTrainCDD [9]	74.65% ± 0.45	75.79% ± 0.63	54.27% ± 0.68	73.06% ± 0.40
TFCLPM [20]	79.50% ± 0.12	**81.71** ± 0.44	65.50 ± 0.16	*78.10* ± 0.08
GAN method [19]	73.94% ± 0.12	70.37% ± 0.43	60.41% ± 0.49	69.44% ± 0.09
Landmark [14]	*79.97%* ± 0.71	79.55% ± 0.66	**67.00%** ± 0.55	77.99% ± 0.20
Last drift [14]	75.97% ± 0.14	74.54% ± 0.75	57.01% ± 0.41	72.70% ± 0.20

The `ImbalancedTasks` dataset aims to investigate whether the frequency of task occurrences affects the method's performance. Table 3 shows that TFCLPM outperforms all other methods with a notably higher average accuracy, demonstrating its effectiveness in scenarios with few tasks and no specific order. CNAPwP follows in second place, indicating an improvement over DynaTrainCDD and the GAN method. However, in Fig. 3 it shows that the frequency of task occurrences might influence the results for all approaches. In the figures illustrating accuracy by event index, each color represents a distinct task, highlighting both the number of tasks and their frequency of occurrence. Initially, all methods exhibit decreased accuracy upon task changes. Subsequently, none of the methods recover the high accuracy observed during the initial tasks, implying a loss of information from Tasks 1, 2, and 3. Task 4 notably impacts the methods, resulting in decreased performance for subsequent occurrences. TFCLPM initially achieves a higher accuracy than the other methods for the first three tasks but ultimately also declines to a lower accuracy. Thus, even though the average accuracy is the highest, the accuracies per event index are not significantly higher after the fourth task is introduced. CNAPwP demonstrates effective adaptation to changing tasks and maintains robust performance across tasks, with fewer accuracy drops compared to other methods.

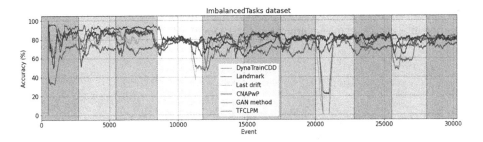

Fig. 3. The accuracy per event for all methods on the ImbalancedTasks dataset.

In Table 3, we observe that CNAPwP maintains the highest accuracy among all methods for the RecurrentTasks and the RandomTasks dataset. In Fig. 4 and Fig. 5, it can be seen that initially, the Last Drift method consistently shows the lowest accuracy declines upon task changes. DynaTrainCDD experiences milder drops in accuracy, but its recovery time is longer compared to CNAPwP. Although CNAPwP occasionally encounters minor accuracy decreases after task changes, it consistently recovers swiftly. The Landmark method manages to prevent accuracy drops following task changes. The method using GANs exhibits better performance on the RecurrentTasks dataset compared to other datasets, but it still faces challenges

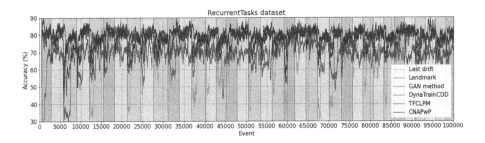

Fig. 4. The accuracy per event for all methods on the RecurrentTasks dataset.

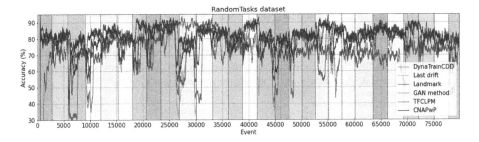

Fig. 5. The accuracy per event for all methods on the RandomTasks dataset.

after initialization. However, when it comes to the RandomTasks dataset, we observe a decline in accuracy as the occurrences of tasks increases.

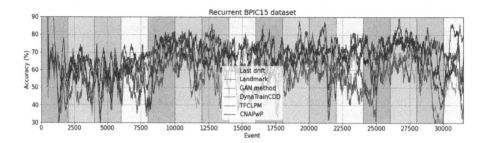

Fig. 6. The accuracy per event for all methods on the Recurrent BPIC2015 dataset.

Table 3 highlights the challenges encountered by all methods when applied to the Recurrent BPIC2015 dataset, which is known for its complexity with 181 unique events. This complexity poses a significant challenge to accurately predict the next activities. All methods take considerable time to achieve approximately 80% accuracy, a benchmark reached by other datasets. The Landmark method achieves the highest accuracy on this dataset, with CNAPwP closely following. In Fig. 6, it is evident that none of the methods maintain stable accuracy throughout the dataset; instead, they exhibit fluctuations following task changes and also during task execution. All methods perform comparably until the reintroduction of previously learned tasks, whereupon there is a noticeable increase in accuracy across all methods with the recurrence of Task 1.

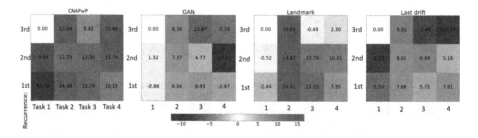

Fig. 7. The task-specific difference in the performance of four methods on the Recurrent BPIC2015 dataset for three recurrences w.r.t. the accuracy of the task first appearance. The x-axis contains the task id, and the y-axis contains the recurrence of each task.

In Fig. 7, task-specific difference in performance is illustrated. In this figure, it can be seen that after the initial occurrences of Tasks 2, 3, and 4, we observe significant increases in delta values for CNAPwP and Landmark. While the accuracy generally decreases for Task 1 across all methods during the data stream, CNAPwP is the only method where accuracy consistently improves for each subsequent task occurrence.

Table 4. Processing time per event and standard deviation after 5 runs of each method over each dataset (in milliseconds).

Method	Dataset			
	RandomTasks	ImbalancedTasks	Recurrent BPIC15	RecurrentTasks
CNAPwP (Ours)	3.29 ± 2.13	2.98 ± 1.42	25.04 ± 1.76	3.16 ± 2.34
DynaTrainCDD [9]	$\mathbf{2.06} \pm 1.24$	$\mathbf{1.90} \pm 1.37$	$\mathbf{9.13} \pm 1.84$	$\mathbf{2.45} \pm 0.87$
GAN [19]	5.08 ± 2.15	5.22 ± 2.79	22.50 ± 1.38	5.23 ± 1.95
Landmark [14]	63.85 ± 6.47	18.45 ± 8.32	229.25 ± 7.68	33.98 ± 9.13
Last drift [14]	3.03 ± 1.96	2.41 ± 1.52	21.26 ± 1.43	2.62 ± 0.93
TFCLPM [20]	2.23 ± 2.31	4.62 ± 2.65	12.14 ± 3.12	2.81 ± 1.72

To assess the feasibility of our approach for real-time implementation, we can calculate the processing time for each event, shown in Table 4. DynaTrainCDD consistently demonstrates the lowest running time per event across all datasets. Generally, CNAPwP does not emerge as the fastest method. The more complex the dataset, the longer CNAPwP takes to execute. Nevertheless, the processing time per event remains relatively low, keeping the approach close to real-time performance.

6 Conclusion and Outlook

In this work, we propose CNAPwP, a novel approach for continual next-activity prediction aimed at mitigating catastrophic forgetting. We evaluated its performance using various metrics, including a novel measure called task-specific forgetting, which quantifies the method's memory retention. Experiments conducted on several datasets indicated that CNAPwP achieves the highest average accuracy on two of the four datasets. In one dataset, it ranks second, with Landmark performing the best but being highly inefficient. Therefore, CNAPwP is still regarded as the superior option. Furthermore, analyses of accuracy per event index and task-specific forgetting indicate that our approach exhibits minimal forgetting compared to alternative methods.

Detecting the concept drifts was outside the scope of the paper. In the future, it is crucial to explore areas such as integrating a robust concept drift detection mechanism, possibly for both sudden and gradual drifts. Additionally, exploring alternative methods for task comparison might offer sharper, faster and more efficient way of the task similarity detection part.

References

1. Chrysakis, A., Moens, M.F.: Online continual learning from imbalanced data. In: International Conference on Machine Learning, pp. 1952–1961. PMLR (2020)
2. Feldman, Z., Fournier, F., Franklin, R., Metzger, A.: Proactive event processing in action: a case study on the proactive management of transport processes. In: DEBS, pp. 97–106 (2013)

3. Ferilli, S., Angelastro, S.: Activity prediction in process mining using the WoMan framework. J. Intell. Inf. Syst. **53**(1), 93–112 (2019). https://doi.org/10.1007/s10844-019-00543-2

4. Gama, J., Žliobaitė, I., Bifet, A., Pechenizkiy, M., Bouchachia, A.: A survey on concept drift adaptation. ACM Comput. Surv. (CSUR) **46**(4), 1–37 (2014)

5. Hou, S., Pan, X., Loy, C.C., Wang, Z., Lin, D.: Lifelong learning via progressive distillation and retrospection. In: Proceedings of the European Conference on Computer Vision (ECCV), pp. 437–452 (2018)

6. Huete, J., Qahtan, A.A., Hassani, M.: PrefixCDD: effective online concept drift detection over event streams using prefix trees. In: COMPSAC, pp. 328–333 (2023)

7. Hurtado, J., Salvati, D., Semola, R., Bosio, M., Lomonaco, V.: Continual learning for predictive maintenance: overview and challenges. Intell. Syst. Appl. **19**, 200251 (2023)

8. Kirkpatrick, J., et al.: Overcoming catastrophic forgetting in neural networks. CoRR abs/1612.00796 (2016)

9. Kosciuszek, T., Hassani, M.: Online next activity prediction under concept drifts. In: Advanced Information Systems Engineering Workshops, pp. 335–346 (2024)

10. Lesort, T., Caselles-Dupré, H., Garcia-Ortiz, M., Stoian, A., Filliat, D.: Generative models from the perspective of continual learning. In: IJCNN, pp. 1–8. IEEE (2019)

11. Li, Z., Hoiem, D.: Learning without forgetting. IEEE Trans. Pattern Anal. Mach. Intell. **40**(12), 2935–2947 (2017)

12. Lopez-Paz, D., Ranzato, M.: Gradient episodic memory for continual learning. Adv. Neural. Inf. Process. Syst. **30**, 6470–6479 (2017)

13. Maaradji, A., Dumas, M., La Rosa, M., Ostovar, A.: Fast and accurate business process drift detection. In: BPM, pp. 406–422 (2015)

14. Pauwels, S., Calders, T.: Incremental predictive process monitoring: the next activity case. In: BPM, pp. 123–140 (2021)

15. Rahaf, A., Lucas, C.: Online continual learning with maximally interfered retrieval. In: NIPS (2019)

16. Rebuffi, S.A., Kolesnikov, A., Sperl, G., Lampert, C.H.: iCaRL: incremental classifier and representation learning, pp. 5533–5542 (2017)

17. Rolnick, D., Ahuja, A., Schwarz, J., Lillicrap, T., Wayne, G.: Experience replay for continual learning. In: Advances in Neural Information Processing Systems, vol. 32 (2019)

18. Rusu, A.A., et al.: Progressive neural networks (2016)

19. Taymouri, F., Rosa, M.L., Erfani, S., Bozorgi, Z.D., Verenich, I.: Predictive business process monitoring via generative adversarial nets: the case of next event prediction. In: BPM, pp. 237–256 (2020)

20. Verbeek, T., Yao, R., Hassani, M.: Task-free continual learning with dynamic loss for online next activity prediction. In: ICPM Workshops (2024, to appear)

21. Wang, Z., et al.: DualPrompt: complementary prompting for rehearsal-free continual learning. In: ECCV, pp. 631–648 (2022)

22. Wang, Z., et al.: Learning to prompt for continual learning. CoRR (2022)

23. Wolters, L., Hassani, M.: Predicting activities of interest in the remainder of customer journeys under online settings. In: ICPM Workshops, pp. 145–157 (2022)

24. Zenke, F., Poole, B., Ganguli, S.: Continual learning through synaptic intelligence. In: International Conference on Machine Learning, pp. 3987–3995. PMLR (2017)

A Decomposed Hybrid Approach to Business Process Modeling with LLMs

Ali Nour Eldin[1,2(✉)], Nour Assy[2], Olan Anesini[2], Benjamin Dalmas[2], and Walid Gaaloul[1]

[1] Telecom SudParis, Institut Polytechnique de Paris, Paris, France
{ali.nour_eldin,walid.gaaloul}@telecom-sudparis.eu
[2] Bonitasoft, Grenoble, France
{ali.nour-eldin,nour.assy,olan.anesini,
benjamin.dalmas}@bonitasoft.com

Abstract. This paper proposes a hybrid and decomposed approach to automate process model generation from textual descriptions using Large Language Models (LLMs). Leveraging LLMs with prompting techniques is promising due to the scarcity of training data. While recent approaches explore LLMs' potential in process modeling, the inherent complexity of this task limits their applicability to real-world scenarios where descriptions by non-experts may be complex or incomplete. Our approach addresses these challenges by modularizing the task into distinct steps within a hybrid pipeline: the LLM analyzes, clarifies, and completes the textual description, and extracts process entities and relationships. The process model is then constructed using a structured algorithm. This hybrid methodology integrates LLMs' natural language understanding with a deterministic approach for robust model creation. Evaluation results demonstrate that our approach uses less tokens, and generates more accurate and understandable models compared to existing methods.

Keywords: Process modeling · BPM · Generative AI · LLMs

1 Introduction

Process modeling is a complex task requiring collaboration among participants and experts to formalize business processes [4]. This involves understanding workflows, activities, and organizational interactions, mapped to formal languages like BPMN. Traditionally, process modeling is done manually through interviews; or automated via process discovery from structured data [3] or extraction from unstructured text [7], each with trade-offs: manual methods are detailed but time-consuming, while automated methods are scalable yet may lack completeness, necessitating sophisticated algorithms for accuracy. In this paper, the focus is on automating process modeling from textual descriptions. This approach is particularly valuable as it reduces the need for traditional interviewing methods; users can simply describe processes in textual form, which are then transformed into process models with minimal manual intervention.

Related Works. Significant research has focused on converting natural language into process representations [7], but extracting processes from text remains unresolved [1,7].

© The Author(s), under exclusive license to Springer Nature Switzerland AG 2025
M. Comuzzi et al. (Eds.): CoopIS 2024, LNCS 15506, pp. 243–260, 2025.
https://doi.org/10.1007/978-3-031-81375-7_14

Over the past decade, proposed approaches have primarily relied on template and rule-based methods [2, 10, 13] or advanced NLP techniques leveraging deep learning [12, 16]. The former lack the flexibility to accommodate diverse writing styles and process domains, while the latter often face challenges due to limited access to large and diverse training datasets. Recent advancements in pre-trained Large Language Models (LLMs) have showcased superior reasoning capabilities across various domains and tasks [19], with prompting techniques offering a cost-effective alternative to fine-tuning [9]. In the field of process modeling, exploration of LLM capabilities is still emerging, with a few recent approaches proposed. Our work falls within this category.

LLM-based approaches typically generate process models in a single step using a single prompt [11, 14, 15]. While effective for simple descriptions, this approach struggles with complex processes, often resulting in hallucinations and illogical structures. For instance, testing ProMoAI [15], which generates Python code to create process models, revealed unstable and illogical outcomes for lengthy, indirect descriptions. This issue arises because process modeling is inherently complex and typically requires a decomposed human approach. Recent research highlights that LLMs perform better in reasoning tasks when they address related subtasks first [20] which is crucial for handling real-world complexities. In contrast, an earlier method proposes a decomposed approach where the LLM is invoked multiple times to extract activities and relations separately [8]. This method decomposes the modeling task into highly fine-grained components, aiming for precision but leading to increased latency due to numerous LLM calls, limiting its applicability in practice. Moreover, this method stops at the extraction stage and does not generate the final process model. Existing approaches also assume complete, expertly articulated process descriptions, which diverge from practical realities and lack human interaction during model generation, hindering understanding and adaptation of the final model.

Contribution. This paper proposes a hybrid and decomposed approach for automated process model generation from textual descriptions using LLMs. The approach comprises two phases. In the first phase, process entities are extracted from the text using an LLM in a decomposed manner, avoiding the limitations of overly fine-grained decomposition as discussed above. The modular pipeline allows end users to validate or update extracted information. It also accommodates the inherent incompleteness and non-expert nature of textual descriptions. In the second phase, we developed an algorithm to construct the process model using BPMN as the modeling language, based on the extracted entities. A comparative evaluation using process descriptions from a public dataset demonstrates improved performance of our approach in terms of token usage, model understandability, and accuracy.

The remainder of this paper is organized as follows: Sect. 2 introduces a motivating example and provides an overview of the proposed methodology. Sections 4 and 5 detail our approach for automated process model generation, including entity extraction by the LLM and model construction phases. Section 6 presents an evaluation of our approach. Finally, Sect. 7 concludes the paper.

2   Approach Overview

Before outlining our approach, we present an example to illustrate the limitations addressed. Consider the process description in Text 1.1, detailing the book publishing process. This narrative-style description uses domain-specific vocabulary and omits steps for handling manuscript rejection.

Existing approaches struggle for several reasons. Non-LLM-based methods using traditional NLP techniques extract activities' names verbatim from the text. LLM-based approaches, like ProMoAI[1], exhibit inconsistent behavior. In tests with GPT-4o/turbo, ProMoAI alternated between extracting activities verbatim and generalizing them to standard terms, resulting in unstable behavior and ambiguous activities like `Green light for publication`, `Piece together the book`, and `Whip out book layout`. Such inconsistencies impact process model usability. Furthermore, all approaches may fail to infer missing steps, like handling rejected manuscripts.

When a manuscript gets the green light for publication, the editors swing into action. If it passes muster, they give a heads-up to the production and design crews. The production team sorts out the printing and binding materials needed for the book, making sure everything's good to go. If they've got what they need in stock, they earmark it for the book project. If not, they fire off orders to their suppliers. They do that for all bits needed to put the book together. Meanwhile, the design squad gets busy whipping up the book layout and cover. Once all that's squared away, they piece together the book just right, following the approved design, before shipping it off to the distribution channels.

Text 1.1. Textual process description of a book publishing process.

LLM-based methods generating models in a single step often produce incorrect behaviors, as LLMs struggle with multiple non-intuitive tasks simultaneously, leading to instability and hallucinations. For example, ProMoAI with GPT-4-turbo sometimes correctly identified activities but duplicated them and added incorrect connections, starting with an erroneous parallel gateway that disrupted the process flow, as shown in Fig. 1.

Involving humans during the generation, rather than only providing post-generation feedback, helps refine the model. This interactive approach allows users to validate intermediary results, enhancing understanding and facilitating refactoring compared to a black-box method. For instance, understanding the model in Fig. 1, identifying errors, and requesting modifications takes time. Involving users during the generation process enhances the accuracy and practicality of the final model, ensuring it closely aligns with user expectations.

To address the aforementioned limitations, we propose an approach that decomposes the process modeling task into multiple sub-tasks, inspired by how a human tackles the process modeling problem. Since some of these sub-tasks can be solved with traditional deterministic algorithms, we created a hybrid pipeline consisting of two modules: an *LLM-based module* and a *structured algorithmic module*, as shown in the general architecture of the proposed approach in Fig. 3.

---

[1] https://promoai.streamlit.app/.

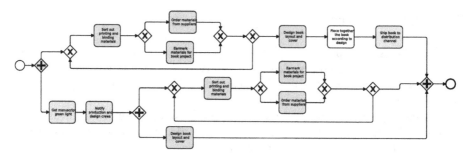

Fig. 1. BPMN model generated by ProMoAI using GPT-4-turbo. Blue activities are illogically repeated. Red elements introduced an incorrect behavior. (Color figure online)

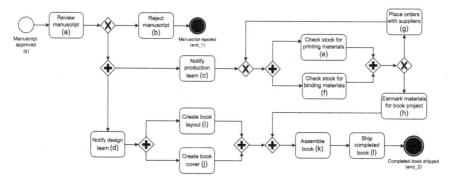

Fig. 2. BPMN model generated with our proposed approach using GPT-4o.

The LLM-based module (Sect. 4) analyzes, if necessary completes the process description, and extracts process entities, like activities and their dependencies, in a decomposed manner. It communicates intermediary results to the user for validation or correction. The structured algorithmic module (Sect. 5) constructs the BPMN diagram from the extracted entities. This approach avoids a black-box process, aids user understanding by sharing intermediary steps, and improves LLM output quality by breaking tasks into smaller steps.

Figure 2 shows the BPMN model generated by our approach using GPT-4o as the LLM[2]. Our approach successfully identified activities without duplication and translated them into a standard vocabulary. It accurately represented the handling of manuscript rejection missing in the text. The model accurately depicts the expected behavior with potential improvements possible in the loop involving activities 'e', 'f', and 'g'.

---

[2] Different executions may yield slightly varied models based on the entities extracted by the LLM, but consistently correct extraction was observed across multiple runs.

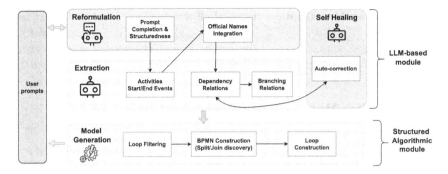

Fig. 3. General architecture of the proposed approach.

3   Preliminaries

This section introduces key definitions essential for subsequent sections. A process model consists of interconnected elements representing process behavior. Using BPMN as our modeling language, we focus on common elements across different modeling languages: activities, start/end events, parallel and exclusive gateways. Two graph structures will be used throughout the paper: a *dependency graph* capturing partial execution order dependencies and a *BPMN model*.

Definition 1 (Dependency Graph). *A dependency graph is defined as a directed graph $DG = (V, E)$, where:*

- *V represents a finite set of vertices, each corresponding to an activity or start/end event.*
- *$E \subseteq V \times V$ represents a set of directed edges, where each edge $(u, v) \in E$ signifies that v can be executed right after the completion of u.*
- *$v_s \in V$ is the starting vertex iff $\nexists (v, v_s) \in E$[3].*
- *$v_e \in V$ is an ending vertex iff $\nexists (v_e, v) \in E$.*
- *For $e = (u, v) \in E$, we use the notations $e.source = u$ and $e.target = v$.*
- *For $v \in V$, the direct successors of v is $\mathrm{Succ}(v) = \{u \in V \mid (v, u) \in E\}$.*

Let $DG = (V, E)$ be a dependency graph.

Definition 2 (Path). *Let $u, v \in V$. A path from u to v, denoted as $P_{u,v} = \langle (v_1, v_2), \dots, (v_{n-1}, v_n) \rangle$, exists if there exists a sequence of unique edges leading from u to v where $n \geq 2$, $v_1 = u$, $v_n = v$, and for all $1 \leq i < n$, $(v_i, v_{i+1}) \in E$. Additionally, there are no repeated edges in the sequence, i.e., $\nexists i \neq j$ such that $(v_i, v_{i+1}) = (v_j, v_{j+1})$.*

Definition 3 (Cycle). *A cycle C_u is a path $P_{u,u} = \langle (u, v_1), \dots, (v_n, u) \rangle$ that starts and ends with u such that $\forall 1 \leq i \leq n, v_i \neq u$.*

---

[3] Since we do not support pools, there is always one source vertex (the start event).

Definition 4 (Branching Relation (Parallel, Exclusive)). *Let* $v \in V$ *such that* $\mathrm{Succ}(v) = \{v_1, \ldots, v_n\}$ *and* $n \geq 2$. *Let* $B = \{\{a, b\} \mid a, b \in \mathrm{Succ}(v) \text{ and } a \neq b\}$ *be the set of all unique pairs of* $\mathrm{Succ}(v)$. *We denote by* $\parallel \; \subseteq B$ *the set of pairs of vertices that are executed in parallel (parallel branching), and by* $\# \subseteq B$ *the set of pairs of vertices that are executed based on a condition (exclusive branching).*

Definition 5 (BPMN Model). *A BPMN model is defined as* $M = (N, G, S)$:

- $N = V$ *is the set of vertices in DG.*
- G *is a finite set of gateways. A gateway* $g \in G$ *can be parallel, represented by* $+$ *or exclusive represented by* $\times$.
- $S \subseteq (N \times G) \cup (N \times G)$ *is a set of directed sequence flows. For each* $s = (u, v) \in S$, *we use the same notations related to source, target and successors as in Definition 1.*

4 LLM-Based Process Entities Extraction

Given the user prompt (i.e. textual process description), this module analyzes and manipulates the input to extract *process entities*. We first define the types of process entities to extract, then detail the different subcomponents.

4.1 Process Entity

Since our aim is to generate a BPMN process model, we initially defined a process entity as a BPMN element, as per Definition 5. After multiple testing iterations evaluating the capabilities of LLMs like GPT-4o/turbo in extracting BPMN elements, we observed that LLMs exhibit the following limitations.

First, LLMs generally struggle to accurately extract *gateways*. While extraction might work for simple examples, more complex or incomplete descriptions often result in hallucinated or inaccurate extractions. Therefore, we excluded gateways as an extracted process entity. Instead, we found the LLM performed better in extracting the same information as a *branching relation* (Definition 4). Second, given that gateways are not explicitly extracted, we updated the way we extract sequence flows. In BPMN, sequence flows are the edges that connect activities and gateways. In the absence of gateways, these sequence flows represent the partial dependency relations between activities, which can be represented as a dependency graph (Definition 1).

Therefore, the process entities extracted by an LLM are activities, start/end events, dependency and branching relations.

4.2 Pipeline Description

Prompt Completion and Structuredness. Upon receiving the user prompt, this component prompts the LLM to reformulate and, if needed, complete the user description into a structured format for easier extraction. Figure 4 illustrates our prompt template, designed following best practices in prompt engineering [18]. The terms in curly brackets serve as placeholders filled with actual values.

All prompts share a consistent structure. *Role play*: Assigns a specific role to the LLM, such as acting as an expert process owner; *Context*: Provides essential information for the LLM, including definitions related to processes and process modeling; *Task & Specific instructions*: Explains the general task such as reformulating and completing missing information, and details task expectations, such as describing termination points and the logical order of steps; *Output format & examples*: Specifies the desired output format, which is simple text for reformulation, and includes examples for the LLM to follow, like process descriptions and their reformulations; *Prompt input*: Provides the input, which is the initial user-provided process description, for the LLM to process.

Role play	You are an experienced process owner in a leading {domain} company.
Context	Considering the context of Business Process Management (BPM) and process modeling: - Process: Describes a sequence or flow of activities in an organization...
Task	You are given a possibly incomplete process description delimited by '''. Analyze the description, then reformulate [...] Your reformulation should be precise, clear and structured ...
Specific instructions	Follow these instructions: - Add all possible termination points. ...
Output format & examples	{format_instruction} Here are some examples: << {examples} >>
Prompt input	Process description: ''' {process_description} '''

Fig. 4. Excerpt of the *Prompt Completeness & Structuredness* prompt template.

Text 1.2 displays a reformulated excerpt from Text 1.1 using GPT-4o. The reformulation adopts standard terminology and fills in missing details concerning the failure of editors' review. This approach accommodates various user scenarios: a well-structured expert description will likely yield a similar output, possibly refined by the LLM. Conversely, if the user's description lacks specificity, such as *"Model a client onboarding process for a bank"*, the LLM generates a comprehensive process description based on its training data. This method enhances entity extraction accuracy and aids in interpreting the logical flow of LLM-generated entities for users. When users provide descriptions in their own words, as seen in Text 1.1, the LLM refines these into clearer, standardized descriptions, ensuring consistent behavior and extraction of activities in standard terminology.

The process begins when a manuscript is approved. The editors then review the manuscript. If the manuscript passes the review, the editors notify the production and design teams [...] If the manuscript does not pass the review, the process ends.

Text 1.2. Excerpt of the reformulated process description by GPT-4o.

Activities and Start/End Events. Following textual reformulation, the next step involves extracting activities and identifying start and end events. Our tests highlighted challenges in LLM-based activity and event extraction, including inconsistencies in adhering to best practices such as starting activity names with verbs, avoiding combining multiple actions into single activities (e.g., "accept or reject order"), using event names to reflect states rather than actions, and ensuring comprehensive coverage without overlooking activities or events.

To address these challenges, we segmented activity and event extraction into a distinct step. We designed a prompt structured according to Fig. 4 to guide the LLM in extracting activities and events while ensuring adherence to desired naming conventions. Instructions were provided for the LLM to emulate a process expert familiar with BPMN standards, with essential definitions related to activity and event characteristics. Specific instructions were established to guide output extraction, emphasizing starting activity names with verbs, maintaining concise and action-focused names, and avoiding combining multiple actions into one activity. Additionally, we instructed the LLM to capture execution preconditions where applicable, enhancing subsequent extraction accuracy.

For the output format, we directed the LLM to return results in a structured JSON following a specific schema, as exemplified by the output in Listing1.1. As input, we passed the reformulation of the previous step. By treating activity extraction as a separate step, we ensure flexibility to incorporate additional attributes, including activity data attributes, and to expand to include intermediate event extraction in future iterations.

```
{"activities": [
    {"activity": "Notify production team", "precondition":
        ↪ "Manuscript passes the review"}, ...]}

{"start_end": [
    {"event": "Manuscript Approved", "type": "start"},
    {"event": "Manuscript Rejected", "type": "end"}, ...]}
```

Listing 1.1. Excerpt of the activities and start/end events extracted by GPT-4o.

Official Names Integration. Before proceeding with extraction, we introduce an additional step to reformulate the textual description by integrating the names of extracted activities and events from the previous step (as shown in Listing 1.1) directly within the description. This adjustment addresses challenges in accurately extracting dependency relations between activities, simplifying the process for the LLM. It ensures that all necessary activity information is readily available in the text, eliminating the need for extensive lookups to associate activity names with their corresponding descriptions. We designed a prompt instructing the LLM to generate a revised description that incorporates the names of extracted activities and events. The input includes the reformulated process description and the names of activities and start/end events from prior steps. Text 1.3 presents an excerpt of the LLM revised description.

Since the output of this step is crucial for accurately extracting the remaining entities, we added interactivity by returning the result to the end user and asking them to validate or propose changes. The user can modify the names of activities and events as well as any other information according to their needs. The validated or updated reformulation is then passed to the subsequent steps.

The process begins with the "Manuscript approved" start event, immediately followed by the "Review manuscript" activity. If the manuscript passes the review, the process continues with the "Notify production team" and "Notify design team" activities [...]

Text 1.3. Revised description by GPT-4o including activities' and events' names

Dependency Relations and Auto-Correction. The revised process description, now integrated with activity and start/end event names, serves as input for the LLM tasked with extracting dependency relations between activities. A single prompt guides the LLM in this task, contrasting with traditional approaches that involve multiple fine-grained calls to extract relations between activity pairs. To ensure correctness and completeness, specific instructions direct the LLM to ensure that start events only act as sources, end events only as targets, and all activities are linked in a path from start to end events.

Given that LLMs are not inherently designed for algorithmic constructions, we implemented a *self-healing mechanism*. This step employs conventional graph-based algorithms to ensure the structural integrity of the dependency graph. If any structural issues are detected, the LLM is prompted to add missing relations, by providing the extracted relations alongside the process description. This process is parameterized to prevent infinite loops. If the LLM cannot resolve all issues, it returns the incomplete relations, allowing the pipeline to proceed to BPMN generation, albeit potentially with missing sequence flows and gateways.

Listing 1.2 shows an excerpt of the dependency relations extracted by GPT-4o.

```
{"relations": [
    {"relation": "Manuscript approved -> Review manuscript"},
    {"relation": "Review manuscript -> Manuscript rejected"},
    ... ]}
```
Listing 1.2. Excerpt of the dependency relations extracted by GPT-4o.

```
{"parallel": [
    {"activity1": "Notify production team", "activity2":
        ↪ "Notify design team", "isParallel": True}, ...]}
```
Listing 1.3. Excerpt of the branching relations classified by GPT-4o.

Branching Relations. The final step of the LLM pipeline involves identifying branching relations for parallel and conditional execution, which will later be represented by gateways in the BPMN construction phase. Using the dependency relations generated in the previous step (defined as a dependency graph in Definition 1), we extract pairs of activities that exhibit branching relations as per Definition 4. These pairs, along with the revised textual description, are then passed to the LLM for classification into parallel or not. For those pairs classified as not parallel, they are automatically identified as conditional without additional instructions to the LLM[4]. Listing 1.3 shows an excerpt of the relations classified as parallel or not returned by GPT-4o.

---

[4] Alternatively, instructing the LLM to classify conditional executions.

5 Structured Algorithm for Model Generation

The dependency relations represented as a dependency graph DG, and the branching relations (parallel $\|$ and exclusive $\#$) returned by the LLM are passed to this component responsible for constructing the BPMN diagram. This step is akin to a process discovery problem [6], where the goal is to accurately translate the relations between activities extracted from an event log into a process model. However, the main difference lies in defining these relations, primarily parallel and exclusive, due to the differing nature of the inputs (unstructured text vs. structured log), rendering existing discovery algorithms inapplicable. Therefore, we proposed an algorithm that constructs the BPMN in three steps, as shown in the *Model Generation* component in Fig. 3. The first step involves analyzing the dependency graph to detect and filter loops, as these are known to pose challenges [5] (Sect. 5.1). Next, an algorithm constructs the BPMN model with a focus on discovering split and join gateways (Sect. 5.2). Finally, the filtered loops are added to the process model (Sect. 5.3)[5].

5.1 Loop Filtering

This step involves removing the loops from DG by detecting and filtering the dependency relations that break the cycles resulting in an acyclic dependency graph. For example, given the dependency graph in Fig. 5, there are four cycles $C_{e1} = \langle (e,e) \rangle$, $C_{e2} = \langle (e,f),(f,e) \rangle$, $C_{f_1} = \langle (f,f) \rangle$ and $C_{f_2} = \langle (f,e),(e,f) \rangle$.

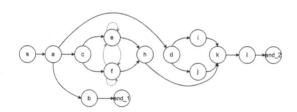

Fig. 5. Dependency graph of the running example with cycles.

Breaking cycles involves removing specific edges, known as *looping edges*, which are the last edges in the paths that create the looping behavior. For example, given the cycle $C_{e2} = \langle (e,f),(f,e) \rangle$, the edge (f,e) creates the loop. It is characterized by the property that, following the path from the graph's start to the edge's source vertex, no other vertices in the cycle are visited before reaching this edge. In this example, the looping edges are (e,e), (f,e), (f,f), and (e,f).

After filtering all the looping edges, we obtain an acyclic dependency graph, DG_A, which is used in the next step to discover split and join gateways.

---

[5] Due to space constraints, a high-level overview of the algorithm is provided. For detailed information, please refer to the technical report: https://github.com/NourEldin-Ali/NaLa2BPMN.

5.2   Split and Join Discovery

Accurately discovering split and join gateways while keeping the model simple is challenging. To simplify model generation, we construct blocks of split/join gateways without enforcing the block-structuredness property. Algorithm 1 outlines the high-level steps. It takes as input the acyclic dependency graph DG_A and the branching parallel relations $\parallel$ and returns as output a BPMN model M.

Initially, we traverse all paths in DG_A from start to all possible ends, ordering them with a depth-first algorithm based on the longest path. This ensures joins are introduced alongside splits, focusing on identifying the maximum number of gateways by analyzing the longest paths first. The result is a list of ordered edges derived from these paths (Line 5). In our example of Fig. 5 (excluding the red looping edges that have been filtered), the ordered depth-first traversal returns the paths ordered $[P_1, P_2, P_3, P_4, P_5]$ where $P_1 = \langle (s,a), (a,c), (c,e), (e,h), (h,k), (k,l), (l,end_2) \rangle$, $P_2 = \langle (s,a), (a,c), (c,f), (f,h), (h,k), (k,l), (l,end_2) \rangle$, $P_3 = \langle (s,a), (a,d), (d,i),$ $(i,k), (k,l), (l,end_2) \rangle$, $P_4 = \langle (s,a),\ (a,d), (d,j), (j,k), (k,l), (l,end_2) \rangle$, and $P_5 = \langle (s,a), (a,b), (b,end_1) \rangle$. The ordered list of unique edges E_O extracted from these paths, respecting their order, is $E_O = [(s,a), (a,c), \ldots, (c,f), (f,h) \ldots]$.

Algorithm 1. BPMN Split/Join Construction.

1: **Input:** Acyclic Dependency Graph $DG_A = (V, E)$, parallel vertices $\parallel$
2: **Output:** Generated BPMN Model $M = (N, G, S)$
3: Initialize M
4: Create a gateway reference $GR = null$
5: $E_O = \text{OrderedDF}(DG_A)$
6: **for all** $e \in E_O$ **do**
7:    **if** $\nexists s', s'' \in S \mid s'.source = e.source \land s''.target = e.target$ **then**
8:       $N \leftarrow N \cup \{e.source, e.target\}$
9:       $S \leftarrow S \cup \{(e.source, e.target)\}$
10:   **else if** $\exists s \in S \mid s.source = e.source \land e.target \notin N$ **then**
11:      **if** $type(s.target) \notin G$ **then**
12:         $AddOneSplitGateway(M, \parallel, e.source, targets)$
13:      **else**
14:         $AddNestingSplitGateway(DG_A, M, \parallel, e.source, e.target)$
15:   **else**
16:      **if** $type(s.source) \notin G$ **then**
17:         $AddOneJoinGateway(M, type(GR), sources, e.target)$
18:      **else**
19:         $AddNestingJoinGateway(M, GR, s, source, e.target)$

The algorithm initializes a gateway reference GR (Line 4) to track the last added split, facilitating the addition of join gateways. It then iterates over the ordered list of edges to begin creating the BPMN elements (Lines 5–6). For each edge, one of three cases is possible: adding a sequence flow, adding a split gateway or adding a join gateway.

Adding a Sequence Flow. If the edge source (respectively target) is not already the source (respectively target) of a sequence flow, the edge is added as a sequence flow. The source and target of the edge are added as BPMN activities (or start/end events) (Lines 7–9). This corresponds to adding the first seven edges of path P_1 in our example.

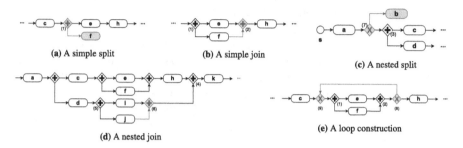

(a) A simple split   (b) A simple join

(c) A nested split

(d) A nested join

(e) A loop construction

Fig. 6. BPMN split/join/loop constructions.

Adding a Split Gateway. If the source of the edge has already been added to the BPMN but not the target, and there is a sequence flow in the BPMN starting with the source, a split gateway needs to be added (Lines 10–14). Two cases are possible. If the sequence flow target is an activity, a simple gateway is added (Lines 11–12). This is illustrated in Fig. 6a where the edge (c, f) needs to be added. Here, c exists but f does not, (c, e) is a sequence flow starting with c, and the target e is an activity. A simple gateway connecting c to both e and f is added. The gateway type is determined by inspecting the relation type between e and f. If they belong to $\|$, then a parallel gateway is added; otherwise, an exclusive gateway is added. If the sequence flow target is a gateway, then nested gateways need to be added (Line 14). This is illustrated in Fig. 6c where (a, b) needs to be added. Here, $(a, +_3)$ is a sequence flow starting with a, and its target $+_3$ is a gateway. In this case, all the gateway's successors are searched, resulting in the extracted list $\{c, d\}^6$. The relationship between the target b and the extracted list $\{c, d\}$ is then analyzed and compared with the gateway $+_3$. Three cases can occur: i) if b is parallel to both c and d, then b is simply connected to the existing $+_3$; ii) if b is not parallel to either c or d as it is the case in Fig. 6c, then a new gateway $\times_7$ is added before the existing gateway and is connected to b; iii) if b is parallel to one of c or d and is exclusive to the other, then an exclusive gateway is added after $+_3$, connecting b to the one with which it has an exclusive relation.

Adding a Join Gateway. If neither of the previous conditions applies, a join gateway needs to be added (Lines 15–19). Similar to the split gateway, there are two cases: adding a simple or a nested gateway by analyzing the predecessors. In Fig. 6b, a simple join is added for the edge (f, h). Since h's predecessor is an activity, a join gateway is added before h. The join gateway type matches the last split gateway tracked by GR. In Fig. 6d, a nested join gateway is added for the edge (j, k) since k's predecessor is

---

^{6} If the successors contain gateways, the gateways' successors are recursively analyzed.

a gateway ($+_4$). The algorithm checks if the last added split gateway which is $+_5$ and join gateway $+_4$ correspond to each other by traversing paths backward from $+_4$ to $+_5$. Three cases can occur: i) if all paths reach $+_5$ and the gateways are the same type, j and k are simply connected through join gateway $+_4$; ii) if the gateways are different types, a new join gateway matching the split type is added after $+_4$ to connect j and k; iii) if not all paths reach $+_5$, as in Fig. 6d, a new join gateway of the same type as $+_5$ is added after the first activities' on the paths that reach $+_5$. In this example, $+_4$ has h and i as predecessors, but only the path from i reaches $+_5$. Therefore, a new join gateway of the same type as $+_5$ is added right after i.

5.3 Loop Construction

In this final step, we add the looping edges that were identified and filtered in the initial step. These edges are incorporated by identifying where the loop should begin and end. To achieve this, we employ two merging algorithms that organize the looping connections based on their sources and target In our example, the set of filtered looping edges is $L = \{(f, f), (e, e), (f, e), (e, f)\}$. The first merge groups looping edges that share the same source and whose targets have common successors in the BPMN. This results in $ML_s = \{(f, \{f, e\}), (e, \{f, e\})\}$. The second merging algorithm, ML, refines ML_s by combining edges that share the same target and whose sources have common predecessors in the BPMN. In our example, this produces $ML = \{(\{f, e\}, \{f, e\})\}$, indicating a loop that starts and ends with the same block $\{f, e\}$.

Adding the loop to the BPMN involves properly incorporating the split/end gateways to the block in ML that preserves the logical flow. First, If a block (source or target) in ML contains multiple elements, the closest common gateway is used. If the block contains a single element, that element is used. The gateway or element then serve as the block entry or exit. Second, four scenarios can occur: i) if both source and target blocks are already connected by sequence flows to other elements in the BPMN, a new gateway is added before the block entry, and another gateway is added after the block exit. This case is illustrated in Fig. 6e; ii) if the target block is connected by a sequence flow but the source block is not, a new gateway is added before block entry, and then it is connected to the block exit; iii) if the source block is connected by a sequence flow but the target block is not, a new gateway is added after block exit, and then it is connected to the block entry; iv) if neither block has a sequence flow, a simple connection is created between the entry and exit without adding gateways.

6 Evaluation

The approach has been implemented and is available at https://nala2bpmn.bonitapps. com/, supporting OpenAI GPT-3.5/4o/4-turbo models. To demonstrate the effectiveness of our approach, we performed a thorough evaluation across several dimensions. This section details our methodology and findings[7].

---

[7] Detailed results, including the generated models, are available at: https://github.com/ NourEldin-Ali/NaLa2BPMN.

Setup. The PET dataset [10] was used, which includes 47 textual descriptions and their BPMN models. Eight descriptions (1.3, 3.2, 3.5, 3.6, 4.1, 5.4, 6.3, and 6.4) were chosen based on alignment with supported BPMN elements. While the number of descriptions is not representative, this subset allows for initial feasibility assessment and comparison with existing approaches. Comparing with existing methods is challenging due to the lack of standardized reproducibility or comparison approaches in the literature, variations in parameters, models, output formats, and unavailability of source code. These issues are particularly relevant in LLM-based approaches, where model versions evolve rapidly. To ensure fair comparison, the most recent LLM-based approach, ProMoAI, with available source code [15] was selected, allowing experiments with identical LLM models and execution environment. For each textual description, we performed two runs of each approach using two models: GPT-4o, and GPT-4-turbo. We used two different API keys and allowed a delay of 2–3 days between each of the two runs to avoid potential biases from cached results on OpenAI's servers.

Evaluation Metrics. The evaluation assessed the feasibility and performance of the two approaches across seven dimensions: *complexity, understandability, correctness, completeness, relevance, ease of updating, and cost.*

Complexity was evaluated using quantitative metrics, including the total number of activities (NA), sequence flows (NSF), gateways (NG), exclusive decisions (NEG), and parallel gateways (NPG).

For the qualitative evaluation, experts in BPMN conducted a case study, including nine practitioners and professional developers from Bonitasoft and three academics specializing in BPM. The participants were given the textual descriptions along with two anonymized models, one from our approach and one from ProMoAI. The less complex model generated by GPT-4 was selected for each approach based on the average of complexity metrics. Participants rated each model on a scale from 1 to 5, where 1 is very poor and 5 is excellent. *Understandability* measured how straightforward and intuitive the BPMN models were to understand. *Correctness* ensured the models accurately represented the described processes. *Completeness* checked for the inclusion of all essential elements, avoiding omissions. *Relevance* ensured the models included only pertinent components, avoiding unnecessary clutter. *Ease of updating* meant the models allowed straightforward modifications with minimal disruption.

Lastly, *cost* analysis measured execution time and API usage costs in terms of tokens, considering the financial implications of using paid LLM APIs.

Results and Discussion. Table 1 shows the average complexity metrics from two runs for models generated by GPT-4o. Results for GPT-4-turbo are not included due to ProMoAI's failures in generating some models. ProMoAI tends to produce models with higher complexity, characterized by more activities and sequence flows. For example, in doc-4.1, ProMoAI features 46 activities compared to 29 in our approach. Similarly, in doc-5.4, ProMoAI includes 55 sequence flows versus 20 in our approach. ProMoAI also utilizes significantly more gateways, especially exclusive gateways, which complicate the process [17]. For instance, in doc-5.4, ProMoAI employs 18 gateways compared to 4 in our approach.

Table 1. Complexity comparison of our approach vs ProMoAI using GPT-4o.

doc	Our Approach					ProMoAI				
	NA	NSF	NG	NPG	NEG	NA	NSF	NG	NPG	NEG
1.3	15	30	9	5	4	12	27	7	3	4
3.2	6	12	4	4	3	7	12	3	1	2
3.5	16	19	1	0	1	19	30	5	3	2
3.6	12	21	5	1	4	12	26	9	0	9
4.1	29	31	0	0	1	46	57	6	5	1
5.4	13	20	4	0	4	26	55	18	8	10
6.3	13	20	4	0	4	9	13	2	1	1
6.4	15	33	10	4	6	15	32	10	1	9

Manual inspection of BPMN models, especially those of 5.4 and 4.1, revealed that ProMoAI tends to duplicate activities when process descriptions are lengthy and not straightforward, which introduces random behavior. For example, Fig. 7a and 7b show the BPMN models generated for description 5.4 by our approach and ProMoAI, respectively. Our approach generates a clear and logical sequence of activities, capturing all essential steps without redundancy. It accurately represents the process of submission, review, and approval or rejection of expense reports, correctly handling cycles of rejection and resubmission. In contrast, the BPMN generated by ProMoAI suffers from redundancy in several activities, such as multiple instances of "Submit expense report" and "Employee edits report", leading to potential confusion and misinterpretation of the process flow. Additionally, parallel gateways are introduced randomly, making the process logic incorrect according to the description.

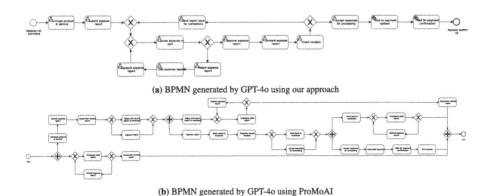

(a) BPMN generated by GPT-4o using our approach

(b) BPMN generated by GPT-4o using ProMoAI

Fig. 7. BPMN models generated for the description 5.4.

The case study results depicted in the boxplots of Fig. 8 validate these observations. Our approach generally received more consistent and higher evaluations across all five

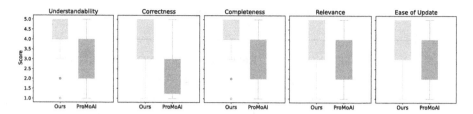

Fig. 8. Case study results.

dimensions compared to ProMoAI. Narrow interquartile ranges and higher medians across these metrics suggest that our models are typically perceived as more understandable, correct, complete, relevant, and easier to update. In contrast, ProMoAI exhibited wider ranges and lower medians, reflecting greater variability and generally lower satisfaction among participants. It is worth noting that our approach did encounter some outliers. For instance, one participant gave a rating of 1 for understandability, citing that the model contained excessively detailed low-level activities. This feedback suggests that consolidating such activities into subprocesses could enhance clarity.

In order to statistically validate these results, a paired t-test was applied to determine the significant differences between the two BPMNs across the five dimensions. The paired t-test compares the means of two related groups – in this case, the evaluations of the participants for both BPMN models. The results are as follows: Understandability (t-statistic = 7.497, p-value = 9.38×10^{-11}); Correctness (t-statistic = 9.164, p-value = 5.78×10^{-14}); Completeness (t-statistic = 9.752, p-value = 4.30×10^{-15}); Relevance (t-statistic = 6.996, p-value = 8.46×10^{-10}); and Ease of Update (t-statistic = 5.714, p-value = 1.99×10^{-7}). These results indicate that for all five dimensions, the differences in evaluations are statistically significant, with our model consistently receiving higher evaluations. The low p-values across all dimensions confirm that the observed differences are unlikely due to random chance and are statistically significant.

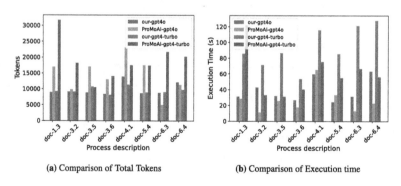

(a) Comparison of Total Tokens   (b) Comparison of Execution time

Fig. 9. Cost Comparison of our approach vs ProMoAI.

Figure 9 displays the cost analysis results averaged over the two runs of each model. Despite requiring at least six API calls, our approach reduces token usage by an average of 40% across various process models compared to ProMoAI, which only needs one call but often fails to generate the process model correctly on the first attempt. Thus, our decomposed approach proves more cost-effective, achieving a 31% reduction in token usage with GPT-4o and a 49% reduction with GPT-4-turbo. However, our approach exhibits a 49% longer execution time, consuming 43% more time with GPT-4 and 55% more time with GPT-4-turbo.

7 Conclusion

We proposed a hybrid approach to process model generation, combining LLMs with a structured algorithm. This method addresses the limitations of existing techniques, which either rely on one-shot generation, resulting in low-quality models, or decompose the task too finely, making it impractical for large models. By breaking down the task into manageable steps, our approach effectively handles complex and incomplete descriptions. Our evaluation demonstrates that this hybrid method reduces token usage and produces more accurate and understandable models compared to the latest approach. Future work will extend this approach to support more BPMN elements and multi-perspective models to create fully executable BPMN models.

References

1. van der Aa, H., Carmona, J., Leopold, H., Mendling, J., Padró, L.: Challenges and opportunities of applying natural language processing in business process management. In: Proceedings of the 27th International Conference on Computational Linguistics, COLING, pp. 2791–2801 (2018)
2. van der Aa, H., Di Ciccio, C., Leopold, H., Reijers, H.A.: Extracting declarative process models from natural language. In: Giorgini, P., Weber, B. (eds.) CAiSE 2019. LNCS, vol. 11483, pp. 365–382. Springer, Cham (2019). https://doi.org/10.1007/978-3-030-21290-2_23
3. van der Aalst, W.M.P.: Process Mining - Data Science in Action, 2nd edn. Springer, Heidelberg (2016)
4. Alotaibi, Y.: Business process modelling challenges and solutions: a literature review. J. Intell. Manuf. **27**(4), 701–723 (2016)
5. Augusto, A., Conforti, R., Dumas, M., Rosa, M.L., Bruno, G.: Automated discovery of structured process models from event logs: the discover-and-structure approach. Data Knowl. Eng. **117**, 373–392 (2018)
6. Augusto, A., et al.: Automated discovery of process models from event logs: review and benchmark. IEEE Trans. Knowl. Data Eng. **31**(4), 686–705 (2019)
7. Bellan, P., Dragoni, M., Ghidini, C.: Process extraction from text: state of the art and challenges for the future. CoRR **abs/2110.03754** (2021)
8. Bellan, P., Dragoni, M., Ghidini, C.: Extracting business process entities and relations from text using pre-trained language models and in-context learning. In: Almeida, J.P.A., Karastoyanova, D., Guizzardi, G., Montali, M., Maggi, F.M., Fonseca, C.M. (eds.) EDOC 2022. LNCS, vol. 13585, pp. 182–199. Springer, Cham (2022). https://doi.org/10.1007/978-3-031-17604-3_11
9. Brown, T.B., et al.: Language models are few-shot learners. In: Advances in Neural Information Processing Systems 33: Annual Conference on Neural Information Processing Systems, NeurIPS, virtual (2020)

.

10. Friedrich, F., Mendling, J., Puhlmann, F.: Process model generation from natural language text. In: Mouratidis, H., Rolland, C. (eds.) CAiSE 2011. LNCS, vol. 6741, pp. 482–496. Springer, Heidelberg (2011). https://doi.org/10.1007/978-3-642-21640-4_36
11. Grohs, M., Abb, L., Elsayed, N., Rehse, J.: Large language models can accomplish business process management tasks. In: De Weerdt, J., Pufahl, L. (eds.) BPM 2023. LNBIP, vol. 492, pp. 453–465. Springer, Cham (2023). https://doi.org/10.1007/978-3-031-50974-2_34
12. Han, X., et al.: A-BPS: automatic business process discovery service using ordered neurons LSTM. In: 2020 IEEE International Conference on Web Services, ICWS, pp. 428–432 (2020)
13. Honkisz, K., Kluza, K., Wiśniewski, P.: A concept for generating business process models from natural language description. In: Liu, W., Giunchiglia, F., Yang, B. (eds.) KSEM 2018. LNCS (LNAI), vol. 11061, pp. 91–103. Springer, Cham (2018). https://doi.org/10.1007/978-3-319-99365-2_8
14. Klievtsova, N., Benzin, J., Kampik, T., Mangler, J., Rinderle-Ma, S.: Conversational process modelling: state of the art, applications, and implications in practice. In: Di Francescomarino, C., Burattin, A., Janiesch, C., Sadiq, S. (eds.) BPM 2023. LNBIP, vol. 490, pp. 319–336. Springer, Cham (2023). https://doi.org/10.1007/978-3-031-41623-1_19
15. Kourani, H., Berti, A., Schuster, D., van der Aalst, W.M.P.: Process modeling with large language models. In: van der Aa, H., Bork, D., Schmidt, R., Sturm, A. (eds.) BPMDS EMMSAD. LNBIP, vol. 511, pp. 229–244. Springer, Cham (2024). https://doi.org/10.1007/978-3-031-61007-3_18
16. Qian, C., et al.: An approach for process model extraction by multi-grained text classification. In: Dustdar, S., Yu, E., Salinesi, C., Rieu, D., Pant, V. (eds.) CAiSE 2020. LNCS, vol. 12127, pp. 268–282. Springer, Cham (2020). https://doi.org/10.1007/978-3-030-49435-3_17
17. Reijers, H.A., Mendling, J.: A study into the factors that influence the understandability of business process models. IEEE Trans. Syst. Man Cybern. Part A 41(3), 449–462 (2011)
18. Sahoo, P., Singh, A.K., Saha, S., Jain, V., Mondal, S., Chadha, A.: A systematic survey of prompt engineering in large language models: Techniques and applications. CoRR abs/2402.07927 (2024)
19. Teubner, T., Flath, C.M., Weinhardt, C., van der Aalst, W.M.P., Hinz, O.: Welcome to the era of chatgpt et al. Bus. Inf. Syst. Eng. 65(2), 95–101 (2023)
20. Wu, Z., et al.: Divide-or-conquer? which part should you distill your llm? CoRR abs/2402.15000 (2024)

Services and Cloud

Self-organising Approach to Anomaly Mitigation in the Cloud-to-Edge Continuum

Bruno Faria[1,2]($\boxtimes$) , David Perez Abreu[1,2] , Karima Velasquez[2] ,
and Marília Curado[2]

[1] Laboratory for Informatics and Systems, Pedro Nunes Institute, Coimbra, Portugal
{bfaria,dabreu}@ipn.pt
[2] CISUC, Department of Informatics Engineering, University of Coimbra, Coimbra, Portugal
{kcastro,marilia}@dei.uc.pt

Abstract. The cloud-to-edge continuum paradigm has permeated various application domains, including critical urban-city safety systems. In these contexts, anomalies can compromise public safety, for example, by disrupting the communication between smart city infrastructure and vehicles, which aims to prevent accidents at pedestrian crossings. Given these environments' heterogeneous and large-scale nature, manual recovery from anomalies is not feasible. Machine Learning techniques have emerged as an alternative, supporting a zero-touch approach that enables self-organising and self-healing solutions for anomaly prediction, detection, and mitigation. This paper proposes an Artificial Intelligence-driven, self-organising approach for anomaly management in the cloud-to-edge continuum, integrating both reactive and proactive mechanisms. We evaluate different Machine Learning models, including Random Forest Classifiers, Neural Networks, and Convolutional Neural Networks, to predict node performance anomalies. The simulation results obtained using the COSCO framework showcase the effectiveness of our method. It achieves an F1 score of 73% for multiclass classification, predicting different levels of anomaly severity, and 87% for binary classification, distinguishing between normal and abnormal states.

Keywords: Cloud-to-edge continuum · Self-X · Zero-touch · Anomaly management · Machine learning · Time-series classification

1 Introduction

Cloud computing provides on-demand access to computational resources, such as storage, networking, and processing capabilities through a communication infrastructure. This enables the development and operation of numerous applications and services, including real-time traffic monitoring, emergency response systems, and autonomous vehicle communication. Edge computing brings resources closer to users, offering lower latency and enhanced privacy. Fog computing serves as an intermediary layer between edge devices and cloud data centres, providing additional processing capabilities and reducing the data transfer load to the cloud. The combination of these paradigms forms the Cloud-to-Edge (C2E) continuum, which provides access to on-demand resources

M. Comuzzi et al. (Eds.): CoopIS 2024, LNCS 15506, pp. 263–279, 2025.
https://doi.org/10.1007/978-3-031-81375-7_15

through diverse devices [15]. This integration creates a complex and dynamic environment characterised by many interconnected and heterogeneous devices [29]. This heterogeneity, the extensive network scale, continuous connectivity and communication, and physical exposure are some of the factors that make the C2E continuum prone to anomalies. These can be caused by unpredictable interactions, hardware faults, software bugs, cyber attacks, intrusions, and physical damage, compromising service availability. In critical application domains, such as urban city services, these anomalies can compromise the communication between city infrastructure like traffic cameras and vehicles, which could cause accidents at crosswalks and put people in danger [25].

In system monitoring and performance management, an anomaly is defined as a significant deviation from normal behaviour [18,26], such as unexpected increases in resource use, which can indicate issues like software bugs, hardware malfunctions, or security breaches. Early anomaly detection is crucial for preventing minor issues from growing into major problems.

Manual anomaly detection and recovery solutions are impractical in complex scenarios as the continuum, as they can introduce additional errors and lead to prolonged recovery times [6]. Artificial Intelligence (AI) and Machine Learning (ML) offer promising alternatives by providing data-driven, intelligent, and automated anomaly detection and mitigation solutions. These technologies enable intelligent decision-making tasks for network management [11], infusing the network with self-organising and self-healing capabilities, reducing the need for human interaction [13]. AI and ML can analyse vast amounts of data from C2E systems to identify patterns, detect anomalies, and take corrective actions autonomously. By using AI and ML, it is possible to develop systems that can detect and predict anomalies before they escalate into significant failures. However, accessing representative datasets that capture the intricacies of real-world C2E deployments to train and test the models remains a key challenge [31].

This work presents a self-organising approach to anomaly detection and mitigation within the C2E continuum, addressing three main challenges: the lack of comprehensive and representative datasets, the effective management of anomalies in a C2E environment, and the identification of future research directions to enhance system resilience and efficiency with self-organising approaches.

To address the first challenge, we utilised the COupled Simulation and Container Orchestration framework (COSCO) for simulation and validation [28], which has been extended to support Service Chains (SCs). This allows the simulation of the flow of containers in the network, stress injection, anomaly detection and prediction, and the capability to generate datasets for anomaly prediction.

For the second challenge, our approach uses detection and prediction components to enable reactive and proactive responses to anomalies. The detection component continuously monitors system metrics to identify abnormal stress levels indicative of potential anomalies, triggering alerts when the impact on resource usage is noticeable. Concurrently, the prediction component tests multiple ML techniques, including Random Forest Classifiers (RFCs), Neural Networks (NNs), and Convolutional Neural Networks (CNNs), to forecast potential anomalies before they become severe. This allows preventive actions to be performed even when resource consumption is low. This dual approach ensures that the system can anticipate and respond to imminent anomalies, thereby maintaining service continuity and reducing the risk of service disruption. Available nodes are used for anomaly recovery and mitigation via container migration, further enhancing the system's resilience.

The third challenge focuses on identifying open issues and possible research paths for future work, as detailed in Sect. 6. Open issues include improving resilience to anomalies and failures using temporal data, developing continuous learning systems, addressing the limitations of centralised approaches, creating models that fit resource-constrained devices, and transitioning from simulation to real testbed environments. Possible approaches to tackle these issues involve exploring advanced time series models, implementing adaptive learning mechanisms, adopting distributed ML techniques, incorporating lightweight and green AI strategies, and validating the system in real-world scenarios.

This paper is structured as follows. Section 2 reviews the state-of-the-art in AI and ML for anomaly detection and mitigation and current challenges in this domain. Section 3 discusses our system's design, detailing its components and metrics used. Section 4 explains the COSCO framework, the simulation setup, and the validation datasets. Section 5 reveals our simulation results, demonstrating our approach's effectiveness. Section 6 looks at current challenges and future research directions. Finally, Sect. 7 concludes the paper.

2 Related Work

ML has proven to be a powerful tool for failure and anomaly detection and prediction [17]. Several approaches have been developed to monitor, detect, and diagnose anomalies in C2E environments.

[9] propose an Anomaly Detection System (ADS) for microservice architectures, addressing challenges in monitoring, detecting, and diagnosing anomalies. The ADS includes monitoring, detection, and fault injection. It collects system metrics like CPU, RAM, and network usage. For detection, they tested Support Vector Machines (SVMs), RFCs, Naive Bayes Classifiers (NBCs), Bayesian Networks (BNs), and k-Nearest Neighbours (k-NN). Their experiments showed k-NN to be the best-performing algorithm, followed by BNs, while SVMs were deemed unsuitable because of the high number of features involved.

[31] explore challenges and solutions for data-driven ML in self-healing systems. They identify five main challenges: (i) data imbalance, (ii) data insufficiency, (iii) cost insensitivity, (iv) non-real-time response, and (v) multisource data fusion. To tackle these, they suggest: (i) data preprocessing (oversampling, undersampling, hybrid sampling, and Synthetic Minority Oversampling Technique (SMOTE)), or algorithmic choice (one-class classifier and cost-sensitive learning), (ii) data preprocessing (oversampling and SMOTE), using either unlabelled data (active, unsupervised, and semi-supervised learning) or transfer learning, (iii) cost-sensitive learning and the introduction of new evaluation metrics (F1 score, precision, recall, G-mean, ROC curve, AUC, among others), (iv) proactive response, and (v) data fusion.

[20] apply various ML techniques, including linear regression, MP5, Reduced Error Pruning Tree (REPTree), SVMs, Least Absolute Selection and Shrinkage Operators

(LASSOs), and Least-Square SVMs, to predict the Remaining Time To Failure (RTTF) of applications. The authors compared the Soft Mean Absolute Errors (SMAEs) of these techniques and found that REPTree and M5P outperformed others in their testbed, although high prediction errors were observed when the system was temporally far from the failure time.

In another study, [12] use Deep Neural Networks (DNNs) with autoencoders to predict the inter-arrival time of faults in a network. They compared this technique against other ML methods, such as autoregressive NNs, linear and nonlinear SVMs, and exponential and linear regression, finding that DNNs with autoencoders provided superior performance.

Large Language Models (LLMs) have also been explored for forecasting and detecting anomalies, as presented by [26]. In their review, the authors examine the challenges and limitations of current LLMs, discussing potential solutions and strategies to overcome these obstacles.

Table 1. Summary of the most relevant works in the state-of-the-art.

Ref	Type	System Metrics	Output	ML Technique	Evaluation
[9]	R	CPU Memory	14 classes: (3 services x 4 fault types) + normal + overload	SVM, RFC, NBC, k-NN	Kubernetes
[31]	R	No	2 classes: Faulty or not	SVM, SVM + SMOTE, SVM + oversampling	Simulation
[20]	P	CPU Memory	RTTF	Linear Regression, M5P, REP-Tree, LASSO, SVM, Least-Square SVM	Simulation
[12]	P	No	Inter-arrival time of faults	DNN with Autoencoders	Real cellular network data
[16]	R	No	Approximation of the output of the sensor node	RNN	Simulation
This work	R+P	CPU Memory Disk Energy	2 classes: Anomalous or not 4 classes: Anomaly Intensity	RFC, NN, CNN	Simulation

Legend: R - Reactive; P - Proactive

Table 1 outlines the works above and their key characteristics and differences. It notes the mechanism type, reactive (triggered after the anomaly) or proactive (triggered before the anomaly), whether system metrics are collected for model training, the predicted outputs, the explored ML algorithms, and the evaluation setup. Notably, both reactive and proactive approaches are covered, although not simultaneously. Common metrics are CPU and RAM usage. SVMs and NNs, along with their variants, are the most popular ML methods. RFC and others are also mentioned. Real testbeds and simulations are employed for evaluation, with simulations often preferred for their scalability and faster setup.

Our work extends this field by combining reactive and proactive approaches to detect and predict anomalies in the C2E continuum. We inform our mechanisms using key system metrics, such as CPU, RAM, disk usage, and energy consumption. By addressing both binary and multiclass classifications of anomalies, our system can identify the presence of anomalies and classify their severity based on the extent of deviation from expected behaviour. This dual capability improves anomaly management, system resilience, and reliability.

3 Self-organising System

This section outlines the proposed strategy to detect and predict anomalies in the C2E continuum. The proposed system comprises two main mechanisms: reactive and proactive. It tracks CPU, RAM, disk usage, and energy consumption, employing ML techniques. Adopting a cloud-native approach, our system uses a microservice architecture deployed using containers, enhancing scalability and flexibility. Each service comprises a chain of microservices, known as an Service Chain, which can spread across different nodes. Given the challenge of limited data, and since simulation has proven to be a helpful tool, simulated environments were used to generate datasets for training and validation.

3.1 System Components

Our system operates as a closed-loop system, as depicted in Fig. 1. The system components are as follows:

- **MANO**: Manage resources and orchestrate services within the system.
- **Monitoring**: Collect data from system sensors.
- **Detection**: Analyse collected data to detect real-time anomalies.
- **Prediction**: Use ML to analyse data and predict anomalies in advance.
- **Decision Making**: Determine the appropriate actions to take when anomalies are detected or predicted.
- **Infrastructure**: The simulated C2E scenario.

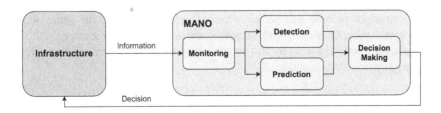

Fig. 1. Self-organising system components.

Our solution employs a centralised Management and Orchestration (MANO) app-roach, where a single node oversees the entire network, taking all decisions. This node aggregates data from all nodes, processes it, and orchestrates the responses to maintain service continuity and performance.

The detection component activates when data hits set thresholds, triggering a response. The prediction component anticipates abnormal behaviour using ML. The decision-making component determines the necessary actions to ensure service conti-nuity upon detecting or predicting an anomaly. One essential action is migrating the heaviest container, the one consuming the most resources, from the affected node to a backup one. This migration process redistributes the workload to maintain performance, prevent service disruption, minimise downtime, mitigate the impact of the detected anomaly, and ensure availability.

3.2 Prediction Models

Three different models were tested for the prediction component:

- **Random Forest Classifier:** A supervised learning algorithm for both classification and regression tasks [3]. It was chosen as the baseline model for its accuracy and quick training. Parameter fine-tuning was performed using grid search with the *Grid-SearchCV* class from the *scikit-learn* library [19].
- **Neural Network:** Four different architectures, each more complex than the previ-ous, were trained with the *Adam* optimiser for up to 100 epochs. They used *cate-gorical_crossentropy* or *binary_crossentropy* loss functions based on the problem. To prevent overfitting and adjust learning rates, *EarlyStopping* and *ReduceLROn-Plateau* callbacks were added. The data was normalised using the *StandardScaler* class from the *scikit-learn* library [19].
- **Convolutional Neural Network:** Although primarily used for image classification, CNNs can also classify time series data. Data preprocessing is a crucial step for CNN training and evaluation. The data was reshaped into a 3-dimensional array and normalised, representing grey-scale images. With this transformation, the CNN can use information from the previous N time stamps. Two normalisation approaches were explored in this work:
  - **Local Normalisation:** Normalised the data according to maximum capacity, excluding the ipscap[1] feature, and normalising according to the maximum number of containers in the host.
  - **Global Normalisation:** Normalised data features according to their maximum values in the training dataset.

It is important to note that resource usages were normalised the same way for both approaches, divided by 100, as usages are presented as percentages. The CNN models were trained for up to 100 epochs using the *Adam* optimiser and *categori-cal_crossentropy* loss function.

---

[1] Node's Million Instructions Per Second (MIPS) maximum capacity. It was removed because, for local normalisation, it would always be a 1.

Different metrics, including accuracy, precision, recall, and F1 score, were used to evaluate and compare the models. Our models were specifically used to predict CPU stress and identify anomalies related to CPU usage. However, they are adaptable to other resources, such as RAM, disk usage, and energy consumption, with minimal adjustments to the input data and normalisation processes. Model architectures and training parameters are detailed in [10].

4   Evaluation Methodology

This section outlines the simulation methodology and tools for validating the proposed solution, starting with the simulator.

4.1   Simulation Tool

Due to its scalability, speed, ease of setup, and low cost, we opted for a simulator over a real environment to generate the datasets needed to train the anomaly prediction system. The chosen simulator was COSCO [28], an AI-based container orchestrator for C2E environments, designed to optimise resource allocation and used to explore various task-scheduling algorithms. As illustrated in Fig. 2, COSCO is divided into two main components: the simulator and the framework, corresponding to simulated and physical environments.

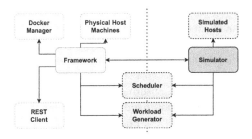

Fig. 2. COSCO high level architecture, adapted from [28].

The simulator emulates hosts, allowing the definition of their characteristics and workloads. The framework runs physical nodes as hosts and instantiates tasks as Docker containers. It communicates with the simulator via REST APIs. This study only used the simulator, with plans to shift to a real testbed with the framework component.

4.2   Extensions to COSCO

Despite COSCO being a valuable tool, it required some modifications to match our research needs since it was initially focused on task placement problems. Our extended version is available in a public repository[2] and is further detailed in [10]. The modifications include:

---

[2] https://github.com/brunofaria1322/COSCO.

- **Addition of Microservice Support, as SCs:** Microservices as containers were supported by COSCO, but there was a lack of interoperability amongst them. To develop services of sequentially running linear chains of microservices, we implemented SCs. For this work, each chain comprised three containers: one on the edge, one on the fog, and one on the cloud, forming an SC with a unidirectional flow from the edge to the cloud.
- **Addition of Replicas:** Redundancy through node replicas was crucial for enhancing the system's resilience. This allows for seamless failover and load balancing in case of anomalies. We modified the simulator to create and manage replicas of each node. These replicas will only receive containers whenever a host is found anomalous, and containers will be migrated to it.
- **Stress Injector:** We needed a mechanism to introduce stress into the system to simulate anomalies, mimicking real-world scenarios in which nodes experience high resource usage or other stress conditions. We developed a stress injector to simulate various stress conditions on numerous targets, such as CPU, RAM, and disk usage spikes. This tool is further detailed in Sect. 4.4.
- **Reduction of Simulation Time Complexity:** The original COSCO simulator had a time complexity of $O(n^2)$, where n is the number of time intervals in the simulation, which was inefficient for large-scale simulations. We pruned and optimised the simulator, reducing its time complexity to linear $O(n)$. This enhancement significantly improved the simulator's performance and scalability, allowing the simulation of more extensive scenarios during larger time intervals in a reasonable time.
- **Use Case:** Considering an urban safety application in a smart city context, edge devices such as cameras and sensors collect real-time data. This data is then processed, and initial decisions are made at the fog layer with intermediate computational capabilities. Finally, the processed data is sent to the cloud for further analysis, statistics, and management tasks. This structure forms an SC with a unidirectional flow from the edge to the cloud, ensuring immediate actions are taken close to the data source. In contrast, the cloud handles more resource-intensive tasks such as long-term analytics and storage [25]. For such a critical application, resilience and availability are paramount since any system downtime could lead to severe consequences, such as accidents at pedestrian crossings. To ensure robustness, stress is injected into the system to mimic unusual behaviours like CPU, memory, and disk usage spikes. These stress conditions can compromise system performance, highlighting the necessity for redundancy. The system can seamlessly handle failover and load balancing by incorporating node replicas. When an anomaly is detected, containers can be migrated from the stressed node to its replicas, maintaining continuous service availability and performance.

4.3 Workload Datasets

To simulate the proposed environment, workloads were defined using datasets created by Azure and BitBrains, built with real-world data. However, these datasets alone were insufficient for anomaly prediction tasks due to their lack of specific anomaly-related data. They only contain resource load information, primarily used to enhance the realism of simulations by providing baseline performance metrics.

The BitBrains dataset [23] was created using metrics from 1750 Virtual Machines (VMs) in a distributed datacenter from Bitbrains[3]. It is organised into two traces: *fastStorage* and *Rnd*. Since *fastStorage* focuses on fast storage machines, the more general *Rnd* trace was chosen, containing the performance metrics of 500 VMs.

The Azure dataset [1,7] is divided into two traces from 2017 and 2019. Only the 2019 trace was used, as it is more recent and contains information about 2 million VMs and 1.9 billion readings.

Workloads were created using the BitBrains dataset as a base and adding the Azure dataset by attributing a percentage of the Azure CPU usage to each VM of the BitBrains dataset for each time interval, as in the work by [28].

4.4 Anomalies and Stress

In this work, a host is considered anomalous by the detection system when resource usage surpasses 90%, as many cloud and edge computing decision-making mechanisms employ this kind of threshold-based decision-making methodology [27]. The prediction component tries to predict the intentional stress applied to the system. This definition is aligned with established fault injection techniques for testing resilience and dependability [9].

To emulate potential environment-related anomalies, a stress injector was developed based on the *stress-ng* tool[4], which is widely used in industry [8,21,22,24], offering various CPU-specific stress tests.

The stress injector generates transparent containers that are invisible to the host but consume its resources, simulating real workloads. Inspired by [24], two types of anomalies were simulated:

– **Recurrent Anomaly:** Occurs at regular intervals, each time with potentially different intensity.
– **Cumulative Anomaly:** Increasing intensity over time, progressively worsening.

The concepts of a fault interval and cooldown interval were adopted from the same work [24]. The fault interval is when stress can be injected, and the cooldown interval is the time between faults, allowing for recovery. Figure 3 depicts the stress injection process for recurrent and cumulative anomalies.

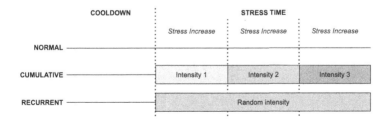

Fig. 3. Types of anomalies that can be injected.

---

[3] http://gwa.ewi.tudelft.nl/datasets/gwa-t-12-bitbrains.
[4] https://manpages.ubuntu.com/manpages/xenial/man1/stress-ng.1.html.

4.5 Simulation Setup

Figure 4 provides a visual overview of the key steps in the simulation process.

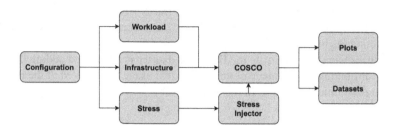

Fig. 4. Experimental methodology.

Table 2 summarises the essential parameters and configurations employed in the simulation, based on [28].

To minimise statistical errors, 30 simulations were run, each with 1000 intervals, resulting in 30, 000 data entries per host. The infrastructure consisted of 50 nodes, generating a random tree-like scenario at the beginning of each simulation. The infrastructure architecture comprises three layers: cloud, fog, and edge. The cloud layer has fewer nodes but more resources and can process data from multiple fog nodes. The fog layer stays between the cloud and the edge, and each fog node can process data from multiple edge nodes. The edge layer is closer to the user and has many more nodes but fewer resources. In our scenario, they are the starting points of the SCs. An example of this architecture is shown in Fig. 5, where we can distinguish these three layers and the flow of information.

Table 2 also includes details about the capacities, ranges, and latencies of the nodes in each layer. Additionally, it covers the characteristics of containers, such as duration, which follows a normal distribution, and the number of arrivals per edge host, following a Poisson distribution. At the end of the table, the stress parameters like cooldown time, stress time, and stress increase time are shown, corresponding to the stress injection process of Fig. 3, as well as the stress probability and the number of containers injected for each stress increase time.

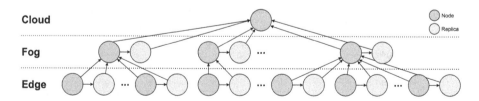

Fig. 5. Example of infrastructure.

Table 2. Simulation parameters.

Element	Parameter	Value (min - max)
Simulation	Number of runs	30
	Number of steps	1000
Infrastructure	Number of cloud nodes	1
	Number of fog + edge nodes	50
Cloud	Resources	∞
	Latency (ms)	76
Fog	CPU capacity (MIPS)	24576–40960
	RAM capacity (GB)	48–80
	Disk capacity (GB)	96–160
	Latency (ms)	20
Edge	CPU capacity (MIPS)	2054–8192
	RAM capacity (GB)	2–8
	Disk capacity (GB)	4–16
	Latency (ms)	3
Containers	Duration (time intervals)	$\mathcal{N}(4, 1^2)$
	Number of arrivals	$\mathcal{P}(2)$
Stress	Cooldown time (time intervals)	14
	Stress time (time intervals)	6
	Stress increase time (time intervals)	2
	Stress probability	0.3
	Number of containers injected	2

5   Results and Discussion

This section presents the results of our simulations and anomaly prediction experiments. The simulation results (Sect. 5.1) show the plots obtained from the simulation, which allow the visualisation of the functioning of the implemented components and the datasets used to develop the ML models. The anomaly prediction results (Sect. 5.2) focus on the performance of different ML models in the multiclass problem, where the models were trained to predict the stress intensity, and the binary problem, where the models were trained to predict whether an anomaly was occurring or not.

5.1   Simulation Results

Initially, COSCO provided metrics regarding the host's CPU, RAM, disk usage, energy consumption, and number of running containers. After implementing the stress injector, stress intensity data was also collected. Table 3 shows a dataset sample for CPU anomalies. The generated dataset contains four different stress intensities, including no stress (intensity 0).

A test was conducted to observe the behaviour of a host and replica node during stress injection and migration using a cooldown time and a stress time of 10 time intervals, and a stress increase time and a stress probability of 1, resulting in 10 different stress intensities. This setup helps provide a clear visualisation of the anomaly detection and mitigation system in action, as illustrated in Fig. 6, where it shows CPU usage and container count on both host and replica nodes fluctuating according to stress levels. When stress reached critical levels, the system initiated container migration to the replica node, increasing container and CPU usage and demonstrating the system's ability to detect anomalies and maintain performance by redistributing workloads.

Table 3. Sample of the dataset for CPU anomalies.

CPU usage	Number of containers	Base IPS	Available IPS	IPS cap	Apparent IPS	Stress intensity
6.6	4	467.1	15643.9	16111.0	1060.0	0
31.7	10	551.3	3477.7	4029.0	1278.0	1
16.2	8	748.0	7354.0	8102.0	1313.0	0
23.8	7	257.7	7844.3	8102.0	1927.0	2
15.3	7	399.8	7702.2	8102.0	1242.0	0

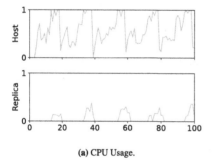

(a) CPU Usage.

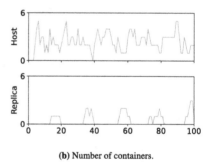

(b) Number of containers.

Fig. 6. Metrics of the fog host and replica during the stress injection test.

5.2 Anomaly Prediction Results

The datasets generated during the simulations were used to train and evaluate the ML models. Three training and testing strategies were initially employed, as shown in Fig. 7: training and testing with the same host (one model per host), training and testing with hosts from the same layer (one model per layer), and training and testing with all nodes (one global model). Ultimately, we adopted the strategy of training and testing with elements of the same layer (one model per layer), as having one model per host is not scalable and consumes excessive resources, and global models cannot adapt to specific host characteristics, resulting in inferior performance. One model per layer allows

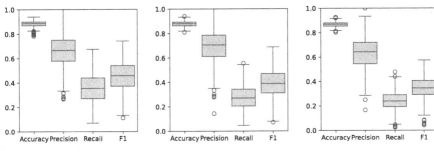

(a) Trained and tested with the same host (local model).

(b) Trained and tested with hosts from the same layer (layer model).

(c) Trained and tested with all the hosts (global model).

Fig. 7. Preliminary results of the RFC for the CPU stress.

each model to adjust to the similarities within the same layer, balancing scalability and specificity.

The data split involved using 70% of the data for training and 30% for testing, or 70% for training, 10% for validation, and the remaining 20% for testing when performing validation. Table 4 summarises the results of the ML experiments.

Table 4. Evaluation results for the most relevant ML models.

	Multiclass				Binary			
	Accuracy	Precision	Recall	F1	Accuracy	Precision	Recall	F1
	Random Forest Classifier							
Fog	0.8913	0.6937	0.4968	0.5519	0.9111	0.7793	0.5460	0.6421
Edge	0.8863	0.6431	0.4897	0.5395	0.9073	0.7635	0.5298	0.6255
	Neural Network							
Fog	0.8991	0.7160	0.5596	0.6188	0.9183	0.8816	0.7622	0.8058
Edge	0.8901	0.6513	0.5947	0.6136	0.9122	0.8544	0.7623	0.7981
	Convolutional Neural Network with Global Normalisation							
Fog	0.9230	0.7548	0.7228	0.7322	0.9363	0.9084	0.8230	0.8584
Edge	0.9265	0.8159	0.6645	0.7267	0.9438	0.9169	0.8485	0.8781

The results show that CNNs achieved the highest performance, with an F1-score of around 73% for the multiclass problem and 87% for the binary problem, both related to CPU anomalies.

Binary classification consistently outperformed the multiclass problem. This suggests that the models are better at predicting the occurrence of anomalies rather than classifying their intensity. This can be attributed to the inherent complexity of distinguishing between multiple levels of fault intensity as opposed to a more straightforward binary decision.

When comparing the *Fog* and *Edge* models, it was observed that *Fog* tends to have slightly higher performance scores compared to *Edge*. The exception was noted in the CNN with global normalisation, where the *Edge* model outperformed the *Fog* model by nearly 2%.

The global normalisation approach yielded the best results among the CNNs. This suggests that uniform data scaling across the entire dataset helped the model better understand and predict the anomalous scenarios.

These findings demonstrate that using ML for anomaly prediction in complex environments like the C2E continuum is a viable approach. By enabling proactive responses to potential failures, the recovery time for critical services can be significantly improved. This proactive failure management is crucial for maintaining the reliability and performance of network infrastructures supporting critical applications.

6   Future Work

This work lays the foundation for future research to enhance the resilience and efficiency of the C2E continuum. Given the generic nature of the AI models and approaches, there is significant room for improvement.

One key area of future work involves improving the performance of anomaly prediction models. Most models presented in this work do not utilise information from previous time steps, and those that do only consider short time frames. To address this, future research will explore advanced time series models such as Long Short-Term Memory (LSTM) networks and transformers.

Another critical area is the continuous learning and adaptation of the models. Since normal behaviour can change over time and with usage, developing systems that can adapt to new patterns and conditions is crucial. This raises challenges in classifying normal and abnormal data, particularly in defining true labels for training. Future work will explore adaptive systems capable of evolving with changing data patterns.

To address the limitations of the centralised model, future research will explore distributed ML approaches [2, 4]. The current centralised approach can lead to single points of failure and scalability issues. Decentralised MANO can distribute decision-making across multiple nodes, enhancing system resilience and scalability while reducing the risk of single points of failure. By performing AI tasks closer to where the data is generated, this approach potentially reduces the need for data transmission, thereby lowering latency, increasing speed, and enhancing the overall performance of the Cloud-to-Thing (C2T) continuum.

However, bringing AI closer to the edge introduces new challenges due to the resource-constrained nature of edge devices. Therefore, future work will incorporate techniques like model pruning and other lightweight strategies to create faster and more efficient models. These approaches aim to reduce the computational load, making AI more suitable for edge environments and promoting a sustainable, energy-efficient future [5, 14, 30].

Extending the scope of simulations to more complex scenarios will also be a critical area of research. This includes deploying the system in real testbed environments and evaluating the impact of the self-organising system on service downtime and availability during anomaly mitigation tasks.

7   Conclusions

This work proposes a self-organising approach for anomaly detection and prediction in the C2E continuum. Our solution integrates proactive and reactive mechanisms to provide a zero-touch approach for self-healing solutions. The ML models developed for this purpose have demonstrated promising results in predicting anomalies, achieving F1 scores of up to 73% for multiclass problems and 87% for binary problems. The simulation platform was extended to validate our approach and generate datasets to train our models. The system effectively combines proactive and reactive anomaly management, helping reduce service downtime and enhancing the overall reliability and robustness of C2E systems.

While this work establishes a solid foundation for anomaly management in C2E environments, it primarily serves as a baseline for future research. The proposed models and methods provide a starting point for more sophisticated and scalable solutions. Future research directions and open challenges have been identified, paving the way for further advancements in the field.

Acknowledgments. This work is funded by the FCT - Foundation for Science and Technology, I.P./MCTES through national funds (PIDDAC), within the scope of CISUC R&D Unit - UIDB/00326/2020 or project code UIDP/00326/2020.

Content produced within the scope of the Agenda "NEXUS - Pacto de Inovação - Transição Verde e Digital para Transportes, Logística e Mobilidade", financed by the Portuguese Recovery and Resilience Plan (PRR), with no. C645112083-00000059 (investment project no. .° 53).

Disclosure of Interests. The authors have no competing interests to declare that are relevant to the content of this article.

References

1. Azure/AzurePublicDataset. Microsoft Azure (2024). https://github.com/Azure/AzurePublicDataset. Accessed 16 June 2023
2. Arzovs, A., Judvaitis, J., Nesenbergs, K., Selavo, L.: Distributed learning in the IoT-edge-cloud continuum. Mach. Learn. Knowl. Extract. **6**(1), 283–315 (2024). https://doi.org/10.3390/make6010015
3. Breiman, L.: Random forests. Mach. Learn. **45**(1), 5–32 (2001). https://doi.org/10.1023/A:1010933404324
4. Chen, M., et al.: Distributed learning in wireless networks: recent progress and future challenges. IEEE J. Sel. Areas Commun. **39**(12), 3579–3605 (2021). https://doi.org/10.1109/JSAC.2021.3118346
5. European Commission: The European Green Deal - European Commission (2021). https://commission.europa.eu/strategy-and-policy/priorities-2019-2024/european-green-deal_en. Accessed 12 Apr 2024
6. Coronado, E., et al.: Zero touch management: a survey of network automation solutions for 5G and 6G networks. IEEE Commun. Surv. Tutor. **24**(4), 2535–2578 (2022). https://doi.org/10.1109/COMST.2022.3212586

7. Cortez, E., Bonde, A., Muzio, A., Russinovich, M., Fontoura, M., Bianchini, R.: Resource central: understanding and predicting workloads for improved resource management in large cloud platforms. In: Proceedings of the 26th Symposium on Operating Systems Principles, SOSP '17, pp. 153–167. Association for Computing Machinery, New York (2017). https://doi.org/10.1145/3132747.3132772

8. Du, Q., He, Yu., Xie, T., Yin, K., Qiu, J.: An approach of collecting performance anomaly dataset for NFV infrastructure. In: Vaidya, J., Li, J. (eds.) ICA3PP 2018. LNCS, vol. 11336, pp. 59–71. Springer, Cham (2018). https://doi.org/10.1007/978-3-030-05057-3_5

9. Du, Q., Xie, T., He, Yu.: Anomaly detection and diagnosis for container-based microservices with performance monitoring. In: Vaidya, J., Li, J. (eds.) ICA3PP 2018. LNCS, vol. 11337, pp. 560–572. Springer, Cham (2018). https://doi.org/10.1007/978-3-030-05063-4_42

10. Faria, B.: Self-organising engine for the cloud-to-edge continuum. Master's thesis, University of Coimbra, Coimbra, Portugal (2023). https://hdl.handle.net/10316/110708

11. Gallego-Madrid, J., Sanchez-Iborra, R., Ruiz, P.M., Skarmeta, A.F.: Machine learning-based zero-touch network and service management: a survey. Digit. Commun. Netw. **8**(2), 105–123 (2022). https://doi.org/10.1016/j.dcan.2021.09.001

12. Kumar, Y., Farooq, H., Imran, A.: Fault prediction and reliability analysis in a real cellular network. In: 2017 13th International Wireless Communications and Mobile Computing Conference (IWCMC), pp. 1090–1095 (2017). https://doi.org/10.1109/IWCMC.2017.7986437

13. Liyanage, M., et al.: A survey on Zero touch network and Service Management (ZSM) for 5G and beyond networks. J. Netw. Comput. Appl. **203**, 103362 (2022). https://doi.org/10.1016/j.jnca.2022.103362

14. Mao, B., Tang, F., Kawamoto, Y., Kato, N.: AI models for green communications towards 6G. IEEE Commun. Surv. Tutor. **24**(1) (2021). https://doi.org/10.1109/COMST.2021.3130901

15. Marchese, A., Tomarchio, O.: Sophos: a framework for application orchestration in the cloud-to-edge continuum. In: Proceedings of the 13th International Conference on Cloud Computing and Services Science - CLOSER, pp. 261–268. SCITEPRESS - Science and Technology Publications, Prague (2023). https://doi.org/10.5220/0011972600003488

16. Moustapha, A.I., Selmic, R.R.: Wireless sensor network modeling using modified recurrent neural networks: application to fault detection. IEEE Trans. Instrum. Measur. **57**(5), 981–988 (2008). https://doi.org/10.1109/TIM.2007.913803

17. Palakurti, N.R.: Challenges and future directions in anomaly detection. In: Practical Applications of Data Processing, Algorithms, and Modeling, pp. 269–284. IGI Global (2024). https://doi.org/10.4018/979-8-3693-2909-2.ch020

18. Pang, G., Shen, C., Cao, L., Hengel, A.V.D.: Deep learning for anomaly detection: a review. ACM Comput. Surv. **54**(2), 38:1–38:38 (2021). https://doi.org/10.1145/3439950

19. Pedregosa, F., et al.: Scikit-learn: machine learning in Python. J. Mach. Learn. Res. **12**, 2825–2830 (2011)

20. Pellegrini, A., Sanzo, P.D., Avresky, D.R.: A machine learning-based framework for building application failure prediction models. In: 2015 IEEE International Parallel and Distributed Processing Symposium Workshop, pp. 1072–1081 (2015). https://doi.org/10.1109/IPDPSW.2015.110

21. Sauvanaud, C., Kaâniche, M., Kanoun, K., Lazri, K., Da Silva Silvestre, G.: Anomaly detection and diagnosis for cloud services: practical experiments and lessons learned. J. Syst. Softw. **139**, 84–106 (2018). https://doi.org/10.1016/j.jss.2018.01.039

22. Sauvanaud, C., Lazri, K., Kaâniche, M., Kanoun, K.: Anomaly detection and root cause localization in virtual network functions. In: 2016 IEEE 27th International Symposium on Software Reliability Engineering (ISSRE), pp. 196–206 (2016). https://doi.org/10.1109/ISSRE.2016.32

23. Shen, S., Van Beek, V., Iosup, A.: Statistical characterization of business-critical workloads hosted in cloud datacenters. In: 2015 15th IEEE/ACM International Symposium on Cluster, Cloud and Grid Computing, pp. 465–474 (2015). https://doi.org/10.1109/CCGrid.2015.60
24. Soualhia, M., Fu, C., Khomh, F.: Infrastructure fault detection and prediction in edge cloud environments. In: Proceedings of the 4th ACM/IEEE Symposium on Edge Computing, SEC '19, pp. 222–235. Association for Computing Machinery, New York (2019). https://doi.org/10.1145/3318216.3363305
25. Sousa, B., et al.: Estudos Preliminares na área do Projeto. Technical report E2.1, Universidade de Coimbra (2021). https://oreos.pt/wp-content/uploads/2022/05/RD-OREOS-17PT-E2.1-EstudosPreliminaresNaA%CC%81reaDoProjeto.pdf
26. Su, J., et al.: Large language models for forecasting and anomaly detection: a systematic literature review (2024). arXiv:2402.10350. https://doi.org/10.48550/arXiv.2402.10350
27. Theodoropoulos, T., Violos, J., Tsanakas, S., Leivadeas, A., Tserpes, K., Varvarigou, T.: Intelligent proactive fault tolerance at the edge through resource usage prediction. ITU J. Future Evolving Technol. 3(3), 761–778 (2022). https://doi.org/10.52953/EHJP3291
28. Tuli, S., Poojara, S.R., Srirama, S.N., Casale, G., Jennings, N.R.: COSCO: container orchestration using co-simulation and gradient based optimization for fog computing environments. IEEE Trans. Parallel Distrib. Syst. 33(1), 101–116 (2022). https://doi.org/10.1109/TPDS.2021.3087349
29. Tusa, F., Clayman, S.: End-to-end slices to orchestrate resources and services in the cloud-to-edge continuum. Future Gener. Comput. Syst. 141, 473–488 (2023). https://doi.org/10.1016/j.future.2022.11.026
30. Verdecchia, R., Sallou, J., Cruz, L.: A systematic review of Green AI. WIREs Data Min. Knowl. Discov. 13(4), e1507 (2023). https://doi.org/10.1002/widm.1507
31. Zhang, T., Zhu, K., Hossain, E.: Data-driven machine learning techniques for self-healing in cellular wireless networks: challenges and solutions. Intell. Comput. 2022, 1–8 (2022). https://doi.org/10.34133/2022/9758169

TALOS: Task Level Autoscaler for Apache Flink

Ourania Ntouni◉ and Euripides G. M. Petrakis(✉)◉

School of Electrical and Computer Engineering, Technical University of Crete (TUC), Chania,
Crete, Greece
ontouni@tuc.gr, petrakis@intelligence.tuc.gr

Abstract. Apache Flink must scale its computational resources at run-time to
comply with the real-time response requirements of fast-paced and changing
workloads. TALOS is a task autoscaler designed to optimize Flink jobs' performance while minimizing infrastructure usage costs in the cloud. Most autoscaling methods solve the resource adaptation problem by allocating new resources
to the entire Flink job (i.e., pipeline). These solutions are suboptimal since not all
tasks are equally stressed and do not need to be scaled, leading to over or under-
provisioning of resources. TALOS monitors each task individually to decide how
to scale the task based on its own data processing needs, without being affected by
the performance of other upstream or downstream tasks. TALOS provides a better performance-to-cost ratio compared to the state-of-the-art Autoscaler of Flink
Kubernetes Operator. Both agents are tested on sophisticated workloads running
a click fraud detection application for several hours.

Keywords: Apache flink · Apache kafka · Flink kubernetes operator · Task
autoscaler

1 Introduction

In today's data-driven landscape, big data platforms are the impulse behind the operations of many enterprises. These platforms empower organizations to manage the mas-
sive volumes of data generated daily for absorbing information, performing analytics,
and making crucial decisions. Big data platforms like Apache Flink [1] are driven to
manage the complexities of real-time data streams. Apache Flink ingests data from a
public-subscribe service like Apache Kafka [12] that ensures prompt delivery and no
data loss. Applications are defined as sequences of operations that run in parallel on different workers (i.e., servers or CPU threads). Individual processing actions are the *tasks*;
the entire sequence of tasks (i.e., the application pipeline) is a *job*. The parallelism of an
application translates to the maximum number of workers. The main problem is to find
the optimal parallelism for a Flink job that maximizes the performance while minimizing application latency and cost (i.e., Apache Flink cloud clients are charged based on
the amount of computing resources they consume). Ideally, parallelism must be scaled
(up or down) automatically to ensure optimal performance and cost-efficiency, especially in the presence of oscillating workloads characterized by rapid fluctuations in
data send rate and processing requirements.

M. Comuzzi et al. (Eds.): CoopIS 2024, LNCS 15506, pp. 280–295, 2025.
https://doi.org/10.1007/978-3-031-81375-7_16

Operations in Apache Flink can be *stateful*. This means that past events can influence how a current event is processed. Stateful processing allows Flink applications to maintain and leverage state information across multiple events. This capability proves essential in applications where understanding the context of events and tracking their evolution over time is necessary. Being distributed and stateful, Apache Flink complicates the scaling (i.e., changing the parallelism) of the application because different workers have to share the same state. Flink's parallelism can be changed by stopping the job, taking a savepoint of the current state of the stream, and then restarting the job with different parallelism from this snapshot. Restoring from a savepoint takes a significant amount of time during which incoming records are not being processed. Once the application is restarted, it should try to catch up on any accumulated records in the input. Downtime refers to the period during which a Flink application is not processing data because it is being updated. Downtime causes records to accumulate in queues, underscoring the inefficiency in the performance.

The options for scaling FLINK are by operator - task, or job level. Job scaling achieves an evenly-balanced load across tasks and operators that minimizes their inter-dependencies and communication [5,19,20]. On the other hand, task scaling offers the advantage of fine-grained resource management, enabling optimization at the level of individual computational tasks to enhance performance. Lately, a few authors have shown interest in creating task scaling agents [9,11,17].

TALOS dynamically adjusts the parallelism of tasks within a pipeline. Each task autonomously determines how to scale based on its own data processing needs, without being influenced by the data processing outcomes of *upstream* (i.e., previous) or *downstream* (i.e., following) operations. This independence between tasks, allows TALOS to effectively handle cases of split data (i.e., when a task sends different portions of data to downstream tasks). Consequently, the parallelism chosen for each task is exclusively based on metrics specific to that task. This ensures that TALOS can react promptly and accurately to workload changes, regardless of how data is partitioned or distributed across different operators within the Apache Flink application. The fundamental monitoring metrics in TALOS are the number of queued records and the throughput of each task individually.

The pioneering efforts for DS2 task autoscaler [9] provided valuable insights and inspiration, catalyzing the development of the initial task autoscaler for Apache Flink. DS2's primary objective is throughput optimization without taking into consideration the infrastructure cost in the cloud (i.e., application users in the cloud are charged by the amount of computational resources they consume). Also, its task monitoring metrics rely on the throughput of upstream operators. This dependency can lead to suboptimal scaling decisions in the case of scenarios where data is split to be routed to different tasks. DS2 and TALOS are evaluated using a fluctuating workload with a high send rate for several hours on the Google Cloud Platform (GCP). The experiments revealed that DS2 scaling actions are limited keeping parallelism at higher values than needed as the algorithm's objective is enhancing throughput. Compared to TALOS, this leads to overprovisioning of resources and higher operational costs over time.

Related work on FLINK autoscaling is discussed in Sect. 2. Issues related to Apache Flink deployment on Kubernetes and scaling are discussed in Sect. 3. TALOS autoscaler solution is presented in Sect. 4 followed by evaluation results in Sect. 5. Conclusions, system extensions, and issues for future research are discussed in Sect. 6.

2   Related Work and Background

Autoscaling is the ability to adjust the resources and the parallelism of a stream processing application according to the workload and the performance requirements. However, Flink autoscaling poses significant challenges in terms of state management, latency, accuracy, and cost. Reactive scaling adjusts resources based on real-time workload changes. Proactive scaling relies on machine learning to predict the changes in the workload and resource needs. TALOS takes a reactive approach by considering the rate of change of the workload and leveraging real-time monitoring metrics to predict scale-up or scale-down decisions.

HYAS [20] is a hybrid job autoscaling controller for Apache Flink. It is inspired by Varga et al. [18] and uses the same metrics to propose a job autoscaler based on performance statistics of individual tasks. It monitors and models the responsiveness of the Flink operators based on their idleness, backpressure, and input record lag, and applies a set of rule and threshold policies to adjust the parallelism of a Flink job. HYAS aims to minimize resources and achieve faster response times. TALOS shares similar ideas with HYAS but takes the method one step forward and proposes a task autoscaler.

DS2 [9] is an automatic task scaling agent for Apache Flink. DS2 uses a general performance model of streaming dataflows and lightweight instrumentation to estimate the true processing time and output rates of individual operators. True processing time refers to the actual time it takes for a system to process a given set of data inputs, from the moment they are received until the final output is produced. Based on these estimates, DS2 decides when and how to scale the tasks of the pipeline to achieve optimal throughput. DS2 optimizes dataflow scaling within a maximum of three steps, preventing excessive fluctuations and reducing the time needed to stabilize. The algorithm has been integrated into the Apache Flink Kubernetes Operator [8].

QAAS [11] is a quick accurate task auto-scaling method for streaming processing jobs in Apache Flink. QAAS uses a nonlinear model to represent the performance of operators, which are the basic units of processing logic in Flink. QAAS divides the operator performance into three stages: non-competition, non-full competition, and full competition. Based on these stages, QAAS can accurately predict the CPU utilization and throughput of operators given their parallelism. QAAS also collects metrics from running Flink jobs and estimates the optimal parallelism for each operator to achieve the target utilization and avoid backpressure. QAAS is a proactive autoscaler, meaning that it anticipates the load changes and adjusts the resources accordingly, rather than reacting to the load changes at the time they occur.

Meces [17] is a method for rescaling stateful distributed stream processing systems, such as Apache Flink, with low latency and high efficiency. It prioritizes the state migration of the most critical operators, which are the ones that have the largest backlog and the highest processing rate. It uses a graph partitioning algorithm to minimize the communication cost and the state migration time. State migration refers to the process of transferring the operational state (data and configuration) of these critical tasks to new or different resources during scaling operations. Meces aims to improve the scalability, reliability, and resource utilization of stream processing applications. Compared to TALOS, Meces focalizes in-state migration, decreasing latency peaks after scaling.

Smilax [5] is a statistical machine learning agent for Apache Flink applications. It predicts the changes in the workload and adjusts the number of workers to match these changes. Each worker runs the entire Flink Job. During online training, it builds a model that maps the performance of the application to the minimum number of workers. It aims to optimize the resource utilization, the latency, and the cost of Flink applications. During the work (optimal) phase, Smilax maintains the performance of the application within acceptable limits (i.e., defined in the form of SLAs) while minimizing the utilization of resources.

Ververica Platform Autopilot [19] is a job scaling agent for Apache Flink that monitors and models the responsiveness of the Flink operators based on their idleness, backpressure, and input record lag. It uses rule and threshold policies to adjust the parallelism of the operators at job level according to the workload and the performance requirements. Ververica Platform Autopilot aims to optimize the resource utilization, the latency, and the cost of Flink applications.

Table 1 summarizes the comparison of all methods. TALOS differs from these works in several aspects, such as the scaling objectives, the scaling granularity, the scaling frequency, and the scaling evaluation. Most importantly, the primary aim of TALOS is to optimize both performance and cost (by minimizing computational resources).

Table 1. Summarization of all methods.

Autoscaler	Task Scaling	Job Scaling	Re-active	Pro-active
TALOS	✓		✓	
HYAS [20]		✓	✓	✓
Smilax [5]		✓		✓
DS2 [9]	✓		✓	
Meces [17]	✓		✓	
QAAS [11]	✓			✓
Ververica [19]		✓	✓	

3   Flink Deployment

Tasks are components of a job in execution. Every task is carried out by a specific number of threads, equivalent to its corresponding level of parallelism. A subtask is a parallel instance of a task. Each task includes at least one operator. If there are multiple operators within the same task, they are considered chained. A chain can be created only if no network action (i.e., *keyBy()*, *shuffle()*, *rebalance()*), redistributing data across different task instances has occurred between the chained operators. Flink has a built-in mechanism to optimize operator chaining (if chaining is not disabled).

Each Task Manager is a JVM process and may execute one or more subtasks in separate threads. A Task Manager may accommodate more than tasks in *task slots*. The number of task slots can define the maximum parallelism, that a Task Manager supports. By default, Flink allows subtasks to share slots even if they are subtasks of different tasks, as long as they are from the same job. The result is that one slot may hold an entire pipeline of the job. The benefit of slot sharing is better resource utilization. Without slot sharing, non-intensive subtasks (e.g., a *sink* operator) would block as many resources as other resource-intensive (e.g., *window*) subtasks.

Each task slot represents a fixed subset of resources of the Task Manager. No CPU isolation happens and subtasks compete with each other for CPU; However, task slots only separate the managed memory of subtasks. A subtask will not compete with subtasks from other jobs for managed memory but instead has a certain amount of reserved memory. By adjusting the number of task slots, users can define how subtasks are isolated from each other. Having one slot per Task Manager means that each task group runs in a separate JVM (which can be started in a separate container or Kubernetes Pod). Having multiple slots means more subtasks share the same JVM. Tasks in the same JVM share TCP connections (via multiplexing) and heartbeat messages. They may also share data sets and data structures, thus reducing the per-task overhead.

3.1   Job and Task Scaling

An operator or a subtask (the parallel instance of a task), is the lowest granularity unit that can be assigned to a task slot, executed on a thread (or machine), and scaled independently. This is the case of task scaling. An alternative is to map the entire job to a task slot. Accordingly, the options for scaling FLINK are by operator-task-subtask or job (pipeline) level. Pipeline scaling achieves an evenly balanced load across tasks and operators, minimizing their interdependencies and communication [16]. Rescaling actions (e.g., adding or removing workers) will modify the parallelism of all operators of a subtask at the same time. HYAS [20] abd Ververica [19] are autoscaler operating at job level.

Figure 1 illustrates a data flow with parallelism 1 (on the left) and the same data flow with parallelism 2 (on its right) after job and task scaling respectively. Before scaling, the Task Manager has one slot that runs the job. After job scaling, the pipeline is replicated. The Task Manager shares its resources between two task slots. Each one executes the entire job in parallel, on a separate thread. The Task Manager will dedicate half of its managed memory to each slot. In that case, the threads are contending for the CPU. Figure 1 (c) is a task scaling example; only *keyby()* operator (i.e., subtask) is replicated leaving resources for other operators (or subtasks) to be placed in the same Task Manager (if stressed). Only parallel instances of different subtasks can be located in the same task slot.

3.2   Flink Deployment on Kubernetes

The Flink Kubernetes (K8s) Operator [8] simplifies the deployment of Apache Flink applications on Kubernetes clusters, providing a declarative way to configure and scale Flink jobs dynamically. Flink deployments are defined in YAML files. Apache Flink K8s Operator has the DS2 [9] autoscaling mechanism pre-installed. Building upon the same idea, the K8s Operator is updated to accommodate TALOS autoscaler too.

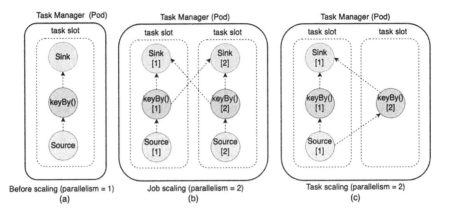

Fig. 1. Flink job and task scaling example.

DS2 and TALOS query the Flink metric system using JMX service and Prometheus [3]. Figure 2 illustrates a Flink deployment with 3 compute nodes (i.e., Task Managers) and TALOS autoscaler (the Control Plane is not shown). Each K8s Pod represents a Task Manager running application tasks. Each K8s Node can run (among other services), TALOS autoscaler and serveral Task Managers on separate Pods. The number of Task Managers may increase if the load grows [7]. In this example, a fourth Task Manager can be added to accommodate new task instances (in response to increasing parallelism) if the existing Task Managers run out of resources. If K8s cluster autoscaler

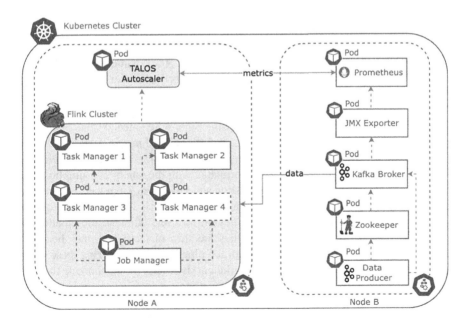

Fig. 2. Apache Flink deployment on Kubernetes.

[6] is enabled, new nodes (i.e., Virtual Machines) will be allocated to accommodate additional Task Managers.

4 TALOS Autoscaler

TALOS, or TaskFlexScaler [14], is designed to efficiently scale the tasks within a Flink job. The TALOS implementation is available online [15]. Operating on a threshold-based approach, the scaling algorithm harnesses multiple metrics to make informed decisions regarding the parallelism of tasks. By incorporating a diverse range of metrics, TALOS ensures a comprehensive evaluation process, thereby enhancing its scalability and adaptability within Flink environments. Tailoring different parallelism levels for each task holds the potential for improved outcomes, as certain tasks may not require extensive resource allocation. This deliberate approach ensures a reflective response to the varying demands of the pipeline, optimizing resource utilization and enhancing overall performance.

By examining various metrics, we gain insights into real-time performance and resource needs, illuminating the relationship between workload dynamics and parallelism adjustments. In the following, metrics for the *source task* (i.e., the first task of the Flink pipeline) and metrics for downstream (intermediate and sink) tasks are discussed separately. The reason is that the source is the only task that communicates with an external service (i.e., Apache Kafka).

4.1 Metrics for Intermediate Tasks

Throughput stands as a pivotal metric in gauging the effectiveness of any Flink job or its tasks, revealing the rate at which records can be processed within a given time frame. TALOS monitors the throughput of individual tasks. Calculating the throughput of intermediate tasks in particular requires two more metrics, namely *recordsInPerSec* and *busyTimeMs*. The *recordsInPerSec* metric represents the number of records the task receives per second and *busyTimeMs* quantifies the duration (in milliseconds) of computation time. Their quotient $\frac{recordsInPerSec}{BusyTimems}$ denotes the average number of records a task can handle within a millisecond of processing time. A heightened value of this metric indicates superior performance. Conversely, a diminished metric value implies that the task handles a smaller data volume, indicating suboptimal performance. Notably, the throughput of source tasks is directly correlated with the rate of consumption from Kafka, reflecting the efficiency of data ingestion and processing from the Kafka source.

The speed at which data can flow through the pipeline is limited by how quickly these downstream tasks can process it. If they are fast and efficient, the pipeline can handle more data per unit of time. But if they are slow or inefficient, they become a bottleneck, limiting the overall throughput of the pipeline. So, optimizing these downstream tasks (making them faster and more efficient) is crucial for maximizing the overall speed and efficiency of the data processing pipeline.

Flink uses *backpressure* [13] to adapt the processing speed of individual operators. An operator can struggle to keep up processing the message volume it receives (e.g., the operation may require more CPU resources or, may wait for I/O operations to complete). If an operator cannot process events fast enough, it builds backpressure in the upstream operators feeding into the slow operator. This causes the upstream operators to slow down, which can further propagate the backpressure to the source and cause the source to adapt to the overall throughput of the application by slowing it down as well. Figure 3 showcases that, the third task in the sequence triggers a backpressure condition for the second task, which in turn extends the backpressure to the first task in the pipeline.

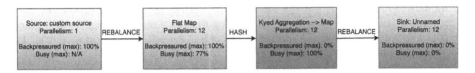

Fig. 3. Flink dataflow example.

To maintain consistent high throughput, Flink uses network buffer queues (also known as in-flight data) on the input and output side of the transmission process. Each subtask has an input queue waiting to consume data and an output queue waiting to send data to the next subtask. A buffer pool in Flink is a collection of buffers that are used to hold data temporarily during the network transmission between tasks in a Flink job. Buffer pools live in the input and in the output of a Flink task feeding or receiving records respectively. Figure 4 illustrates the process of propagating data between tasks. Each task can have more than one input or output buffer, each communicating with other tasks.

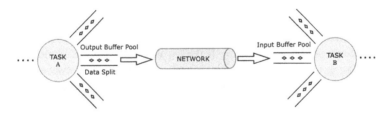

Fig. 4. Data propagation between tasks with input and output buffer pools.

The input buffer pool has an important role in calculating the number of queued records. The lag experienced by an intermediate task corresponds to the records queued. If an operator is backpressured or has low throughput, records accumulate in the input buffers, awaiting processing. Thus, to compute the queued records in the input of intermediate tasks (i.e., except the source), the following buffer pool metric is used

$$queuedRecordsIn = \frac{bufferSize \times inPoolUsage}{avg(bytesPerRecord)}, \tag{1}$$

$$queuedRecordsOut = \frac{bufferSize \times outPoolUsage}{avg(bytesPerRecord)}, \tag{2}$$

where *inPoolUsage* is the percentage of the input buffers usage, *outPoolUsage* is the percentage of the output buffers usage, and *bufferSize* is the size of the input buffer, calculated as the product between the number of buffers in the pool and the size of each buffer in bytes. *inPoolUsage* (or *outPoolUsage*) is *High* if it takes values between $(0.5, 1]$ and *Low* for values between $(0.1, 0.5]$. By monitoring *inPoolUsage* and *outPoolUsage*, the task's "health" (i.e., if the task is backpressured, or it is the bottleneck of the pipeline) can be deduced as follows [10]:

Both Input and Output Buffers Are Full: Output buffers are full, due to the fact that the downstream task is already saturated, preventing the processing of additional records. Likewise, the input buffers are congested as a result of the output buffers being full, thereby impeding further processing. As result, the current task is backpressured by downstream tasks.

Input Buffers Are Full and the Output Buffers' Usage Is Low: When the upstream task experiences backpressure, it signifies that the current task is the bottleneck. This occurs because the upstream task sends data at a high and the current task cannot keep up, due to lower throughput.

Input Buffers' Usage Is Low and Output Buffers Are Full: The current task starts being backpressured by downstream tasks, without upstream tasks being affected, since input buffers' usage is low.

Both Input and Output Buffers' Usage Is Low: The operator can cope with this sending rate and the downstream task is in a healthy condition.

4.2 Metrics for the Source Task

The source task ingests data from Apache Kafka and is the only task connected to an external service. There can be more than one source task reading data from Kafka queues (partitions). The difference between the number of records consumed and the number of records produced is the *lag*. If the lag increases, records accumulate in the queues. The lag is computed from each queue as the difference between the number of records read by the consumer (committed offset) and the total number of records produced (latest offset) at a certain point in time. Figure 5 illustrates an example of Kafka lag on the three partitions of a producer.

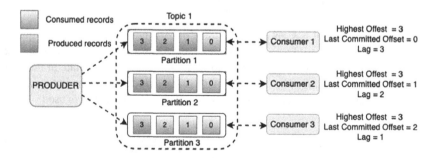

Fig. 5. Scaling example for source and intermediate (downstream) task.

Flink provides *record_lag_max_i* metric which is an upper bound of the lag over all queues read by source task i. The total lag (upper bound) over all queues is calculated using Eq. 3 over 1 min. To ascertain whether Kafka lag grows or drops, TALOS observes the rate of change in Kafka lag relative to *throughput* (i.e., the records consumption rate). For each source task, it is calculated according to Eq. 4 using the *records_consumed_rate* metric of Flink.

$$totalLag = \sum_{i \in instances} \text{record\_lag\_max}_i \quad (records) \tag{3}$$

$$throughput = \sum_{i \in instances} \text{records\_consumed\_rate}_i \quad (records/sec) \tag{4}$$

$$lagChangeRate = \frac{\text{deriv}(totalLag)}{throughput} \tag{5}$$

The rate of change of Kafka lag is computed by Eq. 5. If positive (over 1 min), the parallelism must increase. The reverse is not always true: the application might still need all its source tasks until all records are processed. TALOS takes decisions to scale down based on *idleTimeMsPerSecond* metric of Flink. It represents the amount of time (in milliseconds) an operator is idle (i.e., it has no records to process). It takes values between 0 (for operators processing records at the maximum capacity) and 1,000 (when an operator is idle). The average idle time over all operators of Eq. 6 is used to describe the idle condition of the task as a whole. A value above a (user-defined) threshold, causes Flink to scale down.

$$idleTime = average_{taskOperators}(idleTimeMsPerSecond) \tag{6}$$

An additional condition is backpressure. If the source is backpressured, no scaling action should happen. In this case, the source is not the bottleneck and a downstream task caused the backpressure. Whenever source tasks start being backpressured, Kafka lag is increasing due to the inability to forward records to downstream operators. Therefore, monitoring backpressure on the source task is crucial not to mislead us into incorrect scaling decisions.

4.3 Parallelism Calculation

For scaling up, the new parallelism of a task is calculated by Eq. 7. The number of parallel tasks can be increased by more than one to quickly catch up with the workload and avoid application latency. On constant lag change rate (i.e., *lagChangeRate* = 0) the addition of 1 in Eq. 7 results in the same value of parallelism. If the rate of change of lag equals the parallelism, Eq. 7 suggests doubling the number of tasks. A scale-down action decreases parallelism by 1 always. The rationale for such a preservative decision is to prevent under-provisioning, in case of workload spikes or sudden workload rises.

$$parallelism' = \lceil parallelism \times (lagChangeRate + 1) \rceil \tag{7}$$

Figure 6 illustrates an example Flink pipeline with source and downstream tasks. The parallelism of both tasks is increased by 1 based on metrics observed on each task.

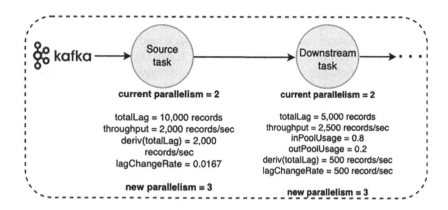

Fig. 6. Scaling example for source and intermediate (downstream) task.

4.4   Task Scaling Algorihtm

Algorithm 1 summarizes the proposed scaling approach. The focus is on identifying tasks that are either under-provisioned and struggling with the workload, or over-provisioned and underutilized and taking effective scaling decisions accordingly. The procedure involves collecting metrics, evaluating them against predetermined

---

Algorithm 1. TALOS scaling algorithm.

1: **while** True **do**
2:     **for** each Task in Flink pipeline **do**
3:         **if** Task is *source* **then**
4:             totalLag = $\sum_{i \in instances}$ record_lag_max$_i$
5:             throughput = $\sum_{i \in instances}$ records_consumed_rate$_i$
6:         **else**
7:             totalLag = $\sum_{i \in instances} \frac{\text{bufferSize} \times \text{inPoolUsage}}{\text{avg(bytesPerRecord)}}$
8:             throughput = $\frac{avg(recordsInPerSec)}{avg(BusyTimems)}$
9:         **end if**

10:        lagChangeRate = $\frac{\text{deriv}(totalLag)}{throughput}$

11:   ▷ conditions must hold over 1 minute
12:   ▷ If task is source *isBottleneck* is always True
13:        **if** lagChangRate>0 **and** busy≥ Threshold **and** *isBottleneck* **then**
14:            $\pi = \lceil currentParallelism \times (lagChangeRate + 1) \rceil$
15:        **end if**

16:        **if** lagChangRate<0 **and** idle≥ Threshold **then**
17:            $\pi = (\text{ currentParallelism - 1 })$
18:        **end if**
19:    **end for**
20: **end while**

---

thresholds, and then adjusting task parallelism for each task separately. The source tasks are handled differently from sinks and intermediate tasks.

isBottleneck is True if, $0.5 < inPoolUsage \leq 1$, and $0.10 < outPoolUsage \leq 0.5$, and the upstream operator starts being backpressured ($backpressure > 500$). The backpressure constraint is important, because low *outPoolUsage* and high *inPoolUsage*, are not enough, to identify a task as the bottleneck. For example, in the case of a filter operation, the job may have a large input throughput, but the output may be empty, due to the failure of the filter condition on the data. The cool-down period between scaling actions is 90 s (i.e., no scaling decisions will be made for this period) to cover the required downtime of Flink when restarting with the new parallelism. The conditions at lines 13–18 must hold for 1 min to avoid unnecessary scaling due to small variations in *lagChangeRate*. The threshold value at line 16 allows control of how quickly the algorithm will reduce parallelism. If no information is available about how smooth the workload is, a threshold value of 500 represents a good balance between having idle tasks and releasing tasks too early when there are still records to process.

5   TALOS Evaluation and Experiments

The Flink Kubernetes (K8s) Operator [8] was used to configure and deploy Apache Flink on the Google Cloud Platform (GCP). Apache Flink deployment comprises three compute nodes, placed in the Europe West 1c zone. Each node was configured as a C2-standard 8 instance, equipped with 8 virtual CPUs (4 cores) and 32 GB of memory. Job Manager and Task Managers are set to allocate 1 CPU, and 1 GB of memory respectively. Apache Kafka was also deployed using Helm [2] featuring a replica count of 1 and 100 GB persistence storage. The input topic was configured with 60 partitions aiming to handle scenarios of high-throughput and distributed data processing challenges. Every message that is published on a topic is placed on a single partition in a round-robin.

TALOS is assessed using a click fraud detection application. Click fraud poses a significant threat to the integrity of online advertising platforms, where malicious actors generate fake clicks to exploit pay-per-click advertising models. The job employs windowing techniques, watermarking, and sliding time windows to identify patterns within specified time intervals. Key functionalities of the application include counting the number of clicks per IP address and user ID, calculating click-through rates (CTR) per user, and identifying instances where CTR surpasses a predefined threshold. Watermarking is utilized for handling event time, and sliding windows are implemented to account for lateness in event arrivals. The Flink job consumes JSON-formatted events from a Kafka topic named "topic" using a Kafka source. The results, highlighting patterns indicative of potential fraudulent activities, are then sent to the "topic-out" Kafka topic. Figure 7 illustrates the pipeline of the Flink job with 8 tasks.

5.1   Experimental Results

The performance of TALOS has been assessed experimentally using a 10-h test with the oscillating workload illustrated in Fig. 8. The same diagram shows how the parallelism

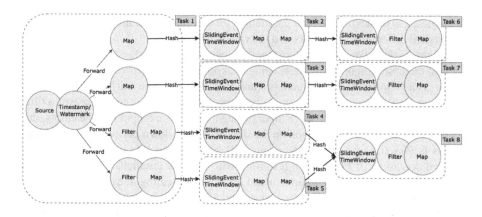

Fig. 7. Click fraud detection pipeline.

of the tasks changes during the experiment. The parallelism is initialized to 2 for all tasks. Parallelism varies as a function of the workload only for tasks 1, 2, and 3. All other tasks scale down at the beginning of the experiment, where the input rate is low and the parallelism stays at 1 for the rest of the experiment. For the source task (task 1) the parallelism increases from 6 to 8 and then decreases again. This happens due to the initial rapid escalation of the workload, possibly caused by a large number of records being queued. Parallelism stabilizes at 3, 1, 1 for tasks 1, 2 and 3 respectively. In the next phase of workload escalation, the parallelism increase is smooth. Notice that the parallelism increases occurred ahead of time (i.e., before the workload reached its peak). Additional experiments with simulated workloads are discussed in [14].

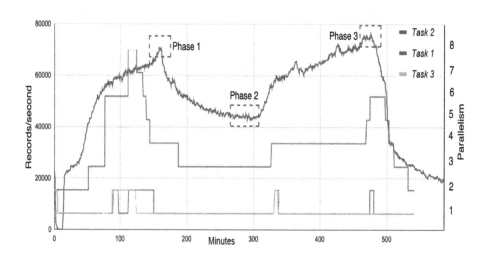

Fig. 8. Workload and Tasks parallelism.

Compared to DS2 (i.e., the default task autoscaler of Kubernetes Operator), TALOS proved more sensitive to variations in the workload. DS2 adjusted the parallelism of Task 1 from 2 to 5 and maintained this value for the whole duration of the experiment. For all other tasks' parallelism changed from 2 to 1 at the start of the experiment. DS2 keeps parallelism at a high value for proactively managing potential workload fluctuations. Moreover, the parallelism decreases when the send rate takes a long-lasting downward turn. As will be explained later, this behavior has disadvantages.

In the following, we observe latency, lag, and throughput in different phases of the workload, notably at phases 1, 2, and 2 depicted on the workload diagram of Fig. 8. These metrics are key indicators of performance. Metrics are only recorded if the system stabilizes, especially after scaling actions, where we ensure a waiting period of at least 1.5 min for the system to settle. The average latency over the 10-h experiments is 173 ms for TALOS. As opposed to 151 ms of DS2, there is a noticeable difference of 22 ms in average latency between the two systems. Nevertheless, this difference is anticipated since the Flink Kubernetes operator opts for a higher parallelism value for a larger portion of the time, in comparison with TALOS.

Table 2 shows measurements of throughput in the two peaks of the workload (depicted as phases 1 and 3 in Fig. 8 respectively) and in the almost stable send-rate phase (depicted as phase 2 in Fig. 8). Throughput is measured by the number of records the pipeline processes per minute and then calculated per second.

Table 2. Throughput at different phases of the experiment for TALOS and DS2.

Phase	TALOS	DS2
1	73,898 rec/sec	71,991 rec/sec
2	44,691 rec/sec	44,945 rec/sec
3	81,359 rec/sec	79,306 rec/sec

During phase 1 the send rate is $\approx 70,000$ records/second. TALOS decided parallelism 4, 1, 1 for tasks 1, 2, 3 respectively. The throughput is 73,898 records/second (i.e., higher than the send rate) due to a previous scaling action and to the higher lag that has to process. DS2 chose parallelism 4, 1, 1 for the same tasks. In phase 2, and for send rate is $\approx 44,000$ records/second; TALOS decided parallelism 3, 1, 1 and DS2 chose 5, 1, 1. Both systems performed equally well in phase 2. In phase 3 and for a send rate of $\approx 76,000$ records/second TALOS has chosen parallelism 6, 1, 1 for tasks 1, 2, 3 respectively, in contrast to DS2 that decided parallelism 5, 1, 1. Both systems can cope with the high sent rate but, compared to DS2, TALOS achieves a higher processing rate at the peaks of the workload due to the higher parallelism for certain tasks. TALOS proved more sensitive than DS2 to workload fluctuations and is capable of adjusting parallelism ahead of time.

The cost of hosting an application on GCP [4] accounts mainly for the number of Virtual Machine (VM) resources consumed (i.e., Apache Flink clients in the cloud are charged by the amount of resources consumed by the application). The dynamic adjustment of Task Managers plays a pivotal role in achieving optimal resource utilization based on the current workload. The increment in the number of Pods, each representing a Task Manager, may lead to a corresponding increase in VMs, if the Kubernetes cluster autoscaler is enabled. This escalation in VMs, while enhancing system capacity, is accompanied by an associated rise in costs.

The experiment was initialized with two VMs and parallelism 2. However, when parallelism is over 4, a third VM is added. Overall, 3 extra VMs were added as the parallelism reached 8. Following the same approach with [20], the cost for the 10-h experiment using TALOS is $9.21 and $10.40 using DS2 (i.e., TALOS is 9,51% less expensive). Presumably, DS2 has opted for a less sensitive parallelism adjustment mechanism and tends to be more conservative in making decisions to scale down. Compared to TALOS, DS2 kept the parallelism of certain Tasks at a higher value that impacts infrastructure (i.e., usage) costs. Overall, TALOS achieves great performance without using redundant resources.

6   Conclusions and Future Work

TALOS is a task autoscaler designed to optimize Apache Flink performance and minimize cloud infrastructure costs. TALOS was benchmarked against DS2 (the default autoscaling system of Apache Flink's Kubernetes Operator). Key observations from the performance evaluation indicate that TALOS dynamically adjusts the parallelization of tasks within the data processing pipeline, significantly enhancing both performance and resource utilization while minimizing usage costs. The TALOS scaling approach enables a more tailored response to workload changes thus protecting the system from sudden workload spikes.

TALOS has left room for further improvements. Currently, TALOS applies a conservative approach to scaling down. In the case of high parallelism, this can cause multiple scaling-down actions by 1 at a time, each one causing downtime. Various software teams report work in progress including an extension to FLINK's adaptive scheduler that would allow the automatic rescaling of a job without the need for redeployment. This could be a good extension to TALOS that would avoid downtime at scaling actions.

Converting TALOS from reactive to proactive would be an interesting extension. TALOS can be trained (using machine learning) to learn the workload. This would allow choosing the ideal parallelism for each task ahead of time (i.e., before the Task is stressed). The decision-making agent is threshold-based, and thresholds need to be defined by the user. While the initial stages of job execution may still rely on a threshold-based algorithm reinforcement learning can be applied to train the autoscaler to calculate thresholds that adapt to the workload.

Acknowledgements. We are grateful to Google for the Google Cloud Platform Education Grants program.

References

1. Apache Flink - Stateful Computations over Data Streams. The Apache Software Foundation (2022). https://flink.apache.org

2. GCP: The Package Manager for Kubernetes. Google Cloud Platform. https://kubernetes.io/docs/tasks/run-application/horizontal-pod-autoscale/
3. GCP: Google Cloud Managed Service for Prometheus (2022). https://cloud.google.com/stackdriver/docs/managed-prometheus
4. GCP: Compute Engine pricing. Google Cloud Platform (2024). https://cloud.google.com/compute/all-pricing
5. Giannakopoulos, P., Petrakis, E.G.M.: Smilax: statistical machine learning autoscaler agent for apache FLINK. In: Barolli, L., Woungang, I., Enokido, T. (eds.) AINA 2021. LNNS, vol. 226, pp. 433–444. Springer, Cham (2021). https://doi.org/10.1007/978-3-030-75075-6_35
6. GKE: About Cluster Autoscaling. Google Kubernetes Engine (2024). https://cloud.google.com/kubernetes-engine/docs/concepts/cluster-autoscaler
7. GKE: Horizontal Pod Autoscaling. Google Kubernetes Engine (2024). https://cloud.google.com/kubernetes-engine/docs/concepts/horizontalpodautoscaler
8. Flink Kubernetes Operator, Version: v1beta1 (2023). https://github.com/apache/flink-kubernetes-operator
9. Kalavri, V., Liagouris, J., Hoffmann, M., Dimitrova, D., Forshaw, M., Roscoe, T.: Three steps is all you need: fast, accurate, automatic scaling decisions for distributed streaming dataflows. In: 13th USENIX Symposium on Operating Systems Design and Implementation (OSDI 2018), Carlsbad, CA, pp. 783–798 (2018). https://www.usenix.org/conference/osdi18/presentation/kalavri
10. Kruber, N., Nowojski, P.: Flink Network Stack Vol. 2: Monitoring, Metrics, and that Backpressure Thing. Apache Flink (2019). https://flink.apache.org/2019/07/23/flink-network-stack-vol.-2-monitoring-metrics-and-that-backpressure-thing/#backpressure
11. Liu, S., et al.: QAAS: quick accurate auto-scaling for streaming processing. Front. Comput. Sci. **18** (2023). https://link.springer.com/content/pdf/10.1007/s11704-022-1706-4.pdf
12. Narkhede, N., Shapira, G., Palino, T.: Kafka the Definitive Guide, Real Time Data and Stream Processing at Scale. O'Reilly Media (2017). https://kafka.apache.org/
13. Nowojski, P.: What is Backpressure. Apache Flink (2021). https://flink.apache.org/2021/07/how-to-identify-the-source-of-backpressure/#what-is-backpressure
14. Ntouni, O.: Optimizing stream processing efficiency and cost: TALOS task level autoscaler for Apache Flink platform. Technical report, ECE School, Technical Univ. of Crete (TUC), Chania, Greece (2024). https://dias.library.tuc.gr/view/99094
15. Ntouni, O.: TALOS: Task Level Autoscaler for Apache Flink (2024). https://github.com/raniantouni/TALOS
16. Paul, F.: Autoscaling Apache Flink with Ververica Platform Autopilot. Ververica Platform (2021). https://www.ververica.com/blog/autoscaling-apache-flink-with-ververica-platform-autopilot
17. Rong, G., Han, Y., Weichang, Z., Chunfeng, Y., Yihua, H.: Meces: latency-efficient rescaling via prioritized state migration for stateful distributed stream processing systems. In: 2022 USENIX Annual Technical Conference (USENIX ATC 22), Carlsbad, CA, pp. 539–556 (2022). https://www.usenix.org/conference/atc22/presentation/gu-rong
18. Varga, B., Balassi, M., Kiss, A.: Towards autoscaling of Apache Flink jobs. Acta Universitatis Sapientiae Informatica **13**(1), 39–59 (2021). https://doi.org/10.2478/ausi-2021-0003
19. Autopilot. Ververica Platform (2022). https://docs.ververica.com/user_guide/application_operations/autopilot.html
20. Zafeirakopoulos, A.N., Petrakis, E.G.: HYAS: hybrid autoscaler agent for Apache Flink. In: International Conference on Web Engineering (ICWE 2023) (2023)

Automating Pathway Extraction from Clinical Guidelines: A Conceptual Model, Datasets and Initial Experiments

Daniel Grathwol[1], Han van der Aa[2], and Hugo A. López[1(✉)]

[1] Technical University of Denmark, DTU Compute, Lyngby, Denmark
`hulo@dtu.dk`
[2] Faculty of Computer Science, University of Vienna, Vienna, Austria
`han.van.der.aa@univie.ac.at`

Abstract. Clinical pathways are structured, multidisciplinary care plans utilized by healthcare providers to standardize the management of specific clinical problems. Designed to bridge the gap between evidence and practice, clinical pathways aim to enhance clinical outcomes and improve efficiency, often reducing hospital stays and lowering healthcare costs. However, maintaining pathways with up-to-date, evidence-based recommendations is complex and time-consuming. It requires the integration of clinical guidelines, algorithmic procedures, and tacit knowledge from various institutions. A critical aspect of updating clinical pathways involves extracting procedural information from clinical guidelines, which are textual documents that detail medical procedures. This paper explores how Large Language Models (LLMs) can facilitate this extraction to support clinical pathway development and maintenance. Concretely, we present a conceptual model for using LLMs in this extraction task, provide a dataset comprising thousands of clinical guidelines for academic research, and share the results of initial experiments demonstrating the efficacy of LLMs in extracting relevant pathway information from these guidelines.

Keywords: Clinical pathways · Clinical guidelines · Large language models · Process extraction · Conceptual model

1 Introduction

Clinical Pathways (CPWs) are structured multidisciplinary care plans used by healthcare providers to describe the care processes with a specific clinical problem [30]. They aim to link evidence to practice, optimize clinical outcomes, and maximize clinical efficiency. Their application can result in reported reductions in length of stay and decreasing hospital costs, among its benefits [30].

Despite their potential to improve the quality and effectiveness of care, it must be recognized that various challenges affect the definition of clinical pathways. Clinical Pathways are established through an interdisciplinary process, including clinical guidelines (CGs) [33], algorithmic processes [35], and tacit knowledge of clinical personnel at each institution [5]. Keeping up-to-date with evidence-based recommendations is a challenge: In just 2023, over 26.000 cancer-related papers were published on

M. Comuzzi et al. (Eds.): CoopIS 2024, LNCS 15506, pp. 296–312, 2025.
https://doi.org/10.1007/978-3-031-81375-7_17

PubMed[1]. When new recommendations affect the pathways used in practice, a change-management plan needs to be established. However, it is documented that revisions and change management plans are not implemented for all institutions [5]. Second, its translation is complex: either the process of interpretation and pathway generation is manual, or supported by algorithms that may bias their understanding of the guidelines based on their expected output (e.g. the semantics of a particular process modeling notation). Third, the process lacks transparency as it is unclear which semantic structures get translated from clinical guidelines to clinical pathways. Finally, the representation of the pathways may not be adequate: traditional notations such as workflows or BPMN are imperative notations that do not capture the discretion and observation-based decision exerted by healthcare practitioners, and, in general, by actors in so-called Knowledge-Intensive Processes [9].

This paper explores how Large Language Models (LLMs) can be helpful in the semantic analysis and extraction of clinical pathways from clinical guidelines. LLMs are generally well-suited for information extraction tasks from unstructured text, representing a considerable part of the long-term goal of transforming CG-to-CPWs. We consider this a long-term goal, yet unrealistic to achieve with the current state of the technology due to several factors. First, the domain-specificity of clinical data makes it more challenging for general-purpose LLMs to produce accurate results (even if this is something that can be improved using fine-tuned or specialized LLMs). Second, the lack of clear semantic structures may lead to false positives in information-extraction tasks, which, given the high-risk impact of healthcare applications, need extra attention according to the AI-Act [10]. Third, there is no consensus on what is the best semantic representation of clinical pathways. While flowcharts and imperative process models are regarded as easier to interpret, they are less apt for capturing context-dependency and discretionary decision-making than declarative process models [11]. Declarative Notations, such as Declare [28] or DCR graphs [17], may capture the flexible nature of clinical work, but they may be harder to comprehend than their imperative counterparts [12]. Even this separation may not be sufficient, as general-purpose notations in process modeling might not cover domain-specific aspects in the transformation pipeline. Finally, clinical guidelines are described in natural language, thus prone to multiple sources of ambiguity that will affect the translation processes [1, 14].

Contributions. This paper reports on the initial steps toward the computational support for clinical pathways. First, we present a dataset of clinical guidelines collected from all the regions in Denmark, which can serve for further semantic annotation and information extraction studies. The dataset comprises more than 90.000 clinical guidelines in 5 regions in Denmark. Second, we develop a conceptual model based on the document analysis of the dataset, to be used for information (e.g. process model) extraction. Third, we document how the conceptual model can be instantiated as a set of guidelines to build an annotated dataset, the challenges in its construction and validation, and

---

[1] https://pubmed.ncbi.nlm.nih.gov/?term=%28%28%222023%2F01%2F01%22%5BDate+-+Publication%5D+%3A+%222023%2F12%2F31%22%5BDate+-+Publication%5D%29%29+AND+%28cancer%29&sort=.

the initial results in the application of LLMs for the extraction of pathway extraction components.

Document Structure: In Sect. 2 we document the process for data collection of the Danish clinical guidelines dataset, and we illustrate the results in Sect. 3. Section 4 introduces the conceptual model for the identification of process-related information in clinical guidelines. In Sect. 5 we validate the conceptual model via the construction of different annotation tasks and illustrate its challenges. Section 6 shows the results of process extraction tasks using SOTA LLMs. In Sect. 7 we present related work and we conclude in Sect. 8.

2   The MedicalInstruks Dataset

In Sect. 2.1 we document the selection criteria used to generate a baseline dataset for clinical guidelines. Section 2.2 documents the filtering process used in the baseline in place, starting from 92.695 unstructured and unmarked documents, to 15 fully annotated clinical descriptions.

2.1   Dataset Construction Criteria

We require a baseline dataset of guidelines to quantify the capabilities of LLMs in extracting clinical pathways. Our main criterion is that our dataset should contain realistic information used in clinical processes. Moreover, we considered the following requirements:

R1. The guidelines must be freely accessible.
R2. The documents in the dataset should all refer to service operating procedures (SOPs) in the medical sector.
R3. The documents should have a consistent format to facilitate automated processing.
R4. The corpus should cover various medical specialties to ensure its relevance to a wide audience, including physicians, nurses, and pharmacists.
R5. If possible, the dataset should include documents in English.

The Danish healthcare sector presents a unique opportunity to create such a dataset. Each of the five regions in Denmark (Syddanmark, Midtjylland, Nordjylland, Sjælland, and Hovedstaden) maintains a centralized guideline document system. These systems aggregate SOPs (locally referred to as *Instruks*) across all regional hospitals and are publicly available. This approach matches selection criteria R1–R4. Concerning criterion R5, the guidelines are only available in Danish. Thus, we needed to add a translation step to benefit from LLMs trained in English. While we considered English alternatives (e.g. [6]), their collection included documents not used in practice, such as PubMed abstracts and papers, thus violating R2. In comparison, constructing a dataset directly from the regional sources in Denmark adds ecological validity to our dataset.

Following individual permissions from each region for research use, we compiled a dataset that based on the crawled documents, forms the cornerstone of our study.

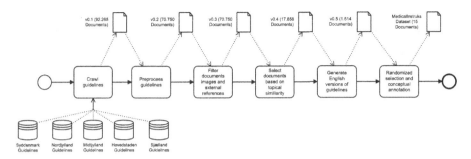

Fig. 1. Process view of the MedicalInstruks dataset construction.

2.2 Data Collection and Refinement Process

This section describes the process followed to build the MedicalInstruks dataset departing from the documentation received from the regions. Our process is summarized in a BPMN diagram in Fig. 1.

The dataset construction process starts with the crawled documents from the regions (v0.1). This version included several non-medical categories that were removed. The remaining medical guidelines were preprocessed (e.g. converted from HTML to Markdown, identifying titles and contents from the crawled documents, removing table of contents, removing empty, incorrect, or duplicated entries, etc.). This constitutes the second version of the dataset and contains 70,750 documents.

Further analysis of the contents in v0.1 of the dataset showed that 12.816 (18, 12%) documents contained references, images, links to internal or external documents, and tables. While process extraction from multimodal artifacts will be exciting research, we proceeded to filter these documents as it will complicate the information extraction task. Multimodal documents were modified to remove references and images. Documents with tables were kept unaltered, as the pilot selection showed them as an important artifact to encode process information. This constituted the v0.2 of the dataset.

The following step included clustering and selection. The 70.750 documents were not evenly distributed among the different areas. For instance, Pediatric Dosage Instructions and Child Healthcare Guidelines included roughly 7.500 documents, while Clinical Practice Standards and Specialist Treatment Guidelines included 90. Moreover, the guidelines included non-medical procedures, such as processes in logistics, human resources, economy, and cleaning. To minimize the risk of undersampling, we used clustering and further refinement based on topic appropriateness for healthcare. Two rounds of clustering (topic/sub-topic) were performed by applying term frequency-inverse document frequency (TF-IDF) transformation, removing terms occurring globally in the dataset. A KMeans clustering algorithm was then applied to the transformation, resulting in a mapping from each document to one cluster in twenty. Clusters obeying inclusion criteria (i.e.: containing clinical process information) were further analyzed via random sampling and analysis of the text contained in the clinical guideline. In addition, we defined minimum and maximum token limits to filter entries that only included links or documents where manual annotation would be unsuitable. Docu-

Table 1. Dataset versions and availability.

Version	Description	Docs.	Lang.	Filters	Annotated	Availability
v0.1	Original Dataset	92.695	Danish	Raw	No	Zenodo [16]
v0.2	Pre-processed Documents	70.750	Danish	Multi-modalities removed	No	hugginface.co/...v0.2
v0.3	Selection based on topical similarity	17.858	Danish	[250, 8.000] tokens/document Selected according to R2 & R4	No	hugginface.co/...v0.3
v0.4	Danish - English translation	1.514	English		No	hugginface.co/...v0.4
v0.5	Annotated Dataset	15	English		Yes	hugginface.co/...v0.5

ments below 250 and over 8.000 tokens were removed. As a result, the clustered dataset in v0.3 included 17.858 documents and 21′814.800 tokens.

Once the documents were clustered and selected, we translated the guidelines into English. We used *DeepL*[2] as it is considered the top-performing translation model [34]. To keep the validation effort feasible for the research team, we randomly selected 1,514 documents from the included entries in v0.4 and translated them into English. The output of the translation was checked for consistency by two native speakers who revised random selections of the translated documents, confirming the validity of the translations[3]. Thus, v0.4 of the dataset constitutes a baseline dataset ideal as a seed for annotation tasks in guideline extraction from text.

The last version of the dataset included the manual annotation phase according to the conceptual model defined in Sect. 4. For this step, 31 documents were randomly assigned for annotation. The annotation step included the refinement of the conceptual model and annotation guidelines and involved the three authors of this paper. This sample also removed 16 documents because they contained information not considered part of the conceptual model and thus could only be partially annotated. The final version of the MedicalInstruks dataset included 15 fully annotated documents, with an average of 1,000 annotated tokens per document.

3   Dataset Results

Table 1 renders public the different versions of the dataset to make the research replicable. In particular, we consider that each version of the dataset has individual merit. v0.1 is the raw material, ensuring traceability to the original guidelines [16]. Moreover, it considers multi-modal process descriptions, a topic seldom explored in NLP4BPM tasks. v0.2 enables the exploration of multimodal extraction of processes including decision and process models. Moreover, it contains process descriptions in classical areas of interest in the BPM community, such as logistics and human resources. v0.4

---

[2] https://www.deepl.com/translator.

[3] Few, negligible cases of mistranslations occurred, for instance, the Danish word "sutten" translates to "Pacifier", but it could be translated to "hickeys", "suckle" or "booze". However, the number of mistranslations was negligible.

contains English descriptions and is independent of any annotation scheme, thus facilitating its use for other annotation purposes, thus it can be used as a benchmark for existing annotation schemes such as [2, 23]. Finally, v0.5 focuses only on clinical guidelines in English and showcases the application of our annotation guidelines. The Medical-ProcessInstruks contains 4.4k tokens, 15 documents, and 270 annotated sentences, with an average token count of 16 per sentence.

4   Conceptual Model

In this section, we propose CGPET, our conceptual model for the annotation of process elements in clinical guidelines. To establish CGPET, we considered three kinds of artifacts: (1) various notations for Computer-Interpretable Guidelines, which define the information that is necessary to represent a CPW, (2) an existing annotation schema for the annotation of process model elements in textual process descriptions, PET [2], and (3) a metamodel for declarative process models [23]. These are complimentary, given that the first provides insights into the need for a target representation (i.e., the CPW), and the latter two provide a starting point to annotate process information using declarative and imperative process semantics. Our proposed CGPET model combines these three artifacts, particularly by extending the PET schema with several (missing) components critical for the representation of computer-interpretable guidelines.

4.1   Key Components in Clinical and Computer-Interpretable Guidelines

Although there is no standardized notation or structure for the description of clinical guidelines, they generally share certain key components. CGPET captures the following elements commonly seen in analyses of pathways and guidelines [8, 13, 19]:

- **Goals:** also referred to as *outcomes*, are essential for guiding the direction of clinical care and evaluating their effectiveness.
- **Indications and Contra-Indications:** Information defining the cases where a particular guideline applies (or not) for a patient.
- **Plan:** a description of tasks, decisions, and time conditions. Tasks and decisions may be sequential or concurrent.
- **Classification Rules:** convert a patient value into a classification further used in the guideline, for example, a SpO2 of 88% is considered *critical* in a Covid-19 guideline.
- **Decision Rules:** logical statements, flowcharts, or tables, defining a set of rules based on input variables coming from the patient's state (e.g., systolic pressure).

4.2   PET Annotation Schema

The PET (Process Extraction from Text) annotation schema was recently proposed [2] as part of an effort to provide a corpus of annotated textual process descriptions that can be used for training and evaluating approaches that extract process information

> The customer office sends the questionnaire to the claimant by email.
> If the questionnaire is received, the office records the questionnaire and the process end.
> Otherwise, a reminder is sent to the customer.

Fig. 2. Text fragment annotated using the entities of the PET schema (adopted from [2], relations omitted for clarity). Legend: *Activity*, *Activity Data*, *Actor*, *Further Specification*, *Gateway*, *Condition Specification*.

from texts. In this sense, its goal is similar to what we want to achieve in our work, although the input and output formats that it focuses on differ from ours.

The core of the PET schema is the *Activity* entity, which corresponds to (the action of) a task performed in a process, e.g., *sends*, *records*, and *sent* in Fig. 2. Each activity can be linked to other kinds of entities, such as *Activity data* to capture objects related to the activity, e.g., the the questionnaire being sent, *Actors* that either perform (The customer office) or are the recipient (the claimant) of the activity, and any *Further specification* that provides details on the execution of the activity, e.g., that the questionnaire is sent by email.

Next to activities, the PET schema defines *Gateway* and *Condition Specification* behavioral entities, which are used, together with the *Flow* relation, to define the control flow of a process, including choices and parallelism. For instance, the words If and Otherwise jointly define a choice (XOR) construct in the process, which PET captures through the *Same Gateway* relation. A *Condition Specification* can be used to annotate a condition that must be satisfied to perform a specific branch of a gateway, for instance, that a the questionnaire is received) before it can be recorded.

4.3   Our Proposal: CGPET

The PET schema provides a valuable starting point for our work. However, it is important to consider that textual process descriptions used as input for PET are simpler than clinical guidelines and lack corresponding elements for our conceptual model. Due to these differences, we identified the need for several adaptations to the PET schema while annotating several clinical guidelines from the MedicalProcessInstruks dataset. This resulted in CGPET, a proposed conceptual model for annotating process information in clinical guidelines, visualized in Fig. 3. The CGPET annotation schema is tailored to how process elements are contained in clinical guidelines. The annotated elements can then be extracted and transformed into a more formalized representation of the procedural information using a language of choice, independent of whether it is an imperative or declarative language, a general-purpose process modeling notation, or a notation specific to CPWs.

- **Activities:** Naturally, the *Activity* entity still plays a central role in CGPET, given that activities form the core of any process. Examples of activities in the dataset are *"Check if the patient has a cavity"* and *"Preparing the CRRT device for treatment"*.

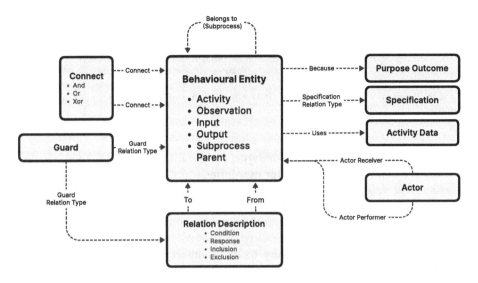

Fig. 3. CGPET Conceptual Model.

- **Activity Purpose:** Next to associating activities with *Activity Data*, *Specification*, and *Actor* entities like in PET, we also define an additional entity: *Purpose Outcome*. This entity captures the underlying reason, goal, objective, or anticipated result of a clinical action, procedure, or recommendation. Figure 4 presents an example of the application of the *Purpose Outcome (PO)* entity. It describes how the Activity i.e. *"Postoperative epidural analgesia"* is performed for *"pain management"*.
- **Observations:** An *Observation* can refer to any information or data that is noted or recorded about a patient's health status, including symptoms, diagnoses, test results, risk factors such as smoking, or contextual information such as the patient's age or condition. Multiple observations can be evidenced in one sentence, for instance, the sentence *"The condition should be suspected in **seizures with increased heart rate, respiration rate, BP and temperature**, as well as **sweating** and **dystonic movements postures** in a **patient with severe acquired brain injury**"* contains 7 different observations ranging from specific symptoms to patient's conditions. Observations do not have a corresponding entity in the PET annotation guidelines.
- **Inputs and Outputs:** An *Input* refers to any word or phrase that denotes a specific type of clinical measurement, score, or value relevant to performing an activity. These include, but are not limited to, physiological measurements, lab test scores, and specific clinical indices. An *Output* entity is its converse. Note that an Input differs from a Guard (see below), since an Input does not represent specific numerical values or thresholds but rather the type of the measurement or value, e.g., *blood pressure* or *heart rate*. Examples of inputs and outputs are "eGFR" and "study is performed without IV contrast" in *"If eGFR < 45 : The study is performed without IV contrast"*
- **Subprocesses:** Clinical guidelines frequently mention higher-level activities, later described in more detail. For example, the sentence *"It may be indicated to **admin-***

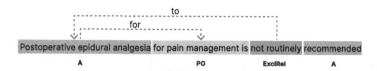

Fig. 4. Annotations of Purpose Outcome (PO) indicating the rationale behind the execution of an activity.

ister morphine to a woman in labor during the dilation phase of labor" describes the existence of the activity **administer morphine**, which is later detailed: *"Regardless of age and weight: Naloxone 0.2 mg svt 0.5 ml. i.m. It can be repeated if needed."*. To capture this behavior we define a *Subprocess* as an entity to annotate higher-level steps, which can subsequently be linked to more specific activities using the *Belongs to the Subprocess* relation.

- **Control-Flow Relations:** Contrary to PET, clinical guidelines are discretionary, meaning that flows can be implicit rather than explicit. We annotate the control flow among activities directly using inter-activity relations, in the form of declarative process constraints [21]. CGPET supports *Condition, Response, No-response, Inclusion*, and *Exclusion* relations between activities. A condition relation describes precedents (e.g. *prescribe medicine* cannot be done unless *confirm diagnose* is done). Responses denote the imposition of obligations (e.g. if a *newborn is assessed to be in pain, a systematic pain assessment* **must** be performed). Its converse relation is No-response. Inclusions/Exclusions denote contextual information (e.g. if a *diagnosis is observed*, then a specific type of treatment *is pertinent*, or, conversely, should not be offered). The annotation example in Fig. 4 uses the *Exclusion* relation to indicate that one activity excludes the other.
- **Guards:** Finally, a key control-flow addition to CGPET is the notion of a *Guard*. A guard refers to a specific type of information that defines conditions, limits, or thresholds in the clinical context. These entities often represent critical values or timeframes that impact clinical decisions, such as dosage limits, duration of treatment, or thresholds for test results. This can include measurements (like volume or concentration), timeframes (like durations or frequencies), or any other quantifiable condition that affects clinical decisions. Note that guards play a similar role as the *Condition Specification* in PET, though with a broader purpose and in line with the terminology used in clinical guidelines (see Sect. 4.1).

5   Validation via Annotated Dataset Construction

The following section discusses the validation of the metamodel using existing clinical guidelines. The conceptual model was instantiated as an annotation guideline for process extraction as it is commonly done in NLP tasks. The guidelines were applied to a randomized selection of clinical guidelines (c.f. dataset construction v0.5 in Sect. 2.2).

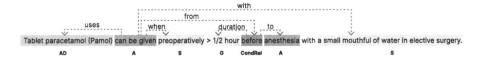

Fig. 5. Ambiguities in Clinical Guidelines: underspecification of timed constraints.

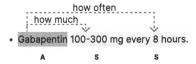

Fig. 6. Example 2 of Guideline Ambiguity.

When uncertainties about the application of the guidelines arose, a lead annotator discussed each of the uncertainties with two senior annotators with experience in NLP and BPM. This process resulted in multiple iterations of the annotation guidelines. When ambiguities arose regarding specific terms that could not be inferred via the context, ChatGPT4 was used for clarification. The annotation process can be broken down into four main phases. First, the annotator must classify each document section according to whether it contains process-related information. Guideline documents are organized into definitions, main chapters, subchapters, and paragraphs, but the hierarchical layout does not necessarily correspond to process-centric information. For example, one of the documents describes an *"ordering guide for 18F-FDG PET Examination"*. Its main paragraphs include *target groups, definitions, procedure, indications, contraindications, patient preparation, execution, interpretations, doses* and *requisitions*. After a closer look at each of the sections it is possible to observe that the *procedure* section is empty, and the process information resides in *indications, contraindications, patient preparation*, and *execution paragraphs*. Thus, the role of the annotator is to parse the document structure and identify the paragraphs containing process-related sentences. Second, once all sentences containing procedural knowledge have been recognized, the annotator labels individual activities. Third, the remaining elements from the metamodel are then annotated according to their relation to labeled activities. Finally, the control-flow relations between activities are labeled.

5.1 Challenges: Textual Ambiguity in Clinical Guidelines

An important finding of the annotation process was how recurrent process-related ambiguities appear inside clinical guidelines. We provide a couple of examples. First, consider the annotations in Fig. 5. They show an ambiguous course of drug administration. On the one hand, several time points are specified (preoperative and 0.5 h before anesthesia). Likewise, the formulations are not exact. Although paracetamol can be administered during this period, it is not obligatory.

The example in Fig. 6 shows an excerpt from a list of activities within the guideline. In this case, a connecting verb (e.g. administer) is missing, which does not create an issue for a human annotator given the reading context, but it may lead to problems

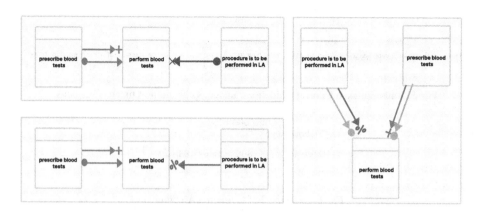

Fig. 7. Ambiguity effects: Three different DCR graphs based on the same description.

when applying automated process extraction, as many approaches [2, 15] use verbs as the main identifier for activities.

Very different process models can emerge from parsing one ambiguous sentence in a clinical guideline. For instance, different ways of parsing relations occurring in *"If the procedure is to be performed in LA, blood tests are not required unless the operator has prescribed otherwise."* resulted in three different process graphs as presented in Fig. 7 (here illustrated as DCR graphs [17]). This example is especially ambiguous as it contains a double condition with the action of performing a blood test. The process at the bottom left describes that a blood test is no longer possible if the procedure is carried out in room LA (exclude relation). On the other hand, a prescription can reactivate the activity. If both conditions are met, a decision problem will occur. In the process on the right side, the condition relation causes a blood test to be executed only if the procedure takes place in room LA, but at the same time, the exclude relation prevents this.

These examples demonstrate the implications of the ambiguities in the annotation process. As posed forward in [14], an ambiguity will take multiple interpretations as valid. In our annotation process, we discussed each ambiguity encountered and left them unchanged as long as one interpretation was correct. The amount of ambiguity and the lack of possibilities for automation made the annotation process extremely difficult and time-consuming. During the beginning of the annotation, one guideline annotation with 70–80 sentences took up to 8 h (on average 6 min. per sentence). This time included noting ambiguities and looking up medical specialties. The refinement of the guidelines and the learning curve improved the efficiency of the annotation process to about 4 h/document. Another factor that makes the process very time-intensive is the amount of layers needed to describe the model. For some of the documents, the time could be reduced to about 2 1/2 h per document, combining manual annotations with a prompting approach where we used Mixtral [18] to semi-automate the annotation process, where a main annotator revised and accepted the outcome. The result of the annotation process became the MedicalInstruks dataset (c.f. v0.5 in Sect. 2.2) and is the first in-depth process-centered annotated corpus of medical clinical guidelines containing information about the current state of medical practice.

6 Initial Experiments on Process Extraction Using LLMs

In this Section, we report on initial experiments using the MedicalProcessInstruks dataset. The process extraction pipeline can benefit from multiple NLP tasks: sentence classification (i.e. does this sentence contain process-related information?), Name-Entity Recognition (i.e. what are the activities in this sentence?) and Relation Extraction (i.e. are these two concepts related?). We focused on Named-Entity-Recognition and relation extraction. In particular, we want to explore whether a pre-trained language model renders process extraction feasible in an automated way. Moreover, we would like to compare its performance against few-shot guideline-based architectures. For the evaluation metrics, we use standard definitions of precision (i.e.: *True Positives*/ (*True Positives + False Positives*)), recall (i.e.: *True Positives*/(*True Positives + False Negatives*)), and F1 (i.e.: $2 \times (Precision \times Recall)/(Precision + Recall)$) scores. For LLM predictions we include hallucination, defined as *Number of wrong predictions*/ *total number of predictions*.

The models selected for this evaluation were sourced from a public repository of pre-trained models[4]. Our initial selection included BioLink-BERT [38] and XLM-Roberta in the `large` model configuration [7], with 355 million parameters. For few-shot learning, we used three models: first, OpenAI NER Model GPT4-0125 Preview with Top_p : 0.9, and $Temperature$: 0.7. Second, Mixtral 8x7b instruct-v0.1 NER. Setup: Top_p : 0.9, temperature: 0.7. Finally, we compared with Guideline Prompting using GoLLIE-34B, an entity and relation extraction finetuned model based on CodeLlama using few-shot prompting combined with a guideline approach [31]. The same parameters were used for the Relation Extraction task. The experiments were carried out on an HPC cluster on two *Tesla A100-PCIE* graphics cards with 40GB memory each and the smaller models (BERT & Roberta) on a *Tesla V100-SXM2* with 32GB memory. Initially, our approach involved document segmentation without contextual information (that is, one sentence at a time), using a 5-fold cross-validation strategy and iterating over 3 epochs. Unfortunately, this strategy did not yield significant accuracy improvements for either BioLinkBERT or XLMRoberta. Subsequently, the models were subjected to an extended training regime of 6 additional epochs with the same 5-fold cross-validation. This phase demonstrated a marginal improvement, particularly with XLM-Roberta, which began to show the first signs of measurable performance. In our final and best approach, we used 10-fold cross-validation.

6.1 Results

We report the best results for both the pre-trained and the guideline approach in Tables 2, 3, and 4. Our initial expectation was that fine-tuned domain-specific models would better extract process elements from clinical guidelines against general-purpose models.

---

[4] Huggingface Transformers Library.

Still, the poor performance of BioLinkBert challenged this. In contrast, XLM-Roberta, a model with a significantly larger general corpus, provided the best results for pre-trained models. Independently of the model and the class, the results of our experiments show an accuracy below random guesses, highlighting process extraction from clinical data as a complex task for pre-trained large language models. They also contrast against the high F1 scores for activity, actor, and specification classes in the PET dataset (0.81, 0.76, 0.19, respectively). The results for the few-shot approaches in Tables 3 and 4 show a difference on the performance against different tasks. While the relation extraction evidenced satisfactory results (particularly in the case of OpenAI), the NER task evidence that most of the entity extraction is below the level of random classifiers, and thus not ready to be used in production for full process extraction pipeline.

Table 2. NER results using XLMRobertaLarge.

	Precision	Recall	F1
Activity	0.5556	0.2170	0.3125
Activity Parent	0.2500	0.5000	0.3300
Actor	0.2600	0.6250	0.3700
Specification	0.4000	0.1100	0.1700
Input	1.0000	0.2500	0.4000
Observation	0.2720	0.3300	0.3000
Overall	**0.3220**	**0.1700**	**0.2260**

Table 3. Results on NER tasks against different LLMs. Hallucination: 0.0% (OpenAI), 3, 61% (Mixtral). Bold means best results.

Class	OpenAI			Mixtral			Gollie		
	Prec.	Rec.	F1	Prec.	Rec.	F1	Prec.	Rec.	F1
Activity	0.4000	0.4819	**0.4372**	0.3125	0.2703	0.2899	0.2266	0.1576	0.1859
Activity Data	0.3592	0.4568	**0.4022**	0.2899	0.2740	0.2817	0.2273	0.0314	0.0552
Actor	0.3077	0.4000	0.3478	0.4500	0.4737	**0.4615**	0.0909	0.0286	0.0435
And	0.3571	0.4545	**0.4000**	0.0000	0.0000	0.0000	0.0000	0.0000	0.0000
Condition Entity	0.3889	0.3889	**0.3889**	0.0556	0.0667	0.0606	0.0000	0.0000	0.0000
Exclusion Entity	0.0000	0.0000	0.0000	0.0000	0.0000	0.0000	0.5000	0.0909	**0.1538**
Guard	0.3182	0.5385	**0.4000**	0.3333	0.0909	0.1429	0.2500	0.1429	0.1818
Inclusion Entity	0.0000	0.0000	0.0000	0.0000	0.0000	0.0000	0.0000	0.0000	0.0000
Input	0.1667	0.0909	0.1176	0.0000	0.0000	0.0000	0.2333	0.2800	**0.2545**
Observation	0.3780	0.3827	**0.3804**	0.2907	0.3247	0.3067	0.3158	0.2264	0.2637
Or	0.1250	0.2000	**0.1538**	0.0000	0.0000	0.0000	0.0000	0.0000	0.0000
Output	0.0000	0.0000	0.0000	0.0000	0.0000	0.0000	0.0000	0.0000	0.0000
Parent Activity	0.1154	0.1875	**0.1429**	0.0323	0.0714	0.0444	0.0000	0.0000	0.0000
Purpose Outcome	0.2308	0.2500	**0.2400**	0.1667	0.0833	0.1111	0.0000	0.0000	0.0000
Response Entity	0.3333	0.1818	**0.2353**	0.1667	0.0909	0.1176	0.0000	0.0000	0.0000
Specification	0,4444	0.2295	**0.3027**	0.3500	0.0648	0.1094	0.1765	0.0147	0.0271
Overall	**0.3426**	**0.3516**	**0.3470**	0.2299	0.1937	0.2103	0.2409	0.0839	0.1245

6.2 Threats to Validity

We are aware of the following limitations of our research. Regarding the annotation process: the annotations were carried out by the annotators with computer science backgrounds. The absence of prior knowledge posed a risk and increased the annotation time. Our mitigation strategy included consultations with medical material, as well as disambiguation using LLMs. Concerning translation errors. The original guidelines were received in Danish, and an additional translation step was required to perform process extraction activities. While mitigation strategies such as random sampling with native speakers were in place, there is the risk that some of the texts may have been unnecessarily altered in the translation phase. Regarding the size of the annotated dataset: the annotated data set may be small to train an encoder-only model, thus having an influence in the low f1 scores reported. As a mitigation strategy, an annotation guideline was developed and every case of ambiguity was discussed among the authors. Further strategies may include inter-annotator agreement and data augmentation strategies for some of the underrepresented classes.

Table 4. Benchmarking LLMs on RE tasks. Hallucination: 4.1825% (OpenAI), 16.11% (Mixtral). Bold means best results.

	OpenAI			Mixtral			Gollie		
Class	Prec.	Rec.	F1	Prec.	Rec.	F1	Prec.	Rec.	F1
Activity Actor-Performer rel.	0.8571	0.8000	**0.8276**	0.2273	0.8333	0.3571	0.0000	0.0000	0.0000
Activity Actor-Receiver rel.	0.6000	0.5000	**0.5455**	0.0000	0.0000	0.0000	0.0000	0.0000	0.0000
Activity Data rel.	0.9063	0.8788	**0.8923**	0.6667	0.7200	0.6923	0.8913	0.1646	0.4481
Activity Guard rel.	0.9231	1.0000	**0.9600**	0.7778	0.6364	0.7000	0.2857	0.1429	0.1905
Activity Parent rel.	0.0000	0.0000	0.0000	0.0000	0.0000	0.0000	0.0000	0.0000	0.0000
Activity Purpose Outcome rel.	0.7273	1.0000	**0.8421**	0.6667	0.6667	0.6667	0.5000	0.1333	0.2105
Activity Specification rel.	0.8144	0.8587	**0.8360**	0.6727	0.5211	0.5873	0.0000	0.0000	0.0000
Actor rel.	0.0000	0.0000	0.0000	0.0000	0.0000	0.0000	0.7500	0.3243	**0.4528**
Condition rel.	0.6842	0.8667	**0.7647**	0.4167	0.6250	0.5000	0.0000	0.0000	0.0000
Condition Response rel.	0.1429	0.3333	**0.2000**	0.0000	0.0000	0.0000	0.0000	0.0000	0.0000
Exclusion rel.	0.8571	0.8571	**0.8571**	0.8333	0.8333	0.8333	0.0000	0.0000	0.0000
Response rel.	1.0000	0,5000	**0.6667**	1.0000	0.4000	0.5714	0.0000	0.0000	0.0000
Inclusion rel.	0,0000	0.0000	0.0000	0.0000	0.0000	0.0000	0.0000	0.0000	0.0000
Overall	**0.7817**	**0.8383**	**0.8090**	0.5320	0.5902	0.5596	0.6087	0.2090	0.3111

7 Related Work

We can divide the related work into three streams: works in datasets for clinical guidelines, works in annotation schemes, and overarching works in process extraction in BPM.

Regarding datasets for clinical guidelines, Pedersen et al. [26] published a set of word embeddings using Standard Operating Procedure (SOP) documents from five Danish regions. Their dataset, MeDa-Bert, includes non-guideline-specific information such as books and Wikipedia entries. To focus on guideline-specific information, we replicated the crawling process and compiled a new dataset using permissions from each region. Compared to [26], we increase the ecological validity of this work by only considering guideline-specific information.

Concerning annotation schemes for clinical guidelines, a broad range of notations for knowledge extraction from Computer-interpretable guidelines has been proposed, for instance, Asbru [24], EON [25], GLIF [27], and PROforma [37]. Each notation uses specific labels and categories for each aspect, with high variability in the covered details. For example, Asbru offers the most developed syntax to formally express a wide range of intentions that can be used to define goals and purposes, whereas the same aspects are left optional in GLIF. By proposing a language-agnostic model, we want to generate as much structured text as possible while being neutral to one specific modeling language.

Concerning general works at the intersection of NLP and BPM, we can report some works on process discovery from unstructured texts. While process discovery from text artifacts has been explored earlier, the inputs have considered business process descriptions [2, 15, 21, 22, 32], e-mail communications [36], cooking recipes [29], or legal documents [20]. To the best of our knowledge, this is the first work exploring the extraction of process elements from the complexity of clinical guidelines. From these works, only [2] provides both a set of annotation guidelines and a dataset for verification, being the closest to our aims (even though the domains are different). For the experimental setup, [3] evaluated few-shot extraction using GPT-3.5, being a good point of comparison. In the medical domain, the recent work by Bombieri et al. [4] studied the sentence classification task to identify procedural knowledge in robotic-assisted surgical text using LLMs. Their approach may be complementary to our work, being sentence classification a pre-condition to the process extraction phase in our extraction workflow.

8   Concluding Remarks

This work is the first of its nature aiming at exploring process extraction from unstructured documents in a highly complex environment, the medical domain. The dataset collected is a legitimate representation of the complex decisions and documents that a knowledge-worker need to deal with. In itself, the dataset (and the different versions from v0.1 to v0.5) evidence multiple challenges when extracting process information, including multiple modalities, long documents, non-standardized layouts, and semantic ambiguities. Moreover, our paper presents a conceptual model of the process-related information found in the documents. Such a conceptual model can be instantiated as a set of clinical guidelines, and it is independent of a specific modeling language, thus allowing hybrid combinations of declarative and imperative approaches. Our validation via annotation of a smaller dataset evidenced the complexity of the tasks for manual annotators, and our experiments using LLMs show ample room for improvement for this complex task. In future work, we would like to enrich the semantic annotations and explore the impact of multi-modal information in process extraction.

Acknowledgments. This work was supported by the research grant "Center for Digital Compliance (DICE)" (VIL57420) from VILLUM FONDEN.

References

1. van der Aa, H., Leopold, H., Reijers, H.A.: Dealing with behavioral ambiguity in textual process descriptions. In: La Rosa, M., Loos, P., Pastor, O. (eds.) BPM 2016. LNCS, vol. 9850, pp. 271–288. Springer, Cham (2016). https://doi.org/10.1007/978-3-319-45348-4_16
2. Bellan, P., van der Aa, H., Dragoni, M., Ghidini, C., Ponzetto, S.P.: Pet: an annotated dataset for process extraction from natural language text tasks. In: BPM Workshops, pp. 315–321. Springer (2022)
3. Bellan, P., Dragoni, M., Ghidini, C.: Leveraging pre-trained language models for conversational information seeking from text (2022)
4. Bombieri, M., Rospocher, M., Dall'Alba, D., Fiorini, P.: Automatic detection of procedural knowledge in robotic-assisted surgical texts. Int. J. Comput. Assist. Radiol. Surg. **16**(8), 1287–1295 (2021). https://doi.org/10.1007/s11548-021-02370-9
5. Burgers, J.S., Grol, R., Klazinga, N.S., Mäkelä, M., Zaat, J.: Towards evidence-based clinical practice: an international survey of 18 clinical guideline programs. Int. J. Qual. Health Care **15**(1), 31–045 (2003)
6. Chen, Z., Cano, A.H., et al., A.R.: Meditron-70b: Scaling medical pretraining for large language models (2023)
7. Conneau, A., Khandelwal, K., Goyal, N., Chaudhary, V., Wenzek, G., Guzmán, F.E.A.: Unsupervised cross-lingual representation learning at scale. In: Proceedingss of the 58th Annual Meeting of the ACL, pp. 8440–8451 (2020)
8. De Bleser, L., Depreitere, R., De Waele, K., Vanhaecht, K., Vlayen, J., Sermeus, W.: Defining pathways. J. Nurs. Manag. **14**(7), 553–563 (2006)
9. Di Ciccio, C., Marrella, A., Russo, A.: Knowledge-intensive processes: characteristics, requirements and analysis of contemporary approaches. J. on Data Sem. **4**, 29–57 (2015)
10. Edwards, L.: The EU AI Act: a summary of its significance and scope. Artif. Intell. (the EU AI Act) **1** (2021)
11. Fahland, D., et al.: Declarative versus imperative process modeling languages: the issue of understandability. In: Halpin, T., et al. (eds.) BPMDS/EMMSAD -2009. LNBIP, vol. 29, pp. 353–366. Springer, Heidelberg (2009). https://doi.org/10.1007/978-3-642-01862-6_29
12. Figl, K., Di Ciccio, C., Reijers, H.A.: Do declarative process models help to reduce cognitive biases related to business rules? In: Dobbie, G., Frank, U., Kappel, G., Liddle, S.W., Mayr, H.C. (eds.) ER 2020. LNCS, vol. 12400, pp. 119–133. Springer, Cham (2020). https://doi.org/10.1007/978-3-030-62522-1_9
13. openEHR Foundation: openehr specification proc. https://specifications.openehr.org/releases/PROC/Release-1.6.0/overview.html#_clinical_practice_guidelines_cpgs. Accessed 15 Jan 2024
14. Franceschetti, M., Seiger, R., López, H.A., Burattin, A., García-Bañuelos, L., Weber, B.: A characterisation of ambiguity in bpm. In: ER, pp. 277–295. Springer (2023)
15. Friedrich, F., Mendling, J., Puhlmann, F.: Process model generation from natural language text. In: Mouratidis, H., Rolland, C. (eds.) CAiSE 2011. LNCS, vol. 6741, pp. 482–496. Springer, Heidelberg (2011). https://doi.org/10.1007/978-3-642-21640-4_36
16. Grathwol, D., van der Aa, H., López, H.A.: Instruks dataset - a dataset of clinical guidelines in Denmark (2024). https://doi.org/10.5281/zenodo.11396622
17. Hildebrandt, T.T., Mukkamala, R.R.: Declarative event-based workflow as distributed dynamic condition response graphs. In: Places (2011)
18. Jiang, A.Q., et al.: Mixtral of experts. arXiv preprint arXiv:2401.04088 (2024)
19. Latina, R., et al.: Towards a new system for the assessment of the quality in care pathways: an overview of systematic reviews. Int. J. Environ. Res Public Health **17**(22) (2020)
20. López, H.A.: Challenges in legal process discovery. In: ITBPM@ BPM, pp. 68–73 (2021)

21. López, H.A., Strømsted, R., Niyodusenga, J.-M., Marquard, M.: Declarative process discovery: linking process and textual views. In: Nurcan, S., Korthaus, A. (eds.) CAiSE 2021. LNBIP, vol. 424, pp. 109–117. Springer, Cham (2021). https://doi.org/10.1007/978-3-030-79108-7_13

22. López, H.A., Marquard, M., Muttenthaler, L., StrÃmsted, R.: Assisted declarative process creation from natural language descriptions. In: EDOC Workshops, pp. 96–99 (2019). https://doi.org/10.1109/EDOCW.2019.00027

23. López A., H.A., Simon, V.: How to (re)design declarative process notations? A view from the lens of cognitive effectiveness frameworks. In: 15th IFIP Working Conference on the Practice of Enterprise Modeling (POEM), pp. 81–97 (11 2022)

24. Miksch, S., Shahar, Y., Johnson, P.: Asbru: a task-specific, intention-based, and time-oriented language for representing skeletal plans. In: Proceedings of KEML-97, pp. 9–19. Milton Keynes, UK (1997)

25. Musen, M.A., Tu, S.W., Das, A.K., Shahar, Y.: EON: a component-based approach to automation of protocol-directed therapy. J. Am. Med. Inform. Assoc. **3**(6), 367–388 (1996)

26. Pedersen, J.S., Laursen, M.S., Vinholt, P.J., Savarimuthu, T.R.: Meda-BERT: a medical danish pretrained transformer model. In: The 24rd Nordic Conference on Computational Linguistics (2023)

27. Peleg, M., et al.: Glif3: the evolution of a guideline representation format. In: Proceedings of the AMIA Symposium, p. 645. American Medical Informatics Association (2000)

28. Pesic, M., Schonenberg, H., Van der Aalst, W.M.: Declare: Full support for loosely-structured processes. In: EDOC, pp. 287–287. IEEE (2007)

29. Qian, C., et al.: An approach for process model extraction by multi-grained text classification. In: Dustdar, S., Yu, E., Salinesi, C., Rieu, D., Pant, V. (eds.) CAiSE 2020. LNCS, vol. 12127, pp. 268–282. Springer, Cham (2020). https://doi.org/10.1007/978-3-030-49435-3_17

30. Rotter, T., et al.: Clinical pathways: effects on professional practice, patient outcomes, length of stay and hospital costs. Cochrane Database Syst. Rev. (3) (2010)

31. Sainz, O., García-Ferrero, I., Agerri, R., de Lacalle, O.L., Rigau, G., Agirre, E.: Gollie: annotation guidelines improve zero-shot information-extraction (2023)

32. Sànchez-Ferreres, J., Burattin, A., Carmona, J., Montali, M., Padró, L.: Formal reasoning on natural language descriptions of processes. In: Hildebrandt, T., van Dongen, B.F., Röglinger, M., Mendling, J. (eds.) BPM 2019. LNCS, vol. 11675, pp. 86–101. Springer, Cham (2019). https://doi.org/10.1007/978-3-030-26619-6_8

33. Schnabel, M., Kill, C., El-Sheik, M., Sauvageot, A., Klose, K., Kopp, I.: From clinical guidelines to clinical pathways: development of a management-oriented algorithm for the treatment of polytraumatized patients in the acute period. Der Chirurg; Zeitschrift fur Alle Gebiete der Operativen Medizen **74**(12), 1156–1166 (2003)

34. Sebo, P., de Lucia, S.: Performance of machine translators in translating french medical research abstracts to english: a comparative study of DeepL, google translate, and CUBBITT. PLoS One **19**(2), e0297183 (2024)

35. Sitter, H., Prünte, H., Lorenz, W.: A new version of the programme algo for clinical algorithms. In: Medical Informatics Europe 1996, pp. 654–657. IOS Press (1996)

36. Soares, D.C., Santoro, F.M., Baião, F.A.: Discovering collaborative knowledge-intensive processes through e-mail mining. J. Netw. Comput. Appl. **36**(6), 1451–1465 (2013)

37. Sutton, D.R., Fox, J.: The syntax and semantics of the PROforma guideline modeling language. J. Am. Med. Inform. Assoc. **10**(5), 433–443 (2003)

38. Yasunaga, M., Leskovec, J., Liang, P.: LinkBERT: pretraining language models with document links. In: Proceedings of the 60th Annual Meeting of the ACL, pp. 8003–8016. ACL, Dublin, Ireland (2022)

Short Papers

IML4DQ: Interactive Machine Learning for Data Quality with Applications in Credit Risk

Elena Tiukhova[1]([✉])(ORCID), Adriano Salcuni[2,3](ORCID), Can Oguz[2], Fabio Forte[2],
Bart Baesens[1,4](ORCID), and Monique Snoeck[1](ORCID)

[1] LIRIS, KU Leuven, Naamsestraat 69, 3000 Leuven, Belgium
elena.tiukhova@kuleuven.be
[2] ING, Belgium, Avenue Marnix 24, 1000 Bruxelles, Belgium
[3] Università degli Studi di Salerno, DISES, Via Giovanni Paolo II, 132, 84084 Fisciano, SA,
Italy
asalcuni@unisa.it
[4] Department of Decision Analytics and Risk, University of Southampton, University Road,
Southampton SO17 1BJ, U.K.

Abstract. Data Quality (DQ) has gained popularity in recent years due to the increasing reliance on data in machine learning (ML). The DQ domain itself can benefit from ML, which is able to learn from large amounts of data, saving time and resources required by manual DQ assurance. To extend the accessibility of ML solutions and incorporate human input, Interactive ML (IML) integrates ML with a user interface (UI) that facilitates a human-in-the-loop approach. Both high-quality data and human involvement are critical in credit risk management (CRM), where poor DQ can lead to incorrect decisions, causing both ethical issues and financial losses. This paper introduces IML4DQ, a novel IML-based solution designed to ensure DQ in CRM through a dedicated UI. The IML4DQ design is grounded in established IML practices and key UI design principles. A rigorous evaluation using behavioral change theories reveals new insights into the significance of instrumental attitude and government- and management-based norms in shaping attitudes towards DQ in CRM, as well as positive attitude towards automating DQ processes with IML.

Keywords: Data quality · Interactive machine learning · Credit risk

1 Introduction

Modern technological advances enabled the collection and analysis of vast amounts of data from various domains. Credit risk management (CRM) features analytics applications ranging from default modeling to managing credit portfolio risk [32]. However, the effectiveness of analytical solutions depends on the quality of the underlying data. This problem is exacerbated in CRM, where inaccurate risk estimates can lead to substantial losses and unjust decisions, making data quality (DQ) a top priority. Since manual data inspection is both time- and resource-consuming, the ability of machine

M. Comuzzi et al. (Eds.): CoopIS 2024, LNCS 15506, pp. 315–326, 2025.
https://doi.org/10.1007/978-3-031-81375-7_18

learning (ML) to learn from data and automate DQ issues identification is an attractive solution [29].

To make ML models more accessible to a broader non-technical audience, they should be complemented by a user-friendly interface that allows a user to interact with the model without explicit programming knowledge. This interaction paradigm, which allows a user to "iteratively build and refine a mathematical model to describe a concept through iterative cycles of input and review", is defined as Interactive Machine Learning (IML) [6]. The IML concept is closely related to the "human-in-the-loop" approach, which assumes human involvement and guidance in ML. IML holds significant potential in fields where non-experts could greatly benefit from ML solutions in their daily tasks. DQ and CRM are such domains, where many practitioners are non-ML experts and can benefit from the intuitive application of ML technologies.

The goal of this study is to design and evaluate a novel prototype IML application aimed at detecting DQ issues in CRM data, designed according to the best practices of IML [6] and core functional UI design principles [25]. To this end, we bridge the IML, DQ, and CRM domains and make the following contributions. First, we develop a novel prototype application designed for an Interactive ML task of identifying DQ issues based on the **ML4DQ** framework [29]. Next, we evaluate the determinants of the intention of potential IML4DQ users to identify DQ issues in general and to use the developed IML solution. To the best of our knowledge, this is the first study that explores the application of IML for boosting DQ in CRM.

2   Related Work

2.1   User Interface Design in Interactive Machine Learning

Traditional ML is concerned with making models accurately learn patterns from data. In many domains, however, involving users in the learning process makes ML models more accessible to a broader audience, including non-experts in ML, and helps ensure that decisions are applied fairly. This is the focus of human-in-the-loop ML (HITL-ML), which aims to combine human and machine intelligence to augment human tasks with ML to increase their accuracy, efficiency, and fairness [19]. IML, a subtype of HITL-ML, balances control between humans and machines by framing training as a human-computer interaction (HCI) task, with humans providing incremental input to the model [6,20]. Initially focused on correcting classifier errors, IML has expanded to include tasks such as feature/model selection and performance evaluation [6].

The defining characteristics of IML systems include (1) active human involvement in the ML loop, (2) diverse human roles, (3) an incremental methodology, and (4) a pivotal emphasis on user interface (UI) design [20]. First, IML suggests that humans and machines should collaborate by doing what each of them does best [23]. Second, IML allows even non-expert ML users to interact with ML solutions in performing real-world tasks as long as they are more efficient than machines. Third, HCI has an iterative nature through cycles of input and review, with even a few iterations being sufficient if user preferences deem it so [13]. Finally, a proper UI design is essential for successful HCI [6,20].

Design. While the UI of a classical ML system is passive, the UI of an IML system is interactive, as it is designed to provide bi-directional feedback [20]. IML system design consists of four main components (Fig. 1) [6]. The *user* is the main driver of the IML process, who has little to no ML knowledge, but significant domain knowledge. The *model* takes inputs provided by the user and determines outputs based on its understanding of the learned concept. The *data* is provided by the user and can be both labeled and unlabeled, depending on the use case. While earlier IML studies neglected user involvement at the feature selection stage, recent research shows a shift towards such user involvement [6]. Finally, the *interface* is the central component of the IML system that enforces the bi-directional feedback between the user and the model [6].

When designing functional UI, key principles such as providing feedback and maintaining consistency are essential [25]. UI design for IML adds new challenges, such as making task goals and constraints explicit, supporting user understanding of model uncertainty, or capturing user intent [6]. The rise of explainable AI (XAI) supports user understanding by making model aspects more transparent [30], further improving mental models of IML systems.

Evaluation. The evaluation of HCI applications differs from the evaluation of conventional ML solutions due to the extensive user involvement (user studies orientation) compared to traditional ML (benchmark test orientation). Evaluation of IML is challenging due to the subjective nature of interaction and the longitudinal nature of studies [6]. Hence, inspiration can be drawn from behavioral change theories, i.e., the Theory of Reasoned Action (TRA) [7], and its extensions, the Theory of Planned Behavior (TPB) [1], and the Technology Acceptance Model (TAM) [5]. Both models have been successfully applied in various domains, including DQ, as illustrated by [8,21] (TPB) and [4,22] (TAM).

2.2 IML: Data Quality and Credit Risk

Interactive (ML) Data Quality. Automated DQ assurance is preferred due to the increasing volumes of data used in ML solutions [29]. However, human expertise remains crucial in complex areas like DQ optimization, where full automation is not feasible due to the importance of expert feedback. Table 1 in Online Appendix A [28] summarizes current IML applications for DQ. These applications leverage statistics and ML to clean and improve DQ, either by focusing solely on the data itself (e.g., [24,26,27,33]) or by integrating these techniques into the entire ML pipeline (e.g., [14]). However, a critical component often missing in these studies is user evaluation. Most systems are assessed using benchmark or real data [26,27], with user evaluation either suggested for future work or omitted altogether [14,24]. Only two studies [4,22] conduct user evaluations, but their DQ frameworks lack the ML component, which excludes them from the IML scope. In addition, existing IML tools generally fail to emphasize explainability, where DQ issues are not only detected and/or remediated with ML but the model reasoning is also explained. Only one study [11] includes an explainer component that elucidates the constraints identified by the ML model.

DQ in CRM. The importance of DQ assessment in CRM is directly related to regulation in the banking sector. After the 2008 crisis, financial institutions were required to strengthen the DQ of their systems [32], with one of the principles being *accuracy*, which requires data to be error-free and reliable. It is common practice in the industry to apply tests to verify that data conforms to certain rules. However, it is not realistic to ensure in advance that these rules cover every case and are error-prone. Advanced techniques are needed to ensure high DQ [17]. ML models allow the identification of errors, which, considering the large amount of data, cannot be detected otherwise [3].

2.3 Research Gap

Most related studies lack rigorous evaluation by system users, a crucial aspect in HCI as IML aims to improve expert efficiency [6]. In addition, many studies overlook explainability, especially for black-box ML models. Finally, to the best of our knowledge, no IML application has been specifically adapted to improve DQ in CRM. To fill these gaps, we propose a novel IML solution to help CRM experts identify DQ issues in CRM data without requiring coding or modeling skills. Our evaluation study combines the TAM and the TRA models, and uses semi-structured interviews to explore the dual intention of experts to detect DQ issues and use the proposed IML solution. We explore this dual intention through the following research questions: *To what extent do the determinants of attitude (RQ1) and subjective norm (RQ2) affect the intention of CRM specialists to detect DQ issues? When it comes to interactive DQ issues detection, what is the intention of CRM specialists to use the proposed IML4DQ solution, and what are the determinants of this intention? (RQ3)*

3   Methodology

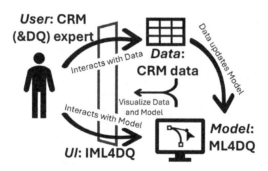

Fig. 1. IML4DQ. Source: own adaption from [6].

In our previous work, we explored the use of ML and XAI to enhance DQ of CRM data [29] (referred to as the ML4DQ framework). The results showed that an ensemble of the Isolation Forest [15] and Autoencoder [10] models effectively identified problematic loan data, and the important features highlighted by the Shapley Additive explanations (SHAP) [2, 16] aligned with expert feedback [29]. More details on the ML4DQ framework can be found in Online Appendix B [28].

The ML4DQ framework serves as a foundation for the IML solution, incorporating three key IML components [6]: data, model, and user. This paper adds the missing UI component (Fig. 1), creating the extended Interactive ML4DQ (IML4DQ) version. The UI increases user flexibility in interacting with the ML model and requires only basic computer skills, making it accessible to non-technical users and expanding its potential audience.

Data. Large financial institutions rely on a variety of local systems to collect data. For analysis and reporting purposes, this data is consolidated in data warehouses, often resulting in DQ problems [17]. In this paper, we use a data from such a data warehouse of an international financial institution that issues loans to other organizations. Since the level of risk of credit portfolios is expressed in terms of risk-weighted assets (RWAs) [32], we select the features that directly affect its calculation (a detailed description of the features and their preprocessing can be found in Online Appendix C, Table 2 [28]).

Model. The model component of IML4DQ is represented by a combination of anomaly detection and XAI, with the model definitions and parameters kept the same as in ML4DQ [29]. The idea of the anomaly detection step is to check whether the data movements have business reasons or are anomalous [29], while the SHAP explanations highlight the features contributing to this abnormality.

User. The IML4DQ supports two levels of user expertise. When used by a DQ expert, the entire pipeline can be managed independently, as the same user both interacts with the IML system and performs the DQ issues checking. A second option requires multiple users: the one who interacts with the IML system (credit risk specialist), e.g. provides the data and controls the model, and the other user who checks the output (DQ expert). Both cases are supported by IML4DQ.

Interface. IML4DQ is a multiscreen desktop application (supplemented by user documentation) developed using the Tkinter framework, a standard Python GUI toolkit with an object-oriented interface. Since it is available as a Python package, its usage comes at no additional software cost. This is important for prototyping, where the application's usefulness needs to be evaluated by stakeholders. The design of the IML4DQ interface is based on both the functional UI principles [25] (outlined in Online Appendix D [28]) and IML principles.

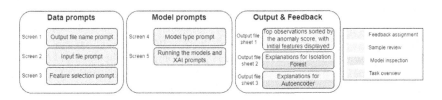

Fig. 2. IML4DQ structure and mapping on the key elements of [6].

In general, the IML interface comprises four key elements [6] (Fig. 2): sample review (reviewing model outputs), feedback assignment (providing user input), model inspection (offering a summative view of model quality), and task overview (informing about task status and termination conditions). Aligning with these elements, the UI of IML4DQ consists of five main screens and an output Excel file. First three screens support the *feedback assignment* task by prompting for the output file name, input data file upload, and feature selection. In addition, there is a separate screen that prompts for the model type. These screens perform the subtasks of selecting features and samples. The labeling subtask is not relevant in the case of IML4DQ, since we are dealing with unsupervised learning, and the labels are assigned ex post, i.e., after the IML4DQ process has been run. The *task overview* step is supported by a screen that displays the progress of the model execution and the status of the generation of XAI explanations. The *sample review* task is supported by the output Excel file: the first sheet lists top abnormal observations, while the other two sheets provide local SHAP explanations [2, 16]. These sheets also support *model inspection* by revealing the model's reasoning in predicting DQ issues with XAI.

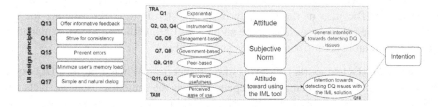

Fig. 3. Evaluation design.

Evaluation. The evaluation aims to understand human intentions in addressing DQ issues through traditional detection and technology-driven automation (Fig. 3). The orange part of the evaluation framework examines the determinants of a general attitude towards detecting DQ problems, inspired by [8], who used the TPB [1], an extension of the TRA model [7], to explore factors influencing data producers' intentions to enter data correctly. Since our interviewees are capable of performing DQ tasks, we apply the original TRA model, excluding the self-efficacy construct of the TPB model used by [8]. Thus, we assume the relationships between attitude, subjective norm, and intention hold, and focus on their antecedents. The green section evaluates users' intentions to interact with the IML system for DQ issues detection. Since we are introducing a new technology, we apply the TAM model [5] to explore technology adoption, assessing perceived ease of use based on key UI principles [25], comprising the third and final (red) part of the evaluation. TAM's relevance stems from its use in interactive DQ solution evaluations [4, 22]. By combining TRA and TAM, we account for DQ domain-specific characteristics, recognizing that automation requires positive user intentions towards the DQ process itself. Further details on the evaluation framework and models can be found in Online Appendix E.1 [28].

4   Results and Discussion

4.1   IML4DQ: User Interface

Figure 4 shows the IML4DQ prototype. Its windows A-C show the data input screens with prompts for output file name, input data file, and input feature selection. To offer informative feedback to the user, window B displays the upload progress bar. Window C shows the columns that are automatically extracted from the file provided in the previous step. To fulfill the principle of preventing errors, we implement checks for the file type and the column types. All the error messages (an example is shown in window E) have a similar layout to fulfill the consistency principle. The same goes for the design of the widgets: the buttons and the progress bars have the same color (orange and green, respectively). Window D shows the model type screen, with a choice between the monthly and daily models (see more details in Online Appendix C [28]).

The main screen of the application is shown in Fig. 4, window F. Initially, sections (5) and (6) are hidden, while the progress bars (2) are displayed in grey; button (4) is unavailable. The topmost labels (1) display the user's previous choices of the model type and selected features, following the principle of minimizing the user's memory load and eliminating the need to remember previous steps. Initially, only the button (3) is available. Once clicked (it becomes unavailable immediately after), a label (5) appears at the bottom of the screen indicating the modeling progress, with the progress bars providing detailed updates on the progress of each modeling step.

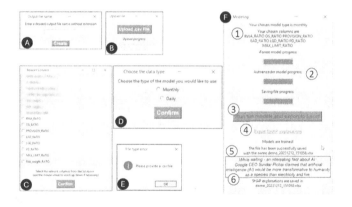

Fig. 4. UI of IML4DQ. (Color figure online)

After the anomaly detection step, section (5) is updated to show this, and a new text is added to show the name of the file where the results are saved, thus reducing memory load. The user can either stop and use the saved results or continue to generate SHAP explanations by clicking the now available button (4). When clicked, two new labels (6) appear: one with an AI fact[1] to engage the user and another with a progress indicator.

---

[1] AI facts are taken from https://www.valuer.ai/blog/75-facts-about-artificial-intelligence.

Once explanations are generated, the indicator updates with the file location, further minimizing memory load.

Finally, the output Excel file comprises three sheets (Online Appendix F, Fig. 3 [28]): one for the anomaly detection results (containing the original input data, sorted in ascending order according to a newly added column, "Final proba"), and the other two containing SHAP explanations.

4.2   Evaluation

Based on the evaluation framework outlined in Sect. 3, we conducted semi-structured, one-hour online interviews with seven potential users from a large financial organization (the interviewees' profiles are outlined in Online Appendices E.2 [28]). Each interview included a five-minute introduction, a 15-minute demonstration, and 15 min for exploration or clarifications. The final 30 min focused on closed and open questions related to the combined model (see Online Appendix E.3 [28]), with responses given on a Likert scale followed by open comments. Due to the small sample size, no causal conclusions were drawn. Instead, the evaluation aims to understand how each construct is established at the intersection of credit risk, DQ, and IML.

General Attitude. Most interviewees found manual DQ issue detection challenging, ranging from moderate to very difficult. Conversely, the automation of DQ issues detection is deemed very important by most respondents (Online Appendix G, Fig. 4 [28], Q1-Q2). Additionally, the impact of DQ issues on credit risk estimation is mostly perceived as high to very high, with many noting that detecting DQ issues is extremely beneficial (Q3-Q4). These findings underscore a generally positive attitude - both instrumental and experiential - towards the task of identifying DQ issues. This aligns with [21] and [8]: the former supports the relationship between attitude and intention, and the latter finds that correct data entry intention is influenced by both types of attitudes. Our study found instrumental attitude more influential than experiential attitude, consistent with the finance sector's emphasis on high-quality data [32], even at the cost of affective aspects. Additionally, [31] noted that clear goals of high DQ, as seen in banking, motivate data collectors to ensure high-quality data.

Subjective Norm. The data shows that government regulations are seen as the most important norms, with all respondents selecting Agree or Strongly Agree (Online Appendix G, Fig. 5, Q7 and Q8 [28]). Management expectations follow, with most respondents acknowledging their role in identifying DQ issues (Q5 and Q6). Peer-based expectations (Q9 and Q10) are considered least important, though most respondents still recognize them as significant. This findings contrast with [18], which found "push" factors less effective than "pull" factors in motivating correct data entry. This difference may have been due to the banking sector's sensitive nature of user data, influencing perceptions of DQ.

Attitude and Intention Towards IML4DQ. Table 1 shows the analysis of the attitude towards IML4DQ and the intention to use it. Regarding the perceived *usefulness*, most interviewees unconditionally agree that IML4DQ can facilitate faster and easier identification of DQ issues and improve DQ. However, some wanted further customization

Table 1. IML4DQ: attitude & intention. Responses were categorized as positive (Yes), positive with requested changes (Condit. Yes), or negative (No).

	Perceived usefulness		Perceived ease of use					Intention
	Q11	Q12	Q13	Q14	Q15	Q16 - rev.	Q17	Q18
Yes	5 (71%)	5 (71%)	5 (71%)	6 (83%)	6 (83%)	5 (67%)	4 (57%)	5 (71%)
Condit. Yes	2 (29%)	2 (29%)	2 (29%)	1 (17%)	1 (17%)	1 (17%)	3 (43%)	2 (29%)
No	0 (0%)	0 (0%)	0 (0%)	0 (0%)	0 (0%)	1 (17%)	0 (0%)	0 (0%)

for specific team use cases, especially regarding data preparation. In terms of *ease of use*, the principles of *striving for consistency* and *preventing errors* are well met. One respondent preferred a more modern layout, while another recommended clearer error messages. Both principles, commonly cited in UI design, align with human psychology [25]. Error prevention also supports the IML design principle of enabling users to reverse mistakes [6]. The principle of *providing informative feedback* is also met, with two respondents suggesting training before use, in line with the recommendation of [31] to set clear goals to enhance user motivation. However, in terms of *minimizing memory load*, two respondents noted difficulty remembering actions and requested more reminders. The principle of *offering simple and natural dialog* mostly met expectations, with one suggestion to move data preparation details from the documentation to the application. Most respondents were satisfied, with 5 out of 7 intending to use IML4DQ and 2 recommending it to others.

Overall, both perceived usefulness and ease of use were highly rated, indicating that the IML4DQ is powerful and user-friendly, and can be considered, according to [12], a "super tool" with high acceptance potential.

Recommendations. Following the design science framework [9], we asked interviewees for suggestions for improvement (Online Appendix H, Fig. 6 [28]). The main recommendation is to enhance the output file with more details about the SHAP framework that are currently only available in the documentation. Some interviewees also suggested simplifying the output by removing unselected original input features and including descriptive statistics on detected DQ issues, in line with the principle of providing efficient data representations to optimize human perception [6]. Some UI improvements were also mentioned: a modern design is requested, with a suggestion to run the application in the cloud. Users also want data preparation details integrated into the UI rather than in separate documentation. In addition, interviewees suggested enhancements to ML4DQ, including incorporating categorical features, extending it to a semi-supervised setting with feedback from previous runs, providing a numerical estimate of the impact of DQ issues on RWA, and linking outputs to transaction-level data.

5   Conclusion

Nowadays, with the rise of data-driven solutions, ensuring high DQ has become a top priority. Automated DQ assurance with ML is effective for managing large volumes of data. To make ML solutions accessible to non-experts, user-friendly interfaces and human-in-the-loop approaches are essential, which is the focus of IML. This study introduced the IML4DQ framework, integrating IML with DQ, and evaluated it in the context of CRM of an international financial institution.

First, attitudes toward detecting DQ issues in CRM are generally positive, with instrumental attitudes being stronger than experiential attitudes. Second, subjective norms, especially governmental and managerial, significantly influence the intention to detect DQ issues in CRM. Finally, attitudes toward the use of IML at the intersection of DQ and CRM are favorable, emphasizing its usefulness and ease of use. IML4DQ adheres to the key functional UI design principles, excelling in feedback and consistency. Stakeholders want more details on the ML components and more interaction with the data in the UI of the IML solution.

Our study has important theoretical and practical implications. We find that IML effectively complements CRM in performing DQ assurance tasks, removing a critical barrier for non-experts to use ML solutions in their daily work. In addition, our research highlights the critical role of attitudes toward DQ in IML adoption, suggesting the importance of maintaining stakeholder motivation regarding the overall importance of DQ. Our findings highlight governmental and managerial norms as influential motivational factors. Nevertheless, it is important to ensure the intrinsic motivation of DQ stakeholders, as recommended by some other studies [18].

There are some limitations to our research. A larger sample size would allow us to move from semi-structured interviews to structured questionnaires using more advanced statistical analysis. Future work includes incorporating feedback from interviews into the next iteration, implementing ML models for daily movements analysis, and expanding the user sample size for evaluation.

References

1. Ajzen, I.: From Intentions to Actions: A Theory of Planned Behavior, pp. 11–39. Springer, Heidelberg (1985)
2. Antwarg, L., Miller, R.M., Shapira, B., Rokach, L.: Explaining anomalies detected by autoencoders using shapley additive explanations. Expert Syst. Appl. **186**, 115736 (2021)
3. Bakumenko, A., Elragal, A.: Detecting anomalies in financial data using machine learning algorithms. Systems **10**(5), 130 (2022)
4. Cho, S., et al.: An interactive fitness-for-use data completeness tool to assess activity tracker data. J. Am. Med. Inform. Assoc. **29**(12), 2032–2040 (2022)
5. Davis, F.D.: Perceived usefulness, perceived ease of use, and user acceptance of information technology. MIS Q. 319–340 (1989)
6. Dudley, J.J., Kristensson, P.O.: A review of user interface design for interactive machine learning. ACM Trans. Interact. Intell. Syst. **8**(2) (2018)
7. Fishbein, M., Ajzen, I.: Belief, attitude, intention, and behavior: an introduction to theory and research. Philos. Rhetor. **10**(2), 130–132 (1977)
8. Haegemans, T., Snoeck, M., Lemahieu, W.: Entering data correctly: an empirical evaluation of the theory of planned behaviour in the context of manual data acquisition. Reliab. Eng. Syst. Saf. **178**, 12–30 (2018)
9. Hevner, A.R., March, S.T., Park, J., Ram, S.: Design science in information systems research. Manag. Inf. Syst. Q. **28**(1), 6 (2008)

10. Hinton, G.E., Salakhutdinov, R.R.: Reducing the dimensionality of data with neural networks. Science **313**(5786), 504–507 (2006)

11. Homayouni, H., Ghosh, S., Ray, I., Kahn, M.G.: An interactive data quality test approach for constraint discovery and fault detection. In: 2019 IEEE International Conference on Big Data (Big Data), pp. 200–205. IEEE (2019)

12. Keil, M., Beranek, P.M., Konsynski, B.R.: Usefulness and ease of use: field study evidence regarding task considerations. Decis. Support Syst. **13**(1), 75–91 (1995)

13. Kleinsmith, A., Gillies, M.: Customizing by doing for responsive video game characters. Int. J. Hum Comput Stud. **71**(7–8), 775–784 (2013)

14. Krishnan, S., Franklin, M.J., Goldberg, K., Wang, J., Wu, E.: Activeclean: an interactive data cleaning framework for modern machine learning. In: Proceedings of the 2016 International Conference on Management of Data, pp. 2117–2120 (2016)

15. Liu, F.T., Ting, K.M., Zhou, Z.H.: Isolation forest. In: 2008 Eighth IEEE International Conference on Data Mining, pp. 413–422 (2008)

16. Lundberg, S.M., et al.: From local explanations to global understanding with explainable AI for trees. Nat. Mach. Intell. **2**(1), 2522–5839 (2020)

17. Moges, H.T., Dejaeger, K., Lemahieu, W., Baesens, B.: A multidimensional analysis of data quality for credit risk management: new insights and challenges. Inf. Manag. **50**(1), 43–58 (2013)

18. Molina, R., Unsworth, K., Hodkiewicz, M., Adriasola, E.: Are managerial pressure, technological control and intrinsic motivation effective in improving data quality? Reliab. Eng. Syst. Saf. **119**, 26–34 (2013)

19. Monarch, R.M.: Human-in-the-Loop Machine Learning: Active learning and annotation for human-centered AI. Simon and Schuster (2021)

20. Mosqueira-Rey, E., Hernández-Pereira, E., Alonso-Ríos, D., Bobes-Bascarán, J., Fernández-Leal, A.: Human-in-the-loop machine learning: a state of the art. Artif. Intell. Rev. **56**(4), 3005–3054 (2022)

21. Murphy, G.D.: Improving the quality of manually acquired data: applying the theory of planned behaviour to data quality. Reliab. Eng. Syst. Saf. **94**(12), 1881–1886 (2009)

22. Pereira, J.L., Fonseca, M.J., Lopes, A., Galhardas, H.: Cleenex: support for user involvement during an iterative data cleaning process. ACM J. Data Inf. Qual. (2024)

23. Porter, R., Theiler, J., Hush, D.: Interactive machine learning in data exploitation. Comput. Sci. Eng. **15**(5), 12–20 (2013)

24. Räth, T., Onah, N., Sattler, K.U.: Interactive data cleaning for real-time streaming applications. In: Proceedings of the Workshop on Human-In-the-Loop Data Analytics, pp. 1–3 (2023)

25. Ruiz, J., Serral, E., Snoeck, M.: Unifying functional user interface design principles. Int. J. Hum. Comput. Interact. **37**(1), 47–67 (2021)

26. Shrivastava, S., et al.: DQA: scalable, automated and interactive data quality advisor. In: 2019 IEEE International Conference on Big Data (Big Data), pp. 2913–2922 (2019)

27. Shrivastava, S., Patel, D., Zhou, N., Iyengar, A., Bhamidipaty, A.: Dqlearn: a toolkit for structured data quality learning. In: 2020 IEEE International Conference on Big Data (Big Data), pp. 1644–1653. IEEE (2020)

28. Tiukhova, E., Salcuni, A., Oguz, C., Forte, F., Baesens, B., Snoeck, M.: IML4DQ: interactive Machine Learning for Data Quality with applications in Credit Risk: Online appendices (2024). https://doi.org/10.5281/zenodo.13898445

29. Tiukhova, E., et al.: Boosting credit risk data quality using machine learning and eXplainable AI techniques. In: Meo, R., Silvestri, F. (eds.) ECML PKDD 2023. CCIS, vol. 2137, pp. 420–429. Springer, Cham (2024). https://doi.org/10.1007/978-3-031-74643-7_30

30. Tiukhova, E., et al.: Explainable learning analytics: assessing the stability of student success prediction models by means of explainable AI. Decis. Support Syst. **182**, 114229 (2024)

31. Unsworth, K., Adriasola, E., Johnston-Billings, A., Dmitrieva, A., Hodkiewicz, M.: Goal hierarchy: improving asset data quality by improving motivation. Reliab. Eng. Syst. Saf. **96**(11), 1474–1481 (2011)
32. Van Gestel, T., Baesens, B.: Credit Risk Management: Basic Concepts: Financial Risk Components, Rating Analysis, Models, Economic and Regulatory Capital. Oxford University Press, Oxford (2009)
33. Naake, T., Huber, W.: MatrixQCvis: shiny-based interactive data quality exploration for omics data. Bioinformatics, 38(4), 1181–1182, Oxford University Press (2022)

Optimizing B-Trees for Memory-Constrained Flash Embedded Devices

Nadir Ould-Khessal⬛, Scott Fazackerley⬛, and Ramon Lawrence(✉)⬛

University of British Columbia, Kelowna, Canada
`ramon.lawrence@ubc.ca`

Abstract. Small devices collecting data for agricultural, environmental, and industrial monitoring enable Internet of Things (IoT) applications. Given their critical role in data collection, there is a need for optimizations to improve on-device data processing. Edge device computing allows processing of the data closer to where it is collected and reduces the amount of network transmissions. The B-tree has been optimized for flash storage on servers and solid-state drives, but these optimizations often require hardware and memory resources not available on embedded devices. The contribution of this work is the development and experimental evaluation of multiple variants for B-trees on memory-constrained embedded devices. Experimental results demonstrate that even the smallest devices can perform efficient B-tree indexing, and there is a significant performance advantage for using storage-specific optimizations.

Keywords: B-tree · Embedded devices · Data indexing and storage · Internet of things

1 Introduction

Devices deployed at the edge of networks are collecting and processing large amounts of data. Processing data on the device before sending it to servers may improve response time and energy efficiency and reduce the amount of data transmitted over the network. The smallest embedded devices have unique hardware and performance characteristics that challenge data processing. These devices may have very small memory between 4 to 64 KB, limited CPUs, and use raw flash storage without a file system. Data processing is dominated by inserts, and there is a limited number of queries related to the collected data.

Implementing a B-tree for a memory-constrained embedded device has unique challenges. Although the data sizes processed are orders of magnitude smaller, the relative RAM versus storage ratio is lower. An embedded device may have less than 1% memory compared to the data size, and the absolute memory size is very small. Every byte counts in this environment. The second factor is with raw flash storage the implementation must handle management of physical memory including wear leveling, page placement, and free space management. Without a flash translation layer (FTL), the algorithm must map logical pages to physical pages while using minimal memory. The CPU is usually single-threaded, the storage device can only respond to one request at a

M. Comuzzi et al. (Eds.): CoopIS 2024, LNCS 15506, pp. 327–337, 2025.
https://doi.org/10.1007/978-3-031-81375-7_19

time, and transferring data on the bus is a bottleneck. I/O performance is limited by the bus speed rather than the storage device bandwidth. The low memory restricts B-trees [7] developed for raw flash that assume memory sizes available on servers.

This work proposes and evaluates optimizations and variants for B-trees in the memory-constrained, embedded environment. The contributions include:

- An approach to reducing write amplification for B-tree updates by using virtual mappings. Virtual mappings allow physical page movements without rebuilding the B-tree index structure.
- A B-tree variant utilizing virtual mappings for raw NAND flash storage.
- A B-tree variant designed for memory supporting page overwriting such as NOR and DataFlash [1].
- An experimental evaluation on two hardware platforms and three memory types showing the benefits of storage-specific B-tree optimizations to maximize performance on hardware with unique characteristics.
- Analysis on the most effective usage for memory for the B-tree index when the memory available is small.

2 Background

The B-tree [2] is a high-performance index structure for database applications. Most implementations use the B$^+$-tree variant [4] where data records are only in the leaf nodes, and interior nodes contain keys for navigation. An example B$^+$-tree is in Fig. 1, where each node contains a maximum of 3 entries.

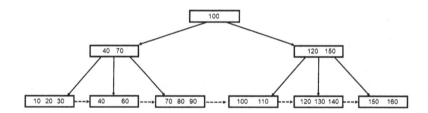

Fig. 1. B$^+$-tree Example.

Graefe [9] provides a discussion of numerous challenges, techniques, and best practices for B-tree implementation. Foster B-trees [10] combine the advantages of several B-tree variants including the write-optimized B-tree [8] to support improved concurrency and efficient page migration in flash storage. Foster B-trees eliminate sibling pointers in the B-tree structure (dashed pointers in the figure) and rely only on parent-children pointers. Bw-trees [14] use a mapping table to convert logical pointers to physical locations. This allows writing a page to any storage location without requiring updating pointers on the complete path from leaf to root. The performance of the mapping table is critical.

The migration from hard drives to flash-based storage and solid-state drives (SSDs) resulted in a renewed emphasis on B-trees and optimization for flash characteristics [7]. B-trees adapted to flash memory properties by favoring reads over writes, using in-memory buffers and logging to reduce the number of writes, and deferring and batching random writes into sequential writes.

To understand a fundamental challenge, consider inserting key 50 into the B-tree in Fig. 1. Key 50 will be inserted into the second leaf node currently containing 40 and 60. On a hard drive, the page containing the node is updated and written back in-place on disk. No modifications to the B-tree structure are required. On an SSD, the B-tree implementation may also overwrite the page logically, but the SSD must use its FTL to write the page to a different physical location as overwriting the same location without erasing is not supported.

For raw flash memory without a file interface, it is not possible to physically over-write an updated page, and writing to a new page location requires updating B-tree pointers. Updating a pointer may require cascading updates to other pages. In our example, inserting 50 and writing the updated page to a new location requires updating the pointer in the parent node containing (40,70) that then triggers an update and write of the root node. Further, if sibling pointers are used, the leaf node containing (10,20,30) would also require updating. Reducing this write amplification is critical to ensure acceptable performance.

A survey on flash based indexing [7] overviews various B-tree implementations. Buffering approaches such as write-optimized trees [3] defer writes by buffering nodes in memory and writing in batches to amortize the write cost. Logging approaches [13] log changes in memory or on the flash data page rather than updating immediately. In our insert key 50 example, a buffering approach may buffer the leaf node and its parent in memory and only write the nodes after many updates have occurred. A logging approach would store the insert 50 as a log record in a separate memory area and defer making changes to the tree. The tree is updated in batch when the log area is full.

Raw flash B-tree implementations often modify the B-tree node structure to reduce the write amplification or exploit flash memory properties such as partial page updates or overwrites [11,12]. B-tree implementations for servers are not executable on memory-constrained embedded devices if they require too much memory. A B-tree implementation [15] for embedded devices that uses limited memory is available but is not optimized for raw flash and relies on file-based storage. Index structures for embedded devices such as SBITS [6] for sequential time series data do not support indexing for non-sequential data like a B-tree.

3   Motivating Environment

The target environment is resource-constrained embedded devices used in logging applications. The device may have a CPU speed of 16 MHz to 128 MHz, between 4 KB and 64 KB RAM, and use NOR, NAND, or SD card storage. The flash storage may not have an FTL. These hardware specifications (see Fig. 2) are comparable to the IBM 360 used in 1970 for the original B-tree experiments.

Device	CPU	RAM	I/O Rate
M0+ SAMD21	48 MHz	32 KB	450 KB/s
PIC24FJ1024	16 MHz	32 KB	200 KB/s
IBM 360/44 [2]	1.6 MHz	32-256 KB	156 KB/s

Fig. 2. Embedded Devices and Original Experimental B-tree Hardware in 1970.

The logging environment domain is characterized by very constrained and specific data access requirements. The devices are typically collecting time series data consisting of a timestamp and a sensed value which is often a small number. Highly efficient inserts are the key consideration. Record inserts are typically append-only in order of record timestamp. Updates and deletes are very rare. Query processing on-device is for performing searches by timestamp or value and aggregate queries over time windows.

The B-tree should adapt to these device properties. There are two distinct use cases for embedded indexing. Indexing the append-only, sorted time series data is for retrieval based on timestamp. Numerous prior index structures that utilize sequential writes, including simple sorted files, demonstrate good performance with minimal memory usage [6]. Even when optimized for sequential data, the B-tree has comparable, but not superior, performance to these specialized index structures [16]. Retrieval by data value in the time series is not as efficiently handled by current embedded index structures. There is no ordering of the data values, and the index must handle random writes to any location. There may also be a considerable amount of duplication in the data set. Further, if the sensor is capturing physical measurements of the environment, the data may be more periodic and follow a function based on the value being measured. As an example, temperature values change slowly over time in a relatively predictable fashion. The focus of this work is on indexing non-sorted data efficiently.

4   B-Tree Optimizations

This section presents B-tree optimizations and implementation variants for embedded systems. Previous work on logging and write-optimized trees are combined and compared with an approach that uses virtual mappings to defer writing nodes when their children pointers change.

4.1   Buffering and Logging

B-tree approaches using buffering have limited use on embedded devices as there is only sufficient memory to buffer the root node and a few nodes in the working path. Thus, a page will not remain in the buffer for long enough to accumulate multiple updates before being written to storage. Logging operations to perform in batch is more memory efficient as the operation is stored rather than the modified page. Previous log-based approaches associated logs with either the entire tree, individual nodes, or based on storage blocks. The most memory efficient is to use a single log for the tree that functions as a write buffer. When the write buffer is full, the operations are sorted, and the inserts are performed in batch. This reduces I/Os by inserting multiple records into a page at a time and has good performance for clustered data. The write buffer optimization performing batch inserts can be applied with any of the other B-tree optimizations. For applications with restrictions on data loss, the write buffer can be sized to require writing after a given amount of time or records have been accumulated.

4.2 Virtual Mappings

Virtual mappings resolve the write amplification issue when writing B-tree nodes on flash storage without an FTL. A virtual mapping is a pair consisting of its previous and new page id *prevPageId → newPageId*. Whenever a page is written to a new location, a virtual mapping is inserted into the mapping table. In the example when inserting key 50, the node containing (40, 60) is updated and written to a new location. The parent node containing (40, 70) requires a pointer update to point to the new location. Rather than modifying the parent node, a virtual mapping is created. Whenever the pointer is traversed, the mapping table is used to lookup if a new location is used.

To minimize the number of mappings, similar to Foster B-trees [10], there are no sibling pointers. With only parent pointers, there is at most one pointer to any given node. Virtual mappings are similar to the mapping table used in Bw-trees [14] except that due to the limited memory, the mapping table size is bounded, and only the required mappings are in the table. Given a page id as a pointer in a B-tree node, if no mapping is found in the table, then the page id provides the node's current physical location. Thus, the mappings are more similar to physical redirects rather than logical to physical mappings. A mapping requires no additional I/Os and will not be chained multiple times. Consider if the node containing (40, 60) is written multiple times at different locations $L_1, L_2, ..., L_N$ and the parent node (40, 70) pointer stores the pointer value L_1. On writing to location L_2, the mapping $L_1 \rightarrow L_2$ is added to the table. Each following write only updates the mapping $L_1 \rightarrow L_3, L_1 \rightarrow L_4, ...,$ to finally $L_1 \rightarrow L_N$. There is no need to store any intermediate mappings as there is only one node that uses the mapping, and it contains the value L_1. Before any I/O is performed, the mapping table is searched to determine if a page's physical location has changed. In all cases, only one I/O is required to retrieve the page.

Virtual mappings must be memory-resident. The mapping table size is configurable but is typically only about 1 to 2 KB. Our implementation uses an in-memory hash table with double hashing to handle collisions. If there is no space to store a mapping, then the node that required the mapping is written to storage. With sufficient space to store all mappings, there is no write amplification. Using virtual mappings allows sequentially writing pages to storage. When a page is updated, it is written to the next sequential page location, and a virtual mapping created. This has performance benefits for some devices, and also simplifies free space management and garbage collection.

4.3 Page Overwriting

Some memory devices allow limited page overwrites which may improve performance [1]. Due to the nature of NOR flash, the entire page can be overwritten but only bit changes from 1 to 0 are supported [1,5]. Overwriting improves write performance and

reduces the number of erases. Our implementation stores the B-tree node in linear insertion order (i.e. not sorted) which works well with overwriting. There are two bits associated with each record: a count bit and a valid bit. Both bit vectors are initialized to 1 s.
When a record is inserted into the page, the count bit is set to 0 from 1. The valid bit
remains as 1. If a record is moved or deleted, its valid bit is set to 0. This allows for all
updates to have writes of 1 to 0. Since keys are no longer sorted, linear search is used.

4.4 Free Space Management and Recovery

Free space management and garbage collection is implemented for raw flash storage,
which is treated as a circular array. Several blocks are erased preceding the current write
location at all times. Before erasing a block, valid pages are determined and buffered
in memory. Once a block is erased, the valid pages are written back to their original
locations in the block so no mappings must be updated. To determine if a page is valid
a free space bit is used for each page.

A page header stores a page id and a previous page id. When writing a new version
of an existing page with ($pageId$, $prevId$), the previous page id for the new page is
$prevId$ if there exists a mapping $prevId \rightarrow pageId$ else it is $pageId$. This allows tracking
the provenance of a page and recovering the virtual mapping table if there is a device
restart. On restart, the storage is scanned backwards from the last page write. When
a page is read with header ($pageId$, $prevId$), search the mapping table for $prevId$. If
no mapping is found, a mapping is added to the mapping table of the form $prevId \rightarrow$
$pageId$. If a mapping $prevId \rightarrow pageId2$ is found and $pageId2 > pageId$, then the $pageId$
page is an older version and is marked as a free page.

4.5 Implementation Variants

The B-tree optimizations are deployed as several implementation variants. The base
B-tree implementation performs update-in-place writing. This implementation is only
executable for storage devices that support a file system interface (with an underlying
FTL) or raw flash memory that supports page-level erase-then-write (such as DataFlash
[1]). The virtual mapping tree, VMTree, uses a virtual mapping table to minimize write
amplification and performs sequential writes to storage. When a logical page is overwritten, the updated page is written to the next sequential page location, and a mapping
is inserted in the mapping table to prevent modifying the parent page. The VMTree-OW
implementation performs physical page overwrites on memory storage that supports the
functionality. A virtual mapping table is not required. All implementations use a page
buffer using a LRU algorithm. The root page is always buffered. Each implementation
may also utilize a write buffer allowing batching of operations.

5 Experimental Results

The B-tree implementations were compared on several hardware platforms for multiple data sets. The hardware platforms and storage devices are in Fig. 3. The data set
characteristics are in Fig. 4. The results are the average of 3 runs.

Device	Storage	Page Size	R (KB/s)	W (KB/s)	R/W Ratio
32-bit SAMD21	SD card	512 bytes	500 ; 400	500 ; 215	1 ; 1.9
32-bit SAMD21	DataFlash	512 bytes	475	35	13.5
16-bit PIC	NAND	2048 bytes	203	187	1.1
16-bit PIC	SD card	2048 bytes	198 ; 194	108 ; 93	1.8 ; 2

Fig. 3. Example Embedded Devices and Memory Configurations.

Data Set	Key Size	Record Size	Description
Random	4 bytes	16 bytes	Random 32-bit integers
Environmental	8 bytes	8 bytes	Time series data from [18]. Indexing data value (temperature, pressure, or wind speed).
Health	8 bytes	8 bytes	WESAD time series data [17] monitoring patient heart, temperature, movement.

Fig. 4. Experimental Data Sets.

In Fig. 3 are device read and write performance with the first value being sequential performance and the second being random performance. The buffer memory allocated to the implementations was $M = 3$ page buffers. The VMTree requires memory for the mapping table. The 32-bit SAMD21 platform used page sizes of 512 bytes, while the PIC platform had page sizes of 2048 bytes. On the SAMD21 platform, total memory consumed was 3141 bytes consisting of 3×512 byte pages, state variables of 330 bytes, bit vector of 251 bytes, and a mapping table of 1024 bytes. On the PIC platform, total memory consumed was 8866 bytes consisting of 3 byte buffer pages, state variables of 547 bytes, bit vector of 127 bytes, and a mapping table of 2048 bytes.

5.1 Random Data

The experiment inserted 10,000 records and then performed 10,000 queries. On the SD card, the VMTree time and I/O is within 3% of the B-tree. There is no advantage in maintaining a virtual mapping table as the SD card has an FTL. The VMTree performs sequential I/O versus random I/O by the B-tree, however, this benefit was not noticeable in the results. VMTree-OW is 8% slower on the SD card which does not support hardware-level overwrites, as its unsorted leaf structure requires more time to process. On the DataFlash, VMTree is about 2% slower than the B-tree. Hardware-level overwrites result in a four times performance improvement for VMTree-OW with its overwrite-friendly page structure.

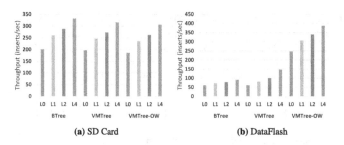

Fig. 5. 32-bit ARM Insert Throughput.

Figure 5 shows the insert throughput for each B-tree variant at various write buffer sizes (e.g. *L1* is 1 write buffer). The write buffer improves all implementations. For queries, the read I/Os is identical for all implementations. The query time is within 2% for VMTree and B-tree. VMTree-OW is 10 to 20% slower due to its unsorted nodes requiring linear search.

On the PIC with SD card storage, VMTree performs 2.2% more reads, 0.5% more writes, and takes 9.1% longer than the B-tree. On NAND memory, VMTree is 14% faster than the B-tree using SD card storage. This is a significant benefit as the NAND chip cost of $2 to $4 is 5 times less expensive than an SD card ($10 to $20) and easier to deploy on small devices. The results demonstrate the advantage of customizing B-tree implementations for storage-specific properties. The addition of a write buffer has substantial performance improvements while not requiring a lot of memory.

5.2 Sensor Data

Two sensor data sets were evaluated: environmental weather station data [6,18] with hourly samples of temperature, precipitation, humidity, and wind speed and the WESAD (wearable stress and affect detection) health data set [17] with sensor measurements including electrocardiogram (ECG), respiration, body temperature, and three-axis acceleration. The B-tree index stores 8-byte index entries consisting of data value (i.e. temperature or ECG) and the record id for retrieval in the time series data set. Although the data is ordered by timestamp, it is not ordered by data value. Data values may have considerable duplication and temporal clustering. The B-tree is a secondary index supporting queries searching on the data value. The buffer memory allocated was $M = 3$ page buffers. The experiment inserted 10,000 records and then ran 10,000 queries on the B-tree.

The insert throughput results on the 32-bit ARM processor for SD card storage and DataFlash are in Fig. 6. The relative performance of the implementations on the SD card is the same as the random data set with VMTree slightly slower than the B-tree. On DataFlash, VMTree-OW has a four times speedup over the B-tree. A write buffer has a larger benefit compared to random data due to clustering. The temperature data is slowly changing, and batching inserts with one write buffer reduces I/O and time by 63–72%.

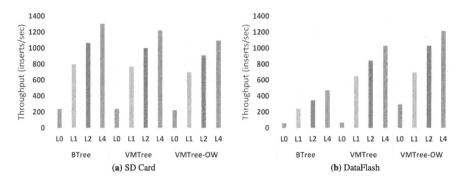

Fig. 6. Insert Throughput Temperature Data (ARM).

The health data and other environmental variables including humidity, pressure, and wind speed displayed similar performance characteristics. Although the percentage I/O savings varies depending on the amount of duplication and temporal clustering, all sensor data demonstrated substantial savings when using the write buffer. The relative performance of the B-tree variants was consistent regardless of the data set and write buffer size.

5.3   Optimizing Memory Usage

There are two uses for additional memory: general page buffers and the write buffer. General page buffers store in RAM pages using an LRU buffer. The write buffer batches operations before performing them on the tree. Experiments used the random and temperature data sets, varied the number of page buffers used from 3 to 10, and compared to using a write buffer with 0 pages or 1 page.

For write throughput, adding page buffers when there is no write buffer increases throughput for the B-tree by 5 to 25% for random data and less than 5% for temperature data. The buffer hit rate for temperature data is quite high and does not improve substantially with more buffers. The VMTree is similar except performance improvement for random data is lower between 3 to 14% due to lower buffer hit rate. Adding more buffers does not change the write I/Os but reduces reads due to more buffer hits. Adding a write buffer has a much larger effect with a significant increase for the temperature data due to clustering.

Read throughput is not affected by a write buffer. Adding page buffers improves read performance by increasing the buffer hit rate. This is noticeable for data with high duplication and clustering like the temperature data. Going from three to four page buffers allows the system to buffer in memory a complete working path from root to leaf, which avoids having to re-read interior nodes on the path to the leaf when performing splits and tree maintenance. When utilizing a write buffer to batch updates is feasible, there is more benefit in dedicating memory to the write buffer compared to general page buffers. Sufficient page buffers to buffer a root-to-leaf path is valuable.

5.4 Discussion

The results demonstrate the advantage of B-tree variants adapting to storage-specific properties. The B-tree implementation is the best choice for file-based storage. The VMTree has competitive performance for certain data sizes, but its additional overhead for managing the storage has no benefit unless the storage has a significant difference in random versus sequential write performance. VMTree executes on raw NAND flash with high performance and uses only 3 to 4 KB of memory. This allows B-trees to be used on small embedded devices where it was not previously possible. For devices that support page ovewriting, VMTree-OW has superior performance, and unlike VMTree, does not need a virtual mapping table. Write buffers enable batch inserts that have significant performance improvements, especially for sensor data. If the use case tolerates buffered data loss, then larger write buffers have the most impact.

6 Conclusions

Small embedded devices are key data collectors in Internet of Things applications. Improving data processing and indexing performance on these memory-constrained devices may reduce energy usage and network transmission. This work developed, implemented, and experimentally evaluated several optimized B-tree variants. The approach of virtual mappings reduces write amplification and allows for efficient B-tree implementations on raw flash memory without requiring a file system interface. The second key optimization was the application of buffering operations. When possible for the application use case, write buffering has a dramatic benefit for many sensor data sets with an insert bandwidth 3 to 5 times faster. Optimizing for memory that supports page overwriting also results in a speedup of 4 times. Overall, the three optimized implementations allow for deployment across a wide-range of devices and memory types and support efficient B-tree indexing while only requiring about 4 KB of memory.

Future work will continue to enhance the optimizations for specific memory types and devices and examine if utilizing other B-tree performance optimizations such as compression have benefit for the sensor data collection environment. The source code is at https://github.com/ubco-db/vmtree.

References

1. Adesto Technologies: AT45DB641E 64-Mbit DataFlash (2024). https://digikey.com/en/htmldatasheets/production/1376615/0/0/1/at45db641e-uun2b-t
2. Bayer, R., McCreight, E.M.: Organization and maintenance of large ordered indices. Acta Informatica **1**, 173–189 (1972). https://doi.org/10.1007/BF00288683
3. Bender, M.A., et al.: An introduction to Bε-trees and write-optimization. Usenix Mag. **40**(5) (2015)
4. Comer, D.: Ubiquitous B-tree. ACM Comput. Surv. **11**(2), 121–137 (1979). https://doi.org/10.1145/356770.356776
5. Fazackerley, S., Penson, W., Lawrence, R.: Write improvement strategies for serial NOR dataflash memory. In: CCECE, pp. 1–6 (2016). https://doi.org/10.1109/CCECE.2016.7726758

6. Fazackerley, S., Ould-Khessal, N., Lawrence, R.: Efficient flash indexing for time series data on memory-constrained embedded sensor devices. In: SENSORNETS, pp. 92–99. SCITEPRESS (2021). https://doi.org/10.5220/0010318800920099

7. Fevgas, A., Akritidis, L., Bozanis, P., Manolopoulos, Y.: Indexing in flash storage devices: a survey on challenges, current approaches, and future trends. VLDB J. **29**(1), 273–311 (2019). https://doi.org/10.1007/s00778-019-00559-8

8. Graefe, G.: Write-optimized B-trees. In: VLDB, pp. 672–683 (2004). https://doi.org/10.1016/B978-012088469-8.50060-7

9. Graefe, G.: A survey of B-tree logging and recovery techniques. ACM TODS **37**(1), 1:1–1:35 (2012). https://doi.org/10.1145/2109196.2109197

10. Graefe, G., Kimura, H., Kuno, H.A.: Foster B-trees. ACM TODS **37**(3), 17:1–17:29 (2012). https://doi.org/10.1145/2338626.2338630

11. Hardock, S., Koch, A., Vinçon, T., Petrov, I.: IPA-IDX: in-place appends for B-tree indices. In: 15th International Workshop on Data Management, pp. 18:1–18:3. ACM (2019). https://doi.org/10.1145/3329785.3329929

12. Kaiser, J., Margaglia, F., Brinkmann, A.: Extending SSD lifetime in database applications with page overwrites. In: 6th International Systems and Storage Conference, pp. 11:1–11:12. ACM (2013). https://doi.org/10.1145/2485732.2485747

13. Kim, B., Lee, D.: LSB-tree: a log-structured b-tree index structure for NAND flash SSDs. Des. Autom. Embed. Syst. **19**(1-2), 77–100 (2015). https://doi.org/10.1007/s10617-014-9139-4

14. Levandoski, J.J., Lomet, D.B., Sengupta, S.: The BW-tree: a B-tree for new hardware platforms. In: ICDE, pp. 302–313. IEEE (2013)

15. Ould-Khessal, N., Fazackerley, S., Lawrence, R.: An efficient B-tree implementation for memory-constrained embedded systems. In: The 19th International Conference on Embedded Systems, Cyber-Physical Systems, and Applications (ESCS 2021) (2021)

16. Ould-Khessal, N., Fazackerley, S., Lawrence, R.: Performance evaluation of embedded time series indexes using bitmaps, partitioning, and trees. In: Sensor Net, vol. 1674, pp. 125–151 (2022). https://doi.org/10.1007/978-3-031-17718-7_7

17. Schmidt, P., Reiss, A., Duerichen, R., Marberger, C., Van Laerhoven, K.: Introducing WESAD, a multimodal dataset for wearable stress and affect detection. In: ICMI 2018, pp. 400–408. ACM (2018). https://doi.org/10.1145/3242969.3242985

18. Zeinalipour-Yazti, D., Lin, S., Kalogeraki, V., Gunopulos, D., Najjar, W.: MicroHash: an efficient index structure for flash-based sensor devices. In: FAST 2005 Conference on File and Storage Technologies, pp. 31–43. USENIX (2005)

Predictive Process Approach for Email Response Recommendations

Ralph Bou Nader[1]([✉]), Marwa Elleuch[1], Ikram Garfatta[1], Walid Gaaloul[1], and Boualem Benatallah[2]

[1] Institut Polytechnique de Paris, Paris, France
ralph.bounader@outlook.com
[2] Dublin City University, Dublin, Ireland

Abstract. Process prediction requires analyzing traces to forecast future activities in a process. Traces can be found in information systems' logs, such as email systems used by business actors. While email traces can aid in process prediction, their unstructured textual nature poses challenges for existing techniques. Additionally, predicting process-oriented emails goes beyond identifying future business process (BP) activities, as it also involves recommending the emails needed for BP actors to perform these activities. Current approaches to email prediction primarily focus on email management, with limited attention to BP contexts, and often only reach the BP discovery or email classification stages. This paper presents an overview of a novel process-activity aware email response recommendation system, designed to enhance both relevance and efficiency in business communications by offering BP knowledge and tailored response templates for incoming emails. The system provides specific recommendations on activities to include in responses, their intent (speech act), and associated business data. Unlike existing approaches, this work uniquely leverages unstructured email data to predict process activities for email responses and incorporates BP knowledge to offer BP-oriented guidance.

Keywords: Business process · Process prediction · Email response recommendation

1 Introduction

Process mining involves techniques for analyzing business process (BP) traces to uncover workflows, identify inefficiencies, and optimize processes [10]. Prediction is a crucial component within this field, leveraging historical data to forecast future process details, such as next activities, remaining time, and costs. These insights help business actors plan and prioritize tasks, thereby enhancing productivity and reducing delays. Accessing BP execution traces, often stored in system logs like emails, is essential for accurate predictions. However, emails present challenges due to their unstructured format, which contrasts with the structured data required for conventional process mining. This highlights a need for innovative approaches tailored to email data within BP contexts.

M. Comuzzi et al. (Eds.): CoopIS 2024, LNCS 15506, pp. 338–345, 2025.
https://doi.org/10.1007/978-3-031-81375-7_20

In email contexts [8], prediction generally focuses on recommending response elements, such as recipients and content. Prior studies, such as those by Fang et al. and Wang et al., explored collaborative filtering and deep learning for email content recommendations but mainly focused on general email management. Other research has linked email management with BP by discovering BP elements in email logs or classifying emails into BP activities, yet process prediction remains largely unexplored. Making accurate predictions in BP-oriented emails involves not only forecasting activities but also suggesting content that enables BP actors to effectively perform these tasks.

Building on previous work [6] that converted unstructured email logs into structured event logs, this paper presents a process-activity-aware email response recommendation system. It predicts BP activities for email responses, including their intentions and relevant business data, and recommends response templates based on historical content aligned with this predicted BP knowledge. This enhances communication by offering tailored recommendations that help business actors respond efficiently. The paper is organized as follows: Sect. 2 reviews related literature, Sect. 3 details our recommendation approach, Sect. 4 covers implementation and evaluation, and Sect. 5 concludes the study.

2   Related Work

Our study bridges two key research domains: process prediction from execution logs and email recommendation techniques. In process prediction, methods like machine learning [2] and statistical approaches [4] are commonly used to forecast activities, times, and risks in business processes (BPs). However, these approaches often assume structured control flows, which are unsuitable for email-driven processes where activities depend on irregular sequences from email threads and interactions. To address this, we introduce a prediction approach tailored to event logs generated from email communication, focusing on predicting activity sequences and business data specific to email-driven BPs.

In email recommendation, techniques fall into field recommendations, question-answer systems, and full response generation. Field recommendations handle metadata like recipients or attachments [5], while question-answer systems use natural language processing to match queries with answers [1]. Full response generation methods, such as Mercure [9] and Google's auto-reply, generate new email content based on past emails. However, most existing systems lack BP integration, with recent efforts primarily focused on BP discovery from emails [3]. Our study addresses this gap by aligning email recommendations with BP contexts, combining process prediction with event logs derived from emails to suggest activity-aware responses tailored to BP needs.

3   The Proposed Approach Overview

This section provides a comprehensive overview of our proposed approach, detailing the methods and strategies employed to address the identified challenges. As illustrated in Fig. 1, the approach focuses on recommending email responses by predicting the BP activities implied by received emails. The figure highlights shaded gray areas, representing the foundational work of Elleuch et al. [6] that this approach builds upon.

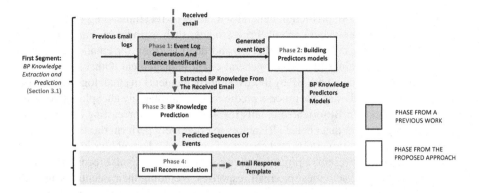

Fig. 1. The proposed approach overview.

Our approach consists of four phases organized into two main segments. The first segment, *BP Knowledge Extraction and Prediction*, encompasses phases 1, 2, and 3, which involve extracting and predicting the BP knowledge necessary for email responses. The second segment, *Response Template Recommendation*, is phase 4, where predicted BP knowledge guides the creation of email response templates. The phases are connected by **blue** arrows representing the recommendation process and *black* arrows for preprocessing steps that develop models and inputs. In BP Knowledge Extraction, email logs are processed into structured event logs containing sender, recipient, timestamp, and content details—essential for predictive modeling (see Sect. 3.1). Using Elleuch et al.'s approach [6], we transform unstructured email logs into structured logs, utilizing algorithms to classify activities, identify BP occurrences, and analyze speech acts to infer sender intent. This structured log then supports BP prediction model development, which forecasts activities, intentions, and data for email responses (Sect. 3.1). For recommendations, the system processes the received email through BP Knowledge Extraction, followed by BP Knowledge Prediction to forecast necessary BP knowledge (Sect. 3.1), and finally **Email Recommendation**, where a response template is suggested based on historical content linked to predicted BP knowledge (Sect. 3.2). Overall, our approach systematically integrates BP knowledge extraction and prediction to generate tailored response templates, enhancing the efficiency and relevance of business email communications.

3.1   First Segment: BP Knowledge Extraction and Prediction

BP Knowledge Extraction Phase 1. This phase serves a dual purpose: (1) creating an event log from an email log to train prediction models, and (2) identifying email instances upon receiving new emails. We employ our unsupervised pattern-based approach from [6] to extract BP knowledge from emails. Figure 3 illustrates an event log example, based on emails like *email1* and *email2* shown in Fig. 2. Each event, represented by Ev_{ID}, contains attributes: (i) **Activity** (*Acto*) with components $ANocc$ and $BDocc$, representing activity name and business data; (ii) **Speech Act (SA)**, indicating the sender's intent (e.g., Request, Intention, Information, Request for Information); (iii) **Performer Indices** (At_{ind}); (iv) **Information Values** (I_{values}); (v) **Email Attributes** (em), including email ID, timestamp, sender, recipients, and conversation ID ($ConvID$); and (vi) **Thread IDs** (Th_{id}) linking to conversations grouped by common business data and email addresses. These threads, illustrated in Fig. 4, approximate BP traces, enabling process-oriented email recommendations by structuring prior email content for model input.

E1	E2
Message-ID: <1552589.1075853972210.JavaMail.evans@thyme> Date: Fri, 10 Nov 2000 06:17:00 -0800 (PST) From: aimee.lannou@enron.com To: daren.farmer@enron.com cc: Subject: Flow w/ no nom Meter 1601 last deal 412219 for 10/00 flowed 11/9 Meter 5192 last deal 454057 for 10/00. flowed 11/3-4	Message-ID: <29717536.1075854150388.JavaMail.evans@thyme Date: Wed, 15 Nov 2000 02:24:00 -0800 (PST) From: daren.farmer@enron.com To: aimee.lannou@enron.com cc: Subject: Re: Flow w/ no nom Rolled deal 454057 to cover flow at mtr 5192. d

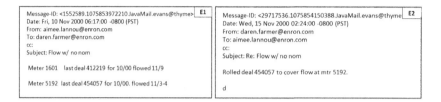

Fig. 2. Emails retrieved from Enron data-set.

Event	Act_n			SA	At_{ind}	I_{values}	em					Th_{id}
Ev_ID	AN_{acc}	BD_{acc}	BC_{acc}				ID	timestamp	Sender	Recipients	ConvIDs	
e_1	('flow deal', ['flowed', 'deal'], [7,4])	[('deal numeric' ,['deal','412219'], [4,5]), ('meter numeric',['meter','1601'], [2,3]), ('deal numeric' ,['deal','45057'], [11,12]), ('meter numeric',['meter','5192'], [9,10])]	[('meter deal', ['meter', deal'], [2,4])]	'information'	[]	['deal numeric_deal 412219'; 'meter numeric_meter 1601', 'deal numeric_deal 45057', 'meter numeric_meter5192']	'<1552589.1075853972210.JavaMail.evans@thyme>'	'Fri, 10 Nov 2000 06:17:00 -0800 (PST)'	'aimee.lannou@enron.com'	['daren.farmer@enron.com']	'C1'	['Th_1']
e_2	('flow deal', ['flowed', 'deal'], [14,11])		()	'information'	[]							
e_3	('roll deal', ['rolled', 'deal'],[2,3])	[('deal numeric' ,['deal','45057'], [3,4]), ('meter numeric',['mtr','5192'], [7,8])]	()	'information'	[]	['deal numeric_deal 45057', 'meter numeric_meter5192']	'<29717536.1075854150388.JavaMail.evans@thyme>'	'Wed, 15 Nov 2000 02:24:00 -0800 (PST)'	'daren.farmer@enron.com'	['aimee.lannou@enron.com']		
e_4	('cover flow', ['cover','flow'],[3,4])			'intention'	[]							

Fig. 3. Example of an event log extract.

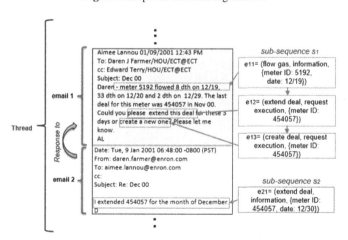

Fig. 4. Sequence of events example extracted from two emails in the same thread.

Building Predictor Models Phase 2. The primary aim of this phase is to train models that forecast BP knowledge for email responses. We convert threads into sequences of events as follows: $S = s_1 \rightarrow s_2 \rightarrow ... \rightarrow s_n$, where s_i represents events within email i, and $s_i \rightarrow s_{i+1}$ indicates temporal order. We develop two LSTM-based models, **"next-bp-knowledge"** and **"sub-sequence"**, optimized with truncated BPTT and hyper-parameter tuning to process these sequences effectively.

BP Knowledge Prediction Phase 3. In this phase, we leverage prediction models to forecast relevant BP knowledge for email responses, expanding beyond basic BP discovery in process-oriented emails. We input the extracted event sub-sequence into the *"next-bp-knowledge"* prediction model, which generates BP knowledge combinations with confidence values, based on overlap with previous emails. The combination with the highest confidence is selected as C_{best}, reflecting the most likely relevant BP knowledge. Each BP knowledge within C_{best} is then processed through the *"sub-sequence"* model to predict an ordered sequence that should appear in the response. For illustration, consider an email from David to Julie about Deal 235670 (Fig. 5), mentioning its expiration and potential extension with Teco Gas Processing. Here, two events stand out: **"Expired Deal"** and **"Extended Deal"**. David mentions, "Deal 235670 has expired", associating BP knowledge with "deal" and "expired," and later states, "we had a successful sale that could be extended," prompting a *"request for information"* tied to "deal" and "extended." As shown in Fig. 6, Phase 3 identifies the most relevant BP knowledge sequence to incorporate into the email response, ensuring it aligns with the context and intent of David's original message.

> Dear Julie,
>
> I hope this email finds you well. I wanted to bring to your attention that Deal # 235670 has expired for Teco Gas Processing as the expiration date was 12/00. However, I wanted to inform you that we had a successful sale in 02/01, which could potentially be extended for Teco Gas Processing. I kindly request you to let me know if we should proceed with extending this deal. This way, I can promptly redraft the sale through Unify.
>
> Thank you, David

Fig. 5. David's Email Correspondence with Julie.

Fig. 6. Predicted sub-sequence of events.

3.2   Second Segment: Response Template Recommendation

Response Template Recommendation Phase 4. In this final phase, we generate an email response template based on the predicted BP knowledge. The response template is constructed as a sequence of sentences, with each term modifiable or static, allowing customization for specific contexts. Templates adhere to three main criteria: alignment with the business context of the original email, inclusion of relevant BP knowledge, and consistency with the author's writing style. Using keywords extraction, we match sentences from past emails to the business context. These sentences are further refined by selecting those with high semantic similarity to the original email's content, filtered through embeddings and classifier analyses. To ensure stylistic coherence, we apply stylometric analysis [7], clustering similar sentences by lexical features. Named entities are then tagged for customization. For example, responding to David's email about Deal #235670, BP knowledge items like *"create deal"* and *"enter deal"* result in sentences such as "I believe it would be advantageous to initiate a new deal with [Company]," and "I will promptly enter the new deal into our system for [Company]," ensuring the response aligns with both context and style, as shown in Fig. 7.

> Dear {name},
> I believe it would be beneficial for us to create a new deal for {company}. I will promptly enter the new deal into our system for {company}.
> Regards, {signature}

Fig. 7. Proposed Email Response Template Tailored for Julie's Communication Style in Reply to David.

4   Experiments and Validation

We evaluated our approach using real emails from the public Enron dataset[1], which contains emails related to online energy trading sent or received by Enron employees. Rather than directly comparing our work to existing studies, we focused on assessing the relevance and coherence of the suggested responses. Our implementation, available on GitHub[2], was benchmarked against fine-tuned *GPT-3* and *GPT-4* models, specifically evaluating BP event inclusion and ordering in email responses. Using 820 Enron email pairs (85% for training, 15% for validation/testing), we fine-tuned *GPT-3* and *GPT-4* with tokenization and optimal hyper-parameters: a learning rate of 1×10^{-5}, batch size of 8, across 3 epochs with the **Adam optimizer**. In our experiments, we analyzed 35 email exchanges, extracting BP knowledge to compare the generated responses from our model and the fine-tuned *GPT-3/4* models based on **precision** and **recall**. As shown in Table 1, our approach achieved a precision of 0.9175, surpassing both *GPT-3*

---

[1] https://www.cs.cmu.edu/~enron/.

[2] https://github.com/ralphbn1995/Predictive-process-approach-for-email-response-recommendations.git.

(0.8789) and *GPT-4* (0.8915), and a recall of 0.9011, higher than *GPT-3* (0.8517) and *GPT-4* (0.8723), indicating stronger relevance and coherence in BP event inclusion and logical flow.

Table 1. Comparing Evaluation Results: Our Approach vs. Fine-tuned GPT-3 vs. Fine-tuned GPT-4 Models.

Model	Events Included (Precision)	Order Accuracy (Recall)
Fine-tuned GPT-3 model	0.8789	0.8517
Fine-tuned GPT-4 model	0.8915	0.8723
Our Approach	**0.9175**	**0.9011**

4.1   Use Case Study

This use case study evaluates the efficiency and quality of email response recommendations using the */response-template-suggestion* endpoint from a Restful API, which leverages our Predictive Process Approach to generate email response templates in JSON format based on email content. We involved 33 participants from diverse backgrounds, including data scientists, software engineers, and Ph.D. students, all skilled in process and data analysis. Participants were split into two groups: an API-assisted group using the endpoint to streamline their response creation and a control group that composed replies manually. The API-assisted group completed tasks significantly faster, with an average response time of 2.2 min compared to 5 min for the control group, resulting in an average time reduction of 18.5%. As shown in Table 2, these results underscore the API's effectiveness in enhancing response efficiency, as the API-assisted group outperformed the control group in all key metrics.

Table 2. Comparison Between Automated and Manual Email Approaches.

Participants	Avg Response Time (s)	Avg Time Reduction (%TR)
33	3764	18.5

These experiments demonstrate the superior performance of our approach compared to *GPT-3/4* models and highlight the API-assisted group's improved response times.

5   Conclusion

This paper presented an overview of a process-activity-aware email response recommendation system that leverages event logs to predict BP knowledge for email responses. Our approach was validated against fine-tuned *GPT-3/4* models. The results showed that our approach consistently outperforms these models in terms of precision and coherence, demonstrating its effectiveness in aligning email recommendations with business process contexts. Future work will focus on expanding the approach with larger datasets and incorporating user feedback to further refine prediction accuracy and enhance the relevance of response templates in real-world applications.

References

1. Arsovski, S., Oladele, M.I., Cheok, A.D., Premčevski, V., Markoski, B.: An approach to email categorization and response generation. Comput. Sci. Inf. Syst. **19**(2), 913–934 (2022)
2. Camargo, M., Dumas, M., González-Rojas, O.: Learning accurate business process simulation models from event logs via automated process discovery and deep learning (2022)
3. Chambers, A.J., et al.: Automated business process discovery from unstructured natural-language documents. In: Del Río Ortega, A., Leopold, H., Santoro, F.M. (eds.) BPM 2020. LNBIP, vol. 397, pp. 232–243. Springer, Cham (2020). https://doi.org/10.1007/978-3-030-66498-5_18
4. Conforti, R., Fink, S., Manderscheid, J., Röglinger, M.: Prism–a predictive risk monitoring approach for business processes. In: Proceedings of the Business Process Management: 14th International Conference, BPM 2016, Rio de Janeiro, Brazil, 18–22 September 2016, pp. 383–400. Springer (2016)
5. Dredze, M., Blitzer, J., Pereira, F.: Sorry, I forgot the attachment: email attachment prediction. In: CEAS (2006)
6. Elleuch, M., Laga, N., Ismaili, O.A., Gaaloul, W.: Multi-perspective business process discovery from messaging systems: state-of-the art. Concurr. Comput. Pract. Exp. **35**(11) (2023). https://doi.org/10.1002/cpe.6642
7. Gómez-Adorno, H., Posadas-Duran, J.P., Ríos-Toledo, G., Sidorov, G., Sierra, G.: Stylometry-based approach for detecting writing style changes in literary texts. Computación y Sistemas **22**(1), 47–53 (2018)
8. Jlailaty, D., Grigori, D., Belhajjame, K.: Mining business process activities from email logs. In: 2017 IEEE International Conference on Cognitive Computing (ICCC), pp. 112–119. IEEE (2017)
9. Lapalme, G., Kosseim, L.: Mercure: towards an automatic e-mail follow-up system. IEEE Comput. Intell. Bull. **2**(1), 14–18 (2003)
10. Van Der Aalst, W.: Process mining: overview and opportunities. ACM Trans. Manag. Inf. Syst. (TMIS) **3**(2), 1–17 (2012)

Achieving Fairness in Predictive Process Analytics via Adversarial Learning

Massimiliano de Leoni and Alessandro Padella$^{(\boxtimes)}$

University of Padua, Padua, Italy
deleoni@math.unipd.it, alessandro.padella@phd.unipd.it

Abstract. Predictive business process analytics has become important for organizations, offering real-time operational support for their processes. However, these algorithms often perform unfair predictions because they are based on biased variables (e.g., gender or nationality), namely variables embodying discrimination. This paper addresses the challenge of integrating a debiasing phase into predictive business process analytics to ensure that predictions are not influenced by biased variables. Our framework leverages on adversarial debiasing is evaluated on four use cases, showing a significant reduction in the contribution of biased variables to the predicted value. The proposed technique is also compared with the state of the art in fairness in process mining, illustrating that our framework allows for a more enhanced level of fairness, while retaining a better prediction quality.

Keywords: Process mining · Deep learning · Predictive process analytics · Adversarial debiasing · Fairness

1 Introduction

Predictive process analytics aims to forecast the outcome of running process instances to identify those requiring specific attention, such as instances risking delays, excessive costs, or unsatisfactory outcomes. By predicting process behavior and outcomes, predictive process analytics enables timely intervention and informed decision-making.

Predictive process analytics naturally needs to rely onto the characteristics of the process being monitored, and performs predictions on their basis. Being that said, this analytics become a problem when predictions are unfair because they are based on characteristics that discriminate in a form that is unacceptable from a legal and/or ethical point of view. For instance, in a loan-application process at a financial institute, one cannot build on the applicant's gender to predict the outcome, namely whether or not the loan is granted. Pohl et al. indicate monitoring, detecting and rectifying biased patterns to be the most significant challenge in Discrimination-Aware Process Mining [5].

Process characteristics are hereafter modelled as process variables. In accordance with the literature terminology [7], we use the term *protected variable* to indicate the variables on which prediction cannot be based. The choice of the set of variables to protect depends on the specific process, and thus needs to be made by the process analysts/stakeholders. Note how simply removing the protected variables from the datasets

M. Comuzzi et al. (Eds.): CoopIS 2024, LNCS 15506, pp. 346–354, 2025.
https://doi.org/10.1007/978-3-031-81375-7_21

would not be effective, because the bias would be simply "hidden under the carpet", as it would be possibly just transferred to other variables that are strongly correlated.

While several researchers acknowledge the importance of ensuring fairness in process predictive analytics, very little research has been carried out on this topic (cf. discussion in Section 2 of the extended version in [2]). This paper proposes a framework based on *adversarial debiasing*, which aims to mitigate bias related to protected variables within the predictive models. In a nutshell, the proposed framework is based on the idea of training the model to predict the process' outcome values, constraining accurately predicting the protected variables and reducing bias in its learned representations.

Compared with the current literature in fairness for process' predictive analytics, adversarial debiasing aims at more accurate predictions through prediction models that also guarantee higher fairness. However, existing research on adversarial debiasing has not focused on process predictive analytics and, more generally, to time series, and cannot be trivially applied in this setting (cf. Section 2 of [2]).

Experiments have been conducted on four use cases to forecast the process-instance total time and whether or not certain activities are going to occur. Protected variables accounted for resources, organization countries, gender, citizenship and spoken languages. The results show that our framework ensures fairness with respect to the chosen protected variables, while the accuracy of the predictive models remains high, also in comparison with the results for comparable research works in literature. Experimental results also highlight that the influence is also reduced for those process variables that are strongly correlated with the protected variables, illustrating that removing the protected variables would just transfer the unfairness to the correlated variables.

2 Preliminaries

The starting point for a prediction system is an *event log*. An event log is a multiset of *traces*. Each trace describes the life-cycle of a particular *process instance* (i.e., a *case*), which is composed by a sequence of *events*, each referring to the execution of a certain activity by a resource at a given timestamps. Additional attributes can be associated to events: the activity cost, outcome, relevant information, etc.

Predictions aims to forecast the outcome value of a running trace, hereafter modelled as an outcome function $\mathcal{K} : \mathcal{E}^* \to \mathcal{O}$, with $\mathcal{O}$ be the set of potential outcome values. Outcome function $\mathcal{K}(\sigma)$ returns the process-instance outcome observed after observing the sequence σ of its events. Predictive analytics aims to build a **process prediction oracle** $\Psi_{\mathcal{K}} : \mathcal{E}^* \to \mathcal{O}$ such that, given a running trace σ' eventually completing in σ_T, $\Psi_{\mathcal{K}}(\sigma')$ is a good predictor of $\mathcal{K}(\sigma_T)$.

The literature proposes several Machine- and Deep-Learning techniques, highlighting LSTM's quality (cf. Section 2 of [3]). We instead opted for fully connected neural networks (FCNNs) [1], which are faster to train than LSTM networks but provide similar accuracy results (see our comparison reported in Section 5.5 of [2]). Also known as Feed-Forward Neural Networks, FCNNs are characterized by having every node in one layer connected to every node in the next layer, meaning that every node in one layer receives input from every node in the previous layer.

The training of FCNN models falls into the problem of supervised learning, which aims to estimate a Machine-Learning (ML) function $\Phi : X_1 \times \ldots \times X_n \to \mathcal{Y}$ where $\mathcal{Y}$

is the domain of variable to predict (a.k.a. dependent variable), and $X_1 \ldots X_n$ are the domains of some independent variables $V_1, \ldots, V_n$, respectively.

To tackle the prediction problem for an outcome function, $\mathcal{Y} = \mathcal{O}$. The values of the independent variables are obtained from the event-log traces: each trace is encoded into a vector element of $X_1 \times \ldots \times X_n$, through a **trace-to-instance encoding function** $\rho_\mathcal{L} : \mathcal{E}^* \rightarrow X_1 \times \ldots \times X_n$. Note that the process prediction oracle is thus implemented as $\Psi_\mathcal{K}(\sigma) = \Phi(\rho_\mathcal{L}(\sigma))$. Section 2 of the extended version of this paper [2] provides further details on how these functions are trained from event logs.

3   An Adversarial Debiasing Framework for Predictive Process Analytics

The overall objective of this paper is to build a process prediction function $\Psi_\mathcal{K}$ whose output values are not influenced by the chosen **protected variables**.

The determination of the protected variable depends on the specific use case under consideration (e.g., the gender or nationality of a loan applicant). It is crucial to note that certain variables may be designated as protected in one use case but not in another (e.g., the variable "Gender" might be designated as a protected variable in the context of a loan application process, but it may not hold the same status in the process of hospital discharge). By carefully selecting the protected variables, we aim to ensure that the predictions do not enforce a discrimination that is not ethically and/or morally acceptable.

The framework is visually depicted in Fig. 1 where the core component is the prediction model that implements the oracle function $\Psi_\mathcal{K}$, capable to of forecasting the outcome of a running trace. Leveraging on neural networks, $\Psi_\mathcal{K}$ is obtained through the composition of the trace-to-instance encoding function ρ_L and an ML function $\Phi : X_1 \times \ldots \times X_n \rightarrow \mathcal{O}$, namely for any trace σ, $\Psi_\mathcal{K}(\sigma) = \Phi(\rho_L(\sigma))$. The most left gray box in Fig. 1 is the encoder ρ_L, which converts the trace into a vector. The second gray box from left depicts the FCNN that implements Φ, along with the decoder represented through the red dot.

Looking from the right in Fig. 1, the first gray box depicts the adversarial FCNN, which tackle the debiasing problem to ensure fairness. In particular, let $\overline{V} = \{\overline{V_1}, \ldots, \overline{V_p}\} \subseteq \{V_1, \ldots, V_n\}$ be the set of the protected variables, which are defined over the domains $Z = \overline{X_1}, \ldots, \overline{X_p}$, respectively. Let $N_1, \ldots, N_q$ are the domains of the output of the q nodes that constitute the last layer of the FCNN implementing Φ. The adversarial FCNN implements a function $\Phi_Z : N_1 \times N_n \rightarrow Z$, which aims to predict the values of the protected variables, using the output of the last layer as input.

In accordance with the literature on adversarial debiasing [7], if the neural network that implements Φ - in our case a FCNN - does not build the prediction on the protected variables, then the adversarial network that implements Φ_Z - in our case another FCNN - is unable to predict the protected-variables values from the output of the network implementing Φ.

More formally, let $\hat{y} = \Phi(x)$ be the predicted value for the running trace σ' that has been encoded $x = \rho_L(\sigma')$. Let σ be the real completion of σ' (i.e. σ' is a prefix of σ), with the real outcome $y = \mathcal{K}(\sigma)$. Let $\boldsymbol{z} = \Phi_Z(\boldsymbol{n})$ be the vector of the values predicted for the protected variables, on the basis of the vector $\boldsymbol{n}$ of the output of the last layer of the neural network that implements Φ. The two neural networks are trained so as to minimize the overall loss function: $L_{\overline{V}}(\hat{y}, y, \boldsymbol{x}, \boldsymbol{z}) = \Delta(\hat{y}, y) - \Delta(\boldsymbol{z}, \pi_{\overline{V}}(\boldsymbol{x}))$. Symbol Δ indicates the normalized difference between two vectors (or two values), and $\pi_{\overline{V}}(\boldsymbol{x})$ is the projection of $\boldsymbol{x}$ over $\overline{V}$, namely retaining the dimensions of $\boldsymbol{x}$ for the protected variables. The normalization in $\Delta(\hat{y}, y)$ is performed by dividing by the largest outcome value $y = \mathcal{K}(\sigma)$ for all traces σ in the training event log. The normalization in $\Delta(\boldsymbol{z}, \pi_{\overline{V}}(\boldsymbol{x}))$ is achieved by dividing by the largest vector $\pi_{\overline{V}}(\rho_L(\sigma))$ for all traces σ in the training event log. Minimizing loss function $L_{\overline{V}}$ implies that prediction accuracy is kept reasonably high while the influence of protected variables is minimized.

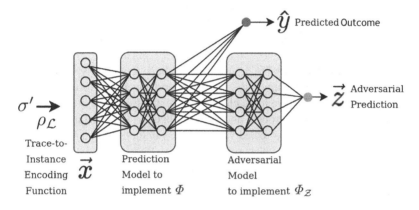

Fig. 1. Overview of our debiasing framework for process' predictive analytics.

The whole framework has been implemented through the training of two FCNNs on a stochastic-gradient-descent based algorithm. The inplementation is in Python and available at https://anonymous.4open.science/r/Fairness-D70B, leveraging on the *PyTorch* package for FCNN's training and *fairlearn* for other debiasing utilities.

4   Evaluation

The evaluation focuses on evaluating how our framework mitigates the influence of protected variables while still ensuring a good quality. The framework evaluation was carried out by training two FCNNs that implement functions Φ and Φ_Z. In particular, we carried out a grid search to tune the hyper-parameters related to the learning rate, layers shape, epochs, and weight decay, so as to prevent over- and under-fitting problems.

Our debiasing framework was evaluated on four use cases, aiming to assess *(i)* the mitigated influence of the protected variables on the prediction, and *(ii)* the extent of the reduction of the prediction accuracy when our framework was employed. Note that a reduction in accuracy is expected when addressing the fairness problem: if the protected variables have some good predictive power, their exclusion has a natural negative impact on the ML-model accuracy. The baseline of comparison is with the only existing framework by Qafari et al. [6].

4.1 Introduction to Use Cases

Our technique was assessed through three process for which we have identified four use cases. The first and the second use case are from Volvo Belgium and refer to a process that focuses on an incident and problem management system called VINST.[1] In the first use case, our aim is to predict the **total time** of an execution that is running, while in the second our aim is to predict **whether or not the activity** *Awaiting Assignment* **will occur** in the future; it is

The third use case refers to the *Hiring* process provided by Pohl et al. in [4]. For this use case we aim to predict the **total time** a running execution.

The last use case is based on the *Hospital* process discussed by Pohl et al. [4]. For this use case our aim is to predict **whether or not the activity** *Treatment unsuccessful* **will occur** in the future.

For each use case, the available process log has been temporarily split into 70% of the traces that were used for training the prediction and adversarial models and 30% for testing. Protected variables have to be clearly different between the different use cases, since their choice depend on process and is also related to specific fairness-preserving considerations. The different protected variables are summarized in the column 3 of the Table 2 the choices for the four use cases.

4.2 Evaluation Metrics

The evaluation's goal is twofold: it aims to assess the mitigation influence of the protected variables on the prediction and the reduction extent of the prediction accuracy.

For the first and third use cases in which we aim to predict the total time of running traces, i.e. a regression problem, the results are provided in terms of **Absolute Percentage Accuracy** (APA), which is defined as 100% minus Mean Absolute Percentage Error, between the actual value and the predicted one. For the second and fourth use cases, we aim to test the accuracy prediction on the occurrence for the activities *Awaiting Assignment* and *Treatment unsuccessful*, respectively. This is a classification problem: hence, we choose **F-score** for assessing the accuracy of our predictions.

To assess the reduction in the influence of protected variables, we employ the theory of Shapley values[2], computing them both when our framework is employed and when it is not: our framework is expected to reduce the absolute Shapley value, which corresponds to a lower influence. For classification problems, we also assess an enhanced fairness through the analysis of the false positive rate (FPR) and true positive rate (TPR), and the verification of the **Equalized Odds** criterion [7]: this criterion states that, if we group the samples in the test set by the values of the protected variables, the FPR and TPR should be somewhat similar in all groups. The rationale behind this criterion is

---

[1] https://data.4tu.nl/articles/dataset/BPI_Challenge_2013_incidents/12693914.

[2] More details on our use of Shapley values are given in Section 3.2 of this paper's extended version [2].

that, splitting the test-set samples based on the values of the protected variables, one obtains groups that are statistically equated, including for false and true positive rates, if the model's prediction are not based on the protected variables.

Table 1. Results achieved by our framework and by Qafari et al. [6], in terms of accuracy.

Process	Outcome	Methodology	Without	With	Δ
VINST	Total Time	Qafari et al. [6]	69%	60%	9%
		Our Framework	78%	74%	4%
VINST	Occurrence of	Qafari et al. [6]	0.71	0.59	0.12
	Awaiting Assignment	Our Framework	0.80	0.72	0.08
Hiring	Total Time	Qafari et al. [6]	79.9%	70.02%	9.88%
		Our Framework	83.6%	81.1%	2.5%
Hospital	Occurrence of	Qafari et al. [6]	0.69	0.58	0.11
	Treatment Unsuccessful	Our Framework	0.78	0.76	0.02

4.3 Evaluation Results

Table 1 illustrates the results in terms of accuracy for the processes, logs and predicted outcomes introduced in Sect. 4.1. The results are based on a test set that is are constructed as discussed in Sect. 4.1, and they refer to the work proposed in this paper, which is then compared with the results that Qafari et al. [6] can achieve, which is considered as baseline. Columns *without* and *within* report on the results when the corresponding techniques doesn't or does aim at achieving fairness, respectively. Column Δ highlights the reduction of accuracy when the techniques aims at fairness. *Our framework consistently obtains higher accuracy for all use cases, if compared with Qafari et al.* [6], *and also the accuracy reduction is significantly more limited.*

The assessment the effectiveness of our fairness framework to reduce the influence of the protected variables, we computed the Shapley values of the protected variables for the four use cases, both when we employed our framework and when we simply used the FCNN predictor that implements Φ (namely excluding the adversarial FCNN for Φ_Z). The results are reported in Table 2. In the use case related the VINST process for predicting the Total-Time outcome, the protected variable *Resource country* is characterized by a Shapley value of 112 h without using the debiasing framework, and 9 h using the framework: the use of our framework brought the Shapley value down to 8% of the value without using our framework, which is a remarkable result, given that the Shapley values are directly correlated with the feature importance in the prediction. For the same process, when the outcome was whether or not activity *Awaiting Assignment Occurrence* is predicted to eventually occur, the protected variable *Organization country* was characterized by a Shapley value that dropped from 1.8 to 0.03,

Table 2. Differences in Shapley Values of protected variables with and without the debiasing framework, for the four use cases.

Process	Outcome	Protected Variable	Without	With	Ratio
VINST	Total Time	Resource country	112 h	9 h	8%
VINST	Occurrence of *Awaiting Assignment*	Organization country	1.8	0.03	1%
Hiring	Total Time	Gender	−463 min	−156 min	20%
		Religious	−447 min	−12 min	3%
Hospital	Occurrence of *Treatment Unsuccessful*	Citizen	0.25	0.04	16%
		german_speaking	0.17	0.06	35%

Table 3. False Positive Rate (FPR) and True Positive Rate (TPR) achieved by the debiasing framework proposed here and by the framework by Qafari et al. for two use cases. The standard deviation of the FPR and TPR among groups is also shown.

		Poland		Sweden		India		Brazil		Usa		Std	
		Without	With	Without	With	Without	With	Without	With	Without	With	Without	With
Qafari et al. [6]	FPR	0.20	0.18	0.13	0.24	0,11	0,12	0,17	0,17	0,32	0,41	0.143	0.086
	TPR	0.91	0.85	0.78	0.89	0.79	0.89	0.98	0.81	0.89	0.83	0.0641	0.0451
Our framework	FPR	0.04	0.08	0.11	0.09	0,14	0,08	0,02	0,06	0,01	0,06	0.153	0.018
	TPR	0.67	0.61	0.72	0.63	0.62	0.63	0.59	0.65	0.59	0.65	0.052	0.024

(a) VINST use case when aiming to predict the eventual occurrence of *Awaiting Assignment*.

		Citizen						german_speaking					
		True		False		Std		True		False		Std	
		without	with	without	with	without	with	without	with	without	with	without	with
Qafari et al. [6]	FPR	0.30	0.35	0.36	0.41	0.03	0.03	0.31	0.35	0.38	0.40	0.035	0.025
	TPR	0.71	0.67	0.62	0.51	0.05	0.08	0.71	0.67	0.62	0.51	0.09	0.16
Our framework	FPR	0.28	0.26	0.22	0.21	0.03	0.025	0.3	0.24	0.22	0.21	0.04	0.015
	TPR	0.82	0.76	0.77	0.74	0.025	0.01	0.82	0.76	0.77	0.74	0.025	0.01

(b) Hospital-process use case, when aiming to predict the eventual occurrence of *Treatment Unsuccessful*

when the debiasing framework was employed: the Shapley value has become 1% of the value without debiasing. Similar results can be observed in Table 2 for the other use cases, yielding the conclusion that *observing the significant drop of the Shapley values of the protected value after applying our debiasing framework, the framework is extremely effective to reduce the influence of the protected variables and, thus, enhance the prediction fairness.*

Space limitation does not allow us to show the whole list of Shapley values for the use cases, which are however available in the extended version [2]. If, e.g., we analyze Shapley values for the VINST use case (cf. Figure 3 in [2]), we can see that, indeed, the Shapley value for the protect variable *resource country* has significantly dropped. One could also observe that the Shapley value for variable *organization country* is also significantly reduced, likely because it is correlated with the protected variable. *If we had simply removed the protected variable, the correlated variable organization country would have gained strong influence onto the predictions: the bias would have simply moved from one sensitive variable to another, leaving the prediction model unfair. Conversely, our debiasing framework can also reduce the influence of the unfair variables that are strongly correlated to the one that has explicitly been stated as protected.*

We complete the section by reporting the results with respect to the criterion of Equalized Odds (cf. Sect. 4.2), which can only be apply to use cases where the set of outcome's values is finite, here namely for the use cases related to VINST process and the Hospital using the activity-occurrence process' outcome.

For the VINST use case related to the occurrence of activity *Awaiting Assignment*, we considered the groups related to top five organization countries, which cover 89% of the instances in the test set (recall that the protected variable is *organization country*): Sweden, Poland, India, Brazil and USA. False positive and negative rates are reported in Table 3a, without and with using the framework, both for our framework and for that of Qafari et al. [6], for all five groups. The last two columns with header *Std* summarizes the standard deviation for FPR and TPR: in case of perfectly meeting the **Equalized Odds** criterion, there would be no difference among the groups, and thus the standard deviation would be zero. For our framework, the introduction of the debiasing phase, the FPR's standard deviation within the five groups is characterized by a 88% drop, moving from 0.153 to 0.018, whereas the TPR's standard deviation shows a 53% drop (from 0.052 to 0.024). *Using the fairness approach by Qafari et al. [6], the FPR's and TPR's standard deviation* within the five groups show a drop of 53% and 29%, which *is nearly half the drop that our debiasing framework achieves.* We conducted the same analysis for the hospital use case, which is reported in Table 3b. FPRs and TPRs are computed for both protected variables. Also for this use case, our debiasing framework guarantees lower FPR's and TPR's standard deviations for both variables, although the reduction is more limited than what achieved for the VINST use case. However, The framework by Qafari et al. [6] does not reduce the FPR's and TPR's standard deviations for any of the two variables, expect for the FPR for variable *german_speaking*. As a matter of fact, their framework increases the TPR's standard deviation for both of variables, certainly going against the criterion of Equalized Odds.

5 Conclusion

Considerable research efforts have been directed towards predictive process analytics. Literature has shown that the fairness problem has generally been overlooked in predictive process analytics (cf. Section 2 of extended version in [2]). This means that predictions may potentially be discriminatory, unethical, and, e.g., targeting certain ethnics, nationalities and religions. This paper proposes a predictive framework that specializes those based on adversarial debiasing so as to allow sequences (i.e., traces) as input.

Experiments were carried out on three processes and four use cases, and the results show that our debasing framework minimizes the influence of the protected variables onto the prediction. At the same time, we illustrates that the reduction of the prediction quality is limited and lower than what is achieved by an existing framework for fairness-preserving process predictive analytics by Qafari et al. [6].

References

1. Krizhevsky, A., Sutskever, I., Hinton, G.E.: Imagenet classification with deep convolutional neural networks. Commun. ACM **60**(6), 84–90 (2017)
2. de Leoni, M., Padella, A.: Achieving Fairness in Predictive Process Analytics via Adversarial Learning (Extended Version) (2024). https://arxiv.org/abs/2410.02618
3. Márquez-Chamorro, A.E., Nepomuceno-Chamorro, I.A., Resinas, M., Ruiz-Cortés, A.: Updating prediction models for predictive process monitoring. In: Advanced Information Systems Engineering, pp. 304–318. Springer, Cham (2022)
4. Pohl, T., Berti, A., Qafari, M.S., van der Aalst, W.M.P.: A collection of simulated event logs for fairness assessment in process mining. In: Proceedings of the Best Dissertation Award, Doctoral Consortium, and Demonstration & Resources Forum at BPM 2023, vol. 3469, pp. 87–91. CEUR-WS.org (2023)
5. Pohl, T., Qafari, M.S., van der Aalst, W.M.P.: Discrimination-aware process mining: a discussion. In: Montali, M., Senderovich, A., Weidlich, M. (eds.) Process Mining Workshops, pp. 101–113. Springer, Cham (2023)
6. Qafari, M.S., van der Aalst, W.: Fairness-aware process mining. In: On the Move to Meaningful Internet Systems: OTM 2019 Conferences, pp. 182–192. Springer (2019)
7. Zhang, B.H., Lemoine, B., Mitchell, M.: Mitigating unwanted biases with adversarial learning. In: Proceedings of the 2018 AAAI/ACM Conference on AI, Ethics, and Society, pp. 335–340. AIES 2018. Association for Computing Machinery, New York (2018)

Enhancing Temporal Knowledge Graph Reasoning with Contrastive Learning and Self-attention Mechanisms

Bao Tran Kim[1,2] and Thanh Le[1,2(✉)]

[1] Faculty of Information Technology, University of Science, Ho Chi Minh City, Vietnam
20120041@student.hcmus.edu.vn, lnthanh@fit.hcmus.edu.vn
[2] Vietnam National University, Ho Chi Minh City, Vietnam

Abstract. Recent advancements in reasoning over Temporal Knowledge Graphs have leveraged historical data to forecast future events more effectively. Traditional models primarily rely on the recurrence and periodicity of events, using past occurrences to predict future ones. These methods often use a self-relation mechanism to account for the influence of timestamps in predictions but typically overlook the significance of interconnected entities within the temporal framework. Addressing this oversight, we introduce a new model called CA-GCN, which is based on a relational graph convolution network. This model not only taps into historical data through a self-attention mechanism but also integrates previously unseen static information. It further extracts insights from the graph's structure using contrastive learning techniques. The embeddings generated by our model are utilized to train a linear binary classifier, aimed at identifying entities crucial for future predictions. Our model demonstrates substantial improvements, showing up to a 5.78% increase in Mean Reciprocal Rank (MRR) and a 10.88% rise in Hits@1 accuracy, when tested across several standard datasets such as ICEWS14, ICEWS18, YAGO, and WIKI. These results indicate that CA-GCN significantly outperforms existing models, providing enhanced predictive accuracy in various evaluation metrics.

Keywords: Temporal knowledge graphs · Graph convolutional networks · Temporal knowledge graph reasoning · Contrastive learning

1 Introduction

Knowledge graphs (KGs) represent facts as triples of *(subject entity, relation, object entity)*, and are integral to applications like recommendation systems [16], and information retrieval [17]. However, these graphs often lack complete information. Traditionally, KGs assume that all facts are static and timeless, leading to challenges in capturing temporal dynamics. To address this, Temporal Knowledge Graphs (TKGs) have been developed. They expand on the standard triple by adding a timestamp, forming quadruples of *(subject entity, relation, object entity, timestamp)*. TKGs essentially serve as a series of snapshots, each representing simultaneous occurrences at specific timestamps.

© The Author(s), under exclusive license to Springer Nature Switzerland AG 2025
M. Comuzzi et al. (Eds.): CoopIS 2024, LNCS 15506, pp. 355–363, 2025.
https://doi.org/10.1007/978-3-031-81375-7_22

These snapshots aid in understanding historical contexts, which is crucial for predicting future events in TKGs.

The primary challenge in TKG reasoning is the persistent issue of missing information, which complicates fact prediction. This study focuses on the extrapolation aspect of TKG reasoning, aiming to predict future facts by completing missing entities in queries formatted as *(subject entity, relation, ?, timestamp)*.

In recent years, various methods have been proposed to integrate structural and temporal information in TKGs for predicting future events. Graph Neural Networks (GNNs) are widely used, employing recurrent mechanisms to capture temporal dynamics. While some models uniformly aggregate historical snapshots, others apply attention mechanisms based on timestamps. Addressing the challenges posed by temporal variations, our model - the **C**ontrastive Learning and Self-**A**ttention **G**raph **C**onvolutional **N**etwork (CA-GCN) - sequences historical data chronologically. This model employs Graph Convolutional Networks (GCNs) combined with self-attention mechanisms to dynamically focus on relevant snapshots, enhancing the analysis of temporal patterns.

Additionally, our framework recognizes the varying relevance of entire TKGs and the distinct roles of individual entities over time. To pinpoint entities closely correlated with accurate predictions, we utilize a contrastive learning module, which enhances query distinction. We address the challenge of evolving and new, unseen entities by incorporating a copy mechanism. This mechanism adjusts scores based on a global static graph, ensuring all relevant entities are considered in the predictions.

Although various models have exploited components of these methods to address link prediction challenges, to our knowledge, no existing framework unifies and maximizes the benefits of all these approaches comprehensively. Our CA-GCN model aims to fill this gap, offering a refined solution for improved link prediction performance.

Our main contributions in this work are as follows:

– We propose a novel CA-GCN framework specifically designed for Temporal Knowledge Graph (TKG) reasoning. This framework integrates Graph Convolutional Networks (GCNs) with self-attention mechanisms, enabling effective capture of temporal dynamics across the graph. To further enhance reasoning capabilities, the framework incorporates both frequency information and a global static graph.
– Additionally, the framework leverages contrastive learning techniques, enabling the model to precisely identify entities that exhibit high correlations with ground truth labels, significantly improving overall predictive accuracy.
– The effectiveness of our proposed framework is validated through extensive experimentation on four benchmark datasets, demonstrating significant performance improvements.

2   Methodology

In this section, we introduce the proposed model, named CA-GCN, for fact/link prediction in TKGs. We start with introduce the model architecture as well as its training and inference procedures.

We define $\mathcal{E}$, $\mathcal{R}$, and $\mathcal{T}$ to represent the entity set, the relation set, and the timestamp set, respectively. A TKG, denoted as $\mathcal{G}$ consists of quadruples (s, r, o, t) where $s, o \in \mathcal{E}$, $r \in \mathcal{R}$, and $t \in \mathcal{T}$.

2.1 Model Overview

As illustrated in Fig. 1, the CA-GCN framework is composed of four main components: evolutionary-attention learning, historical information passing, static unseen information passing, and contrastive learning. Below is a brief explanation of each module's structure, function, and impact:

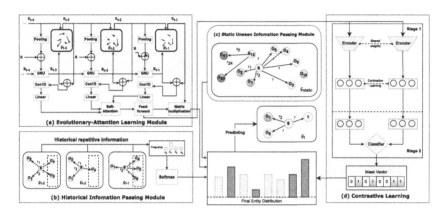

Fig. 1. Overview of the CA-GCN architecture, illustrating the primary components: (a) evolutionary-attention learning module, which adapts to temporal dynamics; (b) historical information passing module, enhancing the impact of repetitive entities; (c) static unseen information passing module, managing new or rare entities by assigning low negative values; and (d) contrastive learning component, which identifies highly correlated entities and outputs a boolean mask vector. The final results are generated through a mask-based inference process that combines these elements.

The evolutionary-attention learning module uses R-GCN [11] to model subgraphs and capture the structural dependencies between them. GRU [3] is applied to aggregate sequential patterns from previous data. Additionally, self-attention [15] and ConvTransE [13] are utilized to score each subgraph based on k preceding subgraphs, allowing the model to learn how the roles of entities change over time. The historical information passing module enhances the influence of past facts, weighting them based on how frequently they occurred before a given timestamp t. The static unseen information passing module leverages a global static graph that includes all triplets (s, r, o) and uses a copy mechanism [18] to adjust scores, reducing them for entities that are not linked, while maintaining scores for entities with existing connections. Finally, the contrastive learning module improves the model's ability to distinguish between queries by undergoing a two-stage training process. Initially, it is trained alongside the evolutionary-attention module with a contrastive learning loss function. In the second stage, it predicts a boolean mask that indicates whether the object entities in a query $(s, r, ?, t)$ have had any prior relationship with s.

2.2   Parameter Learning and Inference

During query processing, we aggregate the scores from three modules: the evolutionary-attention learning module, the historical information passing module, and the static unseen information passing module, denoted as $\mathcal{S}_{EA}$, $\mathcal{S}F$, and $\mathcal{S}U$, respectively. These scores are simultaneously considered to provide a comprehensive assessment:

$$\mathbf{p}_{first}(o|s, r, t) = \mathcal{S}_{EA} + \mathcal{S}_F + \mathcal{S}_U, \tag{1}$$

where $\mathbf{p}_{first}(o|s, r, t)$ represents the probability distribution for each o to be the answer to $q = (s, r, ?, t)$. This probability distribution is utilized in the cross-entropy loss function to compute $\mathcal{L}^{first}$, which is trained alongside the contrastive learning loss $\mathcal{L}^{sup}$ to minimize the overall loss function $\mathcal{L}$:

$$\mathcal{L} = \alpha \cdot \mathcal{L}^{first} + (1 - \alpha) \cdot \mathcal{L}^{sup}, \tag{2}$$

where α is a hyper-parameter between 0 and 1, balancing the two loss terms.

Moreover, $\mathbf{p}_{first}(o|s, r, t)$ is combined with a Boolean mask to yield the final probability distribution $\mathbf{P}(o|s, r, t)$. The object entity $\hat{o}$ with the highest predicted probability is selected from this final distribution:

$$\hat{o} = \underset{o \in \mathcal{E}}{\operatorname{argmax}} \big(\mathbf{P}(o|s, r, t) \big). \tag{3}$$

3   Experiments

In this section, we demonstrate the effectiveness of CA-GCN with four benchmark datasets. We outline the experimental setup, discuss the results, and perform an ablation study to evaluate the importance of different components of CA-GCN.

3.1   Experimental Setup

Datasets. We select four benchmark datasets, comprising two event-based TKGs and two public KGs, each constructed differently. The event-based TKGs include the Integrated Crisis Early Warning System: ICEWS14 [14] and ICEWS18 [2], which contain facts that occurred in 2014 and 2018, respectively. The public KGs, namely WIKI [7] and YAGO [10], consist of temporally associated facts spanning an extended duration. Table 1 provides the statistics for these datasets.

Table 1. Statistics of the datasets.

Dataset	Entities	Relation	Training	Validation	Test
ICEWS14	7,128	230	74,845	8,514	7,371
ICEWS18	23,033	256	373,018	45,995	49,545
WIKI	12,554	24	539,286	67,538	63,110
YAGO	10,623	10	161,540	19,523	20,026

Evaluation Metrics. In our experiments, we use the link prediction task to evaluate the efficacy of the CA-GCN model. We apply standard metrics, including Mean Reciprocal Rank (MRR) and Hits@1/3/10, to assess the rankings of missing ground-truth entities. The mean results for subject and object entity predictions are reported for each query.

We also adopt the raw metrics introduced by Bordes et al. [1]. For each test quadruple (s, r, o, t), we exclude the object $(s, r, ?, t)$ and compute the score assigned by the model to each entity $e \in \mathcal{E}$ as the object in that quadruple. The scores are then sorted in descending order, and we record the rank of the correct entity object. MRR is calculated as the average of the reciprocals of these ranks across all queries in the test set. Hits@k denotes the proportion of correct entities ranked within the top k.

Baselines. CA-GCN undergoes comparison with 9 contemporary knowledge graph reasoning models, encompassing both static and temporal approaches. Among the static methods are ConvTransE [13] and R-GCN [11]. Dynamic reasoning methods include TTransE [5] and HyTE [4]. Certain dynamic methods specialize in modeling historical information and have demonstrated notable performance, such as RGCRN [12], RE-NET [6], CyGNet [18], RE-GCN [8], and DHU-NET [9].

3.2 Results and Discussion

The results of the link prediction task are recorded in Table 2 and Table 3. The evaluation of the proposed model, CA-GCN, is conducted in comparison with various baseline approaches and models, including both static knowledge graphs and temporal knowledge graphs in the reasoning methods.

The CA-GCN model outperforms baseline methods across various evaluation metrics by integrating temporal information and historical dependencies, essential for accurate predictions in dynamic environments. It performs competitively against interpolation-based models like HyTE and TTransE and excels in capturing subgraph evolution over time, especially on the ICEWS14 and ICEWS18 datasets.

CA-GCN uses two recurrent components to learn evolving representations of entities and relations, extracting more information than models like RGCRN. It also incorporates fact frequency and identifies highly relevant neighboring entities, enhancing prediction accuracy. Inspired by DHU-NET, CA-GCN includes an advanced contrastive learning module to differentiate between similar queries, improving its ability to identify correlated entities.

Table 2. Performance (in percentage) for the entity prediction task on ICEWS14 and ICEWS18 with raw metrics. The baseline results are directly obtained from the DHU-NET model [9].

Model	ICEWS14				ICEWS18			
	MRR	Hits@1	Hits@3	Hits@10	MRR	Hits@1	Hits@3	Hits@10
R-GCN	28.03	19.42	31.95	44.83	15.05	8.13	16.49	29.00
ConvTransE	31.50	22.46	34.98	50.03	23.22	14.26	26.13	41.34
HyTE	16.78	2.13	24.84	43.94	7.41	3.10	7.33	16.01
TTransE	12.86	3.14	15.72	33.65	8.44	1.85	8.95	22.38
RGCRN	33.31	24.08	36.55	51.54	23.46	14.24	26.62	41.96
CyGNet	34.68	25.35	38.88	53.16	24.98	15.54	28.58	43.54
RE-NET	35.77	25.99	40.10	54.87	26.17	16.43	29.89	44.37
RE-GCN	41.50	30.86	46.60	62.47	30.55	20.00	34.73	51.46
DHU-NET	62.01	47.74	71.71	88.39	47.44	33.17	54.75	76.17
CA-GCN (ours)	**63.73**	**50.28**	**72.71**	**88.60**	**50.18**	**36.78**	**57.13**	**76.78**

Table 3. Performance (in percentage) for the entity prediction task on WIKI and YAGO with raw metrics. The baseline results are directly obtained from the DHU-NET [9]. Hits@1 results were not provided in the prior work of DHU-NET.

Model	WIKI			YAGO		
	MRR	Hits@3	Hits@10	MRR	Hits@3	Hits@10
R-GCN	13.96	15.75	22.05	20.25	24.01	37.30
ConvTransE	30.89	34.30	41.45	46.67	52,22	62,52
HyTE	25.40	29.16	37.54	14.42	39.73	46.98
TTransE	20.66	23.88	33.04	26.10	36.28	47.73
RGCRN	28.68	31.44	38.58	43.71	48.53	56.98
CyGNet	30.77	33.83	41.19	46.72	52.48	61.52
RE-NET	30.87	33.55	41.27	46.81	52.71	61.93
RE-GCN	50.99	57.34	68.50	62.50	70.24	81.55
DHU-NET	56.18	**64.57**	**82.73**	67.36	76.52	**92.63**
CA-GCN (ours)	**56.54**	64.50	81.77	**68.13**	**77.28**	92.24

While CA-GCN shows promising results, it has lower Hits@10 compared to DHU-NET on the WIKI and YAGO datasets. This may be due to the stronger influence of the global unseen entities module in DHU-NET, which could overshadow the impact of CA-GCN's new contrastive learning module.

3.3 Ablation Study

To understand the model components' effectiveness, we conducted an ablation study on the ICEWS14 dataset using MRR, Hits@1, Hits@3, and Hits@10 metrics. Results are in Table 4. CA-GCN - w/o U causes the most significant decline, with MRR dropping by 25.09%. This shows the importance of unseen entities from the knowledge graph. CA-GCN - w/o F results in a moderate performance drop (MRR by 4.44%). This indicates its role in identifying historically significant entities, though it is less critical than unseen information. The contrastive learning module (CL) has the least impact, leading to a small MRR decrease of 2.72%, suggesting a minor role in differentiating similar queries. Each module plays a distinct role within the model, enabling the combination of modules to achieve the highest score across all metrics compared to other models with ablated components.

Table 4. Results of the ablation study on ICEWS14 are presented as percentages using MRR, Hits@1, Hits@3, and Hits@10 metrics. 'w/o' denotes 'without' for brevity. EA, F, U, and CL represent the evolutionary-attention learning module, historical information passing module, static unseen information passing module, and contrastive learning module, respectively.

Model	MRR	Hit@1	Hit@3	Hit@10
EA	34.11	24.33	38.29	53.14
EA + F	35.06	25.81	38.75	53.62
EA + U	56.53	41.67	65.55	86.15
EA + CL	37.13	26.67	41.98	57.56
CA-GCN - w/o U	38.64	28.60	43.24	58.37
CA-GCN - w/o F	61.05	47.08	70.13	87.27
CA-GCN - w/o CL	62.01	47.74	71.71	88.39
CA-GCN	**63.73**	**50.28**	**72.71**	**88.60**

4   Conclusion

In this paper, we introduce the CA-GCN model for link prediction in TKGs, which captures evolving historical patterns and integrates both global and repetitive temporal information. This comprehensive approach enhances temporal reasoning by employing self-attention mechanisms that prioritize temporally relevant information, facilitating a deeper understanding of historical dynamics. Furthermore, the model incorporates contrastive learning techniques and a binary classifier to discern and highlight dissimilarities between entities, identifying those with high correlation. Our results on four benchmark datasets indicate that CA-GCN performs effectively in temporal reasoning tasks. As future work, we aim to integrate multimodal data sources into the CA-GCN model, which could offer a more nuanced understanding of entity relationships and further improve the model's predictive accuracy across diverse datasets.

Acknowledgments. This research is funded by the University of Science, VNU-HCM, Vietnam under grant number CNTT 2023-13.

References

1. Bordes, A., Weston, J., Collobert, R., Bengio, Y.: Learning structured embeddings of knowledge bases. In: Proceedings of the Twenty-Fifth AAAI Conference on Artificial Intelligence, AAAI 2011, San Francisco, California, USA, 7–11 August 2011, pp. 301–306. AAAI Press (2011). https://doi.org/10.1609/AAAI.V25I1.7917
2. Boschee, E., Lautenschlager, J., O'Brien, S., Shellman, S., Starz, J., Ward, M.: ICEWS Coded Event Data (2015). https://doi.org/10.7910/DVN/28075
3. Cho, K., et al.: Learning phrase representations using RNN encoder–decoder for statistical machine translation. In: Proceedings of the 2014 Conference on Empirical Methods in Natural Language Processing (EMNLP), pp. 1724–1734. Association for Computational Linguistics, Doha, Qatar (2014). https://doi.org/10.3115/v1/D14-1179
4. Dasgupta, S.S., Ray, S.N., Talukdar, P.: HyTE: hyperplane-based temporally aware knowledge graph embedding. In: Proceedings of the 2018 Conference on Empirical Methods in Natural Language Processing, pp. 2001–2011. Association for Computational Linguistics, Brussels, Belgium (2018). https://doi.org/10.18653/v1/D18-1225
5. Jiang, T., et al.: Towards time-aware knowledge graph completion. In: Proceedings of COLING 2016, the 26th International Conference on Computational Linguistics: Technical Papers, pp. 1715–1724. The COLING 2016 Organizing Committee, Osaka, Japan (2016)
6. Jin, W., Qu, M., Jin, X., Ren, X.: Recurrent event network: autoregressive structure inferenceover temporal knowledge graphs. In: Proceedings of the 2020 Conference on Empirical Methods in Natural Language Processing (EMNLP), pp. 6669–6683. Association for Computational Linguistics, Online (2020). https://doi.org/10.18653/v1/2020.emnlp-main.541
7. Leblay, J., Chekol, M.W.: Deriving validity time in knowledge graph. In: Companion of The Web Conference 2018, pp. 1771–1776. International World Wide Web Conferences Steering Committee (2018)
8. Li, Z., et al.: Temporal knowledge graph reasoning based on evolutional representation learning (2021)
9. Liu, K., Zhao, F., Xu, G., Wang, X., Jin, H.: Temporal knowledge graph reasoning via time-distributed representation learning. In: 2022 IEEE International Conference on Data Mining (ICDM), pp. 279–288 (2022). https://doi.org/10.1109/ICDM54844.2022.00038
10. Mahdisoltani, F., Biega, J.A., Suchanek, F.M.: Yago3: a knowledge base from multilingual wikipedias. In: 7th Biennial Conference on Innovative Data Systems Research (CIDR) (2014)
11. Schlichtkrull, M., Kipf, T.N., Bloem, P., van den Berg, R., Titov, I., Welling, M.: Modeling relational data with graph convolutional networks (2017)
12. Seo, Y., Defferrard, M., Vandergheynst, P., Bresson, X.: Structured sequence modeling with graph convolutional recurrent networks (2016)
13. Shang, C., Tang, Y., Huang, J., Bi, J., He, X., Zhou, B.: End-to-end structure-aware convolutional networks for knowledge base completion. In: Proceedings of the AAAI Conference on Artificial Intelligence, vol. 33, no. 01, pp. 3060–3067 (2019). https://doi.org/10.1609/aaai.v33i01.33013060
14. Trivedi, R., Dai, H., Wang, Y., Song, L.: Know-evolve: deep temporal reasoning for dynamic knowledge graphs. In: Proceedings of the 34th International Conference on Machine Learning, ICML 2017, vol. 70, pp. 3462–3471. JMLR.org (2017)
15. Vaswani, A., et al.: Attention is all you need (2023)
16. Wang, X., He, X., Cao, Y., Liu, M., Chua, T.S.: KGAT: knowledge graph attention network for recommendation. In: Proceedings of the 25th ACM SIGKDD International Conference on Knowledge Discovery and Data Mining, pp. 950–958 (2019)

17. Xiong, C., Power, R., Callan, J.: Explicit semantic ranking for academic search via knowledge graph embedding. In: Proceedings of the Twenty-Sixth International Conference on World Wide Web (WWW) (2017)
18. Zhu, C., Chen, M., Fan, C., Cheng, G., Zhang, Y.: Learning from history: modeling temporal knowledge graphs with sequential copy-generation networks. In: Proceedings of the AAAI Conference on Artificial Intelligence, vol. 35, no. 5, pp. 4732–4740 (2021). https://doi.org/10.1609/aaai.v35i5.16604

Graph Convolution Transformer for Extrapolated Reasoning on Temporal Knowledge Graphs

Hoa Dao[1,2], Nguyen Phan[1,2], and Thanh Le[1,2(✉)]

[1] Faculty of Information Technology, University of Science, Ho Chi Minh City, Vietnam
{dnhoa20,ptnguyen20}@clc.fitus.edu.vn, lnthanh@fit.hcmus.edu.vn
[2] Vietnam National University, Ho Chi Minh City, Vietnam

Abstract. Extrapolation on Temporal Knowledge Graphs presents a critical challenge, driven by its applications in predicting future events by analyzing historical data. While recent methods leverage graph structure and temporal dynamics, they often struggle to prioritize neighborhood messages and capture evolving temporal attributes at local and global scales. To address these issues, we introduce a novel forecasting architecture, named Graph Convolution Transformer, which incorporates a time-aware self-attention mechanism. Our approach integrates a Fact Graph Transformer to structure historical data and a Temporal Transformer with advanced position encoding for enhanced time series representation. Also, we propose Query-ConvTransE in the decoder to handle query-based data. Extensive evaluations across six benchmark datasets demonstrate that the model outperforms prior approaches, improving the Mean Reciprocal Rank metric by roughly 2% to 3%, with a notable advancement of 5.23% on the GDELT dataset experiment.

Keywords: Temporal knowledge graph reasoning · Transformer · Graph embedding · Link prediction

1 Introduction

A Knowledge Graph (KG) is a directed, multi-relational graph that structures data in the form of triples to capture interactions among entities. For instance, in Fig. 1, the triple (*Sophia, Infected by, John*) indicates that Sophia was infected with COVID-19 by John. KG are extensively employed in many applications such as recommendation systems [3] and question-answering [1]. Despite their utility, KGs often suffer from incompleteness due to missing informations. Additionally, storing these facts as triples in traditional KGs can result in the loss of crucial temporal information. This creates challenge for Temporal KG Reasoning (TKGR), which focuses on deducing missing events from existing ones. For example, we can predict the quadruple (*Sophia, Infected by, ?*).

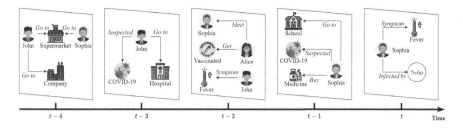

Fig. 1. A TKG shows snapshots in ascending timestamps, with entities and relationships, illustrating the extrapolation process, denoted by *?who* symbol, using historical data to predict the connection: *(Sophia, Infected by, John, t)*.

The effectiveness of extrapolation reasoning in TKGs relies on capturing both structural and temporal dynamics. Combining Graph Neural Networks (GNNs) with Recurrent Neural Networks (RNNs), as in RE-GCN [4], faces challenges. GNNs often fail to prioritize key relations, such as in *(Sophia, Infected by, ?who, t)*, where *(Sophia, Go to, Supermarket, t - 4)* is more relevant than *(Sophia, Met, Alice, t - 2)*. RNNs, though useful for temporal attributes, oftern fail to non-sequential patterns and vanishing gradients.

To tackle the discussed challenges, we propose a novel architecture called Graph Convolution Transformer (GCT). Our main contributions as follows:

- GCT includes a Fact Graph Transformer, which utilizes entity and relation embeddings to extract historical contexts relevant to the query.
- A new position embedding method that captures time series data, using ConvTransE as a decoder to predict future entity and relation likelihoods.
- Through experiments, our model achieves state-of-the-art results on six popular benchmarks, confirming its reliability and effectiveness.

2 Related Work

CyGNET [12] incorporates a copy-generation mechanism to utilize historical vocabulary or repetitive patterns. xERTE [2] utilizes attention propagation and subgraph sampling techniques. Concurrently, TiTer [10] employs reinforcement learning to facilitate multi-step reasoning. One prevalent approach involves combining GNNs with RNNs, as seen in RE-GCN [4]. GNNs, such as RGCN [6], excel at capturing semantic information in multi-relation graphs, while RNNs adeptly handle evolving attributes. Nevertheless, traditional RNNs face scalability issues with increasing timestamps and computational inefficiencies.

Recently, Transformer has proven effective in various fields. Inspired by this, GHT [9], have adopted Transformer-based methods for extracting query-related facts in extrapolation tasks. Although these models have not yet achieved state-of-the-art performance, their results are promising and align with our research objectives.

3   Preliminary

Temporal Knowledge Graph (TKG) is defined as $TKG = \{(s, r, o, t)\}$. Within these quadruplets, s and o represent nodes in TKG, with s as the head, o as the tail, r as the edge connecting them, and t is time. The reverse relation quadruplets (o, r^{-1}, s, t) are also included for completeness.

Extrapolation in TKG involves predicting missing object o for a given query $q = (s, r, ?, t_q)$, using historical information H_{t_q}. We define history as a series of query-related graphs, denoted as $H_{t_q} = \{(s, v, G_t) | t < t_q\}$, where t is a snapshot time before t_q, G_t is sampled KG at snapshot t considering events related to subject s, and v is history entity having relation with s.

4   Methodology

4.1   Fact Graph Transformer

RGT [9] have been introduced to distinguish between neighbor importance. To enhance RGT, we introduce Fact Graph Transformer (FGT), which employs self-attention to aggregate messages, thereby enhancing the query entity s embeddings in each historical snapshot.

The query matrix $\mathbf{Q}_S$ plays a crucial role in the Transformer. Unlike RGT, which excludes the entity embedding $\mathbf{h}_e$ from $\mathbf{Q}_S$ to better handle new entities in extrapolation tasks, FGT incorporates both the entity embedding $\mathbf{h}_e$ and the relation embedding $\mathbf{h}_r$ into $\mathbf{Q}_S$, enabling GCT to capture intensive information.

$$\mathbf{Q}_S = W_{q_S}[\mathbf{h}_s | \mathbf{h}_r] \tag{1}$$

Consider a scenario where n facts are associated with entity s. For each fact $i \in [0, n)$, key and value embeddings, $\mathbf{K}_S[i]$ and $\mathbf{V}_S[i]$, are generated from entity $\mathbf{h}_{e_i}$ and relation $\mathbf{h}_{r_i}$ embedding.

$$\mathbf{V}_S[i] = \text{LeakyReLU}(W_{v_S}[\mathbf{h}_{e_i} | \mathbf{h}_{r_i}]) \tag{2}$$

$$\mathbf{K}_S[i] = W_{k_S}[\mathbf{h}_{e_i} | \mathbf{h}_{r_i}] \tag{3}$$

All queries influence α_S, is derived using Scaled Dot-Product Attention [11] (Fig. 2).

$$\alpha_S = \text{softmax}\left(\frac{\mathbf{Q}_S \mathbf{K}_S^T}{\sqrt{d}}\right) \tag{4}$$

To capture diverse subspaces, Multi-head Attention [11] is used, concatenating each attention head representation, as described in Eq. 5.

$$\mathbf{h}_s' = \prod_{y=1}^{Y} \sum_{i=1}^{n} \alpha_S^y[i] \mathbf{V}_S^y[i] \tag{5}$$

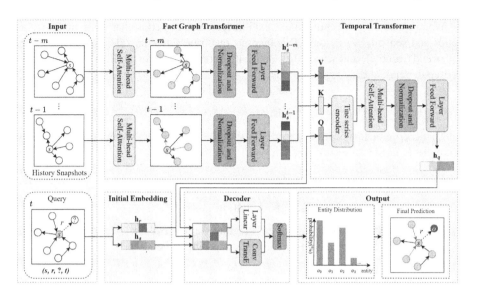

Fig. 2. GCT first uses the Fact Graph Transformer to extract the history graph of query subject s from m previous snapshots. Temporal Transformer processes dynamics between query relation r and entity s, generating the query embedding $\mathbf{h}_q$. It is then combined with initial embeddings of s and r, is used by ConvTransE to compute the final score, with a linear layer refining scores for historical entities, v.

After that, the dimension of $\mathbf{h}'_s$ is reduced through a fully connected layer, and then Layer Normalization $LN(.)$ is applied as follows:

$$\mathbf{h}^l_s = LN(\text{LeakyReLU}(\mathbf{h}'_s W^l_1) + \mathbf{h}^{l-1}_s) \tag{6}$$

4.2 Temporal Transformer

Assuming FGT has learned query entity embedding $\mathbf{h}_s$ in each snapshot t, we propose Temporal Transformer (TT), a module which include time series encoder to better capture historical interactions between s and r. It generates the query $\mathbf{Q}'$, key $\mathbf{K}'$, and value $\mathbf{V}$ matrix as below:

$$\mathbf{Q}' = W_q \mathbf{h}_{r_q} \tag{7}$$

$$\mathbf{K}' = W_k \mathbf{H}_s \tag{8}$$

$$\mathbf{V} = W_v \mathbf{H}_s \tag{9}$$

where history contexts $\mathbf{H}_s \in \mathbb{R}^{m \times d}$ of the query entity s are represented by concatenating all historical embeddings $\mathbf{H}_s = [\mathbf{h}_{s,t_q-m} | \mathbf{h}_{s,t_q-m+1} | \cdots | \mathbf{h}_{s,t_q-1}]$.

We propose that object dynamics exhibit typical time series characteristics, such as trends and seasonal variations. This inspires our time series encoder, which leverages both trend (trend(.)) and seasonality (season(.)) components for a refined representation of time-dependent data.

$$\text{trend}(t) = \tanh(\mathbf{w}_t t) \tag{10}$$

$$\text{season}(t) = \sin(\mathbf{w}_t t) \tag{11}$$

To incorporate this position encoding method, we integrate the trend and seasonality components in the following manner:

$$\mathbf{Q} = [\mathbf{Q}'|\text{trend}(t_q)|\text{season}(t_q)] \tag{12}$$

$$\mathbf{K} = [\mathbf{K}'|\text{trend}(\mathbf{t})|\text{season}(\mathbf{t})] \tag{13}$$

Multi-head attention is then used to integrate single-head query segments, enabling the model to process diverse information streams simultaneously.

$$\mathbf{h}'_q = \prod_{h=1}^{H} \sum_{j=1}^{m} \alpha[j]\mathbf{V}[j] \tag{14}$$

where $\alpha = \text{softmax}\left(\frac{\mathbf{Q}\mathbf{K}^T}{\sqrt{2d}}\right)$ is the influence of history snapshots, $\alpha \in \mathbb{R}^m$. The final embedding $\mathbf{h}_q$ is then obtained as specified in Eq. 15.

$$\mathbf{h}^l_q = LN\left(\text{GeLU}\left(\mathbf{h}'_q W^l_2\right) + \mathbf{h}^{l-1}_q\right) \tag{15}$$

4.3   Decoder

ConvTransE [7] leverages a convolutional network to encapsulate the translational dynamics between entities and relations. Our work introduces Query-ConvTransE, aiming to capture more relevant information which help improve the model's performance in dynamic and complex query scenarios. To elucidate further, the convolution operator functions as follows:

$$\mathbf{m}^p_c = m_c(\mathbf{h}_s, \mathbf{h}_r, \mathbf{h}_q, p)$$
$$= \sum_{\tau=0}^{K-1} \left(w_c(\tau, 0)\hat{\mathbf{h}}_s(p + \tau)\right. \tag{16}$$
$$\left. + w_c(\tau, 1)\hat{\mathbf{h}}_r(p + \tau) + w_c(\tau, 2)\hat{\mathbf{h}}_q(p + \tau)\right)$$

where c is convolution kernel, K is kernel width, w_c is learnable parameter, $p \in [0, d-1]$ is the entries of output vector, and $\hat{\mathbf{h}}_s, \hat{\mathbf{h}}_r, \hat{\mathbf{h}}_q$ the padding version of $\mathbf{h}_s, \mathbf{h}_r, \mathbf{h}_q$ respectively. The output $M_c(\mathbf{h}_s, \mathbf{h}_r, \mathbf{h}_q) = [\mathbf{m}^0_c, \mathbf{m}^1_c, ..., \mathbf{m}^{d-1}_c]$ is then aligned to form a matrix $\mathbf{M}_c \in \mathbb{R}^{c \times d}$. Then, ConvTransE scoring function is applied by employing a feature map operator vec, and a ReLU activation function. This sequence of operations is detailed as follows:

$$\mathbf{score}_{global} = \sigma(\text{ReLU}(vec(\mathbf{M}_c)W_3)\mathbf{H}^T_E) \tag{17}$$

where $\mathbf{H}_E \in \mathbb{R}^{|E| \times d}$ is all entities embedding and $\mathbf{score}_{global} \in \mathbb{R}^{|E|}$.

Additionally, local score is calculated by history entities v as follows:

$$\mathbf{score}_{local} = ([\mathbf{h}_s, \mathbf{h}_r, \mathbf{h}_q] W_4) \mathbf{H}_v^T \tag{18}$$

The calculated probability score is then smoothed using a softplus function:

$$\mathbf{score} = \mathrm{softplus}([\mathbf{score}_{global} | \mathbf{score}_{local}]) \tag{19}$$

4.4 Parameter Learning

Considering entity prediction on TKGs as a multi-classification, a cross entropy loss function, denoted by $\mathcal{L}$, is employed as follow:

$$\mathcal{L} = - \sum_{(s,r,o,t) \in TKG} \sum_{e \in E} y_e \log(\mathbf{score}(e|s,r,t)) \tag{20}$$

where y_e is the label that is 1 if $e = o$, and 0 otherwise.

5   Experiments

5.1   Experimental Setup

Datasets. In our experiments, we employ six TKGs datasets as illustrating in Table 1. The first three ICEWS14, ICEWS18, and ICEWS05-15, are subsets of the ICEWS. GDELT provides event data at 15-minute intervals. YAGO [5] and WIKI are from YAGO3 and Wikipedia, respectively.

Evaluation Metrics. We evaluate performance using MRR and Hits@k metrics. MRR represents the average of the reciprocal ranks of the correctly predicted entities, while Hits@k, where $k \in \{1, 3, 10\}$, measures the proportion of true entities that appear among the top k ranked predictions.

Baselines. In our study, we compare a variety of approaches including GNN-based models like CyGNet [12] and HGAT [8]; path-based models such as xERTE [2] and TiTer [10]; hybrid GNN-RNN model RE-GCN [4]; and the Transformer-based model, GHT [9].

5.2   Results and Discussion

Table 2 and Table 3 present a detailed comparison in the entity prediction task across six datasets, using the metrics MRR and Hits@k, $k \in \{1, 3, 10\}$. The results indicate that our GCT mostly surpasses other methods in all assessed metrics. GCT also shows robustness against variations in time granularity, setting it apart from previous approaches. GCT outperforms many TKGR models due to previous works' limitations. For example, GNN-based model like CyGNet mainly captures repetitive patterns, and

Table 1. Statistics of six different datasets.

#Dataset	#Entities	#Relations	#Timestamps	#Time Granularity	#Train Facts	#Validation Facts	#Test Facts
ICEWS14	7,128	230	365	24 h	63,685	13,823	13,222
ICEWS18	23,033	256	7,272	24 h	373,018	45,995	49,545
ICEWS05-15	10,488	251	4,017	24 h	386,962	46,092	46275
GDELT	7,691	240	8,925	15 mins	1,033,270	238,765	305,241
YAGO	10,623	10	189	1 year	161,54	19,523	20,026
WIKI	12,554	24	232	1 year	2,735,685	341,961	341,961

Table 2. Results for entity prediction task on ICEWS14, ICEWS18, and ICEWS05-15 datasets are presented using metrics MRR and Hits@k, with k $\in \{1, 3, 10\}$. The highest are highlighted in bold, while the second-highest are underlined.

Model	ICEWS14				ICEWS18				ICEWS05-15			
	MRR	Hits@1	Hits@3	Hits@10	MRR	Hits@1	Hits@3	Hits@10	MRR	Hits@1	Hits@3	Hits@10
CyGNet	32.73	23.69	36.31	50.67	24.98	15.54	28.58	43.54	35.46	25.44	40.20	54.47
xERTE	40.79	<u>32.70</u>	45.67	58.44	29.31	21.03	33.51	46.48	46.62	<u>37.84</u>	52.31	63.92
TiTer	41.73	**32.74**	46.46	58.44	29.98	<u>22.05</u>	33.46	44.83	47.70	**38.00**	<u>52.90</u>	65.80
RE-GCN	41.78	31.58	46.65	<u>61.51</u>	<u>30.58</u>	21.01	<u>34.34</u>	48.75	<u>48.03</u>	37.33	**53.85**	<u>68.27</u>
GHT	<u>41.87</u>	31.85	<u>47.21</u>	60.46	30.42	20.83	34.33	<u>49.15</u>	45.07	35.70	50.21	62.66
HGAT	38.90	29.70	42.40	56.40	28.50	19.60	32.70	46.60	-	-	-	-
GCT	**43.01**	30.34	**49.61**	**72.99**	**32.46**	**22.73**	**36.88**	**52.34**	**49.39**	36.65	52.59	**80.94**

HGAT overlooks complex temporal dependencies between historical entities. Additionally, rule-based models such as xERTE and TiTer, despite their effectiveness on ICEWS datasets, suffer from a limited search space.

Performance on TKGR models is notably affected by time granularity, as evidenced in Table 3. This phenomenon occurs because longer time intervals can generate more related historical events, improving prediction accuracy. GCT consistently achieves high performance across both short-granularity datasets like GDELT shows an increase of 5.23% in MRR compared to TiTer and long-granularity datasets like YAGO and WIKI exhibit improvements of 2.99% and 3.25%, respectively; similar enhancements are also observed in the Hits@ metrics across these datasets. These shows GCT's robustness across varying time scales.

5.3 Ablation Study

As recorded in Table 4, we examines each module's impact on ICEWS14. To evaluate the significance of FGT, we substituted it with RGT and RGCN, which resulted in drops of 0.31 and 0.42 in MRR, respectively, highlighting its importance. Additionally, the influence of the Time Series Encoder (TE) was assessed by removing it (GCT - w/o TE), which led to a drop of 0.1 in MRR, 0.26 in Hits@3, 0.37 in Hits@10, demonstrating TE's crucial role in capturing trends and seasonal variations. The most significant performance degradation was observed when the ConvTransE module was excluded (GCT - w/o ConvTransE), which restricted the model to only historical entity sets, diminishing generalization.

Table 3. Results for entity prediction task on GDELT, YAGO, and WIKI datasets are presented using metrics MRR and Hits@k, with k ∈ {1, 3, 10}. The highest are highlighted in bold, while the second-highest are underlined.

Model	GDELT				YAGO				WIKI			
	MRR	Hits@1	Hits@3	Hits@10	MRR	Hits@1	Hits@3	Hits@10	MRR	Hits@1	Hits@3	Hits@10
CyGNet	18.05	11.52	19.57	31.98	52.00	45.30	56.10	63.70	33.89	29.06	36.10	41.86
xERTE	15.46	10.98	15.61	24.31	84.19	80.09	88.02	89.78	71.14	68.05	76.11	79.01
TiTer	20.20	14.10	22.20	31.20	87.47	80.09	89.96	90.27	75.50	72.96	77.49	79.02
RE-GCN	19.80	12.50	21.00	34.00	82.30	78.83	84.27	88.58	78.53	74.50	81.59	84.70
HGAT	-	-	-	-	63.60	59.80	66.00	71.50	56.10	52.90	58.10	61.80
GCT	**25.43**	**14.51**	**24.64**	**54.16**	**90.46**	**87.06**	**94.02**	**94.10**	**81.78**	**77.78**	**85.90**	**89.20**

Table 4. Ablation study on ICEWS14 using MRR and Hits@k, with k ∈ {1, 3, 10}.

Model	MRR	Hits@1	Hits@3	Hits@10
GCT - RGCN	42.59	29.94	50.31	71.85
GCT - RGT	42.70	30.17	49.30	72.06
GCT - w/o TE	42.91	30.14	49.35	72.62
GCT - w/o ConvTransE	38.60	29.03	43.28	56.72
GCT	**43.01**	**30.34**	**49.61**	**72.99**

6 Conclusion

We propose a novel architecture for future forecasting, entitled Graph Convolution Transformer (GCT). GCT addresses two main challenges: capturing the historical facts and integrating evolving temporal patterns. A key feature of GCT is its ability to extract structure and temporal dependencies using two variants of Transformers: FGT and TT with an advanced decoder, Query-ConvTransE, for query-based information. Experimental results on six datasets demonstrate GCT's performance on entity prediction compared to existing methods. Future work will aim to extend GCT to include relation and time prediction tasks.

Acknowledgments. This research is funded by the University of Science, VNU-HCM, Vietnam under grant number CNTT 2023-13.

References

1. Guo, W., et al.: CR-LT-KGQA: a knowledge graph question answering dataset requiring commonsense reasoning and long-tail knowledge (2024)
2. Han, Z., et al.: xerte: explainable reasoning on temporal knowledge graphs for forecasting future links. In: Proceedings of COLING 2016 (2021)
3. Le, et al.: A personalized recommender system based-on knowledge graph embeddings, pp. 368–378 (2023). https://doi.org/10.1007/978-3-031-27762-7_35
4. Li, et al.: Temporal knowledge graph reasoning based on evolutional representation learning. In: Proceedings of the 44th International ACM SIGIR (2021)

5. Rebele, et al.: Yago: a multilingual knowledge base from wikipedia, wordnet, and geonames. In: The Semantic Web – ISWC (2016)
6. Schlichtkrull, M., et al.: Modeling relational data with graph convolutional networks. In: The Semantic Web (2018)
7. Shang, et al.: End-to-end structure-aware convolutional networks for knowledge base completion. In: Proceedings of AAAI Conference on Artificial Intelligence (2019)
8. Shao, P., et al.: Hierarchical graph attention network for temporal knowledge graph reasoning. Neurocomputing **550**, 126390 (2023)
9. Sun, et al.: Graph Hawkes transformer for extrapolated reasoning on temporal knowledge graphs. In: Proceedings of the 2022 Conference on EMNLP (2022)
10. Sun, et al.: TimeTraveler: reinforcement learning for temporal knowledge graph forecasting. In: Proceedings of the 2021 Conference on EMNLP (2021)
11. Vaswani, et al.: Attention is all you need. In: NeurIPS (2017)
12. Zhu, C., et al.: Learning from history: modeling temporal knowledge graphs with sequential copy-generation networks. In: AAAI (2020)

Collaboration Miner: Discovering Collaboration Petri Nets

Janik-Vasily Benzin$^{(\boxtimes)}$ (ID) and Stefanie Rinderle-Ma (ID)

TUM School of Computation, Information and Technology,
Technical University of Munich, Garching, Germany
{janik.benzin,stefanie.rinderle-ma}@tum.de

Abstract. Collaborative discovery techniques mine models that represent behavior of collaborating cases within multiple process orchestrations that interact via collaboration concepts such as organizations, agents, and services. In this work, we rely on collaboration Petri nets as models and propose the Collaboration Miner (CM) to improve the quality of the discovered models. Moreover, CM can discover heterogeneous collaboration concepts and types such as resource sharing and message exchange, resulting in fitting and precise collaboration Petri nets. The evaluation shows that CM achieves its design goals: no assumptions on concepts and types as well as fitting and precise models, based on 26 artificial and real-world event logs.

Keywords: Collaboration mining · Collaboration process discovery · Inter-organizational processes · Multi-agent systems

1 Introduction

A subset of process discovery [4], called *collaboration process discovery* (CPD) [12,15], aims to discover a process model of *collaboration processes* (CP) from a set of process instances correlated by *collaborating cases* [6–8]. Figure 1 depicts a process model of a CP. Since CPs are composed of multiple process orchestrations that jointly achieve a shared business goal and are modeled by *workflow nets* (N_{c_1}, N_{c_2}) [14], its collaborating cases (token in source i) contain multiple cases (tokens in i_1, i_2) each corresponding to a particular process orchestration, i.e., cases and orchestrations are in a 1:1 relationship. Collaboration in a CP is classified into four collaboration types $v \in \Upsilon$ [7,8,12]: Message exchange (v_m), e.g., $p_{ac,2}$ in Fig. 1; handover-of-work as a message that "starts" the receiving process orchestration (v_h) [12,14], e.g., $p_{ac,1}$ and t_{sc} in Fig. 1; resource sharing (v_r), e.g., $p_{r,1}$ in Fig. 1; and activity execution (v_s), e.g., t_{sc} in Fig. 1. Overall, CPD techniques are characterized by targeting different compositional process models that support varying subsets of collaboration types with various assumptions on *interaction patterns*, i.e., how the collaboration between process orchestrations is assumed to occur.

M. Comuzzi et al. (Eds.): CoopIS 2024, LNCS 15506, pp. 373–381, 2025.
https://doi.org/10.1007/978-3-031-81375-7_24

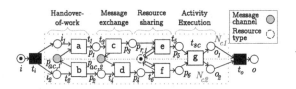

Fig. 1. Collaboration Petri net cPN [6] with all four collaboration types.

By proposing *collaboration Petri nets (cPN)* [6] and designing the new Collaboration Miner (CM) to discover cPN, we answer the following research question: **How can we discover fitting and precise process models of CPs from a single event log?** Our contribution results in a generic CPD technique that mines fitting and precise CP models across domains. CM discovers high quality models for all of the 22 artificial event logs that are recorded from multi-agent systems [13] and inter-organizational processes [9]. Moreover, CM discovers high quality models for the four real-world event logs that are recorded from healthcare CPs [12]. Such that, cPN target supports all four collaboration types and does not assume certain interaction patterns such that model quality is maintained across heterogeneous CPs. Note that we assume a single event log recorded from executing a CP is given, i.e., we abstract from event extraction, merging, and correlation [10] with corresponding clock synchronization issues as well as privacy concerns [9].

The cPN formalism, event log requirements for CM, and a more detailed evaluation are included in our extended version available at [6]. Section 2 presents CM. An empirical evaluation of CM in comparison to existing CPD techniques is reported in Sect. 3. Next, related work is discussed in Sect. 4. Lastly, Sect. 5 concludes and gives an outlook.

2   Collaboration Miner

CM is a technique to discover a cPN from event log L. Table 1 depicts an event log L. Each event records information on the collaborating case ID (case), the executed activity (act), the time, the *collaboration concept* [7] that identifies the executing process orchestration (concept), the shared resource (resource), sent (send_msg) and received messages (receive_msg).

Table 1. Five events (represented by rows) of real-world event log L_{EM} [12].

Event	case	act (activity)	timestamp	c (concept)	rs (resource)	s (send_msg)	r (receive_msg)
e_1	t1	register	2019-12-28T00:20:21	{Emergency}	∅	∅	∅
e_2	t1	rescue	2019-12-28T01:20:21	{Emergency}	{charging system}	∅	
e_3	t1	reserve	2019-12-28T10:20:21	{X_ray}	{charging system}	{acceptance notice}	{reservation form}
e_4	t1	plan imaging	2019-12-28T11:20:21	{Surgical}	∅	{photo form}	{acceptance notice}
e_5	t1	consult	2019-12-28T23:20:21	{Surgical, Cardiovascular}	{diagnosis room}	∅	∅

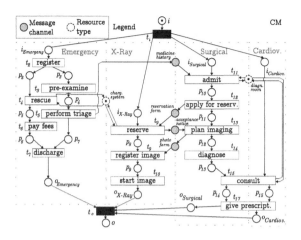

Fig. 2. cPN mined by CM on log EM.

In the following, we define the Collaboration Miner (CM) and illustrate with example event log L_{EM}.

Step 1. Given event log L, the first step determines five sets and three functions by extracting attribute information from each event by traversing traces $\sigma \in L$ (correlated by collaborating cases) and events per trace $e \in \sigma$: The set of collaboration concepts $\mathcal{C} = \bigcup_{\sigma \in L, e \in \sigma} e(c)$, the set of asynchronous message places $P_M = \bigcup_{\sigma \in L, e \in \sigma} e(s) \cup e(r)$, the set of asynchronous resource sharing places $P_{RS} = \bigcup_{\sigma \in L, e \in \sigma} e(rs)$, and the set of activities $\Lambda_L = \bigcup_{\sigma \in L, e \in \sigma} e(act.)$. The function $\Lambda_s(x)$ returns the set of activities that sent message x, $\Lambda_r(x)$ returns the set of activities that received message x, and $\Lambda_{rs}(x)$ returns the set of activities that shared resource x. All three functions are determined by $\Lambda_y(x) = \bigcup_{\sigma \in L, e \in \sigma, e(y)=x} e(act.)$ for $y \in \{s, r, rs\}$.

Example: For Table 1, we have collaboration concepts $\mathcal{C} =\{$Emergency, X-Ray, Surgical, Cardiov.$\}$, asynchronous message places $P_M = \{$photo form, res. form, accept. notice, ...$\}$, asynchronous resource sharing places $P_{RS} = \{$charg. system, diagn. room $\}$, the set of activities $\Lambda_L = \{$ register, ...$\}$, the function returning sending activities per message $\Lambda_s(x) = \{($photo form, $\{$plan imaging$\}$), ...$\}$, the function returning receiving activities per message $\Lambda_r(x) = \{($res. form, $\{$reserve$\}$), (accept. notice, $\{$plan imaging$\}$), ...$\}$, and the function returning resource sharing activities per resource $\Lambda_{rs}(x) = \{($charg. system, $\{$rescue, reserve$\}$), ...$\}$.

Step 2. Project L on collection of event logs $L_{c_1}, \ldots, L_{c_n}$ by filtering events that only refer to collaboration concept $c_1, c_2, \ldots$. Apply a process discovery technique $disc$ on each projected event log L_{c_i} resulting in a collection of WF-nets $N_{c_1}, \ldots, N_{c_n}$. Any technique $disc$ can be applied, as long as it discovers WF-nets. Check if a valid WF-net is discovered on each projected event log. Note that if $disc$ discovers *duplicate labels* [4], the respective transitions will be fused as if they represent synchronous collaboration v_s without an additional label renaming. Construct a workflow collection $WC = (N_c)_{c \in C}$ with $N_c = (P_c, T_c, F_c, l_c, \Lambda_{L, \{\tau\}})$ by renaming place and transition names to avoid name clashes.

Example: For Table 1, we have $L_{c_1} = \{e_1, e_2, \ldots\}$, $L_{c_2} = \{e_3, \ldots\}$, $L_{c_3} = \{e_4, e_5, \ldots\}$, and $L_{c_4} = \{e_5, \ldots\}$. We apply *Inductive Miner* [11] as *disc*, resulting in four valid WF-nets $N_{c_1}, \ldots, N_{c_4}$ as highlighted with blue-dotted rectangles on the left in Fig. 2 (overlapping transitions t_{15}, t_{17} are to be split). Note that the place and transition names are already renamed such that $WC_{ex} = (N_c)_{c \in C}$ is a workflow collection.

Step 3. Apply collaboration discovery *cdisc* to mine collaboration pattern CP as defined in the following. Compute sending transitions $T_s(x) = \{t \in T^u \mid l^u(t) \in \Lambda_s(x)\}^1$, receiving transitions $T_r(x) = \{t \in T^u \mid l^u(t) \in \Lambda_r(x)\}$, resource sharing transitions $T_{rs}(x) = \{t \in T^u \mid l^u(t) \in \Lambda_{rs}(x)\}$, message exchanges $AC' = \{(p_{ac}, T_s(p_{ac}), T_r(p_{ac})) \mid p_{ac} \in P_M \wedge T_s(p_{ac}) \neq \emptyset \wedge T_r(p_{ac}) \neq \emptyset\}$, and resource sharing $AC'' = \{(p_{ac}, T_{rs}(p_{ac}), T_{rs}(p_{ac})) \mid p_{ac} \in P_{RS} \wedge T_{rs}(p_{ac}) \neq \emptyset\}$. If events in L do not contain information on *lifecycles* [4], set $ra(p_r) = 1$ for $p_r \in P_{RS}$, else determine $\max_{p_r}(L)$ the maximum of concurrently running activities sharing p_r and set $ra(p_r) = \max_{p_r}(L)$. Then, define collaboration pattern $CP = (P_{RS} \cup P_M, P_{RS}, ra, AC' \cup AC'', ET)$, where ET is induced by equally-labelled transition subsets of all transitions in WC.

Example: For WC_{ex} (cf. Fig. 2), we have sending transitions $T_s(x) = \{(\text{accept. not.}, \{t_9\}), \ldots\}$, receiving transitions $T_r(x) = \{(\text{res. form}, \{t_9\}), \ldots\}$, resource sharing transitions $T_{rs}(x) = \{(\text{charg. system}, \{t_4, t_9\}), \ldots\}$, message exchanges $AC' = \{(\text{res. form}, \{t_{12}\}, \{t_9\}), \ldots\}$, and resource sharing $AC'' = \{(\text{charg. system}, \{t_4, t_9\}, \{t_4, t_9\}), \ldots\}$. ra is a constant function at value 1, because L_{EM} does not record lifecycles. Then, $CP = (P_{RS} \cup P_M, P_{RS}, ra, AC' \cup AC'', \{(t_{15}, \{t_{15}, t_{16}\}) \ldots\})$.

Step 4. Return $cPN = ((P, T, F, l, \Lambda_{L, \{\tau\}}), m_0) = \biguplus_{c \in C}^{CP} N_c$.

Example: The cPN is depicted in Fig. 2.

Similar to existing CPD techniques, CM applies a divide-and-conquer approach on the collaboration concept in the event log and *disc* on projected event logs (cf. **Step 2**), since a CP is a composition of WF-nets. Conceptually, CM comes with a general formulation of collaboration concepts, no assumptions on the interaction patterns for message exchanges, and supports all four collaboration types (cf. CP in **Step 3** and Sect. 3 for details). Consequently, resulting $cPNs$ are not specialized on certain CPs. Since CM builds on a Petri net theory with activity labels, CM supports all *disc* that discover *duplicate* ($l(t) = l(t')$) and *silent activities* ($l(t) = \tau$). In particular, silent activities are crucial for many control-flow patterns. Both activities are not fused in **Step 4** (cf. **Step 2**). Note that CM projects to the empty trace ϵ for some $c \in C$ in **Step 2**, if a trace does not contain any event with activities executed by c. The design ensures a fitting

---

[1] We denote with $\cdot^u$ the result of merging all respective elements in a workflow collection, e.g., T^u refers to the union of $T_{c_1}, T_{c_2}, \ldots$ [6].

cPN, as without the ability to "skip" a WF-net corresponding traces cannot be perfectly replayed. Thus, this projection conforms to the design goals of CM. The CM implementation is publicly available at https://gitlab.com/janikbenzin/cm and builds on the PM4PY[2] library.

3 Experimental Evaluation

There exist 15 CPD techniques to discover different process models of CPs with different collaboration types [6]. From the 15 CPD techniques, only CCHP [12], Colliery [9], OCPD [2], and Agent Miner [14] have publicly available implementations and can be applied in our evaluation. Nevertheless, Agent Miner is excluded from the evaluation for three reasons. First, the supported collaboration type v_h together with the assumption that only a single concept can execute an activity simultaneously (cf. Def. 4.1 in [14]) means that the Agent Miner cannot be applied to event logs with synchronous collaboration. Second, Agent Miner assumes that every directly-follows pair of events (e_1, e_2) with different concept attributes implies a handover-of-work message between the respective concepts in a trace (cf. Def. 4.2 in [14]), which is violated in all 26 event logs. Third, we still tried to apply Agent Miner on the logs, but were unable to get an output.

We select event logs from literature: 12 artificial event logs from multi-agent systems [13], 10 artificial event logs from BPMN collaborations [9], and 4 real-world event logs from healthcare CPs [12]. For 17/22 artificial event logs (1-A5 in Fig. 2), the *true* process models that generated the respective event log are available or convertible by PM4PY's "BPMN to Petri net" (see True in Fig. 2). For the five artificial event logs R1-R5 conversion with PM4PY is not possible due to the BPMN model structure, so their true process models are not available. Descriptive statistics of the 26 event logs are reported in Fig. 2. The event logs vary along the dimensions: # of collaboration concepts, collaboration types v, and properties describing the respective interaction pattern of message exchanges v_m [5]. Interaction patterns vary along the maximum number of concepts interacting through a message type, i.e., *one*-way and *two*-way bilateral or *multi*lateral, the maximum number of transmissions per type, i.e., *single* or *multi*, and the relation between activities sending/receiving messages per type, i.e., point-to-point (denoted by 1:1), one-to-many (1:n), and many-to-many interaction (m:n).

Each of the 26 event logs is converted to the respective CPD technique's event log input format. We apply CM, CCHP, Colliery, and OCPD on each converted event log with the Inductive Miner [11] for POD *disc* to ensure result differences being caused by the CPD techniques properties, e.g., supported collaboration types, and design choices, e.g., assumptions on the interaction pattern. Inductive Miner is chosen for its formal guarantee to discover perfectly fitting WF-nets such that this design goal can be achieved. We report the model *size* as the sum of the # of places and # of transitions in Fig. 2. We apply *alignment-based fitness* and *precision* [1,3] to measure model quality with PM4PY except for logs ID to SD in Fig. 2 for which we manually computed fitness and precision (annotated

---

[2] https://processintelligence.solutions/pm4py.

Table 2. Model quality metrics of the true model, if available, and discovered by CM, CCHP [12], Colliery [9], and OCPD [2] based on artificial event logs 1-12 [13], A1-A5 & R1-R5 [9], and real-world event logs EM-SD [12], where $\Upsilon_\sigma = \{v_x \mid x \in \sigma\}$.

Event log L		1	2	3	4	5	6	7	8	9	10	11	12	A1
# Events		95052	149988	92668	102404	182452	123322	88068	157098	115000	102548	160000	88089	100
Avg. trace length		19	30	19	20	36	25	18	31	23	21	32	18	8
# Col. concepts		2	2	2	2	2	2	2	3	2	2	2	2	2
Col. types v		v_m	v_m	v_m	v_m	v_m	v_m	v_m	v_m	$\Upsilon_{\langle m,s\rangle}$	$\Upsilon_{\langle m,s\rangle}$	$\Upsilon_{\langle m,s\rangle}$	$\Upsilon_{\langle m,s\rangle}$	v_m
v_m: Max. col. con.		one	one	one	one	two	two	two	two	two	two	two	two	one
v_m: Max. trans.		single	single	single	single	single	single	multi	multi	single	single	single	single	single
v_m: Activity rel.		1:n	m:n	1:1	m:n	1:n	1:n	m:n	m:n	m:n	m:n	1:n	1:n	1:1
True	Precision	0.716	0.401	0.754	0.759	0.39	0.564	0.817	0.481	0.714	0.793	0.495	0.766	0.972
	Size	66	100	88	76	109	113	61	128	105	78	94	86	22
CM	Fitness	1.0	1.0	1.0	1.0	1.0	1.0	1.0	1.0	1.0	1.0	1.0	1.0	1.0
	Precision	0.736	0.351	**0.765**	**0.792**	0.208	0.586	**0.817**	**0.504**	**0.716**	0.781	0.433	**0.758**	**0.972**
	Size	75	125	103	92	167	132	77	148	120	88	125	95	26
CCHP	Fitness	ex	ex	1.0	ex	ex	ex	ex	ex	ex	ex	ex	0.384	1.0
	Precision	ex	ex	**0.765**	ex	ex	ex	ex	ex	ex	ex	ex	0.583	**0.972**
	Size	78	127	**95**	92	165	135	78	150	121	94	128	99	26
Colliery	Fitness	0.867	0.966	1.0	0.71	0.964	0.924	0.667	0.699	0.641	0.707	0.93	0.893	1.0
	Precision	**0.738**	**0.426**	**0.765**	0.747	**0.26**	**0.598**	0.686	0.306	0.5	0.67	**0.465**	0.697	**0.972**
	Size	79	131	103	94	169	136	77	295	130	96	128	104	26
OCPD	Fitness	1.0	1.0	1.0	1.0	1.0	1.0	1.0	1.0	1.0	1.0	1.0	1.0	1.0
	Precision	0.714	0.341	0.719	0.701	0.136	0.545	0.594	0.387	0.677	0.726	0.185	0.717	0.753
	Size	**74**	**123**	101	**90**	**121**	128	**74**	142	118	86	106	93	**24**

Event log L		A2	A3	A4	A5	R1	R2	R3	R4	R5	EM	ID	FP	SD
# Events		100	100	100	100	22	100	100	100	100	18909	50427	37816	4320
Avg. trace length		18	23	6	24	7	15	18	18	13	32	25	25	23
# Col. concepts		2	3	2	4	2	2	3	3	3	6	6	4	4
Col. types v		v_m	$\Upsilon_{\langle m,h\rangle}$	v_m	$\Upsilon_{\langle m,h\rangle}$	v_m	v_m	$\Upsilon_{\langle m,h\rangle}$	$\Upsilon_{\langle m,h\rangle}$	$\Upsilon_{\langle m,h\rangle}$	Υ	$\Upsilon_{\langle m,s,h\rangle}$	$\Upsilon_{\langle m,s,h\rangle}$	$\Upsilon_{\langle m,s,h\rangle}$
v_m: Max. col. con.		two	one	two	two	two	two	two	two	two	two	two	two	two
v_m: Max. trans.		single	single	single	single	single	multi	multi	single	single	single	single	single	single
v_m: Activity rel.		1:1	1:1	1:1	1:1	1:1	1:1	1:1	1:1	1:1	1:1	1:1	1:1	1:1
True	Precision	0.648	0.645	0.998	0.646	n/a	n/a	n/a	n/a	n/a	n/a	n/a	n/a	n/a
	Size	47	59	18	63	n/a	n/a	n/a	n/a	n/a	n/a	n/a	n/a	n/a
CM	Fitness	1.0	1.0	1.0	1.0	1.0	1.0	1.0	1.0	1.0	1.0	1.0	1.0	1.0
	Precision	0.606	0.435	**0.998**	0.44	**0.538**	0.419	0.293	0.649	**0.945**	**0.986**	**0.797***	**0.789***	**0.845***
	Size	50	64	22	75	20	42	80	54	71	95	74	74	65
CCHP	Fitness	0.935	0.958	1.0	0.905	1.0	0.894	0.974	0.889	0.844	ex	1.0	0.943	0.979
	Precision	**0.648**	0.467	**0.998**	0.471	**0.538**	0.422	**0.369**	**0.758**	**0.945**	ex	**0.797***	0.615*	0.777*
	Size	51	65	22	71	20	41	84	55	61	105	74	76	66
Colliery	Fitness	0.935	0.935	1.0	0.888	0.6	0.894	0.846	0.757	0.785	0.918	0.865	0.88	0.857
	Precision	**0.648**	**0.645**	**0.998**	**0.646**	0.333	**0.439**	0.333	0.638	0.814	0.253	0.233	0.176	0.229
	Size	51	63	22	67	**12**	43	82	48	61	81	**62**	67	**51**
OCPD	Fitness	1.0	1.0	1.0	0.971	1.0	1.0	0.995	1.0	0.868	1.0	1.0	1.0	1.0
	Precision	0.598	0.399	0.703	0.314	**0.538**	0.253	0.193	0.201	0.251	0.148	0.409*	0.530*	0.509*
	Size	**48**	**60**	**20**	**65**	20	**30**	66	**41**	**59**	**76**	68	**66**	58

with *) using the more efficient ProM plugin with similar parameters, as PM4PY exceeds a space limit of >58GB.

Considering fitness, CM is the only CPD technique that always discovers a cPN that perfectly fits event log L (cf. Fig. 2). CCHP discovers Petri nets whose final markings are unreachable for event logs 1, 2, and 4-11, as CCHP implicitly assumes a point-to-point (1:1) activity relation, but still adds an interaction for each unique activity pair, e.g., a 2:2 relation yields four activity pairs. As resource places are not discovered as self-loop places by CCHP, the only log EM with resource sharing results in a Petri net with unreachable final marking. Since support for synchronous collaboration v_s is not implemented in CCHP, Petri nets discovered on event logs with v_s have a lower fitness similar to Colliery that does not support v_s by design. Considering precision, CM and Colliery discover the most precise models for 15/26 and 12/26 event logs respectively, i.e., either CM or Colliery discover the most precise model with the exception of CCHP for R3 and R4. In particular, the most precise model is in the same range as the true model's precision. CM can discover most precise models across all three different event log groups and, thus, across multi-agent systems, inter-organizational processes and healthcare CPs. CCHP discovers the most precise model for 9/26 event logs due to the final marking being unreachable for 11/26 event logs. OCPD usually discovers the least precise model due to the low precision of parallelly executed WF-nets without any message exchange. Considering size, OCPD regularly discovers the smallest model, since it does not discover asynchronous places. CCHP, Colliery, and CM are typically in the same range of size. Overall, the sizes of discovered models are close to each other and usually in the range of 1.2x the true model size.

To sum up, the results show that support for synchronous collaboration increases fitness, support for asynchronous collaboration increases precision, and violated assumptions on interaction patterns significantly decrease fitness and precision and can lead to models in which the final marking is not reachable. The experimental evaluation with 26 artificial and real-world event logs with a diverse set of CPs, collaboration types, and interaction patterns shows that CM achieves its design goals of precise and fitting process models without assumptions on concepts, types or patterns.

4   Related Work

To start with, we elaborate on our differences in detail to CCHP [12] that is the CPD technique closest to CM. CCHP [12] shows multiple inconsistencies between paper and implementation; hence we use CCHP sources https://github.com/ promworkbench/ShandongPM/ as substitute for parts that are undefined, e.g., *cdisc*. While CCHP has a similar divide-and-conquer approach and modelling of collaboration types, it differs in several aspects in which CM improves CCHP as shown in Sect. 3. CCHP does not allow empty traces in projected logs, which lead to reduced fitness. It assumes a one-to-one activity relation per message channel, resulting in unreachable final markings. v_s is only theoretically discovered and v_r is practically not discovered as self-loop places. CCHP does not discover resource allocations and does not specify event log requirements, which leaves an early decision of applicability to the user. Lastly, CCHP is not defined with activity labels such that duplicate and silent activities are always fused. Hence, POD techniques such as the Inductive Miner lead to undesirable results. Overall, CM generalizes, improves, and extends CCHP. Regarding collaboration types, this work provides a global view on the CP to reduce redundancies and separates the process orchestrations (intra-process) from the collaborations (inter-process) to simplify the discovery of CPs. Not separating intra-process from inter-process behavior as done in the RM_WF_nets [16] requires to simultaneously discover both behaviors for each collaboration concept. As collaborations are nonetheless discovered, collaborations are discovered multiple times. In general, CM advances CPD techniques in the direction of a generalized formulation, fewer assumptions, discovery of resource allocations, support of all four collaboration types, of silent activities, and of more techniques *disc*.

5   Conclusion and Outlook

We propose Collaboration Miner (CM) to discover fitting and precise process models of CPs. Among the heterogeneous set of existing target model classes proposed to model CPs, CM proposes collaboration Petri nets (*cPN*). CM generalizes over domains and their CPs through collaboration concepts, types, and event log requirements. In addition, *cdisc* eliminates assumptions of existing techniques on the interaction patterns in the event log. CM's ability to discover high-quality models across domains and interaction patterns is empirically shown on 26 artificial and real-world event logs. Future directions are towards providing soundness guarantees, discovering multiplicities between collaboration concept instances, and supporting *the Pub/Sub communication model* [9] for collaboration type v_m. Extending CM to also discover process models that can represent multiplicities between concept instances necessitates an extension to *cPN*s that would bring collaboration and object-centric process mining closer together.

References

1. van der Aalst, W.M.P., Adriansyah, A., van Dongen, B.: Replaying history on process models for conformance checking and performance analysis. WIREs Data Min. Knowl. Discov. **2**(2), 182–192 (2012)
2. van der Aalst, W.M.P., Berti, A.: Discovering object-centric Petri nets. Fundamenta Informaticae **175**(1–4), 1–40 (2020)
3. Adriansyah, A., Munoz-Gama, J., Carmona, J., Van Dongen, B.F., Van Der Aalst, W.M.: Measuring precision of modeled behavior. Inf. Syst. E-Bus. Manag. **13**(1), 37–67 (2015)
4. Augusto, A., et al.: Automated discovery of process models from event logs: review and benchmark. IEEE Trans. Knowl. Data Eng. **31**(4), 686–705 (2019)
5. Barros, A., Dumas, M., ter Hofstede, A.H.M.: Service interaction patterns. In: BPM, pp. 302–318 (2005)
6. Benzin, J.V., Rinderle-Ma, S.: Collaboration miner: discovering collaboration petri nets (extended version) (2024). arXiv:2401.16263 [cs]
7. Benzin, J.V., Rinderle-Ma, S.: Petri net classes for collaboration mining: assessment and design guidelines. In: PM Workshops (2024)

8. Benzin, J.V., Rinderle-Ma, S.: Towards standardized modeling of collaboration processes in collaboration process discovery. In: PM Workshops (2025, accepted)
9. Corradini, F., Pettinari, S., Re, B., Rossi, L., Tiezzi, F.: A technique for discovering BPMN collaboration diagrams. SoSyM (2024)
10. Diba, K., Batoulis, K., Weidlich, M., Weske, M.: Extraction, correlation, and abstraction of event data for process mining. Data Min. Knowl. Disc. **10**(3) (2020)
11. Leemans, S.J.J., Fahland, D., van der Aalst, W.M.P.: Discovering block-structured process models from event logs - a constructive approach. In: PETRI NETS 2013, pp. 311–329 (2013)
12. Liu, C., Li, H., Zhang, S., Cheng, L., Zeng, Q.: Cross-department collaborative healthcare process model discovery from event logs. IEEE Trans. Autom. Sci. Eng. **20**(3), 2115–2125 (2023)
13. Nesterov, R., Bernardinello, L., Lomazova, I., Pomello, L.: Discovering architecture-aware and sound process models of multi-agent systems: a compositional approach. SoSyM **1**, 351–375 (2023)
14. Tour, A., Polyvyanyy, A., Kalenkova, A., Senderovich, A.: Agent miner: an algorithm for discovering agent systems from event data. In: BPM, pp. 284–302 (2023)
15. Zeng, Q., Duan, H., Liu, C.: Top-down process mining from multi-source running logs based on refinement of Petri nets. IEEE Access **8**, 61355–61369 (2020)
16. Zeng, Q., Sun, S., Duan, H., Liu, C., et al.: Cross-organizational collaborative workflow mining from a multi-source log. Decis Support Syst. **54**, 1280–1301 (2013)

Discovering Order-Inducing Features in Event Knowledge Graphs

Christoffer Olling Back[1,2]([email]) and Jakob Grue Simonsen[1]

[1] University of Copenhagen, Copenhagen, Denmark
{back,simonsen}@di.ku.dk
[2] ServiceNow Denmark ApS, Aarhus, Denmark

Abstract. Event knowledge graphs (EKG) extend the classical notion of a trace to capture multiple, interacting views of a process execution. In this paper, we tackle the open problem of automating EKG discovery from uncurated data through a principled, probabilistic framing based on featured-derived partial orders on events. We derive an EKG discovery algorithm based on statistical inference rather than an ad-hoc or heuristic-based strategy, or manual analysis from domain experts.

This approach comes at the computational cost of exploring a large, non-convex hypothesis space. In particular, solving the likelihood term involves counting the number of linear extensions of posets, which in general is #P-complete. Fortunately, bound estimates suffice for model comparison, and admit incorporation into a bespoke branch-and-bound algorithm. We show that the posterior probability as defined is antitonic w.r.t. search depth for branching rules that are monotonic w.r.t. model inclusion. This allows pruning of large portions of the search space, which we show experimentally leads to rapid convergence toward optimal solutions that are consistent with manually built EKGs.

Keywords: Bayesian inference · Branch and bound · Event knowledge graphs · Linear extension · Partial order · Process mining

1 Introduction

Event knowledge graphs (EKGs) capture the temporal ordering of events associated with entities and objects via so-called local directly-follows paths (df-path), resulting in an intertwined web of event sequences, synchronized at shared events. Automating the process of identifying, "relevant structural relations between entities" is a stated open problem, currently requiring domain knowledge [12,13].

We present a theoretically principled method for automatically identifying event-level features to include as entities in the EKG, defining the structure of its df-paths. Our approach rests on a natural Bayesian formulation which reduces the task to its core elements. Features are analyzed w.r.t. the df-paths

Supported by Innovation Fund Denmark through the DIREC research consortium.

Table 1. Event table adapted from [13].

Event	Activity	Actor	Order	S.O.	Invoice	Payment
e_1	Create Order	R_1	O_1			
e_2	Create Order	R_1	O_2			
e_3	Place S.O.	R_1		A		
e_4	Place S.O.	R_3		B		
e_5	Create Invoice	R_3	O_2		I_2	
e_6	Receive S.O.	R_2		A		
e_7	Update S.O.	R_1	O_2	B		
e_9	Update Invoice	R_2		A	I_2	
e_{18}	Create Invoice	R_3	O_1		I_1	
e_{19}	Receive S.O.	R_2		B		
e_{28}	Ship Order	R_4	O_1			
e_{29}	Receive Payment	R_5				P_1
e_{30}	Clear Invoice	R_5			I_1 I_2	P_1
e_{34}	Ship Order	R_4	O_2			

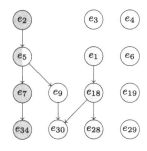

Fig. 1. Transitive reduction of poset induced by feature relations.

they induce, which taken together define a partial order on events. The resulting poset is the cornerstone of our probabilistic approach to model evaluation. We take a maximum likelihood approach, seeking the model that maximizes the probability of the observed sequence of events. This is by definition one linear extension permitted by the event poset, so the task is to identify features that most narrow the remaining outcome space. The likelihood term requires a limiting factor to avoid overfitting [14]. We introduce an entropy-based measure of *feature informativeness* as a prior probability over models which favors informative models, disfavors models that are trivial or add unnecessary complexity.

Calculating the likelihood term relies on counting the number of linear extensions of the event poset, which is #P-complete [6]. However, poset structure can be exploited to establish bounds on posterior odds between models, which is sufficient for comparing models. We incorporate this model comparison strategy into a bespoke branch and bound algorithm for exploring feature combinations that can prune large portions of the search space, making the overall task tractable.

1.1 Related Work

EKGs were introduced by Fahland et al. [12,13], and reflect a growing recognition in the process mining community of the shortcomings of the classical trace concept based on a single case identifier [1,2]. Even when a classical event log is sufficient, extracting event traces from raw data still tends to be an expensive, ad-hoc process relying on domain expert input [5]. While some work has been done on automating this task for classical event logs [10], for novel representations like EKGs, it remains unaddressed [13]. Calculating the number of linear extensions of a poset has been explored by mathematicians for decades as a problem in its own right [7]; as well as by computer scientists, typically in the context of sorting and other comparison-based algorithms [6]. It also arises in a number of other applications such as convex rank tests [16], structure learning for graphical models [19], measuring flexibility of partial-order plans [17], sequence analysis [15], and is equivalent to counting topological sorts on an acyclic graph [20]. Branch and bound algorithms have long been used for feature selection in general [8,18], model selection [21] and maximum likelihood estimation in particular [9]. For proofs and examples relevant to the remainder we refer the reader to [3].

1.2 Preliminaries

We will draw on elements from basic combinatorics, order theory, probability theory, and set theory. We denote by $[S]^{\leq n} :- \{S' \subseteq S \mid n \geq |S'|\}$ the set of subsets of S containing n or fewer elements.

An event is a unique execution of some activity at a certain point in time, and associated with (potentially empty) features. Each row in Table 1 represents an event. We denote by E a nonempty set of events, by D a total order on E called the observed data, by $\mathcal{D} :- \{D_1, \ldots, D_N\}$ a set of N independent observations. We denote by X_i a feature associated with events, i.e., a column in an event table, and by $X_i(e)$ the set of values of X_i associated with event e. The set of all features is denoted by $\mathcal{F} :- \{X_1, \ldots, X_M\}$. Singleton sets of features are called *atomic*, whereas sets containing exactly two features are called *derived*, following [13]. These *sets* of features are denoted $\mathcal{X}$, with $\mathcal{X} \in [\mathcal{F}]^{\leq 2}$, and constitute the building blocks of models and, by extension, partial orders.

A model $\mathcal{M} \subseteq [\mathcal{F}]^{\leq 2}$ is a collection of sets of features. For example, the model $\{\{X_1\}, \{X_2, X_3\}\}$ contains one atomic and one derived feature. An ordering relation $\prec$ when paired with a set, $P :- (E, \prec)$, is called a partially ordered set or poset. The set of linear extensions of poset P is written $\mathcal{E}_P$, and represents all total orders on E that respect the partial order $\prec$.

2   Event Knowledge Graph as Poset

EKGs are not per se process models with execution semantics, but rather a representation of one execution trace. Each event is unique and local *df*-paths are not order relations in the sense of rules or constraints of a *model* that defines a language of traces. Nevertheless, it can be shown that EKGs are equivalent to posets [3]. After establishing definitions, we show how an observed order is reduced w.r.t. a model. In our case, the original poset will be a total order (an event table) and the resulting poset interpreted as the *df*-paths of an EKG.

Definition 1 (Atomic Feature Relation). *Events* $a, b \in E$ *are related by* $\mathcal{X} :- \{X\}$ *if they share values for* $\mathcal{X}$. *Formally,* $\overset{X}{\sim} :- \{ (a,b) \mid X(a) \cap X(b) \neq \emptyset \}$.

Definition 2 (Derived Feature Relation). *Events* $a, d \in E$ *are related by* $\mathcal{X} :- \{X_i, X_k\}$ *if they are related by* X_i *or* X_k, *or if there exists* $X_j \in \mathcal{F} \setminus \{X_i, X_k\}$ *and distinct events* $b, c \in E$ *that relate* a *and* b *transitively by* X_i, X_j, X_k. *Formally,* $\overset{X_i, X_k}{\sim} :- \overset{X_i}{\sim} \cup \overset{X_k}{\sim} \cup \{ (a,d) \mid \exists X_j, b, c. \ X_j \notin \{X_i, X_k\} \wedge a \overset{X_i}{\sim} b \overset{X_j}{\sim} c \overset{X_k}{\sim} d \}$.

We write $\overset{\mathcal{X}}{\sim}$ in general. The following defines a subset of order relations in D if the elements are also feature-related w.r.t. some feature in model $\mathcal{M}$.

Definition 3 (*df*-path Generator). *Given partial order* $D :- (E, \prec)$, *model* $\mathcal{M}$, *then the df-path generator is* $g_{\mathcal{M}}(D) :- \{ (a, b) \mid a \prec b \land \exists \mathcal{X} \in \mathcal{M}. \, a \overset{\mathcal{X}}{\sim} b \}$.

3   A Probabilistic (Bayesian) Formulation

Our aim is to identify the set of features $\mathcal{M}$ that provides the most information about the observed sequence of events w.r.t. the poset induced by $\mathcal{M}$ via *df*-path generator $g_{\mathcal{M}}$. We seek to find the model $\mathcal{M}$ most strongly indicated by data D by *posterior* $\mathbb{P}(\mathcal{M} \mid D)$ i.e.: $\arg\max_{\mathcal{M}} \mathbb{P}(\mathcal{M} \mid D) = \arg\max_{\mathcal{M}} \frac{\mathbb{P}(\mathcal{M})\mathbb{P}(D|\mathcal{M})}{\mathbb{P}(D)}$.

3.1   Maximum Likelihood

Recall the outcome space of $\mathcal{M}$ w.r.t. observation D is the set of linear extensions of the poset P. We can then write $\mathbb{P}(D \mid P) = \mathbb{P}(D \mid D \in \mathcal{E}_P) \, \mathbb{P}(D \in \mathcal{E}_P)$ for the likelihood, i.e., the probability of selecting the observed sequence D from all linear extensions of P. This formulation allows us to consider posets for which D is not, or is not *known to be*, a linear extension of P, but by Definition 3 we have $D \in \mathcal{E}_P$ by construction. Assuming a uniform distribution over $\mathcal{E}_P$ - which is a common [15] though not universal [4] assumption - gives the likelihood:

$$\mathbb{P}(D \mid D \in \mathcal{E}_P) \, \mathbb{P}(D \in \mathcal{E}_P) = \frac{1}{|\mathcal{E}_P|} \tag{1}$$

3.2   Model Priors

Maximum likelihood is not a sufficient criterion since it can always be increased with an increasingly narrowly fitted model. It is common when working with parametric models to assume a uniform distribution over *models*, though not necessarily parameters [14]. Our models are non-parametric, and uniform model priors would reduce our objective function to likelihood $(1/|\mathcal{E}_P|)$ alone, potentially resulting in degenerate models. Typically, overly simplistic models *underfit* the data: $\mathbb{P}(D \mid \mathcal{M})$ will tend to be low for seen as well as unseen data since the probability mass is spread thin across the outcome space. Our task has an idiosyncratic property that trivial models may maximize likelihood, despite being completely *uninformative*. For example, a feature with one outcome across events would induce total order D, on seen and likely on unseen data. This is akin to a prediction task in which a copy of the target variable has been included in the data, leading to a trivial classifier. This can be avoided by explicitly expressing a preference against both degenerate and unnecessarily complex models. We propose distribution based on the product of normalized entropies for features in the model. The per-feature score penalizes features with deterministic distributions, while the product of $[0, 1)$ bounded scores discourages the addition of superfluous features.

Definition 4 (Normalized Shannon entropy). *Let Ω_X denote the outcome space of discrete random variable X, and $H(X)$ the Shannon entropy of X. The normalized Shannon entropy of X is* $\eta(X) :- \frac{H(X)}{1+\max H(X)} = \frac{-\sum_{x\in\Omega_X}\mathbb{P}(x)\log\mathbb{P}(x)}{1+\log|\Omega_X|}.$

Definition 5 (η-Based Model Prior). *Given model $\mathcal{M} \subseteq [\mathcal{F}]^{\leq 2}$, we define*

$$\mathbb{P}(\mathcal{M}) :- \frac{\prod_{\mathcal{X}\in\mathcal{M}}\eta(\mathcal{X})}{\sum_{\mathcal{M}\subseteq[\mathcal{F}]^{\leq 2}}\prod_{\mathcal{X}\in\mathcal{M}}\eta(\mathcal{X})} \tag{2}$$

That is, $\eta(X) \in [0,1)$ is the ratio of the entropy of X to its upper bound with a padding factor to guarantee $\eta(X) < 1$. It ranges from a deterministic/degenerate (zero surprise) to a uniform (maximal surprise) distribution. A model $\mathcal{M}$ containing a trivial feature $\mathcal{X}$ s.t. $\eta(\mathcal{X}) \approx 0$ will have $\mathbb{P}(\mathcal{M}) \approx 0$ due to the product in Eq. 2, which also penalizes additional features since $\eta(\mathcal{X}) < 1$.

3.3 Posterior Odds Objective Function

Combining Eqs. 1 and 2 gives a posterior balancing likelihood against our preference for parsimonious and informative models. For readability we write $\mathcal{E}_{\mathcal{M}}^D$ in place of $\mathcal{E}_{g_{\mathcal{M}}(D)}$, the linear extensions of the poset defined by $\mathcal{M}$ on D. For independent observations, $\mathcal{D} :- \{D_1, \ldots, D_i, \ldots, D_N\}$, by conditional independence:

$$\mathbb{P}(\mathcal{M}|\mathcal{D}) = \frac{\mathbb{P}(\mathcal{M})\prod_{i=1}^N\mathbb{P}(D_i|\mathcal{M})}{\mathbb{P}(\mathcal{D})} = \frac{1}{\mathbb{P}(\mathcal{D})}\frac{\prod_{\mathcal{X}\in\mathcal{M}}\eta(\mathcal{X})}{\sum_{\mathcal{M}\subseteq[\mathcal{F}]^{\leq 2}}\prod_{\mathcal{X}\in\mathcal{M}}\eta(\mathcal{X})}\prod_{i=1}^N\frac{1}{|\mathcal{E}_{\mathcal{M}}^{D_i}|}$$

Since we are interested in the *relative* fitness of models, it suffices to calculate *posterior odds*, in which case $\mathbb{P}(\mathcal{D})$ and the normalizing constant cancel To determine $\mathbb{P}(\mathcal{M}_1|\mathcal{D}) < \mathbb{P}(\mathcal{M}_2|\mathcal{D})$ we harness bounds on the individual terms.

4   Branch and Bound for Model Selection

To avoid exact computation, we can use properties of posets and linear extension count to construct a greedy, divide-and-conquer strategy for establishing bounds and incorporate this into a branch-and-bound algorithm for model selection.

4.1 Bounding Linear Extension Count

Let $P :- (E, \prec)$ be a poset: if it is a total order, there is one linear extension; if $\prec\ = \emptyset$, all permutations of E are linear extensions hence $1 \leq |\mathcal{E}_P| \leq |E|!$. We combine this bound with the following recursive decomposition rules. Figure 2 shows how decomposition rules can be recursively applied, substituting new bound estimates as posets shrink in size: by element removal, or by splitting.

Theorem 1 (Disjoint decomposition). *Given poset P partitioned by $\{P_1, P_2\}$ s.t. no $a \in P_1$ is comparable to any $b \in P_2$, then $|\mathcal{E}_P| = \binom{|P|}{|P_1|}|\mathcal{E}_{P_1}||\mathcal{E}_{P_2}|$.*

$$4.1 \times 10^5 < |\mathcal{E}_P| < 1.5 \times 10^{11} \qquad 8.2 \times 10^5 < |\mathcal{E}_P| < 3.3 \times 10^{10} \qquad 2.1 \times 10^7 < |\mathcal{E}_P| < 8.3 \times 10^9$$

Fig. 2. Repeated application of decomposition with bounds from Corollary 1 and 2.

Corollary 1. *Given a poset P as in Theorem 1, applying naïve bounds we can establish that $\binom{|P|}{|P_1|} \leq \binom{|P|}{|P_1|}|\mathcal{E}_{P_1}||\mathcal{E}_{P_2}| \leq \binom{|P|}{|P_1|}|P_1|!|P_2|!$.*

Theorem 2 (Minimal Element Decomposition). *Given poset P s.t. $|P| > 1$ with set of minimal elements $\min P$, then $|\mathcal{E}_P| = \sum_{x \in \min P} |\mathcal{E}_{P \setminus \{x\}}|$.*

Corollary 2. *Given poset P as in Theorem 2, applying naïve bounds we can establish that $|\min P| = \sum_{x \in \min P} 1 \leq \sum_{x \in \min P} |\mathcal{E}_{P \setminus \{x\}}| \leq \sum_{x \in \min P} |P \setminus \{x\}|!$*

4.2 Bounds for Pruning

The search space over models is exponential in feature count and calculating $\mathbb{P}(\mathcal{M}|D)$ for each model is expensive due to the $|\mathcal{E}_{P_\mathcal{M}}|$ term. Two factors, respectively, help tackle these challenges: pruning model space, and quick model evaluation using bounds onlinear extension counts. When maximizing an objective function f, pruning in branch and bound requires a bounding function that provides a closer and closer upper bound on f as more constraints are added to set of candidate solutions (models), and agrees with f for solutions at the end of the search space.Our full objective function $\mathbb{P}(\mathcal{M}|D)$ is intentionally non-convex, with opposing terms $\mathbb{P}(\mathcal{M})$ and $\mathbb{P}(D|\mathcal{M})$.Nevertheless, we can formulate a convex bounding function that takes advantage of upper bounds on each term, assuming a monotone branching rule w.r.t. model inclusion, i.e. child states in our search space are generated by adding features to a candidate model.

Theorem 3 ($\mathbb{P}(\mathcal{M})$ Is Strictly Antitonic). $\mathbb{P}(\mathcal{M}_i) > \mathbb{P}(\mathcal{M}_j)$ *for $\mathcal{M}_i \subset \mathcal{M}_j$.*

The following bound on $\mathbb{P}(D|\mathcal{M})$ assumes that from the state associated with $\mathcal{M}$, the set of features in models reachable from this state is known, allowing us to determine the most restrictive reachable poset.

Theorem 4 (Upper Bound on $\mathbb{P}(D|\mathcal{M})$ Is Antitonic). *Let $S_\mathcal{M}$ denote the search space reachable from state$\mathcal{M}$, with $\mathcal{M} \subseteq \mathcal{M}'$ for any $\mathcal{M}' \in S_\mathcal{M}$ and define $\mathcal{M}^* :- \bigcup_{\mathcal{M}' \in S_\mathcal{M}} \mathcal{M}'$. Then, $\mathbb{P}(D|\mathcal{M}) \leq \frac{1}{|\mathcal{E}_{\mathcal{M}^*}|}$ and $\frac{1}{|\mathcal{E}_{\mathcal{M}_i^*}|} \geq \frac{1}{|\mathcal{E}_{\mathcal{M}_j^*}|}$ for $\mathcal{M}_i \subset \mathcal{M}_j$.*

Corollary 3. *Let $S_\mathcal{M}$ be defined as in Theorem 4, then $\mathbb{P}(\mathcal{M})\mathbb{P}(D|\mathcal{M}) < \frac{\mathbb{P}(\mathcal{M})}{|\mathcal{E}_{\mathcal{M}^*}^D|}$ and $\frac{\mathbb{P}(\mathcal{M}_i)}{|\mathcal{E}_{\mathcal{M}_i^*}^D|} > \frac{\mathbb{P}(\mathcal{M}_j)}{|\mathcal{E}_{\mathcal{M}_j^*}^D|}$ for $\mathcal{M}_i \subset \mathcal{M}_j$, extending naturally to multiple observations.*

4.3 Bounds for Model Evaluation

When pruning is not possible, we can harness bounds on $\mathbb{P}(\mathcal{M})\,\mathbb{P}(\mathcal{D}\mid\mathcal{M})$ to minimize model evaluation time. Three cases arise: updating current best score and model when its lower bound is above the current best score, marking a model to be revisited when current best score lies between its upper and lower bound, dismissing a model once its upper bound is below the current best score.

Eagerly updating the lower bound estimate on the best possible score helps improve the convergence rate. Quickly marking models (by extension portions of search space) for revisit and moving on means when models are revisited, they are more likely to be dismissed when compared to the now improved best score, or to require less precision in bound estimation before eventual dismissal.

5   Experiments

We evaluate model quality and runtime on the BPIC 2017 event log [11], commonly used in EKG literature and for which hand-built EKGs exist. It contains 19 features, resulting in 524,288 possible models built from atomic features, to which we restrict this preliminary implementation. The algorithm is implemented using a prefix-based, breadth-first branching rule for exploring model space, which satisfies the monotonic condition on branching rules in Theorem 4. The subroutine for estimating bounds on linear extensions is a depth-first approach with iterative deepening with a stopping condition based on time elapsed

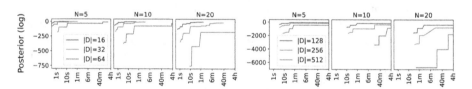

Fig. 3. Convergence across number ($5 \leq N \leq 20$) and size ($16 \leq |D| \leq 512$) of samples/posets. Lines begin at first completed estimate and end if finished.

To assess runtime, we monitored increase in current best score (see Fig. 3). Sample *size* can have drastic impact on the complexity of calculating bounds on linear extensions, but *number* of independent samples will have a linear impact. Increased sample size has the downstream effect of delaying establishment of bounds early on which via pruning and model dismissal allows rapid convergence.

To assess model quality, we compare to hand-built models from [12]. Figure 4 shows EKGs for application 681547497. At the bottom is the EKG for model {{EventOrigin},{ApplicationType},{LoanGoal}} which shows a correspondence with the hand-built EKG above. In particular, EventOrigin is a core entity in the hand-built model defining the three colored "swimlanes". Our algorithm does fail to select feature OfferID, causing offers to be combined into one *df*-path.

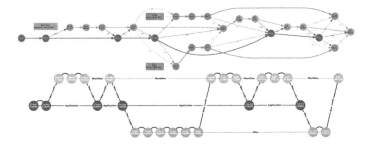

Fig. 4. EKGs for application 681547497 from BPIC 2017 event log. Top: hand-built EKG from [12]. Bottom: EKG discovered by our algorithm.

6 Conclusion

We presented the first algorithm for automatic EKG discovery from uncurated data, showing it discovers models congruent with hand-built EKGs in reasonable time. We use a principled, probabilistic framing with outcome space the linear extensions admitted by the EKG as poset. This lays a foundation for extensions including: alternative model priors; and redefined outcome spaces, such as pairwise event orders - a ubiquitous concept in linear extension research. Finally, it is crucial to outline objective approaches for evaluating discovered models.

References

1. Adams, J.N., Schuster, D., Schmitz, S., Schuh, G., van der Aalst, W.: Defining cases and variants for object-centric event data. In: ICPM, pp. 128–35. IEEE (2022)
2. Back, C.O., Manataki, A., Papanastasiou, A., Harrison, E.: Stochastic workflow modeling in a surgical ward: towards simulating and predicting patient flow. In: Biomedical Engineering Systems and Tech, pp. 565–591. Springer, Cham (2021)
3. Back, C.O., Simonsen, J.G.: Posets and bounded probabilities for discovering order-inducing features in event knowledge graphs. arXiv:2410.06065 (2024)
4. Banks, J., Garrabrant, S.M., Huber, M.L., Perizzolo, A.: Using tpa to count linear extensions. J. Discrete Algorithms **51**, 1–11 (2018)
5. Berti, A., Park, G., Rafiei, M., Van Der Aalst, W.: A generic approach to extract object-centric event data from databases supporting SAP ERP. JIIS (2023)
6. Brightwell, G., Winkler, P.: Counting linear extensions. Order **8**(3), 225–242 (1991)
7. Butler, K.K.H.: The number of partially ordered sets. JCTB **13**(3), 276–289 (1972)
8. Chen, X.w.: An improved branch and bound algorithm for feature selection. Pattern Recogn. Lett. **24**(12), 1925–1933 (2003)
9. Decani, J.S.: A branch and bound algorithm for maximum likelihood paired comparison ranking. Biometrika **59**(1), 131–135 (1972)
10. Diba, K., Batoulis, K., Weidlich, M., Weske, M.: Extraction, correlation, and abstraction of event data for process mining. WIREs DMKD **10**(3), e1346 (2020)
11. van Dongen, B.: Bpi challenge 2017 event log (2017)
12. Esser, S., Fahland, D.: Multi-dimensional event data in graph databases. J. Data Seman. 109–141 (2021). https://doi.org/10.1007/s13740-021-00122-1

13. Fahland, D.: Process mining over multiple behavioral dimensions with event knowledge graphs. In: Process Mining Handbook, pp. 274–319. Springer (2022)
14. MacKay, D.J.: Information theory, inference and learning algorithms. CUP (2003)
15. Mannila, H., Meek, C.: Global partial orders from sequential data. In: Proceedings of the 6th ACM International Conference on Knowledge Discovery and Data Mining, pp. 161–68. ACM, Boston (2000)
16. Morton, J., Pachter, L., Shiu, A., Sturmfels, B., Wienand, O.: Convex rank tests and semigraphoids. SIAM J. Discrete Math. **23**(3), 1117–1134 (2009)
17. Muise, C., Beck, J.C., McIlraith, S.A.: Optimal partial-order plan relaxation via MaxSAT. J. Artif. Intell. Res. **57**, 113–149 (2016)
18. Nakariyakul, S., Casasent, D.P.: Adaptive branch and bound algorithm for selecting optimal features. Pattern Recogn. Lett. **28**(12), 1415–1427 (2007)
19. Niinimäki, T., Parviainen, P., Koivisto, M.: Structure discovery in Bayesian networks by sampling partial orders. J. Mach. Learn. Res. **17**(57), 1–47 (2016)
20. Robinson, R.W.: Counting unlabeled acyclic digraphs, pp. 28–43 (1977)
21. Thakoor, N., Gao, J.: Branch-and-bound for model selection and its computational complexity. IEEE Trans. Knowl. Data Eng. **23**(5), 655–668 (2011)

LabelIT: A Multi-cloud Resource Label Unification Tool

Jeremy Mechouche(⊠), Marwa Mokni, and Yann Ramusat

Devoteam Research, 1 Rue Galvani, 91300 Massy, France
{jeremy.mechouche,marwa.mokni,yann.ramusat}@devoteam.com

Abstract. In cloud environments, labels are often defined by cloud architects to categorise and describe their resources, such as virtual machines, storage and network components. These labels play a crucial role in organising, managing and tracking resources, making it easier to identify and analyse them. However, these labels are often inconsistent, abbreviated, or misspelled, leading to potential mismanagement of cloud resources. In this demonstration, we present LABELIT Kubernetes-based tool designed to standardize resource labels for improved cloud resource management. The label unification tool system is built using NLP (Natural Language Processing) based analysis methods that combine syntactic and semantic similarity processing for accurate unification.

Keywords: Cloud computing · Multi-cloud · Labels · Cloud resource management · Natural language processing

1 Introduction

Cloud computing resources are characterised by labels that are essential for their management. A label consists of a key-value pair that aids in the organization and management of resources within the cloud environment [7]. Labels provide metadata for categorizing, identifying, and grouping assets. While cloud service providers automatically generate labels that describe technical aspects, cloud architects manually create functional labels related to business needs, such as organizational units or projects. However, human input in manual labeling often leads to errors like typos or misinterpretation, which can cause mismanagement, improper access controls, and cost-tracking issues. For instance, two cloud operators aiming to associate their resources to a project might use different labels such as 'Proj,' 'Project,' or 'Projet'. These inaccuracies can disrupt cloud operations, impacting overall efficiency and performance. Tag management in the cloud is supported by both native tools from cloud providers and advanced third-party solutions that manage tags across multiple clouds [1–3,8]. **AWS Tag Editor**, **Google Cloud Resource Manager**, and **Azure Resource Manager** are tools provided by Amazon Web Service (AWS), Google Cloud, and Microsoft Azure, respectively, for managing resource labels within their ecosystems. However, these tools are specific to their platforms and may not address the needs of a multi-cloud environment. For broader functionality, third-party tools like CloudHealth [5], Turbot (https://turbot.com/), CloudCheckr(https://spot.io/product/cloudcheckr/), Apptio Cloudability

M. Comuzzi et al. (Eds.): CoopIS 2024, LNCS 15506, pp. 391–397, 2025.
https://doi.org/10.1007/978-3-031-81375-7_26

(https://apptio.com/products/cloudability/), and Finout (https://finout.io/) offer comprehensive label management, including features for cost tracking, policy enforcement, and compliance across various cloud providers. These solutions help streamline resource management and optimize costs in multi-cloud infrastructures. However, although these tools leverage cloud resources labels, none of them enable the automatic correction of inconsistent labels.

In this demonstration, we present the LABELIT tool designed to correct mislabeled cloud resources by leveraging Natural Language Processing (NLP) techniques widely adopted by state-of-the-art solutions [4]. The use of NLP aims to unify labels both semantically and syntactically, improving the consistency and reliability of cloud resource management.

2   Foundations

In this section, we define the core terms used in the composition of our tool LABELIT. These terms provide a structured foundation for understanding how various components interact within the system.

A **cloud resource** $ResourceCloud = (Id, Kind, Labels)$ refers to any computational or storage resource within a cloud environment, characterized by three key attributes, namely, an Id is a unique identifier for each resource, a $Kind$ is the type of resource, such as compute, Network, and $Labels$ is a list of labels associated with the resource. A **label** is identified by a key-value pair. Each cloud resource is associated with a set of key-value pairs, where the key represents a specific attribute or property, and the value corresponds to the value of that attribute. In our work, we adopt the same definition of a label as the standards, where each $label\ in\ Labels$ is defined as $label = (Key : Value)$.

The **Local Repository** is a comprehensive JSON file that encapsulates the configuration of all extracted cloud resources. Each resource entry in the local repository includes key attributes such as the resource's ID, type (Kind), and associated labels. The **Global Repository** is a CSV file containing a set of consistent and well-formulated labels that adhere to industry best practices and established business rules.

3   System Overview

The LABELIT system is proposed with different phases, namely the extraction of local data which is implemented with a cloud asset inventory. Next, the corrective approach is implemented using python and state-of-the-art Natural Language Processing libraries. The Fig. 1 illustrates the architecture of the proposed tool system.

In the initial phase, the system architecture aims to establish a **local repository** using the data extracted from the cloud architecture. To extract these data, we use a cloud asset inventory tool, such as **Resoto** (https://resoto.com/). In fact, cloud asset inventory tools are used regarding their abilities of gathering a comprehensive information about infrastructure setup and relevant parameters.

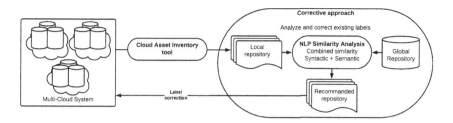

Fig. 1. Architecture of the tool system.

The **global repository** is created by a cloud architect based on our proposed recommendations. Subsequently, our tool advances to application of the combined similarity method (syntactic and semantic), which has been proposed to amplify the coherence among labels.

The proposed tool creates a harmonious union between semantic similarity and syntactic similarity, providing an overview of the relationships between texts. Estimated semantic and syntactic similarities are skilfully combined, and each element is gracefully weighted to reflect its own relevance. The result resembles a symphony of knowledge in which syntactic structure and semantic meaning combine to form a unique similarity score. The weights are carefully defined to reflect their respective contributions.

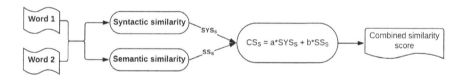

Fig. 2. Proposed workflow for combined similarity method.

The Fig. 2 details the multi-step process involved in the comparison of two words using the combined similarity method, ultimately leading to the identification of the best match for the given input words: **word 1** and **word 2**. The combined similarity involves both syntactic and semantic analysis. The syntactic analysis evaluates the structural similarity between the words, focusing on their form, spelling, and phonetic resemblances. On the other hand, the semantic analysis assesses the meaning and context of the words, identifying relationships such as synonyms, antonyms, and context-based similarities. By combining these two approaches, the method achieves a more accurate comparison, capturing nuances in both word structure and meaning. The syntactic and semantic analysis phase produces a list of similarity results. The match with the highest score is selected for combined aggregation. The semantic similarity score SS_S and syntactic similarity score SYS_S contribute to the combined similarity final score CS_S. This final score, incorporating predefined weights (a and b), calculates the combined similarity score as defined in Eq. 1.

$$CS_S = a * SYS_S + b * SS_S \tag{1}$$

Where, CS_S is the aggregated score of the semantic similarity score SS_S and syntactic similarity score SYS_S. a is the weight given to the syntactic similarity and b is the weight given to the semantic similarity.

In the context of label unification in cloud computing, we adopt the method of combined similarity as a means to generate recommended labels based on the provided input labels. Figure 3 illustrates the adoption of the combined similarity method.

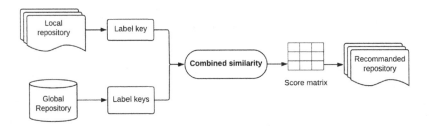

Fig. 3. Combined similarity method for label management.

In this context, we are currently treating the input word as the key of the label within our label unification approach. However, it is important to note that our methodology could be readily adapted to consider the label's value instead. This means that rather than focusing solely on the key (the input word), we could shift our attention to the value associated with the label. We extract the input label keys from both the local repository and the global repository, subjecting them to assessment through the combined similarity method. Every label key within the local repository undergoes a comprehensive evaluation in relation to its combined similarity with the entire set of label keys contained within the global repository. From each combined similarity calculation, the highest combined similarity final score CS_S is selected. Each label from the global repository that possesses the chosen score is subsequently included in the repository of recommended labels.

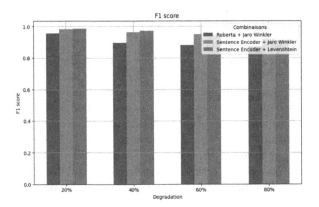

Fig. 4. Results of analysis combination in terms of F1 score.

For the tool's implementation, we carried out a comparison of NLP methods in terms of F1 score in order to identify the most precise and accurate methods. This experiment is based on the dataset presented in the interface of our tool which has been degraded at different frequencies (20%, 40%, 60%, and 80%) in order to test the similarity methods and their robustness. We implemented different well-known similarity analysis methods. For this test, we selected the most performing ones, namely **RoBERTa** and **sentence encoder** for semantic analysis, and **Jaro winkler** and **Levenshtien** for syntactic analysis. In Fig. 4, The results show that the combination of the sentence encoder with RoBERTa yields the lowest F1 score, while the combination with Levenshtein provides the best performance. Based on the obtained results, we argue that the combination of the sentence encoder with Jaro-Winkler and Levenshtein are recommanded for label uniformization.

4 Demonstration

In order to demonstrate the novelty and applicability of our approach, our demonstration scenario will give a quick tour of LABELIT's functionalities and will focus on the main benefits it offers to a Cloud Architect in managing a multi-cloud system.

In the cloud system managed by our Cloud Architect, developers have already independently deployed resources on several cloud providers. Developer 1 deployed two resources on Cloud Service Provider A (CSP A). Resource 1 is labeled with ("Proj.": "A" and "env": "Dev") and Resource 2 with ("Proj.": "A" and "env": "Dev"). Meanwhile, Developer 2 deployed two resources on Cloud Service Provider B (CSP B). Resource 3 is labeled with ("Project": "B" and "Env": "Dev") and Resource 4 with ("Project": "C" and "Env": "Prod").

This system is managed by label-based engine rules for operations, security and FinOps. Therefore, the cloud architect defined rules such as *"resources of project A cannot communicate with resources from project B"*. These rules rely on labels, but as seen in the deployed resources, the concept of a project is described using two different terms: "Proj." and "Project". Consequently, no simple label-based rule can cover all resources associated with a project and a poor labeling would limit the use of state-of-the-art label-based DevOps tools, inducing difficulties in managing resources.

For the purpose of the demonstration, sample resources were deployed on several service providers such as AWS and GCP, simulating developers in independent teams deploying resources. These multi-cloud resources were extracted in the first part of our pipeline using **Resoto** (https://resoto.com/) – Fig. 5 (a). The Cloud Architect can now trigger from our tool's web interface – Fig. 5 (b), the computation of the similarities between the labels found in the resources and a curated list of label (the global repository) he or she provides. The Cloud Architect can select an algorithm from a comprehensive list of algorithms supporting semantic and syntactic corrections to compute the similarities between the extracted labels and the labels in the global repository; visualize key metrics assessing the relevance of the recommendations; and download the results for further inspection.

For a fully automated process, the Cloud Architect can also call our library using our CLI toolkit to compute the recommended labels, and then automatically update the labels of the already deployed resources using the **Crossplane** (https://www.crossplane.io/) orchestrator running on the top of **Kubernetes** (https://kubernetes.io/) – Fig. 5 (c).

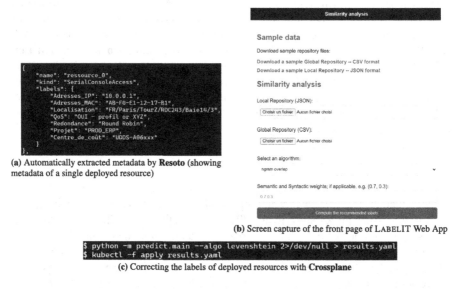

(a) Automatically extracted metadata by **Resoto** (showing metadata of a single deployed resource)

(b) Screen capture of the front page of LABELIT Web App

(c) Correcting the labels of deployed resources with **Crossplane**

Fig. 5. Overview of the demonstration platform.

5   Maturity and Future Work

The LABELIT tool offers a combined approach leveraging Natural Language Processing for label unification which relies on syntactic and semantic analysis of labels to ensure consistency and homogeneity. It is implemented in Python, leveraging state-of-the-art libraries for NLP such as e.g., nltk [6] and spaCy [9] (semantic similarities) and utilizing several reference implementations of prominent algorithms for fuzzy matching such as Levenshtein and Jaro Winkler (syntactic similarities). This tool already offers technical collaborators working within our private cloud a solution to automatically correct poorly formatted labels in their deployments, and to streamline the shared use of labels among developers and cloud operators without requiring prior synchronization. We further plan to present the results of our comprehensive experimental study which compares the robustness of the proposed approaches under diverse syntactic and semantic degradation types. As part of planned future work, we will study improving the accuracy of recommendations based on the analysis of resource-related contextual data such as their technical properties functional or not, and their observed interactions in live deployments.

Unfortunately, the source code of our application has to follow a long mandatory auditing process by lead engineers before being accepted for open-sourcing, but we plan to make it available in a public repository such as GITHUB in the very next future. Nevertheless, we provide public access (http://labelit.devolab.cloud) to a part of the web interface, a **Flask** application, included along with our tool. A detailed presentation of the usage of the whole tool is available in the accompanying video (https://drive.google.com/file/d/1XG1rnF88HlbJK9GzLk8wx-JdIqO9z-te/view?usp=sharing).

References

1. De Lucia, A., Di Penta, M., Oliveto, R., Panichella, A., Panichella, S.: Using IR methods for labeling source code artifacts: Is it worthwhile? In: 2012 20th IEEE ICPC, pp. 193–202 (2012)
2. De Lucia, A., Di Penta, M., Oliveto, R., Panichella, A., Panichella, S.: Labeling source code with information retrieval methods: an empirical study. ESE **19**, 1383–1420 (2014)
3. Deng, S., et al.: Cloud-native computing: a survey from the perspective of services. In: Proceedings of the IEEE (2024)
4. Gašpar, A., Grubišić, A., Šarić-Grgić, I.: Evaluation of a rule-based approach to automatic factual question generation using syntactic and semantic analysis. LRE **57**(4), 1431–1461 (2023)
5. Gu, D., et al.: Tracking knowledge evolution in cloud health care research: knowledge map and common word analysis. JI **22**(2) (2020)
6. Hardeniya, N., Perkins, J., Chopra, D., Joshi, N., Mathur, I.: Natural Language Processing: Python and NLTK. Packt Publishing Ltd, Birmingham, UK (2016)
7. Kang, J.M., Lee, J., Nagendra, V., Banerjee, S.: Lms: label management service for intent-driven cloud management. In: 2017 IFIP/IEEE IM, pp. 177–185 (2017)
8. Niu, N., Reddivari, S., Mahmoud, A., Bhowmik, T., Xu, S.: Automatic labeling of software requirements clusters. In: 2012 4th International Workshop on Search-Driven Development: Users, Infrastructure, Tools, and Evaluation (SUITE), pp. 17–20 (2012)
9. Vasiliev, Y.: NLP with Python and spaCy: A Practical Introduction. No Starch Press, San Francisco, CA, USA (2020)

Nala2BPMN: Automating BPMN Model Generation with Large Language Models

Ali Nour Eldin[1,2(✉)], Nour Assy[2], Olan Anesini[2], Benjamin Dalmas[2], and Walid Gaaloul[1]

[1] Telecom SudParis, Institut Polytechnique de Paris, Paris, France
{ali.nour_eldin,walid.gaaloul}@telecom-sudparis.eu
[2] Bonitasoft, Grenoble, France
{ali.nour-eldin,nour.assy,olan.anesini,
benjamin.dalmas}@bonitasoft.com

Abstract. Nala2BPMN is a web-based tool that automates the generation of business process models from textual descriptions using large language models (LLMs). It employs a hybrid approach, breaking down tasks into steps to improve accuracy and reduce errors. The tool efficiently handles both simple and complex descriptions, as well as incomplete inputs. A qualitative evaluation by experts found Nala2BPMN to produce accurate and understandable models, highlighting its effectiveness in dealing with diverse process description complexities.

Keywords: Process modeling · BPM · Generative AI · LLMs

1 Introduction

Business process modeling is essential for organizations to formalize, analyze, and improve workflows [2]. BPMN (Business Process Model and Notation) diagrams are widely used for this purpose, but their creation traditionally requires significant manual effort and expertise. While manual modeling can be accurate, it is time-consuming, and automating BPMN diagram generation poses several challenges. One key issue is handling complex or incomplete descriptions. Textual descriptions of business processes, often provided by non-experts, tend to be ambiguous or lack crucial details, which makes it difficult for current automated tools to interpret them accurately.

Existing solutions in this domain have utilized Natural Language Processing (NLP) techniques to automatically generate process models from textual descriptions [3]. These approaches often depend on rule-based templates [1] or deep learning methods [6] to extract process-related information. Although effective for well-structured text, such methods face difficulties in handling diverse writing styles, domain-specific terminology, and the ambiguity typically found in informal descriptions [9]. Additionally, these methods require large, high-quality datasets for training, which are often scarce or difficult to obtain [4]. Consequently, NLP-based techniques may fail to capture the full complexity of business processes or generate incomplete models.

Recently, Large Language Models (LLMs) have been applied to business process modeling, given their advanced capabilities in comprehending and generating human-like text [7]. LLM-based approaches aim to generate process models in a single step

M. Comuzzi et al. (Eds.): CoopIS 2024, LNCS 15506, pp. 398–404, 2025.
https://doi.org/10.1007/978-3-031-81375-7_27

by converting textual descriptions directly into formal process representations. While promising, these methods also face substantial challenges, as LLMs are prone to generating hallucinations—introducing or misinterpreting information—especially in complex situations. Furthermore, when handling lengthy or vague process descriptions, LLMs tend to produce unstable or illogical structures, reducing their reliability for real-world business applications.

In response to these challenges, we introduce Nala2BPMN, a web-based tool designed to automate the generation of BPMN models from textual descriptions using Large Language Models (LLMs). Nala2BPMN addresses the limitations of previous approaches by employing a hybrid method that breaks the model generation process into manageable steps, ensuring higher accuracy and logical consistency. The tool is capable of handling both simple and complex process descriptions, including incomplete or ambiguous inputs, by interpreting the text in stages to ensure that key elements are captured accurately. Nala2BPMN is available online for public use[1] and includes a video tutorial to explain its functionality[2].

2 Design and Main Features

Nala2BPMN adopts a hybrid approach that integrates the reasoning capabilities of LLMs with deterministic algorithms, handling the complexity of converting unstructured text into a formalized BPMN model in distinct phases. This approach ensures higher accuracy and logical consistency, minimizing errors like hallucinations or entity extraction issues common in fully LLM-driven methods.

System Architecture. The architecture of Nala2BPMN consists of two primary modules: the LLM-based module and the structured algorithmic module. The system is designed to separate the natural language processing phase from the model construction phase, thereby minimizing errors and inconsistencies. The key components of the architecture are:

– **LLM-Based Module:** This module is responsible for text understanding and entity extraction. It leverages the LangChain framework[3] to manage prompt generation, allowing the tool to handle incomplete or ambiguous descriptions effectively.
– **Structured Algorithmic Module:** After extracting key entities such as tasks, events, and gateways, this module constructs a BPMN model based on BPMN 2.0 standards. It ensures that loops, branches, and other BPMN-specific structures are accurately represented[4].

The overall architecture is illustrated in Fig. 1, which outlines how these modules interact with each other to generate BPMN models from textual descriptions.

---

[1] Tool available here: https://nala2bpmn.bonitapps.com/.

[2] Video available here: https://github.com/NourEldin-Ali/NaLa2BPMN.

[3] https://github.com/langchain-ai.

[4] Details of the structured algorithm available here: https://github.com/NourEldin-Ali/NaLa2BPMN.

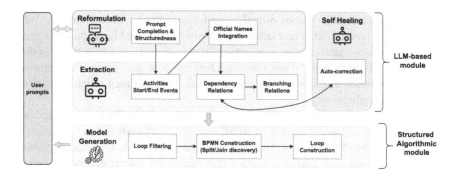

Fig. 1. General architecture of Nala2BPMN.

In addition to the core modules, the backend is built using Flask[5], which manages communication between the frontend and the LLM processing module. The frontend is developed with Vite[6], ensuring a fast and user-friendly interface. The visualization of the BPMN models is handled by the *bpmn-visualization* library[7], which provides interactive representations of the generated BPMN models.

Prompt Completion and Structuredness. Upon receiving the user prompt, this component prompts the LLM to reformulate and, if needed, complete the user description into a structured format for easier extraction. Figure 2 illustrates our prompt template, designed following best practices in prompt engineering [8]. The terms in curly brackets serve as placeholders filled with actual values.

All prompts share a consistent structure. *Role play*: Assigns a specific role to the LLM, such as acting as an expert process owner; *Context*: Provides essential information for the LLM, including definitions related to processes and process modeling; *Task & Specific instructions*: Explains the general task such as reformulating and completing missing information, and details task expectations, such as describing termination points and the logical order of steps; *Output format & examples*: Specifies the desired output format, which is simple text for reformulation, and includes examples for the LLM to follow, like process descriptions and their reformulations; *Prompt input*: Provides the input, which is the initial user-provided process description, for the LLM to process.

Text Understanding and Entity Extraction. In the first phase, Nala2BPMN processes textual descriptions using an LLM to extract key elements such as tasks, events, and gateways. The LangChain framework manages prompt generation and response flow[8], allowing for better handling of incomplete or ambiguous inputs. Extracted elements are then structured into a logical flow, which ensures completeness before proceeding to the next phase.

Role play	You are an experienced process owner in a leading {domain} company.
Context	Considering the context of Business Process Management (BPM) and process modeling: - Process: Describes a sequence or flow of activities in an organization...
Task	You are given a possibly incomplete process description delimited by '''. Analyze the description, then reformulate [...] Your reformulation should be precise, clear and structured ...
Specific Instructions	Follow these instructions: - Add all possible termination points. ...
Output format & examples	{format_instruction} Here are some examples: << {examples} >>
Prompt input	Process description: ''' {process_description} '''

Fig. 2. Excerpt of the *Prompt Completeness & Structuredness* prompt template.

Scalability and Flexibility. Nala2BPMN is versatile and flexible, adapting to a variety of input types, from well-defined descriptions to incomplete or ambiguous inputs. In cases where information is missing, our first step is to reformulate and complete the missing information in the textual description.

Interactive User Validation. One of the key features of Nala2BPMN is its interactive validation functionality. Users can review the extracted process elements before finalizing the BPMN model by modifying the reformulated textual description.

Visualization and Export. The tool incorporates the *bpmn-visualization* library to visualize the generated BPMN models, allowing users to interact with and review them. Users can download the final models in BPMN 2.0 format, making it easier to integrate the diagrams into any Business Process Management Suite (BPMS) for further refinement or execution.

3 Tool Maturity

Nala2BPMN has reached a mature stage of development and has been tested extensively with real-world business process descriptions. The tool has been evaluated against publicly available datasets such as the PET dataset, which includes complex process descriptions commonly found in real business environments. Nala2BPMN has proven its capability to generate accurate and coherent BPMN models, and its modular architecture makes it efficient and cost-effective for organizations.

3.1 Performance Evaluation

During testing, Nala2BPMN demonstrated strong performance in terms of accuracy, token efficiency, model completeness, and cost efficiency. Compared to ProMoAI [7], Nala2BPMN produced more coherent BPMN models while using fewer tokens, making it a cost-effective solution for organizations relying on paid API services[9].

A comprehensive evaluation was conducted with BPM professionals and academics using textual descriptions from the publicly available PET dataset [5], which includes

---

[9] https://openai.com/api/pricing/.

47 textual descriptions and their corresponding BPMN models. A subset of eight descriptions (1.3, 3.2, 3.5, 3.6, 4.1, 5.4, 6.3, and 6.4) was selected for testing, and Nala2BPMN consistently outperformed other tools in both qualitative and quantitative evaluations.

Key results from the qualitative evaluation include:

- **Understandability:** Nala2BPMN received an average score of 4.5/5, compared to 3.2 for ProMoAI.
- **Correctness:** Nala2BPMN scored 4.6/5, while ProMoAI scored 3.1, with fewer logical errors observed in Nala2BPMN's models.
- **Completeness:** Nala2BPMN averaged a score of 4.4/5, outperforming ProMoAI's score of 3.0.
- **Relevance:** Nala2BPMN received a score of 4.5/5, compared to 3.3 for ProMoAI, for including only relevant elements.
- **Ease of Updating:** Nala2BPMN was rated 4.7/5, while ProMoAI scored 3.0, with experts noting the ease of modifying Nala2BPMN's models.

In the quantitative evaluation, Nala2BPMN demonstrated a 40% reduction in token usage compared to ProMoAI based on the same process descriptions mentioned below, which translates to significant cost savings when using paid APIs such as OpenAI's GPT models. This efficiency makes Nala2BPMN a more economical choice for organizations, particularly those generating multiple BPMN models.

These results confirm that Nala2BPMN not only produces more accurate and logically sound models but also reduces costs, making it an ideal tool for both small and large scale business process modeling[10].

3.2 Web Deployment and Availability

Nala2BPMN is available as a web-based application, providing users with easy access to the tool without the need for installation or configuration. The web interface (see Fig. 3) is designed to offer a seamless experience for users who need to quickly convert text descriptions into BPMN models. It allows users to generate, review, and refine models efficiently. Additionally, the tool supports the export of BPMN diagrams in standard formats, making it easy to integrate the models into any Business Process Management Suite (BPMS) for further use.

The tool operates using OpenAI's API keys[11], and users can connect their own OpenAI key to access different versions of GPT models (GPT-3.5, GPT-4-turbo, GPT-4o). This flexibility allows users to choose the model that best fits their needs, balancing cost and performance. For users looking to reduce costs, Nala2BPMN enables the use of smaller models for simpler tasks through its decomposed approach.

---

[10] More details available here: https://github.com/NourEldin-Ali/NaLa2BPMN.

[11] https://openai.com/index/openai-api/.

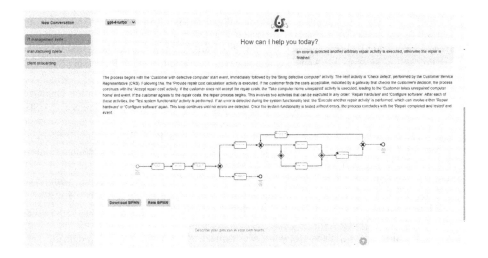

Fig. 3. Screenshot of Nala2BPMN tool.

4 Conclusion and Future Works

Nala2BPMN offers a powerful and efficient solution for automating BPMN model generation from textual descriptions. By combining the language understanding capabilities of LLMs with a structured algorithmic approach, the tool addresses many challenges associated with fully automated BPMN generation, such as logical inconsistencies and incomplete model extraction. Its interactive interface ensures that users remain in control of the modeling process, enabling them to refine and adjust extracted entities before finalizing the BPMN diagram. The decomposed approach also opens the door to assigning the divided tasks based on their complexity to smaller LLM models, reducing costs.

Moving forward, we plan to extend the capabilities of Nala2BPMN by incorporating additional BPMN elements, such as data objects, message flows, and swimlanes, which are not yet covered in the current version. This will make the tool even more versatile and applicable to more complex process modeling scenarios. Another area of focus will be improving the tool's integration with existing BPM platforms. By enabling direct execution of the generated models within BPM software suites, we aim to provide users with a more seamless transition from process modeling to process execution and analysis.

References

1. van der Aa, H., Ciccio, C.D., Leopold, H., Reijers, H.A.: Extracting declarative process models from natural language. In: Advanced Information Systems Engineering - 31st International Conference, CAiSE. Lecture Notes in Computer Science, vol. 11483, pp. 365–382 (2019)
2. Alotaibi, Y.: Business process modelling challenges and solutions: a literature review. J. Intell. Manuf. **27**(4), 701–723 (2016)

3. Bellan, P., Dragoni, M., Ghidini, C.: Process extraction from text: state of the art and challenges for the future. CoRR **abs/2110.03754** (2021)

4. Brown, T.B., et al.: Language models are few-shot learners. In: Advances in Neural Information Processing Systems 33: Annual Conference on Neural Information Processing Systems, NeurIPS, virtual (2020)

5. Friedrich, F., Mendling, J., Puhlmann, F.: Process model generation from natural language text. In: Advanced Information Systems Engineering - 23rd International Conference, CAiSE. Lecture Notes in Computer Science, vol. 6741, pp. 482–496 (2011)

6. Han, X., Hu, L., Mei, L., Dang, Y., Agarwal, S., Zhou, X., Hu, P.: A-BPS: automatic business process discovery service using ordered neurons LSTM. In: 2020 IEEE International Conference on Web Services, ICWS. pp. 428–432 (2020)

7. Kourani, H., Berti, A., Schuster, D., van der Aalst, W.M.P.: Process modeling with large language models. In: Enterprise, Business-Process and Information Systems Modeling - 25th International Conference, BPMDS. Lecture Notes in Business Information Processing, vol. 511, pp. 229–244 (2024)

8. Sahoo, P., Singh, A.K., Saha, S., Jain, V., Mondal, S., Chadha, A.: A systematic survey of prompt engineering in large language models: Techniques and applications. CoRR **abs/2402.07927** (2024)

9. Teubner, T., Flath, C.M., Weinhardt, C., van der Aalst, W.M.P., Hinz, O.: Welcome to the era of chatgpt et al. Bus. Inf. Syst. Eng. **65**(2), 95–101 (2023)

TeaPie: A Tool for Efficient Annotation of Process Information Extraction Data

Julian Neuberger[1]([⊠])[iD], Jannic Herrmann[1], Martin Käppel[1][iD], Han van der Aa[2][iD], and Stefan Jablonski[1]

[1] University of Bayreuth, Universitätsstraße 30, 95444 Bayreuth, Germany
{julian.neuberger,jannic.herrmann,martin.kaeppel,
stefan.jablonski}@uni-bayreuth.de
[2] University of Vienna, Universitätsring 1, 1010 Vienna, Austria
han.van.der.aa@univie.ac.at

Abstract. Machine-learning based generation of process models from natural language text process descriptions is severely restrained by a lack of datasets. This lack of data can be attributed to, among other things, an absence of proper tool assistance for dataset creation, resulting in high workloads and inferior data quality. We address these shortcomings with a tool for annotating textual process descriptions. Compared to other, existing data annotation tools, ours implements a multi-step workflow specifically designed for extracting process information, including supporting features that have been shown to reduce workloads and improve data quality.

Keywords: Process information extraction · Text annotation · Business process management

1 Introduction

Organizations looking to utilize the benefits of Business Process Management (BPM) initially have to model their internal business processes. These so-called as-is process models are expensive to create, as it is a time consuming task, usually performed by BPM experts together with process experts of the organization [3]. To accelerate this initial step, approaches using Natural Language Processing (NLP) have been proposed. These extract the process-relevant information contained in textual process descriptions of various sources, such as quality management handbooks, standard operating procedures, or employee notes [2]. In a subsequent step, this information is transformed into formal models, e.g., in the BPMN modeling standard (see https://www.omg.org/bpmn/).

While approaches based on machine learning became more common in recent years [5,13], Process Information Extraction (PIE) still has not adopted the state-of-the-art machine learning techniques and architectures used in other fields of information extraction, even though the tasks share many similarities [4]. These approaches need vast amounts of annotated training data, which is not yet available in BPM in general [9], and especially for PIE [13], where the currently largest available dataset (PET [6]) contains just 45 process descriptions. Approaches based on Large Language

M. Comuzzi et al. (Eds.): CoopIS 2024, LNCS 15506, pp. 405–410, 2025.
https://doi.org/10.1007/978-3-031-81375-7_28

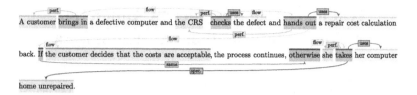

Fig. 1. Example for the high information density of PIE data. Of 40 tokens total, only six (15%) are not directly relevant for the process. The text is a fragment of *doc-1.2* of the PET dataset.

Models (LLM) circumvent this issue, as they are pretrained on out-of-domain data, and only need marginal amounts of data for in-context learning [5]. However, they are hard to optimize for this task, cause considerable costs, and have a poor ecological footprint, making them a suboptimal solution. Accordingly, approaches specifically trained for PIE are preferable.   To provide appropriate training data for this, it is necessary to annotate large amounts of natural language text. Although annotating text is a common task in machine learning research and is supported by various tools to enhance efficiency and productivity, most existing tools are not suited for annotating *process description* text. This is primarily due to three reasons: First, process descriptions have a very high density of information (cf. Fig. 1). As a result, identifying, annotating, and displaying information quickly becomes confusing, which hampers completeness and correctness. Second, annotation of process information is very susceptible to errors, which invalidate the resulting process entirely. Such errors include, but are not limited to accidentally reversing control-flow, disjointed process models, or missing decision points in the process (*XOR-Gates*). We argue, supporting the user with proper visualizations while they annotate yields more complete and correct process models. Third, annotation of process descriptions is often ambiguous. This means that there is more than one arguably correct set of annotations, which makes annotating process descriptions mentally demanding, as many possibilities have to be considered at any given time. The validity of these issues is underlined by other work in the same context, such as the tool Model Judge [8], which facilitates the training of novice modelers in the text-to-model task. To this end, the user's model is compared to a gold standard model and discrepancies are highlighted. While the means of Model Judge are very similar, the ends differ fundamentally—most notably, there is no gold standard during data annotation to which an annotation could be compared to. To address these issues, we present TeaPie, a tool for efficient process information annotation[1].

2   System Overview

To facilitate the extraction of process information from textual descriptions, we developed a modular annotation tool comprising three main components: the front-end web application, the annotation backend and the visualization server. Fig. 2 shows a high-level overview of the architecture of TeaPie.

---

[1] See https://github.com/JulianNeuberger/assisted-process-annotation for code, video, and live demo. Credentials: *coopis* (user), *processes2024* (password).

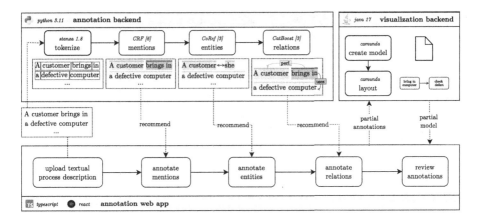

Fig. 2. Overview of the modular architecture of TeaPie.

The front-end web application is implemented using TypeScript and React[2]. It serves as the primary interface for annotators to interact with the system, guiding them through the annotation workflow.

The annotation backend server is built with Python 3.11 and handles various NLP tasks required for generating annotation suggestions. After a user submits a process description, it is tokenized using the Stanza package[3]. The resulting tokens are then fed into three prediction models, to generate annotation recommendations for the user. First a Conditional Random Fields model from Bellan et al. [5] identifies and extracts mentions of process-relevant entities. Following this, the pre-trained neural co-reference resolution model presented in [13] clusters mentions referring to the same entity throughout the process description. Finally, we use the CatBoost model presented in [13] to extract relation. Models are trained on 80% of the PET dataset, while the remaining 9 documents were set aside for the user study.

The visualization server is developed in Java 17 and utilizes the Camunda Model API[4] to generate graphical models for the front-end. The graphical model updates whenever annotations are modified.

3   Key Innovations

One of TeaPie's three core innovation lies in its six-step workflow, which is specifically designed to reduce the complexity of PIE, both for expert, as well as for beginner annotators. As such, for each piece of process information (mentions, entities, relations) annotations are first recommended by TeaPie, reviewed by the annotator, and subsequently amended with missing annotations. During early prototyping iterations, we found that annotators often would recognize additional mentions during annotation of

---

[2] See https://www.typescriptlang.org/ and https://react.dev/ respectively.
[3] See https://stanfordnlp.github.io/stanza/pipeline.html.
[4] See https://docs.camunda.org/manual/7.21/user-guide/model-api/.

entities and relations, which is why we added a final review step, where all information is presented at once and annotations can be rectified before finalizing.

The second innovation that sets TeaPie apart from other annotation tools, is the visualization of the current state of annotated process information. This visualization is generated as soon as the first process relevant entity mention is annotated, and regenerated, whenever the annotations change. This gives users immediate feedback on the information they annotated so far, which helps them understand the impact of certain annotations on the over all process model. This was especially helpful for annotators familiar with BPMN, who compared the graphical process model with their expectations.

The third innovation of TeaPie are machine learning based recommendations. While other text annotation tools support recommendations of annotations, TeaPie generates recommendations for all three types of PIE data end-to-end. These recommendations have been shown to improve the quality of annotations beyond what either humans or recommendation system in isolation could achieve, while at the same time making the annotation process cognitively less taxing [11]. Furthermore, recommendations help to bridge the experience gap between annotators, which makes it easier to assemble teams [11].

4 Maturity

We evaluated TeaPie in a controlled user study where we asked 31 participants to annotate fragments of textual process descriptions and recorded their feedback regarding TeaPie's practicality. Note that 19 of the 31 participants (61.3%) had no prior experience in BPMN. These users are potential data annotators, currently unable to contribute to PIE annotation projects, due to their inherent complexity and ambiguity [1]. For this reason their feedback is particularly valuable to us. In the following we present a brief analysis focused on usability. A detailed analysis of metrics like annotation accuracy, mental workload, or time per document can be found in the full paper of our user study [11]

We found that the workflow we implemented was well suited to how most users extract process relevant information from text. Fig. 4 shows the how much users agreed with statements regarding certain aspects of the workflow implemented in TeaPie. Most users felt the speed with which they were able to complete their tasks was satisfactory (Fig. 4a), understood their task in each extraction step (Fig. 4b), and agreed with the order of extraction steps (Fig. 4c). All users were satisfied with the way the workflow was implemented (Fig. 4d,e). This is especially encouraging, as first time BPMN users agree with experts in this matter, leading us to believe the workflow provides good guidelines for novice users, while not being overly restrictive for experienced ones.

Limitations. We currently see two main limitations with TeaPie. First, the process generation algorithm we use is a very rough prototype and sometimes results in confusing or incomplete process models. This results in many users rating the visualization as less useful, preferring annotation recommendations over the visualization of currently extracted information (see Fig. 5c). We plan to use an improved visualization algorithm to further improve the usefulness of the process model visualization. Second,

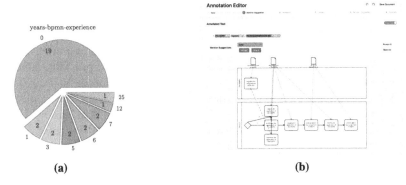

Fig. 3. Years of experience with BPMN of user study participants (left), and a screenshot of TeaPie (right).

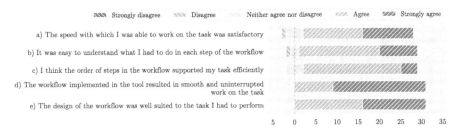

Fig. 4. User feedback regarding the workflow implemented in TeaPie.

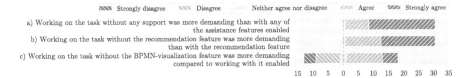

Fig. 5. User preferences regarding the supporting features of TeaPie.

TeaPie only supports the PET data annotation schema. We are actively working on the dynamic definition of annotation schemas in a graphical user interface integrated into TeaPie. This will make TeaPie useful in data annotation projects for various modelling languages, e.g., DCR graphs [10], as well as different paradigms, e.g., Object-Centric modelling.

Future Work. Besides the future work mentioned during our discussion of current limitations, we plan to extend TeaPie with additional features for large-scale data annotation projects. First, we want to integrate features to support the collaboration of multiple annotators. These features include, among others, the automatic calculation of inter-annotator agreement, i.e., how well the annotations of two or more annotators align. Process descriptions where annotators disagree, will be assigned to a referee annotator. This concept proved useful for other text annotation projects [7] and results in higher data quality. Next, TeaPie will provide annotation statistics, such as linguistic variability of process elements, preliminary results of training extraction models, or the percentage of process relevant text in documents. Such statistics are often included in articles presenting new datasets (cf. PET [6]). Additionally, providing automatic conversion of other modalities to text, such as image-to-text, or audio-to-text, could enable new applications of TeaPie. Furthermore, we plan to experiment with different approaches towards generating annotation recommendations. The current approach uses very few learnt parameters, which makes it efficient, but less effective compared to LLMs, which outperform shallow machine learning approaches [12]. Finally, we plan to provide a publicly accessible instance of TeaPie for use in annotation projects of the BPM research community.

References

1. van der Aa, H., Leopold, H., Mannhardt, F., Reijers, H.A.: On the fragmentation of process information: challenges, solutions, and outlook. In: BPMDS (2015)
2. Ackermann, L., et al.: Recent advances in data-driven business process management (2024)
3. Ackermann, L., Neuberger, J., Jablonski, S.: Data-driven annotation of textual process descriptions based on formal meaning representations. In: CAiSE (2021)
4. Ackermann, L., Neuberger, J., Käppel, M., Jablonski, S.: Bridging research fields: an empirical study on joint, neural relation extraction techniques. In: CAiSE (2023)
5. Bellan, P., Dragoni, M., Ghidini, C.: Extracting business process entities and relations from text using pre-trained language models and in-context learning. In: EDOC (2022)
6. Bellan, P., Ghidini, C., Dragoni, M., Ponzetto, S.P., van der Aa, H.: Process extraction from natural language text: the PET dataset and annotation guidelines. In: NL4AI (2022)
7. Brants, T.: Inter-annotator agreement for a German newspaper corpus. In: LREC, Citeseer (2000)
8. Delicado Alcántara, L., Sanchez-Ferreres, J., Carmona Vargas, J., Padró, L.: The model judge: a tool for supporting novices in learning process modeling. In: BPMTracks. CEUR-WS. org (2018)
9. Käppel, M., Schönig, S., Jablonski, S.: Leveraging small sample learning for business process management. Inf. Softw. Technol. **132**, 106472 (2021)
10. López, H.A., Strømsted, R., Niyodusenga, J.M., Marquard, M.: Declarative process discovery: linking process and textual views. In: CAiSE (2021)
11. Neuberger, J., van der Aa, H., Ackermann, L., Buschek, D., Herrmann, J., Jablonski, S.: Assisted data annotation for business process information extraction from textual documents (2024)
12. Neuberger, J., Ackermann, L., van der Aa, H., Jablonski, S.: A universal prompting strategy for extracting process model information from natural language text using large language models. arXiv preprint arXiv:2407.18540 (2024)
13. Neuberger, J., Ackermann, L., Jablonski, S.: Beyond rule-based named entity recognition and relation extraction for process model generation from natural language text. In: CoopIS (2023)

Author Index

© The Editor(s) (if applicable) and The Author(s), under exclusive license
to Springer Nature Switzerland AG 2025
M. Comuzzi et al. (Eds.): CoopIS 2024, LNCS 15506, pp. 411–412, 2025.
https://doi.org/10.1007/978-3-031-81375-7

Printed in the United States
by Baker & Taylor Publisher Services